Software Engineering Standards: Third Edition

- ANSI/IEEE Std 729-1983
  Glossary of Software Engineering Terminology

- ANSI/IEEE Std 730-1984
  Software Quality Assurance Plans

- ANSI/IEEE Std 828-1983
  Software Configuration Management Plans

- ANSI/IEEE Std 829-1983
  Software Test Documentation

- ANSI/IEEE Std 830-1984
  Software Requirements Specifications

- IEEE Std 982.1-1988
  Standard Dictionary of Measures to Produce Reliable Software

- IEEE Std 982.2-1988
  Guide for the Use of IEEE Standard Dictionary of Measures
  to Produce Reliable Software (IEEE Std 982.1-1988)

- ANSI/IEEE Std 983-1986
  Software Quality Assurance Planning

- ANSI/IEEE Std 990-1987
  Ada* As a Program Design Language

- ANSI/IEEE Std 1002-1987
  Taxonomy for Software Engineering Standards

- ANSI/IEEE Std 1008-1987
  Software Unit Testing

- ANSI/IEEE Std 1012-1986
  Software Verification and Validation Plans

- ANSI/IEEE Std 1016-1987
  Software Design Descriptions

- IEEE Std 1028-1988
  Standard for Software Reviews and Audits

- ANSI/IEEE Std 1042-1987
  Guide to Software Configuration Management

- ANSI/IEEE Std 1058.1-1987
  Standard for Software Project Management Plans

- ANSI/IEEE Std 1063-1987
  Standard for Software User Documentation

Published by
The Institute of Electrical and Electronics Engineers, Inc

*Ada is a registered trademark of the US Government (Ada Joint Program Office).

Guidance from the Experts at IEEE Standards Seminars

Software Engineering

The IEEE currently offers Seminars on Software Engineering standards throughout the year.
Our Seminars include:
- Software Reviews and Audits
- Software Testing
- Software Project Management Planning
- Software Verification and Validation
- Software Quality Assurance
- Software Requirements Specification
- Software Configuration Management

Local Area Networks (LANs)

The IEEE offers a new, one-day seminar based on IEEE Std 802.5-1989, Standard for Local Area Networks: Token Ring Access Method. In this seminar, you'll learn the underlying principles of token ring operation and physical design, and how to plan the physical wiring and configuration in accordance with the IEEE standard. If you're planning networks, building wiring for networks, or if you're involved in the physical design and implementation of networks in various applications environments, make sure you sign up for our LAN seminar.

POSIX

The IEEE offers a new, two-day seminar based on IEEE P1003.0, Guide to POSIX Open Systems Environments, and other IEEE projects that deal with open systems. In this seminar, you'll learn about frameworks and profiles for Information Technology (IT) standards, and how they apply to your organization. The seminar introduces methods for creating profiles to satisfy the specific needs of an organization, program, or project.

Special team discounts are available. IEEE-sponsored seminars may also be brought to your plant. For details, write to the IEEE Standards Seminar Manager, 445 Hoes Lane, PO Box 1331, Piscataway, NJ 08855-1331 USA. Or call us Toll Free in the U.S. and Canada at 1-800-678-IEEE and ask for Standards Seminars and Training Programs. Outside the U.S. and Canada, please call 908-562-3805.

Fourth Printing
August 1990

Contains corrected versions of IEEE Std 982.2-1988 and IEEE Std 1028-1988. IEEE Std 730.1-1989 is the revision of IEEE Std 730-1984 and is available individually. It will be included in the Fourth Edition of this collection.

ISBN 1-55937-008-4

Library of Congress Catalog Card Number 89-084469

© Copyright 1989 by

**The Institute of Electrical and Electronics Engineers, Inc
345 East 47th Street, New York, NY 10017, USA**

Software Engineering Standards: Third Edition

- ANSI/IEEE Std 729-1983
  Glossary of Software Engineering Terminology
  729

- ANSI/IEEE Std 730-1984
  Software Quality Assurance Plans
  730

- ANSI/IEEE Std 828-1983
  Software Configuration Management Plans
  828

- ANSI/IEEE Std 829-1983
  Software Test Documentation
  829

- ANSI/IEEE Std 830-1984
  Software Requirements Specifications
  830

- IEEE Std 982.1-1988
  Standard Dictionary of Measures to Produce Reliable Software
  982.1

- IEEE Std 982.2-1988
  Guide for the Use of IEEE Standard Dictionary of Measures
  to Produce Reliable Software (IEEE Std 982.1-1988)
  982.2

- ANSI/IEEE Std 983-1986
  Software Quality Assurance Planning
  983

- ANSI/IEEE Std 990-1987
  Ada As a Program Design Language
  990

- ANSI/IEEE Std 1002-1987
  Taxonomy for Software Engineering Standards
  1002

- ANSI/IEEE Std 1008-1987
  Software Unit Testing
  1008

- ANSI/IEEE Std 1012-1986
  Software Verification and Validation Plans
  1012

- ANSI/IEEE Std 1016-1987
  Software Design Descriptions
  1016

- IEEE Std 1028-1988
  Standard for Software Reviews and Audits
  1028

- ANSI/IEEE Std 1042-1987
  Guide to Software Configuration Management
  1042

- ANSI/IEEE Std 1058.1-1987
  Standard for Software Project Management Plans
  1058.1

- ANSI/IEEE Std 1063-1987
  Standard for Software User Documentation
  1063

Software Engineering Standards: Third Edition

Introduction by
John W. Horch

For the last nearly 100 years, the Institute of Electrical and Electronics Engineers (IEEE) has been involved in the generation and promulgation of standards. IEEE standards represent the formalization of current norms of professional practice, through the process of obtaining the consensus of concerned, practicing professionals in the given field. Today, the IEEE Computer Society is the fastest growing area of IEEE standardization efforts.

Software engineering has emerged as a specific engineering field in recent years, and those involved have increasingly recognized the need for standards. As a result, the Computer Society of the IEEE formed a subcommittee to codify these norms of professional software engineering practice into standards by means of the consensus process. This book presents a continuation of the accumulated results of these efforts and provides, in a single volume, the first seventeen standards developed for software engineering using the consensus process.

(1) ANSI/IEEE Std 729-1983, IEEE Standard Glossary of Software Engineering Terminology
(2) ANSI/IEEE Std 730-1984, IEEE Standard for Software Quality Assurance Plans
(3) ANSI/IEEE Std 828-1983, IEEE Standard for Software Configuration Management Plans
(4) ANSI/IEEE Std 829-1983, IEEE Standard for Software Test Documentation
(5) ANSI/IEEE Std 830-1984, IEEE Guide to Software Requirements Specifications
(6) IEEE Std 982.1-1988, IEEE Standard Dictionary of Measures to Produce Reliable Software
(7) IEEE Std 982.2-1988, IEEE Guide for the Use of IEEE Standard Dictionary of Measures to Produce Reliable Software (IEEE Std 982.1-1988)
(8) ANSI/IEEE Std 983-1986, IEEE Guide for Software Quality Assurance Planning
(9) ANSI/IEEE Std 990-1986, IEEE Recommended Practice for Ada* As a Program Design Language
(10) ANSI/IEEE Std 1002-1987, IEEE Standard Taxonomy for Software Engineering Standards
(11) ANSI/IEEE Std 1008-1987, IEEE Standard for Software Unit Testing
(12) ANSI/IEEE Std 1012-1986, IEEE Standard for Software Verification and Validation Plans
(13) ANSI/IEEE Std 1016-1987, IEEE Recommended Practice for Software Design Descriptions
(14) IEEE Std 1028-1988, IEEE Standard for Software Reviews and Audits
(15) ANSI/IEEE Std 1042-1988, IEEE Guide to Software Configuration Management
(16) ANSI/IEEE Std 1058.1-1987, IEEE Standard for Software Project Management Plans
(17) ANSI/IEEE Std 1063-1987, IEEE Standard for Software User Documentation

Standards have been written as reference documents and, therefore, text of a tutorial nature has been omitted. Background material and the rationale for making certain choices are provided in the Guides and Recommended Practices, as they provide alternative approaches or selectable options in their areas. This accurately reflects the current consensus that documentation of software requirements is a fast-moving field, and that knowledgeable tradeoffs are required.

Each IEEE software engineering standard is prepared with two goals in mind:

(1) The standard must fit with all other IEEE software engineering standards; that is, it must be compatible with and not contradict any of the other existing standards.

(2) The standard must be capable of being used without other IEEE standards. Since all IEEE standards are "voluntary use" in nature, the compliance with one software engineering standard does not require or imply compliance with any other.

---

*Ada is a registered trademark of the US Government (Ada Joint Program Office).

Historical Perspective

For an overall viewpoint, the creation of software engineering standards has been an evolutionary process. The early standards provided a common vocabulary (ANSI/IEEE Std 729-1983) and an initial framework of relationship (ANSI/IEEE Std 730-1984) for the subsequent standardization efforts. More recently, a Taxonomy of Software Engineering Standards (IEEE Std 1002-1987) was developed to effectively map standards needs to availability and application.

Additional standards efforts are underway to build on this foundation. The first effort is to continue the definition and expansion of the requirements contained in ANSI/IEEE Std 730-1984 and the framework presented in IEEE Std 1002-1987. A second is to move from Standards and Recommended Practices to Guides; this provides additional tutorial material for guidance in further implementations. The third goes from a product standard (for example, a document) to a process standard (for example, testing). The last is the expansion of the terminology, both to include additional terms themselves and to define associated metrics (for example, productivity metrics).

Throughout all of this work there have been several themes, the first of which has been consensus. These standards have been averaging a ballot return of over 85%. And over 90% of the returned ballots have been approvals.

The second theme has been timeliness. The best standards in the world will not help if they are not provided in a timely manner. The time from project approval to approval of the resulting standard is slightly over three years. This reflects the efforts to attain consensus of concerned, practicing professionals in the field.

Synopses of the Standards

The main motivation behind the creation of these IEEE Standards has been to provide recommendations reflecting the state-of-the-art in the application of engineering principles to the development and maintenance of software. For those that are new to software engineering, these standards are an invaluable source of carefully considered advice, brewed in the cauldron of a consensus process of professional discussion and debate. For those that are on the leading edge of the field, these standards serve as a baseline against which advances can be communicated and evaluated.

The following are synopses of each of the standards included in this volume:

ANSI/IEEE Std 729. ANSI/IEEE Std 729 establishes definitions for most of the software engineering terms in general usage. It contains definitions for more than 500 terms and therefore establishes the basic vocabulary of software engineering. Building on a foundation of American National Standard Institute (ANSI) and International Standards Organization (ISO) terms, it promotes clarity and consistency in the vocabulary of software engineering and associated fields.

ANSI/IEEE Std 730. This Standard has as its basic rationale legal liability. It is directed toward the development and maintenance of critical software, that is, where failure could impact safety or cause large financial or social losses. The orientation is toward delineating all of the planned and systematic actions on a particular project that would provide adequate confidence that the software product conforms to established technical requirements.

The Standard establishes a required format and a set of minimum contents for Software Quality Assurance Plans. The description of each of the required elements is sparse and thus provides a template for development of further standards, each expanding on a specific section of this document.

ANSI/IEEE Std 828. This Standard is similar in format to ANSI/IEEE Std 730, but deals with the more limited subject of Software Configuration Management. The Standard identifies requirements for configuration identification, configuration control, configuration status accounting and reporting, and configuration audits and reviews. The implementation of these requirements provides a means by which the evolution of the software product items are recorded, communicated, and controlled. This provides assurance of the integrity and continuity of the software product items as they evolve through the Software Development and Maintenance Life Cycle.

ANSI/IEEE Std 829. This Standard defines the content and format of eight documents that cover the entire testing process.

The test plan prescribes the scope, approach, resources, and schedule of the testing activities. It identifies the items to be tested, the features to be tested, the testing tasks to be performed, the personnel responsible for each task, and the risks associated with the plan.

Test specification is covered by three document types, while test reporting is covered by four document types.

The Standard shows the relationships of these documents to one another as they are developed, and to the test process they document.

ANSI/IEEE Std 830. This Guide describes alternate approaches to good practice in the specification of software requirements. To enable the reader to make knowledgeable choices, extensive tutorial material is provided. This covers the attributes of a good software requirements specification itself, as well as specification methodologies and associated formats.

IEEE Std 982.1 This standard provides a dictionary of the definitions of selected measures. The measures are intended for use throughout the software development life cycle in order to produce reliable software. The standard does not specify nor require the use of any of the measures. Its intent is to describe the individual measures and their use.

IEEE Std 982.2 IEEE Std 982.2 is a companion to IEEE Std 982.1 and provides guidance in the use of the measures in 982.1. It provides information needed by industry to make the best use of 982.1.

ANSI/IEEE Std 983. This Guide is intended to explain and clarify the contents of each section of a Software Quality Assurance Plan. It is directed at the requirements in ANSI/IEEE Std 730-1984.

ANSI/IEEE Std 990. This Recommended Practice provides recommendations reflecting the state-of-the-art and alternate approaches to good practice for characteristics of Program Design Languages (PDLs) based on the syntax and semantics of the Ada Programming Language. In this document, these are referred to as Ada PDLs.

ANSI/IEEE Std 1002. This Standard describes the form and content of a software engineering standards taxonomy. Applicability is not restricted by software application, size, complexity, criticality, or hardware environment. This taxonomy applies to standards (from the related disciplines of engineering management, systems engineering, computer hardware engineering, computer science, and information science) with which a software engineer would be reasonably acquainted. It is application independent. For example, an accounting test standard would be placed under test standards, but the qualifier, accounting, has no significance. The Standard explains the various types of software engineering standards, their functional and external relationships, and the role of various functions participating in the software life cycle. The taxonomy may be used as a method for planning the development or evaluation of standards for an organization. It could also serve as a basis for classifying a set of standards or for organizing a standards manual.

ANSI/IEEE Std 1008. Software unit testing is a process that includes the performance of test planning, the development of a test set, and the measurement of a test unit against its requirements. Measuring entails the use of sample data to exercise the unit and the comparison of the unit's actual behavior with its required behavior as specified in the unit's requirements documentation.

This Standard defines an integrated approach to systematic and documented unit testing. The approach uses unit design and unit implementation information, in addition to unit requirements, to determine the completeness of the testing. The Standard describes a testing process composed of a hierarchy of phases, activities, and tasks. Further, it defines a minimum set of tasks for each activity, although additional tasks may be added to any activity.

ANSI/IEEE Std 1012. This Standard has a threefold purpose:
(1) To provide, for both critical and noncritical software, uniform and minimum requirements for the format and content of Software Verification and Validation Plans (SVVPs).
(2) To define, for critical software, specific minimum verification and validation (V&V) tasks and their required inputs and outputs that shall be included in SVVPs.
(3) To suggest optional V&V tasks to be used to tailor SVVPs as appropriate for the particular V&V effort.

ANSI/IEEE Std 1016. A software design description is a representation of a software system. It is used as a medium for communicating software design information. This Recommended Practice describes that documentation of software designs. It specifies the necessary information content and the recommended organization for a software design description.

IEEE Std 1028. Software Reviews and Audits are a basic part of the ongoing evaluation of software products as they pass along the software development life cycle. This standard provides direction to the reviewer or auditor on the conduct of evaluations. Included are processes applicable to both critical and non-critical software and the procedures required for the execution of reviews and audits.

ANSI/IEEE Std 1042. The purpose of this Guide is to provide guidance in planning Software Configuration Management (SCM) practices that are compatible with ANSI/IEEE Std 828-1983. The Guide focuses on the process of SCM planning and provides a broad perspective for the understanding of software configuration management.

ANSI/IEEE Std 1058.1. IEEE Std 1058.1 specifies the format and contents of software project management plans. It does not specify the procedures or techniques to be used in the development of project plans, nor does it provide examples of project management plans. The Standard sets a foundation for an organization to build its own set of practices and procedures for developing project management plans.

ANSI/IEEE Std 1063. This Standard provides minimum requirements on the structure and information content of User Documentation. It applies primarily to technical substance rather than to style. Users of this Standard may develop their own style manual for use within their organizations to implement the requirements of this Standard.

Summary

The evolution of software engineering as a recognized scientific discipline has been rapid, and not always without conflict. The work represented in this volume is an outgrowth of that evolution and represents, in many cases, the resolution of some of the evolutionary conflicts. By seeking the consensus of the concerned, practicing professionals in the field, the best, most up-to-date statements of the current norms of professional practices are developed.

Additional software engineering standards are in process, and the seventeen IEEE standards contained herein will themselves be revisited, no less often than every five years, to ensure their continued applicability. In this way, through timely, consensus-based standards, the IEEE will continue to foster and support the evolution of the software engineering discipline.

An American National Standard

IEEE Standard Glossary of Software Engineering Terminology

Sponsor

Software Engineering Technical Committee
of the
IEEE Computer Society

Approved September 23, 1982
IEEE Standards Board

Approved August 9, 1983
American National Standards Institute

Foreword

(This Foreword is not a part of ANSI/IEEE Std 729-1983, IEEE Standard Glossary of Software Engineering Terminology.)

Software engineering is an emerging field. New terms are continually being generated, and new meanings are being adopted for existing terms. The Glossary of Software Engineering Terminology was undertaken to document this vocabulary. Its purpose is to identify terms currently used in software engineering and to present the current meanings of these terms. It is intended to serve as a useful reference for software engineers and for those in related fields and to promote clarity and consistency in the vocabulary of software engineering. It is recognized that software engineering is a dynamic area; thus the standard will be subject to appropriate change as becomes necessary.

This glossary was prepared by the Terminology Task Group of the Software Engineering Standards subcommittee of the Software Engineering Technical Committee of the IEEE Computer Society.

Comments are welcome and should be directed to:

The Secretary
IEEE Standards Board
345 East 47th Street
New York, NY 10017

At the time this standard was approved, the Terminology Task Group had the following members:

Shirley A. Gloss-Soler, *Chairperson*

Steering Committee:

Russell J. Abbott	Glenn C. Hughes, II	Jane W. Radatz
Joan P. Bateman	John M. Ives	Marilyn J. Stewart
Stephen R. Beason	John J. McKissick, Jr	Alan N. Sukert
Milton E. Boyd, Jr	Albrecht J. Neumann	Donald A. Woodmancy
Kurt F. Fischer	John N. Postak	David Yablon

Other members:

Duane C. Abbey	Raymond Houghton	William E. Russell
Allen Troy Acree, Jr	William B. Humphrey	David J. Schultz
Lynn Beckwith	F.T. James	Lee Shaw
Peter C. Belford	Tom Kallai	Stanley Siegel
Edward H. Bersoff	Edwin Kammerer	Gene Sievert
Grady Booch	Kathleen A. Kenney	Ronald C. Sivertson
John B. Bowen	Brij M. Khandelwal	John Smart
Martha A. Branstad	Ronald Klobert	Mark K. Smith
John R. Brown	K. Peter Koschewa	I. Richard Smook
Fletcher J. Buckley	O.J. Krten	Joseph Spellman
E. Jane Cameron	James C. Landerkin	James D. Stringer
Joseph Cavano	John B. Lane	E. Burton Swanson
James V. Cellini, Jr	Myron Lipow	Douglas B. Tabor
Karl E. Christen	Benn Manny	Barbara J. Taute
Tom Clark	Harvey Marks	Linda T. Taylor
Michele J. DiFranza	Neldon Marshall	Alex Terentiev
Paul Doelger	James A. McCall	Richard H. Thayer
Edward H. Ely	Siba Mohanty	Rinaldo A. Vaccaro
B. Dale Farrar	Dennis B. Mulcare	Don F. Utter
Carolyn Gannon	John Nissen	Keith Waters
David Gelperin	John O'Rourke	Andrew H. Weigel
R.R. Gordon	R. Poston	Herb Weiner
Robert M. Gross	Stephen Pozgaj	Peter J. Weyman
David A. Gustafson	J.A. (Jock) Rader	Terry Wolf
Virl Haas	Geraldine (Burke) Rajcula	Yvonne Wong
George B. Hawthorne	Jean C. Rault	Ralph Worrest
Herbert Hecht	R. Ravichandran	Martin Young
Robert E. Hite	Donald J. Reifer	Peter F. Zoll
Daniel E. Hocking	Debra J. Richardson	Jean Cochrane Zolnowski

At the time it approved this glossary, the Software Engineering Standards Subcommittee had the following membership:

Fletcher J. Buckley, *Chairperson*

Russell J. Abbott	Andre Fortier	William M. Lively	R. Waldo Roth
Peter G. Anderson	Heinz H. Frey	Alan Cheuk-Wai Ma	Clarence W. Rutter, III
William L. Anderson	Morris Frimer	G. H. MacEwen	Burnett H. Sams
Joan P. Bateman	M. Galinier	Andy K. Mahindru	Norman F. Schneidewind
Leo Beltracchi	G. W. Gates	Ben Manny	Harvey E. Shock, Jr
Moredechai Ben-Menachem	David Gelperin	Philip C. Marriott	Roger W. Scholten
Richard L. Bernstein	Edward L. Gibbs	W. R. Mattersdorff	Leonard W. Seagren
Edward H. Bersoff	Shirley A. Gloss-Soler	Lawrence J. Mazlack	I. Lee Shaw
Barry W. Boehm	Amrit L. Goel	James A. McCall	Stanley Siegel
John B. Bowen	Jack A. Goetz	John McIntosh	Roy L. Skelton
Martha A. Branstad	John J. Greene	John McKissick, Jr	Orval N. Skousen
A. Winsor Brown, Jr	Robert M. Gross	Bertrand Meyer	Marian P. Smith
Fletcher J. Buckley	H. Mark Grove	Edward F. Miller, Jr	I. Richard Smook
Brian H. Burger	Russell T. Gustin	Siba N. Mohanty	Harry M. Sneed
James V. Cellini, Jr	Paul E. Haddon	M. F. Moon	Al R. Sorkowitz
John Center	Thomas L. Hannan	Gene T. Morun	D. Steinberg
Won L. Chung	George B. Hawthorne	David G. Mullens	Edward A. Straker
Antonio M. Cicu	Joel J. Hebert	Walter G. Murch	Alan N. Sukert
Bruce M. Clay	Herbert Hecht	John D. Musa	Douglas B. Tabor
Marlene Conklin	Leslie R. Heselton, III	Myron L. Nack	Barbara J. Taute
Guy L. Copeland	Charles P. Hollocker	Saied Najafi	Daniel Thalmann
Jack Cowan	Grace M. Hopper	Geraldine Neidhart	Rush Thompson
Stewart G. Crawford	Sam Horvitz	John O. Neilson	George D. Tice, Jr
George Darling	Glenn C. Hughes, II	Albrecht J. Neumann	Terrence L. Tillmanns
James R. Dildine	Donald J. Humcke	Leon Osterweil	George W. Trever
James V. Dinkey	Shuenn-Chang Hwang	Donald J. Ostrom	William S. Turner, III
Walter Du Blanica	Jim H. Ingram	Thomas Pittman	R.L. Van Tilburg
Lorraine Duvall	John M. Ives	John N. Postak	Robert D. Vavra
Robert E. Dwyer	Dwayne L. Knirk	Robert M. Poston	Udo Voges
Mary L. Eads	George Konomos	Patricia B. Powell	Dale R. Webdale
John D. Earls	Richard W. Kubica	Jane W. Radatz	Andrew H. Weigel
Leo G. Egan, Jr	Thomas M. Kurihara	Steven R. Rakitin	Peter J. Weyman
Richard E. Fairley	Dominic V. LaRosa	Jean C. Rault	Farrell L. White
Chungpeng Fan	Gregory N. Larsen	T.L. Regulinski	Paul A. Willis
Dennis W. Fife	Arvid G. Larson	Hans Reiche	Saul A. Zaveler
Kurt F. Fischer	Albert M. Lerner	Donald J. Reifer	Jean C. Zolnowski
Joel J. Forman	Paul J. Levine, Jr	R. San Roman	

Special representatives to the Software Engineering Subcommittee were as follows:

American Society for Quality Control: **A. Ferlan**
Wayne Kost

ANSI Z1: **J. Milandin**

EDP Auditors Association: **Roy Pritchett**

The Group wishes to acknowledge the close coordination and assistance of the American National Standard Committee X3K5 Subcommittee.

The following organizations supported the development of this standard:

Advanced Data Management
The Aerospace Corporation
Air Force Weapons Laboratory
Airmics, U.S. Army
Amdahl Corporation
American Society for Quality Control
Auto-trol Technology Corporation
Bell-Northern Research
Bell Laboratories
Boeing Computer Services Co.
Boeing Commercial Airplane Company
CTEC, Inc.
California State University, Northridge
Cameron Programming Consultants
Computer Sciences Corporation
Computron Systems, Inc.
Coopers and Lybrand
Data Analysis Center for Software
Digital Equipment Corporation
Doty Associates, Inc.
EG&G, Idaho
Edinboro State College
Electronics Corporation of America

GEC Telecommunications, LTD
GTE Laboratories
General Electric Company
General Research Corporation
Georgia Institute of Technology
Greatermans Management Services, LTD
Honeywell, Inc.
Hughes Aircraft Company
Human Computing Resources Corporation
Identicon Corporation
IIT Research Institute
Informatics, Inc.
Institute DeRecherche D'Informatique
    Et D'Automatique
Johnson Controls, Inc.
Kansas State University
Lockheed - Georgia Company
Logicon, Inc.
MRI Systems Corporation
Martin Marietta Labs
Microdate Corporation
NCR Corporation
National Bureau of Standards

Paul Revere Life Insurance Co.
Perkin Elmer Co.
Programming Environments, Inc.
QYX - Intelligent Typewriter Systems
RCA
Rome Air Development Center
Sacramento State University
Smart Communications, Inc.
SoHaR, Inc
Software Management Consultants
Sperry Systems Management
Super Valu Stores, Inc.
System Development Corporation
TRW
Tektronix, Inc.
Teledyne Brown Engineering
Time, Inc.
U.S. Air Force Academy
UCLA
United States Army Signal Corps
University of Massachusetts
Westinghouse Electric Company

When the IEEE Standards Board approved this standard on September 23, 1982, it had the following membership:

I. N. Howell, Jr, *Chairman*   **Irving Kolodny,** *Vice Chairman*

Sava I. Sherr, *Secretary*

G. Y. R. Allen
J. J. Archambault
James H. Beall
John T. Boettger
J. V. Bonucchi
Edward Chelotti
Edward J. Cohen

Len S. Corey
D. C. Fleckenstein
Jay Forster
Kurt Greene
Joseph L. Koepfinger
John E. May

Donald T. Michael*
A. R. Parsons
J. P. Riganati
Robert W. Seelbach
Jay A. Stewart
Clifford O. Swanson
Robert E. Weiler

*Member emeritus

An American National Standard

IEEE Standard Glossary of Software Engineering Terminology

1. Scope

This glossary defines terms in general use in the software engineering field.

A term was excluded from the glossary if it was considered to be:

(1) Parochial to one particular group or organization.

(2) A company proprietary term.

(3) A standard term in some other well defined discipline, although terms used in software engineering were repeated in this glossary to avoid conflicts.

(4) A multi-word term whose meaning could be inferred from definitions of the component terms.

(5) A term whose meaning for software engineering could be directly inferred from its standard English meaning.

2. Glossary Structure

The structure of the glossary is as follows.

(1) Entries in the glossary are arranged alphabetically.

(2) If a term has more than one definition, the definitions are listed with numerical prefixes.

(3) Where necessary, examples have been added to clarify the definitions.

(4) The following crossreferences have been used to show a term's relationship to other terms in the glossary.

(a) *Compare with* refers to a complementary term.

(b) *Contrast with* refers to a term with an opposite or substantially different meaning.

(c) *Synonymous with* refers to a synonymous term.

(d) *See* refers the reader to a preferred or highly related term.

(e) *See also* refers to a related term.

(f) Words which appear in bold face type within a definition are defined elsewhere in the glossary. When a phrase is in bold face type, the glossary may define either the entire phrase or its component words.

3. Sources

In order to avoid conflict with accepted standards, American National Standards Institute (ANSI) and International Organization for Standardization (ISO) definitions that have relevance to software engineering are included. In those cases where the ANSI or ISO definitions do not fully reflect current software engineering usage, additional definition(s) are provided.

Sources are identified as follows.

(1) Definitions extracted from the ANSI Technical Report, American National Dictionary for Information Processing, X3/TR-1-77, September 1977, are identified by (ANSI) following the definition.

(2) Definitions developed by Technical Committee 97, (Information Systems), Subcommittee 1, (Vocabulary) of The International Organization for Standardization are identified by (ISO) following the definition.

(3) Definitions appearing in other standards are identified by that standard number following the definition. See Appendix A for complete identification of these references.

4. Terms

abort. To terminate a **process** prior to completion.

absolute machine code. Machine language code that must be loaded into fixed storage locations at each use and may not be relocated. Contrast with **relocatable machine code.**

abstract machine. (1) A representation of the characteristics of a **process** or machine.
(2) A **module** that processes inputs as though it were a machine.

abstraction. (1) A view of a problem that extracts the essential information relevant to a par-ticular purpose and ignores the remainder of the informa-/·ion.
(2) The process of forming an abstraction.

acceptance criteria. The criteria a **software product** must meet to successfully complete a **test phase** or meet **delivery requirements.**

acceptance testing. Formal testing conducted to determine whether or not a **system** satisfies its **acceptance criteria** and to enable the customer to determine whether or not to accept the system. See also **qualification testing, system testing.**

accessibility. The extent to which **software** facilitates selective use or **maintenance** of its **components.**

access-control mechanism. Hardware or **software** features, operating **procedures,** or management procedures designed to permit authorized access and prevent unauthorized access to a **computer system.**

accuracy. (1) A quality of that which is free of **error.** (ISO)
(2) A qualitative assessment of freedom from **error,** a high assessment corresponding to a small error. (ISO)
(3) A quantitative measure of the magnitude of **error,** preferably expressed as a function of the relative error, a high value of this measure corresponding to a small error. (ISO)
(4) A quantitative assessment of freedom from **error.**
Contrast with **precision.**

actual parameter. An argument or expression used within a call to a **subprogram** to specify **data** or **program** elements to be transmitted to the subprogram. Contrast with **formal parameter.**

adaptability. The ease with which **software** allows differing **system** constraints and user needs to be satisfied.

adaptive maintenance. Maintenance performed to make a **software product** usable in a changed environment.

address. (1) A character or group of characters that identifies a register, a particular part of storage, or some other **data** source or destination. (ISO)
(2) To refer to a device or an item of **data.** (ISO)

address space. The range of **addresses** available to a **computer program.**

algorithm. (1) A finite set of well-defined rules for the solution of a problem in a finite number of steps; for example, a complete specification of a sequence of arithmetic operations for evaluating sin x to a given **precision.** (ISO)
(2) A finite set of well-defined rules that gives a sequence of operations for performing a specific task.

algorithm analysis. The examination of an **algorithm** to determine its **correctness** with respect to its intended use, to determine its operational characteristics, or to understand it more fully in order to modify, simplify, or improve it.

alias. (1) An additional name for an item.
(2) An alternate **label.** For example, a label and one or more aliases may be used to refer to the same **data** element or point in a **computer program.** (ANSI)

analysis phase. See **requirements phase.**

analytical model. A representation of a **process** or phenomenon by a set of solvable equations. Contrast with **simulation.**

application-oriented language. (1) A computer-oriented language with facilities or notations applicable primarily to a single application area; for example, a language for statistical analysis or machine design.

(2) A problem-oriented language whose statements contain or resemble the terminology of the occupation or profession of the user. (ANSI)

application software. **Software** specifically produced for the functional use of a **computer system;** for example, software for navigation, gun fire control, payroll, general ledger. Contrast with **system software.**

architecture. See **program architecture, system architecture.**

architectural design. (1) The **process** of defining a collection of **hardware** and **software components** and their **interfaces** to establish a framework for the development of a **computer system.**

(2) The result of the architectural design process.

artificial language. See **formal language.**

assemble. To translate a **program** expressed in an **assembly language** into a **machine language** and perhaps to link **subroutines.** Assembling is usually accomplished by substituting machine language operation codes for assembly language operation codes and by substituting absolute addresses, immediate addresses, relocatable addresses, or virtual addresses for symbolic addresses. Contrast with **compile, interpret.**

assembler. A **computer program** used to **assemble.** (ISO) Contrast with **compiler, interpreter.** Synonymous with assembly **program.**

assembly language. (1) A computer-oriented language whose **instructions** are usually in one-to-one correspondence with **computer** instructions and that may provide facilities such as the use of **macroinstructions.** (ISO) Contrast with **machine language, higher order language.** See also **assemble, assembler.**

(2) A machine-specific language whose **instructions** are usually in one-to-one correspondence with **computer** instructions.

assertion. A logical expression specifying a **program** state that must exist or a set of conditions that program **variables** must satisfy at a particular point during program **execution;** for example, *A is positive and A is greater than B.* See also **input assertion, output assertion.**

assignment statement. An **instruction** used to express a sequence of operations, or used to assign **operands** to specified **variables,** or symbols, or both. (ANSI)

audit. (1) An independent review for the purpose of assessing compliance with **software requirements, specifications, baselines,** standards, **procedures,** instructions, codes, and contractual and licensing requirements. See also **code audit.**

(2) An activity to determine through investigation the adequacy of, and adherence to, established **procedures, instructions, specifications,** codes, and standards or other applicable contractual and licensing requirements, and the effectiveness of **implementation.** (ANSI N45.2.10-1973)

automated design tool. A **software tool** that aids in the synthesis, analysis, modeling, or **documentation** of a software **design.** Examples include **simulators,** analytic aids, design representation processors, and documentation generators.

automated test case generator. See **automated test generator.**

automated test data generator. See **automated test generator.**

automated test generator. A **software tool** that accepts as input a **computer program** and test criteria, generates test input **data** that meet these criteria, and, sometimes, determines the expected results.

automated verification system. A **software tool** that accepts as input a **computer program** and a representation of its **specification,** and produces, possibly with human help, a **correctness proof** or disproof of the **program.** See also **automated verification tools.**

automated verification tools. A class of **software tools** used to evaluate products of the **software development process.** These **tools** aid in the **verification** of such characteristics as **cor-**

rectness, completeness, consistency, traceability, testability, and adherence to standards. Examples include design analyzers, automated verification systems, static analyzers, dynamic analyzers, and standards enforcers.

availability. (1) The probability that software will be able to perform its designated system function when required for use.

(2) The ratio of system up-time to total operating time.

(3) The ability of an item to perform its designated function when required for use. (ANSI/ASQC A3-1978)

availability model. A model used for predicting, estimating, or assessing availability.

back-up. Provisions made for the recovery of data files or software, for restart of processing, or for use of alternative computer equipment after a system failure or a disaster.

backup programmer. The assistant leader of a chief programmer team; a senior-level programmer whose responsibilities include contributing significant portions of the software being developed by the team, aiding the chief programmer in reviewing the work of the other team members, substituting for the chief programmer when necessary, and having an overall technical understanding of the software being developed.

baseline. (1) A specification or product that has been formally reviewed and agreed upon, that thereafter serves as the basis for further development, and that can be changed only through formal change control procedures.

(2) A configuration identification document or a set of such documents formally designated and fixed at a specific time during a configuration item's life cycle. Baselines, plus approved changes from those baselines, constitute the current configuration identification. For configuration management there are three baselines, as follows:

  (a) Functional baseline. The initial approved functional configuration.

  (b) Allocated baseline. The initial approved allocated configuration.

  (c) Product baseline. The initial approved or conditionally approved product configuration identification. (DoD-STD 480A)

begin-end block. A sequence of design or programming statements bracketed by *begin* and *end* delimiters and characterized by a single entrance and single exit.

binding. The assigning of a value or referent to an identifier; for example, the assigning of a value to a parameter or the assigning of an absolute address, virtual address, or device identifier to a symbolic address or label in a computer program. See also dynamic binding, static binding.

bit. A contraction of the term *binary digit*; a unit of information represented by either a zero or a one.

block. (1) A string of records, a string of words, or a character string, formed for technical or logic reasons to be treated as an entity. (ISO)

(2) A collection of contiguous records recorded as a unit. Blocks are separated by interblock gaps and each block may contain one or more records. (ANSI)

(3) A group of bits or N-ary digits, transmitted as a unit. An encoding procedure is generally applied to the group of bits or N-ary digits for error-control purposes. (ANSI)

(4) A set of things, such as words, characters, or digits, handled as a unit. (ANSI)

(5) See program block.

block diagram. A diagram of a system, a computer, or a device in which the principal parts are represented by suitably annotated geometrical figures to show both the basic functions of the parts and their functional relationships. (ISO) Contrast with flowchart.

block-structured language. A design or programming language in which sequences of statements are demarcated, usually with *begin* and *end* delimiters. See also program block.

bootstrap. (1) A short computer program that is permanently resident or easily loaded into a computer, whose execution brings another, larger program, such as an operating system or its loader, into memory.

(2) A set of instructions that causes additional instructions to be loaded until the complete computer program is in storage. (ISO)

(3) A technique or device designed to bring itself into a desired state by means of its own action; for

example, a machine **routine** whose first few **instructions** are sufficient to bring the rest of itself into the **computer** from an input device. (ANSI)

(4) That part of a **computer program** used to establish another version of the computer program. (ANSI)

(5) To use a bootstrap. (ISO)

bootstrap loader. An input **routine** in which preset **computer** operations are used to load a **bootstrap.** (ISO)

bottom-up. Pertaining to an approach that starts with the lowest level **software components** of a **hierarchy** and proceeds through progressively higher levels to the top level component; for example, **bottom-up design,** bottom-up programming, bottom-up **testing.** Contrast with **top-down.**

bottom-up design. The **design** of a **system** starting with the most basic or primitive **components** and proceeding to higher level components that use the lower level ones. Contrast with **top-down design.**

bug. See **fault.**

bug seeding. See **fault seeding.**

build. An operational version of a **software product** incorporating a specified subset of the capabilities that the final product will include.

building block. An individual unit or **module** that is utilized by higher-level **programs** or modules.

byte. (1) A binary character **string** operated upon as a unit and usually shorter than a **computer word** (ISO).

(2) A group of adjacent binary digits operated on as a unit and usually shorter than a computer word (frequently connotes a group of eight **bits**). (ANSI/IEEE Std 488-1978)

case. A multi-branch conditional statement that allows for selective **execution** of bounded groups of **program** statements depending upon the value of a control expression. See also **control structure.**

certification. (1) A written guarantee that a **system** or **computer program** complies with its specified **requirements.**

(2) A written authorization that states that a **computer system** is secure and is permitted to operate in a defined environment with or producing sensitive information.

(3) The formal demonstration of **system** acceptability to obtain authorization for its **operational** use.

(4) The process of confirming that a **system, software subsystem,** or **computer program** is capable of satisfying its specified **requirements** in an operational environment. Certification usually takes place in the field under actual conditions, and is utilized to evaluate not only the software itself, but also the **specifications** to which the software was constructed. Certification extends the process of **verification** and **validation** to an actual or simulated operational environment.

(5) The procedure and action by a duly authorized body of determining, verifying, and attesting in writing to the qualifications of personnel, **processes, procedures,** or items in accordance with applicable **requirements.** (ANSI/ASQC A3-1978)

chained list. A **list** in which the items may be dispersed but in which each item contains an **identifier** for locating the next item. (ISO) Synonymous with **linked list.**

change control. The process by which a change is proposed, evaluated, approved or rejected, scheduled, and tracked.

chief programmer. The leader of a **chief programmer team;** a senior-level programmer whose responsibilities include producing key portions of the **software** assigned to the team, coordinating the activities of the team, reviewing the work of the other team members, and having an overall technical understanding of the software being developed.

chief programmer team. A **software** development group that consists of a **chief programmer,** a **backup programmer,** a **secretary/librarian,** and additional programmers and specialists as needed, and that employs support **procedures** designed to enhance group communication and to make optimum use of each member's skills.

code. (1) A set of unambiguous rules specifying the manner in which **data** may be represented in a discrete form. (ISO)

(2) To represent **data** or a **computer program** in a symbolic form that can be accepted by a processor. (ISO)

(3) To write a **routine.** (ANSI)

(4) Loosely, one or more **computer programs,** or part of a computer program.

(5) An encryption of **data** for **security** purposes.

code audit. An independent review of source **code** by a person, team, or **tool** to verify compliance with **software design documentation** and programming standards. **Correctness** and **efficiency** may also be evaluated. See also **audit, static analysis, inspection, walk-through.**

code generator. A **program** or program **function,** often part of a **compiler,** that transforms a **computer program** from some intermediate level of representation (often the output of a parser) into a lower level representation such as assembly **code** or machine code.

code inspection. See **inspection.**

code walk-through. See **walk-through.**

cohesion. The degree to which the tasks performed by a single **program module** are functionally related. Contrast with **coupling.**

command language. A set of procedural **operators** with a related **syntax,** used to indicate the **functions** to be performed by an **operating system.** Synonymous with control language. (ISO)

comment. (1) Information embedded within a **computer program, command language,** or set of **data** that is intended to provide clarification to human readers and that does not effect machine interpretation.

(2) A description, reference, or explanation added to or interspersed among the statements of the **source language,** that has no effect in the **target language.** (ISO)

comparator. A **software tool** used to compare two **computer programs, files,** or sets of **data** to identify commonalities or differences. Typical ob-

jects of comparison are similar versions of source **code,** object code, **data base** files, or test results.

compatibility. The ability of two or more **systems** to exchange information. Compare with **interoperability.**

compile. To translate a **higher order language program** into its **relocatable** or **absolute machine code** equivalent. Contrast with **assemble, interpret.**

compiler. A **computer program** used to **compile.** (ISO) Contrast with **assembler, interpreter.**

compiler generator. A **translator** or an **interpreter** that is used to construct **compilers.** (ISO) Synonymous with **metacompiler.**

compiler compiler. See **compiler generator.**

complexity. The degree of complication of a **system** or system **component,** determined by such factors as the number and intricacy of **interfaces,** the number and intricacy of conditional branches, the degree of **nesting,** the types of **data structures,** and other system characteristics.

component. A basic part of a **system** or **program.**

computer. (1) A **functional unit** that can perform substantial computation, including numerous arithmetic operations or logic operations, without intervention by a human operator during a run. (ISO).

(2) A functional programmable unit that consists of one or more associated processing units and peripheral equipment, that is controlled by internally stored **programs,** and that can perform substantial computation, including numerous arithmetic operations or logic operations, without human intervention.

computer data. **Data** available for communication between or within **computer** equipment. Such data can be external (in computer-readable form) or resident within the computer equipment and can be in the form of analog or digital signals.

computer network. A complex consisting of two or more interconnected **computers.** (ANSI)

computer program. A sequence of **instructions** suitable for processing by a **computer.** Processing may include the use of an **assembler,** a **compiler,** an **interpreter,** or a **translator** to prepare the **program** for **execution** as well as to execute it. (ISO) See also **program.**

computer program abstract. A brief description of a **computer program,** providing sufficient information for potential users to determine the appropriateness of the computer program to their needs and resources.

computer program annotation. See **comment.**

computer program certification. See **certification.**

computer program configuration identification. See **configuration identification.**

computer program development plan. See **software development plan.**

computer program validation. See **validation.**

computer program verification. See **verification.**

computer system. A **functional unit,** consisting of one or more **computers** and associated **software,** that uses common storage for all or part of a **program** and also for all or part of the **data** necessary for the **execution** of the program; **executes** user-written or user-designated programs; performs user-designated data manipulation, including arithmetic operations and logic operations; and that can execute programs that modify themselves during their execution. A computer system may be a standalone unit or may consist of several interconnected units. Synonymous with ADP system, computing system. (ISO)

concurrent processes. Processes that may execute in parallel on multiple processors or asynchronously on a single processor. Concurrent processes may interact with each other, and one process may suspend **execution** pending receipt of information from another process or the occurrence of an external event. Contrast with **sequential processes.**

conditional control structure. A programming **control structure** that allows alternative **flow of control** in a **program** depending upon the fulfillment of specified conditions; for example, **case,** if...then... else...

configuration. (1) The arrangement of a **computer system** or **network** as defined by the nature, number, and the chief characteristics of its **functional units.** More specifically, the term configuration may refer to a **hardware** configuration or a **software** configuration. (ISO)

(2) The **requirements, design,** and **implementation** that define a particular version of a **system** or system **component.**

(3) The functional and/or physical characteristics of **hardware/software** as set forth in technical **documentation** and achieved in a product. (DoD-STD 480A)

configuration audit. The process of verifying that all required **configuration items** have been produced, that the current version agrees with specified **requirements,** that the technical **documentation** completely and accurately describes the configuration items, and that all change requests have been resolved.

configuration control. (1) The process of evaluating, approving or disapproving, and coordinating changes to **configuration items** after formal establishment of their **configuration identification.**

(2) The systematic evaluation, coordination, approval or disapproval, and **implementation** of all approved changes in the **configuration** of a **configuration item** after formal establishment of its **configuration identification.** (DoD-STD 480A)

configuration control board. The authority responsible for evaluating and approving or disapproving proposed engineering changes, and ensuring **implementation** of the approved changes.

configuration identification. (1) The process of designating the **configuration items** in a **system** and recording their characteristics.

(2) The approved **documentation** that defines a **configuration item.**

(3) The current approved or conditionally approved technical **documentation** for a **configuration item** as set forth in **specifications,** drawings and associated lists, and **documents** referenced therein. (DoD-STD 480A)

configuration item. (1) A collection of **hardware** or **software** elements treated as a unit for the purpose of **configuration management.**

(2) An aggregation of **hardware/software,** or any of its discrete portions, that satisfies an end use **function** and is designated for **configuration management.** Configuration items may vary widely in **complexity,** size, and type from an aircraft, electronic or ship **system** to a test meter or round of ammunition. During development and initial production, Configuration items are only those specification items that are referenced directly in a contract (or an equivalent in-house agreement). During the operation and maintenance period, any reparable item designated for separate procurement is a configuration item. (DoD-STD 480A)

configuration management. (1) The process of identifying and defining the **configuration items** in a **system,** controlling the release and change of these items throughout the system life cycle, recording and reporting the status of configuration items and change requests, and verifying the completeness and **correctness** of configuration items. See also **change control, configuration identification, configuration control, configuration status accounting, configuration audit.**

(2) A discipline applying technical and administrative direction and surveillance to (a) identify and document the functional and physical characteristics of a **configuration item,** (b) control changes to those characteristics, and (c) record and report change processing and **implementation** status. (DoD-STD 480A)

configuration status accounting. The recording and reporting of the information that is needed to manage a **configuration** effectively, including a listing of the approved **configuration identification,** the status of proposed changes to the configuration, and the **implementation** status of approved changes. (DoD-Std 480A)

confinement. (1) Prevention of unauthorized alteration, use, destruction, or release of **data** during authorized access. See also **integrity.**

(2) Restriction on **programs** and **processes** so that they do not access or have influence on **data,** programs, or processes other than that allowed by specific authorization.

connection. (1) A reference in one part of a **program** to the **identifier** of another part (that is, something found elsewhere). See also **interface.**

(2) An association established between **functional units** for conveying information. (ISO)

control data. Data that selects an operating mode or submode in a **program,** directs the sequential flow, or otherwise directly influences the operation of **software.**

control statement. A **programming language** statement that affects the order in which operations are performed.

control structure. A construct that determines the **flow of control** through a **computer program.** See also **conditional control structure.**

conversational. Pertaining to an **interactive** system that provides for interaction between a user and a **system** similar to a human dialog.

conversion. Modification of existing **software** to enable it to operate with similar functional capability in a different environment; for example, converting a **program** from FORTRAN to Ada, converting a program that runs on one **computer** to run on another computer.

coroutines. Two or more **modules** that can call each other, but that are not in a superior to subordinate relationship.

corrective maintenance. Maintenance performed specifically to overcome existing **faults.** (ISO) See also **software maintenance.**

correctness. (1) The extent to which **software** is free from **design** defects and from coding defects; that is, **fault** free.

(2) The extent to which **software** meets its specified **requirements**.

(3) The extent to which **software** meets user expectations.

correctness proof. See **proof of correctness.**

coupling. A measure of the interdependence among **modules** in a **computer program.** Contrast with **cohesion.**

critical piece first. Pertaining to an approach to **software** development that focuses on implementing the most critical aspects of a software **system** first. The critical piece may be defined in terms of services provided, degree of risk, difficulty, or some other criterion.

critical section. A **segment** of **code** to be **executed** mutually exclusively with some other segment of code that is also called a critical section. Segments of code are required to be executed mutually exclusively if they make competing uses of a **computer** resource or **data** item.

criticality. A classification of a **software error** or **fault** based upon an evaluation of the degree of impact of that error or fault on the development or operation of a **system** (often used to determine whether or when a fault will be corrected).

cross-assembler. An **assembler** that executes on one **computer** but generates object **code** for a different computer.

cross-compiler. A **compiler** that executes on one **computer** but generates assembly **code** or object code for a different computer.

data. A representation of facts, concepts, or **instructions** in a formalized manner suitable for communication, interpretation, or processing by human or automatic means. (ISO) See also **computer data, control data, error data, reliability data, software experience data.**

data abstraction. The result of extracting and retaining only the essential characteristic properties of **data** by defining specific **data types** and their associated functional characteristics, thus separating and hiding the representation details. See also **information hiding.**

data base. (1) A set of **data,** part or the whole of another set of data, and consisting of at least one **file** that is sufficient for a given purpose or for a given data processing **system.** (ISO)

(2) A collection of **data** fundamental to a **system.** (ANSI)

(3) A collection of **data** fundamental to an enterprise. (ANSI)

data dictionary. (1) A collection of the names of all **data** items used in a **software system,** together with relevant properties of those items; for example, length of data item, representation, etc.

(2) A set of definitions of **data** flows, data elements, **files, data bases,** and **processes** referred to in a leveled **data flow diagram** set.

data flow chart. See **data flow diagram.**

data flow diagram. A graphic representation of a **system,** showing **data** sources, data sinks, storage, and **processes** performed on data as **nodes,** and logical flow of data as links between the nodes. Synonymous with **data flow graph, data flow chart.**

data flow graph. See **data flow diagram.**

data structure. A formalized representation of the ordering and accessibility relationships among **data** items without regard to their actual storage configuration.

data type. A class of **data** characterized by the members of the class and the operations that can be applied to them; for example, integer, real, logical.

debugging. The process of locating, analyzing, and correcting suspected **faults.** Compare with **testing.**

debugging model. See **error model.**

decision table. (1) A **table** of all contingencies that are to be considered in the description of a problem together with the actions to be taken for each set of contingencies. (ISO)

(2) A presentation in either matrix or tabular form of a set of conditions and their corresponding actions. (ANSI)

defect. See **fault.**

definition phase. See **requirements phase.**

delivery. (1) The point in the **software development cycle** at which a product is released to its intended user for **operational** use.

(2) The point in the **software development cycle** at which a product is accepted by its intended user.

design. (1) The process of defining the **software architecture, components, modules, interfaces,** test approach, and **data** for a software **system** to satisfy specified **requirements.**

(2) The result of the design process.

design analysis. (1) The evaluation of a **design** to determine **correctness** with respect to stated **requirements,** conformance to design standards, **system efficiency,** and other criteria.

(2) The evaluation of alternative **design** approaches. See also **preliminary design.**

design analyzer. An **automated design tool** that accepts information about a **program's design** and produces such outputs as **module hierarchy** diagrams, graphical representations of control and **data structure,** and **lists** of accessed **data blocks.**

design inspection. See **inspection.**

design language. A language with special constructs and, sometimes, **verification** protocols used to develop, analyze, and **document** a **design.**

design methodology. A systematic approach to creating a **design,** consisting of the ordered application of a specific collection of **tools,** techniques, and guidelines.

design phase. The period of time in the **software life cycle** during which the **designs** for **architecture,** software **components, interfaces,** and **data** are created, documented, and verified to satisfy **requirements.**

design requirement. Any **requirement** that impacts or constrains the **design** of a **software system** or software system **component;** for example, **functional requirements, physical requirements, performance requirements,** software development standards, **software quality assur**ance standards. See also **requirements specification.**

design review. (1) A formal meeting at which the preliminary or **detailed design** of a **system** is presented to the user, customer, or other interested parties for comment and approval.

(2) The formal review of an existing or proposed **design** for the purpose of detection and remedy of design deficiencies that could affect fitness-for-use and environmental aspects of the product, process or service, and/or for identification of potential improvements of **performance,** safety and economic aspects. (ANSI/ASQC A3-1978)

design specification. A **specification** that **documents** the **design** of a **system** or system **component; for example, a software configuration item.** Typical contents include **system** or component **algorithms,** control logic, **data structures, data** set-use information, input/output formats, and **interface** descriptions. See also **requirements specification.**

design verification. See **verification.**

design walk-through. See **walk-through.**

desk checking. The manual **simulation** of **program execution** to detect **faults** through step-by-step examination of the source **code** for **errors** in logic or **syntax.** See also **static analysis.**

detailed design. (1) The process of refining and expanding the **preliminary design** to contain more detailed descriptions of the processing logic, **data structures,** and **data** definitions, to the extent that the **design** is sufficiently complete to be **implemented.**

(2) The result of the detailed design process.

development cycle. See **software development cycle.**

development life cycle. See **software development cycle.**

development methodology. A systematic approach to the creation of **software** that defines development phases and specifies the activities, products, **verification procedures,** and completion criteria for each phase.

development specification. Synonymous with **requirements specification.** (DOD usage).

diagnostic. (1) A message generated by a **computer program** indicating possible **faults** in another **system component;** for example, a **syntax** fault flagged by a **compiler.**

(2) Pertaining to the detection and isolation of **faults** or **failures.**

digraph. See **directed graph.**

directed graph. A **graph** whose edges are unidirectional.

document. (1) A **data** medium and the data recorded on it, that generally has permanence and that can be read by man or machine. (ISO) Often used to describe human readable items only, for example, technical documents, **design** documents, version description documents.

(2) To create a document.

documentation. (1) A collection of **documents** on a given subject. (ISO) See also **user documentation, software documentation, system documentation.**

(2) The management of **documents** which may include the actions of identifying, acquiring, processing, storing, and disseminating them. (ISO)

(3) The process of generating a **document.**

(4) Any written or pictorial information describing, defining, specifying, reporting or certifying activities, **requirements, procedures,** or results. (ANSI N45.2.10-1973)

documentation level. See **level of documentation.**

driver. A **program** that exercises a **system** or system **component** by simulating the activity of a higher level component. See also **test driver.**

dual coding. A development technique in which two functionally identical versions of a **program** are developed from the same **specification** by different programmers or different programming teams. The resulting source **code** may be in the same or different languages. The purpose of dual coding is to provide for **error** detection, increase **reliability,** provide additional **documentation,** or reduce the probability of systematic programming errors or **compiler** errors influencing the end result.

dummy parameter. See **formal parameter.**

dump. (1) **Data** that have been dumped. (ISO)

(2) To write the contents of a storage, or of part of a storage, usually from an internal storage to an external medium, for a specific purpose such as to allow other use of the storage, as a safeguard against **faults** or **errors,** or in connection with **debugging.** (ISO)

dynamic allocation. The allocation of addressable storage and other resources to a **program** while the program is executing.

dynamic analysis. The process of evaluating a **program** based on **execution** of the program. Contrast with **static analysis.**

dynamic analyzer. A **software tool** that aids in the evaluation of a **computer program** by monitoring **execution** of the **program.** Examples include **instrumentation tools, software monitors,** and **tracers.** Contrast with **static analyzer.**

dynamic binding. Binding performed during **execution** of a **program.** Contrast with **static binding.**

dynamic restructuring. (1) The process of changing **software components** or structure while a **system** is running.

(2) The process of restructuring a **data base** or **data structure** during **program execution.**

editor. A **computer program** that permits selective revision of **computer**-stored **data.**

efficiency. The extent to which **software** performs its intended **functions** with a minimum consumption of computing resources.

egoless programming. An approach to **software** development based upon the concept of team responsibility for **program** development. Its purpose is to prevent the programmer from identifying so closely with his or her output that objective evaluation is impaired.

embedded computer system. A **computer system** that is integral to a larger system whose primary purpose is not computational; for example, a computer system in a weapon, aircraft, command and control, or rapid transit system.

embedded software. **Software** for an **embedded computer system.**

emulation. The imitation of all or part of one **computer system** by another, primarily by **hardware,** so that the imitating computer system accepts the same **data,** executes the same **programs,** and achieves the same results as the imitated system. (ISO)

emulator. **Hardware, software,** or **firmware** that performs **emulation.**

encapsulation. The technique of isolating a **system function** within a **module** and providing a precise **specification** for the module. See also **information hiding.**

error. (1) A discrepancy between a computed, observed, or measured value or condition and the true, specified, or theoretically correct value or condition. (ANSI)

(2) Human action that results in **software** containing a **fault.** Examples include omission or misinterpretation of user **requirements** in a software **specification,** incorrect translation or omission of a requirement in the **design specification.** This is not a preferred usage.
See also **failure, fault.**

error analysis. (1) The process of investigating an observed **software fault** with the purpose of tracing the fault to its source.

(2) The process of investigating an observed **software fault** to identify such information as the cause of the fault, the phase of the development process during which the fault was introduced, methods by which the fault could have been prevented or detected earlier, and the method by which the fault was detected.

(3) The process of investigating **software errors, failures,** and **faults** to determine quantitative rates and trends.

error category. One of a set of classes into which an **error, fault,** or **failure** might fall. Categories may be defined for the cause, **criticality,** effect, life cycle phase when introduced or detected, or other characteristics of the error, fault, or failure.

error data. A term commonly (but not precisely) used to denote information describing **software** problems, **faults, failures,** and changes, their characteristics, and the conditions under which they are encountered or corrected.

error model. A mathematical **model** used to predict or estimate the number of remaining **faults, reliability,** required test time, or similar characteristics of a **software system.** See also **error prediction.**

error prediction. A quantitative statement about the expected number or nature of **software** problems, **faults,** or **failures** in a software **system.** See also **error model.**

error prediction model. See **error model.**

error recovery. See **failure recovery.**

error seeding. See **fault seeding.**

exception. An event that causes suspension of normal **program execution.**

execution. The process of carrying out an **instruction** or the instructions of a **computer program** by a computer. (ISO)

execution time. (1) The amount of actual or central processor time used in executing a **program.**

(2) The period of time during which a **program** is executing.
See also **run time.**

execution time theory. A theory that uses cumulative **execution time** as the basis for estimating **software reliability.**

executive program. See **supervisory program.**

exit. (1) Any **instruction** in a **computer program,** in a **routine,** or in a **subroutine,** after the

18

execution of which control is no longer exercised by that computer program, that routine, or that subroutine. (ISO)

(2) The point beyond which control is no longer exercised by a **routine.**

failure. (1) The termination of the ability of a **functional unit** to perform its required **function.** (ISO)

(2) The inability of a **system** or system **component** to perform a required **function** within specified limits. A failure may be produced when a **fault** is encountered.

(3) A departure of **program** operation from program **requirements.**

failure category. See **error category.**

failure data. See **error data.**

failure rate. (1) The ratio of the number of **failures** to a given unit of measure; for example, failures per unit of time, failures per number of transactions, failures per number of **computer** runs.

(2) In **reliability** modeling, the ratio of the number of **failures** of a given category or severity to a given period of time; for example, failures per second of **execution time,** failures per month. Synonymous with **failure ratio.**

failure ratio. See **failure rate.**

failure recovery. The return of a **system** to a reliable operating state after **failure.**

fault. (1) An accidental condition that causes a **functional unit** to fail to perform its required **function.** (ISO)

(2) A manifestation of an **error(2)** in **software.** A fault, if encountered, may cause a **failure.** Synonymous with **bug.**

fault category. See **error category.**

fault insertion. See **fault seeding.**

fault seeding. The process of intentionally adding a known number of **faults** to those already in a **computer program** for the purpose of estimating the number of **indigenous faults** in the **program.** Synonymous with **bug seeding.**

fault tolerance. The built-in capability of a **system** to provide continued correct **execution** in the presence of a limited number of **hardware** or **software faults.**

file. A set of related **records** treated as a unit. (ISO) See also **logical file.**

finite state machine. A computational **model** consisting of a finite number of states, and transitions between these states.

firmware. (1) **Computer programs** and **data** loaded in a class of memory that cannot be dynamically modified by the **computer** during processing. See also **microcode, microprogram.**

(2) **Hardware** that contains a **computer program** and **data** that cannot be changed in its user environment. The computer programs and data contained in firmware are classified as **software;** the circuitry containing the computer program and data is classified as **hardware.**

(3) **Program instructions** stored in a read-only storage.

(4) An assembly composed of a **hardware** unit and a **computer program** integrated to form a functional entity whose **configuration** cannot be altered during normal operation. The computer program is stored in the hardware unit as an integrated circuit with a fixed logic configuration that will satisfy a specific application or operational **requirement.**

flag. (1) An indicator that signals the occurrence of an **error,** state, or other specified condition.

(2) Any of various types of indicators used for identification; for example, a **word** mark. (ANSI)

(3) A character that signals the occurrence of some condition, such as the end of a **word.** (ANSI)

(4) To indicate an **error,** state, or other specified condition in a **program.**

flow of control. The sequence of operations performed in the **execution** of an **algorithm.**

flowchart. A graphical representation of the definition, analysis, or solution of a problem in which symbols are used to represent operations, **data,** flow, and equipment. Contrast with **block diagram.** (ISO)

formal language. A language whose rules are explicitly established prior to its use. Synonymous with **artificial language.** Examples include **programming languages,** such as FORTRAN and Ada, and mathematical or logical languages, such as predicate calculus. Contrast with **natural language.**

formal parameter. A **variable** used in a **subprogram** to represent **data** or **program** elements to be transmitted to the subprogram by a calling **routine.** Synonymous with **dummy parameter.** Contrast with **actual parameter.**

formal specification. (1) A **specification** written and approved in accordance with established standards.

(2) In **proof of correctness,** a description in a **formal language** of the externally visible behavior of a **system** or system **component.**

formal testing. The process of conducting **testing** activities and reporting results in accordance with an approved **test plan.**

function. (1) A specific purpose of an entity or its characteristic action. (ANSI)

(2) A **subprogram** that is invoked during the evaluation of an expression in which its name appears and that returns a value to the point of invocation. Contrast with **subroutine.**

functional decomposition. A method of designing a **system** by breaking it down into its **components** in such a way that the components correspond directly to system **functions** and subfunctions. See also **hierarchical decomposition.**

functional design. The **specification** of the working relationships among the parts of a **data processing system.** (ISO) See also **preliminary design.**

functional requirement. A **requirement** that specifies a **function** that a **system** or system **component** must be capable of performing.

functional specification. A **specification** that defines the functions that a **system** or system **component** must perform. See also **performance specification.**

functional unit. An entity of **hardware, software,** or both capable of accomplishing a specified purpose. (ISO)

graph. A **model** consisting of a finite set of **nodes** having connections called edges or arcs.

hardware. Physical equipment used in **data** processing, as opposed to **computer programs, procedures,** rules, and associated **documentation.** Contrast with **software.** (ISO)

hierarchical decomposition. A method of designing a **system** by breaking it down into its **components** through a series of **top-down** refinements. See also **functional decomposition, modular decomposition, stepwise refinement.**

hierarchy. A structure whose **components** are ranked into **levels** of subordination according to a specific set of rules.

high level language. Synonymous with **higher order language.**

higher order language. A **programming language** that usually includes features such as nested expressions, user defined **data types,** and **parameter** passing not normally found in lower order languages, that does not reflect the structure of any one given **computer** or class of computers, and that can be used to write machine independent **source programs.** A single, higher-order, language statement may represent multiple machine operations. Contrast with **machine language, assembly language.**

host machine. (1) The **computer** on which a **program** or **file** is installed.

(2) A **computer** used to develop **software** intended for another computer. Contrast with **target machine.**

(3) A **computer** used to **emulate** another computer. Contrast with **target machine.**

(4) In a **computer network,** a **computer** that provides processing capabilities to users of the **network.**

identifier. (1) A symbol used to name, indicate, or locate. Identifiers may be associated with such things as **data structures, data** items, or **program** locations.

(2) A character or group of characters used to identify or name an item of **data** and possibly to indicate certain properties of that data. (ISO)

imperfect debugging. In **reliability** modeling, the assumption that attempts to correct or remove a detected **fault** are not always successful.

implementation. (1) A realization of an **abstraction** in more concrete terms; in particular, in terms of **hardware, software,** or both.
(2) A machine executable form of a **program,** or a form of a program that can be translated automatically to machine executable form.
(3) The process of translating a **design** into **code** and **debugging** the code.

implementation phase. The period of time in the **software life cycle** during which a **software product** is created from **design documentation** and debugged. See also **installation and checkout phase, test phase.**

implementation requirement. Any **requirement** that impacts or constrains the **implementation** of a **software design;** for example, design descriptions, software development standards, **programming language** requirements, software **quality assurance** standards.

independent verification and validation.
(1) **Verification** and **validation** of a **software product** by an organization that is both technically and managerially separate from the organization responsible for developing the product.
(2) **Verification** and **validation** of a **software product** by individuals or groups other than those who performed the original **design,** but who may be from the same organization. (10 CFR 50). The degree of independence must be a function of the importance of the **software.**

indigenous fault. A **fault** existing in a **computer program** that has not been inserted as part of a **fault seeding** process.

inductive assertion method. A **proof of correctness** technique in which **assertions** are written describing **program** inputs, outputs, and intermediate conditions, a set of theorems is developed relating satisfaction of the **input assertions** to satisfaction of the **output assertions,** and the theorems are proved to be true.

information hiding. The technique of **encapsulating software design** decisions in **modules** in such a way that the module's **interfaces** reveal as little as possible about the module's inner workings; thus, each module is a "black box" to the other modules in the **system.** The discipline of information hiding forbids the use of information about a module that is not in the module's **interface specification.** See also **encapsulation.**

input assertion. A logical expression specifying one or more conditions that **program** inputs must satisfy in order to be valid.

inspection. (1) A formal evaluation technique in which **software requirements, design,** or **code** are examined in detail by a person or group other than the author to detect **faults,** violations of development standards, and other problems. Contrast with **walk-through.** See also **code audit.**
(2) A phase of quality control that by means of examination, observation or measurement determines the conformance of materials, supplies, components, parts, appurtenances, **systems, processes** or structures to predetermined **quality requirements.** (ANSI N45.2.10-1973)

installation and checkout phase. The period of time in the **software life cycle** during which a **software product** is integrated into its **operational** environment and tested in this environment to ensure that it performs as required.

instruction. (1) A **program** statement that causes a **computer** to perform a particular operation or set of operations.
(2) In a **programming language,** a meaningful expression that specifies one operation and identifies its **operands,** if any. (ISO)

instruction set. The set of **instructions** of a **computer,** of a **programming language,** or of the programming languages in a programming **system.** (ISO)

instruction set architecture. An **abstract machine** characterized by an **instruction set.**

instruction trace. See **trace.**

instrumentation. See **program instrumentation.**

instrumentation tool. A **software tool** that generates and inserts counters or other probes at strategic points in another **program** to provide statistics about program **execution,** such as how thoroughly the program's **code** is exercised.

integration. The process of combining **software** elements, **hardware** elements, or both into an overall **system.**

integration testing. An orderly progression of **testing** in which **software** elements, **hardware** elements, or both are combined and tested until the entire **system** has been integrated. See also **system testing.**

integrity. The extent to which unauthorized access to or **modification** of **software** or **data** can be controlled in a **computer system.** See also **security.**

interactive. Pertaining to a **system** in which each user entry causes a response from the system. See also **conversational.**

interface. (1) A shared boundary. An interface might be a **hardware component** to link two devices or it might be a portion of storage or registers accessed by two or more **computer programs.** (ANSI)
(2) To interact or communicate with another **system component.**

interface requirement. A **requirement** that specifies a **hardware, software,** or **data base** element with which a **system** or system **component** must **interface,** or that sets forth constraints on formats, timing, or other factors caused by such an interface.

interface specification. A **specification** that sets forth the **interface requirements** for a **system** or system **component.**

interface testing. Testing conducted to ensure that **program** or **system components** pass information or control correctly to one another.

interoperability. The ability of two or more **systems** to exchange information and to mutually use the information that has been exchanged. Compare with **compatibility.**

interpret. To translate and to execute each **source language** statement of a **computer program** before translating and executing the next statement. (ISO) Contrast with **assemble, compile.**

interpreter. (1) **Software, hardware,** or **firmware** used to **interpret computer programs.** Contrast with **compiler, assembler.**
(2) A **computer program** used to **interpret.** (ISO)

interrupt. A suspension of a **process** such as the **execution** of a **computer program,** caused by an event external to that process, and performed in such a way that the process can be resumed. Synonymous with interruption. (ISO)

iteration. (1) The process of repeatedly executing a given sequence of **programming language** statements until a given condition is met or while a given condition is true.
(2) A single execution of a **loop.**

kernel. (1) A nucleus or core, as in the kernel of an **operating system.**
(2) An **encapsulation** of an elementary **function.** Kernels can be combined to form some or all of an **operating system** or set of **firmware.**
(3) A **model** used in **computer** selection studies to evaluate computer **performance.**

key. One or more characters, within a set of **data,** that contains information about the set, including its identification. (ISO)

label. (1) One or more characters, within or attached to a set of **data,** that contain information about the set, including its identification. (ISO)
(2) In **computer** programming, an **identifier** of an **instruction.** (ISO)
(3) An identification **record** for a tape or disk **file.**

language processor. (1) A **computer program** that performs such **functions** as translating, interpreting, and other tasks required for processing a specified **programming language;** for example, a FORTRAN processor, a COBOL processor. (ISO)
(2) A **software tool** that performs such **functions** as translating, **interpreting,** and other

tasks required for processing a specific language, such as a **requirements specification language,** a **design language,** or a **programming language.**

level. (1) The degree of subordination of an item in a hierarchical arrangement. (ISO)

(2) A rank within a **hierarchy.** An item is of the lowest level if it has no subordinates and of the highest level if it has no superiors.

level of documentation. A description of required **documentation** indicating its scope, content, format, and **quality.** Selection of the level may be based on project cost, intended usage, extent of effort, or other factors.

librarian. See **software librarian.**

library. See **software library, system library.**

life cycle. See **software life cycle.**

linkage editor. A **computer program** used to create one **load module** from one or more independently translated object modules or load modules by resolving cross-references among the object modules, and possibly by relocating elements. (ANSI) Note that not all object modules require linking prior to execution.

linked list. See **chained list.**

list. (1) An ordered set of items of **data.** (ISO)

(2) To print or otherwise display items of **data** that meet specified criteria. (ANSI)

(3) See **chained list.**

list processing. A method of processing **data** in the form of **lists.** Usually, **chained lists** are used so that the logical order of items can be changed without altering their physical locations. (ISO)

listing. (1) A **computer** output in the form of a human-readable **list.**

(2) A human-readable, textual **computer** output.

load map. A **computer** generated **list** that identifies the location or size of all or selected parts of a memory-resident **computer program** or of memory-resident **data.**

load module. A **program** unit that is suitable for loading into main storage for **execution;** it is usually the output of a **linkage editor.** (ISO)

loader. (1) A **routine** that reads an **object program** into main storage prior to its **execution.**

(2) A **routine,** commonly a **computer program,** that reads **data** into main storage. (ANSI)

logical file. A **file** independent of its physical environment. Portions of the same logical file may be located in different physical files, or several logical files or parts of logical files may be located in one physical file.

logical record. A **record** independent of its physical environment. Portions of the same logical record may be located in different physical records, or several logical records or parts of logical records may be located in one physical record. (ANSI)

loop. A set of **instructions** that may be executed repeatedly while a certain condition prevails. (ISO) See also **iteration.**

machine language. A representation of **instructions** and **data** that is directly executable by a **computer.** Contrast with **assembly language, higher order language.**

macro. (1) A predefined sequence of **instructions** that is inserted into a **program** during assembly or compilation at each place that its corresponding **macroinstruction** appears in the program.

(2) Synonymous with **macroinstruction.**

macroinstruction. An **instruction** in a **source language** that is to be replaced by a defined sequence of instructions in the same source language. The macroinstruction may also specify values for **parameters** in the instructions that are to replace it. (ISO)

macroprocessor. The portion of some **assemblers** and **compilers** that allows a programmer to define and use **macros.**

maintainability. (1) The ease with which **software** can be maintained.

(2) The ease with which **maintenance** of a **functional unit** can be performed in accordance with prescribed **requirements.** (ISO)

(3) Ability of an item under stated conditions of use to be retained in, or restored to, within a given period of time, a specified state in which it can perform its required **functions** when **maintenance** is performed under stated conditions and while using prescribed **procedures** and resources. (ANSI/ASQC A3-1978).

maintenance. See **software maintenance**.

maintenance phase. See **operation and maintenance phase**.

maintenance plan. A **document** that identifies the management and technical approach that will be used to maintain **software products**. Typically included are topics such as **tools,** resources, facilities, and schedules.

map program. A **compiler** or **assembler** feature that generates a **load map**.

master library. A **software library** containing formally released versions of **software** and documentation. Contrast with **production library**.

metacompiler. See **compiler generator**.

metalanguage. A language used to specify a language or languages.

microcode. (1) A symbolic representation of a **microprogram**.
(2) The internal representation of a **microprogram** in its storage medium. See also **firmware**.

microprogram. A sequence of elementary **instructions** that corresponds to a **computer** operation, that is maintained in special storage, and whose **execution** is initiated by the introduction of a computer instruction into an instruction register of a computer. (ISO) Microprograms are often used in place of hard-wired logic. See also **firmware**.

milestone. A scheduled event for which some project member or manager is held accountable and that is used to measure progress; for example, a formal review, issuance of a **specification,** product **delivery**.

mnemonic symbol. A symbol chosen to assist the human memory; for example, an abbreviation such as *"mpy"* for *"multiply"*. (ISO)

model. A representation of a real world **process,** device, or concept. See also **analytical model, availability model, debugging model, error model, reliability model, simulation, statistical test model**.

modification. (1) A change made to **software**.
(2) The process of changing **software**.

modular decomposition. A method of designing a **system** by breaking it down into **modules**. See also **hierarchical decomposition**.

modular programming. A technique for developing a **system** or **program** as a collection of **modules**.

modularity. The extent to which **software** is composed of discrete **components** such that a change to one component has minimal impact on other components.

module. (1) A **program** unit that is discrete and identifiable with respect to compiling, combining with other units, and loading; for example, the input to, or output from, an **assembler, compiler, linkage editor,** or executive **routine**. (ANSI)
(2) A logically separable part of a **program**.

module strength. See **cohesion**.

multilevel security. A mode of operation permitting **data** at various **security levels** to be concurrently stored and processed in a **computer system,** when at least some users have neither the clearance nor the need-to-know for all data contained in the system.

multiprogramming. (1) A mode of operation that provides for the interleaved **execution** of two or more **computer programs** by a single processor. (ISO)
(2) Pertaining to the concurrent **execution** of two or more **computer programs** by a computer. (ANSI)
(3) The concurrent **execution** of two or more **functions** as though each function operates alone.

mutation. See **program mutation**.

N-ary. (1) Characterized by a selection, choice, or condition that has n possible different values or states. (ISO)

(2) Of a fixed radix numeration system, having a radix of n. (ISO)

natural language. A language whose rules are based on current usage without being explicitly prescribed. (ISO) Examples include English, Chinese, French, and Swahili. Contrast with **formal language.**

nest. (1) To incorporate a structure or structures of some kind into a structure of the same kind. For example, to nest one **loop** (the nested loop) within another loop (the nesting loop); to nest one **subroutine** (the nested subroutine) within another subroutine (the nesting subroutine). (ISO)

(2) To place **subroutines** or **data** in other subroutines or data at a different hierarchical **level** so that subroutines can be executed as recursive subroutines or so that the data can be accessed recursively.

network. (1) An interconnected or interrelated group of **nodes.**

(2) In connection with a disciplinary or problem oriented qualifier, the combination of material, **documentation,** and human resources that are united by design to achieve certain objectives; for example, a social science network, a science information network.

node. (1) An end point of any branch of a **network** or **graph,** or a junction common to two or more branches.

(2) In a tree structure, a point at which subordinate items of **data** originate. (ANSI)

(3) In a **network,** a point where one or more **functional units** interconnect transmission lines. (ISO)

(4) The representation of a state or an event by means of a point on a diagram. (ANSI)

object program. A fully **compiled** or **assembled program** that is ready to be loaded into the **computer.** (ISO) Contrast with **source program.**

operand. (1) An entity on which an operation is performed. (ISO)

(2) That which is operated upon. An operand is usually identified by an **address** part of an **instruction.** (ANSI)
See also **operator.**

operating system. Software that controls the **execution** of **programs.** An operating system may provide services such as resource allocation scheduling, input/output control, and **data** management. Although operating systems are predominantly software, partial or complete **hardware implementations** are possible. (ISO) An operating system provides support in a single spot rather than forcing each program to be concerned with controlling hardware. See also **system software.**

operation and maintenance phase. The period of time in the **software life cycle** during which a **software product** is employed in its **operational** environment, monitored for satisfactory **performance,** and modified as necessary to correct problems or to respond to changing **requirements.**

operational. Pertaining to the status given a **software product** once it has entered the **operation and maintenance phase.**

operational reliability. The **reliability** of a **system** or **software subsystem** in its actual use environment. Operational reliability may differ considerably from reliability in the specified or test environment.

operational testing. Testing performed by the end user on **software** in its normal operating environment. (DoD usage)

operator. (1) In symbol manipulation, a symbol that represents the action to be performed in an operation. (ISO) Examples of operators are +,-,*,/.

(2) In the description of a **process,** that which indicates the action to be performed on **operands.** (ANSI)

(3) A person who operates a machine. (ANSI)
See also **operand.**

output assertion. A logical expression specifying one or more conditions that **program** outputs must satisfy in order for the program to be correct.

overlay. (1) In a **computer program,** a **segment** that is not permanently maintained in internal storage. (ISO)

(2) The technique of repeatedly using the same areas of internal storage during different stages of a **program.** (ANSI)

(3) In the **execution** of a **computer program,** to load a **segment** of the computer program in a storage area hitherto occupied by parts of the computer program that are not currently needed. (ISO)

parameter. (1) A **variable** that is given a constant value for a specified application and that may denote the application. (ISO)

(2) A **variable** that is used to pass values between **program routines.** See also **actual parameter, formal parameter.**

parse. To determine the syntactic structure of an **artificial** or **natural language** unit by decomposing the unit into more elementary subunits and establishing the relationships among the subunits; for example, **blocks,** statements, and expressions may be decomposed into statements, expressions, and **operators** and **operands.**

partial correctness. In **proof of correctness,** a designation indicating that a **program's output assertions** follow logically from its **input assertions** and processing steps. Contrast with **total correctness.**

patch. (1) A **modification** to an **object program** made by replacing a portion of existing machine **code** with modified machine code.

(2) To modify an **object program** without recompiling the **source program.**

path analysis. Program analysis performed to identify all possible paths through a program, to detect incomplete paths, or to discover portions of the program that are not on any path.

path condition. A set of conditions that must be met in order for a particular **program** path to be executed.

path expression. A logical expression indicating the input conditions that must be met in order for a particular **program** path to be executed.

perfective maintenance Maintenance performed to improve **performance, maintainability,** or other **software** attributes. See also **adaptive maintenance, corrective maintenance.**

performance. (1) The ability of a **computer system** or **subsystem** to perform its **functions.**

(2) A measure of the ability of a **computer system** or **subsystem** to perform its **functions;** for example, response time, **throughput,** number of transactions. See also **performance requirement.**

performance evaluation. The technical assessment of a **system** or system **component** to determine how effectively operating objectives have been achieved.

performance requirement. A **requirement** that specifies a **performance** characteristic that a **system** or system **component** must possess; for example, speed, **accuracy,** frequency.

performance specification. (1) A **specification** that sets forth the **performance requirements** for a **system** or system **component.**

(2) Synonymous with **requirements specification.** (U.S. Navy usage)
See also **functional specification.**

Petri net. An abstract, formal **model** of information flow, showing static and dynamic properties of a **system.** A Petri net is usually represented as a **graph** having two types of **nodes** (called places and transitions) connected by arcs, and markings (called tokens) indicating dynamic properties. See also **state diagram.**

physical requirement. A **requirement** that specifies a physical characteristic that a **system** or system **component** must possess; for example, material, shape, size, weight.

pointer. (1) An **identifier** that indicates the location of an item of **data.** (ANSI)

(2) A **data** item whose value is the location of another data item.

portability. The ease with which **software** can be transferred from one **computer system** or environment to another.

precision. (1) A measure of the ability to distinguish between nearly equal values; for example, four-place numerals are less precise than six-place numerals; nevertheless, a properly computed four-place numeral may be more accurate than an improperly computed six-place numeral. (ISO)

(2) The degree of discrimination with which a quantity is stated; for example, a three-digit numeral discriminates among 1000 possibilities. (ISO)
Contrast with **accuracy.**

precompiler. A **computer program** that preprocesses source **code,** part of which may be unacceptable to a **compiler,** to generate equivalent code acceptable to the compiler; for example, a **preprocessor** which converts structured FORTRAN to ANSI-standard FORTRAN.

preliminary design. (1) The process of analyzing **design** alternatives and defining the **software architecture.** Preliminary design typically includes definition and structuring of **computer program components** and **data,** definition of the **interfaces,** and preparation of timing and sizing estimates.
(2) The result of the preliminary design process. See also **design analysis, functional design.**

preprocessor. A **computer program** that effects some preliminary computation or organization. (ISO) See also **precompiler.**

privileged instruction. An **instruction** that may be used only by a **supervisory program.** (ISO)

procedure. (1) A portion of a **computer program** which is named and which performs a specific task. Compare with **subroutine, subprogram, function, module.**
(2) The course of action taken for the solution of a problem. (ISO)
(3) The description of the course of action taken for the solution of a problem. (ANSI)
(4) A set of manual steps to be followed to accomplish a task each time the task is to be done.

process. (1) In a **computer system,** a unique, finite course of events defined by its purpose or by its effect, achieved under given conditions. (ISO)
(2) To perform operations on **data** in process. (ISO)

product certification. See **certification.**

product specification. Synonymous with **design specification.** (DoD usage)

production library. A **software library** containing **software** approved for current **operational** use.

program. (1) A **computer program.**
(2) A schedule or plan that specifies actions to be taken.
(3) To **design,** write, and test **computer programs.** (ISO)

program architecture. The structure and relationships among the **components** of a **computer program.** The program architecture may also include the program's **interface** with its operational environment.

program block. In problem-oriented languages, a **computer program** subdivision that serves to group related statements, delimit **routines,** specify storage allocation, delineate the applicability of **labels,** or **segment** paths of the computer program for other purposes. (ANSI)

program correctness. See **correctness.**

program design language. See **design language.**

program extension. An **enhancement** made to existing **software** to increase the scope of its capabilities.

program instrumentation. (1) Probes, such as **instructions** or **assertions,** inserted into a **computer program** to facilitate **execution** monitoring, **proof of correctness,** resource monitoring, or other activities.
(2) The process of preparing and inserting probes into a **computer program.**

program library. An organized collection of **computer programs.** (ISO) See also **software library, system library.**

program mutation. (1) A **program** version purposely altered from the intended version to evaluate the ability of program **test cases** to detect the alteration. Synonymous with program mutant.
(2) The process of creating program mutations in order to evaluate the adequacy of **program test data.**

program protection. The application of internal or external controls to preclude any unauthorized access or **modification** to a **computer program.**

program specification. (1) Any **specification** for a **computer program.** See **design specification, functional specification, performance specification, requirements specification.**
(2) Synonymous with **design specification.**

program support library. See **software development library.**

program synthesis. The use of **software tools** to aid in the transformation of a **program specification** into a **program** that realizes that **specification.**

program validation. Synonymous with **computer program validation.** See **validation.**

programming language. An **artificial language** designed to generate or express **programs.** (ISO)

programming support environment. An integrated collection of **tools** accessed via a single **command language** to provide programming support capabilities throughout the **software life cycle.** The environment typically includes tools for designing, editing, compiling, loading, **testing, configuration management,** and project management.

project file. See **project notebook.**

project notebook. A central repository of written material such as memos, plans, technical reports, etc., pertaining to a project. Synonymous with **project file.** See also **software development notebook.**

project plan. A management **document** describing the approach that will be taken for a project. The plan typically describes the work to be done, the resources required, the methods to be used, the **configuration management** and **quality assurance** procedures to be followed, the schedules to be met, the project organization, etc.

prompt. (1) A message informing a user that a **system** is ready for the next command, message, or other user action.

(2) To inform a user that a **system** is ready for the next command, element, or other input.

proof of correctness. (1) A formal technique used to prove mathematically that a **program** satisfies its **specifications.** See also **partial correctness, total correctness.**
(2) A **program** proof that results from applying this technique.

protection. An arrangement for restricting access to or use of all, or part, of a **computer system.** (ISO)

protocol. (1) A set of conventions or rules that govern the interactions of **processes** or applications within a **computer system** or **network.**
(2) A set of rules that govern the operation of **functional units** to achieve communication. (ISO)

pseudo code. A combination of **programming language** and **natural language** used for **computer program design.**

pushdown storage. A storage device that handles **data** in such a way that the next item to be retrieved is the most recently stored item still in the storage device; i.e., last-in-first-out (LIFO). (ISO) See also **stack.**

qualification testing. **Formal testing,** usually conducted by the developer for the customer, to demonstrate that the **software** meets its specified **requirements.** See also **acceptance testing, system testing.**

quality. (1) The totality of features and characteristics of a product or service that bears on its ability to satisfy given needs. (ANSI/ASQC A3-1978)
(2) See **software quality.**

quality assurance. A planned and systematic pattern of all actions necessary to provide adequate confidence that the item or product conforms to established technical **requirements.** (ANSI/IEEE Std 730-1981)

quality metric. A quantitative measure of the degree to which **software** possesses a given attribute that affects its **quality.**

queue. A **list** that is accessed in a first-in, first-out manner. Contrast with **stack.**

real time. (1) Pertaining to the processing of **data** by a **computer** in connection with another **process** outside the computer according to time requirements imposed by the outside process. This term is also used to describe **systems** operating in **conversational** mode, and processes that can be influenced by human intervention while they are in progress. (ISO)

(2) Pertaining to the actual time during which a physical **process** transpires; for example, the performance of a computation during the actual time that the related physical process transpires, in order that results of the computation can be used in guiding the physical process. (ANSI)

record. A collection of related **data** or **words** treated as a unit. (ISO) See also **logical record.**

recursive routine. A **routine** that may be used as a **subroutine** of itself, calling itself directly or being called by another subroutine, one that it itself has called. The use of a recursive routine usually requires the keeping of records of the status of its unfinished uses in, for example, a pushdown **list.**

redundancy. The inclusion of duplicate or alternate **system** elements to improve **operational reliability** by ensuring continued operation in the event that a primary element fails.

regression testing. Selective retesting to detect **faults** introduced during **modification** of a **system** or system **component,** to verify that modifications have not caused unintended adverse effects, or to verify that a modified system or system component still meets its specified **requirements.**

reliability. (1) The ability of an item to perform a required **function** under stated conditions for a stated period of time. (ANSI/ASQC A3-1978)

(2) See **software reliability.**

reliability, numerical. The probability that an item will perform a required **function** under stated conditions for a stated period of time. (ANSI/ASQC A3-1978)

reliability assessment. The process of determining the achieved level of **reliability** of an existing **system** or system **component.**

reliability data. Information necessary to assess the **reliability** of **software** at selected points in the **software life cycle.** Examples include **error data** and time data for **reliability models, program** attributes such as **complexity,** and programming characteristics such as development techniques employed and programmer experience.

reliability evaluation. See **reliability assessment.**

reliability growth. The improvement in **software reliability** that results from correcting **faults** in the **software.**

reliability model. A **model** used for predicting, estimating, or assessing **reliability.** See also **reliability assessment.**

relocatable machine code. Machine language code that requires relative **addresses** to be translated into absolute addresses prior to **computer execution.** Contrast with **absolute machine code.**

rendezvous. The interaction that occurs between two parallel tasks when one task has called an entry of the other task, and a corresponding accept statement is being executed by the other task on behalf of the calling task.

repeatability. See **test repeatability.**

requirement. (1) A condition or capability needed by a user to solve a problem or achieve an objective.

(2) A condition or capability that must be met or possessed by a **system** or system **component** to satisfy a contract, standard, **specification,** or other formally imposed **document.** The set of all requirements forms the basis for subsequent development of the system or system component. See also **requirements analysis, requirements phase, requirements specification.**

requirements analysis. (1) The process of studying user needs to arrive at a definition of **system** or **software requirements.**

(2) The **verification** of **system** or **software requirements.**

requirements inspection. See **inspection.**

requirements phase. The period of time in the **software life cycle** during which the **requirements** for a **software product,** such as the functional and **performance** capabilities, are defined and documented.

requirements specification. A **specification** that sets forth the **requirements** for a **system** or system **component;** for example, a **software configuration item.** Typically included are **functional requirements, performance requirements, interface requirements, design requirements,** and development standards.

requirements specification language. A **formal language** with special constructs and **verification** protocols used to specify, verify, and **document requirements.**

requirements verification. See **verification.**

retirement phase. The period of time in the **software life cycle** during which support for a **software product** is terminated.

reusability. The extent to which a **module** can be used in multiple applications.

review. See **design review.**

robustness. The extent to which **software** can continue to operate correctly despite the introduction of invalid inputs.

root compiler. A **compiler** whose output is a machine independent, intermediate-level representation of a **program.** A root compiler, when combined with a machine-dependent **code generator,** comprises a full compiler.

routine. (1) A **computer program segment** that performs a specific task. See also **function, procedure, subroutine, subprogram.**

(2) A **program,** or a sequence of **instructions** called by a program, that may have some general or frequent use. (ISO)

run time. (1) A measure of the time expended to execute a **program.** While run time ordinarily reflects the expended central processor time, run time may also include peripheral processing and peripheral accessing time; for example, a run time of 5 hours.

(2) The instant at which a **program** begins to execute.
See also **execution time.**

secretary/librarian. The **software librarian** on a **chief programmer team.**

security. The **protection** of **computer hardware** and **software** from accidental or malicious access, use, **modification,** destruction, or disclosure. Security also pertains to personnel, **data,** communications, and the physical protection of computer installations.

security kernel. A small, self-contained collection of key **security**-related statements that works as a privileged part of an **operating system.** All criteria specified by the **kernel** must be met for a **program** or **data** to be accessed.

seeding. See **fault seeding.**

segment. (1) A self-contained portion of a **computer program** that may be executed without the entire **computer program** necessarily being maintained in internal storage at any one time. (ISO) See also **component, module, subprogram.**

(2) The sequence of **computer program** statements between two consecutive branch points. See also **path analysis.**

(3) To divide a **computer program** into segments. (ISO)

semantics. (1) The relationships of characters or groups of characters to their meanings, independent of the manner of their interpretation and use. (ISO)

(2) The relationships between symbols and their meanings. (ANSI)

(3) The discipline of expressing the meanings of **computer** language constructs in **metalanguages.**
See also **syntax.**

semaphore. A shared **variable** used to synchronize **concurrent processes** by indicating whether an action has been completed or an event has occurred.

sequential processes. Processes that execute in such a manner that one must finish before the next begins. Contrast with **concurrent processes.**

severity. See **criticality.**

side-effect. Processing or activities performed, or results obtained, secondary to the primary **function** of a **program, subprogram,** or operation.

simulation. The representation of selected characteristics of the behavior of one physical or abstract **system** by another system. In a digital **computer system,** simulation is done by **software;** for example, (a) the representation of physical phenomena by means of operations performed by a computer system, (b) the representation of operations of a computer system by those of another computer system. (ISO) Contrast with **analytical model.**

simulator. A device, **data** processing **system,** or **computer program** that represents certain features of the behavior of a physical or abstract system. (ANSI)

sizing. The process of estimating the amount of **computer** storage or the number of source lines that will be required for a **system** or system **component.**

software. (1) **Computer programs, procedures,** rules, and possibly associated **documentation** and **data** pertaining to the operation of a **computer system.** See also **application software, system software.**
(2) **Programs, procedures,** rules, and any associated **documentation** pertaining to the operation of a **computer system.** (ISO)
Contrast with **hardware.**

software configuration management. See **configuration management.**

software data base. A centralized **file** of **data** definitions and present values for data common to, and located internal to, an **operational software system.**

software development cycle. (1) The period of time that begins with the decision to develop a **software product** and ends when the product is delivered. This cycle typically includes a **requirements phase, design phase, implementation phase, test phase,** and sometimes, **installation** and **checkout phase.** Contrast with **software life cycle.**
(2) The period of time that begins with the decision to develop a **software product** and ends when the product is no longer being enhanced by the developer.
(3) Sometimes used as a synonym for **software life cycle.**

software development library. A **software library** containing **computer** readable and human readable information relevant to a **software** development effort.

software development notebook. A collection of material pertinent to the development of a given **software module.** Contents typically include the **requirements, design,** technical reports, **code listings, test plans,** test results, problem reports, schedules, notes, etc., for the module. See also **project notebook.**

software development plan. A **project plan** for the development of a **software product.** Synonymous with **computer program development plan.**

software development process. The process by which user needs are translated into **software requirements,** software requirements are transformed into **design,** the design is implemented in **code,** and the code is tested, documented, and certified for **operational** use.

software documentation. Technical **data** or information, including **computer listings** and printouts, in human-readable form, that describe or specify the **design** or details, explain the capabilities, or provide operating instructions for using the **software** to obtain desired results from a software system. See also **documentation, system documentation, user documentation.**

software engineering. The systematic approach to the development, operation, **maintenance,** and retirement of **software.**

software experience data. Data relating to the development or use of **software** that could be useful in developing **models, reliability** predictions, or other quantitative descriptions of software.

software librarian. The person responsible for establishing, controlling, and maintaining a **software library.**

software library. A controlled collection of **software** and related **documentation** designed to aid in software development, use, or **maintenance.** Types include **software development library, master library, production library, program library,** and **software repository.** See also **system library.**

software life cycle. The period of time that starts when a **software product** is conceived and ends when the product is no longer available for use. The software life cycle typically includes a **requirements phase, design phase, implementation phase, test phase, installation and checkout phase, operation and maintenance phase,** and sometimes, **retirement phase.** Contrast with **software development cycle.**

software maintenance. (1) **Modification** of a **software product** after **delivery** to correct **faults.**

(2) **Modification** of a **software product** after **delivery** to correct **faults,** to improve **performance** or other attributes, or to adapt the product to a changed environment. See also **adaptive maintenance, corrective maintenance, perfective maintenance.**

software monitor. A **software tool** that executes concurrently with another **computer program** and that provides detailed information about the **execution** of the other **program.**

software product. A **software** entity designated for **delivery** to a user.

software quality. (1) The totality of features and characteristics of a **software product** that bear on its ability to satisfy given needs; for example, conform to **specifications.**

(2) The degree to which **software** possesses a desired combination of attributes.

(3) The degree to which a customer or user perceives that **software** meets his or her composite expectations.

(4) The composite characteristics of **software** that determine the degree to which the software in use will meet the expectations of the customer.

software quality assurance. See **quality assurance.**

software reliability. (1) The probability that **software** will not cause the **failure** of a **system** for a specified time under specified conditions. The probability is a function of the inputs to and use of the system as well as a function of the existence of **faults** in the software. The inputs to the system determine whether existing faults, if any, are encountered.

(2) The ability of a **program** to perform a required **function** under stated conditions for a stated period of time.

software repository. A **software library** providing permanent, archival storage for **software** and related **documentation**.

software sneak analysis. A technique applied to **software** to identify latent (sneak) logic control paths or conditions that could inhibit a desired operation or cause an unwanted operation to occur.

software tool. A **computer program** used to help develop, test, analyze, or maintain another computer program or its **documentation;** for example, **automated design tool, compiler,** test **tool, maintenance tool.**

source language. (1) A language used to write **source programs.**

(2) A language from which statements are translated. (ISO) Contrast with **target language.**

source program. (1) A **computer program** that must be **compiled, assembled,** or **interpreted** before being executed by a **computer.**

(2) A **computer program** expressed in a **source language.** Contrast with **object program.** (ISO)

specification. (1) A **document** that prescribes, in a complete, precise, verifiable manner, the **requirements, design,** behavior, or other characteristics of a **system** or system **component**. See also **design specification, formal specification, functional specification, interface specification, performance specification, requirements specification.**

(2) The process of developing a specification.

(3) A concise statement of a set of **requirements** to be satisfied by a product, a material or **process** indicating, whenever appropriate, the **procedure** by means of which it may be determined whether the requirements given are satisfied. (ANSI N45.2.10-1973)

specification language. A language, often a machine-processable combination of **natural** and **formal language,** used to specify the **requirements, design,** behavior, or other characteristics of a **system** or system **component**. See also **design language, requirements specification language.**

specification verification. See **verification.**

stability. (1) The ability to continue unchanged despite disturbing or disruptive events.

(2) The ability to return to an original state after disturbing or disruptive events.

stack. A **list** that is accessed in a last-in, first-out manner. Contrast with **queue.**

standards enforcer. A **software tool** that determines whether prescribed development standards have been followed. The standards may include **module** size, module structure, commenting conventions, use of certain statement forms, and **documentation** conventions.

state diagram. A **directed graph** in which **nodes** correspond to internal states of a **system,** and edges correspond to transitions; often used for describing a system in terms of state changes. See also **Petri net.**

static analysis. The process of evaluating a **program** without executing the program. See also **desk checking, code audit, inspection, static analyzer, walk-through.** Contrast with **dynamic analysis.**

static analyzer. A **software tool** that aids in the evaluation of a **computer program** without executing the **program**. Examples include **syntax** checkers, **compilers,** cross-reference generators, **standards enforcers,** and flowcharters. Contrast with **dynamic analyzer.**

static binding. **Binding** performed prior to **execution** of a **program** and not subject to change during execution. Contrast with **dynamic binding.**

statistical test model. A **model** that relates **program faults** to the input **data** set (or sets) which cause them to be encountered. The model also gives the probability that these faults will cause the program to fail.

stepwise refinement. A **system development methodology** in which **data** definitions and processing steps are defined broadly at first and then with increasing detail. See also **hierarchical decomposition, top-down, bottom-up.**

string. A linear sequence of entities such as characters or physical elements. (ISO)

strong typing. A **programming language** feature that requires the **data type** of each **data** object to be declared, and that precludes the application of **operators** to inappropriate data objects and, thereby, prevents the interaction of data objects of incompatible **types.**

structured design. A disciplined approach to **software design** that adheres to a specified set of rules based on principles such as **top-down design, stepwise refinement,** and **data** flow analysis.

structured program. A **program** constructed of a basic set of **control structures,** each one having one entry point and one exit. The set of control structures typically includes: sequence of two or more **instructions,** conditional selection of one of two or more instructions or sequences of instructions, and repetition of an instruction or a sequence of instructions.

structured programming. (1) A well-defined **software** development technique that incorporates **top-down design** and **implementation** and strict use of **structured program** control constructs.

(2) Loosely, any technique for organizing and coding **programs** that reduces **complexity,** improves clarity, and facilitates **debugging** and **modification.**

structured programming language. A **programming language** that provides the **structured program** constructs and that facilitates the development of structured programs.

stub. (1) A dummy **program module** used during the development and **testing** of a higher-level module.

(2) A **program** statement substituting for the body of a program unit and indicating that the unit is or will be defined elsewhere.

subprogram. A **program** unit that may be invoked by one or more other program units. Examples are **procedure, function, subroutine.**

subroutine. (1) A sequenced set of statements that may be used in one or more **computer programs** and at one or more points in a computer program. (ISO)

(2) A **routine** that can be part of another routine. (ANSI)

(3) A **subprogram** that is invoked by a calling statement, that may or may not receive input values, and that returns any output values through **parameter** names, **program variables,** or mechanisms other than the subroutine name itself. Contrast with **function.** See also **procedure.**

subsystem. A group of assemblies or **components** or both combined to perform a single **function.** (ANSI N45.2.10-1973)

supervisor. See **supervisory program**

supervisory program. A **computer program,** usually part of an **operating system,** that controls the **execution** of other computer programs and regulates the flow of work in a **data** processing **system.** Synonymous with **executive program, supervisor.** (ISO)

symbolic execution. A **verification** technique in which **program execution** is simulated using symbols rather than actual values for input **data,** and program outputs are expressed as logical or mathematical expressions involving these symbols.

syntax. (1) The relationship among characters or groups of characters, independent of their meanings or the manner of their interpretation and use. (ISO)

(2) The structure of expressions in a language. (ANSI)

(3) The rules governing the structure of a language. (ANSI)
See also **semantics.**

system. (1) A collection of people, machines, and methods organized to accomplish a set of specific **functions.**

(2) An integrated whole that is composed of diverse, interacting, specialized structures and subfunctions.

(3) A group or **subsystem** united by some interaction or interdependence, performing many duties but functioning as a single unit. (ANSI N45.2.10-1973)

system architecture. The structure and relationship among the **components** of a **system.** The system architecture may also include the system's **interface** with its operational environment.

system design. (1) The process of defining the **hardware** and **software** architectures, **components, modules, interfaces,** and **data** for a **system** to satisfy specified system **requirements.**

(2) The result of the system design process.

system documentation. Documentation conveying the **requirements, design** philosophy, design details, capabilities, limitations, and other characteristics of a **system.** Contrast with **user documentation.**

system library. A controlled collection of **system-**resident **software** that can be accessed for use or incorporated into other **programs** by reference, for example, a group of **routines** that a **linkage editor** can incorporate into a program as required. See also **software library.**

system reliability. The probability that a **system,** including all **hardware** and **software subsys-**

tems, will perform a required task or mission for a specified time in a specified environment. See also **operational reliability, software reliability.**

system software. Software designed for a specific **computer system** or family of computer systems to facilitate the operation and **maintenance** of the computer system and associated **programs,** for example, **operating systems, compilers,** utilities. Contrast with **application software.**

system testing. The process of **testing** an integrated **hardware** and **software system** to verify that the system meets its specified **requirements.** See also **acceptance testing, qualification testing.**

system validation. See **validation.**

system verification. See **verification.**

table. (1) An array of **data,** each item of which may be unambiguously identified by means of one or more arguments. (ISO)
　(2) A collection of **data** in which each item is uniquely identified by a **label,** by its position relative to the other items, or by some other means. (ANSI)

target language. A language into which source statements are translated. (ANSI) Contrast with **source language.**

target machine. (1) The **computer** on which a **program** is intended to operate.
　(2) The **computer** being emulated by another computer.
Contrast with **host machine.**

termination proof. In **proof of correctness,** the demonstration that a **program** will terminate under all specified input conditions.

test bed. (1) A test environment containing the **hardware, instrumentation tools, simulators,** and other support **software** necessary for **testing** a **system** or system **component.**
　(2) The repertoire of **test cases** necessary for **testing** a **system** or system **component.**

test case. A specific set of **test data** and associated **procedures** developed for a particular objective,

such as to exercise a particular **program** path or to verify compliance with a specific **requirement.** See also **testing.**

test case generator. See **automated test generator.**

test data. Data developed to test a **system** or system **component.** See also **test case.**

test data generator. See **automated test generator.**

test driver. A **driver** that invokes the item under test and that may provide test inputs and report test results.

test log. A chronological record of all relevant details of a **testing** activity.

test phase. The period of time in the **software life cycle** during which the **components** of a **software product** are evaluated and integrated, and the software product is evaluated to determine whether or not **requirements** have been satisfied.

test plan. A **document** prescribing the approach to be taken for intended **testing** activities. The plan typically identifies the items to be tested, the testing to be performed, test schedules, personnel requirements, reporting requirements, evaluation criteria, and any risks requiring contingency planning.

test procedure. Detailed instructions for the set-up, operation, and evaluation of results for a given test. A set of associated **procedures** is often combined to form a test procedures **document.**

test repeatability. An attribute of a test indicating whether the same results are produced each time the test is conducted.

test report. A **document** describing the conduct and results of the **testing** carried out for a **system** or system **component.**

test validity. The degree to which a test accomplishes its specified goal.

testability. (1) The extent to which **software** facilitates both the establishment of test criteria and the evaluation of the software with respect to those criteria.

(2) The extent to which the definition of **requirements** facilitates analysis of the requirements to establish test criteria.

testing. The process of exercising or evaluating a **system** or system **component** by manual or automated means to verify that it satisfies specified **requirements** or to identify differences between expected and actual results. Compare with **debugging.**

throughput. A measure of the amount of work performed by a **computer system** over a period of time; for example, number of jobs per day. (ISO)

time sharing. (1) An operating technique of a **computer system** that provides for the interleaving in time of two or more **processes** in one processor. (ISO)

(2) Pertaining to the interleaved use of time on a computing **system** that enables two or more users to execute **computer programs** concurrently. (ANSI)

timing analyzer. A **software tool** that estimates or measures the **execution time** of a **computer program** or portions of a computer program either by summing the execution times of the **instructions** in each path, or by inserting probes at specific points in the **program** and measuring the execution time between probes.

tolerance. The ability of a **system** to provide continuity of operation under various abnormal conditions.

tool. (1) See **software tool.**

(2) A **hardware** device used to analyze **software** or its **performance.**

top-down. Pertaining to an approach that starts with the highest level **component** of a **hierarchy** and proceeds through progressively lower **levels**; for example, **top-down design,** top-down programming, **top-down testing.** Contrast with **bottom-up.**

top-down design. The process of designing a **system** by identifying its major **components,** decomposing them into their lower **level** components, and iterating until the desired level of detail is achieved. Contrast with **bottom-up design.**

top-down testing. The process of checking out hierarchically organized **programs,** progressively, from top to bottom, using **simulation** of lower level **components.**

total correctness. In **proof of correctness,** a designation indicating that a **program's output assertions** follow logically from its **input assertions** and processing steps, and that, in addition, the program terminates under all specified input conditions. Contrast with **partial correctness.**

trace. (1) A record of the **execution** of a **computer program**; it exhibits the sequences in which the **instructions** were executed. (ANSI)

(2) A record of all or certain classes of **instructions** or **program** events occurring during **execution** of a **computer program.**

(3) To produce a **trace.**

tracer. A **software tool** used to **trace.**

translator. A **program** that transforms a sequence of statements in one language into an equivalent sequence of statements in another language. See also **assembler, compiler, interpreter.**

tree. An abstract **hierarchical** structure consisting of **nodes** connected by branches, in which: (a) each branch connects one node to a directly subsidiary node, and (b) there is a unique node called the root that is not subsidiary to any other node, and (c) every node besides the root is directly subsidiary to exactly one other node.

type. See **data type.**

user documentation. Documentation conveying to the end user of a **system** instructions for using the system to obtain desired results; for example, a user's manual. Contrast with **system documentation.**

utility software. Computer programs or routines designed to perform some general support **function** required by other **application soft-**

ware, by the **operating system,** or by **system** users.

validation. The process of evaluating **software** at the end of the **software development process** to ensure compliance with software **requirements.** See also **verification.**

variable. (1) A quantity that can assume any of a given set of values. (ISO)

(2) In programming, a character or group of characters that refers to a value and, in the **execution** of a **computer program,** corresponds to an **address.** (ANSI)

verification. (1) The process of determining whether or not the products of a given phase of the **software development cycle** fulfill the **requirements** established during the previous phase. See also **validation.**

(2) Formal proof of **program** correctness. See **proof of correctness.**

(3) The act of reviewing, inspecting, **testing,** checking, auditing, or otherwise establishing and documenting whether or not items, **processes,** services, or **documents** conform to specified **requirements.** (ANSI/ASQC A3-1978).

verification system. See **automated verification system.**

virtual machine. A functional **simulation** of a **computer** and its associated devices.

virtual memory. See **virtual storage.**

virtual storage. The storage space that may be regarded as addressable main storage by the user of a **computer system** in which virtual **addresses** are mapped into real addresses. The size of virtual storage is limited by the addressing scheme of the computer system and by the amount of auxiliary storage available and not by the actual number of main storage locations. (ISO)

walk-through. A review process in which a designer or programmer leads one or more other members of the development team through a **segment** of **design** or **code** that he or she has written, while the other members ask questions and make comments about technique, style, possible **errors,** violation of development standards, and other problems. Contrast with **inspection.**

word. (1) An ordered set of **bits** or characters that is the normal unit in which information may be stored, transmitted, or operated upon within a given **computer.**

(2) A character **string** or **bit** string considered as an entity. (ANSI)

5. Software Life Cycle

The software life cycle consists of a set of discrete activities occurring in a given order during the development and use of software and software systems. The time periods during which these activities occur are referred to as phases. At the current time a consensus has not developed as to which phases comprise the software life cycle. The following diagram (Figure 1) provides an example illustration of the relationship among the life cycle phases. Each of the phases shown in the figure is defined in the glossary.

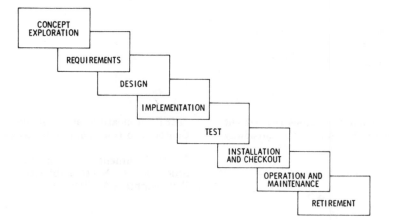

Figure 1. An Example Software Life Cycle

Appendix 1

Reference Identification

(This Appendix is not part of IEEE Std 729-1982, IEEE Standard Glossary of Software Engineering Terminology).

The following provides complete identification of the short references provided after specific terms.

(1) ANSI/ASQC A3-1978 Quality Systems Terminology.[1]

(2) ANSI N45.2.10-1973, Quality Assurance Terms and Definitions.

(3) ANSI/IEEE Std 488-1978, IEEE Standard Digital Interface for Programmable Instrumentation.[2]

(4) ANSI/IEEE Standard 730-1981, IEEE Standard for Software Quality Assurance Plans.

(5) DoD-STD 480A, Configuration Control -Engineering Changes, Deviation and Waivers.[3]

(6) Title 10, Code of Federal Regulations, Chapter 50.

---

[1] ANSI publications are available from Sales Department, Amercian National Standard Institute, 1430 Broadway, New York, NY 10018.

[2] IEEE publications are available from the IEEE Service Center, 445 Hoes Lane, Piscataway, NJ 08854.

[3] DoD documents are available from the DoD Single Stock Point, Naval Publications and Forms Center, Philadelphia, PA 19120.

ANSI/IEEE
Std 730-1984
(Revision of ANSI/IEEE
Std 730-1981)

An American National Standard

IEEE Standard for
Software Quality Assurance Plans

730

Sponsor

**Software Engineering Technical Committee
of the
IEEE Computer Society**

Approved June 14, 1984

IEEE Standards Board

Approved December 17, 1984

American National Standards Institute

Foreword

(This Foreword is not a part of IEEE Std 730-1984, IEEE Standard for Software Quality Assurance Plans.)

This standard assists in the preparation and content of Software Quality Assurance Plans and provides a standard against which such plans can be prepared and assessed. It is directed toward the development and maintenance of critical software, that is, where failure could impact safety or cause large financial or social losses.

There are three groups to whom this standard applies: the user, the developer, and the public.

(1) The user, who may be another element of the same organization developing the software, has a need for the product. Further, the user needs the product to meet the requirements identified in the specification. The user thus cannot afford a "hands-off" attitude toward the developer and rely solely on a test to be executed at the end of the software development time period. If the product should fail, not only does the same need still exist but also a portion of the development time has been lost. The user therefore needs to obtain a reasonable degree of confidence that the product is in the process of acquiring required attributes during software development.

(2) The developer needs an established standard against which to plan and to be measured. It is unreasonable to expect a complete reorientation from project to project. Not only is it not cost-effective, but unless there exists a stable framework on which to base changes, improvements cannot be made.

(3) The public may be affected by the users' use of the product. These users include, for example, depositors at a bank and passengers using a reservation system. Users have requirements, such as legal rights, which preclude haphazard development of software. At some later date, the user and the developer may be required to show that they acted in a reasonable and prudent professional manner to ensure that required software attributes were acquired.

This standard was prepared by the Software Engineering Standards Subcommittee of the Software Engineering Technical Committee of the IEEE Computer Society and initially approved for "trial-use" by the IEEE Standards Board in December 1979. The subsequent revision was approved by the IEEE Standards Board in September of 1981 as a "full-use" standard. At the time that it approved this revision, the subcommittee had the following membership:

F. J. Buckley, *Chairperson*

R. J. Abbott	J. T. Deignan	S. A. Gloss-Soler	R. A. C. Lane
W. R. Adrion	F. A. Denbrock	A. L. Goel	G. N. Larson
T. Armbruster	P. A. Denny	R. W. Graves	R. C. Lewis
R. L. Aurbach	M. J. Devlin	J. J. Greene	F. C. Lim
W. F. Bangs	J. V. Dinkey	K. Greene	A. J. Lindabury
V. R. Basili	F. M. Discenzo	J. Greenhill	G. S. Lindsay
R. W. Bass	A. Dniestrowski	J. W. Grigsby	M. Lipow
M. Ben-Menachem	D. C. Coty	H. M. Grove	J. Long
L. Beltrachi	W. DuBlancia	D. A. Gustafson	A. C. Ma
M. A. Branstad	R. H. Dunn	R. T. Gustin	A. J. Maher
W. C. Brantly	R. E. Dwyer	V. E. Haas	A. K. Mahindru
W. L. Bryan	M. L. Eads	T. Hannan	H. Malec
D. W. Burt	J. D. Earls	D. A. Heath	W. A. Mandeville
H. C. Carney	L. G. Egan, Jr	J. J. Herbert	B. Manny
C. L. Carpenter	D. Eller	G. H. Heblinger	P. C. Marcondes
J. Center	W. J. Ellis	L. S. Heselton	P. C. Marriott
R. L. Chilausky	B. W. Englar	G. Hokel	R. J. Martin
W. L. Chung	R. J. Felker	C. J. Hornback	R. F. Martini
M. A. Cohn	K. F. Fisher	S. Horvitz	C. F. Martiny
C. M. Cooke	J. J. Forman	H. B. Boyle	J. A. McCall
G. G. Cooke	J. Forster	P. Hung	M. P. McDonald
J. D. Cooper	S. J. Foster	M. Jennings	J. McKissick, Jr
A. J. Cote	C. R. Fredrick	L. M. Johmann	D. C. McMann
J. W. Cowan	M. Frimer	L. V. Kaleda	B. Menkus
S. G. Crawford	L. Gagner	R. Kessler	D. F. Meronek
J. W. Currier	M. Galinier	J. J. Klock	E. F. Miller, Jr
M. A. Daniels	L. B. Gardner	R. W. Kubica	G. S. Morris
G. Darling	D. Gelperin	T. M. Kurihara	G. T. Morun
J. A. Darling	E. W. Gibbs	J. W. Kyle	W. G. Murch
C. Davis	J. L. Gildersleeve	D. V. La Rosa	B. Mutafelelja

J. Nebb	J. A. Ronback	J. E. Skeen, Jr	G. D. Tice, Jr
G. R. Neidhart	S. M. Rowan	R. L. Skelton	T. L. Tillmanns
W. J. Newsom	A. Rudeseal	J. C. Stucki	E. A. Ulbrich, Jr
P. C. Olsen	F. Salvia	M. P. Smith	D. L. Ulery
D. E. Peercy	R. San-Roman	W. Smith	D. Usechak
M. T. Perkins	C. Sanchex III	H. M. Sneed	R. L. Van Tilburg
D. J. Pfeiffer	R. E. Sandborgh	R. L. Spear	U. Voges
R. M. Poston	N. F. Schneidewind	E. A. Straker	A. Weigel
P. B. Powell	H. A. Shock, Jr	W. B. Strigel	M. L. Weisbein
R. P. Pritchett	R. Scholten	D. B. Tabor	B. B. White
S. J. Raddue	R. G. Schuppert	B. J. Taute	W. M. Wong
J. R. Rault	D. J. Schultz	E. F. Testa	W. Woo
L. K. Reed	E. P. Shaughnessy	R. H. Thayer	C. Wortz
D. J. Reifer	C. L. Shermer	J. R. Thompson	V. L. Wright
G. S. Robinson	D. S. Simkins	P. U. Thompson	J. C. Zolnowski

Special representatives to the Software Engineering Standards Subcommittee were as follows:

H. R. Berlack: Electronic Industry Association
N. C. Farr: Nuclear Power Engineering Committee,
  IEEE Power Engineering Society
A. Ferlan: American Society for Quality Control
S. R. Jarocki: EDP Auditors Association
J. Milandin: ANSI Z1
W. E. Perry: Data Processing Manufacturers Association
T. L. Regulinski: IEEE Reliability Society

The working group had the following members:

F. J. Buckley, *Chairperson*
R. J. Felker, *Co-Chairperson*

M. J. Berg	R. L. Evans	R. M. Poston
D. Boehm	C. Fan	H. Reeves
R. H. Brickley	N. Farr	B. J. Taute
R. L. Chilausky	E. L. Gibbs	E. F. Testa
G. G. Cooke	J. Gilbert	J. Thomas
S. G. Crawford	C. P. Hollocker	N. Thomas
J. T. Deignan	R. A. Kessler	D. Usechak
R. Dumas	J. J. Klock	N. P. Wilburn
J. Edwards	G. Pedrocchi	M. J. Wise
R. F. Ely, Jr	R. E. Pingleton	J. C. Zolnowski

Comments on this standard are welcomed and should be addressed to:
Secretary
IEEE Standards Board
345 East 47th Street
New York, NY 10017

At the time this standard was approved on June 14, 1984, the IEEE Standards Board had the following membership:

Contents

IEEE Standard for
Software Quality Assurance Plans

1. Scope

The purpose of this standard is to provide uniform, minimum acceptable requirements for preparation and content of Software Quality Assurance Plans (SQAP).

In considering adoption of this standard, regulatory bodies should be aware that specific application of this standard may already be covered by one or more IEEE or ANSI standards documents relating to quality assurance, definitions, or other matters. It is not the purpose of IEEE Std 730 to supersede, revise or amend existing standards directed to specific industries or applications.

This standard applies to the development and maintenance of critical software; for example, where failure could impact safety or cause large financial or social losses. For non-critical software, or for software already developed, a subset of the requirements of this standard may be applied.

The existence of this standard should not be construed to prohibit additional content in a Software Quality Assurance Plan. An assessment should be made for the specific software product item to assure adequacy of coverage. Where this standard is invoked for a project engaged in producing several software items, the applicability of the standard should be specified for each of the software product items encompassed by the project.

2. Definition and Acronyms

2.1 Definition.
The definition listed below establishes meaning in the context of this standard. Other definitions can be found in ANSI/ IEEE Std 729-1983, IEEE Standard Glossary of Software Engineering Terminology, or latest revision thereof. For the purpose of this standard, the term *Software* includes documentation and data, and execution control statements (e.g., command files, Job Control Language, etc.).

quality assurance. A planned and systematic pattern of all actions necessary to provide adequate confidence that the item or product conforms to established technical requirements.

2.2 Acronyms.
The following alphabetical contractions appear within the text of this standard:

CDR   critical design review
PDR   preliminary design review
SDD   software design description
SQA   software quality assurance
SQAP software quality assurance plan
SRR   software requirements review
SRS   software requirements specification
SVVP software verification and validation plan
SVVR software verification and validation report

3. Software Quality Assurance Plan

The organization responsible for Software Quality Assurance shall prepare a Software Quality Assurance Plan (also referred to as the Plan) that includes the sections listed below. The sections should be ordered in the described sequence. If there is no information pertinent to a section, the following shall appear below the section heading, *This section is not applicable to this plan*, together with the appropriate reasons for the exclusion.

(1) Purpose
(2) Reference Documents
(3) Management
(4) Documentation
(5) Standards, Practices, and Conventions
(6) Reviews and Audits
(7) Software Configuration Management
(8) Problem Reporting and Corrective Action
(9) Tools, Techniques, and Methodologies
(10) Code Control
(11) Media Control
(12) Supplier Control
(13) Records Collection, Maintenance, and Retention

Additional sections may be added at the end, as required. Some of the material may appear in other documents. If so, then reference to those documents should be made in the body of the plan.

This plan shall be authenticated by the chief operating officer of each unit of the organization having responsibilities defined within this plan.

Details for each outline paragraph are described in 3.1 through 3.13 of this standard.

3.1 Purpose (Section 1 of the Plan). This section shall delineate the specific purpose and scope of the particular Software Quality Assurance Plan (SQAP). It shall list the name(s) of the software product items covered by the SQAP and the intended use of the software.

3.2 Reference Documents (Section 2 of the Plan). This section shall provide a complete list of documents referenced elsewhere in the text of the plan.

3.3 Management (Section 3 of the Plan). This section shall describe the organization, tasks, and responsibilities.

3.3.1 Organization. This paragraph shall depict the organizational structure that influences the quality of the software. This shall include a description of each major element of the organization together with the delegated responsibilities. Organizational dependence or independence of the elements responsible for SQA from those responsible for software development and use shall be clearly described or depicted.

3.3.2 Tasks. This paragraph shall describe the tasks associated with that portion of the software life cycle covered by this plan with special emphasis on software quality assurance activities. The sequence of the tasks shall be indicated.

3.3.3 Responsibilities. This paragraph shall identify the specific organizational elements responsible for each task.

3.4 Documentation (Section 4 of the Plan).
3.4.1 Purpose. This section shall:
(1) Identify the documentation governing the development, verification and validation, use, and maintenance of the software.

(2) State how the documents are to be checked for adequacy. The statement shall include identification of the review or audit by which the adequacy of each document shall be confirmed, with reference to Section 6 of the Plan.

3.4.2 Minimum Documentation Requirements. To ensure that the implementation of the software satisfies the requirements, the following documentation is required as a minimum:

3.4.2.1 *Software Requirements Specification* (SRS). The SRS shall clearly and precisely describe each of the essential requirements (functions, performances, design constraints, and attributes) of the software and the external interfaces. Each requirement shall be defined such that its achievement is capable of being objectively verified and validated by a prescribed method, for example, inspection, analysis, demonstration, or test.

3.4.2.2 *Software Design Description* (SDD). The SDD shall describe the major components of the software design including data bases and internal interfaces. An expansion of this description shall be included to describe each subcomponent of the major components.

3.4.2.3 *Software Verification and Validation Plan* (SVVP). The SVVP shall describe the methods (for example, inspection, analysis, demonstration, or test) to be used:
(1) To verify that:
(a) The requirements in the SRS are implemented in the design expressed in the SDD.
(b) The design expressed in the SDD is implemented in the code.

(2) To validate that the code, when executed, complies with the requirements expressed in the SRS.

3.4.2.4 *Software Verification and Validation Report* (SVVR). The SVVR shall describe the results of the execution of the SVVP. This shall include the results of all reviews, audits, and tests required by the SQA plan.

3.4.2.5 *User Documentation.* The User Documentation (e.g., manual, guide, etc.) shall specify and describe the required data and control inputs, input sequences, options, program limitations and other activities/items necessary for successful execution of the software. All error messages shall be identified and corrective actions described. A method of describing user-identified errors/problems to the developer/owner of the software shall be described. (Embedded software that has no direct user interaction has no need for User Documentation and is therefore exempted from this requirement.)

3.4.3 Other. Other documentation may include the following:

(1) Software Development Plan
(2) Software Configuration Management Plan
(3) Standards and Procedures Manual

3.5 Standards, Practices, and Conventions (Section 5 of the Plan).

3.5.1 Purpose. This section shall:

(1) Identify the standards, practices, and conventions to be applied.

(2) State how compliance with these items is to be monitored and assured.

3.5.2 Content. The subjects covered shall include the basic technical, design, and programming activities involved, such as documentation naming and coding, programming languages, and unit testing. As a minimum the following information shall be provided:

(1) Documentation standards
(2) Logic structure standards
(3) Coding standards
(4) Commentary standards

3.6 Review and Audits (Section 6 of the Plan).

3.6.1 Purpose. This section shall:

(1) Define the technical and managerial reviews and audits to be conducted.

(2) State how the reviews and audits are to be accomplished.

3.6.2 Minimum Requirements. As a minimum, the following reviews shall be conducted:

3.6.2.1 *Software Requirements Review* (SRR). The SRR is held to ensure the adequacy of the requirements stated in the Software Requirements Specification.

3.6.2.2 *Preliminary Design Review* (PDR). The PDR is held to evaluate the technical adequacy of the preliminary design of the software as depicted in a preliminary version of the Software Design Description.

3.6.2.3 *Critical Design Review* (CDR). The CDR is held to determine the acceptability of the detailed software designs as depicted in the Software Design Description in satisfying the requirements of the Software Requirements Specification.

3.6.2.4 *Software Verification and Validation Review.* The Software Verification and Validation Review is held to evaluate the adequacy and completeness of the verification and validation methods defined in the SVVP.

3.6.2.5 *Functional Audit.* This audit is held prior to the software delivery to verify that all requirements specified in the Software Requirements Specifications have been met.

3.6.2.6 *Physical Audit.* This audit is held to verify that the software and its documentation are internally consistent and are ready for delivery.

3.6.2.7 *In-Process Audits.* In-process audits of a sample of the design are held to verify consistency of the design, including:

(1) Code versus design documentation
(2) Interface specifications (hardware and software)
(3) Design implementations versus functional requirements
(4) Functional requirements versus test descriptions

3.6.2.8 *Managerial Reviews.* These reviews are held periodically to assess the execution of this plan. These reviews shall be held by an organizational element independent of the unit being audited, or by a qualified third party.

3.7 Software Configuration Management (Section 7 of the Plan). This section shall document the methods to be used for identifying the soft-

ware product items, controlling and implementing changes, and recording and reporting change implementation status. This documentation shall either be provided explicitly in this section or by reference to an existing software configuration management plan.

3.8 Problem Reporting and Corrective Action (Section 8 of the Plan).
This section shall:

(1) Describe the practices and procedures to be followed for reporting, tracking, and resolving software problems.

(2) State the specific organizational responsibilities concerned with their implementation.

3.9 Tools, Techniques, and Methodologies (Section 9 of the Plan). This section shall identify the special software tools, techniques, and methodologies employed on the specific project that support Quality Assurance, state their purposes, and describe their use.

3.10 Code Control (Section 10 of the Plan). This section shall define the methods and facilities used to maintain and store controlled versions of identified software. This may be implemented in conjunction with a Computer Program Library.

3.11 Media Control (Section 11 of the Plan). This section shall state the methods and facilities to be used to protect computer program physical media from unauthorized access or inadvertent damage or degradation.

3.12 Supplier Control (Section 12 of the Plan). This section shall state the provisions for assuring that vendor-provided and subcontractor-developed software meets established technical requirements. As a minimum the supplier shall be required to prepare and implement a Software Quality Assurance Plan in accordance with this standard.

3.13 Records Collection, Maintenance and Retention (Section 13 of the Plan). This section shall identify the SQA documentation to be retained, shall state the methods and facilities to be used to assemble, safeguard and maintain this documentation and shall designate the retention period.

ANSI/IEEE Std 828-1983

An American National Standard

828

IEEE Standard for
Software Configuration Management Plans

Sponsor

**Software Engineering Technical Committee
of the
IEEE Computer Society**

Approved June 23, 1983

IEEE Standards Board

Approved December 17, 1984

American National Standards Institute

Foreword

(This Foreword is not a part of ANSI/IEEE Std 828-1983, IEEE Standard for Software Configuration Management Plans.)

Software Configuration Management (SCM) is a formal engineering discipline which provides software developers and users with the methods and tools to identify the software developed, establish baselines, control changes to these baselines, record and track status, and audit the product. SCM is the means through which the integrity and continuity of the software product are recorded, communicated, and controlled. The application of SCM, together with Hardware Configuration Management and overall Systems Configuration Management, benefits all phases of the life cycle of a system containing software components and is a matter of good engineering practice. Without SCM, the reliability and the quality of the software cannot be assured.

This standard assists in the preparation of SCM plans for all environments; for example, large-scale ADP systems, embedded computer systems, control processors, etc, and provides a standard against which such plans can be prepared and assessed. It is directed toward the development and maintenance of all software, including critical software, that is, software whose failure could impact safety or cause large financial or social losses.

There are three groups served by this standard: the users, the developers, and the public.

(1) It aids the users in obtaining and supporting a software product consistent with the users' evolving needs. It assists the users in obtaining a reasonable degree of confidence that the product is in the process of acquiring required attributes as the software is being developed and maintained.

(2) It aids the developers by providing an established standard against which a cost-effective solution to SCM needs can be planned and measured throughout the applicable portions of the software life cycle.

(3) It aids the public by enhancing the likelihood that a software product will perform as expected. The public has legal rights which preclude haphazard control of software development and maintenance. At some later date, the users and developers may be required to show that they acted in a reasonable and prudent manner to ensure that adequate controls were applied.

This standard is consistent with ANSI/IEEE Std 730-1981, IEEE Standard for Software Quality Assurance Plans and IEEE Std 729-1983, IEEE Standard Glossary of Software Engineering Terminology. This standard may be applied in conjunction with those standards, or independently.

This standard was prepared by a working group of the Software Engineering Subcommittee of the Technical Committee on Software Engineering of the IEEE Computer Society. The working group had the following members:

R. Frederick, *Chairman*

H. R. Berlack	J. Granton	J. Postak
E. Bersoff	N. Hill	R. M. Poston
F. J. Buckley	J. H. Johnston	P. B. Powell
R. Clingan	C. Kolb	S. Siegel
D. Dorazio	T. M. Kurihara	L. Starbuck
R. Evans	W. A. Mandeville	B. Taute
A. Ets	J. Miguel	A. Terentiev
J. J. Forman	J. Neilson	N. Thomas
J. Fonj	D. Paster	R. L. Van Tilburg
N. P. Ginex	R. Phillips	J. Williamson

At the time the Software Engineering Standards Subcommittee approved the standard, it had the following members:

F. J. Buckley, *Chairman*

R. J. Abbott	R. A. Felker	T. M. Kurihara	L. B. Robertson
A. F. Ackerman	J. W. Fendrich	J. A. Kyle	R. E. Sandborgh
R. L. Aurbach	J. Flourney	D. V. LaRosa	M. J. Schindler
J. P. Bateman	J. J. Forman	R. C. Lane	N. F. Schneidewind
N. G. Biasi	R. Fredrick	G. N. Larson	R. W. Scholten
E. G. Booch	M. Galinier	A. C. Ma	L. W. Seagren
M. A. Branstead	A. Ganz	A. J. Maher	C. L. Shermer
W. A. Bryan	F. K. Gardner	A. K. Mahindru	D. J. Simkins
D. C. Burt	D. Gelperin	W. A. Mandeville	J. E. Skeen, Jr
H. C. Carney	M. J. Gooding	P. C. Marriott	J. M. Smith
M. Carney	S. Gloss-Soler	C. F. Martiny	H. N. Sneed
C. L. Carpenter	R. W. Graves	G. T. Morun	T. Q. Stevenson
J. V. Cellini	B. W. Greene	W. G. Murch	D. B. Tabor
J. W. Center	J. J. Greene	S. Najafi	K. C. Tai
E. R. Comer	J. W. Grigsby	J. Nebb	B. Taute
J. D. Cooper	R. M. Gross	G. R. Neidhart	J. R. Thompson
A. J. Cote, Jr	R. T. Gustin	D. J. Ostrom	P. U. Thompson
R. Cotter	V. E. Haas	D. E. Peercy	G. D. Tice, Jr
J. W. Currier	T. L. Hannan	M. T. Perkins	T. L. Tillmanns
P. W. Daggett	L. R. Hestelton, III	D. J. Pfeiffer	H. J. Trochesset
G. Darling	C. P. Hollocker	R. M. Poston	C. L. Troyanowski
P. A. Denny	S. Horvitz	M. A. Potter	W. S. Turner, III
A. Dniestrowski	H. B. Hoyle	P. B. Powell	E. A. Ulbrich, Jr
J. A. Dobbins	S. Hwang	S. J. Raddue	R. L. Van Tilburg
W. DuBlancia	J. H. Ingram	S. R. Rakitin	A. H. Weigel
R. E. Dwyer	J. M. Ives	J. Rault	P. J. D. Weyman
M. L. Eads	R. M. Jacobs	H. Reiche	W. M. Wong
J. W. Earls	G. Konomos	D. J. Reifer	A. W. Yonda
			P. F. Zoll

Special representatives to the Software Engineering Standards Subcommittee were:

H.R. Berlack	*Electronic Industries Association*
J. Milandin	*ANS Z1*
W. Perry	*Data Processing Management Association*
R. Pritchett	*EDP Auditors Association*
T. L. Regulinski	*IEEE Reliability Society*

At the time the IEEE Standards Board approved this standard on June 23, 1983, it had the following members:

James H. Beall, *Chairman*   **Edward Chelotti,** *Vice Chairman*

Sava I. Sherr, *Secretary*

J. J. Archambault	Donald H. Heirman	John P. Riganati
John T. Boettger	Irvin N. Howell	Frank L. Rose
J. V. Bonucchi	Joseph L. Koepfinger*	Robert W. Seelbach
Rene Castenschiold	Irving Kolodny	Jay A. Stewart
Edward J. Cohen	George Konomos	Clifford O. Swanson
Len S. Corey	John E. May	Robert E. Weiler
Donald C. Fleckenstein	Donald T. Michael*	W. B. Wilkens
Jay Forster		Charles J. Wylie

*Member emeritus

Contents

An American National Standard
IEEE Standard for
Software Configuration Management Plans

Note

In considering adoption of this standard, regulatory bodies should be aware that specific application of this standard may already be covered by one or more IEEE or ANSI standards documents relating to quality assurance, definitions, or other matters. It is not the purpose of IEEE Std 828-1983 to supersede, revise, or amend existing standards directed to specific industries or applications.

1. Scope and References

1.1 Scope. This standard provides minimum requirements for preparation and content of Software Configuration Management (SCM) Plans. SCM Plans document the methods to be used for identifying software product items, controlling and implementing changes, and recording and reporting change implementation status.

This standard applies to the entire life cycle of critical software; for example, where failure could impact safety or cause large financial or social losses. For noncritical software, or for software already developed, a subset of the requirements may be applied.

This standard identifies those essential items that shall appear in all Software Configuration Management Plans. In addition to these items, the users of this standard are encouraged to incorporate additional items into the plan, as appropriate, to satisfy unique configuration management needs, or to modify the contents of specific sections to fully describe the scope and magnitude of the software configuration management effort. Where this standard is invoked for a project engaged in producing several software items, the applicability of the standard shall be specified for each of the software product items encompassed by the project.

Examples are incorporated into the text of this standard to enhance clarity and to promote understanding. Examples are either explicitly identified as such, or can be recognized by the use of the verb *may*. Examples shall not be construed as mandatory implementations.

NOTE: For application to nuclear power generating stations, see IEEE Std 1033-1985, IEEE Recommended Practice for Application of IEEE Std 828 to Nuclear Power Generating Stations [4].[1]

1.2 References. The standards listed here should be considered when applying this standard. The latest revisions shall apply.

[1] ANSI/IEEE Std 730-1981, IEEE Standard for Software Quality Assurance Plans.[2]

[2] IEEE Std 729-1983, IEEE Standard Glossary of Software Engineering Terminology.

[3] IEEE Std 829-1983, IEEE Standard for Software Test Documentation.

[4] IEEE Std 1033-1985, IEEE Recommended Practice for Application of IEEE Standard 828 to Nuclear Power Generating Stations.

2. Definitions and Acronyms

2.1 Definitions. The definition listed here establishes meaning in the context of this standard. Other definitions can be found in IEEE Std 729-1983 [2]. See specifically: **baseline, configuration item, configuration management, configuration control, configuration control board, configuration audit, configuration identification, configuration status accounting,** and **software library.**

interface control. The process of: (1) Identifying all functional and physical characteristics relevant to the interfacing of two or more configuration items provided by one or more organizations. (2) Ensuring that proposed changes to these characteristics are evaluated and approved prior to implementation.

2.2 Acronyms. The following acronyms are referred to within the text of this standard:

CCB   Configuration Control Board
SCM   Software Configuration Management
SCMP   Software Configuration Management Plan

---

[1] The numbers in brackets correspond to references in 1.2.

[2] ANSI standards are available from the Sales Department, American National Standards Institute, 1430 Broadway, New York, NY 10018.

3. Software Configuration Management Plans

The organization or person responsible for Software Configuration Management shall prepare a Software Configuration Management Plan (hereafter referred to as the Plan) that includes the sections and subsections listed below. The sections and subsections shall be ordered in the described sequence (if there is no information pertinent to a section or subsection, the following information shall appear below the section or subsection heading: **There is no pertinent information for this section** together with the appropriate reasons for the exclusion).

(1) Introduction
    (a) Purpose
    (b) Scope
    (c) Definitions and acronyms
    (d) References
(2) Management
    (a) Organization
    (b) SCM responsibilities
    (c) Interface control
    (d) SCMP implementation
    (e) Applicable policies, directives and procedures
(3) SCM activities
    (a) Configuration identification
    (b) Configuration control
    (c) Configuration status accounting
    (d) Audits and reviews
(4) Tools, techniques, and methodologies
(5) Supplier control
(6) Records collection and retention

Additional sections may be added at the end, as required. Some of the material may appear in other documents. If so, reference to those documents shall be made in the body of the plan.

The cover page of the plan shall identify the plan and the project to which the plan pertains. As a minimum, the plan shall be signed by the chief operating-officer of each unit having responsibilities defined within the SCMP.

Detailed requirements for each portion of the Plan are described in 3.1 through 3.6 of this standard.

3.1 Introduction (Section 1 of the Plan). This section shall provide an overview of the plan.

3.1.1 Purpose (1.1 of the Plan). This subsection shall delineate the specific purpose of the particular Software Configuration Management Plan.

3.1.2 Scope (1.2 of the Plan). This subsection shall identify the software items to be produced and used, the organizations, the activities, and the phases of the software life cycle to which the plan applies.

3.1.3 Definitions and Acronyms (1.3 of the Plan). This subsection shall define or provide a reference to the definitions of all terms and acronyms required to properly interpret the SCMP.

3.1.4 References (1.4 of the Plan). This subsection shall:

(1) Provide a complete list of all documents referenced elsewhere in the SCMP.

(2) Identify each document by title, report number, if applicable, date, and publishing organization.

(3) Specify the sources from which the referenced documents can be obtained.

3.2 Management (Section 2 of the Plan). This section shall describe the organization, and associated responsibilities.

3.2.1 Organization (2.1 of the Plan). This subsection shall describe the organizational structure that influences the configuration management of the software during the development and the operation and maintenance phases. This shall:

(1) Describe each major element of the organization together with the delegated responsibilities. Organizational dependence or independence of the elements responsible for SCM from those responsible for software development and use shall be clearly described or depicted.

(2) Include an organizational chart or list for the project which illustrates the structure for program/project/system management.

(3) Describe the organization responsible for SCM during the operation and maintenance phase.

(4) Describe the interface between the developing organization and the using organization, if any, with particular emphasis on the transfer of SCM functions in the operation and maintenance phase.

(5) Specifically cover the organizational relationships with the Configuration Control Board

in the development and the operation, and maintenance phases.

3.2.2 SCM Responsibilities (2.2 of the Plan). This subsection shall describe:

(1) The organizational responsibilities for each SCM task; for example, identification, control, status accounting, and reviews and audits.

(2) The relationships with software quality-assurance, software development, and other functional organizations required to ensure delivery of the approved final product configuration.

(3) The responsibilities of the users and developer/maintenance activity in the review, audit, and approval process during each phase of the life cycle indicated in 1.2 of the Plan.

(4) Any SCM responsibilities of the representatives from each organization participating in the product development.

(5) The overall responsibility of the Configuration Control Board.

(6) Any unusual responsibilities such as special approval requirements necessary to meet SCM requirements.

3.2.3 Interface Control (2.3 of the Plan). This subsection shall describe the methods to be utilized to:

(1) Identify interface specifications and control documents.

(2) Process changes to released interface specifications and documents.

(3) Provide follow-up on action items scheduled to be accomplished on items pertaining to SCM.

(4) Maintain status of interface specifications and control documents.

(5) Control the interface between software and the hardware on which it is running.

3.2.4 SCMP Implementation (2.4 of the Plan). This subsection shall establish the major milestones for implementation of the SCMP.

Example milestones include the establishment of:

(1) The configuration control board

(2) Each configuration baseline

(3) Schedules and procedures for SCM reviews and audits

(4) Configuration management of related software development, test, and support tools

3.2.5 Applicable Policies, Directives, and Procedures (2.5 of the Plan). This subsection shall:

(1) Identify all applicable SCM policies, directives, and procedures which are to be implemented as part of this plan. The degree of implementation of each shall be stated

(2) Describe any SCM policies, directives, and procedures that are to be written and implemented for this project

Examples of material which may be covered by policies, directives, and procedures are:

(a) Identification of levels of software in a hierarchical tree

(b) Program and module naming conventions

(c) Version level designations

(d) Software product identification methods

(e) Identification of specifications, test plans and procedures, programming manuals, and other documents

(f) Media identification and file management identification

(g) Document release process

(h) Turnover or release of software products to a library function

(i) Processing of problem reports, change requests, and change orders

(j) Structure and operation of configuration control boards

(k) Release, and acceptance of software products

(l) Operation of software library systems to include methods of preparing, storing, and updating modules

(m) Auditing of SCM activities

(n) Problem report, change request or change order documentation requirements describing purpose and impact of a configuration change, or both

(o) Level of testing required prior to entry of software into configuration management

(p) Level of quality assurance; for example, verification against development standards, required prior to entry of software into configuration management

3.3 SCM Activities (Section 3 of the Plan). This section shall describe how the following requirements for SCM shall be satisfied:

(1) Configuration identification

(2) Configuration control

(3) Configuration status accounting and reporting

(4) Configuration audits and reviews

3.3.1 Configuration Identification (3.1 of the Plan). This subsection shall:

3.3.1.1 Identify the software project baselines (that is, the initial approved configuration identifications) and correlate them to the specific life-cycle phases defined in 1.2 of the Plan. For each baseline, the following shall be described:

3.3.1.1.1 The items which form each baseline (for example, software requirements specification, deliverable software, etc).

3.3.1.1.2 The review and approval events, and the acceptance criteria associated with establishing each baseline.

3.3.1.1.3 The users' and developers' participation in establishing baselines.

The following are example baselines which may be established as indicated:

(1) *Functional Baseline.* The agreement between the developers and the users that defines all the system level functions and the system test criteria.

(2) *Allocated Baseline.* The agreement between the developers and the users that identifies all the software requirements to include design constraints and user-required standards.

(3) *Product Baseline.* The agreement between the developer and the user that defines the exact version of the software product which is to be accepted. Elements of this baseline definition might include the following:

(a) Product name and nomenclature

(b) Product identification number

(c) For each new version release, the version release number, a description of the new changes, the change release vehicle, the changes to any support software, and the changes to the associated documentation

(d) Installation instructions

(e) Known faults and failures

(f) Software media and media identification

3.3.1.2 Delineate the project titling, labeling, numbering, and cataloging procedures for all software code and documentation.

As an example, for code:

3.3.1.2.1 The compilation date may be indicated as a part of the identification for each delivered module.

3.3.1.2.2 The sequence numbering of all source lines of code in a module may be structured so that future changes to any module can be properly noted.

3.3.2 Configuration Control (3.2 of the Plan). This subsection shall:

3.3.2.1 Describe the level of authority for change approval to be used in each of the life cycle phases identified in 1.2 of the Plan.

3.3.2.2 Define the methods to be used to process change proposals to established configurations. As a part of this, this section shall:

(1) Identify the routing of change proposals during each of the software life cycle phases identified in 1.2 of the Plan. This may be provided in chart form with narrative support.

(2) Describe the methods of implementing approved change proposals (to include changes in source and object code, and documentation).

(3) Describe the procedures for software library control including those procedures which provide for:

(a) Access control

(b) Read and write protection for applicable baselines

(c) Member protection

(d) Member identification

(e) Archive maintenance

(f) Change history

(g) Disaster recovery

(4) If patches must be used to change object code, describe the methods for identification and control

3.3.2.3 For each CCB and other change management bodies:

(1) Define the role of each; for example, change review authority

(2) Specify their authority and responsibility

(3) Identify the chairperson and the membership in the organizations, if the organizations have been formed

(4) State how the chairperson and the members (and alternates) are to be appointed, if the organizations have not yet been formed

(5) State the relationships of the developers and the users to the CCB(s)

3.3.2.4 State the methods to be used for configuration control of interfaces with programs/projects beyond the scope of this SCMP. If the software changes are required to be reviewed by other boards or teams prior to or in addition to the CCB(s), this subsection shall describe these boards (or teams, or both) and their relationship to the CCB(s) and to each other.

3.3.2.5 State the control procedures for associated special software products, such as nonreleased software, off-the-shelf software, user-furnished software, and in-house support software.

3.3.3 Configuration Status Accounting (3.3 of the Plan). This subsection shall:

(1) Delineate how information on the status of configuration items is to be collected, verified, stored, processed, and reported

(2) Identify the periodic reports to be provided, and their distribution

(3) State what dynamic inquiry capabilities, if any, are to be provided

(4) Describe the means to be used to implement any special status accounting requirements specified by the user

Some examples of information normally desired is as follows:

(a) Status of specifications

(b) Status of proposed changes

(c) Reports of approved changes

(d) Status of product versions or revisions

(e) Reports of the implementation of installed updates or releases

(f) Status of user-furnished property; for example, user-furnished operating systems

3.3.4 Audits and Reviews (3.4 of the Plan). This subsection shall:

(1) Define the SCM role in audits and reviews to be performed at specified points in the software life cycle defined in 1.2 of the SCMP

(2) Identify the configuration items to be covered at each of these audits and reviews

(3) State the procedures to be used for the identification and resolution of problems occurring during these audits and reviews

3.4 Tools, Techniques, and Methodologies (Section 4 of the Plan). This section shall identify, state the purposes, and describe (within the developers' scope of proprietary rights) the use of the specific software tools, techniques, and methodologies to be employed to support SCM on the specific project. This shall include the tools, techniques, and methodologies used to:

(1) Identify software media and media documentation

(2) Bring documentation and media under SCM control and formally release it to a user

As examples, it may:

(a) Provide a description of the tools, methodologies, and techniques to be used for source and object control within the software libraries, to include a description of the Database Management System, if used

(b) State how the software library tools, methodologies, and techniques are to be used to process software products for release

(3) Document the status of changes made to software and associated documentation. It shall further define the tools, methodologies, and techniques to be used to prepare reports for various levels of management, such as the project manager, CCB, SCM, and the user.

3.5 Supplier Control (Section 5 of the Plan). This section shall state the provisions for assuring that vendor-provided and subcontractor-developed software meet established SCM requirements. As a part of this, this section shall:

(1) Indicate the proposed methods for control of subcontractors and vendors insofar as it impacts on the execution of this SCMP

(2) Explain the methods to be used:

(a) To determine the SCM capability of subcontractors and vendors

(b) To monitor their adherence to the requirements of this SCMP

As a minimum, the supplier shall be required to prepare and implement a SCM plan in accordance with this standard.

3.6 Records Collection and Retention (Section 6 of the Plan). This section shall:

(1) Identify the SCM documentation to be retained

(2) State the methods and facilities to be used to assemble, safeguard, and maintain this documentation. As part of this, identify any off-site backup facilities to be used

(3) Designate the retention period

An American National Standard

IEEE Standard for
Software Test Documentation

829

Sponsor

**Software Engineering Technical Committee
of the
IEEE Computer Society**

Approved December 3, 1982

IEEE Standards Board

Approved August 19, 1983

American National Standards Institute

Foreword

(This Foreword is not a part of ANSI/IEEE Std 829-1983, IEEE Standard for Software Test Documentation.)

Purpose

The purpose of this standard is to describe a set of basic software test documents. A standardized test document can facilitate communication by providing a common *frame of reference* (for example, a customer and a supplier have the same definition for a test plan). The content definition of a standardized test document can serve as a completeness checklist for the associated testing process. A standardized set can also provide a baseline for the evaluation of current test documentation practices. In many organizations, the use of these documents significantly increases the manageability of testing. Increased manageability results from the greatly increased visibility of each phase of the testing process.

This standard specifies the form and content of individual test documents. It does not specify the required set of test documents. It is assumed that the required set of test documents will be specified when the standard is applied. Appendix B contains an example of such a set specification.

Overview

The documents outlined in this standard cover test planning, test specification, and test reporting.

The test plan prescribes the scope, approach, resources, and schedule of the testing activities. It identifies the items to be tested, the features to be tested, the testing tasks to be performed, the personnel responsible for each task, and the risks associated with the plan.

Test specification is covered by three document types:

(1) A test-design specification refines the test approach and identifies the features to be covered by the design and its associated tests. It also identifies the test cases and test procedures, if any, required to accomplish the testing and specifies the feature pass/fail criteria.

(2) A test-case specification documents the actual values used for input along with the anticipated outputs. A test case also identifies any constraints on the test procedures resulting from use of that specific test case. Test cases are separated from test designs to allow for use in more than one design and to allow for reuse in other situations.

(3) A test procedure specification identifies all steps required to operate the system and exercise the specified test cases in order to implement the associated test design. Test procedures are separated from test-design specifications as they are intended to be followed step by step and should not have extraneous detail.

Test reporting is covered by four document types:

(1) A test item transmittal report identifies the test items being transmitted for testing in the event that separate development and test groups are involved or in the event that a formal beginning of test execution is desired.

(2) A test log is used by the test team to record what occurred during test execution.

(3) A test incident report describes any event that occurs during the test execution which requires further investigation.

(4) A test summary report summarizes the testing activities associated with one or more test-design specifications.

Figure 1 shows the relationships of these documents to one another as they are developed and to the testing process they document.

Terminology

The words *shall*, *must*, and the imperative form identify the mandatory material within this standard. The words *should* and *may* identify optional material.

Appendixes

The examples found in Appendix A are meant to clarify the intent of the document descriptions found in the standard. Some suggestions about implementing and using the standard are in Appendix B. Appendix C contains references to related test documentation standards. Appendix D contains references to testing-related documents of general interest which are not focused on test documentation.

Fig 1
Relationship of Test Documents to Testing Process

Audience

The standard should be of interest to software users and software procurement personnel; to development, test, and maintenance personnel; to operations and acquisition support managers; to software quality assurance personnel and auditors; and to participants in the legal system.

History

The development of this standard began from discussions within the Software Engineering Standards Subcommittee in 1977. Some initial work was done by a group including Joan Bateman, Leonard Birns, Herb Hecht, and Bob Poston and resulted in an early draft outline. The project authorization request for this effort was approved by the IEEE Standards Board in May, 1980. Following authorization, a series of ten meetings which were held across the country from September, 1980 to May, 1982 produced the first draft submitted for balloting.

Suggestions for improvement of the standard will be welcome. They should be sent to:
Secretary
IEEE Standards Board
Institute of Electrical and Electronics Engineers
345 East 47th Street
New York, NY 10017.

At the time this standard was approved on December 3, 1982, the IEEE Standards Board had the following membership:

Irvin N. Howell, *Chairman*   **Edward Chelotti,** *Vice Chairman*

Sava I. Sherr, *Secretary*

G. Y. R. Allen	D. C. Fleckenstein	A. R. Parsons
J. J. Archambault	Jay Forster	J. P. Riganati
James H. Beall	Kurt Greene	Frank L. Rose
John T. Boettger	Joseph L. Koepfinger	Robert W. Seelbach
J. V. Bonucchi	Irving Kolodny	Jay A. Stewart
Edward J. Cohen	John E. May	Clifford O. Swanson
Len S. Corey	Donald T. Michael*	Robert E. Weiler

*Member emeritus

This standard was completed by a working group with the following members:

David Gelperin, *Chairman*

Rick Adrion	Tom Gilb	Art Pollari
Jules Aronson	Loretta Guarino	Robert Poston
Joan Bateman	John Hawthorne	Sam Redwine
Charlie Bates	Herb Hecht	Charles Schult
A. Birnbaum	Mike Hennell	David Schultz
Leonard Birns	Dan Hocking	Dennis Sharp
John Bowen	Mark Holthouse	Jerry Smith
Martha Branstad	Ray Houghton	Wayne Smith
Fletcher Buckley	Paul Howley	Joan Spalding
Douglas Burt	John Kalasky	Bob Stewart
Ian Burton	Jason Kazarian	S. L. Stewart
John Cain	Ed Kit	Sarah Swales
John Center	Denise Krauss	Barbara Taute
George Chapman	Joseph Krupinski	J. R. Taylor
Santosh Chokhani	Tom Kurihara	Rudolf Van Megen
Bruce Clay	Costa J. Labovites	David Vatsaas
D. L. Cooper	Paula Levinton	John Walter
Doc Craddock	Leo Lippman	Andrew Weigel
James Cridge	Alex Long	Jonathon Wexler
Patricia Daggett	Mable Love	Paul White
Bill Dupras	Ben Manny	Bruce Wilkins
Mary Eads	Albrecht Newmann	Harry Wilkinson
Sharon Freid	Bill Newsom	F. T. Woodall
Tom Frost	C. Donald Ostler	Fred Yonda
	Varsha Pai	

The standard was approved by the Software Engineering Standards Subcommittee of the IEEE Computer Society. At the time it approved this standard, the subcommittee had the following membership:

Fletcher J. Buckley, *Chairman*

Russell J. Abbott
A. Frank Ackerman
Leo Beltracchi
Richard L. Bernstein
Nestore G. Biasi
Dennis W. Bragg
Douglas W. Burt
Homer C. Carney
John Center
Won L. Chung
Anonio M. Cicu
Lori A. Clarke
Gilmore G. Cooke
A. J. Cote, Jr
Patricia W. Daggett
George Darling
B. Dasarathy
Noah S. Davids
James A. Dobbins
Mary L. Eads
John D. Earls
Leo G. Egan, Jr
John W. Fendrich
Dennis W. Fife
Joel J. Forman
M. Galinier
Forrest Karl Gardner
David Gelperin
Gary Gladden
Shirley A. Gloss-Soler
John J.Greene
Jack W. Grigsby
Robert M. Gross
David A. Gustafson

Russell T. Gustin
Thomas L. Hannan
Herbert Hecht
Leslie R. Heselton, III
Sam Horvitz
Paul Howley
Shuenn-Chang Hwang
Jim H. Ingram
John P. Kalasky
Laurel V. Kaleda
Thomas M. Kurihara
Domenic V. La-Rosa
Robert A. C. Lane
Gregory N. Larsen
Geoffrey R. Lewis
A. Lip Lim
G. S. Lindsay
Myron Lipow
William M. Lively
Marvin Lubofsky
Don Lundquist
Alan Cheuk-Wai Ma
Andy K. Mahindru
Philip C. Marriott
Mike McCollough
Belden Menkus
Edward F. Miller, Jr
G. Scott Morris
Gene T. Morun
Walter G. Murch
Jack Nebb
Geraldine Rajcula Neidhart
Michael A. Neighbors

Leon Osterweil
Donald J. Ostrom
William E. Perry
Donald J. Pfeiffer
Robert M. Poston
Patricia B. Powell
Farzad Raji
Jean Claude Rault
Samuel T. Redwine
T. L. Regulinski
William E. Riddle
Clarence W. Rutter, III
Norman F. Schneidewind
Antonia D. Schuman
Leonard W. Seagren
Wayne Smith
Harry M. Sneed
Lee Sprague
Edward A. Straker
Kou Chung Tai
Barbara J. Taute
George D. Tice, Jr
Terrence L. Tillmanns
William S. Turner, III
Edwin A. Ulbrich, Jr
Udo Voges
John P. Walter
Andrew H. Weigel
N. P. Wilburn
Martin Wong
David C. Wood
Ted Workman
Alfred W. Yonda
Peter F. Zoll

Special representatives to the Software Engineering Subcommittee were as follows:

William E. Perry, *DPMA*
Roy P. Pritchett, Jr, *EDP Auditors Association*
John Milandin, *ANSI Z1*

Contents

An American National Standard

IEEE Standard for Software Test Documentation

1. Scope

This standard describes a set of basic test documents which are associated with the dynamic aspects of software testing (that is, the execution of procedures and code). The standard defines the purpose, outline, and content of each basic document. While the documents described in the standard focus on dynamic testing, several of them may be applicable to other testing activities (for example, the test plan and test incident report may be used for design and code reviews).

The standard may be applied to commercial, scientific, or military software which runs on any digitial computer. Applicability is not restricted by the size, complexity, or criticality of the software. However, the standard does *not* specify any class of software to which it must be applied. The standard addresses the documentation of both initial development testing and the testing of subsequent software releases. For a particular software release, it may be applied to all phases of testing from module testing through user acceptance. However, since all of the basic test documents may not be useful in each test phase, the particular documents to be used in a phase are *not* specified. Each organization using the standard will need to specify the classes of software to which it applies and the specific documents required for a particular test phase.

The standard does *not* call for specific testing methodologies, approaches, techniques, facilities, or tools, and does *not* specify the documentation of their use. Additional test documentation may be required (for example, code inspection checklists and reports). The standard also does *not* imply or impose specific methodologies for documentation control, configuration management, or quality assurance. Additional documentation (for example, a quality assurance plan) may be needed depending on the particular methodologies used.

Within each standard document, the content of each section (that is, the text which covers the designated topics) may be tailored to the particular application and the particular testing phase. In addition to tailoring content, additional documents may be added to the basic set, additional sections may be added to any document and additional content to any section. It may be useful to organize some of the sections into subsections. Some or all of the contents of a section may be contained in another document which is then referenced. Each organization using the standard should specify additional content requirements and conventions in order to reflect their own particular methodologies, approaches, facilities, and tools for testing, documentation control, configuration management, and quality assurance.

The standard applies to documentation on electronic media as well as paper. Paper must be used for documents requiring approval signatures, unless the electronic documentation system has a secure approval annotation mechanism and that mechanism is used.

2. Definitions

This section contains key terms as they are used in the standard.

design level. The design decomposition of the software item (for example, system, subsystem, program, or module).

pass/fail criteria. Decision rules used to determine whether a software item or a software feature passes or fails a test.

software feature. A distinguishing characteristic of a software item (for example, performance, portability, or functionality).

software item. Source code, object code, job control code, control data, or a collection of these items.

test. (1) A set of one or more test cases, or

(2) A set of one or more test procedures, or
(3) A set of one or more test cases and procedures.

test case specification. A document specifying inputs, predicted results, and a set of execution conditions for a test item.

test design specification. A document specifying the details of the test approach for a software feature or combination of software features and identifying the associated tests.

test incident report. A document reporting on any event that occurs during the testing process which requires investigation.

test item. A software item which is an object of testing.

test item transmittal report. A document identifying test items. It contains current status and location information.

test log. A chronological record of relevant details about the execution of tests.

test plan. A document describing the scope, approach, resources, and schedule of intended testing activities. It identifies test items, the features to be tested, the testing tasks, who will do each task, and any risks requiring contingency planning.

test procedure specification. A document specifying a sequence of actions for the execution of a test.

test summary report. A document summarizing testing activities and results. It also contains an evaluation of the corresponding test items.

testing. The process of analyzing a software item to detect the differences between existing and required conditions (that is, bugs) and to evaluate the features of the software item.

3. Test Plan

3.1 Purpose. To prescribe the scope, approach, resources, and schedule of the testing activities. To identify the items being tested, the features to be tested, the testing tasks to be performed, the personnel responsible for each task, and the risks associated with this plan.

3.2 Outline. A test plan shall have the following structure:

1. Test-plan identifier
2. Introduction
3. Test items
4. Features to be tested
5. Features not to be tested
6. Approach
7. Item pass/fail criteria
8. Suspension criteria and resumption requirements
9. Test deliverables
10. Testing tasks
11. Environmental needs
12. Responsibilities
13. Staffing and training needs
14. Schedule
15. Risks and contingencies
16. Approvals

The sections shall be ordered in the specified sequence. Additional sections may be included immediately prior to *Approvals*. If some or all of the content of a section is in another document, then a reference to that material may be listed in place of the corresponding content. The referenced material must be attached to the test plan or available to users of the plan.

Details on the content of each section are contained in the following sections.

3.2.1 Test-Plan Identifier. Specify the unique identifier assigned to this test plan.

3.2.2 Introduction. Summarize the software items and software features to be tested. The need for each item and its history may be included.

References to the following documents, when they exist, are required in the highest-level test plan:

Project authorization
Project plan
Quality assurance plan
Configuration management plan
Relevant policies
Relevant standards

In multilevel test plans, each lower-level plan must reference the next higher-level plan.

3.2.3 Test Items. Identify the test items including their version/revision level. Also specify characteristics of their transmittal media which impact hardware requirements or indicate the need for logical or physical transformations before testing can begin (for example, programs must be transferred from tape to disk).

Supply references to the following item documentation, if it exists:

Requirements specification
Design specification
Users guide
Operations guide
Installation guide

Reference any incident reports relating to the test items.

Items which are to be specifically excluded from testing may be identified.

3.2.4 Features to be Tested. Identify all software features and combinations of software features to be tested. Identify the test-design specification associated with each feature and each combination of features.

3.2.5 Features Not to be Tested. Identify all features and significant combinations of features which will not be tested and the reasons.

3.2.6 Approach. Describe the overall approach to testing. For each major group of features or feature combinations, specify the approach which will ensure that these feature groups are adequately tested. Specify the major activities, techniques, and tools which are used to test the designated groups of features.

The approach should be described in sufficient detail to permit identification of the major testing tasks and estimation of the time required to do each one.

Specify the minimum degree of comprehensiveness desired. Identify the techniques which will be used to judge the comprehensiveness of the testing effort (for example, determining which statements have been executed at least once). Specify any additional completion criteria (for example, error frequency). The techniques to be used to trace requirements should be specified.

Identify significant constraints on testing such as test-item availability, testing-resource availability, and deadlines.

3.2.7 Item Pass/Fail Criteria. Specify the criteria to be used to determine whether each test item has passed or failed testing.

3.2.8 Suspension Criteria and Resumption Requirements. Specify the criteria used to suspend all or a portion of the testing activity on the test items associated with this plan. Specify the testing activities which must be repeated, when testing is resumed.

3.2.9 Test Deliverables. Identify the deliverable documents. The following documents should be included:

Test plan

Test design specifications
Test case specifications
Test procedure specifications
Test item transmittal reports
Test logs
Test incident reports
Test summary reports

Test input data and test output data should be identified as deliverables.

Test tools (for example, module drivers and stubs) may also be included.

3.2.10 Testing Tasks. Identify the set of tasks necessary to prepare for and perform testing. Identify all intertask dependencies and any special skills required.

3.2.11 Environmental Needs. Specify both the necessary and desired properties of the test environment. This specification should contain: the physical characteristics of the facilities including the hardware, the communications and system software, the mode of usage (for example, stand-alone), and any other software or supplies needed to support the test. Also specify the level of security which must be provided for the test facilities, system software, and proprietary components such as software, data, and hardware.

Identify special test tools needed. Identify any other testing needs (for example, publications or office space). Identify the source for all needs which are not currently available to the test group.

3.2.12 Responsibilities. Identify the groups responsible for managing, designing, preparing, executing, witnessing, checking, and resolving. In addition, identify the groups responsible for providing the test items identified in 3.2.3 and the environmental needs identified in 3.2.11.

These groups may include the developers, testers, operations staff, user representatives, technical support staff, data administration staff, and quality support staff.

3.2.13 Staffing and Training Needs. Specify test staffing needs by skill level. Identify training options for providing necessary skills.

3.2.14 Schedule. Include test milestones identified in the Software Project Schedule as well as all item transmittal events.

Define any additional test milestones needed. Estimate the time required to do each testing task. Specify the schedule for each testing task and test milestone. For each testing resource (that is, facilities, tools, and staff), specify its periods of use.

11

3.2.15 Risks and Contingencies. Identify the high-risk assumptions of the test plan. Specify contingency plans for each (for example, delayed delivery of test items might require increased night shift scheduling to meet the delivery date).

3.2.16 Approvals. Specify the names and titles of all persons who must approve this plan. Provide space for the signatures and dates.

4. Test-Design Specification

4.1 Purpose. To specify refinements of the test approach and to identify the features to be tested by this design and its associated tests.

4.2 Outline. A test-design specification shall have the following structure:

(1) Test-design-specification identifier
(2) Features to be tested
(3) Approach refinements
(4) Test identification
(5) Feature pass/fail criteria

The sections shall be ordered in the specified sequence. Additional sections may be included at the end. If some or all of the content of a section is in another document, then a reference to that material may be listed in place of the corresponding content. The referenced material must be attached to the test-design specification or available to users of the design specification.

Details on the content of each section are contained in the following sections.

4.2.1 Test-Design-Specification Identifier. Specify the unique identifier assigned to this test-design specification. Supply a reference to the associated test plan, if it exists.

4.2.2 Features to be Tested. Identify the test items and describe the features and combinations of features which are the object of this design specification. Other features may be exercised, but need not be identified.

For each feature or feature combination, a reference to its associated requirements in the item requirement specification or design description should be included.

4.2.3 Approach Refinements. Specify refinements to the approach described in the test plan. Include specific test techniques to be used. The method of analyzing test results should be identified (for example, comparator programs or visual inspection).

Specify the results of any analysis which provides a rationale for test-case selection. For example, one might specify conditions which permit a determination of error tolerance (for example, those conditions which distinguish valid inputs from invalid inputs).

Summarize the common attributes of any test cases. This may include input constraints that must be true for every input in the set of associated test cases, any shared environmental needs, and any shared special procedural requirements, and any shared case dependencies.

4.2.4 Test Identification. List the identifier and a brief description of each test case associated with this design. A particular test case may be identified in more than one test design specification. List the identifier and a brief description of each procedure associated with this test-design specification.

4.2.5 Feature Pass/Fail Criteria. Specify the criteria to be used to determine whether the feature or feature combination has passed or failed.

5. Test-Case Specification

5.1 Purpose. To define a test case identified by a test-design specification.

5.2 Outline. A test-case specification shall have the following structure:

(1) Test-case-specification identifier
(2) Test items
(3) Input specifications
(4) Output specifications
(5) Environmental needs
(6) Special procedural requirements
(7) Intercase dependencies

The sections shall be ordered in the specified sequence. Additional sections may be included at the end. If some or all of the content of a section is in another document, then a reference to that material may be listed in place of the corresponding content. The referenced material must be attached to the test-case specification or available to users of the case specification.

Since a test case may be referenced by several test-design specifications used by different groups over a long time period, enough specific information must be included in the test-case specification to permit reuse.

Details on the content of each section are contained in the following sections.

5.2.1 Test-Case-Specification Identifier. Specify the unique identifier assigned to this test-case specification.

5.2.2 Test Items. Identify and briefly describe the items and features to be exercised by this test case.

For each item, consider supplying references to the following item documentation.
(1) Requirements specification
(2) Design specification
(3) Users guide
(4) Operations guide
(5) Installation guide

5.2.3 Input Specifications. Specify each input required to execute the test case. Some of the inputs will be specified by value (with tolerances where appropriate), while others, such as constant tables or transaction files, will be specified by name. Identify all appropriate data bases, files, terminal messages, memory resident areas, and values passed by the operating system.

Specify all required relationships between inputs (for example, timing).

5.2.4 Output Specifications. Specify all of the outputs and features (for example, response time) required of the test items. Provide the exact value (with tolerances where appropriate) for each required output or feature.

5.2.5 Environmental Needs.

5.2.5.1 Hardware. Specify the characteristics and configurations of the hardware required to execute this test case (for example, 132 character × 24 line CRT).

5.2.5.2 Software. Specify the system and application software required to execute this test case. This may include system software such as operating systems, compilers, simulators, and test tools. In addition, the test item may interact with application software.

5.2.5.3 Other. Specify any other requirements such as unique facility needs or specially trained personnel.

5.2.6 Special Procedural Requirements. Describe any special constraints on the test procedures which execute this test case. These constraints may involve special set up, operator intervention, output determination procedures, and special wrap up.

5.2.7 Intercase Dependencies. List the identifiers of test cases which must be executed prior to this test case. Summarize the nature of the dependencies.

6. Test-Procedure Specification

6.1 Purpose. To specify the steps for executing a set of test cases or, more generally, the steps used to analyze a software item in order to evaluate a set of features.

6.2 Outline. A test-procedure specification shall have the following structure:
(1) Test-procedure-specification identifier
(2) Purpose
(3) Special requirements
(4) Procedure steps

The sections shall be ordered in the specified sequence. Additional sections, if required, may be included at the end. If some or all of the content of a section is in another document, then a reference to that material may be listed in place of the corresponding content. The referenced material must be attached to the test-procedure specification or available to users of the procedure specification.

Details on the content of each section are contained in the following sections.

6.2.1 Test-Procedure-Specification Identifier. Specify the unique identifier assigned to this test-procedure specification. Supply a reference to the associated test-design specification.

6.2.2 Purpose. Describe the purpose of this procedure. If this procedure executes any test cases, provide a reference for each of them.

In addition, provide references to relevant sections of the test item documentation (for example, references to usage procedures).

6.2.3 Special Requirements. Identify any special requirements that are necessary for the execution of this procedure. These may include prerequisite procedures, special skills requirements, and special environmental requirements.

6.2.4 Procedure Steps. Include the following steps as applicable:

6.2.4.1 Log. Describe any special methods or formats for logging the results of test execution, the incidents observed, and any other events pertinent to the test (see Test Log, Section 8 and Test Incident Report, Section 9).

6.2.4.2 Set Up. Describe the sequence of actions necessary to prepare for execution of the procedure.

6.2.4.3 Start. Describe the actions necessary to begin execution of the procedure.

6.2.4.4 Proceed. Describe any actions necessary during execution of the procedure.

6.2.4.5 Measure. Describe how the test

measurements will be made (for example, describe how remote terminal response time is to be measured using a network simulator).

6.2.4.6 Shut Down. Describe the actions necessary to suspend testing, when unscheduled events dictate.

6.2.4.7 Restart. Identify any procedural restart points and describe the actions necessary to restart the procedure at each of these points.

6.2.4.8 Stop. Describe the actions necessary to bring execution to an orderly halt.

6.2.4.9 Wrap Up. Describe the actions necessary to restore the environment.

6.2.4.10 Contingencies. Describe the actions necessary to deal with anomolous events which may occur during execution.

7. Test-Item Transmittal Report

7.1 Purpose. To identify the test items being transmitted for testing. It includes the person responsible for each item, its physical location, and its status. Any variations from the current item requirements and designs are noted in this report.

7.2 Outline. A test-item transmittal report shall have the following structure:

(1) Transmittal-report identifier
(2) Transmitted items
(3) Location
(4) Status
(5) Approvals

The sections shall be ordered in the specified sequence. Additional sections may be included just prior to *Approvals.* If some or all of the content of a section is in another document, then a reference to that material may be listed in place of the corresponding content. The referenced material must be attached to the test-item transmittal report or available to users of the transmittal report.

Details on the content of each section are contained in the following sections.

7.2.1 Transmittal-Report Identifier. Specify the unique identifier assigned to this test-item transmittal report.

7.2.2 Transmitted Items. Identify the test items being transmitted, including their version/revision level. Supply references to the item documentation and the test plan relating to the transmitted items. Indicate the people responsible for the transmitted items.

7.2.3 Location. Identify the location of the transmitted items. Identify the media that contain the items being transmitted. When appropriate, indicate how specific media are labeled or identified.

7.2.4 Status. Describe the status of the test items being transmitted. Include deviations from the item documentation, from previous transmittals of these items, and from the test plan. List the incident reports which are expected to be resolved by the transmitted items. Indicate if there are pending modifications to item documentation which may affect the items listed in this transmittal report.

7.2.5 Approvals. Specify the names and titles of all persons who must approve this transmittal. Provide space for the signatures and dates.

8. Test Log

8.1 Purpose. To provide a chronological record of relevant details about the execution of tests.

8.2 Outline. A test log shall have the following structure:

(1) Test log identifier
(2) Description
(3) Activity and event entries

The sections shall be ordered in the specified sequence. Additional sections may be included at the end. If some or all of the content of a section is in another document, then a reference to that material may be listed in place of the corresponding content. The referenced material must be attached to the test log or available to users of the log.

Details on the content of each section are contained in the following sections.

8.2.1 Test-Log Identifier. Specify the unique identifier assigned to this test log.

8.2.2 Description. Information which applies to all entries in the log except as specifically noted in a log entry should be included here. The following information should be considered.

(1) Identify the items being tested including their version/revision levels. For each of these items, supply a reference to its transmittal report, if it exists.

(2) Identify the attributes of the environments in which the testing is conducted. Include facility identification, hardware being used (for example, amount of memory being

used, CPU model number, and number and model of tape drives, and/or mass storage devices), system software used, and resources available such as the amount of memory available.

8.2.3 Activity and Event Entries. For each event, including the beginning and end of activities, record the occurrence date and time along with the identity of the author.

The following information should be considered:

8.2.3.1 Execution Description. Record the identifier of the test procedure being executed and supply a reference to its specification. Record all personnel present during the execution including testers, operators, and observers. Also indicate the function of each individual.

8.2.3.2 Procedure Results. For each execution, record the visually observable results (for example, error messages generated, aborts, and requests for operator action). Also record the location of any output (for example, reel number). Record the successful or unsuccessful execution of the test.

8.2.3.3 Environmental Information. Record any environmental conditions specific to this entry (for example, hardware substitutions).

8.2.3.4 Anomalous Events. Record what happened before and after an unexpected event occurred (for example, *A summary display was requested and the correct screen displayed, but response seemed unusually long. A repetition produced the same prolonged response*). Record circumstances surrounding the inability to begin execution of a test procedure or failure to complete a test procedure (for example, a power failure or system software problem).

8.2.3.5 Incident-Report Identifiers. Record the identifier of each test-incident report, whenever one is generated.

9. Test-Incident Report

9.1 Purpose. To document any event that occurs during the testing process which requires investigation.

9.2 Outline. A test-incident report shall have the following structure:

(1) Test-incident-report identifier
(2) Summary
(3) Incident description
(4) Impact

The sections shall be ordered in the specified sequence. Additional sections may be included at the end. If some or all of the content of a section is in another document, then a reference to that material may be listed in place of the corresponding content. The referenced material must be attached to the test-incident report or available to users of the incident report.

Details on the content of each section are contained in the following sections.

9.2.1 Test-Incident-Report Identifier. Specify the unique identifier assigned to this test incident report.

9.2.2 Summary. Summarize the incident. Identify the test items involved indicating their version/revision level. References to the appropriate test-procedure specification, test-case specification, and test log should be supplied.

9.2.3 Incident Description. Provide a description of the incident. This description should include the following items:

Inputs
Expected results
Actual results
Anomalies
Date and time
Procedure step
Environment
Attempts to repeat
Testers
Observers

Related activities and observations that may help to isolate and correct the cause of the incident should be included. For example, describe any test-case executions that might have a bearing on this particular incident and any variations from the published test procedure.

9.2.4 Impact. If known, indicate what impact this incident will have on test plans, test-design specifications, test-procedure specifications, or test-case specifications.

10. Test-Summary Report

10.1 Purpose. To summarize the results of the designated testing activities and to provide evaluations based on these results.

10.2 Outline. A test-summary report shall have the following structure:

(1) Test-summary-report identifier
(2) Summary
(3) Variances
(4) Comprehensive assessment
(5) Summary of results
(6) Evaluation
(7) Summary of activities
(8) Approvals

The sections shall be ordered in the specified sequence. Additional sections may be included just prior to *Approvals.* If some or all of the content of a section is in another document, then a reference to that material may be listed in place of the corresponding content. The referenced material must be attached to the test-summary report or available to users of the summary report.

Details on the content of each section are contained in the following sections.

10.2.1 Test-Summary-Report Identifier. Specify the unique identifier assigned to this test-summary report.

10.2.2 Summary. Summarize the evaluation of the test items. Identify the items tested, indicating their version/revision level. Indicate the environment in which the testing activities took place.

For each test item, supply references to the following documents if they exist: test plan, test-design specifications, test-procedure speci-

fications, test-item transmittal reports, test logs, and test-incident reports.

10.2.3 Variances. Report any variances of the test items from their design specifications. Indicate any variances from the test plan, test designs, or test procedures. Specify the reason for each variance.

10.2.4 Comprehensiveness Assessment. Evaluate the comprehensiveness of the testing process against the comprehensiveness criteria specified in the test plan (3.2.6) if the plan exists. Identify features or feature combinations which were not sufficiently tested and explain the reasons.

10.2.5 Summary of Results. Summarize the results of testing. Identify all resolved incidents and summarize their resolutions. Identify all unresolved incidents.

10.2.6 Evaluation. Provide an overall evaluation of each test item including its limitations. This evaluation must be based upon the test results and the item level pass/fail criteria. An estimate of failure risk may be included.

10.2.7 Summary of Activities. Summarize the major testing activities and events. Summarize resource consumption data, for example, total staffing level, total machine time, and total elapsed time used for each of the major testing activities.

10.2.8 Approvals. Specify the names and titles of all persons who must approve this report. Provide space for the signatures and dates.

Appendixes

(The following Appendixes are not a part of IEEE Std 829-1983, IEEE Standard for Software Test Documentation.)

A. Examples

The following examples are taken from commercial data processing. This should not imply any limitations on the applicability of the standard to other classes of software.

Contents

A1. Corporate Payroll-System Test Documentation

A1.1. Introduction

A1.1.1. Scope. The system test documentation example presented here is done in accordance with the IEEE Standard for Software Test Documentation. Each document is represented as it might be used for the system test of a payroll system.

The payroll system used in this example contains the following major functions:

(1) Maintain employee information
(2) Maintain payroll history information
(3) Prepare payroll checks
(4) Prepare payroll tax reports
(5) Prepare payroll history reports

A Phase 2.0 development plan exists for the payroll system which will be started at some future time. This phase covers, primarily, a personnel reporting system.

A1.1.2. Assumptions. The following assumptions were made when preparing this example:

(1) System testing activities assume that *module* and *integration* testing have been done. This implies that single program functionality has been comprehensively tested. System level testing, therefore, focuses on the testing of multiprogram functionality (for example, year-end processing) as well as external interfaces, security, recovery, and performance. In addition, operator and user procedures are tested.

(2) The payroll system will be system tested at only one site.

A1.1.3. Naming Conventions. The naming conventions which follow are used throughout the payroll-system example.

Corporate Payroll System

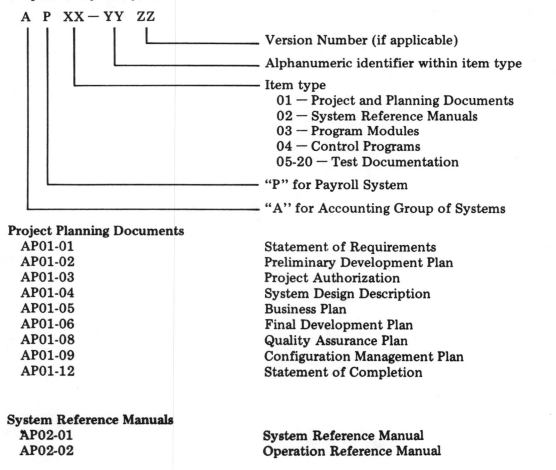

Project Planning Documents

AP01-01	Statement of Requirements
AP01-02	Preliminary Development Plan
AP01-03	Project Authorization
AP01-04	System Design Description
AP01-05	Business Plan
AP01-06	Final Development Plan
AP01-08	Quality Assurance Plan
AP01-09	Configuration Management Plan
AP01-12	Statement of Completion

System Reference Manuals

AP02-01	System Reference Manual
AP02-02	Operation Reference Manual

| AP02-03 | Module Reference Manual |
| AP02-04 | User Transaction Reference Manual |

Program Modules

| AP03- | Program Modules |

Control Programs

| AP04- | Control Programs, Utilities, Sorts |

Test Documentation

AP05-YYZZ	Test Plan
AP06-YYZZ	Test Design Specification
AP07-YYZZ	Test Case Specification
AP08-YYZZ	Test Procedure Specification
AP09-YY	Test Log
AP10-00	Test Incident Report Log*
AP11-YY	Test Incident Report
AP12-YY	Test Summary Report
AP13-YY	Test Item Transmittal Report

---

*Note: This *test* document is not specified by this standard.

A.1.2

System Test Plan
for the
Corporate Payroll System

XYZ Corporation

AP05-0101

Prepared by
Manager, System Test Group
Manager, Corporate Payroll Department

January 21, 1982

System Test Plan
Corporate Payroll System

Contents

1. Test Plan Identifier

AP05-0103

2. Introduction

2.1 Objectives. A system test plan for the corporate payroll system should support the following objectives.

(1) To detail the activities required to prepare for and conduct the system test.

(2) To communicate to all responsible parties the tasks which they are to perform and the schedule to be followed in performing the tasks.

(3) To define the sources of the information used to prepare the plan.

(4) To define the test tools and environment needed to conduct the system test.

2.2 Background. Last year the XYZ Corporate Systems and Programming Department developed a new General Ledger System at the request of the Corporate Accounting Department. A request was made at the same time for a new corporate payroll system to be developed which would interface with the general ledger system.

The Management Systems Review Committee approved the request for the payroll system in September of 1981 and named a corporate payroll system advisory group to decide on the system requirements. The group finished a Statement of Requirements (AP01-01) and a Preliminary Development Plan (AP01-02) in December, 1981.

2.3 Scope. This test plan covers a full systems test of the corporate payroll system. This includes operator and user procedures, as well as programs and job control. In addition to comprehensively testing multiprogram functionality, external interfaces, security, recovery, and performance will also be evaluated.

2.4 References. The following documents were used as sources of information for the test plan.

Corporate Payroll System Preliminary Development Plan (AP01-02)
Corporate Payroll System Authorization (AP01-03)
Corporate Payroll System Final Development Plan (AP01-06)
Corporate Payroll System Quality Assurance Plan (AP01-08)
Corporate Payroll System Configuration Management Plan (AP01-09)
XYZ Corporate Systems Development Standards and Procedures (XYZ01-0100)
Corporate General Ledger System Design Description (AG01-04)
Corporate General Ledger System Test Plan (AG05-01)

3. Test Items

All items which make up the corporate payroll system will be tested during the system test. The versions to be tested will be placed in the appropriate libraries by the configuration administrator. The administrator will also control changes to the versions under test and notify the test group when new versions are available.

The following documents will provide the basis for defining correct operation.

Corporate Payroll System Statement of Requirements (AP01-01)
Corporate Payroll System Design Description (AP01-04)
Corporate Payroll System Reference Manual (AP02-01)
Corporate Payroll System Module Reference Manual (AP02-03)
The items to be tested are:

3.1 Program Modules. The program modules to be tested will be identified as follows:

Type	Library	Member Name
Source Code	SOURLIB1	AP0302
		AP0305

Executable Code	MACLIB1	AP0301
	SYSLIB1	AP0302
		AP0305

3.2 Job-Control Procedures. The control procedures for application programs, sorts, and utility programs will be identified as follows:

Type	Library	Member Name
Application Programs	PROCLIB1	AP0401
Sorts	PROCLIB1	AP0402
Utility Programs	PROCLIB1	AP0403

3.3 User Procedures. The online procedures specified in the Corporate Payroll Sytem User Transaction Reference Manual (AP02-04) will be tested.

3.4 Operator Procedures. The system test includes the procedures specified in the Corporate Payroll System Operation Reference Manual (AP02-02).

4. Features to be Tested

The following list describes the features that will be tested.

Test Design Specification Number	Description
AP06-01	Data base conversion
AP06-02	Complete payroll processing for salaried employees only
AP06-03	Complete payroll processing for hourly employees only
AP06-04	Complete payroll processing for all employees
AP06-05	Periodic reporting
AP06-06	General Ledger transaction building
AP06-07	Security
AP06-08	Recovery
AP06-09	Performance

5. Features not to be Tested

The following features will not be included in the system tests because they are not to be used when the system is initially installed.

Equal Employment Opportunity Commission Compliance Reports

Internal Training Schedule Reports

Salary/Performance Review Reports

The development Phase 2.0 documentation will contain a test plan for these features.

The test cases will not cover all possible combinations of options within the transaction or report being tested. Only combinations that are known to be required for current XYZ Corporate Payroll processing will be tested.

6. Approach

The test personnel will use the system documentation to prepare all test design, case, and procedure specifications. This approach will verify the accuracy and comprehensiveness of the information in the documentation in those areas covered by the tests.

Personnel from the Payroll and Corporate Accounting Departments will assist in developing the test designs and test cases. This will help ensure that the tests represent the production use of the system.

In order to ensure privacy, all test data extracted from production files will have privacy sensitive fields changed.

6.1 Conversion Testing. In addition to counting the input and output records, the validity of the converted data base will be verified in two ways. The first verification method involves the use of a *data base auditor* which must be built by the development group. When run against the converted data base, the data base auditor will check value ranges within a record and the required relationships between records.

The second verification method involves the random selection of a small subset of old records and than a direct comparison against a corresponding subset of the new records. The number of direct comparisons, c, and the number of old records, r, must be specified. A set of c random numbers will be generated from the range 1 to r. This set will be sorted and used during the conversion process to drive the selection of records for direct comparison.

NOTE: This same two-pronged verification approach should be used during the actual conversion.

6.2 Job Stream Testing. A comprehensive set of records of salaried employees, hourly employees, and a merged set of these two should be used to test payroll processing. The standard job stream testing approach should be used.

Run each of the periodic reporting job streams at least once.

6.3 Interface Testing. In order to test the interface between the payroll and general-ledger systems, the payroll system will build a comprehensive set of general-ledger transactions. These transactions will then be input to the general-ledger test system. The resulting general-ledger entries must be extracted, printed, and compared with a printout of the general-ledger transactions prepared by the payroll system.

6.4 Security Testing. Attempted access without a proper password to the online data entry and display transactions will be tested.

6.5 Recovery Testing. Recovery will be tested by halting the machine during stand alone time and then following the recovery procedures.

6.6 Performance Testing. Performance will be evaluated against the performance requirements (AP01-01) by measuring the run times of several jobs using production data volumes.

6.7 Regression. It is assumed that several iterations of the system test will be done in order to test program modifications made during the system test period. A regression test will be performed for each new version of the system to detect unexpected impact resulting from program modifications.

The regression test will be done by running all of the tests on a new version that were run on the previous version and then comparing the resulting files. The standard comparator program, UT08-0100, will be used to compare all system outputs.

6.8 Comprehensiveness. Each of the system features described in the Corporate Payroll System Reference Manual (AP02-01) will have at least one associated test-design specification. Each of the user procedures specified in the Corporate Payroll-System User Transaction Reference Manual (AP02-04) will be tested at least once. Each of the operating procedures specified in the Corporate Payroll-System Operation Reference Manual (AP02-02) also will be tested at least once. In addition, each job control procedure will be executed at least once.

A coverage matrix will be used to related test-design specifications to each of the areas described above.

6.9 Constraints. A final implementation date of August 31, 1982 has been planned for the Corporate Payroll System. It will be necessary to meet this date because the new ABC Division begins full operation on September 1, and they must have this payroll system to pay their employees.

7. Item Pass/Fail Criteria

The system must satisfy the standard requirements for system pass/fail stated in the XYZ Corporate Systems Development Standards and Procedures (XYZ01-0100).

The system must also satisfy the following requirements:

Memory requirements must not be greater than 64K of real storage

Consistency of user procedures with other accounting systems must satisfy the Payroll Supervisor

8. Suspension Criteria and Resumption Requirements

8.1 Suspension Criteria. Inability to convert the Employee Information Data Base will cause suspension of all testing activities.

8.2 Resumption Requirements. When a new version of the system is transmitted to the test group after a suspension of testing has occurred, a regression test as described in 6.7 will be run.

9. Test Deliverables

The following documents will be generated by the system test group and will be delivered to the configuration management group after test completion.

Test Documentation:

System Test Plan

System Test Design Specifications

System Test Case Specifications

System Test Procedure Specifications

System Test Logs

System Test Incident Report Log

System Test Incident Reports

System Test Summary Report

Test Data:

(1) Copies of all data entry and inquiry screens and the reply screens are to be attached to the related test case document.

(2) Copies of the input and output test files should be delivered to the configuration management group.

(3) Microfiche copies of the printed output from the final execution of each test procedure are to be delivered to the configuration management group along with the test documentation.

10. Testing Tasks

See Task List, Attachment A, page 28.

11. Environmental Needs

11.1 Hardware. The testing will be done on the XYZ hardware configuration.

Since most testing must be done during prime operating hours, 3 on-line terminals must be available to the test group during this period.

11.2 Software

11.2.1 Operating System. The production operating system will be used to execute these tests.

11.2.2 Communications Software. All on-line programs will be tested under the control of the test communication software.

11.3 Security. Security will be limited to existing controls.

11.4 Tools. The following test tools are required to develop and evaluate the system tests.

(1) Test Data Generator (UT09-0200). This program will be used to generate the majority of the test data. It is located in the standard system library, SYSLIBA.

(2) Comparator Program (UT08-0100). This program will be used to compare system results during the regression tests. It is located in the standard system library, SYSLIBA.

(3) Data Base Auditor. This program audits value ranges and interrecord relationships in the data base. It must be supplied by the development group.

11.5 Publications. The following documents are required to support systems testing.

Corporate Payroll System Statement of Requirements (AP01-01)
Corporate Payroll System Design Description (AP01-04)
Corporate Payroll System Reference Manual (AP02-01)
Corporate Payroll Operation Reference Manual (AP02-02)
Corporate Payroll System Module Reference Manual (AP02-03)
Corporate Payroll System User Transaction Reference Manual (AP02-04)

12. Responsibilities

The following groups have responsibility for segments of the testing.

12.1 System Test Group. This group provides the overall management of the testing and the technical testing expertise.

12.2 Corporate Payroll Department. This group is the end user of the Corporate Payroll System and will provide assistance to the test group in the following activities:

Reviewing the test-design specifications.
Executing the on-line tests.
Checking output screens and reports.

12.3 Development Project Group. This group transmits the system to be tested and responds to the System Test Incident Reports. This group does any program debugging that is required. It also supplies the data-base auditor.

13. Staffing and Training Needs

13.1 Staffing. The following staff is needed to carry out this testing project.

    13.1.1 Test Group.

Test Manager	1
Senior Test Analyst	1
Test Analysts	2
Test Technician	1

    13.1.2 Payroll Department.

Payroll Supervisor	1

13.2 Training. The Corporate Payroll Department personnel must be trained to do the data entry transactions. The User Transaction Reference Manual (AP02-04) will be the basis of this training.

14. Schedule

See attached Task List (Attachment A).

Hardware, software, and test tools will be used for testing during the period from June 1, 1982 through August 1, 1982.

15. Risks and Contingencies

If the testing schedule is significantly impacted by system failure, the development manager has agreed to assign a full-time person to the test group to do debugging.

If one payroll supervisor is not sufficiently available for testing, then the payroll manager has agreed to identify a second supervisor.

If hardware problems impact system availability during the day, then the test group will schedule their activities during the evening.

The first production runs of the Corporate Payroll System must be checked out in detail before the payroll checks are distributed, and any checks in error must be corrected manually.

16. Approvals

Test Manager	Date
Development Project Manager	Date
Quality Assurance Manager	Date

ANSI/IEEE
Std 829-1983

Attachment — A. Task List

Task	Predecessor Tasks	Special Skills	Responsibility	Effort	Finish Date
(1) Prepare test plan.	Complete payroll system design description (AP01-04) and preliminary development plan (AP01-02)		Test manager Senior test analyst	4	01-21-82
(2) Prepare test-design specifications.	Task 1	Knowledge of corporate payroll procedures	Senior test analyst	9	04-01-82
(3) Prepare test-case specifcations.	Complete corresponding test designs (Task 2)		Test analyst	4	04-15-82
(4) Prepare test-procedure specifications.	Complete corresponding test cases (Task 3)		Test analyst	6	05-15-82
(5) Build the initial employee-information data base.	Task 4		Test analyst	6	06-01-82
(6) Complete test-item transmittal and transmit the corporate payroll system to the test group.	Complete integration testing		Development project manager		06-01-82
(7) Checkout all job-control procedures required to execute the system.	Task 6	Job control experience	Test technician	1	06-08-82
(8) Assemble and link the corporate payroll system.	Task 6		Test technician	1	06-08-82
(9) Execute data-entry test procedures.	Task 5 Task 8		Test analyst	1	06-22-82
(10) Execute batch test procedures.	Task 5 Task 8		Test technician	3	06-30-82
(11) Check out batch test results.	Task 10	Knowledge of payroll-report requirements	Test analyst	1	07-02-82
(12) Resolve test-incident reports.	Task 9 Task 11		—Development group manager —System test-group manager —Corporate payroll department manager	2	07-16-82
(13) Repeat tasks (6)—(12) until all test procedures have succeeded.	Task 12			2	07-30-82
(14) Write the system test summary report.	Task 13		—System test-group manager —Corporate payroll-department manager	1	08-06-82
(15) Transmit all test documentation and test data to the configuration management group.	Task 14		System test group	1	08-06-82

A1.3. Corporate Payroll
System Test-Procedure Specification

1. Test-Procedure Specification Identifier

AP08-0101 March 5, 1982

2. Purpose

This procedure describes the steps necessary to perform the test specified in the test-design specification for data-base conversion (AP06-0101). The procedure describes the execution of the test
case described in System Test-Case Specification AP07-0101. (NOTE: Neither the test-design specification nor test-case specification are included in this set of system test examples). This test will
exercise the Employee Information Data Base Conversion Procedures specified in the Corporate
Payroll System Reference Manual (AP02-01) and the conversion program (AP03-07) described in
the Corporate Payroll System Module Reference Manual (AP02-03).

3. Special Requirements

In order to execute this procedure, the "random subset" program, the old data extract program,
the new data extract program, and the data base auditor specified in AP06-0101 must be available.

4. Procedure Steps

4.1 Log. Record the execution of this procedure on a standard test log (AP09-YY).

4.2 Set Up
   (1) Generate a test version of the old employee data base according to the test-case specification
in AP07-0101 using the test data generator (UT09-0200).
   (2) Execute the random subset program requesting 50 random numbers in the range 1 to 500.
   (3) Sort the random number file into an increasing sequence.
   (4) Execute the old data extract program with the test version of the old employee-information
data base using the sorted random number file.
   (5) Print the extracted records.

4.3 Proceed. Execute the conversion program with the test version of the old data base generating
the new employee information data base.

4.4 Measure
   (1) Execute the data-base auditor with the new employee information data base. Report violations in test-incident reports.
   (2) Execute the new data extract program with the new data base using the sorted random-
number file.
   (3) Print the extracted records.
   (4) Compare the extracted old records with the extracted new records. Report differences in test-
incident reports.

4.5 Wrap Up. Delete both extracted files and the random number file.

A1.4. Corporate Payroll
System Transmittal Report

1. Transmittal Report Identifier

AP13-03 June 24, 1982

2. Transmitted Items

A new version of the data conversion program (AP03-0702) is being transmitted.

The program is described in the Module Reference Manual (AP02-0305). The associated conversion procedures are specified in the System Reference Manual (AP02-0109). The transmitted program is associated with system test plan AP05-0103.

Communication about this program should be directed to the manager of the payroll system development project.

3. Location

The transmitted code is located as follows:

Source Code   SOURLIB1 (AP0307)
Object Code   SYSLIB1 (AP0307)

The system documentation and test plans are available in the documentation library.

4. Status

The conversion program has been fully retested at the unit and integration levels. The three incident reports (AP11-15, 16, and 17) generated by the June 10th execution of AP08-0101 are resolved by this new version.

The *invalid department code* messages (AP11-15) and the *blank home addresses* (AP11-16) resulted from insufficient logic in the conversion program. Additional logic was added. The *number of dependents* field processing problem (AP11-17) resulted from an imprecise program specification. The logic has been changed and comments have been added for clarity.

5. Approvals

_____   _____
Development Manager   Date

_____   _____
Test Manager   Date

31

A1.5 Corporate Payroll-System Test Log

1. Test Log Identifier

AP09-04 June 10, 1982

2. Description

The first version of the data conversion program (AP03-0701) is being tested. The program was transmitted (AP13-01) to the test group along with the entire payroll system.

This batch testing is being conducted using the standard corporate data-center facilities.

This log records the execution of the data conversion test procedure (AP08-0101). The tests are being submitted to background processing through a CRT by a senior test analyst.

3. Activities and Event Entries

June 10, 1982		Incidents
2:00 PM —	Dick J. started testing.	
2:15 PM —	Began to generate the old test data base.	
3:30 PM —	Discovered a possible bug in the test data generator. Filled out an incident report and worked around the problem.	AP11-14
6:00 PM —	Completed the old test data base generation. It is located on TEST1.	
6:15 PM —	Dick J. stopped testing.	

June 11, 1982		Incidents
9:45 AM —	Dick J. started testing.	
10:00 AM —	Began to create the random number file.	
10:45 AM —	Generated a sorted random number file.	
11:30 AM —	Selected and printed a random subset of records from the old test data base.	
12:30 PM —	Dick J. stopped testing.	
12:45 PM —	Jane K. started testing.	
1:00 PM —	Ran the conversion program against the old test data base. The new data base is on TEST2. The status report from the run contained 3 messages warning of invalid data in the department code field. The three records were checked and the values appeared valid. An incident report was generated.	AP11-15
3:30 PM —	Ran the data-base auditor against the new data base. The auditor reported multiple instances of blank home addresses. A check found these addresses nonblank in the old data base. The incident was reported.	AP11-16
4:00 PM —	Jane K. stopped testing.	

June 12, 1982   Incidents

    8:15 AM — Jane K. started testing.

    8:30 AM — Selected and printed the random subset of   AP11-17
                records from the new data base. In one case,
                the *number of dependents* field was changed
                from three to zero (possibly because no names
                were present). The incident was reported.

  11:30 AM — The extract and random number files were
                deleted.

  11:45 AM — Jane K. stopped testing.

A1.6. Corporate Payroll
System Test Incident Report

1. Report Identifier

AP11-17 June 12, 1982

2. Summary

Changes in the *number of dependents* field were found by comparing records from the new employee data base created by the conversion program (AP03-0701) with those from the old data base. Test log AP09-04 records this incident. The incident occurred during execution of test procedure AP08-0101.

3. Incident Description

June 12, 1982   8:30 AM   Jane K.

A test version of the old employee data base was converted to its new format. The value in the *number of dependents* field was not expected to change during this process. This field value changed in the record indicated on the attached printouts.

Note that although the dependent count is three in the original record, none of the names appear. The number of names matches the count in all of the other records.

Perhaps the program is counting the names and forcing consistency.

4. Impact

Testing activity is suspended until this incident is resolved.

A2. Normalize Numeric Expression
Module-Test Documentation

The following example describes the testing of a module which reformats a numeric expression entered on a CRT. The module removes all commas, the sign, and the decimal point. It also checks the validity of the input expression.

A2.1 Introduction

General Requirements. To provide user-friendly entry of numeric data on a CRT, a system permits the keying of numeric expressions containing optional non-numeric symbols such as commas, a decimal point, and a leading sign. Any of the following examples would be valid entries:

```
+0
1234.
- .012
12,345.6
```

To facilitate editing of such input, a routine is required to normalize the numeric expression to a decimal point aligned value and to describe it. An expression is described by various character-istics such as:

Includes sign
Includes commas
Includes decimal point
Number of fractional digits and
Number of integer digits

A return code should identify the specific nature of any edit error.
The routine will be accessed by COBOL programs.

Functional Design.
Input: A character string of length 25 called NUMERIC-EXPRESSION contains a numeric ex-pression. The expression must contain at least 1 digit. It may contain no more than 14 integer digits and no more than 4 fractional digits. It may contain valid combinations of
Leading sign
Decimal point and
Grouping commas.
A valid entry field may have spaces on the left, the right, or both. Interior spaces are invalid.
Process: The input expression is edited and if invalid an error condition is recorded in the return code. If valid, any signs, decimal points, and commas are removed and the resulting numeric value is decimal-point aligned in a signed field. In addition, a set of input descriptors is calculated.
Output: A decimal-point aligned, signed numeric value in a PIC S9(14)V9(4) field called ALIGNED-NUMERIC-VALUE
A set of input descriptors

INTEGER-DIGIT-COUNT	(0 - 14)
FRACTIONAL-DIGIT-COUNT	(0 - 4)
WAS-SIGN-FOUND	(N-0, YES)
WERE-COMMAS-FOUND	(N-0, YES)
WAS-DECIMAL-POINT-FOUND	(N-0, YES)

A RETURN-CODE with the following values
· NORMALIZATION-OK
· INVALID-FIRST-CHAR
First character is other than a digit, period, or sign
· INVALID-NONFIRST-CHAR
Nonfirst character is other than a digit, period, or comma

· NO-DIGIT-FOUND

No numeric character was entered

· TOO-MANY-INTEGER-DIGITS

More than 14 consecutive digits without a decimal point

· TOO-MANY-FRACTIONAL-DIGITS

More than 4 digits to the right of a decimal point

· TOO-MANY-DECIMAL-POINTS

More than 1 decimal point

· COMMA-RIGHT-AFTER-SIGN

Comma immediately follows a sign

· INVALID-COMMA-INTERVAL

Less than 3 consecutive-digits following a comma

More than 3 consecutive digits preceding or following a comma

· COMMA-AFTER-POINT

Comma appears to the right of a decimal point

If the value of RETURN-CODE is *not* NORMALIZATION-OK, then the values of the other output fields are *undefined.*

TECHNICAL DESIGN.

LANGUAGE: COBOL

ACCESS: PERFORM of included sub-routine

HIERARCHY: Normalize-Numeric-Exp
CHART   Left-justify Expression
       Find Right-most Non-space
       Validate Expression
         Initialize Descriptor Fields
         Set Return OK
         Do Validation Scan
         Wrap Up Validation Scan
       Normalize Valid Expression
         Save Digit
         Delete Specials
         Align Output Value
         Establish Sign

NOTES:

Output Fields	Setting Procedures
Return Code (Error)	Do Validation Scan Wrap Up Validation Scan
Return Code (OK)	Set Return OK
Input Descriptors	Initialize Description Fields Do Validation Scan Wrap Up Validation Scan
ALIGNED-NUMERIC-VALUE	Align Output Value Establish Sign

ANSI/IEEE
Std 829-1983

Module Test Documentation for Normalize Numeric Expression

- Test Design Specification
- Test Case Specification
- Test Summary Report

Prepared by Module Developer
March 23, 1982

A2.2. Normalize Numeric Expression
Module Test-Design Specification

1. Test-Design Specification Identifier

NNE.TD.01.05   15 March 1981

NOTE: No test plan is associated with this module, because its development was not associated with any particular application project (so there is no project level test plan) and because the special projects manager decided that a specific module test plan was unnecessary. The quality support manager concurred.

2. Features to be Tested

Individual Features
    2.1 Digits Only Processing
    2.2 Sign Processing
    2.3 Decimal Point Processing
    2.4 Commas Processing
Combinations
    2.5 Sign and Decimal Point
    2.6 Sign and Commas
    2.7 Decimal Point and Commas
    2.8 Sign, Decimal Point and Commas

All of these features are specified in the functional design description contained in the *common routines* section of the programmer's guide.

3. Approach Refinements

The individual processing features of the module will be tested first with valid and invalid input. All of the combinations will then be used.

A program will be written to drive the module. A file will be created with each record containing a single input value and fields to store the resulting values. The driver program will read a record, pass the corresponding input value to the module, store the resulting values in the record and rewrite it. The current version id of the module should be stored in each rewritten record.

Before testing begins, a test-case file will be generated in the same format as the driver file. The records will contain the input values along with the *predicted* resulting values. Following a test run, the driver file will be compared with the case file. The file comparison utility program will report any differences.

Since generation of all possible input values is impractical, test-set comprehensiveness will be evaluated based upon the following criteria:

(1) Requirements coverage — has each of the requirements been satisfied?

(2) Design coverage — has each of the functional design specifications been satisfied?

(3) Domain coverage — has each of the input constraints (for example, maximum of one decimal point) been tested? Have representative values been included? Have all error messages been generated?

(4) Branch coverage — has every branch been taken at least once?

(5) Statement coverage — has every statement been executed at least once?

Appropriate checklists will be generated to evaluate criteria 1-3. Existing code instrumentation tools will be used to evaluate 4 and 5.

The test set must satisfy each component of the five criteria specified above at least once.

Test Case Selection Rationale

Input constraints

(1) No more than 14 integer digits

(2) No more than 4 fractional digits

(3) No more than one decimal point

(4) Between 1 and 3 contiguous digits to the left of each comma

(5) Exactly 3 contiguous digits to the right of each comma

(6) No commas after the decimal point

There are no relevant internal or output constraints.

Common Test-Case Characteristics

All test cases require a module driver.

4. Test Identification

Cases

Digits Only
  Valid

14 integer digits	NNE.TC.001
centered 6 integer digits	NNE.TC.002
left justified 1 integer digit	NNE.TC.003

  Invalid

15 integer digits	NNE.TC.010
digit string with imbedded space	NNE.TC.011
digit string with leading invalid character	NNE.TC.012
digit string with imbedded invalid character	NNE.TC.013
digit string with trailing invalid character	NNE.TC.014

Sign
  Valid

right justified + signed 14 integers	NNE.TC.020
— signed integers	NNE.TC.021

  Invalid

imbedded sign	NNE.TC.030
trailing sign	NNE.TC.031
sign alone without digits	NNE.TC.032
2 leading signs	NNE.TC.033
2 separated signs	NNE.TC.034

Decimal Point
  Valid

leading point with 4 fractional digits	NNE.TC.040
embedded point with 1 fractional digit	NNE.TC.041
trailing point with 14 integers	NNE.TC.042

Cases
    Invalid
        5 fractional digits   NNE.TC.050
        2 points   NNE.TC.051
        point without digits   NNE.TC.052

Commas
    Valid
        1 comma   NNE.TC.060
        4 commas with 14 integer digits   NNE.TC.061
    Invalid
        leading comma   NNE.TC.070
        4 digits to left of a comma   NNE.TC.071
        2 digits to right of a comma   NNE.TC.072
        4 digits to right of a comma   NNE.TC.073
        trailing comma   NNE.TC.074
        comma without digits   NNE.TC.075
        15 integer digits   NNE.TC.076

Sign and Decimal Point
    Valid
        sign and trailing point with 1 digit   NNE.TC.080
        sign adjacent to point with 1 digit   NNE.TC.081
        sign and point with 14 digits   NNE.TC.082
    Invalid
        sign and point without digits   NNE.TC.090

Sign and Commas
    Valid
        sign and comma with 14 digits   NNE.TC.100
        sign and comma with 4 digits   NNE.TC.101
    Invalid
        sign adjacent to comma   NNE.TC.110

Decimal Point and Commas
    Valid
        comma with 14 integer digits and 4 fractional
          digits   NNE.TC.120
        one comma with 4 digits and trailing point NNE.TC.121
    Invalid
        no digits between comma and point   NNE.TC.130
        4 digits between comma and point   NNE.TC.131
        comma following point   NNE.TC.132

Sign, Decimal Point and Commas
    Valid
        longest valid expression   NNE.TC.140
        shortest valid expression   NNE.TC.141
        representative valid expression   NNE.TC.142
    Invalid
        15 integer and 4 fractional digits   NNE.TC.150
        14 integer and 5 fractional digits   NNE.TC.151

Procedures. There are no *formal* test procedures associated with this design.

The procedure for using the module driver is in the *test tools* section of the programmer's guide.

5. Feature Pass/Fail Criteria

Each feature must pass all of its test cases in order to pass this test.

ANSI/IEEE
Std 829-1983

A2.3. Normalize Numeric Expression
Module Test-Case Specification

1. Test Case Specification Identifier

NNE.TC.121.01   17 March 1981
One comma with 4 digits and trailing point.

2. Test Items

Normalized Numeric Expression Subroutine — This routine strips signs, commas, and decimal points from numeric expressions.

The requirements, functional design, and technical design specifications are contained in the *common routines* section of the programmer's guide.

3. Input Specifications

1,234. in NUMERIC-EXPRESSION

4. Output Specifications

+12340000 in ALIGNED-NUMERIC-VALUE
NORMALIZATION-OK in RETURN-CODE
4 in INTEGER-DIGIT-COUNT
0 in FRACTIONAL-DIGIT-COUNT
N-0 in WAS-SIGN-FOUND
YES in WERE-COMMAS-FOUND
YES in WAS-DECIMAL-POINT-FOUND

5. Environmental Needs

A module driver is required to execute this case.

6. Special Procedural Requirements

The procedure for using the module driver is in the *test tools* section of the programmer's guide.

7. Intercase Dependencies

None.

A2.4. Normalize Numeric Expression
Module Test Summary Report

1. Test Summary Report Identifier

NNE.TS.01 23 March 1981

2. Summary

After correcting three faults, the Normalize Numeric Expression Module (Revision 5) passed all tests. The routine was tested using a module driver.

The following test documents are associated with this module.

(1) Module Test Design Specification
    NNE.TD.01.05
(2) Module Test Case Specifications
    NNE.TC.001 − .151

3. Variances

Conditions identified during testing resulted in enhancements to the set of invalid conditions described in the original functional design. This in turn resulted in the specification of eleven additional test cases. All of these changes are included in the current documentation.

4. Comprehensiveness Assessment

The attached (but not included with example) checklists and execution trace reports demonstrate that the minimum comprehensiveness requirements specified in the test design specification have been satisfied.

5. Summary of Results

Three of the test cases (071, 073, and 131) exposed faults involving insufficient logic. Additional logic was added, some new test cases were defined and the test set was rerun. All features passed their tests.

6. Evaluation

The module passed comprehensive testing with only three faults being detected. No more than one additional fault in the first six months of use is specified.

ANSI/IEEE
Std 829-1983

7. Summary of Activities

Begin Testing 03/12/82	Est	Actual
Test Design (including cases)	2.0 days	3.0 days
Module Driver Development	1.0 days	1.5 days
Test Execution	2.0 days	2.0 days
Module Revision	2.0 days	1.5 days
Test Reporting	0.5 days	0.5 days
End Testing 03/23/82	7.5 days	8.5 days

8. Approvals

_____   _____

Development Project Manager   Date

Appendix B
Implementation and Usage Guidelines

B1. Implementation Guidelines

When the standard is adopted by an organization, it is recommended that it be implemented in phases.

(1) Initial Phase. Begin by introducing the planning and reporting documents. The test plan will provide a foundation for the whole testing process. The reporting documents will encourage the testing organization to record the appropriate data in an organized manner.

Begin by implementing test documentation at the system level. The need for rigor and control during system testing is critical. System test documentation is a key element in meeting this need.

(2) Subsequent Phases. Introduce the balance of the documents in subsequent phases. Their sequence of introduction will depend upon the results of prior phases.

The test documentation eventually will form a document hierarchy corresponding to the design hierarchy, that is, system test documentation, subsystem test documentation, and module test documentation.

B2. Additional Test-Documentation Guidelines

Develop guidelines for the documentation of the specific testing techniques used in your organization (for example, code inspections or simulation). This documentation will supplement the basic documents of the standard.

B3. Usage Guidelines

(1) In the project plan or the organization's standards, identify which test documents are required during which testing activities. Provide guidelines for using these documents in your organization.

Figure B1 (below) is an example of a specification for the test documents required for various testing activities. The amount of documentation required will vary from organization to organization.

(2) Add sections and material within sections in order to tailor each document to a particular test item and a particular test environment.

(3) Consider documenting sets of modules at the module test level. For example, if might be useful to develop a module test design specification for a set of modules which generate reports. While different test cases would be required, a common test procedure specification might be appropriate.

Documents Activities	Test Plan	Test Design Spec	Test Case Spec	Test Proc Spec	Test Item Trans Report	Test Log	Test Incident Report	Test Summary Report
Acceptance	X	X	X	X	X		X	X
Field	X	X			X		X	X
Installation	X	X	X	X	X		X	X
System	X	X	X	X	X	X	X	X
Subsystem		X	X	X	X	X	X	X
Program		X	X					X
Module		X	X					X

Fig B1
Example of a Required Test Documentation Specification

Appendix C
Related Documentation Standards

Several other standards which relate to test documentation are described below. Related testing standards can be found in Appendix D.

C1. National Standards

These references establish nationally recognized requirements for software documentation.

ANSI N413-1974, American National Standard Guidelines for the Documentation of Digital Computer Programs.[1]

ANSI/IEEE Std 100-1977, IEEE Standard Dictionary of Electrical and Electronics Terms.[2]

ANSI/IEEE Std 730-1981, Standard for Software Quality Assurance Plans.

IEEE Std 729-1983, IEEE Standard Glossary of Software Engineering Terminology.

Guide for Technical Documentation of Computer Projects, American National Standards Institute Technical Committee X3. Technical Report no 6, New York: June 1982.[3]

C2. Federal Standards

These references include standards and guidelines adopted for use by Federal agencies.

Guidelines for Documentation of Computer Programs and Automated Data Systems. Federal Information Processing Standards Pub 38. National Bureau of Standards, (FIPS PUB 38), February 1976.

C3. Military Standards

These references include standards and guidelines which may be invoked in Department of Defense contracts.

Automated Data Systems Documentation Standards, Standard 7935.1-S, Department of Defense, Sept 1977.

Tactical Digital Systems Documentation Standards SECNAVINST 3560.1, Department of the Navy, 1974.

WWMCCS CCTC Test Package Development Guidelines, Technical Memorandum TM 241-80, Defense Communications Agency, Nov 1980.

---

[1] ANSI standards are available from the Sales Department of American National Standards Institute, 1430 Broadway, New York, NY 10018.

[2] IEEE standards are available from the Institute of Electrical and Electronics Engineers, IEEE Service Center, 445 Hoes Lane, Piscataway, NJ 08854.

[3] This document is available from ANSI X3 Secretary, CBEMA, 311 1st Street NW, Suite 500, Washinton, DC 20001.

Appendix D
Annotated Bibliography

This bibliography contains two kinds of references. One set of references identifies a set of basic sources on software verification and testing. The objective is to identify a few basic references on testing for those who wish information on techniques and tools. The second set of references identifies some military testing standards which might serve as source material for those developing testing standards within their organization. These standards focus on testing rather than documentation.

D1 Basic Sources

ADRION, W.R., BRANSTAD, M.A. and CHERNIAVISKY, J.C. *Validation, Verification and Testing of Computer Software.* National Bureau of Standards: NBS Special Pub 500-75 1980.

This survey discusses testing and analysis techniques that can be used to validate software. Verification throughout the development process is stressed. Specific tools and techniques are described.

BARRY, M. *Airborne Systems Software Acquisition Engineering Guidebook for Software Testing and Evaluation.* TRW: 30323-6011-TU-00 1980.

This guidebook describes the planning and testing activities necessary to a successful software testing effort. It presents checklists and references to supplemental information in government documents and to summarized data from professional journals and books.

DEUTSCH, M.S. *Software Verification and Validation.* Prentice-Hall: 1982.

This book describes a testing methodology based upon techniques used at the Hughes Aircraft Company. It describes the application of automated verification systems and summarizes the verification activities used throughout the software life cycle. It provides insight into one effective approach to dealing with the verification of large software systems.

GLASS, R. *Software Reliability Guidebook.* Prentice-Hall: 1979.

This book defines reliability as the degree to which a software system both satisfies its requirements and delivers usable services. The book surveys many methodologies that are supposed to increase software reliability. These methodologies span the software life cycle requirements, design, implementation, checkout, and maintenance. The handbook rates each methodology as to its value, as a function of the degree of reliability required for the software program. The book is written for the practitioner but includes an annotated bibliography at the end of each chapter for readers desiring a more academic discussion of the topics. The section devoted to the checkout phase (testing) contains almost as much material as all the other life cycle sections combined. Test plans, procedures and reports are briefly described.

GUNTHER, R. *Management Methodology for Software Product Engineering.* John Wiley and Sons: Wiley-Interscience, 1978.

This book was selected for inclusion from the many management oriented books on software development because of its chapter devoted to managing the software product test. This chapter maps the product test groups activities into the traditional software life cycle phases. The chapter discusses software test documentation and even presents a table of contents for test plans and test logs. The author writes from his experience as a product planning manager for Amdahl Corporation.

HETZEL, W.C. Ed. *Program Test Methods.* Prentice-Hall: 1973.

This book is a collection of papers from a testing symposium held in 1972. It covers testing concepts, design of programs to facilitate testing, design of languages to facilitate testing, testing mathematical software, and testing large software systems. The book contains a comprehensive bibliography.

MILLER, E. and HOWDEN, W.E. *Tutorial: Software Testing and Validation Techniques (2nd Ed).* IEEE Computer Society Press: Catalog no EHO 180-0, 1981.

This IEEE Tutorial is a collection of papers that represent new developments in program structure analysis, test coverage, test results analysis, test project management techniques, and test tools. The publication also includes an extensive bibliography on testing.

MYERS, G. *The Art of Software Testing.* Wiley — Interscience, John Wiley and Sons: 1979.

This book is based upon material from Software Reliability: Principles and Practices by the same author. The book emphasizes testing as an activity which tries to find errors in a program, not an activity that attempts to show that a program works. The book expands this thesis into a set of testing principles. Testing techniques and methodology are covered along with a survey of existing tools. Test documentation is not addressed. The book does a good job of defining testing terms and classifying testing techniques.

PERRY, W. *Effective Methods of EDP Quality Assurance.* Wellesly Massachusetts: QED Systems, 1977.

This handbook contains the following four sections: The Quality Assurance Function, Planning The Quality Assurance Function, Quality Assurance Reviews, and Relationships and Other QA Tests. The appendix presents a sample software QA manual. Software testing is presented as one activity requiring a QA review. The handbook presents what points should be addressed by a detailed test plan as well as the test result report. The handbook's strength is its broad coverage of all the aspects of a well organized QA group. The book addresses software testing as an important activity in software development that should be reviewed by a QA function.

POWELL, P.B. Ed. *Planning for Software Validation, Verification and Testing.* National Bureau of Standards: NBS Special Pub 1982.

The document is for those who direct and those who implement computer projects. It explains the selection and use of validation, verification, and testing (VV and T) tools and techniques. It explains how to develop a plan to meet specific software VV and T goals.

POWELL, P.B. Ed. *Software Validation, Verification, and Testing Technique and Tool Reference Guide.* National Bureau of Standards: NBS Special Pub 1982.

Thirty techniques and tools for validation, verification, and testing (VV and T) are described. Each description includes the basic features of the technique or tool, the input, the output, an example, an assessment of the effectiveness and of the learning time and training, an estimate of the needed resources, and references.

WOOLRIDGE, S. *Systems and Programming Standards.* New York: Petrocelli/Charter, 1977.

The author's major purpose is to outline the contents of a programming standards manual. Chapter 8 addresses system testing and presents the table of contents for a system test plan as well as a checklist for system testing. The presentation differs from the other references because of the book's focus on standards and procedures as contrasted to testing philosophies and software QA techniques. The book shows that testing procedures can be integrated into general software development procedures.

YEH, R. *Current Trends in Programming Methodology.* vol II Program Validation. Prentice-Hall, 1977.

This book is a selection of papers published during the first half of the seventies. The collection of papers is indexed and the volume also includes an extensive annotated bibliography. Test documentation is not covered but the book provides a reference point to theoretical treatments of software testing.

D2. Military Testing Standards

Acquisition and Support Procedures for Computer Resources in Systems. AF Regulation 800-14, vol 2, Department of the Air Force, 1975.

The volume defines the Air Force procedures for the acquisition of computer programs used in military systems. It defines a software acquisition life cycle. In chapter four, it defines the required types, levels and phases of software testing and their relationship to this life cycle. It specifies policy for software testing at the following levels: informal testing, preliminary qualification testing, formal qualification testing, and system level testing. This volume identifies the required contents for test plans and procedures and it also discusses general methods for computer program verification and validation.

Testing of Computer Software Systems. Technical Bulletin, TB 18-104, Department of the Army, September 1981.

This technical bulletin defines the Army's computer software testing methodology. It identifies required tests and test documentation. It also identifies a variety of participants in the testing process and their responsibilities.

Weapon System Software Development. MIL-STD-1679. Department of the Navy, 1978.

This specification requires quality assurance procedures at each stage of development to validate accuracy, correctness, and performance of the product programs and to verify the accuracy and conformance of program documentation. In the area of software trouble reporting, the specification requires the development and implementation of procedures for handling and reporting software problems. Section 5.8 describes various testing requirements.

ANSI/IEEE
Std 830-1984

An American National Standard

IEEE Guide to Software Requirements Specifications

830

Sponsor

**Software Engineering Technical Committee
of the
IEEE Computer Society**

Approved September 30, 1983

IEEE Standards Board

Approved July 20, 1984

American National Standards Institute

Foreword

(This Foreword is not a part of IEEE Std 830-1984, IEEE Guide to Software Requirements Specifications.)

This guide describes alternate approaches to good practice in the specification of software requirements. The requirements may be explicitly stated by the user or they may be allocated to computer software (that is, programs) by the system requirements analysis process. This guide does not suggest that a hierarchy of software requirements specifications exists, of which each, in turn, defines a smaller subset of requirements.

As a guide, this document should help:

(1) Software customers to accurately describe what they wish to obtain.

(2) Software suppliers to understand exactly what the customer wants.

(3) Individuals to accomplish the following goals:

(a) Develop standard software requirements specifications (SRS) outline for their own organizations.

(b) Define the form and content of their specific software requirements specifications.

(c) Develop additional local supporting items such as an SRS quality checklist, or an SRS writer's handbook.

To the customers, suppliers and other individuals, a good SRS provides several specific benefits. It will accomplish the following goals:

(1) Establish the basis for agreement between the customers and the suppliers on what the software product is to do. The complete description of the functions to be performed by the software specified in the SRS will assist the potential user, to determine if the software specified meets their needs or how the software must be modified to meet their needs.

(2) Reduce the development effort. The preparation of the SRS forces the various concerned groups in the customer's organization to consider rigorously all of the requirements before design begins and reduces later redesign, recoding, and retesting. Careful review of the requirements in the SRS can reveal omissions, misunderstandings, and inconsistencies early in the development cycle when these problems are easier to correct.

(3) Provide a basis for estimating costs and schedules. The description of the product to be developed as given in the SRS is a realistic basis for estimating project costs and can be used to obtain approval for bids or price estimates. The SRS also provides a clear description of the required software and makes it easier to estimate and plan the necessary resources. The requirements which, together with a development plan, can be used to measure progress.

(4) Provide a baseline for validation and verification. Organizations can develop their validation and verification plans much more productively from a good SRS. As a part of the development contract, the SRS provides a baseline against which compliance can be measured. (However, that the converse is not true; a standard legal contract cannot be used as an SRS. Such documents rarely contain the detail required and are often incomplete.)

(5) Facilitate transfer. The SRS makes it easier to transfer the software product to new users or new machines. Customers thus find it easier to transfer the software to other parts of their organization, and suppliers find it easier to transfer it to new customers.

(6) Serves as a basis for enhancement. Because the SRS discusses the product but not the project that developed it, the SRS serves as a basis for later enhancement of the finished product. The SRS may need to be altered, but it does provide a solid foundation for continued production evolution.

This guide is based on a model in which the result of the software requirements specification process is an unambiguous and complete specification document. In principle, the SRS can be mechanically translated into the specified software program directly. As such, the resulting SRS document itself is the specified software, and the supplier's only duty (after completing the SRS) would be the mechanical compilation of the SRS into machine code for the target computer. The present state of the art does not support such a compiler with an optimizer of such efficiency to make it practical but this limitation need not, and should not, restrict the intermediate objective of an unambiguous SRS.

This guide is consistent with IEEE Std 729-1983, IEEE Standard Glossary of Software Engineering Terminology; ANSI/IEEE Std 730-1981, IEEE Standard for Software Quality Assurance Plans; and IEEE Std 829-1983, IEEE Standard for Software Test Documentation. This guide may be used in conjunction with those standards or separately.

This guide was prepared by the Software Requirements Working Group of the Software Engineering Standards Subcommittee of the Technical Committee on Software Engineering of the IEEE Computer Society.

At the time the guide was approved, the Software Requirements Working Group had the following membership:

A. M. Davis, *Chairperson*

M. Bariff	R. A. C. Lane	G. R. Niedhart
H. Berlack	R. Lechner	J. Russell
F. Buckley	E. Levinson	A. Salwin
E. Byrne	P. Lindemann	N. B. Schneidewind
F. Calm	S. Mroczek	D. Schultz
K. Foster	A. J. Neumann	R. W. Szczech
S. Frankel	W. Newson	A. Weigel
T. L. Hannan	D. Paster	P. Willis
P. W. Kendra	B. Pope	H. Willman
T. M. Kurinara	P. B. Powell	A. W. Yonda

At the time that it approved this guide, the Software Engineering Standards Subcommittee had the following membership:

F. J. Buckley, *Chairperson*

R. J. Abbott	L. R. Heselton, III	D. J. Pfeiffer
A. F. Ackerman	S. Horvitz	R. M. Poston
L. Beltracchi	P. Howley	P. B. Powell
D. W. Bragg	R. N. Hurwitz	J. W. Radatz
D. W. Burt	S. Hwang	J. C. Rault
E. R. Byrne	J. H. Ingram	S. T. Redwine
H. Carney	J. P. Kalasky	L. K. Reed
J. W. Center	R. Kessler	W. E. Riddle
A. M. Cicu	T. M. Kurinara	C. W. Rutter, III
G. G. Cooke	D. V. LaRosa	P. E. Schilling
A. J. Cote, Jr	R. A. C. Lane	N. F. Schniedewind
P. W. Daggett	G. R. Lewis	A. D. Schuman
G. Darling	F. C. Lim	L. W. Seagren
B. Dasarathy	G. S. Lindsay	R. L. Skelton
A. M. Davis	M. Lipow	W. Smith
P. A. Denny	W. M. Lively	H. M. Sneed
J. A. Dobbins	M. Lubofsky	K. C. Tai
M. L. Eads	D. Lindquist	B. J. Taute
J. D. Earls	A. K. Manhindru	R. H. Thayer
L. G. Egan, Jr	P. C. Marriott	G. D. Tice, Jr
D. W. Fife	C. F. Martiny	T. L. Tillmans
J. Flournoy	M. McCollough	W. S. Turner, III
J. J. Forman	B. Menkus	E. A. Ulbrich, Jr
F. K. Gardner	B. Meyer	D. Usechak
D. Gelperin	E. F. Miller, Jr	U. Voges
E. L. Gibbs	G. S. Morris	R. Wachter
G. Gladden	G. T. Morun	J. P. Walter
S. A. Gloss-Soler	W. G. Murch	D. Webdale
J. W. Grigsby	J. Nebb	A. H. Weigel
R. M. Gross	G. R. Niedhart	N. P. Wilburn
D. A. Gustafson	M. A. Neighbors	W. M. Wong
R. T. Gustin	J. O. Neilson	T. Workman
T. L. Hannan	D. J. Ostrom	A. W. Yonda
H. Hecht		P. F. Zoll

Special representatives to the software engineering standards subcommittee were:

J. Milandin: ANSI Z1
W. G. Perry: Data Processing Manufacturers Association
R. Pritchett: EDP Auditors Association
T. L. Regulinski: IEEE Reliability Society
N. C. Farr: Nuclear Power Engineering Committee, IEEE Power Engineering Society

Suggestions for improvement of this guide are welcome. They should be provided to:

The Secretary
IEEE Standards Board
345 East 47th St
New York, New York 10017

At the time the IEEE Standards Board approved this standard on September 20, 1983 it had the following members:

James H. Beall, *Chairman*   **Edward Chelotti,** *Vice Chairman*

Sava I. Sherr, *Secretary*

J. J. Archambault	Donald H. Heirman	John P. Riganati
John T. Boettger	Irvin N. Howell	Frank L. Rose
J. V. Bonucchi	Joseph L. Koepfinger*	Robert W. Seelbach
Rene Castenschiold	Irving Kolodny	Jay A. Stewart
Edward J. Cohen	George Konomos	Clifford O. Swanson
Len S. Corey	John E. May	Robert E. Weiler
Donald C. Fleckenstein	Donald T. Michael*	W. B. Wilkens
Jay Forster		Charles J. Wylie

*Member emeritus

Contents

IEEE Guide to Software Requirements Specifications

1. Scope and Organization

1.1 Scope. This is a guide for writing software requirements specifications. It describes the necessary content and qualities of a good Software Requirements Specification (SRS) and presents a prototype SRS outline.

This guide does not specify industry-wide SRS standards nor state mandatory SRS requirements. This guide is written under the premise that the current state of the art does not warrant or support such a formal standards document.

This guide is applicable to in-house and commercial software products. Special care, however, should be used in its application because:

(1) This guide is aimed at specifying requirements of software to be developed. Application of this material to already-developed software is counter-productive.

(2) This guide does not cover the specification of requirements for software being developed using the techniques of rapid prototyping.

1.2 Organization. The remainder of this guide is organized as follows:

(1) Section 2 provides the references used throughout the guide.

(2) Section 3 provides definitions of specific terms used throughout the guide.

(3) Section 4 provides background information for writing a good SRS.

(4) Section 5 provides specific guidance for expressing software requirements.

(5) Section 6 discusses each of the essential parts of an SRS and provides alternate prototype outlines.

2. References

[1] ANSI/IEEE Std 100-1977, IEEE Standard Dictionary of Electrical and Electronics Terms.

[2] ANSI/IEEE Std 730-1981, IEEE Standard for Software Quality Assurance Plans.

[3] ANSI/IEEE Std 729-1983, IEEE Standard Glossary of Software Engineering Terminology.

[4] BRUSAW, C. T., ALRED, G. and OLIU, W., *Handbook of Technical Writing*, New York, St. Martin's Press, 1976.

[5] DASARATNY, B., *Timing Constraints of Real-Time Systems: Constructs for Expressing Them*, IEEE Real-Time Systems Symposium, Dec 1982.

[6] DAVIS, A., The Design of a Family of Applications-Oriented Requirements Languages, *IEEE Computer*, 15, 5 May 1982, pp 21–28.

[7] FREEDMAN, D. and WEINBERG, G., Handbook of Walkthroughs, *Inspections and Technical Reviews*, 3rd Ed, Little and Brown Publishers, New York.

[8] KAIN, R., Automata Theory: Machines and Languages, McGraw Hill, New York, 1972.

[9] KOHAVI, Z., Switching and Finite Automata Theory, McGraw Hill, New York, 1970.

[10] KRAMER, J., Editor, Application Oriented Specifications Glossary of Terms, *European Workshop on Industrial Computer Systems (EWICS)*, Imperial College, London, England, May 6, 1981.[1]

---

[1]Copies of this document are available from EWICS, c/o G. R. Koch, BIOMATIK Gmbh, Carl-Mez Str 81–83, D-7800 Freiburg, Federal Republic of Germany.

[11] MILLS, G., and WALTER, J., *Technical Writing*, New York, Holt, Rinehart and Winston, 4th Ed, 1978.

[12] PETERSON, J., *Petri Nets*, ACM Computing Surveys, 9, 4, Dec 1977, pp 223–252.

[13] RAMAMOORHY, C. and SO, H. H., *Software Requirements and Specifications: Status and Perspectives*, Tutorial: Software Methodology, RAMAMOORTHY, C. and YEH, R. T., Editors. IEEE Catalog no EHO 142-0, 1978, pp 43–164.

[14] TAGGART, W. M. Jr, and THARP, M. O., *A Survey of Information Requirements Analysis Techniques*, ACM Computing Surveys, 9, 4, Dec 1977, pp 273–290.

[15] TEICHROEW, D., *A Survey of Languages for Stating Requirements for Computer-Based Information Systems*, 1972 Fall Joint Computer Conference, 1972, pp 1203–1224.

3. Definitions

Except for the definitions listed below, the definitions of all terms used in this guide conform to the definitions provided in IEEE Std 729-1983 [3][2], for example, the terms requirement, requirements specification. If a term used in this guide does not appear in that Standard, then ANSI/IEEE Std 100-1977 [1], applies.

The terms listed in this section have been adopted from Section 2, [10].

contract. A legally binding document agreed upon by the customer and supplier. This includes the technical, organizational, cost and schedule requirements of a product.

customer. The person, or persons, who pay for the product and usually (but not necessarily) decides the requirements. In the context of this document the customer and the supplier may be members of the same organization.

language. A means of communication, with syntax and semantics, consisting of a set of representations, conventions and associated rules used to convey information.

partitioning. Decomposition; the separation of the whole into its parts.

supplier. The person, or persons, who produce a product for a customer. In the context of this document, the customer and the supplier may be members of the same organization.

user. The person, or persons, who operate or interact directly with the system. The user(s) and the customer(s) are often not the same person(s).

4. Background Information for Writing a Good SRS

This section provides background information necessary for writing an SRS. This includes:
  (1) Examination of the nature of the SRS
  (2) Environmental considerations surrounding the SRS
  (3) Characteristics required for a good SRS
  (4) Recommendations for joint preparation of an SRS
  (5) Evolutionary aspects of the SRS
  (6) The use of automated tools to develop an SRS

4.1 The SRS. The SRS is a specification for a particular software product, program, or set of programs that does certain things. See ANSI/IEEE Std 730-1981 [2], 3.4.2.1.

The description places two basic requirements on the SRS:
  (1) It must say certain things. For example, software developed from an SRS that fails to specify that error messages will be provided, will probably fail to satisfy the customer.
  (2) It must say those things in certain ways. For example, software developed from an SRS that fails to specify the format and content of error messages and instead is developed from a vague and non-quantifiable requirement such as *All error messages will be helpful*, will probably be unsatisfactory. What is *helpful* for one person can be a severe aggravation to another person.

For recommended contents of an SRS see Section 6.

4.2 Environment of the SRS. It is important to consider the part that the SRS plays in the total software project. The provisions in ANSI/IEEE Std 730-1981 [2], define the minimum required documents for a software project. See [2], 3.4.2.

ANSI/IEEE Std 730-1981 [2] also identifies the other useful documents. See [2], 3.4.3.

---
[2]Numbers in brackets correspond to those of the references in Section 2.

Since the SRS has a definite role to play in this documentation scheme, SRS writers should be careful not to go beyond the bounds of that role. This means the following requirements should be met:

(1) The SRS must correctly define all of the software requirements, but no more.

(2) The SRS should not describe any design, verification, or project management details, except for required design constraints.

Such a properly written SRS limits the range of valid solutions but does not specify any particular design and thus provides the supplier with maximum flexibility.

4.3 Characteristics of A Good SRS. The previous sections describe the types of information that should be contained in an SRS. The following concepts deal with particular characteristics. A good SRS is:

(1) Unambiguous
(2) Complete
(3) Verifiable
(4) Consistent
(5) Modifiable
(6) Traceable
(7) Usable during the Operation and Maintenance Phase

4.3.1 Unambiguous. An SRS is unambiguous if — and only if — every requirement stated therein has only one interpretation.

(1) As a minimum, this requires that each characteristic of the final product be described using a single unique term.

(2) In cases where a term used in a particular context could have multiple meanings, the term must be included in a glossary where its meaning is made more specific.

4.3.1.1 Natural Language Pitfalls. Requirements are often written in a natural language (for example, English). SRS writers who use a natural language must be especially careful to review their requirements for ambiguity. The following examples are taken from Section 2, [7].

(1) The specification *The data set will contain an end of file character*, might be read as:

(a) There will be one and only one end of file character

(b) Some character will be designated as an end of file character

(c) There will be at least one end of file character

(2) The specification *The control total is taken from the last record*, might be read as:

(a) The control total is taken from the record at the end of the file

(b) The control total is taken from the latest record

(c) The control total is taken from the previous record

(3) The specification *All customers have the same control field*, might be read as:

(a) All customers have the same value in their control field

(b) All customer control fields have the same format

(c) One control field is issued for all customers

(4) The specification *All files are controlled by a file control block*, might be read as:

(a) One control block controls the entire set of files

(b) Each file has its own block

(c) Each file is controlled by a control block, but one control block might control more than one file

4.3.1.2 Formal Requirements Specifications Languages. One way to avoid the ambiguity inherent in natural language is to write the SRS in a formal requirements specification language.[3]

(1) One major advantage in the use of such languages is the reduction of ambiguity. This occurs, in part, because the formal language processors automatically detect many lexical, syntactic, and semantic errors.

(2) One major disadvantage in the use of such languages is the length of time required to learn them.

4.3.2 Complete. An SRS is complete if it possesses the following qualities:

(1) Inclusion of all significant requirements, whether relating to functionality, performance, design constraints, attributes or external interfaces.

(2) Definition of the responses of the software to all realizable classes of input data in all realizable classes of situations. Note that it is important to specify the responses to valid and invalid input values.

(3) Conformity to any SRS standard that applies to it. If a particular section of the standard is not applicable, the SRS should

---

[3]For detailed discussion on this topic, suggested readings are [6], [13], [14], and [15].

include the section number and an explanation of why it is not applicable.

(4) Full labeling and referencing of all figures, tables, and diagrams in the SRS and definition of all terms and units of measure.

4.3.2.1 Use of TBDs. Any SRS that uses the phrase *to be determined* (TBD) is not a complete SRS.

(1) The TBD is, however, occasionally necessary and should be accompanied by:

(a) A description of the conditions causing the TBD (for example, why an answer is not known) so that the situation can be resolved.

(b) A description of what must be done to eliminate the TBD.

(2) Any project documents that are based on an SRS that contains TBDs, should:

(a) Identify the version or state the specific release number of the SRS associated with that particular document.

(b) Exclude any commitments dependent upon the sections of the SRS that are still identified as TBDs.

4.3.3 Verifiable. An SRS is verifiable if and only if every requirement stated therein is verifiable. A requirement is verifiable if and only if there exists some finite cost-effective process with which a person or machine can check that the software product meets the requirement.

(1) Examples of nonverifiable requirements include statements such as:

(a) *The product should work well*, or *The product should have a good human interface.* These requirements cannot be verified because it is impossible to define the terms *good* or *well*.

(b) *The program shall never enter an infinite loop.* This requirement is non-verifiable because the testing of this quality is theoretically impossible.

(c) *The output of the program shall usually be given within 10 s.* This requirement is non-verifiable because the term *usually* cannot be measured.

(2) An example of a verifiable statement is *The output of the program shall be given within 20 s of event* X, *60% of the time; and shall be given within 30 s of event* X, *100% of the time.* This statement can be verified because it uses concrete terms and measurable quantities.

(3) If a method cannot be devised to determine whether the software meets a particular requirement, then that requirement should be removed or revised.

(4) If a requirement is not expressible in verifiable terms at the time the SRS is prepared, then a point in the development cycle (review, test plan issue, etc) should be identified at which the requirement must be put into a verifiable form.

4.3.4 Consistent. An SRS is consistent if and only if no set of individual requirements described in it conflict. There are three types of likely conflicts in an SRS:

(1) Two or more requirements might describe the same real world object but use different terms for that object. For example, a program's request for a user input might be called a *prompt* in one requirement and a *cue* in another.

(2) The specified characteristics of real world objects might conflict. For example:

(a) The format of an output report might be described in one requirement as *tabular* but in another as *textual*.

(b) One requirement might state that all lights shall be green while another states that all lights shall be blue.

(3) There might be a logical or temporal conflict between two specified actions. For example:

(a) One requirement might specify that the program will add two inputs and another specify that the program will multiply them.

(b) One requirement might state that A must always follow B, while another requires that A and B occur simultaneously.

4.3.5 Modifiable. An SRS is modifiable if its structure and style are such that any necessary changes to the requirements can be made easily, completely, and consistently. Modifiability generally requires an SRS to:

(1) Have a coherent and easy-to-use organization, with a table of contents, an index, and explicit cross-referencing.

(2) Not be redundant; that is, the same requirement should not appear in more than one place in the SRS.

(a) Redundancy itself is not an error, but it can easily lead to errors. Redundancy can occasionally help to make an SRS more readable, but a problem can arise when the redundant document is updated. Assume, for instance, that a certain requirement is stated in two places. At some later time, it is determined that the requirement should be altered, but the change is made in only one of the two locations. The SRS then becomes inconsistent.

(b) Whenever redundancy is necessary, the SRS should include explicit cross-references to make it modifiable.

4.3.6 Traceable. An SRS is traceable if the origin of each of its requirements is clear and if it facilitates the referencing of each requirement in future development or enhancement documentation. Two types of traceability are recommended:

(1) Backward traceability (that is, to previous stages of development) depends upon each requirement explicitly referencing its source in previous documents.

(2) Forward traceability (that is, to all documents spawned by the SRS) depends upon each requirement in the SRS having a unique name or reference number.

When a requirement in the SRS represents an apportionment or a derivative of another requirement, both forward and backward traceability should be provided. Examples include:

4.3.6.1 The allocation of response time to a data base function from the overall user response time requirement.

4.3.6.2 The identification of a report format with certain functional and user interface requirements.

4.3.6.3 A software product that supports legislative or administrative needs (for example, tax computations, reporting of an overhead ratio). In this case, the exact legislative or administrative document that is being supported should be identified.

The forward traceability of the SRS is especially important when the software product enters the operation and maintenance phase. As code and design documents are modified, it is essential to be able to ascertain the complete set of requirements that may be affected by those modifications.

4.3.7 Usable During the Operation and Maintenance Phase. The SRS must address the needs of the operation and maintenance phase, including the eventual replacement of the software.

(1) Maintenance is frequently carried out by personnel not associated with the original development. Local changes (corrections) can be implemented by means of a well-commented code. For changes of wider scope, however, the design and requirements documentation is essential. This implies two actions

(a) The SRS should be modifiable as indicated in 4.3.5.

(b) The SRS should contain a record of all special provisions that apply to individual components such as:

(i) Their criticality (for example, where failure could impact safety or cause large financial or social losses).

(ii) Their relation to only temporary needs (for example, to support a display that may be retired soon).

(iii) Their origin (for example, function X is to be copied from an existing software product in its entirety).

(2) Knowledge of this type is taken for granted in the developing organization but is frequently missing in the maintenance organization. If the reason for or origin of a function is not understood, it is frequently impossible to perform adequate software maintenance on it.

4.4 Joint Preparation of the SRS. The software development process begins with supplier and customer agreement on what the completed software must do. This agreement, in the form of an SRS, should be jointly prepared. This is important because usually neither the customer nor the supplier is qualified to write a good SRS by himself.

(1) Customers usually do not understand the software design and development process well enough to write a usable SRS.

(2) Suppliers usually do not understand the customer's problem and field of endeavor well enough to specify requirements for a satisfactory system.

The customer and the supplier need to work together to produce a well written and completely understood SRS.[4]

4.5 SRS Evolution. The SRS may need to evolve as the development of the software product progresses.

(1) It may be impossible to specify some details at the time the project is initiated. For example, it may be impossible to define during the Requirements Phase, all of the screen formats for an interactive program in a manner that guarantees that they will not be altered later.

(2) Additional changes may ensue as deficien-

---

[4]This guide does not specifically discuss style, language usage, or techniques of good writing. It is quite important, however, that an SRS be well written; for guidance, please refer to general technical writing guides such as [1] and [11].

cies, shortcomings, and inaccuracies are discovered in the SRS, as the product evolves.

Two major considerations in this process are:

4.5.1 The requirements should be specified as completely and thoroughly as possible, even if evolutionary revisions can be forseen as inevitable. For example, the desired screen formats should be specified as well as possible in the SRS as a basis for later design.

4.5.2 A formal change process should be initiated to identify, control, track, and report projected changes, as soon as they are initially identified. Approved changes in requirements should be incorporated in the SRS in such a way as to:

(1) Provide an accurate and complete audit trail of changes.

(2) Permit the review of current and superseded portions of the SRS.

4.6 Tools for Developing an SRS. The most obvious way to create an SRS is to write it in a natural language (for example, English). But because natural languages are rich, although imprecise, a number of more formal methods have been devised to assist SRS writers.

4.6.1 Formal Specification Methodologies. The degree to which such formal methodologies may be useful in preparing an SRS depends upon a number of factors:

(1) The size and complexity of the program

(2) Whether a customer contract requires it

(3) Whether the SRS is a vehicle for contracts or merely an internal document

(4) Whether the SRS document will become the top level of the design document

(5) What computer facilities are available to support such a methodology

No attempt is made here to describe or endorse any particular tool.[5]

4.6.2 Production Tools. A computer-based word processor is a most useful production aid. Usually, an SRS will have several authors, will undergo several revisions, and will have several reorganizations. A word processor that manages the text as a computer file facilitates this process.

Almost all computer systems have a word processor and often a document preparation package is associated with it. This automates paragraphing and referencing, the printing of headings and subheadings, the compilation of tables of contents and indexes, etc, all of which help in the production of a more readable SRS.

4.6.3 Representation Tools. Some words in the SRS, especially nouns and verbs, refer specifically to entities and actions in the system. There are several advantages to identifying them as such.

(1) It is possible to verify that an entity or action always has the same name everywhere in the SRS. Thus *calculate trajectory* would not co-exist with *determine flight path*.

(2) It is possible to identify every place in the specification where a particular entity or action is described.

In addition, it may be desirable to formalize the English structure in some way to allow automated processing of the content of the SRS. With such constraints it becomes possible to:

4.6.3.1 Display the requirements in some tabular or graphical way.

4.6.3.2 Automatically check the SRS requirements in hierarchical layers of detail, where each layer is complete in itself but may also be expanded upon in a lower hierarchical layer or be a constituent of an upper hierarchical layer.

4.6.3.3 Automatically check that the SRS possesses some or all of the characteristics described in 4.3.

5. Software Requirements

Each software requirement in an SRS is a statement of some essential capability of the software to be developed. The following subsections describe:

(1) Methods used to express software requirements

(2) Annotation of the software requirements

(3) Common pitfalls encountered in the process

5.1 Methods Used To Express Software Requirements. Requirements can be expressed in a number of ways:

(1) Through input/output specifications

(2) By use of a set of representative examples

(3) By the specification of models

5.1.1 Input/Output Specifications. It is often effective to specify the required behavior of a software product as a sequence of inputs and outputs.

---

[5]For detailed discussion on this topic, see, for example, [6], [13], [14], and [15].

5.1.1.1 Approaches. There are at least three different approaches based on the nature of the software being specified:

(1) Some software products (such as reporting systems) are best specified by focusing on required outputs. In general, output-focused systems operate primarily on data files. User input usually serves to provide control information and trigger data file processing.

(2) Others are best specified by focusing on input/output behavior. Input/output-focused systems operate primarily on the current input. They are required to generate the *matching* output (as with data conversion routines or a package of mathematical functions).

(3) Some systems (such as process control systems) are required to remember their behavior so that they can respond to an input based on that input and past inputs; that is, behave like a finite state machine. In this case the focus is on both input/output pairs and sequences of such pairs.

5.1.1.2 Difficulties. Most software products can receive an infinite number of sequences as input. Thus, to completely specify the behavior of the product through input/output sequences would require that the SRS contain an infinitely long set of sequences of inputs and required outputs. With this approach, therefore, it may be impossible to completely specify every conceivable behavior that is required of the software.

5.1.2 Representative Examples. One alternative is to indicate what behavior is required by using representative examples of that behavior. Suppose, for example, that the system is required to respond with a "1" every time it receives a "0". Clearly, a list of all possible sequences of inputs and outputs would be impossible. However, by using representative sequences one might be able to fully understand the system's behavior. This system's behavior might be described by using this representative set of four dialogues: [6]

0101
010101010101
01
010101

These dialogues provide a good idea of the required inputs and outputs but they do not specify the system's behavior completely.

5.1.3 Models. Another approach is to express the requirements in the form of a model. [7] This can be an accurate and efficient way to express complex requirements.

At least three generalized types of models are in common usage:

(1) Mathematical
(2) Functional
(3) Timing

Care should be taken to distinguish between the model for the application; that is, a linear programming model (with a set of linear inequalities and an objective function) and the model for the software which is required to implement the application model. See 5.1.3.5.

5.1.3.1 Mathematical Models. A mathematical model is a model that uses mathematical relations to describe the software's behavior. Mathematical models are especially useful for particular application areas, including navigation, linear programming, econometrics, signal processing and weather analysis.

A mathematical model might specify the response discussed in 5.1.2 like this:

(01)∗

where ∗ means that the parenthesized character string is repeated one or more times.

5.1.3.2 Functional Models. A functional model is a model that provides a mapping from inputs to outputs. Functional models, for example, finite state machines or Petri nets can help identify and define various features of the software or can demonstrate the intended operation of the system.

A functional model might specify the response, previously described by the mathematical model, in the form of a finite state machine as shown in Fig 1. In this figure, the incoming arrow points to the starting state. The double lined box represents the accepting state. The notation X/Y on the lines indicates that when X is accepted as an input, Y is produced as an output.

5.1.3.3 Timing Models. A timing model is a model that has been augmented with timing constraints. Timing models are quite useful for specifying the form and details of the software's behavior, particularly for real-time systems or for human factors of any system.

---

[6] Each of the four sample dialogues given here (one per line) represents a sequence of one-character user inputs and one-character system outputs.

[7] For details on using modeling techniques, see [5], [8], [9], and [12].

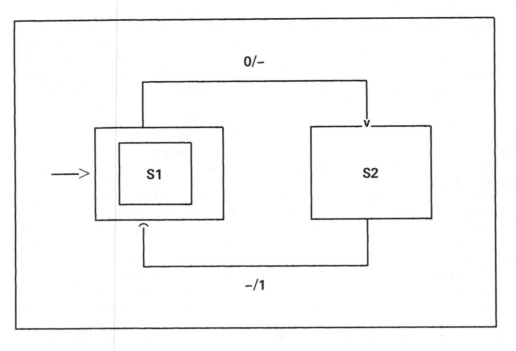

Fig 1
A Functional Model Specifying Any Sequence of Alternating 0s and 1s

A timing model might add these constraints to the model shown in Fig 1.

(1) The stimulus 0 will occur within 30 s of the arrival in state S1

(2) The response 1 will occur within 2 s of the arrival in state S2

5.1.3.4 Other Models. In addition to the aforementioned, specific applications have particularly helpful models. For example, a compiler specification might employ attribute grammars, or a payroll system might use tables. It is to be noted that the use of a formal requirements language for an SRS usually implies a need for the use of a particular model.

5.1.3.5 Cautions. Whatever type of model is used:

(1) It must be rigorously defined, either in the SRS or in a document referenced in the SRS. This definition should specify

(a) The required ranges of the model's parameters

(b) The values of constraints it uses

(c) The required accuracy of results

(d) The load capacity

(e) The required execution time

(f) Default or failure response

(2) Care must be taken to keep a model definition within the domain of requirements.

Whenever an SRS uses a model:

(a) It means that the model provided an especially efficient and accurate way to specify the requirements

(b) It does not mean that the implementation of the software product must be based on that model.

A model that works effectively for explaining requirements in a written document may not be optimal for the actual software implementation.

5.2 Annotation of the Software Requirements. Typically, all of the requirements that relate to a software product are not equally important. Some requirements may be essential, especially for life-critical applications, while others may be just *nice to have*.

(1) Each requirement in the SRS should be annotated to make these differences in relative importance clear and explicit.

(2) Annotating the requirements in this manner, helps:

(a) Customers to give more careful consideration to each requirement, which often clarifies any hidden assumptions they may have.

(b) Developers to make correct design decisions and devote appropriate levels of effort to the different parts of the software product.

5.2.1 Stability. One method of annotating requirements uses the dimension of stability. A requirement may be considered *stable* when it is thought that the needs which it addresses will not change during the expected life of the software, or it may be considered *volatile* and subject to change.

5.2.2 Degree of Necessity. Another way to annotate is to distinguish classes of requirements as mandatory, desirable, and optional.

(1) Mandatory implies that the software will not be acceptable unless these requirements are provided in an agreed manner.

(2) Desirable implies that these are requirements that would enhance the software product, but would not make it unacceptable if they are absent.

(3) Optional implies a class of functions that may or may not be worthwhile, which gives the supplier the opportunity to propose something which exceeds the SRS.

5.2.3 Annotation Caution. Prior to annotating the requirements, a thorough understanding of the contractual implications of such annotations, should be obtained.

5.3 Common Pitfalls Encountered in Expressing Requirements. An essential point about the SRS is that it should specify the results that must be achieved by the software, not the means of obtaining those results.

(1) The basic issues that the requirements writer must address are these:

(a) *Functionality* — what the software is supposed to do

(b) *Performance* — the speed, availability, response time, recovery time of various software functions, etc

(c) *Design Constraints Imposed on an Implementation* — any required standards in effect, implementation language, policies for data base integrity, resource limits, operating environment(s), etc

(d) *Attributes* — considerations of portability, correctness, maintainability, security, etc

(e) *External Interfaces* — interactions with people, hardware, other software and other hardware

(2) The requirements writer should avoid placing either design or project requirements in the SRS. The requirements writer should clearly distinguish between identifying required design constraints and projecting a design.

5.3.1 Embedding Design in the SRS. Embedding design specifications in the SRS unduly constrains the software designs and artificially places potentially dangerous requirements in the SRS.

(1) The SRS must specify what functions are to be performed on what data to produce what results at what location for whom. The SRS should focus on the services to be performed. The SRS should not normally specify design items such as

(a) Partitioning the software into modules

(b) Allocating functions to the modules

(c) Describing the flow of information or control between modules

(d) Choosing data structures

(2) It is not always practical to consider the design as being completely isolated from the SRS. Security or safety considerations may impose requirements that reflect directly into design constraints; for example, the need to

(a) Keep certain functions in separate modules

(b) Permit only limited communication between some areas of the program

(c) Compute check sums for critical quantities

In general, it must be considered that the selection of an appropriate high-level design for the software may require vast amounts of resources (perhaps as much as 10% to 20% of the total product development cost). There are two alternatives:

(1) Ignore the warning in this guide and specify the design in the SRS. This will mean that either a potentially inadequate design is stated as a requirement (because insufficient time was spent in arriving at it), or an exorbitant amount of time is spent during the requirements phase (because an entire design analysis is performed before SRS completion).

(2) Use the advice in 5.1.3 of this guide. State the requirements using a *model* design used solely to assist in the description of the requirements and not intended to serve as the actual design.

5.3.2 Embedding Project Requirements in the SRS. The SRS should address the software product, not the process of producing the software product.

(1) Project requirements represent an understanding between a customer and a supplier about the contractual matters pertaining to the production of software (and thus should not be

included in the SRS). These normally include such items as:

 (a) Cost
 (b) Delivery schedules
 (c) Reporting procedures
 (d) Software development methods
 (e) Quality assurance
 (f) Validation and verification criteria
 (g) Acceptance procedures

(2) Project requirements are specified in other documents, typically in a computer program development plan or a statement of work. The requirements for only the software product itself are given in the SRS.

6. An SRS Prototype Outline

This section discusses each of the essential parts of the SRS. These parts are arranged in Table 1 in an outline that can serve as a prototype for any SRS.

Software suppliers and customers should tailor the content requirements of this guide based on the particular package being specified, and individual companies might base their own SRS standards upon it. Remember that while an SRS does not have to follow this outline or use the names for its parts, any good SRS must include all of the information discussed here.

6.1 Introduction (Section 1 of the SRS). The following subsections of the SRS should provide an overview of the entire SRS.

Table 1
Prototype SRS Outline

Table of Contents
1. Introduction
 1.1 Purpose
 1.2 Scope
 1.3 Definitions, Acronyms, and Abbreviations
 1.4 References
 1.5 Overview
2. General Description
 2.1 Product Perspective
 2.2 Product Functions
 2.3 User Characteristics
 2.4 General Constraints
 2.5 Assumptions and Dependencies
3. Specific Requirements
 (See 6.3.2 of this guide for alternate organizations of this section of the SRS.)
Appendixes
Index

6.1.1 Purpose (1.1 of the SRS). This subsection should accomplish the following:

(1) Delineate the purpose of the particular SRS

(2) Specify the intended audience for the SRS

6.1.2 Scope (1.2 of the SRS). This subsection should:

(1) Identify the software product(s) to be produced by name; for example, Host DBMS, Report Generator, etc

(2) Explain what the software product(s) will, and, if necessary, will not do

(3) Describe the application of the software being specified. As a portion of this, it should:

 (a) Describe all relevant benefits, objectives, and goals as precisely as possible. For example, to say that one goal is to provide *effective reporting capabilities* is not as good as saying *parameter-driven, user-definable reports with a 2 h turnaround and on-line entry of user parameters.*

 (b) Be consistent with similar statements in higher-level specifications (for example, the System Requirement Specification), if they exist.

6.1.3 Definitions, Acronyms, and Abbreviations (1.3 of the SRS). This subsection should provide the definitions of all terms, acronyms, and abbreviations required to properly interpret the SRS. This information may be provided by reference to one or more appendixes in the SRS or by reference to other documents.

6.1.4 References (1.4 of the SRS). This subsection should:

(1) Provide a complete list of all documents referenced elsewhere in the SRS, or in a separate, specified document.

(2) Identify each document by title, report number — if applicable — date, and publishing organization.

(3) Specify the sources from which the references can be obtained.

This information may be provided by reference to an appendix or to another document.

6.1.5 Overview (1.5 of the SRS). This subsection should:

(1) Describe what the rest of the SRS contains

(2) Explain how the SRS is organized

6.2 The General Description (Section 2 of the SRS). This section of the SRS should describe the general factors that affect the product and its requirements.

18

This section usually consists of five subsections, as follows:
(1) Product Perspective
(2) Product Functions
(3) User Characteristics
(4) General Constraints
(5) Assumptions and Dependencies

It should be made clear that this section does not state specific requirements; it only makes those requirements easier to understand.

6.2.1 Product Perspective (2.1 of the SRS). This subsection of the SRS puts the product into perspective with other related products or projects.

(1) If the product is independent and totally self-contained, it should be stated here.

(2) If the SRS defines a product that is a component of a larger system or project — as frequently occurs — then this subsection should:

(a) Describe the functions of each component of the larger system or project, and identify interfaces

(b) Identify the principal external interfaces of this software product.

NOTE: This is not a detailed description of these interfaces; the detailed description is provided elsewhere in the SRS.

(c) Describe the computer hardware and peripheral equipment to be used.

NOTE: This is an overview description only.

A block diagram showing the major components of the larger system or project, interconnections, and external interfaces can be very helpful.

This subsection should not be used to impose a specific design solution or specific design constraints on the solution. This subsection should provide the reasons why certain design constraints are later specified as part of the Specific Requirements Section of the SRS.

6.2.2 Product Functions (2.2 of the SRS). This subsection of the SRS should provide a summary of the functions that the software will perform. For example, an SRS for an accounting program might use this part to address *customer account maintenance, customer statement and invoice preparation* without mentioning the vast amount of detail that each of those functions requires.

Sometimes the function summary that is necessary for this part can be taken directly from the section of the higher-level specifica-tion (if one exists) that allocates particular functions to the software product. Note that, for the sake of clarity:

(1) The functions should be organized in a way that makes the list of functions understandable to the customer or to anyone else reading the document for the first time.

(2) Block diagrams showing the different functions and their relationships can be helpful. Remember, however, that such a diagram is not a requirement on the design of a product itself; it is simply an effective explanatory tool.

This subsection should not be used to state specific requirements. This subsection should provide the reasons why certain specific requirements are later specified as part of the Specific Requirements Section(s) of the SRS.

6.2.3 User Characteristics (2.3 of the SRS). This subsection of the SRS should describe those general characteristics of the eventual users of the product that will affect the specific requirements.

Many people interact with a system during the operation and maintenance phase of the software life cycle. Some of these people are users, operators, and maintenance and systems personnel. Certain characteristics of these people, such as educational level, experience, and technical expertise impose important constraints on the system's operating environment.

If most users of the system are occasional users, a resulting specific requirement might be that the system contains reminders of how to perform essential functions rather than assuming that the user will remember these details from the last session or from reading the user's guide.

This subsection should not be used to state specific requirements or to impose specific design constraints on the solution. This subsection should provide the reasons why certain specific requirements or design constraints are later specified as part of the Specific Requirements Section(s) of the SRS.

6.2.4 General Constraints (2.4 of the SRS). This subsection of the SRS should provide a general description of any other items that will limit the developer's options for designing the system. These can include:

(1) Regulatory policies
(2) Hardware limitations; for example, signal timing requirements
(3) Interfaces to other applications
(4) Parallel operation
(5) Audit functions

(6) Control functions

(7) Higher-order language requirements

(8) Signal handshake protocols; for example, XON –XOFF, ACK – NACK.

(9) Criticality of the application

(10) Safety and security considerations

This subsection should not be used to impose specific requirements or specific design constraints on the solution. This subsection should provide the reasons why certain specific requirements or design constraints are later specified as part of the Specific Requirements Section of the SRS.

6.2.5 Assumptions and Dependencies (2.5 of the SRS). This subsection of the SRS should list each of the factors that affect the requirements stated in the SRS. These factors are not design constraints on the software but are, rather, any changes to them that can affect the requirements in the SRS. For example, an assumption might be that a specific operating system will be available on the hardware designated for the software product. If, in fact, the operating system is not available, the SRS would then have to change accordingly.

6.3 The Specific Requirements (Section 3 of the SRS). This section of the SRS should contain all the details the software developer needs to create a design. This is typically the largest and most important part of the SRS.

(1) The details within it should be defined as individual specific requirements, following the guidelines described in Section 3 of this guide (verifiable, unambiguous, etc)

(2) Background should be provided by cross-referencing each specific requirement to any related discussion in the Introduction, General Description, and Appendixes portions of the SRS, whenever possible.

(3) One way to classify the specific requirements is as follows:

    (a) Functional Requirements

    (b) Performance Requirements

    (c) Design Constraints

    (d) Attributes

    (e) External Interface Requirements

The important points to be recognized are that:

(1) Specific requirements should be organized in a logical and readable fashion.

(2) Each requirement should be stated such that its achievement can be objectively verified by a prescribed method.

6.3.1 Information Required as Part of the Specific Requirements

6.3.1.1 Functional Requirements. This subsection of the SRS should specify how the inputs to the software product should be transformed into outputs. It describes the fundamental actions that must take place in the software.

For each class of function or sometimes for each individual function, it is necessary to specify requirements on inputs, processing, and outputs. These are usually organized with these four subparagraphs:

(1) Introduction. This subparagraph should provide a description of the purpose of the function and the approaches and techniques employed. It should contain any introductory or background material which might clarify the intent of the function.

(2) Inputs. This subparagraph should contain:

    (a) A detailed description of all data input to this function to include:

        (i) The sources of the inputs

        (ii) Quantities

        (iii) Units of measure

        (iv) Timing

        (v) The ranges of the valid inputs to include accuracies and tolerances.

    (b) The details of operator control requirements should include names and descriptions of operator actions, and console or operator positions. For example, this might include required operator activities such as form alignment — when printing checks.

    (c) References to interface specifications or interface control documents where appropriate.

(3) Processing. This subparagraph should define all of the operations to be performed on the input data and intermediate parameters to obtain the output. It includes specification of:

    (a) Validity checks on the input data

    (b) The exact sequence of operations to include timing of events

    (c) Responses to *abnormal* situations, for example:

        (i) Overflow

        (ii) Communication failure

        (iii) Error handling

    (d) Parameters affected by the operations

    (e) Requirements for degraded operation

    (f) Any methods (for example, equations, mathematical algorithms, and logical operations) which must be used to transform the system inputs into corresponding outputs. For example, this might specify:

(i) The formula for computing the withholding tax in a payroll package

(ii) A least squares curve fitting technique for a plotting package

(iii) A meteorological model to be used for a weather forecasting package

(g) Validity checks on the output data

(4) Outputs. This subparagraph should contain:

(a) A detailed description of all data output from this function to include:

(i) Destinations of the outputs

(ii) Quantities

(iii) Units of measure

(iv) Timing

(v) The range of the valid outputs is to include accuracies and tolerances

(vi) Disposition of illegal values

(vii) Error messages

(b) References to interface specifications or interface control documents where appropriate

In addition, for those systems whose requirements focus on input/output behavior, the SRS should specify all of the significant input/output pairs and sequences of pairs. Sequences will be needed when a system is required to remember its behavior so that it can respond to an input based on that input and past behavior; that is, behave like a finite state machine.

6.3.1.2 Performance Requirements. This subsection should specify both the static and the dynamic numerical requirements placed on the software or on human interaction with the software, as a whole.

(1) Static numerical requirements may include:

(a) The number of terminals to be supported

(b) The number of simultaneous users to be supported

(c) Number of files and records to be handled

(d) Sizes of tables and files

Static numerical requirements are sometimes identified under a separate section entitled *capacity.*

(2) Dynamic numerical requirements may include, for example, the numbers of transactions and tasks and the amount of data to be processed within certain time periods for both normal and peak workload conditions.

All of these requirements should be stated in measurable terms, for example, *95% of the transactions shall be processed in less than 1 s,*

rather than, *operator shall not have to wait for the transaction to complete.*

NOTE: Numerical limits applied to one specific function are normally specified as part of the processing subparagraph description of that function.

6.3.1.3 Design Constraints. Design constraints can be imposed by other standards, hardware limitations, etc.

6.3.1.3.1 Standards Compliance. This subsection should specify the requirements derived from existing standards or regulations. They might include:

(1) Report format

(2) Data naming

(3) Accounting procedures

(4) Audit Tracing. For example, this could specify the requirement for software to trace processing activity. Such traces are needed for some applications to meet minimum government or financial standards. An audit trace requirement might, for example, state that all changes to a payroll data base must be recorded in a trace file with before and after values.

6.3.1.3.2 Hardware Limitations. This subsection could include requirements for the software to operate inside various hardware constraints. For example, these could include:

(1) Hardware configuration characteristics (number of ports, instruction sets, etc)

(2) Limits on primary and secondary memory

6.3.1.4 Attributes. There are a number of attributes that can place specific requirements on the software. Some of these are indicated below. These should not be interpreted to be a complete list.

6.3.1.4.1 Availability. This could specify the factors required to guarantee a defined availability level for the entire system such as checkpoint, recovery and restart.

6.3.1.4.2 Security. This could specify the factors that would protect the software from accidental or malicious access, use, modification, destruction, or disclosure. Specific requirements in this area could include the need to:

(1) Utilize certain cryptographical techniques

(2) Keep specific log or history data sets

(3) Assign certain functions to different modules

(4) Restrict communications between some areas of a program

(5) Compute checksums for critical quantities

6.3.1.4.3 Maintainability. This could specify the requirements to ensure that the software could be maintained. For example, as a part of this,

(1) Specific coupling metrics for the software modules could be required

(2) Specific data/program partitioning requirements could be specified for micro-devices

6.3.1.4.4 Transferability/Conversion. This could specify the user procedures, user interface compatibility constraints (if any) etc, required to transport the software from one environment to another.

6.3.1.4.5 Caution. It is important that required attributes be specified so that their achievement can be objectively verified by a prescribed method.

6.3.1.5 External Interface Requirements

6.3.1.5.1 User Interfaces. This should specify:

(1) The characteristics that the software must support for each human interface to the software product. For example, if the user of the system operates through a display terminal, the following should be specified:

(a) Required screen formats

(b) Page layout and content of any reports or menus

(c) Relative timing of inputs and outputs

(d) Availability of some form of programmable function keys

(2) All the aspects of optimizing the interface with the person who must use the system. This may simply comprise a list of do's and don'ts on how the system will appear to the user. One example might be a requirement for the option of long or short error messages. Like all others, these requirements should be verifiable and for example, *a clerk typist grade 4 can do function X in Z min* after 1 h *of training* rather than *a typist can do function X.* (This might also be specified in the Attributes section under a section titled *Ease of Use.*)

6.3.1.5.2 Hardware Interfaces. This should specify the logical characteristics of each interface between the software product and the hardware components of the system. It also covers such matters as what devices are to be supported, how they are to be supported, and protocols. For example, terminal support might specify full screen support as opposed to line by line.

6.3.1.5.3 Software Interfaces. This should specify the use of other required software products (for example, a data management system, an operating system, or a mathematical package), and interfaces with other application systems (for example, the linkage between an accounts receivable system and a general ledger system).

For each required software product, the following should be provided:

(1) Name

(2) Mnemonic

(3) Specification number

(4) Version number

(5) Source

For each interface, this part should:

(1) Discuss the purpose of the interfacing software as related to this software product.

(2) Define the interface in terms of message content and format. It is not necessary to detail any well-documented interface, but a reference to the document defining the interface is required.

6.3.1.5.4 Communications Interfaces. This should specify the various interfaces to communications such as local network protocols, etc.

6.3.1.6 Other Requirements. Certain requirements may, due to the nature of the software, the user organization, etc, be placed in separate categories as indicated below.

6.3.1.6.1 Data Base. This could specify the requirements for any data base that is to be developed as part of the product. This might include:

(1) The types of information identified in 6.3.1.1

(2) Frequency of use

(3) Accessing capabilities

(4) Data element and file descriptors

(5) Relationship of data elements, records and files

(6) Static and dynamic organization

(7) Retention requirements for data

NOTE: If an existing data base package is to be used, this package should be named under *Interfaces to Software* and details of using it specified there.

6.3.1.6.2 Operations. This could specify the normal and special operations required by the user such as:

(1) The various modes of operations in the user organization; for example, user-initiated operations

(2) Periods of interactive operations and periods of unattended operations

(3) Data processing support functions

(4) Backup and recovery operations

NOTE: This is sometimes specified as part of the User Interfaces section.

6.3.1.6.3 Site Adaptation Requirements. This could:

(1) Define the requirements for any data or initialization sequences that are specific to a given site, mission, or operational mode, for example, grid values, safety limits, etc.

(2) Specify the site or mission-related features that should be modified to adapt the software to a particular installation.

6.3.2 Organizing The Specific Requirements. This subsection is often the largest and most complex of all the parts of the SRS.

(1) It may be necessary to organize this section into subdivisions according to the primary classes of functions to be performed by the software. For example, consider a large interactive accounting system. This may be broken down at the top level into operational software (which supports near-real-time transactions), support software (logging functions, disk backup, loading tapes, etc), and diagnostic software (primarily hardware and communications support), and at the next level into accounts receivable, accounts payable, etc.

(2) It should be remembered, however, that the purpose of this subdivided organization is to improve the readability of the SRS, not to define the high level design of the software being specified.

The best organization for Section 3, Specific Requirements, in an SRS, depends on the application area and the nature of the software product being specified. Tables 2 through 4 show four possible organizations.

(1) In Prototype Outline 1 (Table 2), all the Functional Requirements are specified, then the four types of interface requirements are specified, and then the rest of the requirements are specified.

(2) Prototype Outline 2 (Table 3) shows the four classes of interface requirements applied to each individual Functional Requirement. This is followed by the specification of the rest of the requirements.

(3) In Prototype Outline 3 (Table 4), all of the issues addressed by the Functional Requirements are specified, then the other requirements that apply to them are specified. This pattern is then repeated for each of the External Interface Requirement Classifications.

Table 2
Prototype Outline 1 for SRS Section 3

```
3.  Specific Requirements
    3.1  Functional Requirements
         3.1.1  Functional Requirement 1
                3.1.1.1  Introduction
                3.1.1.2  Inputs
                3.1.1.3  Processing
                3.1.1.4  Outputs
         3.1.2  Functional Requirement 2
         . . . .
         3.1.n  Functional Requirement n
    3.2  External Interface Requirements
         3.2.1  User Interfaces
         3.2.2  Hardware Interfaces
         3.2.3  Software Interfaces
         3.2.4  Communications Interfaces
    3.3  Performance Requirements
    3.4  Design Constraints
         3.4.1  Standards Compliance
         3.4.2  Hardware Limitations
         . . . .
    3.5  Attributes
         3.5.1  Security
         3.5.2  Maintainability
         . . . .
    3.6  Other Requirements
         3.6.1  Data Base
         3.6.2  Operations
         3.6.3  Site Adaptation
         . . . .
```

Table 3
Prototype Outline 2 for SRS Section 3

```
3.  Specific Requirements
    3.1  Functional Requirements
         3.1.1  Functional Requirement 1
                3.1.1.1  Specification
                         3.1.1.1.1  Introduction
                         3.1.1.1.2  Inputs
                         3.1.1.1.3  Processing
                         3.1.1.1.4  Outputs
                3.1.1.2  External Interfaces
                         3.1.1.2.1  User Interfaces
                         3.1.1.2.2  Hardware
                                    Interfaces
                         3.1.1.2.3  Software
                                    Interfaces
                         3.1.1.2.4  Communication
                                    Interfaces
         3.1.2  Functional Requirement 2
         . . . .
         3.1.n  Functional Requirement n
    3.2  Performance Requirements
    3.3  Design Constraints
    3.4  Attributes
         3.4.1  Security
         3.4.2  Maintainability
         . . . .
    3.5  Other Requirements
         3.5.1  Data Base
         3.5.2  Operations
         3.5.3  Site Adaption
         . . . .
```

Table 4
Prototype Outline 3 for SRS Section 3

```
3.  Specific Requirements
    3.1  Functional Requirements
         3.1.1  Functional Requirement 1
                3.1.1.1  Introduction
                3.1.1.2  Inputs
                3.1.1.3  Processing
                3.1.1.4  Outputs
                3.1.1.5  Performance Requirements
                3.1.1.6  Design Constraints
                         3.1.1.4.1  Standards
                                    Compliance
                         3.1.1.4.2  Hardware
                                    Limitations
                         . . . .
                3.1.1.7  Attributes
                         3.1.1.7.1  Security
                         3.1.1.7.2  Maintainability
                         . . . .
                3.1.1.8  Other Requirements
                         3.1.1.8.1  Data Base
                         3.1.1.8.2  Operations
                         3.1.1.8.3  Site Adaption
                         . . . .
         3.1.2  Functional Requirement 2
         . . . .
         3.1.n  Functional Requirement n
    3.2  External Interface Requirements
         3.2.1  User Interfaces
                3.2.1.1  Performance Requirements
                3.2.1.2  Design Constraints
                         3.2.1.2.1  Standards
                                    Compliance
                         3.2.1.2.2  Hardware
                                    Limitations
                         . . . .
                3.2.1.3  Attributes
                         3.2.1.3.1  Security
                         3.2.1.3.2  Maintainability
                         . . . .
                3.2.1.4  Other Requirements
                         3.2.1.4.1  Data Base
                         3.2.1.4.2  Operations
                         3.2.1.4.3  Site Adaption
                         . . . .
         3.2.2  Hardware Interfaces
         3.2.3  Software Interfaces
         3.2.4  Communications Interfaces
```

Table 5
Prototype Outline 4 for SRS Section 3

```
3.  Specific Requirements
    3.1  Functional Requirement 1
         3.1.1  Introduction
         3.1.2  Inputs
         3.1.3  Processing
         3.1.4  Outputs
         3.1.5  External Interfaces
                3.1.5.1  User Interfaces
                3.1.5.2  Hardware Interfaces
                3.1.5.3  Software Interfaces
                3.1.5.4  Communication Interfaces
         3.1.6  Performance Requirements
         3.1.7  Design Constraints
         3.1.8  Attributes
                3.1.8.1  Security
                3.1.8.2  Maintainability
                . . . .
         3.1.9  Other Requirements
                3.1.9.1  Data Base
                3.1.9.2  Operations
                3.1.9.3  Site Adaption
                . . . .
    3.2  Functional Requirement 2
    . . . .
    3.n  Functional Requirement n
```

(4) In Prototype Outline 4 (Table 5), the interface requirements and the rest of the requirements are specified as they pertain to each Functional Requirement.

The organization of the Specific Requirements Section of the SRS should be chosen with the goal of properly specifying the requirements in the most readable manner.

6.4 Supporting Information. The supporting information; that is, the Table of Contents, the Appendixes, and the Index, make the SRS easier to use.

(1) The Table of Contents and Index are quite important and should follow the generally accepted rules for good documentation practices.[8]

(2) The Appendixes are not always considered part of the actual requirements specification and are not always necessary. They might include:

(a) Sample I/O formats, descriptions of cost analysis studies, or results of user surveys.

(b) Supporting or background information that can help the readers of the SRS.

(c) A description of the problems to be solved by the software.

(d) The history, background, experience and operational characteristics of the organization to be supported.

(e) A cross-reference list, arranged by milestone, of those incomplete software requirements that are to be completed by specified milestones. (See 4.3.2 and 4.3.3 (4).)

(f) Special packaging instructions for the code and the media to meet security, export, initial loading, or other requirements.

(3) When Appendixes are included, the SRS should explicitly state whether or not the Appendixes are to be considered part of the requirements.

---

[8] See, for example: [4] and [11].

IEEE Standard Dictionary of Measures to Produce Reliable Software

982.1

Sponsor

**Software Engineering Standards Subcommittee
of the
Technical Committee on Software Engineering
of the
IEEE Computer Society**

Approved June 9, 1988

IEEE Standards Board

Foreword

(This Foreword is not a part of IEEE Std 982.1-1988, IEEE Standard Dictionary of Measures to Produce Reliable Software.)

This standard provides a set of measures indicative of software reliability that can be applied to the software product as well as to the development and support processes. It was motivated by the need of software developers and users who are confronted with a plethora of models, techniques, and measures. There is a need for measures that can be applied early in the development process that may be indicators of the reliability of the delivered product. This standard provides a common, consistent definition of a set of measures that may meet those needs.

This standard is intended to serve as the foundation on which researchers and practitioners can build consistent methods. This document is designed to assist management in directing product development and support toward specific reliability goals. Its purpose is to provide a common set of definitions through which a meaningful exchange of data and evaluations can occur. Successful application of the measures is dependent upon their use as intended in the specific environments.

There is both a process goal and a product goal for this document:

(1) The process goal is to provide measures that may be applicable throughout the life cycle and may provide the means for continual self-assessment and reliability improvement.

(2) The product goal is to increase the reliability of the software in its actual use environment during the operations and support phases.

This standard is intended to be of interest to design, development, evaluation (for example, auditors, procuring agency) and maintenance personnel; software quality and software reliability personnel; and to operations and acquisition support managers. This document contains four sections:

Section 1: Scope, establishes the goals and boundaries of the standard.

Section 2: Definitions, serves as a central location for key terms used throughout the body of the document.

Section 3: Functional Classification of Measures, provides a taxonomy with respect to measure objectives.

Section 4: Measures for Reliable Software, presents the measures ordered in general by complexity.

The Software Reliability Measurement Working Group Steering Committee had the following membership:

James Dobbins, *Chairman*

Ray Leber, *Co-Chairman*   **Ted Workman,** *Co-Chairman*

Peter Bright	Laura Good	Frank Salvia
Antonio Cicu	Nancy Hall	David Siefert
Carlo Cucciati	Philip Marriott	Raghu Singh
Walter Ellis	Roger Martin	Vijaya Srivastava
William Farr	Walter Murch	Henry Trochesset
Stuart Glickman	Patricia Powell	William Wilson

The Software Reliability Measurement Working Group had the following membership:

The following persons were on the balloting committee that approved this document for submission to the IEEE Standards Board:

When the IEEE Standards Board approved this standard on June 9, 1988, it had the following membership:

Donald C. Fleckenstein, *Chairman*   **Marco Migliaro**, *Vice Chairman*

Andrew G. Salem, *Secretary*

Arthur A. Blaisdell	John W. Horch	L. Bruce McClung
Fletcher J. Buckley	Jack M. Kinn	Donald T. Michael*
James M. Daly	Frank D. Kirschner	Richard E. Mosher
Stephen R. Dillon	Frank C. Kitzantides	L. John Rankine
Eugene P. Fogarty	Joseph L. Koepfinger*	Gary S. Robinson
Jay Forster*	Irving Kolodny	Frank L. Rose
Thomas L. Hannan	Edward Lohse	Helen M. Wood
Kenneth D. Hendrix	John E. May, Jr.	Karl H. Zaininger
Theodore W. Hissey, Jr.	Lawrence V. McCall	Donald W. Zipse

*Member Emeritus

Contents

List of Symbols

Symbol	Meaning	Measures Used	Primitive/ Metric
A	(1) Number of arrivals during time period T	37	P
	(2) Reliability growth factor	26	M
$A_{existing}$	Number of ambiguities in a program remaining to be eliminated	6	P
$A(t)$	System availability	39	M
A_{tot}	Total number of ambiguities identified	6	P
α	Test accuracy	36	M
AQ	Average queue length	37	M
AS	Average service time	37	P
B	Software science measure (number of errors)	14	M
B_1	Number of functions not satisfactorily defined	35	P
B_2	Number of functions	35	P
B_3	Number of data references not having an origin	35	P
B_4	Number of data references	35	P
B_5	Number of defined functions not used	35	P
B_6	Number of defined functions	35	P
B_7	Number of referenced functions not defined	35	P
B_8	Number of referenced functions	35	P
B_9	Number of decision points not using all conditions, options	35	P
B_{10}	Number of decision points	35	P
B_{11}	Number of condition options without processing	35	P
B_{12}	Number of condition options	35	P
B_{13}	Number of calling routines with parameters not agreeing with defined parameters	35	P
B_{14}	Number of calling routines	35	P
B_{15}	Number of condition options not set	35	P
B_{16}	Number of set condition options having no processing	35	P
B_{17}	Number of set condition options	35	P
B_{18}	Number of data references having no destination	35	P
β	Observed hardware failure rate	39	P
C	Complexity metric (static, dynamic, cyclomatic)	15, 16	M
c_i	Complexity for program invocation and return along each edge e_i as determined by the user	15	P
CE	Cause and effect measure	6	M
CM	Completeness measure	35	M
D	Software science measure (program difficulty)	14	M
d_k	Complexity for allocation of resource k as determined by the user	15	P

Symbol	Meaning	Measures Used	Primitive/ Metric
D_i	Total number of unique defects detected during the ith design or code inspection process or the ith life cycle phase	2, 8	P
DD	Defect density	2	M
DEs	Decomposition elements	23	P
DI	Defect index	8	M
DSM	Design structure metric	19	M
datain	Number of data structures from which the procedure retrieves data	25	P
dataout	Number of data structures that the procedure updates	25	P
E	(1) Number of edges	15, 16, 17	P
	(2) Software science measure (effort)	14	M
e_i	Number of entry points for the ith module	13	P
F or F_i	Total number of unique faults found in a given time interval resulting in failures of a specified severity level	1	P
f or f_i	Total number of failures of a given severity level in a given time interval	3, 20, 21, 27, 31	P
F_d	Fault density	1	M
f_{ij}	Frequency execution of intermodule transfer from module i to j	38	P
F_a	Number of software functions (modules) in the current delivery that are additions in the current delivery	10	P
F_c	Number of software functions (modules) in the current delivery that include internal changes from a previous delivery	10	P
FD	Fault days metric	4	M
FD_i	Fault days for the ith fault	4	P
F_{del}	Number of software functions (modules) in the previous delivery that are deleted in the current delivery	10	P
FE	Number of the software functional (modular) requirements for which all test cases have been satisfactorily completed	5	P
F_{it}	Total number of faults detected to date in software integration testing	29	P
F_{pit}	Number of faults detected prior to software integration testing	29	P
FT	Total number of software functional (modular) test requirements	5	P
Γ	Average rate of jobs	37	M
Υ	Observed hardware repair rate	39	P
I	Total number of inspections to date	2, 11	P
IFC	Information flow complexity	25	M
J	Total number of jobs completed	37	P
K	Number of resources	15	P

Symbol	Meaning	Measures Used	Primitive/ Metric
k	Number of runs for the specified period of time	18	P
$KSLOC$	Number of source lines of executable code and nonexecutable data declarations in thousands	1, 2, 8	P
$KSLOD$	Number of source lines of design statements in thousands that have been inspected to date	2, 8	P
L	Software science measure (observed program length)	14	M
l	Software science measure (program vocabulary)	14	M
Ll	Software science measure (program level)	14	M
$\lambda(t)$	Failure rate function	31	M
λ	Observed software failure rate	39	P
length	Number of source statements in a procedure	25	P
lfi	Local flows into a procedure	25	P
lfo	Local flows from a procedure	25	P
M	Manhours per major defect detected	11	M
M_i	Number of medium defects found	8	P
m_i	Number of entry and exit points for module i	13	M
MD	Number of modules	38	P
$ME(i)$	Measure effectiveness for the ith issue	34	P
M_{it}	Number of modules integrated	29	M
M_T	Number of software functions (modules) in the current delivery	10	M
M_{tot}	Total number of modules in final configuration	29	M
MTTF	Mean-time-to-failure	30	M
μi	Observed software fault correction rate with i faults in the software	39	P
N	Number of nodes	15, 16, 17	P
nc	Number of correct runs in a given test sample	18, 26	P
NF	Total number of faults within a program	29, 39	M
NF_{rem}	Total number of faults remaining within a program	22, 29	M
NF_{rem} (%)	Percentage of faults remaining within a program	36	M
n_F	Number of faults found that were not intentionally seeded	22	P
NR	Number of runs (or test cases) in a given test sample	18, 26	P
NS	Total number of stages	26	P
N_s	Number of seeded faults	22, 36	P
n_s	Number of seeded faults found	22	P
$N1$	Total number of occurrences of the operators in a program	14	P
$n1$	Number of distinct operators in a program	14	P

Symbol	Meaning	Measures Used	Primitive/ Metric
$N2$	Total number of occurrences of the operands in a program	14	P
$n2$	Number of distinct operands in a program	14	P
N_1	Number of errors detected using SVDs due to inconsistencies	23	P
N_2	Number of errors detected using SVDs due to incompleteness	23	P
N_3	Number of errors detected using SVDs due to misinterpretation	23	P
P	Probability measure over the sample space	18	P
p_n	Probability of repairing a hardware failure correctly	39	P
P_i	(1) Probability that the ith run is selected from the sample space	18, 38	P
	(2) Probability that the ith process that can be generated in a user environment is selected	39	P
P_s	Probability of correcting a software fault when detected	39	P
$P_{N,n}(t)$	System upstate probabilities	39	P
PI_i	Phase index metric for the ith life cycle phase	8	M
PL	Purity level	21	M
PS	Product size	8	P
$P1$	Total number of modules in the program	19	P
$P2$	Number of modules dependent on the input or output	19	P
$P3$	Number of modules dependent on prior processing	19	P
$P4$	Number of database elements	19	P
$P5$	Number of nonunique database elements	19	P
$P6$	Number of database segments (partition of the state)	19	P
$P7$	Number of modules not single entrance/single exit	19	P
Q	Queue length distribution	37	P
q_i	Probability that P_i will be generated in a user environment	38	P
R	(1) Total response time for each functional job	37	M
	(2) Reliability of the system	38	M
R_i	Reliability of the ith module	38	P
R_k	Run reliability at a specified stage	18, 26	M
$R(t)$	Reliability function	31	M
r_i	Flag to denote if the ith process generates the correct software system output	38	P
r_{ki}	Resource status array indicator flags	15	P
RG	Number of regions	16, 17	P
$RK(i)$	Risk factor for the ith measure	34	M
RT	Response time distribution	37	P
$R1$	Number of requirements met by the architecture	7	P

Symbol	Meaning	Measures Used	Primitive/ Metric
$R2$	Number of original requirements	7	P
S	Sample space of possible input patterns and states	18	P
S_i	Point from the sample space of possible inputs	18	P
s_i	Number of serious defects found	8, 11	P
SB	Total amount of time server is busy	37	P
SE	Server's efficiency	37	M
SN	Number of splitting nodes	16, 17	P
SMI	Software maturity index	10	M
ST	Service time distribution	37	P
T	(1) Time period over which measurements are made	37	P
	(2) Time	14	M
T_i	Number of trivial defects found	8	P
t_i	Observed times between failures of a given severity level	20, 21, 27 28, 30, 31	P
TC	Test coverage	24	M
TM	Traceability measure	7	M
T_1	Time expended by the inspection team in preparation for design or code inspection meeting	11	P
T_2	Time expended by the inspection team in conduct of a design or code inspection meeting	11	P
U	Utilization	37	P
V	Software science measure (program volume)	14	M
VR	Number of requests per functional job for each server during time period T	37	P
W_i	Weighting distribution	8, 19, 34	P
WT	Waiting time distribution	37	P
X	Throughput	37	P
x_i	Number of exit points for the ith module	13	P

NOTE: P stands for primitive
M stands for derived metric

IEEE Standard Dictionary of Measures to Produce Reliable Software

1. Introduction

1.1 Scope. The objective of this standard is to provide the software community with defined measures currently used as indicators of reliability. The predictive nature of these measures is dependent on correct application of a valid model.

This standard presents a selection of applicable measures, the proper conditions for using each measure, the methods of computation, and the framework for a common language among users. It moreover provides the means for continual assessment of the process, as well as the products, at each phase of the life cycle. By emphasizing early reliability assessment, this standard supports methods through measurement to improve the product reliability. Successful application of the measures is dependent upon their use as intended in the specified environments.

Applicability is not restricted by the size, type, complexity, or criticality of the software. Typical life cycle phases based upon ANSI/IEEE Std 729-1983 [1],[1] are used to illustrate when each of the measures may be applied.

Errors, faults, and failures serve as primitive units for the majority of the measures.

1.2 References. The following publications shall be used in conjunction with this standard:

[1] ANSI/IEEE Std 729-1983, IEEE Standard Glossary of Software Engineering Terminology.[2]

[2] Software Maintainability — Evaluation Guide, AFOTEC Pamphlet 800-2, vol 3, Mar 1987.[3]

2. Definitions

Most of the definitions listed below can be found in ANSI/IEEE Std 729-1983 [1], IEEE Standard Glossary of Software Engineering Terminology. The definitions of the terms *concept phase, defect, measure, primitive,* and *software management* are not present in ANSI/IEEE Std 729-1983 [1], and establish meaning in the context of this standard. The acronym ISO (International Organization for Standardization) indicates that the definition is also accepted by ISO.

concept phase. The period of time in the software life cycle during which system concepts and objectives needed by the user are identified and documented. Precedes the requirements phase.

defect. A product anomaly. Examples include such things as (1) omissions and imperfections found during early life cycle phases and (2) faults contained in software sufficiently mature for test or operation. See also **fault.**

error. Human action that results in software containing a fault. Examples include omission or misinterpretation of user requirements in a software specification, incorrect translation, or omission of a requirement in the design specification (ANSI/IEEE Std 729-1983 [1]).

failure. (1) The termination of the ability of a functional unit to perform its required function (ISO; ANSI/IEEE Std 729-1983 [1]).

---

[1] The numbers in brackets correspond to those of the references listed in 1.2.

[2] ANSI/IEEE publications are available from the Sales Department, American National Standards Institute, 1430 Broadway, New York, NY 10018, or from the Institute of Electrical and Electronics Engineers, Service Center, 445 Hoes Lane, P.O. Box 1331, Piscataway, NJ 08854-1331.

[3] AFOTEC publications are available from the Air Force Operational Test and Evaluation Center (AFOTEC/DAP), Kirtland Air Force Base, NM 87117-7001.

(2) An event in which a system or system component does not perform a required function within specified limits. A failure may be produced when a fault is encountered (ANSI/IEEE Std 729-1983 [1]).

fault. (1) An accidental condition that causes a functional unit to fail to perform its required function (ISO; ANSI/IEEE Std 729-1983 [1]).

(2) A manifestation of an error in software. A fault, if encounterred, may cause a failure. Synonymous with **bug** (ANSI/IEEE Std 729-1983 [1]).

measure. A quantitative assessment of the degree to which a software product or process possesses a given attribute.

primitive. Data relating to the development or use of software that is used in developing measures or quantitative descriptions of software. Primitives are directly measurable or countable, or may be given a constant value or condition for a specific measure. Examples include: error, failure, fault, time, time interval, date, number of noncommentary source code statements, edges, and nodes.

software reliability. The probability that software will not cause the failure of a system for a specified time under specified conditions. The probability is a function of the inputs to and use of the system as well as a function of the existence of faults in the software. The inputs to the system determine whether existing faults, if any, are encountered (ANSI/IEEE Std 729-1983 [1]).

software reliability management. The process of optimizing the reliability of software through a program that emphasizes software error prevention, fault detection and removal, and the use of measurements ot maximize reliability in light of project constraints such as resources (cost), schedule, and performance.

3. Functional Classification of Measures

The measures can be divided into two functional categories: product and process (Table 3-1). Product measures are applied to the software objects produced and are divided into six subcategories. Process measures are applied to the activities of development, test, and maintenance. Process measures are divided into three subcategories.

3.1 Product Measures. The product measures address cause and effect of the static and dynamic aspects of both projected reliabilty prior to operation, and operational reliability. As an example, reliability may change radically during the maintenance effort, due to the complexity of the system design. These product measures cover more than the correctness aspect of reliability; they also address the system utility aspect of reliability. The following six product measure subcategories address these dimensions of reliability:

(1) Errors; Faults; Failures — Count of defects with respect to human cause, program bugs, observed system malfunctions.
(2) Mean-Time-to-Failure; Failure Rate — Derivative measures of defect occurrence and time.
(3) Reliability Growth and Projection — The assessment of change in failure-freeness of the product under testing and in operation.
(4) Remaining Product Faults — The assessment of fault-freeness of the product in development, test, or maintenance.
(5) Completeness and Consistency — The assessment of the presence and agreement of all necessary software system parts.
(6) Complexity — The assessment of complicating factors in a system.

3.2 Process Measures. The three process measure subcategories are directly related to process management:

(1) Management Control — The assessment of guidance of the development and maintenance processes.
(2) Coverage — The assessment of the presence of all necessary activities to develop or maintain the software product.
(3) Risk; Benefit; Cost Evaluation — The assessment of the process tradeoffs of cost, schedule, and performance.

The measure classification matrix (Table 3-1) is a cross index of the measures and functional categories and can be used to select measures applicable to each category.

4. Measures for Reliable Software

4.1 Fault Density
4.1.1 Application. This measure can be used to
(1) Predict remaining faults by comparison with expected fault density.

Table 3-1
Measure Classification Matrix

MEASURE CATEGORIES / Measures	PRODUCT MEASURES						PROCESS MEASURES		
	Errors; Faults; Failures	Mean-Time-to-Failure; Failure Rate	Reliability Growth & Projection	Remaining Product Faults	Completeness & Consistency	Complexity	Management Control	Coverage	Risk Benefit; Cost Evaluation
1. Fault density	X								
2. Defect density	X								
3. Cumulative failure profile	X								
4. Fault – days number	X						X		
5. Functional test coverage					X			X	X
6. Cause and effect graphing					X			X	X
7. Requirements traceability	X				X			X	
8. Defect indices	X						X		
9. Error distribution(s)	X						X		
10. Software maturity index			X						X
11. Man hours per major defect detected	X						X		X
12. Number of conflicting requirements					X			X	
13. Number of entries/exits per module						X			
14. Software science measures				X		X			X
15. Graph-theoretic complexity for architecture						X			
16. Cyclomatic complexity					X	X			
17. Minimal unit test case determination					X	X			
18. Run reliability			X						
19. Design structure						X	X		
20. Mean time to discover the next K faults							X		X
21. Software purity level			X						X
22. Estimated number of faults remaining (seeding)				X					X
23. Requirements compliance	X				X			X	
24. Test coverage					X			X	
25. Data or information flow complexity						X			
26. Reliability growth function			X						
27. Residual fault count				X					X
28. Failure analysis using elapsed time			X	X					
29. Testing sufficiency			X					X	
30. Mean-time-to-failure		X							
31. Failure rate		X							X
32. Software documentation & source listings					X			X	
33. RELY (Required Software Reliability)								X	X
34. Software release readiness								X	X
35. Completeness					X			X	
36. Test accuracy				X	X			X	
37. System performance reliability			X						
38. Independent process reliability			X						
39. Combined HW/SW system operational availability			X						

(2) Determine if sufficient testing has been completed based on predetermined goals for severity class.

(3) Establish standard fault densities for comparison and prediction.

4.1.2 Primitives. Establish the severity levels for failure designation.

F = total number of unique faults found in a given time interval resulting in failures of a specified severity level

KSLOC = number of source lines of executable code and nonexecutable data declarations in thousands

4.1.3 Implementation. Establish severity, failure types, and fault types.

(1) Failure types might include I/O and user. Fault types might result from design, coding, documentation, and initialization.

(2) Observe and log each failure.

(3) Determine the program fault(s) that caused the failure. Classify the faults by type. Additional faults may be found resulting in total faults being greater than the number of failures observed. Or one fault may manifest itself by several failures. Thus, fault and failure density may both be measured.

(4) Determine total lines of executable and nonexecutable data declaration source code (KSLOC).

(5) Calculate the fault density for a given severity level as

$$F_d = F/K\text{SLOC}$$

4.2 Defect Density

4.2.1 Application. The defect density measure can be used after design and code inspections of new development or large block modifications. If the defect density is outside the norm after several inspections, it is an indication that the inspection process requires further scrutiny.

4.2.2 Primitives. Establish severity levels for defect designation.

D_i = total number of unique defects detected during the ith design or code inspection process

I = total number of inspections

KSLOD = in the design phase, the number of source lines of design statements in thousands

KSLOC = in the implementation phase, the number of source lines of executable code and nonexecutable data declarations in thousands

4.2.3 Implementation. Establish a classification scheme for severity and class of defect. For each inspection, record the product size, and the total number of unique defects. For example, in the design phase, calculate the ratio

$$DD = \frac{\sum\limits_{i=1}^{I} D_i}{K\text{SLOD}}$$

This measure assumes that a structured design language is used. However, if some other design methodology is used, then some other unit of defect density has to be developed to conform to the methodology in which the design is expressed.

4.3 Cumulative Failure Profile

4.3.1 Applications. This is a graphical method used to

(1) Predict reliability through the use of failure profiles.

(2) Estimate additional testing time to reach an acceptability reliable system.

(3) Identify modules and subsystems that require additional testing.

4.3.2 Primitives. Establish the severity levels for failure designation.

f_i = total number of failures of a given severity level in a given time interval, $i=1, \ldots$

4.3.3 Implementation. Plot cumulative failures versus a suitable time base. The curve can be derived for the system as a whole, subsystems, or modules.

4.4 Fault-Days Number

4.4.1 Application. This measure represents the number of days that faults spend in the software system from their creation to their removal.

4.4.2 Primitives

(1) Phase when the fault was introduced in the system.

(2) Date when the fault was introduced in the system.

(3) Phase, date, and time when the fault is removed.

FD_i = fault days for the ith fault

NOTE: For more meaningful measures, the time unit can be made relative to test time or operational time.

4.4.3 Implementation. For each fault detected and removed, during any phase, the number of days from its creation to its removal is determined (fault-days).

The fault-days are then summed for all faults detected and removed, to get the fault-days number at system level, including all faults detected/ removed up to the delivery date. In cases when the creation date for the fault is not known, the fault is assumed to have been created at the middle of the phase in which it was introduced.

In Fig 4.4.3-1 the fault-days for the design fault for module A can be accurately calculated because the design approval date for the detailed design of module A is known. The fault introduced during the requirements phase is assumed to have been created at the middle of the requirement phase because the exact knowledge of when the corresponding piece of requirement was specified, is not known.

The measure is calculated as shown in Fig 4.4.3-1.

4.5 Functional or Modular Test Coverage

4.5.1 Application. This measure is used to quantify a software test coverage index for a software delivery. The primitives counted may be either functions or modules. The operational user is most familiar with the system functional requirements and will report system problems in terms of functional requirements rather than module test requirements. It is the task of the evaluator to obtain or develop the functional requirements and associated module cross reference table.

4.5.2 Primitives
FE = number of the software functional (modular) requirements for which all test cases have been satisfactorily completed
FT = total number of software functional (modular) requirements

4.5.3 Implementation. The test coverage index is expressed as a ratio of the number of software functions (modules) tested to the total number of software functions (modules) that make up the users (developers) requirements. This ratio is expressed as

$$\text{FUNCTIONAL (MODULAR) TEST COVERAGE INDEX} = \frac{FE}{FT}$$

4.6 Cause and Effect Graphing

4.6.1 Application. Cause and effect graphing aids in identifying requirements that are incomplete and ambiguous. This measure explores the inputs and expected outputs of a program and identifies the ambiguities. Once these ambiguities are eliminated, the specifications are considered complete and consistent.

Cause and effect graphing can also be applied to generate test cases in any time of computing application where the specification is clearly stated (that is, no ambiguities) and combinations of input conditions can be identified. It is used in developing and designing test cases that have a

Fig 4.4.3-1
Calculation of Fault-Days

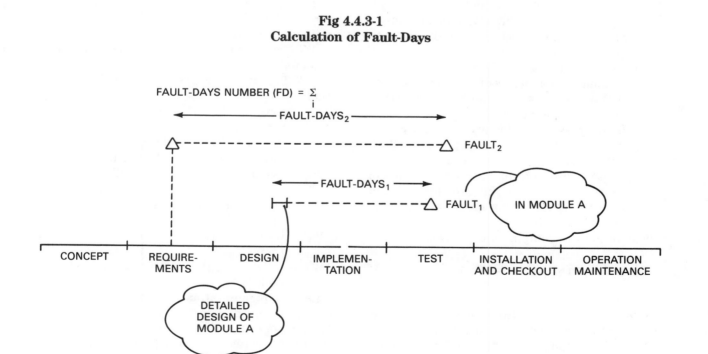

high probability of detecting faults that exist in programs. It is not concerned with the internal structure or behavior of the program.

4.6.2 Primitives

List of causes: distinct input conditions

List of effects: distinct output conditions or system transformation (effects are caused by changes in the state of the system)

A_{existing} = number of ambiguities in a program remaining to be eliminated

A_{tot} = total number of ambiguities identified

4.6.3 Implementation. A cause and effect graph is a formal translation of a natural language specification into its input conditions and expected outputs. The graph depicts a combinatorial logic network.

To begin, identify all requirements of the system and divide them into separate identifiable entities. Carefully analyze the requirements to identify all the causes and effects in the specification. After the analysis is completed, assign each cause and effect a unique identifier. For example, E1 for effect one or I1 for input one.

To create the cause and effect graph:

(1) Represent each cause and each effect by a node identified by its unique number.

(2) Interconnect the cause and effect nodes by analyzing the semantic content of the specification and transforming it into a Boolean graph. Each cause and effect can be in one of two states: true or false. Using Boolean logic, set the possible states of the causes and determine under what conditions each effect will be present.

(3) Annotate the graph with constraints describing combinations of causes and effects that are impossible because of semantic or environmental constraints.

(4) Identify as an ambiguity any cause that does not result in a corresponding effect, any effect that does not originate with a cause as a source, and any combination of causes and effects that are inconsistent with the requirement specification or impossible to achieve.

The measure is computed as follows:

$$CE(\%) = 100 \times \left(1 - \frac{A_{\text{existing}}}{A_{\text{tot}}} \right)$$

To derive test cases for the program, convert the graph into a limited entry decision table with "effects" as columns and "causes" as rows. For each effect, trace back through the graph to find all combinations of causes that will set the effect to be TRUE. Each combination is represented as a column in the decision table. The state of all other effects should also be determined for each such combination. Each column in the table represents a test case.

4.7 Requirements Traceability

4.7.1 Application. This measure aids in identifying requirements that are either missing from, or in addition to, the original requirements.

4.7.2 Primitives

$R1$ = number of requirements met by the architecture

$R2$ = number of original requirements

4.7.3 Implementation. A set of mappings from the requirements in the software architecture to the original requirements is created. Count each requirement met by the architecture ($R1$) and count each of the original requirements ($R2$). Compute the traceability measure (TM):

$$TM = \frac{R1}{R2} \times 100\%$$

4.8 Defect Indices

4.8.1 Application. This measure provides a continuing, relative index of how correct the software is as it proceeds through the development cycle. This measure is a straightforward phase dependent, weighted, calculation that requires no knowledge of advanced mathematics or statistics. This measure may be applied as early in the life cycle as the user has products that can be evaluated.

4.8.2 Primitives. For each phase in the life cycle:

D_i = total number of defects detected during the ith phase

S_i = number of serious defects found

M_i = number of medium defects found

PS = size of the product at the ith phase

T_i = number of trivial defects found

W_1 = weighting factor for serious defects (default is 10)

W_2 = weighting factor for medium defects (default is 3)

W_3 = weighting factor for trivial defects (default is 1)

4.8.3 Implementation. The measure is generated as a sum of calculations taken throughout development. It is a continuing measure applied to the software as it proceeds from design through final tests.

At each phase of development, calculate the phase index (PI_i) associated with the number and severity of defects.

$$PI_i = W_1 \frac{S_i}{D_i} + W_2 \frac{M_i}{D_i} + W_3 \frac{T_i}{D_i}$$

The defect index (DI) is calculated at each phase by cumulatively adding the calculation for PI_i as the software proceeds through development:

$$DI = \sum_i (i * PI_i)/PS$$

$$= (PI_1 + 2PI_2 + 2PI_3 + \ldots + iPI_i + \ldots)/PS$$

where each phase is weighted such that the further into development the software has progressed, such as phase 2 or 3, the larger the weight (that is, 2 or 3, respectively) assigned.

The data collected in prior projects can be used as a baseline figure for comparison.

4.9 Error Distribution(s)

4.9.1 Application. The search for the causes of software faults and failures involves the analysis of the defect data collected during each phase of the software development. Distribution of the errors allows ranking of the predominant failure modes.

4.9.2 Primitives. Error description:
(1) Associated faults
(2) Types
(3) Severity
(4) Phase introduced
(5) Preventive measure
(6) Discovery mechanism, including reasons for earlier nondetection of associated faults

4.9.3 Implementation. The primitives for each error are recorded and the errors are counted according to the criteria adopted for each classification. The number of errors are then plotted for each class. Examples of such distribution plots are shown in Fig 4.9.3-1. In the three examples of Fig 4.9.3-1, the errors are classified and counted by phase, by the cause, and by the cause for deferred fault detection. Other similar classification could be used such as the type of steps suggested to prevent the reoccurrence of similar errors or the type of steps suggested for earlier detection of the corresponding faults.

4.10 Software Maturity Index

4.10.1 Application. This measure is used to quantify the readiness of a software product. Changes from a previous baseline to the current baseline are an indication of the current product stability. A baseline can be either an internal release or an external delivery.

4.10.2 Primitives
M_T = number of software functions (modules) in the current delivery
F_c = number of software functions (modules) in the current delivery that include internal changes from a previous delivery
F_a = number of software functions (modules) in the current delivery that are additions to the previous delivery
F_{del} = number of software functions (modules) in the previous delivery that are deleted in the current delivery

4.10.3 Implementation. The software maturity index (SMI) may be calculated in two different ways depending on the available data (primitives).

4.10.3.1 Implementation #1
(1) For the present (just delivered or modified) software baseline, count the number of functions (modules) that have been changed (F_c).
(2) For the present software baseline, count the number of functions (modules) that have been added (F_a) or deleted (F_{del}).
(3) For the present software baseline, count the number of functions (modules) that make up that baseline (M_T).

Calculate the maturity index:

$$\text{MATURITY INDEX} = \frac{\begin{pmatrix} \text{NUMBER OF} \\ \text{CURRENT} \\ \text{FUNCTIONS} \\ \text{(MODULES)} \end{pmatrix} - \begin{pmatrix} \text{NUMBER OF} \\ \text{CURRENT BASELINE} \\ \text{FUNCTIONS (MODULES)} \\ \text{THAT HAVE BEEN} \\ \text{ADDED} \end{pmatrix} + \begin{pmatrix} \text{NUMBER OF} \\ \text{FUNCTIONS} \\ \text{(MODULES)} \\ \text{CHANGED} \end{pmatrix} + \begin{pmatrix} \text{NUMBER OF} \\ \text{CURRENT BASELINE} \\ \text{FUNCTIONS (MODULES)} \\ \text{THAT HAVE BEEN} \\ \text{DELETED} \end{pmatrix}}{\text{NUMBER OF CURRENT FUNCTIONS (MODULES)}}$$

that is

$$SMI = \frac{M_T - (F_a + F_c + F_{del})}{M_T}$$

Notice that the total number of current functions (modules) equals the number of previous functions (modules) plus the number of current baseline functions (modules) that were added to the previous baseline minus the number of functions (modules) that were deleted from the previous baseline. In the software maturity index calculation, the deletion of a function (module) is treated the same as an addition of a function (module).

4.10.3.2 Implementation #2. The software maturity index may be estimated as

$$SMI = \frac{M_T - F_c}{M_T}$$

The change and addition of functions (modules) is tracked and the maturity index is calculated

(a) **Error Distribution by Phase**

(b) **Error by Cause Category**

(c) **Suggested Causes for Error Detection Deferral**

Fig 4.9.3-1
Error Analysis

for each baseline. Problem reports that would result in a software update subsequent to the tracking period are included in the maturity analysis by estimating the configuration of the subsequent baselines.

4.11 Manhours per Major Defect Detected

4.11.1 Application. The design and code inspection processes are two of the most effective defect removal processes available. The early removal of defects at the design and implementation phases, if done effectively and efficiently, significantly improves the reliability of the developed product and allows a more controlled test environment. This measure provides a quantitative figure that can be used to evaluate the efficiency of the design and code inspection processes.

4.11.2 Primitives

T_1 = time expended by the inspection team in preparation for design or code inspection meeting

T_2 = time expended by the inspection team in conduct of a design or code inspection meeting

S_i = number of major (nontrivial) defects detected during the ith inspection

I = total number of inspections to date

4.11.3 Implementation. At each inspection meeting, record the total preparation time expended by the inspection team. Also, record the total time expended in conducting the inspection meeting. All defects are recorded and grouped into major/minor categores. (A major defect is one which must be corrected for the product to function within specified requirements.)

The inspection times are summarized and the defects are cumulatively added. The computation should be performed during design and code. If the design is not written in a structural design language, then this measure can be only applied during the implementation phase.

The manhours per major defect detected is

$$ M = \frac{\sum\limits_{i=1}^{I} (T_1 + T_2)_i}{\sum\limits_{i=1}^{I} S_i} $$

This computation should be initiated after approximately 8000 lines of detailed design or code have been inspected.

4.12 Number of Conflicting Requirements

4.12.1 Application. This measure is used to determine the reliability of a software system, resulting from the software architecture under consideration, as represented by a specification based on the entity-relationship-attribute model.

4.12.2 Primitives

(1) List of the inputs
(2) List of the outputs
(3) List of the functions performed by the program

4.12.3 Implementation. The mappings from the software architecture to the requirements are identified. Mappings from the same specification item to more than one differing requirement are examined for requirements inconsistency. Mappings from more than one specification item to a single requirement are examined for specification inconsistency.

4.13 Number of Entries and Exits per Module

4.13.1 Application. This measure is used to determine the difficulty of a software architecture, as represented by entry and exist points identified in a modular specification or design language.

4.13.2 Primitives

e_i = number of entry points for the ith module

x_i = number of exit points for the ith module

4.13.3 Implementation. The number of entry points and exit points for each module is

$$ m_i = e_i + x_i $$

4.14 Software Science Measures

4.14.1 Application. These measures apply the Halstead Software Science to the properties and structure of computer programs. They provide measures of the complexity of existing software, predict the length of a program, and estimate the amount of time an average programmer can be expected to use to implement a given algorithm.

This measure computes the program length by counting "operators" and "operands." The measure suggests that the difficulty of a given program can be derived, based on the above counts.

4.14.2 Primitives

$n1$ = number of distinct operators in a program

$n2$ = number of distinct operands in a program

$N1$ = total number of occurrences of the operators in a program

$N2$ = total number of occurrences of the operands in a program

4.14.3 Implementation. Once the source code has been written, this measure can be applied to predict the program difficulty and other derived quantities using the following equations:

Program vocabulary: $l = n1 + n2$

Observed program length: $L = N1 + N2$

Estimated program length: $L = n1\ (\log_2 n1) + n2\ (\log_2 n2)$

Program volume: $V = L\ (\log_2 n)$

Program difficulty: $D = (n1/2)\ (N2/n2)$

Program level: $L1 = 1/D$

Effort: $E = \dfrac{V}{L1}$

Number of errors: $B = \dfrac{V}{3000} \simeq \dfrac{E^{2/3}}{3000}$

Time: $T = E/S$ (S = Stroud number; typical value is 18 elementary mental discriminations per second)

An alternate expression to estimate the program length is the factorial length estimator:

$$\hat{L} = \log_2((n1)!) + (\log_2((n2)!)$$

4.15 Graph-Theoretic Complexity for Architecture

4.15.1 Application.
Complexity measures can be applied early in the product life cycle for development trade-offs as well as to assure system and module comprehensibility adequate for correct and efficient maintenance. Many system faults are introduced in the operational phase by modifications to systems that are reliable but difficult to understand. In time, a system's entropy increases making a fault insertion more likely with each new change. Through complexity measures the developer plans ahead for correct change by establishing initial order and thereby improves the continuing reliability of the system throughout its operational life.

There are three graph-theoretic complexity measures for software architecture:

(1) Static Complexity — A measure of software architecture, as represented by a network of modules, useful for design trade-off analyses. Network complexity is a function based on the countable properties of the modules (nodes) and intermodule connections (edges) in the network.

(2) Generalized Static Complexity — A measure of software architecture, as represented by a network of modules and the resources used. Since resources are acquired or released when programs are invoked in other modules, it is desirable to measure the complexity associated with allocation of those resources in addition to the basic (static) network complexity.

(3) Dynamic Complexity — A measure of software architecture, as represented by a network of modules during execution, rather than at rest, as is the case for the static measures. For example, modules may execute at different frequencies.

4.15.2 Primitives

K = number of resources, index by $K = 1, ..., K$

E = number of edges, indexed by $i = 1, ..., E$

N = number of nodes, indexed by $j = 1, ..., N$

c_i = complexity for program invocation and return along each edge e_i as determined by the user (such as operating system complexity)

Resource status array $R(K,E)$

$r_{ki} = \begin{cases} 1 & \text{if } k\text{th resource is required for the } i\text{th edge } (e_i) \\ 0 & \text{otherwise} \end{cases}$

d_k = complexity for allocation of resource k as determined by the user (for example, complexity associated with a procedure used to gain exclusive access to common data)

4.15.3 Implementation.
Using nodes and edges, a strongly connected graph of the network is required. A strongly connected graph is one in which a node is reachable from any other node. This is accomplished by adding an edge between the exit node and the entry node. Each node represents a module that may or may not be executed concurrently with another module. Each edge represents program invocation and return between modules. In this case the edges are called single paths.

(1) Static Complexity — Once a strongly connected graph is constructed, with modules as nodes, and transfer of control as edges, the static complexity is calculated as

$$C = E - N + 1$$

(2) Generalized Static Complexity — Resources (storage, time, logic complexity, or other measurable factors) are allocated when programs are invoked in other modules. Given a network and resources to be controlled in the network, the generalized static complexity associated with allocation of these resources is

$$C = \sum_{i=1}^{E} \left(c_i + \sum_{k=1}^{K} (d_k * r_{ki}) \right)$$

(3) Dynamic Complexity — A change in the number of edges may result from module interruption due to invocations and re-

turns. An average dynamic network complexity can be derived over a given time period to account for the execution of modules at different frequencies and also for module interruption during execution. Dynamic complexity is calculated using the formula for static complexity at various points in time. The behavior of the measure (ex. time average) is then used to indicate the evolution of the complexity of the software.

4.16 Cyclomatic Complexity

4.16.1 Application. This measure may be used to determine the structural complexity of a coded module. The use of this measure is designed to limit the complexity of a module, thereby promoting understandability of the module.

4.16.2 Primitives

N = number of nodes (sequential groups of program statements)

E = number of edges (program flows between nodes)

SN = number of splitting nodes (nodes with more than one edge emanating from it)

RG = number of regions (areas bounded by edges with no edges crossing)

4.16.3 Implementation. Using regions, or nodes and edges, a strongly connected graph of the module is required. A strongly connected graph is one in which a node is reachable from any other node: this is accomplished by adding an edge between the exit node and the entry node. Once the graph is constructed, the measure is computed as follows:

$$C - E - N + 1$$

The cyclomatic complexity is also equivalent to the number of regions (RG) or the number of splitting nodes plus one ($SN + 1$). If a program contains an N-way predicate, such as a CASE statement with N cases, the N-way predicate contributes $N-1$ to the count of SN.

4.17 Minimal Unit Test Case Determination

4.17.1 Application. This measure determines the number of independent paths through a module so that a minimal number of covering test cases can be generated for unit test. It is applied during unit testing.

4.17.2 Primitives

N = number of nodes; a sequential group of program statements

E = number of edges; program flow between nodes

SN = number of splitting nodes; a node with more than 1 edge emanating from it

RG = number of regions; in a graph with no edges crossing, an area bounded by edges

4.17.3 Implementation. The cyclomatic complexity is first computed using the cyclomatic complexity measure described in 4.16. The complexity of the module establishes the number of distinct paths. The user constructs test cases along each path so all edges of the graph are traversed. This set of test cases forms a minimal set of cases that covers all paths through the module.

4.18 Run Reliability. Run reliability (R_k) is the probability that k randomly selected runs (corresponding to a specified period of time) will produce correct results.

4.18.1 Application. The run reliability measure may be applied at any phase in the life cycle when the set of possible discrete input patterns and states can be identified. The sequence is randomly selected based on the probability assigned to selection of any one of them.

4.18.2 Primitives

NR = number of runs made in a given test sample

nc = number of correct runs in a given test sample

k = number of runs for the specified period of time

S = sample space of possible input patterns and states; $\{S_i, i = 1...\}$ are elements in the sample space (for each input pattern and state there is a unique output pattern and state; thus, S_i designates a given ((input, state), (output state)), which constitutes a run)

P = probability measure over the sample space

P_i = probability that the ith run is selected from the sample space

4.18.3 Implementation

4.18.3.1 Sample Space (S). The sample space is viewed as the set of possible inputs into the program. In the early phases of the life cycle, the sample space consists of operational scenarios. For instance, in the early requirements phase the inputs and states are the listed requirements for the program. In the later phases of the life cycle, the sample space consists of all detailed input and state conditions of the program. For a given life cycle phase, a single sample space (S) is determined and a probability measure (P) is assigned. Runs are then generated by randomly choosing input patterns and states from the sample space according to the assigned probability P.

4.18.3.2 Probability Measure (P). For each possible run i, a number p_i (between zero and one inclusive) must be assigned so that the sum of all the p_i's is 1. The simplest case is the assumption of a uniform probability distribution. However, in the operational environment some runs are more likely to occur than others and should be weighted appropriately.

4.18.3.3 Test *NR* Randomly Selected Runs. The accuracy of the measure R_k is determined by the number of runs NR used for estimation. The runs are randomly selected according to the probability distribution. The results of each run are examined for correctness. The number of correct runs is nc.

4.18.3.4 Probability of a Successful Run (P_r). The probability of a randomly selected run being correct (P_r) is estimated by the sum of the probabilities for the correct runs, divided by the sum of the probabilities for all runs. In the case of a uniform distribution $P_r = nc/NR$.

4.18.3.5 Run Reliability (R_k). Given k randomly selected runs during the specified period of time, the probability that all k runs give correct results is $R_k = P_r^k$.

4.19 Design Structure

4.19.1 Application. This measure is used to determine the simplicity of the detailed design of a software program. Also, the values determined for the associated primitives can be used to identify problem areas within the software design.

4.19.2 Primitives

$P1$ = total number of modules in the program
$P2$ = number of modules dependent on the input or output
$P3$ = number of modules dependent on prior processing (state)
$P4$ = number of database elements
$P5$ = number of nonunique database elements
$P6$ = number of database segments (partition of the state)
$P7$ = number of modules not single entrance/ single exit

4.19.3 Implementation. The design structure measure is the weighted sum of six derivatives determined by using the primitives given above. The six derivatives are

$D1$ = design organized top down (Boolean)
$D2$ = module dependence ($P2/P1$)
$D3$ = module dependent on prior processing ($P3/P1$)
$D4$ = database size ($P5/P4$)

$D5$ = database compartmentalization ($P6/P4$)
$D6$ = module single entrance/single exit ($P7/ P1$)

The design structure measure (DSM) can be expressed as

$$DSM = \sum_{i=1}^{6} W_i D_i$$

The weights (W_i) are assigned by the user based on the priority of each associated derivative. Each W_i has a value between 0 and 1 ($\Sigma\ W_i = 1.0$).

4.20 Mean Time to Discover the Next K Faults

4.20.1 Application. This measure can be used to project the average length of time until the next K faults are discovered. This can provide an indication of how much time would be required until a desired level of reliability is achieved.

4.20.2 Primitives

f = number of failures found from the beginning of testing to the present
t_i = observed time between the $(i-1)$st and ith failure for a given severity level, $i = 1, \ldots$

4.20.3 Implementation. The mean-time-to-failure (see 4.30) should be used to estimate the mean time to discover the next K faults in the software. This estimate can then be expressed as

$$\begin{array}{l}\text{mean time to discover} \\ \text{the next } K \text{ faults}\end{array} = \sum_{i=f}^{f+K-1} \widehat{\text{MTTF}}_i$$

where MTTF_i is an estimate of the mean-time-to-failure between the ith and $(i+1)$st failure.

The estimate of the mean-time-to-failure between the ith and $(i+1)$st failure can be calculated using any of the software models based upon time between failures. Suppose that estimate is

$$\text{MTTF}_i = \hat{E}\ \{\text{time between the } i\text{th and the} \\ (i+1)\text{st failures}\}\ f \le i \le f+K-1$$

Notice that if $K=1$, then we simply have the estimate of the MTTF (see 4.30) between the fth and $(f+1)$st failure. Then the estimate is

$$\begin{pmatrix}\text{mean time to} \\ \text{discover the} \\ \text{next } K \text{ faults}\end{pmatrix} = \sum_{i=n}^{f+K-1} \hat{E} \begin{Bmatrix}\text{time between} \\ \text{the } i\text{th and the} \\ (i+1)\text{st failures}\end{Bmatrix}$$

By estimating the mean-time-to-failure, one can then estimate how much additional time will be required to discover all, or a subset, of the estimated remaining faults. One can judge how long it will take before the software achieves a desired level of reliability.

4.21 Software Purity Level

4.21.1 Application. The software purity level provides an estimate of the relative fault-freeness of a computer program at any specified point in time during the operational phase.

4.21.2 Primitives

t_i = observed times between failures (for example, execution time) for a given severity level

f = total number of failures in a given time interval

4.21.3 Implementation. Suppose f failures have occurred during the operational phase of the life cycle of the program. Suppose also the length of time in this phase when the fth failure is detected is t_f. Then the estimate of the purity level of the program at that point in time is

$$PL = \frac{\hat{Z}(t_0) - \hat{Z}(t_f)}{\hat{Z}(t_0)}$$

where t_0 is the start of the operations and maintenance phase and $\hat{Z}(t)$ is the estimated hazard (or failure) rate at time t. The hazard rate is defined as the conditional probability that a software failure happens in an interval of time $(t, t+\Delta t)$ given that the software has not failed up to time t. It is derived from any of the software reliability models that use time between failure data t_i. PL denotes the relative change in the hazard rate function from the beginning of the operations and maintenance phase to the time of the fth failure detection.

4.22 Estimated Number of Faults Remaining (by Seeding)

4.22.1 Application. The estimated number of faults remaining in a program is related to the reliability of the program. There are many sampling techniques that estimate this number. This section describes a simple form of seeding that assumes a homogeneous distribution of a representative class of faults.

This measure can be applied to any phase of the software life cycle. The search for faults continues for a determined period of time that may be less than that required to find all seeded faults. The measure is not computed unless some nonseeded faults are found.

4.22.2 Primitives

N_s = number of seeded faults

n_s = number of seeded faults found

n_F = number of faults found that were not intentionally seeded

4.22.3 Implementation. A monitor is responsible for error seeding. The monitor inserts (seeds) N_s faults representative of the expected indigenous faults. The test team reports to the monitor the faults found during a test period of predetermined length.

Before seeding, a fault analysis is needed to determine the types of faults and their relative frequency of occurrences expected under a particular set of software development conditions. Although an estimate of the number of faults remaining can be made on the basis of very few inserted faults, the accuracy of the estimate (and hence the confidence in it) increases as the number of seeded faults increases.

Faults should be inserted randomly throughout the software. Personnel inserting the faults should be different and independent of those persons later searching for the faults. The process of searching for the faults should be carried out without knowledge of the inserted faults. The search should be performed for a previously determined period of time (or effort) and each fault reported to the central monitor.

Each report fault should be reviewed to determine if it is in the class of faults being studied and, if so, if it is a seeded or an indigenous fault. The maximum likelihood estimate of the number of indigenous (unseeded) faults in the specified class is

$$\widehat{NF} = \frac{n_F N_s}{n_s}$$

where $\widehat{NF}$ is truncated to the integer value. The estimate of the remaining number of faults is then

$$\widehat{NF}_{rem} = \widehat{NF} - n_F$$

The probability of finding n_F of NF indigenous faults and n_F of N_s seeded faults, given that there are $(n_F + n_s)$ faults found in the program is $C(N_s, n_s)C(NF, n_F)/C(NF+N_s, n_F+n_s)$, where the function $C(x,y) = x!/(x-y)!y!$ is the combination of "x" things taken at "y" at a time. Using this relation one can calculate confidence intervals.

4.23 Requirements Compliance

4.23.1 Application. This analysis is used to verify requirements compliance by using system verification diagrams (*SVD*s), a logical interconnection of stimulus response elements (for example, stimulus and response), which detect inconsistencies, incompleteness, and misinterpretations.

4.23.2 Primitives

*DE*s = decomposition elements:

Stimulus — external input

Function — defined input/output process

Response — result of the function
Label — numerical *DE* identifier
Reference — specification paragraph number
Requirement errors detected using *SVD*s:

N_1 = number due to inconsistencies
N_2 = number due to incompleteness
N_3 = number due to misinterpretation

4.23.3 Implementation. The implementation of an *SVD* is composed of the following phases:

(1) The decomposition phase is initiated by mapping the system requirement specifications into stimulus/response elements (*DE*s). That is, all keywords, phrases, functional and/or performance requirements and expected outputs are documented on decomposition forms (see Fig 4.23.3-1).

(2) The graph phase uses the *DE*s from the decomposition phase and logically connects them to form the *SVD* graph.

(3) The analysis phase examines the *SVD* from the graph phase by using connectivity and reachability matrices. The various requirement error types are determined by examining the system verification diagram and identifying errors as follows:

(a) Inconsistencies — Decomposition elements that do not accurately reflect the system requirement specification.

(b) Incompleteness — Decomposition elements that do not completely reflect the system requirement specification.

(c) Misinterpretation — Decomposition elements that do not correctly reflect the system requirement specification. These errors may occur during translation of the requirements into decomposition elements, constructing the *SVD* graph, or interpreting the connectivity and reachability matrices.

An analysis is also made of the percentages for the various requirement error types for the respective categories: inconsistencies, incompleteness, and misinterpretation.

$$\text{Inconsistencies } (\%) = (N_1/(N_1+N_2+N_3)) \times 100$$
$$\text{Incompleteness } (\%) = (N_2/(N_1+N_2+N_3)) \times 100$$
$$\text{Misinterpretation } (\%) = (N_3/(N_1+N_2+N_3)) \times 100$$

This analysis can aid also in future software development efforts.

4.24 Test Coverage

4.24.1 Application. Test coverage is a measure of the completeness of the testing process from both a developer and a user perspective. The measure relates directly to the development, integration and operational test stages of product development, in particular, unit, functional, system and acceptance tests. Developers, using the program class of primitives, can apply the measure in unit test to obtain a measure of thoroughness of structural tests. System testers can apply the measure in two ways. First, by focusing on requirements primitives, the system tester can gain a user-view of the thoroughness of functional tests. Second, by focusing on the program class of primitives, the system tester can determine the amount of implementation in the operational environment.

4.24.2 Primitives. The primitives for test coverage are in two classes, program and requirements. For program, there are two types: functional and data. The program functional primitives are either modules, segments, statements, branches (nodes), or paths. Program data primitives are equivalence classes of data. Requirements primitives are either test cases or functional capabilities.

4.24.3 Implementation. Test coverage (*TC*) is the percentage of requirements primitives implemented times the percentage of primitives executed during a set of tests. A simple interpretation of test coverage can be expressed by the following formula:

$$TC(\%) = \frac{(\text{implemented capabilities})}{(\text{required capabilities})}$$
$$\times \frac{(\text{program primitives tested})}{(\text{total program primitives})} \times 100$$

4.25 Data or Information Flow Complexity

4.25.1 Application. This is a structural complexity or procedural complexity measure that can be used to evaluate:

(1) The information flow structure of large scale systems

(2) The procedure and module information flow structure

Fig 4.23.3-1
Decomposition Form

STIMULUS	LABEL	RESPONSE
	FUNCTION	
	SPEC. REFERENCE	

(3) The complexity of the interconnections between modules

Moreover, this measure can also be used to indicate the degree of simplicity of relationships between subsystems and to correlate total observed failures and software reliability with data complexity.

4.25.2 Primitives

lfi = local flows into a procedure

datain = number of data structures from which the procedure retrieves data

lfo = local flows from a procedure

dataout = number of data structures that the procedure updates

length = number of source statements in a procedure (excludes comments in a procedure)

4.25.3 Implementation.
Determine the flow of information between modules and/or subsystems by automated data flow techniques, HIPO charts, etc.

A local flow from module A to B exists if one of the following occurs:

(1) A calls B,

(2) B calls A and A returns a value to B that is passed by B, or

(3) Both A and B are called by another module that passes a value from A to B.

Values of primitives are obtained by counting the data flow paths directed into and out of the modules.

fanin   = lfi + datain
fanout = lfo + dataout

The information flow complexity (IFC) is IFC = (fanin $\times$ fanout)^2.

weighted IFC = length $\times$ (fanin $\times$ fanout)^2

4.26 Reliability Growth Function

4.26.1 Application. This measure provides an estimate (or prediction) of the time or stage of testing when a desired failure rate or fault density goal will be achieved. It is an indicator of the level of success of fault correction.

4.26.2 Primitives

NR_k = total number of test cases during the kth stage

NS = total number of stages

nc_k = total number of successful test cases during the kth stage

4.26.3 Implementation. Good record keeping of failure occurrences is needed to accurately document at which stage the failure occurred. Detailed failure analysis is required to determine

if a fault was inserted by previous correction efforts. This will be used to calculate the reinsertion rate of faults (r), which is the ratio of the number of faults reinserted to the total number of faults found.

A test sequence of software is conducted in N stages (periods between changes to the software being tested). The reliability for the kth stage is

$$R(k) = R(u) - A/k \qquad \text{(Eq 4.26-1)}$$

where

$$R(u) = R(k) \text{ as } k \rightarrow \infty$$

The unknown parameter A represents the growth parameter of the model. An $A > 0$ indicates the reliability is increasing as a function of the testing stage; an $A < 0$ indicates it is decreasing. The estimation of $R(u)$ and A is done using least squares estimates. The two equations used to derive the estimates are

$$\sum_{k=1}^{NS} \left(\frac{nc_k}{NR_k} - R(u) + \frac{A}{k} \right) = 0 \qquad \text{(Eq 4.26-2)}$$

$$\sum_{k=1}^{NS} \left(\frac{nc_k}{NR_k} - R(u) + \frac{A}{k} \right) \frac{1}{k} = 0 \qquad \text{(Eq 4.26-3)}$$

The simultaneous solution of these two equations provides the estimates. If failure analysis was performed to determine a fault reinsertion rate (r), a third equation can be used in conjunction with Eq 4.26-2 and Eq 4.26-3 to estimate the fault insertion rate, r:

$$\sum_{k=1}^{NS} \left(\frac{nc_k}{NR_k} - R(u) + \frac{A}{k(1-r)} \right) \frac{1}{k(1-r)} = 0$$

$$\text{(Eq 4.26-4)}$$

4.27 Residual Fault Count

4.27.1 Application. This measure provides an indication of software integrity.

4.27.2 Primitives

t_i = observed time between the ith and $(i-1)$st failure of a given severity level

f_i = number of failures during the ith time interval of a given severity level

4.27.3 Implementation. The failure-rate class of models can be used to predict the remaining faults. This class of models is used to estimate the shape of a hypothesized hazard function from which an estimate of the number of remaining faults can be obtained.

4.28 Failure Analysis Using Elapsed Time

4.28.1 Application. This measure can be used to determine reliability growth based on the estimated number of remaining faults and software reliability. It can be used to

(1) Predict the total number of faults in the software
(2) Predict the software reliability
(3) Estimate required testing time for reliability goal
(4) Estimate required resource allocation

4.28.2 Primitives

t_i = observed time between failures of a given severity level (for example, execution time)

4.28.3 Implementation. Observed failures should be recorded and the associated faults identified. The time between failures (CPU or other unit that represents actual execution time of the software) should also be recorded.

Using the maximum likelihood estimation, the method of least squares, or the Newton–Raphson optimizing scheme, the parameters and normalizing constants of candidate models can be estimated. These can be interpreted as initial fault content (N_o), normalizing constants, and initial mean-time-to-failure (M_o) based on the model selected. Once a model has been successfully fitted to the data using any of the well-known statistical tests (for example, goodness-of-fit), then the model can be used to estimate the remaining faults (N), MTTF (M), and reliability (R).

4.29 Testing Sufficiency

4.29.1 Application. This measure assesses the sufficiency of software-to-software integration testing by comparing actual to predicted faults.

4.29.2 Primitives

$\widehat{NF}$ = total number of faults predicted in the software

F_{it} = total number of faults detected to date in software integration testing
F_{pit} = number of faults detected prior to software integration testing
M_{it} = number of modules integrated
M_{tot} = total number of modules in final configuration

4.29.3 Implementation. The fault density (see 4.1) should be used to calculate the estimated total number of faults (NF) in the software. The number of faults remaining in the integrated portion of the software can then be estimated using

$$NF_{\text{rem}} = (NF - F_{pit})\, M_{it}/M_{\text{tot}}$$

Maximum and minimum tolerance coefficients (l_1 and l_2) should be established based on user experience. Values of 0.5 and 1.5 are suggested for use as the default values.

The guidelines shown in Table 4-1 assume that all scheduled integration tests have been run.

4.30 Mean-Time-to-Failure

4.30.1 Application. This measure is used for hypothesis testing a specified MTTF requirement.

4.30.2 Primitives. Mean-time-to-failure is the basic parameter required by most software reliability models. Computation is dependent on accurate recording of failure time (t_i), where t_i is the elapsed time between the ith and the $(i-1)$st failure. Time units used should be as precise as feasible. CPU execution time provides more resolution than wall-clock time. Thus CPU cycles would be more appropriate for a software development environment. For an operational environment that might require less resolution, an estimate based on wall-clock time could be used.

4.30.3 Implementation. Detailed record keeping of failure occurrences that accurately track the time (calendar or execution) at which the faults manifest themselves is essential. If weighting or organizing the failures by complexity, severity, or the reinsertion rate is desired, detailed

Table 4-1
Guidelines for Integration Testing Sufficiency

Measure Result	Interpretation	Recommended Action	Comments
$l_1 NF_{\text{rem}} < F_{it} < l_2 NF_{\text{rem}}$	Testing sufficiency is adequate	Proceed	—
$F_{it} > l_2 NF_{\text{rem}}$	Detected more faults than expected	Proceed, but apply fault density measure for each integrated module	Error-ridden modules may exist that should be replaced by a redesigned module
		Recalculate F_p	
$F_{it} < l_1 NF_{\text{rem}}$	Detected less faults than expected	Apply test coverage measure (see 4.24) before proceeding	May not have designed adequate number or variety of tests

failure analysis must be performed to determine the severity and complexity. Prior failure experience or model fitting analysis (for example, goodness-of-fit test) can be used to select a model representative of a failure process, and to determine a reinsertion rate of faults.

4.31 Failure Rate

4.31.1 Application. This measure can be used to indicate the growth in the software reliability as a function of test time.

4.31.2 Primitives

t_i = observed times between failures (for example, execution time) for a given severity level, i=1, ...

f_i = number of failures of a given severity level in the ith time interval

4.31.3 Implementation. The failure rate $\lambda(t)$ at any point in time can be estimated from the reliability function, $R(t)$, which in turn can be obtained from the cumulative probability distribution, $F(t)$, of the time until the next failure using any of the software reliability growth models such as the nonhomogeneous Poisson process (NHPP) or a Bayesian type model. The failure rate is

$$\lambda(t) = -\frac{1}{R(t)}\left[\frac{dR(t)}{dt}\right]$$

where

$$R(t) = 1 - F(t)$$

4.32 Software Documentation and Source Listings

4.32.1 Application. The primary objective of this measure is to collect information to identify the parts of the software maintenance products that may be inadequate for use in a software maintenance environment. Two questionnaires are used to examine the format and content of the documentation and source code attributes from a maintainability perspective.

4.32.2 Primitive. The questionnaires examine the following primitive product characteristics:

(1) Modularity
(2) Descriptiveness
(3) Consistency
(4) Simplicity
(5) Expandability
(6) Testability

Subcharacteristics include format, interface, math models, and data/control.

4.32.3 Implementation. Two questionnaires, the Software Documentation Questionnaire and

the Software Source Listing Questionnaire, are used to evaluate the software products in a desk audit. The questionnaires are contained in "Software Maintainability — Evaluation Guide [2]." The guide can be ordered from the Air Force Operational Test and Evaluation Center.

For the *software documentation evaluation*, the resource documents should include those that contain the program design specifications, program testing information and procedures, program maintenance information, and guidelines used in preparation of the documentation. These documents may have a variety of physical organizations depending upon the particular source, application, and documentation requirements. The documentation will in general consist of all documents that reveal the software design and implementation. A single evaluation of all the documents is done. Typical questions from the Software Documentation Questionnaire include the following:

(1) The documentation indicates that data storage locations are not used for more than one type of data structure.
(2) Parameter inputs and outputs for each module are explained in the documentation.
(3) Programming conventions for I/O processing have been established and followed.
(4) The documentation indicates the resource (storage, timing, tape drives, disks, consoles, etc) allocation is fixed throughout program execution.
(5) The documentation indicates that there is a reasonable time margin for each major time-critical program function (rate group, time slice, priority level, etc).
(6) The documentation indicates that the program has been designed to accommodate software test probes to aid in identifying processing performance.

For the *software source listings evaluation*, the program source code is evaluated. The source code may be either a high order language or assembler. Multiple evaluations using the questionnaire are conducted for the unit (module) level of the program. The units (modules) selected should represent a sample size of at least 10% of the total source code. Typical questions from the Source Listing Questionnaire include the following:

(1) Each function of this module is an easily recognizable block of code.
(2) The quantity of comments does not detract from the legibility of the source listings.

(3) Mathematical models as described/derived in the documentation correspond to the mathematical equations used in the module's source listing.

(4) Esoteric (clever) programming is avoided in this module.

(5) The size of any data structure that affects the processing logic of this module is parameterized.

(6) Intermediate results within this module can be selectively collected for display without code modification.

4.33 RELY (Required Software Reliability)

4.33.1 Application. RELY provides at the early planning phases of a project a measure that makes visible the trade-offs of cost and degree of reliability. It is recognized that reliability may vary relative to the system purpose. Man-rated software in space applications, for example, has higher reliability requirements than game software. The development processes for high reliability software especially integration and test should correspondingly be greater than that of average software.

4.33.2 Primitives. Required Reliability Rating:

Very low — The effect of a software failure is simply the inconvenience incumbent on the developers to fix the fault. Typical examples are a demonstration prototype of a voice typewriter or an early feasibility phase software simulation mode.[4]

Low — The effect of a software failure is a low level, easily-recoverable loss to users. Typical examples are a long range planning model or a climate forecasting model.[5]

Nominal — The effect of a software failure is a moderate loss to users, but a situation from which one can recover without extreme penalty. Typical examples are management information systems or inventory control systems.[6]

High — The effect of a software failure can be a major financial loss or a massive human inconvenience. Typical examples are banking systems and electric power distribution systems.[7]

Very high — The effect of a software failure can be the loss of human life. Examples are military command and control systems or nuclear reactor control systems.[8]

4.33.3 Implementation. Depending on the required reliability rating, the effort required for each phase of the development cycle can be adjusted to include the processes necessary to ensure that the product achieves the reliability goal. Figure 4.33.3-1[9] shows the effort factors relative to nominal required to achieve each of the required reliabililty ratings.

This technique can be used conversely to provide a reliability rating for a product through examination of the processes used to develop it (Fig 4.33.3-2).[10]

4.34 Software Release Readiness

4.34.1 Application. This measure is used to quantify the user and supporter (consumer) risk of ownership, based on either quantitative or subjective assessments of user and supporter issues. Given a number of issues, one can combine them to obtain a composite risk assessment. Although the primitives described here are designed for the Operational Test and Evaluation phases, the risk assessment method is applicable during any phase of the life cycle by the identification of appropriate issues and the selection or design of corresponding measures for assessment.

4.34.2 Primitives. The measurements of effectiveness, $ME(i)$, $i=1, ..., I$, for issues relating to software risk assessment. Example issues are

(1) Functional test coverage
(2) Software maturity
(3) Software source code listings quality factors
(4) Documentation quality factors
(5) Software operator-machine interface
(6) Software support resources assessments

4.34.3 Implementation. This measure assumes that I issues can be combined to assess the readiness of the software for release and the attendant consumer risk. For each issue i the measure $ME(i)$ is converted into an associated risk $RK(i)$ as it relates to the user and supporter. This risk is subjectively assigned by the evaluators and is defined to be in the range of 0 to 1.0, where zero denotes no risk and one denotes extreme risk. For the functional test coverage, maturity, and quality

---

[4] Definition of primitives and figures from Barry W. Boehm, *Software Engineering Economics* © 1981, pp 374–376. Reprinted by permission of Prentice-Hall, Inc., Englewood Cliffs, NJ.

[5] See footnote 4.

[6] See footnote 4.

[7] See footnote 4.

[8] See footnote 4.

[9] See footnote 4.

[10] See footnote 4.

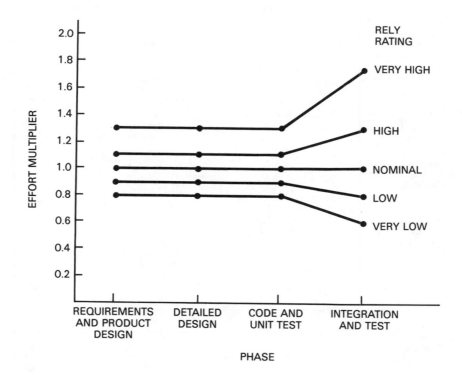

Fig 4.33.3-1
Effort Multipliers by Phase: Required Software Reliability
(Reprinted by permission of Prentice-Hall, Inc., Englewood Cliffs, NJ.)

factor primitives, the associated risk is determined by

$$RK(i) = 1.0 - ME(i)$$

Furthermore, each of the primitives $ME(i)$ is assigned a subjective, relative weight that represents its importance to the user (supporter). For each $ME(i)$ value, there is a corresponding $RK(i)$ risk and a $W(i)$ relative importance weight. All the relative weights $W(i)$ fo all user (supporter) measures sum to 1.0. Furthermore, there is an influence matrix [S] that provides a modification factor to the risk $RK(i)$ when a measure $ME(i)$ is influenced by another measure $ME(j)$. For example, consider the influence between software maturity (the fraction of software modified and added during a test [see 4.10]) and functional test coverage (the fraction of code demonstrated during a test [see 4.5]). It is clear that incomplete testing would reduce the confidence in the resulting maturity score because of incomplete demonstration of the software functions. The influence matrix $S(i,j)$ coefficients are assigned values that are representative of the dependence between $ME(i)$ and $ME(j)$.

The following steps are used in calculating this measure:

(1) Evaluate each primitive $ME(i)$.
(2) Assign a risk value $RK(i)$ to the $ME(i)$ measure such that $RK(i)$ is between zero and one [for example, $RK(i) = 1.0 - ME(i)$]. Or for subjective assessments:
    Low risk   = 0.0 to 0.33
    Medium risk = 0.34 to 0.66
    High risk   = 0.67 to 1.0
(3) For each measure $ME(i)$, determine the weighting $W(i)$ that reflects the importance of the measure to the total user (supporter). A suggested default value is $1/I$ giving equal weight to all issues.
(4) For each pair of measures $ME(i)$ and $ME(j)$, assign a value for the $S(i,j)$ influence coefficient that represents the subjective or quantified influence between the measures. The $S(i,j)$ coefficients vary between zero and one, where zero represents no influence (low correlation) and one represents high dependence (high correlation). Coefficient $S(i,j)$ is the measured or subjective value of measure $ME(i)$'s depen-

31

Rating	Requirements and Product Design	Detailed Design	Code and Unit Test	Integration and Test
Very high	Little detail Many TBDs Little Verification Minimal Quality Assurance (QA), Configuration Management (CM) draft user manual, test plans Minimal Program Design Review (PDR)	Basic design information Minimum QA, CM, draft user manual, test plans Informal design inspections	No test procedures Minimal path test, standards check Minimal QA, CM Minimal I/O and off-nominal tests Minimal user manual	No test procedures Many requirements untested Minimal QA, CM Minimal stress, off-nominal tests Minimal as-built documentation
Low	Basic information, verification Frequent TBDs Basic QA, CM, standards, draft user manual, test plans	Moderate detail Basic QA, CM, draft user manual, test plans	Minimal test procedures Partial path test, standards check Basic QA, CM, user manual Partial I/O and off-nominal tests	Minimal test procedures Frequent requirements untested Basic QA, CM, user manual Partial stress off-nominal tests
Nominal	Nominal project V & V			
High	Detailed verification, QA, CM, standards, PDR, documentation Detailed test plans, procedures	Detailed verification, QA, CM, standards, CDR, documentation Detailed test plans, procedures	Detailed test procedures, QA, CM, documentation Extensive off-nominal tests	Detailed test procedures, QA, CM, documentation Extensive stress, off-nominal tests
Very high	Detailed verification, QA, CM, standards, PDR, documentation IV & V interface Very detailed test plans, procedures	Detailed verification, QA, CM, standards, CDR, documentation Very thorough design inspections Very detailed test plans, procedures IV & V interface	Detailed test procedures, QA, CM, documentation Very thorough code inspections Very extensive off-nominal tests IV & V interface	Very detailed test procedures, QA, CM, documentation Very extensive stress, off-nominal tests IV & V interface

Fig 4.33.3-2
Projected Activity Differences Due to Required Software Reliability
(Reprinted by permission of Prentice-Hall, Inc., Englewood Cliffs, NJ.)

dence on measure $ME(j)$. Usually matrix $[S]$ is symmetric.

Let the apportioned risk $RK'(i)$ for measure i in relation to the other measures be:

$$RK'(i) = \frac{\sum\limits_{j=1}^{I} RK(i) \times S(i,j)}{\sum\limits_{j=1}^{I} S(i,j)}$$

Then combined user (supporter) risk is

$$R_{(user/supporter)} = \sum\limits_{i=1}^{I} RK'(i) \times W(i)$$

4.35 Completeness

4.35.1 Application. The purpose of this measure is to determine the completeness of the soft-

ware specification during the requirements phase. Also, the values determined for the primitives associated with the completeness measure can be used to identify problem areas within the software specification.

4.35.2 Primitives. The completeness measure consists of the following primitives:

B_1 = number of functions not satisfactorily defined

B_2 = number of functions

B_3 = number of data references not having an origin

B_4 = number of data references

B_5 = number of defined functions not used

B_6 = number of defined functions

B_7 = number of referenced functions not defined

B_8 = number of referenced functions

B_9 = number of decision points not using all conditions, options

B_{10} = number of decision points

B_{11} = number of condition options without processing

B_{12} = number of condition options

B_{13} = number of calling routines with parameters not agreeing with defined parameters

B_{14} = number of calling routines

B_{15} = number of condition options not set

B_{16} = number of set condition options having no processing

B_{17} = number of set condition options

B_{18} = number of data references having no destination

4.35.3 Implementation. The completeness measure (CM) is the weighted sum of ten derivatives expressed as

$$CM = \sum_{i=1}^{10} w_i D_i$$

where for each $i=1, ..., 10$, each weight w_i has a value between 0 and 1, the sum of the weights is equal to 1, and each D_i is a derivative with a value between 1 and 0.

To calculate the completeness measure

(1) The definitions of the primitives for the particular application must be determined.

(2) The priority associated with the derivatives must also be determined. This prioritization would affect the weights used to calculate the completeness measure.

Each primitive value would then be determined by the number of occurrences related to the definition of the primitive.

Each derivative is determined as follows:

$D_1 = (B_2 - B_1)/B_2$ = functions satisfactorily defined

$D_2 = (B_4 - B_3)/B_4$ = data references having an origin

$D_3 = (B_6 - B_5)/B_6$ = defined functions used

$D_4 = (B_8 - B_7)/B_8$ = referenced functions defined

$D_5 = (B_{10} - B_9)/B_{10}$ = all condition options at decision points

$D_6 = (B_{12} - B_{11})/B_{12}$ = all condition options with processing at decision points are used

$D_7 = (B_{14} - B_{13})/B_{14}$ = calling routine parameters agree with the called routine's defined parameters

$D_8 = (B_{12} - B_{15})/B_{12}$ = all condition options that are set

$D_9 = (B_{17} - B_{16})/B_{17}$ = processing follows set condition options

$D_{10} = (B_4 - B_{18})/B_4$ = data references have a destination

4.36 Test Accuracy

4.36.1 Application. This measure can be used to determine the accuracy of the testing program in detecting faults. With a test coverage measure, it can be used to estimate the percentage of faults remaining.

4.36.2 Primitives

N_s = number of seeded faults

$\hat{N}_s$ = estimated number of detectable seeded faults

4.36.3 Implementation. The software to be tested is seeded with faults. The number of seeded faults detected in each testing time interval is recorded along with time to detect faults, and a mathematical model is selected to represent the cumulative seeded faults detected across the total testing period. The cumulative seeded faults detected at time infinity is then estimated and test accuracy is calculated:

$$ALPHA = \hat{N}_s/N_s$$

4.37 System Performance Reliability

4.37.1 Application. This measure assesses the system's performance reliability, the probability that the value of each performance requirement be less than or equal to a predefined threshold value. The specific performance requirements addressed in this measure are:

U = utilization

X = throughput

Q = queue length distribution

WT = waiting time distribution

SE = mean server's efficiency

RT = response time distribution

ST = service time distribution

The application of these derived measures will ensure that

(1) Reliability planning functions are done by all inter- and intra-organizations.

(2) Periodic reliability estimations during the software life cycle are done to track reliability development.

(3) Verification and validation are done on the system capacity.

4.37.2 Primitives. The following primitives quantify the basic performance attributes that are measured over a time period of length T.

A = number of arrivals (functional jobs) during the time period T

SB = total amount of time "server" is busy

J = number of jobs completed during T

VR = number of requests (visits) per functional job for each server during time period T

T = time period over which measurements are made

4.37.3 Implementation. These measures are applicable to operating systems and networks. Based upon the measured primitives the derived quantifiable measures are

Γ = A/T, average arrival rate of jobs

X = J/T, average throughput rate

U = SB/T, average utilization

AS = SB/J, average service time

WT = $f(\Gamma, U, AS, VR$, waiting time distribution (expressed as a function of arrival rate, utilization, service time, and visit rate)

SE = $A/(AS+W)$, server's efficiency of each job

$$R = \sum_{i=1}^{k} (VR \times S)_i + \sum_{i=1}^{k} (VR \times W)_i,$$

total response time for each functional job over the k servers

AQ = $W \times \Gamma$, the average queue length

(Eq 4.37-1)

Using any of these measures, one can derive the corresponding probability distribution of the measure under the stated assumptions of the system. The distribution can then be used to calculate the probability that the measure will achieve a desired level.

The following step by step process can be followed to achieve this.

(1) Determine the infrastructure of the performance model. This involves identifying the critical system resources and the system's underpinning connections in the form of a Queueing Network Model (QNM). The basic idea of the model is that the "essential" part of the system's architecture is represented by a network of "servers" and queues that are connected by transition paths. Jobs circulate through the network, the flow being controlled by the transition probabilities.

(2) Define, qualify, and quantify the workload classes. This is to identify the resource demand characteristics of the different classes of jobs and their dynamic performance attribute matrix. This determines the

apportionment of the utilization of each server by each work class.

(3) Measure the resource demands for each work class. The service time, arrival rate, visit ratios of each system resource are measured for each class of job.

(4) Solve the QNM. The approximation algorithms in analytic queueing theory and operations research techniques are used to solve the model.

(5) Perform the reliability evaluation. For example, suppose the response time R must meet the goal of $R \leq R_o$, where R is given by Eq 4.37-1. Calculate the system performance reliability as Reliability = Prob $\{R \leq R_o\}$ for stated assumptions during time period of length T. The system performance is not achieved if the desired reliability is not attained.

4.38 Independent Process Reliability

4.38.1 Application. This measure provides a direct method to compute reliability (R) of certain types of software systems such as telephone switching and business transaction systems in which the programs have no loops and no local dependencies exist. This is a measure of the reliability of service that a software system provides.

4.38.2 Primitives

f_{ij} = frequency of execution of intermodule transfer from module i to j

MD = number of modules

P_i = ith process, which can be generated in a user environment

q_i = probability that P_i will be generated in a user environment

r_i = random variable equal to 1 if the process P_i generates the correct software system output and zero otherwise

R_i = reliability of the ith module

4.38.3 Implementation. This measure assumes that a large program is composed of logically independent modules that can be designed, implemented, and tested independently.

Let L = set of processes P_i that can be generated by the software system corresponding to different input values. Then the reliability R of the software system can be computed from

$$R = \sum_{\forall P_i \, \epsilon L} q_i \, r_i$$

In large programs it is infeasible to evaluate r_i and q_i for each process P_i because L could be large. To circumvent this difficulty, a simple Markov model is developed with intermodule probabilities, (f_{ij}), as the user profiles. The reliability parameters of the program are expressed in terms of transitional probability parameters between states. The reliability R of the software system is defined as the probability of reaching the correct state [after module n] from the initial state [from module 1] of the Markov process, that is,

$$R = S\,(1, MD)\,R_n$$

where

$$S = [I-Q]^1$$

Q is the state transition matrix spanning the entire Markov graph program and I is the identity matrix.

Elements of the matrix, $f_{ij}R_i$ represent the probability that execution of module i produces the correct result and transfers control to module j. R_i is determined from experimentation as the ratio of the number of output sets generated by module i to the number of input sets when the software system is tested by samples of representative valid input.

4.39 Combined Hardware and Software (System) Operational Availability

4.39.1 Application. This measure provides a direct indication of system dependability, that is, if it is operating or operable when required by the user.

4.39.2 Primitives

λ = observed software failure rate

β = observed hardware failure rate

μ_i = observed software fault correction rate with i faults in the software

γ = observed hardware repair rate

NF = estimated number of remaining software faults

P_s = probability of correcting a software fault when detected $(0 \le P_s \le 1)$

P_h = probability of correctly repairing a hardware failure $(0 \le P_h \le 1)$

4.39.3 Implementation. Tha basic Markovian model is used for predicting combined hardware and software (system) availability as a function of operating time. System upstate probabilities $P_{NF,n}(t)$ with n remaining faults, given that there were NF software faults at the commissioning $(t=0)$ of the system, is computed for $n=0, 1, 2, ..., N$.

$$\text{System Availability } A(t) = \sum_{n=0}^{NF} P_{N,n}(t)$$

The expression for $P_{NF,n}(t)$, $n=1, ..., NF$ is derived as

$$P_{NF,n}(t) = G_{NF,n}(t) - \sum_{j=1}^{K}$$

$$\cdot \frac{\prod_{i=n+1}^{K} (P_s\lambda_i\mu_i)(-x_jP_h\gamma)^{NF-n}A(-x_j)(1-e^{-x_jt})}{x_j \prod_{\substack{i=1 \\ i\neq j}}^{K}(-x_j+x_i)}$$

where

$G_{NF,n}(t)$ = cumulative distribution function of the first passage time for operational state with NF faults to operational state with n faults and is expressed as

$$\sum_{j=1}^{K} \frac{\prod_{i=n+1}^{NF}(P_s\lambda_i\mu_i)(-x_j+P_h\gamma)^{NF-n}}{\prod_{\substack{i=1 \\ i\neq j}}^{K}(-x_j+x_i)}\frac{1}{-x_j}(e^{-x_jt}-1)$$

$\lambda_i = i\lambda$

$\mu_i = i_\mu$

$K = 3\,(NF-n)$

$x_1 = x_{1,(n+1)}$

$x_2 = x_{2,(n+1)}$

$x_3 = x_{3,(n+1)}$

$x_4 = x_{1,(n+2)}$

$x_5 = x_{2,(n+2)}$

$x_6 = x_{3,(n+2)}$

$\cdot$

$\cdot$

$\cdot$

$x_{1,(NF-n)} = x_{1,NF}$

$x_{2,(NF-n)} = x_{2,NF}$

$x_{3,(NF-n)} = x_{3,NF}$

$-x_{1,i}$, $-x_{2,i}$, and $-x_{3,i}$ $(i=n+1, ..., NF)$ are the roots of the polynomial:

$$S^3 + S^2\,(\lambda_i + \mu_i + \beta + P_h\gamma)$$
$$+ S(P_s\lambda_i\mu_i + \beta\mu_i + \lambda_iP_h\gamma) + \mu_iP_h\gamma)$$
$$+ P_sP_h\gamma\lambda_i\mu_i$$

Also

$$A(-x_j) = (-x_j\beta)\,(-x_j + \mu_n)$$
$$+ \lambda_n(-x_j + P_s\mu_n)\,(-x_j + P_h\gamma)$$

Acknowledgment

The following organizations supported the development of this standard:

Aerospace Corporation
Apple Computer, Inc.
Argonne National Laboratory
Bechtel Group, Inc.
Bell Canada
Boeing Aerospace
Computer Sciences Corp.
CTA, Inc.
Digital Equipment Corp.
Dynamics Research Corp.
EG&G
Federal Aviation Administration
General Dynamics
General Electric
Hewlett-Packard
Honeywell
Hughes Aircraft Co.
IBM
INTEL Corporation
International Bureau Software Test
ITT Telecom
Martin-Marietta
McDonnell Douglas
NASA

National Bureau of Standards
National Centre of Systems Reliability
NCR Corporation
Norden Systems
PRC
Product Assurances Consulting
RCA
Sanders Associates
Satellite Business Systems
SOFTECH Microsystems
SoHaR, Incorporated
Sperry
Stromberg Carlson
Tadiran, Ltd.
Tandem Computers
Teledyne Brown Engineering
Transport Canada
TRW
U.S. Air Force
U.S. Army
U.S. Navy
University of Southwestern Louisiana
Xerox Corporation

ANSI/IEEE
Std 982.2-1988

An American National Standard

IEEE Guide for the Use of IEEE Standard Dictionary of Measures to Produce Reliable Software

Sponsor

**Software Engineering Technical Subcommittee
of the
Technical Committee on Software Engineering
of the
IEEE Computer Society**

982.2

Approved September 27, 1988

IEEE Standards Board

Approved August 10, 1989

American National Standards Institute

Corrected Edition

October 23, 1989

NOTE: A black bar has been placed in the margin next to each correction to aid in identifying the changes made to this printing.

Foreword

(This Foreword is not a part of IEEE Std 982.2-1988, IEEE Guide for the Use of IEEE Standard Dictionary of Measures to Produce Reliable Software.)

This guide provides the underlying concepts and motivation for establishing a measurement process for reliable software, utilizing IEEE Std 982.1-1988, IEEE Standard Dictionary of Measures to Produce Reliable Software. This guide contains information necessary for application of measures to a project. It includes guidance for the following:

(1) Applying product and process measures throughout the software life cycle, providing the means for continual self-assessment and reliability improvement;

(2) Optimizing the development of reliable software, beginning at the early development stages, with respect to constraints such as cost and schedule;

(3) Maximizing the reliability of software in its actual use environment during the operation and maintenance phases;

(4) Developing the means to manage reliability in the same manner that cost and schedule are managed.

The guide is intended for design, development, evaluation (eg, auditing or procuring agency) and maintenance personnel; software quality and software reliability personnel; and operations and acquisition support managers. It is organized to provide input to the planning process for reliability management.

This document contains six sections and one appendix.

Section 1, "Scope and References," establishes the goals and boundaries of the guide.

Section 2, "Definitions," serves as a central location for key terms used throughout the body of the document.

Section 3, "Measures to Produce Reliable Software," contains guidance for measure selection and application.

Section 4, "Measure Organization and Classification," provides both functional and software life cycle taxonomies of the measures.

Section 5, "Framework for Measures," refines the measurement process to nine stages for effective implementation.

Section 6, "Errors, Faults, and Failures Analysis for Reliability Improvement," provides further definition of the interrelationship of these concepts.

Appendix A, "Measures for Reliable Software," contains the standard set of measures.

The goal of IEEE Std 982.2-1988, IEEE Guide for the Use of Standard Dictionary of Measures to Produce Reliable Software is to generate a dialogue on the use and effectiveness of selected measures. This dialogue should result in the evolution of existing measures and the development of new measures that evaluate and promote software reliability. In this way, the body of knowledge of and experience with software reliability can be improved and expanded.

This is one of a series of integrated IEEE Software Engineering Standards. This guide is consistent with ANSI/IEEE Std 729-1983, Glossary of Software Engineering Terminology; ANSI/IEEE Std 730-1984, IEEE Standard for Software Quality Assurance Plans; ANSI/IEEE Std 828-1983, IEEE Standard for Software Configuration Management Plans; and ANSI/IEEE Std 1012-1986, IEEE Standard for Software Verification and Validation Plans. This guide may be applied either independently or in conjunction with those standards.

The following persons were on the balloting committee that approved this document for submission to the IEEE Standards Board:

F. Ackerman	L. Good	D. Pfeiffer
W. Boll	D. Gustavson	R. Poston
J. Bowen	V. Haas	P. Powell
P. Bright	C. Hay	N. Schneidewind
F. Buckley	H. Hecht	W. Schnoege
H. Carney	L. Kaleda	R. Schueppert
J. Chung	T. Kurihara	R. Shillato
F. Coallier	G. Larsen	D. Siefert
P. Denny	F. C. Lim	D. Simkins
J. Dobbins	B. Lindberg	R. Singh
D. Doty	M. Lipow	V. Srivastava
R. Dwyer	B. Livson	A. Sukert
W. Ellis	P. Marriott	K. Tai
W. Farr	R. Martin	R. Thibodeau
D. Favor	J. McCall	P. Thompson
J. Fendrich	J. Mersky	D. To. n
G. Fields	W. Murch	H. Trochesset
J. Forster	J. Navlakha	R. van Tilburg
D. Gelperin	D. Nickle	P. Wolfgang
S. Glickman	D. Peercy	T. Workman
S. Gloss-Sloer	W. Perry	N. Yopconka
	P. Petersen	

The Software Reliability Measurement Working Group had the following membership:

B. Andrews	W. Goss	K. Oar
S. Beason	S. Gray	R. Panchal
R. Berlack	F. Gray	R. Pikul
M. Berry	V. Haas	E. Presson
N. Beser	C. Harrison	R. Prudhomme
J. Bieman	S. Hartman	H. Richter
J. Blackman	L. Hearn	M. Richter
J. Bowen	H. Hecht	L. Sanders
M. Bruyere	R. Hood	R. Sandborgh
F. Buckley	J. Horch	H. Schock
N. Chu	D. Hurst	D. Simkins
G. Chisholm	N. Johnson, Jr	O. Smith
G. Clow	R. Kenett	R. Spear
J. Corrinne	R. Kessler	E. Soistman
W. Covington	R. Kumar	L. Sprague
W. Daney	M. Landes	A. Stone
B. Daniels	R. Lane	D. Sudbeck
F. DeKalb	J. Latimer	R. Sulgrove
I. Doshay	L. Lebowitz	D. Town
E. Dunaye	M. Lipow	R. Wamser
F. Fisk	C. McPherson	J. Wang
A. Florence	A. Moseley	D. Winterkorn
D. Frevert	S. Nemecek	J. Wujek
D. Gacke	K. Nidiffer	B. Zamastil

The Software Reliability Measurement Working Group Steering Committee had the following members:

James Dobbins, Chairman

Ray Leber, *Cochairman*   **Ted Workman,** *Cochairman*

P. Bright	L. Good	F. Salvia
A. Cicu	N. Hall	D. Siefert
C. Cucciati	P. Marriott	R. Singh
W. Ellis	R. Martin	V. Srivastava
W. Farr	W. Murch	H. Trochesset
S. Glickman	P. Powell	W. Wilson

When the IEEE Standards Board approved this standard on September 27, 1988, it had the following membership:

Donald C. Fleckenstein, *Chairman*   **Marco Migliaro**, *Vice Chairman*

Andrew G. Salem, *Secretary*

Comments on this guide are welcome and should be addressed to:

James Dobbins
Director, Software Quality Engineering
AMS, Inc.
1525 Wilson Boulevard, 3rd Floor
Arlington, VA 22209

Contents

Figures

Tables

Appendix A
Measures for Reliable Software

APPENDIX FIGURES

APPENDIX TABLES   PAGE

List of Symbols

Symbol	Meaning	Measures Used	Primitive/Metric
A	(1) Number of arrivals during time period T	37	P
	(2) Reliability growth factor	26	M
$A_{existing}$	Number of ambiguities in a program remaining to be eliminated	6	P
$A(t)$	System availability	39	M
A_{tot}	Total number of ambiguities identified	6	P
α	Test accuracy	36	M
AQ	Average queue length	37	M
AS	Average service time	37	P
B	Software science measure (number of errors)	14	M
B_1	Number of functions not satisfactorily defined	35	P
B_2	Number of functions	35	P
B_3	Number of data references not having an origin	35	P
B_4	Number of data references	35	P
B_5	Number of defined functions not used	35	P
B_6	Number of defined functions	35	P
B_7	Number of referenced functions not defined	35	P
B_8	Number of referenced functions	35	P
B_9	Number of decision points not using all conditions, options	35	P
B_{10}	Number of decision points	35	P
B_{11}	Number of condition options without processing	35	P
B_{12}	Number of condition options	35	P
B_{13}	Number of calling routines with parameters not agreeing with defined parameters	35	P
B_{14}	Number of calling routines	35	P
B_{15}	Number of condition options not set	35	P
B_{16}	Number of set condition options having no processing	35	P
B_{17}	Number of set condition options	35	P
B_{18}	Number of data references having no destination	35	P
β	Observed hardware failure rate	39	P
C	Complexity metric (static, dynamic, cyclomatic)	15, 16	M
C_i	Complexity for program invocation and return along each edge e_i as determined by the user	15	P
CE	Cause and effect measure	6	M
CM	Completeness measure	35	M
D	Software science measure (program difficulty)	14	M
d_k	Complexity for allocation of resource k as determined by the user	15	P

Symbol	Meaning	Measures Used	Primitive/ Metric
D_i	Total number of unique defects detected during the ith design or code inspection process or the ith life cycle phase	2, 8	P
DD	Defect density	2	M
DEs	Decomposition elements	23	P
DI	Defect index	8	M
DSM	Design structure metric	19	M
datain	Number of data structures from which the procedure retrieves data	25	P
dataout	Number of data structures that the procedure updates	25	P
E	(1) Number of edges	15, 16, 17	P
	(2) Software science measure (effort)	14	M
e_i	Number of entry points for the ith module	13	P
F or F_i	Total number of unique faults found in a given time interval resulting in failures of a specified severity level	1	P
f or f_i	Total number of failures of a given severity level in a given time interval	3, 20, 21, 27, 31	P
F_d	Fault density	1	M
f_{ij}	Frequency execution of intermodule transfer from module i to j	38	P
F_a	Number of software functions (modules) in the current delivery that are additions in the current delivery	10	P
F_c	Number of software functions (modules) in the current delivery that include internal changes from a previous delivery	10	P
FD	Fault days metric	4	M
FD_i	Fault days for the ith fault	4	P
F_{del}	Number of software functions (modules) in the previous delivery that are deleted in the current delivery	10	P
FE	Number of the software functional (modular) requirements for which all test cases have been satisfactorily completed	5	P
F_{it}	Total number of faults detected to date in software integration testing	29	P
F_{pit}	Number of faults detected prior to software integration testing	29	P
FT	Total number of software functional test requirements (modular)	5	P
Γ	Average rate of jobs	37	M
Υ	Observed hardware repair rate	39	P
I	Total number of inspections to date	2, 11	P
IFC	Information flow complexity	25	M
J	Total number of jobs completed	37	P
K	Number of resources	15	P

Symbol	Meaning	Measures Used	Primitive/ Metric
k	Number of runs for the specified period of time	18	P
$KSLOC$	Number of source lines of executable code and nonexecutable data declarations in thousands	1, 2, 8	P
$KSLOD$	Number of source lines of design statements in thousands that have been inspected to date	2, 8	P
L	Software science measure (observed program length)	14	M
l	Software science measure (program vocabulary)	14	M
Ll	Software science measure (program level)	14	M
$\lambda(t)$	Failure rate function	31	M
λ	Observed software failure rate	39	P
length	Number of source statements in a procedure	25	P
lfi	Local flows into a procedure	25	P
lfo	Local flows from a procedure	25	P
M	Manhours per major defect detected	11	M
M_i	Number of medium defects found	8	P
m_i	Number of entry and exit points for module i	13	M
MD	Number of modules	38	P
$ME(i)$	Measure effectiveness for the ith issue	34	P
M_{it}	Number of modules integrated	29	M
M_T	Number of software functions (modules) in the current delivery	10	M
M_{tot}	Total number of modules in final configuration	29	M
MTTF	Mean-time-to-failure	30	M
μ_i	Observed software fault correction rate with i faults in the software	39	P
N	Number of nodes	15, 16, 17	P
nc	Number of correct runs in a given test sample	18, 26	P
NF	Total number of faults within a program	29, 39	M
NF_{rem}	Total number of faults remaining within a program	22, 29	M
NF_{rem} (%)	Percentage of faults remaining within a program	36	M
n_F	Number of faults found that were not intentionally seeded	22	P
NR	Number of runs (or test cases) in a given test sample	18, 26	P
NS	Total number of stages	26	P
N_s	Number of seeded faults	22, 36	P
n_s	Number of seeded faults found	22	P
$N1$	Total number of occurrences of the operators in a program	14	P
$n1$	Number of distinct operators in a program	14	P

Symbol	Meaning	Measures Used	Primitive/ Metric
$N2$	Total number of occurrences of the operands in a program	14	P
$n2$	Number of distinct operands in a program	14	P
N_1	Number of errors detected using SVDs due to inconsistencies	23	P
N_2	Number of errors detected using SVDs due to incompleteness	23	P
N_3	Number of errors detected using SVDs due to misinterpretation	23	P
P	Probability measure over the sample space	18	P
p_n	Probability of repairing a hardware failure correctly	39	P
P_i	(1) Probability that the ith run is selected from the sample space	18, 38	P
	(2) Probability that the ith process that can be generated in a user environment is selected	39	
P_s	Probability of correcting a software fault when detected	39	P
$P_{N,n}(t)$	System upstate probabilities	39	P
PI_i	Phase index metric for the ith life cycle phase	8	M
PL	Purity level	21	M
PS	Product size	8	P
$P1$	Total number of modules in the program	19	P
$P2$	Number of modules dependent on the input or output	19	P
$P3$	Number of modules dependent on prior processing	19	P
$P4$	Number of database elements	19	P
$P5$	Number of nonunique database elements	19	P
$P6$	Number of database segments (partition of the state)	19	P
$P7$	Number of modules not single entrance/single exit	19	P
Q	Queue length distribution	37	P
q_i	Probability that P_i will be generated in a user environment	38	P
R	(1) Total response time for each functional job	37	M
	(2) Reliability of the system	38	M
R_i	Reliability of the ith module	38	P
R_k	Run reliability at a specified stage	18, 26	M
$R(t)$	Reliability function	31	M
r_i	Flag to denote if the ith process generates the correct software system output	38	P
r_{ki}	Resource status array indicator flags	15	P
RG	Number of regions	16, 17	P
$RK(i)$	Risk factor for the ith measure	34	M
RT	Response time distribution	37	P
$R1$	Number of requirements met by the architecture	7	P

Symbol	Meaning	Measures Used	Primitive/Metric
$R2$	Number of original requirements	7	P
S	Sample space of possible input patterns and states	18	P
S_i	Point from the sample space of possible inputs	18	P
s_i	Number of serious defects found	8, 11	P
SB	Total amount of time server is busy	37	P
SE	Server's efficiency	37	M
SN	Number of splitting nodes	16, 17	P
SMI	Software maturity index	10	M
ST	Service time distribution	37	P
T	(1) Time period over which measurements are made	37	P
	(2) Time	14	M
T_i	Number of trivial defects found	8	P
t_i	Observed times between failures of a given severity level	20, 21, 27 28, 30, 31	P
TC	Test coverage	24	M
TM	Traceability measure	7	M
T_1	Time expended by the inspection team in preparation for design or code inspection meeting	11	P
T_2	Time expended by the inspection team in conduct of a design or code inspection meeting	11	P
U	Utilization	37	P
V	Software science measure (program volume)	14	M
VR	Number of requests per functional job for each server during time period T	37	P
W_i	Weighting distribution	8, 19, 34	P
WT	Waiting time distribution	37	P
X	Throughput	37	P
x_i	Number of exit points for the ith module	13	P

NOTE: P stands for primitive
      M stands for derived metric

IEEE Guide for the Use of IEEE Standard Dictionary of Measures to Produce Reliable Software

1. Scope and References

1. Scope. This guide provides the conceptual insights, implementation considerations, and assessment suggestions for the application of IEEE Std 982.1-1988, IEEE Standard Dictionary of Measures to Produce Reliable Software [2].[1] The Dictionary, by its very nature, is limited in what it may contain. While this is necessary for standardization, abbreviation of detail might be detrimental to the most effective use of the Dictionary. This guide is written to provide a bridge between IEEE Std 982.1-1988 and the user, so that full benefit may be derived from the application of the standard to a software project.

1.2 References. This guide shall be used in conjunction with the following publications:

[1] ANSI/IEEE 729-1983, IEEE Standard Glossary of Software Engineering Terminology.[2]

[2] IEEE Std 982.1-1988, IEEE Standard Dictionary of Measures to Produce Reliable Software.[3]

2. Definitions

Most of the definitions listed below can be found in ANSI/IEEE Std 729-1983, IEEE Standard Glossary of Software Engineering Terminology [1]. The definitions of the terms "concept phase," "defect," "measure," "primitive," "software reliability management" are not present in ANSI/

IEEE Std 729-1983, and establish meaning in the context of this guide. The acronym ISO (International Organization for Standardization) indicates that the definition is also accepted by ISO.

concept phase. The period of time in the software life cycle during which system concepts and objectives needed by the user are identified and documented. Precedes the requirements phase.

defect. A product anomaly. Examples include such things as (1) omissions and imperfections found during early life cycle phases and (2) faults contained in software sufficiently mature for test or operation. See also "fault."

error. Human action that results in software containing a fault. Examples include omission or misinterpretation of user requirements in a software specification, and incorrect translation or omission of a requirement in the design specification (see ANSI/IEEE Std 729-1983 [1]).

failure. (1) The termination of the ability of a functional unit to perform its required function. (ISO; ANSI/IEEE Std 729-1983 [1]). (2) An event in which a system or system component does not perform a required function within specified limits. A failure may be produced when a fault is encountered [1].

fault. (1) An accidental condition that causes a functional unit to fail to perform its required function. (ISO; ANSI/IEEE Std 729-1983 [1]). (2) A manifestation of an error in software. A fault, if encountered, may cause a failure. Synonymous with bug [1].

measure. A quantitative assessment of the degree to which a software product or process possesses a given attribute.

primitive. Data relating to the development or use of software that is used in developing measures or quantitative descriptions of software.

---

[1] The numbers in brackets correspond to those of the references in 1.2; numbers in brackets preceded by an "A" correspond to references in the Appendix.

[2] ANSI/IEEE publications are available from the Sales Department, American National Standards Institute, 1430 Broadway, New York, NY 10018, or from the IEEE Service Center, 445 Hoes Lane, P.O. Box 1331, Piscataway, NJ 08854-1331.

[3] IEEE publications are available from the IEEE Service Center, 445 Hoes Lane, P.O. Box 1331, Piscataway, NJ 08854-1331.

Primitives are directly measurable or countable, or may be given a constant value or condition for a specific measure. Examples include error, failure, fault, time, time interval, date, number of noncommentary source code statements, edges, nodes.

software reliability. The probability that software will not cause the failure of a system for a specified time under specified conditions. The probability is a function of the inputs to, and use of, the system as well as a function of the existence of faults in the software. The inputs to the system determine whether existing faults, if any, are encountered [1].

software reliability management. The process of optimizing the reliability of software through a program that emphasizes software error prevention, fault detection and removal, and the use of measurements to maximize reliability in light of project constraints such as resources (cost), schedule, and performance.

3. Measures to Produce Reliable Software

This guide addresses two major topics. The first is the rationale for the document IEEE Std 982.1-1988, IEEE Standard Dictionary of Measures to Produce Reliable Software. The guide presents the measure selection criteria. It address these questions: "To whom is the standard directed?" "When should the standard be applied?" and "Why was the standard created?"

The second topic is the application of these measures to product, project, and industry. For each measure the guide provides further definition, examples, interpretation, and references. The questions addressed include: "How can the standard be used effectively?" "How should results be interpreted?" and "How should objectives be set?"

The goal of the Dictionary is to support software developers, project managers, and system users in achieving optimum reliability levels in software products. It was designed to address the needs of software developers and customers who are confronted with a plethora of models, techniques, and measures in the literature, but who lack sufficient guidance to utilize them effectively. The standard addresses the need for a uniform interpretation of these and other indicators of reliability.

The Dictionary assumes an intimate relationship between the reliability of a product and the process used to develop that product. The reliable product provides confirmation of a successful process; the unreliable product provides a lesson for process change. It is in this general spirit that the measures selected give visibility to both process and product so that the essential facts necessary for process evaluation and change are available.

The measures were selected to provide information throughout the life cycle of a product. They can be used to make optimum operational reliability levels and to provide a *post factum* measurement of reliability levels achieved. The basic goal is to provide the elements of a measurement program that support a constructive approach for achieving optimum reliability of the end product.

The selected measures are related to various product and process factors that may have an impact on software reliability and that are observable throughout the entire life cycle. The Dictionary provides, even in the early life cycle phases, a means for continual assessment of the evolving product and the process. Through early reliability assessment, the Dictionary supports constructive optimization of reliability within given performance, resource, and schedule constraints.

The Dictionary focuses on measures of the potential causes of failure throughout the software life cycle, rather than just on measures of the effect of poor reliability of nearly completed products. The intent is to produce software that is reliable, rather than just an estimate of the failure-freeness of a nearly completed and possibly unreliable product. Both the traditional approach of measuring reliability and the constructive approach of building in reliability are placed in context in this document.

The primitives to be used and the method of computation are provided for each measure. The standard calibrates the rulers, the measurement tools, through the use of common units and a common language. It promotes the use of a common database in the industry. Through commonality the standard provides the justification for building effective tools for the measurement process itself.

The standard and this guide are intended to serve as the foundation on which researchers and practitioners can build consistent methods. These documents are designed to assist management in directing product development and support toward specific reliability goals. The purpose is to provide a common set of definitions through which a meaningful exchange of data and evaluations can occur. Successful application of the measures is dependent upon their use as intended in the specified environments.

The future study of extensive sets of basic data collected through the application of this standard will make it feasible to understand causal relationships, if any, between reliability indicators obtained during the process and operational reliability of a completed product. It will also promote the refinement of existing models and the development of new models based on this consistent data.

3.1 Constructive Approach to Reliable Software. An analysis of the relationship between the software development and maintenance processes and software reliability is provided. The purpose is to clarify the criteria used in the selection of measures.

Software reliability measurement is the determination of the probability that software will not cause the failure of a system for a specified time under specified conditions. The probability is a function of the inputs to, and use of, the system as well as a function of the existence of faults in the software. The inputs to the system determine whether existing faults, if any, are encountered [1].

3.1.1 Constructive Approach. Reliability is an estimation of system failure-freeness. System failures that are caused by software are a valid concern of the software community. A constructive approach to reliable software seeks to remove the root causes of this class of system failures (Fig 3.1.1-1) through software development and support processes that promote fault avoidance, early fault detection, appropriately prompt removal, and system-designed fault tolerance (Fig 3.1.1-2).

The analysis of the errors, faults, and failures from previous development and support processes can lead to improved future processes. While the exact functional relationships are not proven, it is through experience that the majority of failures are related to their origins. Examples include the following:

(1) Incompletely defined user needs and requirements
(2) Omissions in the design and coding process
(3) Improper usage of the system
(4) Excessive change activity

The error, fault, and failure analysis is detailed further in Section 6.

A process strategy to achieve reliable software includes activities, methods, tools, and measurements. Figure 3.1.1-3 shows the process strategy

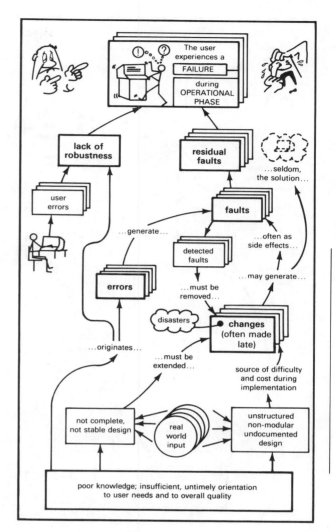

Fig 3.1.1-1
Causes of Failures

and the integrated role of measurements as the control window through which the quality of the product and of the process are monitored.

While Fig 3.1.1-3 is in large part self-explanatory, it is worthwhile to emphasize the major drivers for the process strategy. The strategy does not itself contain new techniques or new methodologies. It is a collection of known concepts, activities, and techniques, that can be used to drive a project toward better reliability.

The driving criteria of this constructive process strategy are as follows:

3.1.1.1 Do It Right the First Time. This approach stresses the use of all means necessary to define and build a product with no faults. "Doing it right the first time" must stress error prevention and fault avoidance through the following practices:

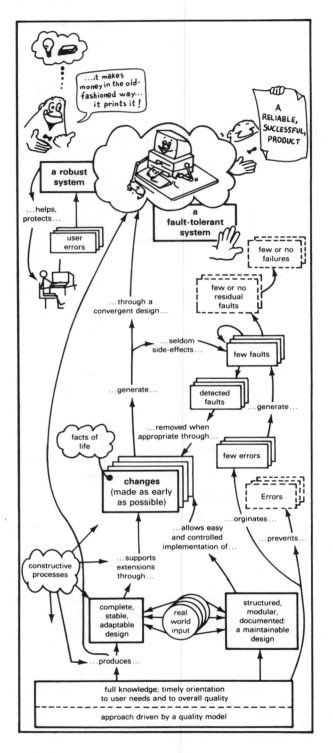

Fig 3.1.1-2
Constructors of a Reliable Product

(1) Employment of skilled, competent personnel is of foremost importance in building reliable products. It is important in all phases of development, especially the identification of user requirements and needs in the concept phase. The strategy stresses the necessity of intensely studying the stated and unstated needs of the user application, and of having sufficient experience in solving similar problems to apply to the present problem. For this reason, the concept phase is considered a major life cycle component toward a complete and stable definition of the objectives of a project. Quality work requires extensive knowledge of the application, which is often forgotten in the intermediate design phases, and remembered only when the user realizes some important features are missing during operation and maintenance.

(2) Early user involvement in the conception of the product through techniques such as prototyping must be stressed to ensure that usability matches failure-freeness in importance.

(3) Modern methods, languages and automated tools should be selected to promote productivity and quality in the activities of specification, design, coding and configuration management. The selected languages and tools must also support the verification activities through automation of requirements tracing, completeness and consistency analysis, performance simulation, complexity measurements, and configuration definition and control. Automation significantly reduces the risk of human errors.

3.1.1.2 Detect It Early; Fix It as Soon as Practicable. Detection and repair should be properly planned activities. Verification [1] is the process of determining whether or not the products of a given phase of the software development cycle fulfill the requirements established during the previous phase. Validation [1] is the process of evaluating software at the end of the software development process to ensure compliance with software requirements.

Early detection of faults throughout the life cycle through reviews, inspections, prototyping, simulation, or proof of correctness of the product will improve reliability. During the operations and maintenance phase, faults do not necessarily have to be fixed immediately. The severity of the problem, the frequency of occurrence of the problem, and the opportunity to manage and test the new configuration should weigh in the decision of when to fix a fault.

18

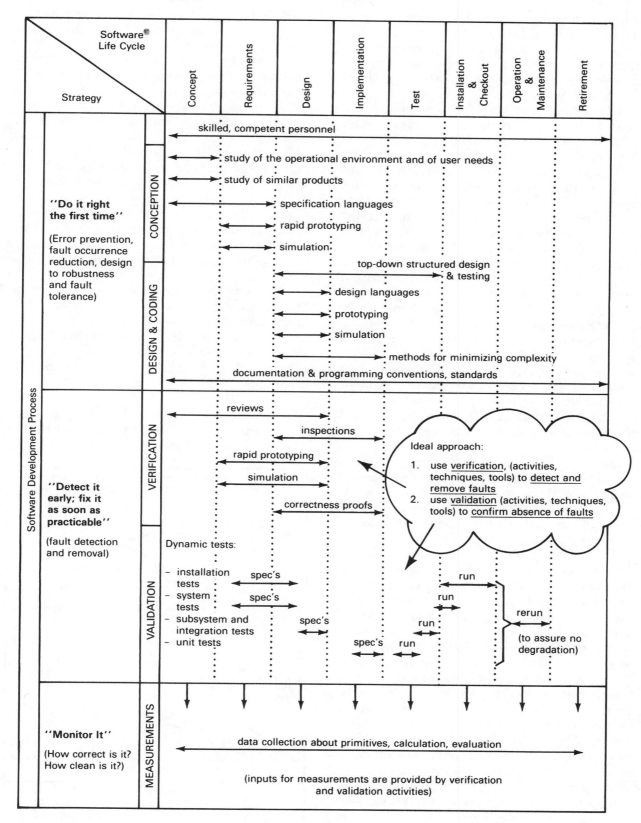

Fig. 3.1.1-3
Strategy of the Constructive Approach for Development of Reliable Software

Timely design of software tests, plans, and procedures is necessary to determine required resources and schedule. Early design of tests contributes to earlier detection of consistency and completeness faults, and ensures the testability of the requirements.

Reliability cannot be tested into a product. More testing does not necessarily mean better reliability. However, dynamic tests, the main tool for validation, have to be used cost-effectively with measures to provide the widest test coverage of a product. In the light of a constructive approach to reliable software, dynamic tests should be viewed as a tool for confirming the absence of faults rather than as the preferred tool for detecting them. When system test design is driven by user requirements, and when test samples are randomly selected based on defined probabilities of product inputs, testing contributes effectively to this constructive approach by providing an independent assessment of the software execution in representative operating environments. The costs of early verification efforts can be offset by savings from less repetition of dynamic tests, because most faults should be detected during verification.

3.1.1.3 Monitor It. Primitive data should be collected and evaluated throughout the life cycle.

Inegration between measurements and verification and validation activities is of paramount importance. There cannot be good measurements without a well-organized verification and validation process that provides the input data for measurements.

Measurements evaluation is used not only for software quality evaluation, but also for fault detection. Each instance where the criterion used for evaluation indicates a "below threshold" value should be considered an instance of a software fault. For example, measures of processing times higher than a given value may be sufficient reason to reject the implemented code and to redesign it.

3.1.2 Reliability Optimization within Project Constraints. Software reliability should not be considered separately from other major factors: resources (cost), performance, and schedules. Software reliability should be optimized with respect to the project constraints. For example, if reliability and cost are considered as a ratio in which to attempt to increase the reliability and minimize the cost, then the project should seek the more efficient fault detection and removal activities. If reliability and schedule are jointly considered, early fault detection should be empha-

sized. Each project should assign priorities to these project factors and seek to optimize reliability within these constraints.

The cost of fixing faults rises significantly from the time they are generated to the time they are detected. It is more efficient to dedicate resources to fault detection and removal as soon after fault insertion as possible. Total cost comparisons for various levels of verification and validation efforts have shown that the savings of a verification and validation program are substantial. Figure 3.1.2-1 illustrates these considerations. Cases A and B have an equal cumulative amount of costs but different distribution of costs in time. In Case B the verification program puts greater emphasis, hence more resources, in early reviews, inspections, prototyping, and dynamic test design than in Case A.

3.1.3 Software Reliability in the Context of Product Quality. An analysis of the relationship of software reliability to other quality objectives is provided. The purpose of this discussion is to clarify the relationship among selected measures, software reliability and other quality objectives in general.

**Fig 3.1.2-1
Different Approaches in Verification and
Validation Programs**

3.1.3.1 Quality Models for Adaptability and Reliability.

Change, a fact of life for system developers and maintainers, is one of the major indirect causes of faults in a software system. Change can impact not only reliability but the other major project drivers—schedule and cost.

A program to construct reliable software must consider not only the initial correctness of the product, but also the plan for accommodating change. It is important to strive to minimize reasons for change during the life cycle. Design stability and product stability are extremely important. But it is a reality that unforeseen changes in requirements, market forces, and other factors may introduce change into the process.

Change most often occurs in response to unmet quality objectives (such as, ease-of-use, maintainability, or portability) that were not given proper attention during design. Therefore, there is a need for a quality model that defines user-oriented needs. This model must be evolved during the same time period as function and performance objectives (Fig 3.1.3.1-1). Such a quality model is the premise for both a complete and an adaptable design that can easily absorb changes due to unforeseen new requirements.

Software reliability is a major quality objective. Rarely is medium or low reliability acceptable. Software reliability is both an individual quality attribute and one that is interdependent on other user quality attributes. It is because of this duality that we must consider software reliability in context with other user quality objectives. It is for this reason that user quality objectives are within the scope of this guide.

3.1.3.2 User Quality Objectives and Reliability.

User quality objectives should influence the system design and serve as criteria both for intermediate verification and for system validation and acceptance. The defined user quality objectives give the most direct means for fault search and detection. Examples of user quality objectives are ease-of-use for a word processor; ultra-high reliability for a telephone exchange plant; reliability and security for a banking application; safety and robustness for a nuclear power plant system.

User quality objectives are reached through intermediate software engineering objectives, which are achieved in the earlier phases of system development. Examples of intermediate software engineering objectives include complexity, traceability, modularity, topological coverage, defect index, and fault-days. These intermediate software engineering objectives are rarely of direct interest to the user. They constitute the tactics through which the software engineer achieves user quality objectives. Figure 3.1.3.2-1 gives a global, but not exhaustive, view of the mix of both user and software engineering objectives that have an impact on software reliability. The figure presents a schema for organizing quality objectives in each life cycle phase. Specific attention should be given to those intermediate quality objectives that directly affect project selected user quality objectives.

A software reliability management program requires the establishment of a balanced set of user quality objectives, and identification of intermediate quality objectives that will assist in achieving the user quality objectives. Resources should be spent commensurate with priority of objectives. Methods for measuring intermediate quality objectives related to reliability are identified in the Appendix of this guide.

A similar approach is applicable for the larger class of quality objectives in general and the maintenance activity specifically. Once software is delivered, the maintenance activity applied to that software has many of the same attributes that are associated with a new development effort. Thus, many of the same quality and reliability objectives are applicable.

A balanced quality program is both necessary and instrumental for a constructive approach to reliable software.

3.2 Measurement Environment.

Measurement is the comparison of a property of an object to a similar property of a standard reference. Measurements are effective when they are used either to orient decisions, to define corrective actions, or to get a better understanding of causal relationships between intended expectations and observed facts. If there is no prestated objective on how the results will be used, there should be no measurements.

When measurements are used as process diagnostics, there must be a proper environment for data collection, analysis, and corrective action in a closed loop system. Measurement information must flow throughout the process, supporting integration of both technical and managerial activities (Fig 3.2-1).

The building blocks for deriving more complex measures from collected data are called primitives. Some primitives are derived directly from the product (specifications, source code, object code). Examples of these are statements, edges, nodes, branches, changes, capabilities, networks,

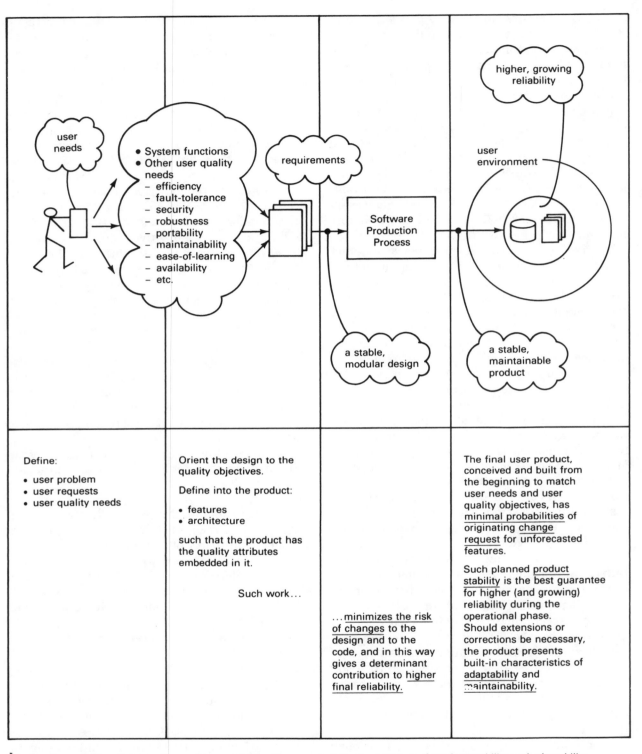

*During the operational phase, the quality model for software reliability is a function of product stability and adaptability.

Fig 3.1.3.1-1
Quality Model for Software Reliability

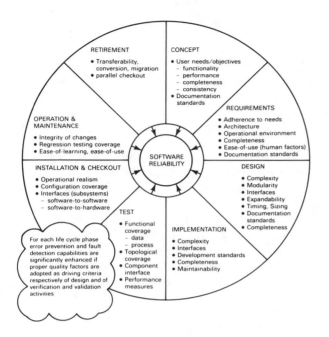

Fig 3.1.3.2-1
Quality Factors Impacting Software Reliability

Fig 3.2-1
Measurement Information Flow: An Integral
Part of Development Process

and goals. Other primitives, produced by verification and validation activities, include errors, faults and failures.

A two-step process is recommended to prepare for data collection:

(1) For each potential measure selected from IEEE Std 982.1-1988 [2], determine the data needed to perform the measurement from the list of primitives.

(2) Develop project practices for organizing data so information related to events during the development effort can be stored in a data base and retained for historical purposes and analysis. Automated tools integrated with the development environment should be considered.

Patient, accurate data collection and recording is the key to producing accurate measurements. If not well-organized, data collection can become very expensive. To contain these costs, the information gathering should be integrated with verification and validation activities. Appropriate mechanisms, such as forms or direct terminal entry, should be used to record the results of reviews. Use of automated tools for data retrieval and data entry can also reduce costs. Properly augmented configuration change control systems may furnish an ideal support environment for recording and evaluating most of the data for reliability assessment.

An important outgrowth of implementing a measurement effort is the ability to evaluate the results of collected data, develop measures, and apply analysis of the results to the end product. By tracking progress and evaluating the results, the measurement effort can be used to assess product reliability growth as well as the effectiveness of the development and support processes.

3.3 Measurement Selection Criteria. Current technology in software reliability is limited largely to the use of models that rely exclusively on test data applied to software at the end of development. The measures selected for the standard were extracted from available literature and from the collective experience of practitioners in the field. The primary emphasis was to identify a varied set of measures that cover the many aspects of the concept of reliability. This led to the inclusion of faults and failures as well as models for the traditional reliability calculations.

The constructive approach expanded the search to measures that promote reliability by minimizing residual faults through error prevention and early fault detection and removal. Therefore, the standard includes product measures to determine how carefully a product was verified (eg, completeness and traceability) and complexity measures to accommodate the possibility of change to the system.

Careful consideraton was given to the selection of process measures that monitor the quality of the development process and identify the need to make changes early in the process. Some process measures monitor the accuracy and completeness of development and test activities through examination of product properties (such as completeness and consistency). Other process measures monitor the efficiency of the activities (eg, error distribution). The process measures have the potential to stimulate adoption of good engineering practices at the proper project phase, specifically encouraging early fault detection.

A key consideration in the selection of the measures was to address the full range of the life cycle, a varied audience of both users and software and systems engineers, and a range of audience skills in reliability measurement.

The user class, which may include the owner, the operator and the recipient of the system capability, is more interested in measures related to system availability and operability, such as mean time to failure. The software engineer is more interested in software faults that cause excessive failure rates.

Reliability measures take on both aspects — system failures and software faults. The user can focus on system availability and capability; whereas the engineer can focus on the fault in the software product. Other measures, such as complexity, are of interest to managers and developers, assisting them to improve processes and control costs, schedules, personal productivity, and professional skills.

From the point of view of skill required, the measures are arranged in increasing order of difficulty. This allows individuals with little knowledge of computational methodologies to start making meaningful measurements. Subsequent measures depend upon increasing experience and sophistication with computational methodologies and automated assists.

4. Measure Organization and Classification

The measures in this guide are organized by the two basic objectives of reliability. The first objective is product maturity assessment — a certification of product readiness for operation (including an estimation of support necessary for corrective maintenance). The second objective of reliability is process maturity assessment — an ongoing evaluation of a software factory's capability to produce products of sufficient quality for user needs.

Process maturity assessement includes product maturity assessment with the objective of process repair when necessary.

With hardware factories, process maturity assessment is usually performed through the technique of statistical process control. In software, this technique has been hampered by the lack of clearly defined measurables to relate product quality deficiencies to process cause. The measures in this guide provide the means to apply statistical process control to software.

The software life cycle can be modeled and refined into a sequence of subprocesses. Each subprocess has inputs that should meet well-defined entry criteria and outputs that should meet well-defined exit criteria.

An assessment of the product at the completion of a subprocess (the output against the exit criteria) not only evaluates the readiness of that individual product to enter the next subprocess, it serves as an indicator of the quality of the subprocess itself. It should be noted that failure of a product to pass the established exit criteria is a signal for further analysis. Either the subprocess could be defective or the criteria could be too stringent. Corrective action should be taken only after sufficient analysis (Fig 4-1).

For each measure the following topics are detailed in the Appendix: implementation, interpretation, considerations, training, an example, benefits, experience, and references.

Fig 4-1
Generalized Process Control

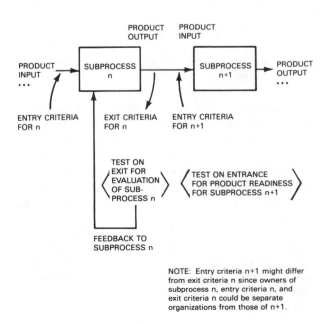

NOTE: Entry criteria n+1 might differ from exit criteria n since owners of subprocess n, entry criteria n, and exit criteria n could be separate organizations from those of n+1.

These measures can be divided into two functional categories: product and process. Product measures are applied to the software objects produced and are divided into six subcategories. Process measures are applied to the life cycle activities of development, test and maintenance and are divided into three subcategories.

The functional categories are as follows:

Product Measures

Errors, faults, and failures
Mean time to failure; failure rate
Reliability growth and projection
Remaining product faults
Completeness and consistency
Complexity

Process Measures

Management control
Coverage
Risk, benefit, cost evaluation

In addition to the functional classification, the measures are also classified by the software life cycle phases in which their use is appropriate. Typical software life cycle phases based upon IEEE Std 729-1983, IEEE Standard Glossary of Software Engineering Terminology [1] are used to illustrate when each of the measures may be applied. The life cycle phases are as follows:

Concepts
Requirements
Design
Implementation
Test
Installation and Checkout
Operation and Maintenance
Retirement

Finally, the measures can be classified as indicators or predictors.

4.1 Functional Classification. The measure classification matrix (Table 4.1-1) is a cross index of measures and functional categories. It can be used to select measures applicable to each category. For each functional category, a matrix is presented that cross-references the measures with the phases of the software life cycle in which they are applicable (Tables 4.2-1 through 4.2-9).

Table 4.1-1 includes an experience rating of 0, 1, 2, or 3. A "0" indicates that the measure has been formalized but has not been sufficiently validated to have operational experience. A "1" means that the measure has had limited use in the software community. This could be because the measure has been used only within an organization and has not had industry-wide exposure, or because the measure is not sufficiently well known to have been used on many projects. A "2" means that the measure has had moderate experience and a "3" means that it has had extensive experience. In no way does the experience rating imply that one measure is better than another.

Table 4-1
Category: Errors, Faults, Failures Counting

| | Life Cycle Phase | | | | | | | |
Measures	Concept	Requirements	Design	Implementation	Test	Installation & Checkout Installation	Operation & Maintenance	Retirement
1. Fault density	Δ	Δ	Δ	Δ	Δ	Δ	Δ	Δ
2. Defect density	Δ	Δ	Δ	Δ	Δ	Δ	Δ	Δ
3. Cumulative failure profile	Δ	Δ	Δ	Δ	Δ	Δ	Δ	Δ
4. Fault-days number	Δ	Δ	Δ	Δ	Δ	Δ	Δ	Δ
7. Requirements traceability		Δ	Δ				Δ	
8. Defect indices	Δ	Δ	Δ	Δ	Δ	Δ	Δ	Δ
12. Number of conflicting requirements		Δ					Δ	
23. Requirements compliance		Δ					Δ	

Table 4.1-1
Measure Classification Matrix

Measures (Experience)	Product Measures						Process Measures		
	Errors, Faults, Failures	Mean Time to Failure; Failure Rate	Reliability Growth & Projection	Remaining Product Faults	Completeness & Consistency	Complexity	Management Control	Coverage	Risk, Benefit, Cost Evaluation
1. Fault density (2)	X								
2. Defect density (3)	X								
3. Cumulative failure profile (1)	X								
4. Fault-days number (0)	X						X		
5. Functional or modular test coverage (1)					X			X	X
6. Cause and effect graphing (2)					X			X	
7. Requirements traceability (3)	X				X			X	
8. Defect indices (1)	X						X		
9. Error distribution(s) (1)	X						X		
10. Software maturity index (1)			X						
11. Man hours per major defect detected (2)	X				X		X		X
12. Number of conflicting requirements (2)					X			X	X
13. Number of entries/exits per module (1)						X			
14. Software science measures (3)						X			
15. Graph-theoretic complexity for architecture (1)				X		X			
16. Cyclomatic complexity (3)					X	X			
17. Minimal unit test case determination (2)					X	X			
18. Run reliability (2)			X						
19. Design structure (1)						X			X
20. Mean time to discover the next K faults (3)									X
21. Software purity level (1)			X	X					
22. Estimated number of faults remaining (seeding) (2)	X								
23. Requirements compliance (1)					X			X	
24. Test coverage (2)					X			X	
25. Data or information flow complexity (1)						X			
26. Reliability growth function (2)			X						
27. Residual fault count (1)				X					
28. Failure analysis using elapsed time (3)			X	X					
29. Testing sufficiency (0)			X				X		
30. Mean-time-to-failure (3)		X							
31. Failure rate (3)		X							
32. Software documentation & source listings (2)					X				
33. RELY – (Required Software Reliability) (1)								X	X
34. Software release readiness (0)								X	X
35. Completeness (2)					X				
36. Test accuracy (1)				X	X			X	
37. System performance reliability (2)			X						
38. Independent process reliability (0)			X						
39. Combined HW/SW system operational availability (0)			X						

4.1.1 Product Measures. The product measures address cause and effect of the static/dynamic aspects of both projected reliability prior to operation, and operational reliability. As an example, reliability may change radically during the maintenance effort, due to the complexity of the system design. The six product measure subcategories address these dimensions of reliability.

(1) Errors, faults, failures — Count of defects with respect to human cause, program bugs, and observed system malfunctions.

(2) Mean-time-to-failure; failure rate — Derivative measures of defect occurrence and time.

(3) Reliability growth and projection — The assessment of change in failure-freeness of the product under testing and in operation.

(4) Remaining products faults — The assessment of fault-freeness of the product in development, test, or maintenance.

(5) Completeness and consistency — The assessment of the presence and agreement of all necessary software system parts.

(6) Complexity — The assessment of complicating factors in a system.

4.1.2 Process Measures. The process measures address cause and effect of both the static and dynamic aspects of the development and support management processes necessary for maximizing quality and productivity. The three process measure subcategories address the process dimension of reliability.

(1) Management control measures address the quantity and distribution of error and faults and the trend of cost necessary for defect removal.

(2) Coverage measures allow one to monitor the ability of developers and managers to guarantee the required completness in all the activities of the life-cycle and support the definition of corrective actions to carry the coverage indicators to the desired levels.

(3) Risks, benefits, and cost evaluation measures support delivery decisions based both on technical and cost criteria. Risk can be assessed based on residual faults present in the product at delivery and the cost associated with the resulting support activity.

Table 4.2-1
Life Cycle Classification Matrix: Errors, Faults, Failures Counting

Measures	Concept	Requirements	Design	Implementation	Test	Installation & Checkout Installation	Operation & Maintenance	Retirement
1. Fault density	Δ	Δ	Δ	Δ	Δ	Δ	Δ	Δ
2. Defect density	Δ	Δ	Δ	Δ	Δ	Δ	Δ	Δ
3. Cumulative failure profile	Δ	Δ	Δ	Δ	Δ	Δ	Δ	Δ
4. Fault-days number	Δ	Δ	Δ	Δ	Δ	Δ	Δ	Δ
7. Requirements traceability		Δ	Δ				Δ	
8. Defect indices	Δ	Δ	Δ	Δ	Δ	Δ	Δ	Δ
12. Number of conflicting requirements		Δ					Δ	
23. Requirements compliance		Δ					Δ	

Table 4.2-2
Life Cycle Classification Matrix: Mean-Time-to-Failure; Failure Rate

					Life Cycle Phase		
Measures	Concept	Requirements	Design	Implementation	Test	Installation & Checkout Installation	Operation & Maintenance	Retirement
30. Mean time to failure					Δ	Δ	Δ	
31. Failure rate					Δ	Δ	Δ	

Table 4.2-3
Life Cycle Classification Matrix: Reliability Growth and Projection

					Life Cycle Phase		
Measures	Concept	Requirements	Design	Implementation	Test	Installation & Checkout Installation	Operation & Maintenance	Retirement
10. Software maturity index	Δ	Δ	Δ			Δ	Δ	
18. Run reliability					Δ	Δ	Δ	
21. Software purity level					Δ	Δ	Δ	
26. Reliability growth function					Δ	Δ	Δ	
28. Failure analysis using elapsed time					Δ	Δ	Δ	
29. Testing sufficiency					Δ	Δ		
30. Mean time to failure					Δ	Δ	Δ	
37. System performance reliability		Δ	Δ	Δ	Δ	Δ	Δ	
38. Independent process reliability						Δ	Δ	
39. Combined HW/SW operational availability					Δ	Δ	Δ	

Table 4.2-4
Life Cycle Classification Matrix: Remaining Faults Estimation

| | Life Cycle Phase | | | | | | |
Measures	Concept	Requirements	Design	Implementation	Test	Installation & Checkout Installation	Operation & Maintenance	Retirement
14. Software science measures				Δ			Δ*	
22. Estimated number of faults remaining (seeding)					Δ	Δ	Δ	
27. Residual fault count					Δ	Δ	Δ	
28. Failure analysis using elapsed time					Δ	Δ	Δ	
36. Test accuracy					Δ			

*If source code is changed

Table 4.2-5
Life Cycle Classification Matrix: Completeness, Consistency

| | Life Cycle Phase | | | | | | |
Measures	Concept	Requirements	Design	Implementation	Test	Installation & Checkout Installation	Operation & Maintenance	Retirement
5. Functional or modular test coverage					Δ	Δ	Δ	
6. Cause and effect graphing		Δ	Δ	Δ	Δ		Δ	
7. Requirements traceability		Δ	Δ				Δ	
12. Number of conflicting requirements		Δ					Δ	
16. Cyclomatic complexity (testing phase)				Δ	Δ		Δ	
23. Requirements compliance		Δ					Δ	
24. Test coverage		Δ	Δ		Δ	Δ	Δ	
32. Software documentation and source listings				Δ	Δ	Δ	Δ	
35. Completeness		Δ	Δ				Δ	
36. Test accuracy					Δ			

Table 4.2-6
Life Cycle Classification Matrix: Complexity

Measures	Concept	Requirements	Design	Implementation	Test	Installation & Checkout Installation	Operation & Maintenance	Retirement
13. Number of entries/exits per module			Δ	Δ			Δ	
14. Software science measures				Δ			Δ	
15. Graph-theoretic complexity for architecture		Δ	Δ				Δ	
16. Cyclomatic complexity			Δ	Δ			Δ	
17. Minimal test case determination				Δ	Δ		Δ	
19. Design structure			Δ				Δ	
25. Data or information flow complexity			Δ	Δ			Δ	

Table 4.2-7
Life Cycle Classification Matrix: Management Control

Measures	Concept	Requirements	Design	Implementation	Test	Installation & Checkout Installation	Operation & Maintenance	Retirement
4. Fault-days number	Δ	Δ	Δ	Δ	Δ	Δ	Δ	
8. Defect indices		Δ	Δ	Δ	Δ	Δ	Δ	
9. Error distribution(s)		Δ	Δ	Δ	Δ	Δ	Δ	
11. Man-hours per major defect detected		Δ	Δ	Δ	Δ	Δ	Δ	
20. Mean time to discover next K faults					Δ	Δ	Δ	

30

Table 4.2-8
Life Cycle Classification Matrix: Coverage

Measures	Concept	Requirements	Design	Implementation	Test	Installation & Checkout Installation	Operation & Maintenance	Retirement
5. Functional or modular test coverage					Δ	Δ	Δ	
6. Cause and effect graphing		Δ	Δ	Δ	Δ		Δ	
7. Requirements traceability		Δ	Δ				Δ	
12. Number of conflicting requirements		Δ					Δ	
23. Requirements compliance		Δ					Δ	
24. Test coverage		Δ	Δ	Δ	Δ	Δ	Δ	
29. Testing sufficiency					Δ		Δ	
32. Software documentation & source listings				Δ	Δ	Δ	Δ	
33. RELY – Required Software Reliability	Δ	Δ	Δ	Δ	Δ	Δ	Δ	
35. Completeness		Δ	Δ				Δ	
36. Test accuracy					Δ			

Table 4.2-9
Life Cycle Classification Matrix: Risk, Benefit, and Cost Evaluation

Measures	Concept	Requirements	Design	Implementation	Test	Installation & Checkout Installation	Operation & Maintenance	Retirement
5. Functional or modular test coverage					Δ	Δ	Δ	
10. Software maturity index	Δ	Δ	Δ			Δ	Δ	
11. Man-hours per major defect detected		Δ	Δ	Δ	Δ	Δ	Δ	
14. Software science measures				Δ			Δ	
18. Run reliability					Δ	Δ	Δ	
19. Design structure			Δ					
20. Mean time to discover the next K faults					Δ	Δ	Δ	
21. Software purity level					Δ	Δ	Δ	
27. Residual fault count					Δ	Δ	Δ	
31. Failure rate					Δ	Δ	Δ	
33. RELY – Required Software Reliability	Δ	Δ	Δ	Δ	Δ	Δ	Δ	
34. Software release readiness					Δ	Δ		

4.2 Life Cycle Classification. To assist the user in more practical considerations, such as "When are the measures applied?" the life cycle classification (Fig 4.2-1) has been developed. The life cycle has been divided into early, middle, and late segments. In the early segment, the measures relate to the potential causes of system reliability. The middle segment measures relate to the reduction of process errors that can improve the efficiency of software development. The late segment measures relate to actual system performance reliability.

For each life cycle phase a set of possible measures that might be applied during the development effort should be identified. Selection need not be limited to one measure per development phase, but on the other hand, it is expected that overzealous selection of measures would not benefit a project.

4.2.1 Early Life Cycle Segment. The early segment—concepts, requirements, and design—is the period when many of the characteristics of the system, including potential reliability, are determined. Problems in these early phases tend to result from premature constraints on the system design that limit system solution alternatives and affect the real system objectives, which include reliability. Emphasis and focus of the measures in the early stages are on the goals and objectives of the system. The concrete feedback they provide aids in achieving completeness and consistency in the definition of user requirements as well as the design.

4.2.2 Middle Life Cycle Segment. The middle segment of the software life cycle includes imple-

mentation, test, installation and checkout. The software engineer's goal in this segment is to develop fault-free software efficiently. The objectives of reliability measurement in this segment include not only reliability projection, but also guidance of the process so that fault-free software is developed efficiently. For reliability projection, faults found in this segment can relate directly to operational failures, expecially when development activity is halted prematurely. These faults, in fact, can be used to determine software readiness. For the process evolution objective, these faults can be considered process errors and can be directly related to the effectiveness and efficiency of the previously applied processes. Cause-analysis can relate the fault to that point in the process where the error was made. Proper process-control techniques applied to these measures can indicate if and when action should be taken to change the process.

4.2.3 Late Life Cycle Segment. The late segment of the software life cycle — operation, maintenance, and retirement — is where system performance, as an expression of reliability and availability, can be directly measured using the traditional software reliability measures. Current software product performance can be used to project future performance. In addition, future development can be improved by relating the problems in the current software product to the steps in the development process that produced them.

In this segment there are two audiences for software reliability measures—the user and the software engineer. The users are the owner, the operator, and the recipient of the end product of the system capability. The software engineers include both the original developer and the subsequent maintainer. In most cases, the user is more interested in system availability and operability; the software engineer is more interested in the origins of software faults that cause failures. The user focuses on the capability of the system; the software engineer focuses on the faults in the restricted software domain.

Reliability measures should address both system failures and software faults to provide useful information to both user and software engineer. There are traditional measures of software performance that provide both a user and a software engineer view of system reliability. Many of these measures—for example, mean-time-to-failure (user) and software fault discovery rate (software engineer)—serve as primitives for reliability projections based on modeling techniques.

**Fig 4.2-1
Life Cycle Classification**

LIFE CYCLE SEGMENTS

EARLY { CONCEPTS, REQUIREMENTS, DESIGN

MIDDLE { IMPLEMENTATION, TEST, INSTALLATION AND CHECKOUT

LATE { OPERATIONS AND MAINTENANCE, RETIREMENT

4.3 Indicators and Predictors. Measures can also be organized with respect to their primary function as indicators or predictors. Indicator measures provide an assessment of reliability at the point in time the measurement is taken. Predictor measures project forecasted behavior as suggested by past behavior. Historical data based upon consistently applied indicator measures are the basic input for predictor measures. The higher the integrity and quantity of the historical record, the better results can be expected from the predictor measures. Note that some measures are both predictor and indicator in nature.

Indicator measures can be used to determine completion of activities throughout the life cycle. In this context, established goals are considered successfully achieved based on the value of the indicator measure. Using the history of indicator measurements, future behavior can be determined based upon predictor measures.

Table 4.3-1 provides a cross reference of measures—first, to the object or events that are subjects of measurement, and second, to the primary indicator or predictor nature of the measure.

5. Framework for Measures

Software reliability measurements take place in an environment that includes user needs and requirements, a process for developing products meeting those needs, and user environment within which the delivered software satisfies those needs. This measurement environment establishes a framework for determining and interpreting indicators of software reliability.

5.1 Measurement Process. In this section, a measurement process is detailed that can constructively affect the delivered reliability of software through the selection and interpretation of indicators of software reliability. This process formalizes the data collection practices in both development and support. It provides for product evaluation at major milestones in the life cycle. Furthermore, it relates measures from one life cycle phase to another. In summary, this process provides the basis for reliability measurement of a product.

5.2 Stages of a Measurement Process. The software reliability measurement process can be described in nine stages (Fig 5.2-1). These stages may overlap or occur in different sequences depending on organization needs. These stages

**Table 4.3-1
Indicator/Predictor Measure Classification**

Object/Event	Measure
Requirements	
Indicator	4.6, 4.7, 4.12, 4.23, 4.33, 4.35
Predictor	—
Design	
Indicator	4.13, 4.15, 4.19, 4.25
Predictor	—
Source code	
Indicator	4.16, 4.17
Predictor	4.14
Test set	
Indicator	4.5, 4.24
Predictor	—
Any product	
Indicator	4.32
Predictor	—
Software faults	
Indicator	4.1, 4.2, 4.4, 4.8, 4.9, 4.11
Predictor	4.22, 4.29, 4.36
Software failures	
Indicator	4.3
Predictor	4.18, 4.20, 4.21, 4.26, 4.27, 4.28, 4.30, 4.31, 4.39
Release package	
Indicator	4.10, 4.34
Predictor	—
Performing object code	
Indicator	4.37
Predictor	—
Tested object modules	
Indicator	4.38
Predictor	—

provide a useful model for describing measurement process issues. Each of these stages in the measurement process influences the production of a delivered product with the potential for high reliability. Other factors influencing the measurement process include the following: a firm management commitment to continually assess product and process maturity, or stability, or both during the project; use of trained personnel in applying the measures to the project in a useful way; software support tools; and a clear understanding of the distinctions among errors, faults, and failures.

5.2.1 Stage 1: Plan Organizational Strategy. Initiate a planning process. Form a planning group and review reliability constraints and objectives, giving consideration to user needs and requirements. Identify the reliability characteristics of a software product necessary to achieve

33

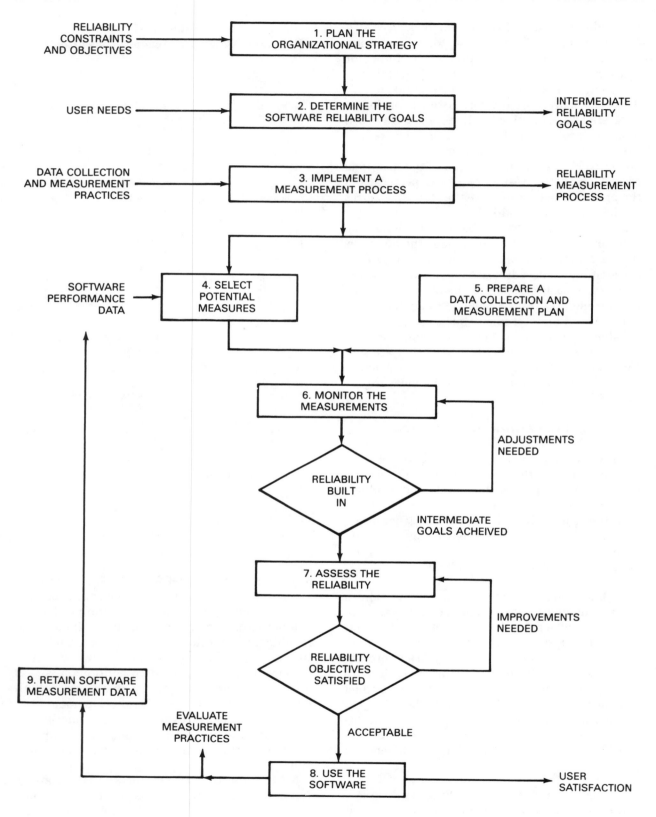

Fig 5.2-1
Reliability Measurement Process

these objectives. Establish a strategy for measuring and managing software reliability. Document practices for conducting measurements.

5.2.2 Stage 2: Determine Software Reliability Goals. Define the reliability goals for the software being developed in order to optimize reliability in light of realistic assessments of project constraints, including size, scope, cost, and schedule.

Review the requirements for the specific development effort, in order to determine the desired characteristics of the delivered software. For each characteristic, identify specific reliability goals that can be demonstrated by the software or measured against a particular value or condition. Establish an acceptable range of values. Consideration should be given to user needs and requirements, including user perception of software reliability and the system environment in which the software must interact.

Establish intermediate reliability goals at various points in the development effort to assist in achieving the reliability goals.

5.2.3 Stage 3: Implement Measurement Process. Establish a software reliability measurement process that best fits an organization's needs.

Review the process described in stages 4 through 8 and select those stages that best lead to optimum reliability. Add to or enhance these stages as needed to reflect the specific work environment. Consider the following suggestions when establishing the measurement process:

(1) Select appropriate data collection and measurement practices designed to optimize software reliability.

(2) Document the measures required, the intermediate and final milestones when measurements are taken, the data collection requirements, and the acceptable values for each measure.

(3) Assign responsibilities for performing and monitoring measurements, and provide necessary support for these activities from across the internal organization.

(4) Initiate a measure selection and evaluation process.

(5) Prepare educational materials for training personnel in concepts, principles, and practices of software reliability and reliability measures.

After selecting and establishing the steps of the measurement process, reduce it to an organization operation procedure. Maintain complete records of the measurement process to provide a historical perspective so that future reliability measurement programs may benefit.

5.2.4 Stage 4: Select Potential Measures. Identify potential measures that would be helpful in achieving the reliability goals established in Stage 2.

Once the organization software reliability goals are established, select the measures best suited to the development and support environments.

Use the classification scheme described in Section 4 to determine which category or categories of reliability measurements would be most useful to the project. When possible, measures should be chosen within a particular category to show a continuous relationship between early indicators and the final software reliability achieved at delivery.

Measures should be selected to span categories and development phases. Selection need not be limited to one measure per category or phase. However, overzealous selection of measures should be avoided.

The classification scheme assists in identifying and applying related measures across a development project (commonality) or in applying the same measure(s) to several projects (comparison).

5.2.5 Stage 5: Prepare Data Collection and Measurement Plan. Prepare a data collection and measurement plan for the development and support effort. For each potential measure, determine the primitives needed to perform the measurement. Data should be organized so that information related to events during the development effort can be properly recorded in a data base and retained for historical purposes.

For each intermediate reliability goal identified in Stage 2, identify the measures needed to achieve the goal. Identify the points during development when the measurements are to be taken. Establish acceptable values or a range of values to assess whether the intermediate reliability goals are achieved.

Include in the plan an approach for monitoring the measurement effort itself. The responsibility for collecting and reporting data, verifying its accuracy, computing measures, and interpreting the results should be described. Use historical data where possible.

5.2.6 Stage 6: Monitor Measurements. Once the data collection and reporting begins, monitor the measurements and the progress made during development, so as to manage the reliability and thereby achieve the goals for the delivered product. The measurements assist in determining whether the intermediate reliability goals are achieved and whether the final goal is achieveable. Analyze the measures and determine if the results are sufficient to satisfy the reliability goals. Decide whether a measure result assists in affirming the reliability of the product or process being measured. Take corrective action as necessary to improve the desired characteristics of the software being developed.

5.2.7 Stage 7: Assess Reliability. Analyze measurements to ensure that reliability of the delivered software satisfies the reliability objectives and that the reliability, as measured, is acceptable.

Identify assessment steps that are consistent with the reliability objectives documented in the data collection and measurement plan. Check the consistency of acceptance criteria and the sufficiency of tests to satisfactorily demonstrate that the reliability objectives have been achieved. Identify the organization responsible for determining final acceptance of the reliability of the software. Document the steps involved in assessing the reliability of the software.

Ensure that reliability improvements in the software have been made. Demonstrate satisfactory achievement of all reliability goals by reliability measurements and internal tests and by field reliability measurements during use.

5.2.8 Stage 8: Use Software. Assess the effectiveness of the measurement effort and perform necessary corrective action. Conduct a follow-up analysis of the measurement effort to evaluate reliability assessment and development practices, record lessons learned, and evaluate user satisfaction with the reliability of the software. Identify practices that are ineffective and requirements that indicate a need to develop and refine future measurement efforts.

5.2.9 Stage 9: Retain Software Measurement Data. Retain measurement data on the software throughout the development and operation phases for use by future projects. This data provides a baseline for reliability improvement and an opportunity to compare the same measures across completed projects. This information can assist in developing future guidelines and standards.

6. Errors, Faults, and Failures Analysis for Reliability Improvement

Reliability is a high-level indicator of the operational readiness of a system. Measurement for reliability need not be viewed as a passive score to be achieved, but rather as an active means of improving the processes used to build and maintain systems.

A key to reliability improvement is the maintenance of an accurate history of errors and faults associated with failure events. This section presents an introduction to the dynamics of errors, faults, and failures, with the goal of improving reliability by minimizing future failure events through error analysis and process control.

6.1 Dynamics of Errors, Faults, and Failures. Errors, faults, and failures can be viewed as a series of cause and effect relationships (Fig 6.1-1). The source of errors is either developers or users. Those developer errors resulting in undetected faults in the product directly affect reliability. User errors, usually misunderstandings, can affect perceived reliability.

Failures may occur when a fault is encountered (for example, in the code or the user documentation), or when a how-to-use error is made by the user. Faults exist in the product due to errors made by the designer or programmer during the development process. How-to-use errors are originated by either human factor faults within the product, or by the user misunderstanding the product application.

Lacks within the product exist when a desired feature or characteristic is incomplete or missing from the software. These lacks or weaknesses are a subclass of faults.

While features due to how-to-use errors may be caused by the interaction of the product and user, or by the actions of the user alone, they are often perceived by the average user as a failure of the product.

These interactions must be clearly understood in order to measure and control the development and support processes.

6.2 Analysis of Error, Fault, Failure Events

6.2.1 Failure Analysis. The purpose of failure analysis is to acquire knowledge of the most important "failure modes" of the product in the user environment. It is important to distinguish between failure due to product faults and failure due to user error. Failures due to user error may be caused by the following:

- lack of clear, well-structured user documentation
- complex user interfaces
- lack of training
- lack of support
- insufficient user educational or systems background

*Product lacks (or weaknesses) could also be seen as a subclass of faults.

**Fig 6.1-1
The Error, Fault, Failure Chain**

- insufficient user awareness of the operational environment or product purpose
- inconsistencies between product specifications and the user's application environment
- inadequate hardware configuration
- inadequate system performance.

An analysis of these failures can improve the human factors of the product based on a better understanding of the user's needs. The developer can improve documentation, application support, and system support. Further, the developer can suggest a tailored user assistance and training program. In order to prevent reoccurrence, the developer can monitor this failure type.

6.2.2 Fault Analysis. Failures due to developer or maintainer error are caused by product faults.

The purpose of fault analysis is to gather historical information on product faults in order to evaluate reliability, perform error analysis, sensitize defect removal processes, and identify fault-prone subsystems. This analysis is performed mainly with product measures.

6.2.3 Error Analysis. The purpose of error analysis is to gather historical information about error types in order to acquire insight into typical individual and organizational behavior in a software engineering environment. This information can be used to address human weaknesses in the development process.

Error analysis is usually performed with process measures. This analysis mainly aids in improvement of the review and testing activities.

6.3 Minimizing Failure Events. Reliability can be improved by minimizing future failure events. This requires that specific attention be given throughout the life cycle to fault avoidance, fault detection, and fault removal.

It is obvious that failures can be minimized by avoiding errors that generate the corresponding faults. Furthermore, once faults have been generated in development, it is more productive to strive for early detection and efficient removal. For faults discovered in support processes, it is important to determine the testing necessary to recertify the repaired system. In this case, prompt fault removal may not be as productive as periodic batched updates to the system.

6.4 Summary. Improved reliability, the end objective, can be achieved with an accurate history of errors, faults, and failures. An analysis of failures, and the faults and errors that cause them, provides a basis for improving the development and support processes. At the same time, this history provides a performance projection of future systems to be developed with these processes. The accuracy of this projection and the success of process improvements is directly related to the accuracy of the record of errors, faults, and failures. The measures in this document assume errors, faults, and failures as primitive objects or events to be counted.

Measures for Reliable Software

(This Appendix is not a part of IEEE Std 982.2-1988, IEEE Guide for the Use of IEEE Standard Dictionary of Measures to Produce Reliable Software.)

A1. Fault Density

A1.1 Application. This measure can be used to perform the following functions:

(1) Predict remaining faults by comparison with expected fault density;

(2) Determine if sufficient testing has been completed, based on predetermined goals for severity class;

(3) Establish standard fault densities for comparison and prediction.

A1.2 Primitives. Establish the severity levels for failure designation.

F = Total number of unique faults found in a given time interval resulting in failures of a specified severity level

KSLOC = Number of source lines of executable code and non-executable data declarations in thousands

A1.3 Implementation. Establish severity, failure types and fault types.

(1) Failure types might include I/O (input, output, or both) and user. Fault types might result from design, coding, documentation, and initialization.

(2) Observe and log each failure.

(3) Determine the program fault(s) that caused the failure. Classify the faults by type. Additional faults may be found resulting in total faults being greater than the number of failures observed, or one fault may manifest itself by several failures. Thus, fault and failure density may both be measured.

(4) Determine total lines of executable and non-executable data declaration source code (KSLOC).

(5) Calculate the fault density for a given severity level as:

$$F_d = F/K\text{SLOC}$$

A1.4 Interpretation. Comparison of fault density measurements made on similar systems can give some indication of whether the current system has been sufficiently tested. Software reliability may be qualitatively assessed from this information. In earlier phases of the life cycle, when KSLOC is unavailable, some other normalizing factor (eg, thousands of words of prose) agreed upon for that life cycle phase could be used.

A1.5 Considerations

(1) Test results must be thoroughly analyzed to ensure that faults, not just failures, are identified. Test coverage must be comprehensive.

(2) KSLOC must be consistently calculated (executable code and data).

(3) It should be recognized when comparing products that expected fault densities and measured fault densities have class and severity.

A1.6 Training. Minimal training is required for the use of this measure. Previous software testing experience, however, is required to establish fault and failure classifications. Good record keeping techniques and a source counting tool are essential.

A1.7 Example

(1) Sample data collection form:

Failure/Fault Log   Date: / /

Software Tested: ____ Version: ____ KSLOC: _____

Test Suite:_____ Recorder:_____

Hardware Configuration:_____

Software Configuration:_____

Failure #	Fault #	Date	Description	Severity
.	.	.	.	.
.	.	.	.	.
.	.	.	.	.

(2) Sample calculation:

Let the number of failures be 21, the number of unique faults from the 21 failures be $F = 29$, and the number of lines of source code be 6000. Then the fault density is

F_d = $F/KSLOC$ = 29/6 = 4.8 faults/$KSLOC$.

A1.8 Benefits. This measure is simple to use and provides a first approximation for reliability estimates. Collected data can be used to calculate other measures.

A1.9 Experience. Many organizations are using this measure and have developed their own guidelines but have not published their results. See the references for published examples.

A1.10 References

[A1] BOWEN, J. B. A Survey of Standards and Proposed Metrics for Software Quality Metrics. *Computer*, 1979, 12 (8), pp 37–41.

[A2] SHOOMAN, M. L. *Software Engineering Design/Reliability/Management.* New York: McGraw Hill, 1983, pp 325–329.

A2. Defect Density

A2.1 Application. The defect density measure can be used after design and code inspections of new development or large block modifications. If the defect density is outside the norm after several inspections, it is an indication that the inspection process requires further scrutiny.

A2.2 Primitives. Establish severity levels for defect designation.

D_i = total number of unique defects detected during the ith design, or code inspection process, or the ith life cycle phase;

I = total number of inspections to date;

$KSLOD$ = In the design phase, the number of source lines of design statements in thousands;

$KSLOC$ = In the implementation phase, the number of source lines of executable code and non-executable data declarations in thousands.

A2.3 Implementation. Establish a classification scheme for severity and class of defect. For each inspection, record the product size and the total number of unique defects.

For example, in the design phase calculate the ratio

$$DD = \frac{\sum\limits_{i=1}^{I} D_i}{KSLOD}$$

This measure assumes that a structured design language is used. However, if some other design methodology is used, then some other unit of defect density has to be developed to conform to the methodology in which the design is expressed.

A2.4 Interpretation. This measure has a degree of indeterminism. For example, a low value may indicate either a good process and a good product or it may indicate a bad process. If the value is low compared to similar past projects, the inspection process should be examined. If the inspection process is found to be adequate, it should then be concluded that the development process has resulted in a relatively defect-free product.

If the measurement value is too high compared to similar past projects, the development process should be examined to determine if poor programming practices have resulted in poor software products. In such a case, a breakdown of defects by type and severity should be made into defect categories such as design, logic, standards, interface, commentary, requirements, etc. The significance of the defect density can then be determined and management action taken. For example, if the defects are high due to requirements, it would be appropriate to halt development, at least in one area, until the requirements are corrected. If, on the other hand, the development process is judged to be adequate, then the inspection process is serving a valuable pretest function.

After significant experience with this measure, it may be appropriate to establish lower values as goals in order to ensure continued reliability growth of the software development process.

A2.5 Considerations. This measure assumes a knowledge of the design and code inspection process. It further assumes consistent and standard data collection and recording. The inspection process should prove effective if strongly committed to and supported by management. The earlier the inspection data can be derived and assessed, the greater the benefit.

A2.6 Training. Although little or no training is needed for calculation of the measure, training in the inspection process is required.

A2.7 Example. Suppose, in the design phase,

I = 7
$KSLOD$ = 8

$$\sum_{i=1}^{7} D_i = 78 \text{ (total defects found)}$$

Then,

$$DD = \frac{78}{8} = 9.8 \text{ (estimated defect density)}$$

A2.8 Benefits. The measure is easy to compute and it serves as one of the parameters to evaluate the effectiveness of the inspection process. Deviations from the norm serve as an indicator that immediate management attention is required, and therefore gives the developer a chance to make whatever corrections are necessary to maintain significant product control, reliability, and correctness.

A2.9 Experience. The analysis of this measure in several studies [A3, A4] has shown the utilization of the inspection process and the measurement of the collected data to be a highly effective management tool for software development and defect removal. In addition, the results have been highly consistent and the impact on error profiles during test has been seen.

A2.10 References

[A3] DOBBINS, J., and BUCK, R. Software Quality in the 80's. *Trends and Applications Proceedings*, IEEE Computer Society, 1981.

[A4] DOBBINS, J., and BUCK, R. Software Quality Assurance. *Concepts, Journal of the Defense Systems Management College*, Autumn, 1982.

[A5] FAGAN, MICHAEL E. Design and Code Inspection to Reduce Errors in Program Development. *IBM Systems Journal*, vol 15, no 3, Jul 1976, pp 102–211.

A3. Cumulative Failure Profile

A3.1 Applications. This is a graphical method used to:
(1) Predict reliability through the use of failure profiles;
(2) Estimate additional testing time to reach an acceptably reliable system;
(3) Identify modules and subsystems that require additional testing.

A3.2 Primitives. Establish the severity levels for failure designation. f_i = total number of failures of a given severity level in a given time interval, $i=1, \ldots$

A3.3 Implementation. Plot cumulative failures versus a suitable time base. The curve can be derived for the system as a whole, subsystems, or modules.

A3.4 Interpretation. The shape of the cumulative failure curve can be used to project when testing will be complete, provided that test coverage is sufficiently comprehensive. The curve gives an assessment of software reliability. It can provide an indication of clustering of faults in modules, suggesting a further concentration of testing for those modules. The total failures for each testing phase may be estimated by the asymptotic nature of the curve. A non-asymptotic curve indicates the need for continued testing.

A3.5 Considerations. Failures must be observed and recorded, and must be distinct. The failure curve may be compared with open SPR curves (Software Problem Report) or other measures. Several shapes for curves are proposed in the literature [A6, A9]. Profiles may be organized on a system, subsystem, or module basis. Test coverage must be both comprehensive and random.

A3.6 Training. Previous software testing experience is required if classification of severity and of failures is to be established. Good recordkeeping techniques are essential. Knowledge of the modular structure of the program and how it correlates with the test base is required in order to assess if the testing has been comprehensive.

A3.7 Example

**Fig A3.7-1
Failure Profile**

INT TEST = START OF INTEGRATION TEST.
MPT = MIDPOINT OF TESTING.
ACC TEST = START OF ACCEPTANCE TESTING.
SEE [A4, A6, A8, A9] FOR INTERPRETATIONS.

A3.8 Benefits. This measure is simple to use. Data can also be used as input to published reliability models.

A3.9 Experience. Many companies are using this measure and have developed their own guidelines but have not published their results [A8].

A3.10 References. See also Dobbins [A3, A4].

[A6] MENDIS, K. S. Quantifying Software Quality. *Quality Progress*, May 1982, pp 18-22.

[A7] MUSA, J. D., IANNINO, A., and OKUMOTO, K. *Software Reliability: Measurement, Prediction, Application.* New York: McGraw-Hill, 1987.

[A8] SHOOMAN, M. L. *Software Engineering Design/Reliability/Management.* New York: McGraw Hill, 1983, pp 329-335.

[A9] TRACHTENBERG, M. Discovering How to Ensure Software Reliability. *RCA Engineer*, vol 27, no 1, Jan/Feb 1982, pp 53-57.

A4. Fault-Days Number

A4.1 Application. This measure represents the number of days that faults spend in the software system from their creation to their removal.

A4.2 Primitives
(1) Phase when the fault was introduced in the system.

(2) Date when the fault was introduced in the system.
(3) Phase, date, and time when the fault is removed.

FD_i = Fault days for the ith fault

NOTE: For more meaningful measures, time units can be made relative to test time or operational time.

A4.3 Implementation. For each fault detected and removed, during any phase, the number of days from its creation to its removal is determined (fault-days).

The fault-days are then summed for all faults detected and removed, to get the fault-days number at system level, including all faults detected/removed up to the delivery date. In cases when the creation date for the fault is not known, the fault is assumed to have been created at the middle of the phase in which it was introduced.

In Fig A4.3-1 the fault-days for the design fault for module A can be accurately calculated because the design approval date for the detailed design of module A is known. The fault introduced during the requirements phase is assumed to have been created at the middle of the requirement phase because the exact time that the corresponding piece of requirement was specified is not known.

The measure is calculated as follows:

$$\text{Fault days number } (FD) = \sum_i FD_i$$

Fig A4.3-1
Calculation of Fault-Days

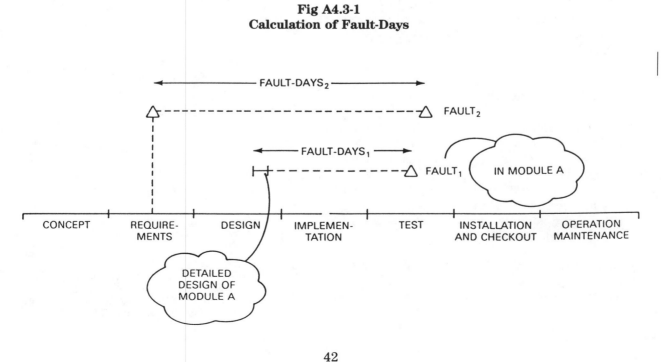

A4.4 Interpretation. The effectiveness of the software design and development process depends upon the timely removal of faults across the entire life cycle. This measure is an indicator of the quality of the software system design and of the development process. For instance, a high number of fault days indicates either many faults (probably due to poor design, indicative of product quality), or long-lived faults, or both (probably due to poor development effort, indicative of process quality).

A4.5 Considerations. Careful collection of primitive data is essential to the successful use of this measure.

A4.6 Training. In order to improve the effectiveness of the software design and development process and to lower development costs (by timely detection and removal of faults), it is essential for personnel to become aware of the importance of recording data that would be needed to generate fault-birth information for each phase across the entire software life cycle phase (for example, date of module creation, changes, deletions, integration, etc, during the design phase).

A4.7 Example. Table 4.7-1 (extracted from Mills [A10], gives fault day information for two systems (A and B). These systems were developed with the same specifications and acceptance conditions, and had the same number of known faults at delivery time. However, the two systems possess very different histories in terms of faults. In this case, the knowledge of fault-days would have helped in predicting their very different behavior in terms of faults detected during acceptance.

These systems, built with the same specifications and subjected to the same acceptance testing, are not the same even though each has no known faults.

A4.8 Benefits. This measure encourages timely inspections and testing and can also assist management in improving the design and development process.

A4.9 Experience. Although limited published experience is available, this measure can be used in a software reliability program to monitor the quality of process and product development effort.

A4.10 Reference

[A10] MILLS, HARLAN D. Software Development. *IEEE Transactions on Software Engineering*, vol SE-4, no 4, Dec 1976.

A5. Functional or Modular Test Coverage

A5.1 Application. This measure is used to quantify a software test coverage index for a software delivery. The primitives counted may be either functions or modules. The operational user is most familiar with system functional requirements and will report system problems in terms of functional requirements rather than module test requirements. It is the task of the evaluator to obtain or develop the functional requirements and associated module cross reference table.

A5.2 Primitives

FE = number of the software functional (modular) requirements for which all test cases have been satisfactorily completed.

FT = total number of software functional (modular) requirements.

Table A4.7-1
Fault Days

During Development	A	Fault Days	B	Fault Days
Lines of code	50 000		50 000	
Faults fixed				
day old	100	100	500	500
week old	10	50	50	250
month old	5	100	50	1000
year old	5	1250	20	5000
Known faults	0		0	
Fault-days (total)		1500		6750
During acceptance				
Faults fixed	10		50	
Known faults	0		0	

A5.3 Implementation. The test coverage index is expressed as a ratio of the number of software functions (modules) tested to the total number of software functions (modules) that make up user (developer) requirements. This ratio is expressed as:

$$\text{Functional (modular) test coverage index} = \frac{FE}{FT}$$

A5.4 Interpretation. The test coverage index can be compared with the status of planned testing and the impact that functional (modular) changes are having on schedule and resources.

A5.5 Considerations. Additional data required to support the test coverage index include:
  (1) Software version identification and date of release.
  (2) The functions (modules) delivered, changed, and added for each release.
  (3) Test results treated as additional primitives.

A5.6 Training. Training is important in methods that identify functions and modules. Examples of such methods are given in Ceriani, Cicu, and Maiocchi [A11].

A5.7 Example. Table A5.7-1 depicts an example of the proposed test data and resulting test coverage index for a series of software releases.

A5.8 Benefit. The test coverage index provides a measure of the percentage of software tested at any time. For many applications programs, the function (modular) test coverage index might always be relatively low because of the system application (eg, automatic test equipment) and the restrictions of the test environment (eg, electronic warfare systems).

A5.9 Experience. Application references for the test coverage index are contained in Henderson [A12] and Maiocchi, Mazzetti, and Villa [A13].

A5.10 References

[A11] CERIANI, M., CICU, A., and MAIOCCHI, M. A Methodology for Accurate Software Test Specification and Auditing. *Computer Program Testing*, B. Chandrasekaran and S. Radicchi, eds, North Holland Publishing Company, 1981.

[A12] HENDERSON, JAMES B. Hierarchical Decomposition: Its Use in Testing. *Testing Techniques Newsletter*, vol 3, no 4, San Francisco: Software Research Associate, Nov 1980.

[A13] MAIOCCHI, M., MAZZETTI, A., and VILLA, M. TEFAX: An Automated Test Factory for Functional Quality Control of Software Projects. Colloque de Genie Logiciel #2, Nice, 1984.

[A14] MILLER, E. Coverage Measure Definition Reviewed. *Testing Techniques Newsletter*, vol 3, no 4, San Francisco: Software Research Associate, Nov 1980.

Table A5.7-1
Example of Software Test Coverage Index Evaluation

Release:	1	2	3	4	5	6	7
Date:	3/82	5/82	8/82	12/82	2/83	5/83	Prod
Identification of deficiency corrected	n/a	n/a	#3	#15 #16	#17	#20	#25
Modules:	99	181	181	181	183	184	185
Changes:	13	6	2	36	23	Est(6)	Est(4)
Additions:	82	0	0	2	1	Est(1)	Est(0)
Deletions:	0	0	0	0	0	Est(0)	Est(0)
Module testing completed: (FE)	0	50	100	100	110	TBD	TBD
Module requirements: (FT)	181	181	181	183	184	Est(185)	Est(185)
Test coverage index	0	.28	.55	.55	.60	TBD	TBD

NOTE: This table uses modules as the counted quantities instead of user functions. A similar table would be generated for user functions as the quantities counted.

A6. Cause and Effect Graphing

A6.1 Application. Cause and effect graphing aids in identifying requirements that are incomplete and ambiguous. This measure explores the inputs and expected outputs of a program and identifies the ambiguities. Once these ambiguities are eliminated, the specifications are considered complete and consistent.

Cause and effect graphing can also be applied to generate test cases in any type of computing application where the specification is clearly stated (ie, no ambiguities) and combinations of input conditions can be identified. It is used in developing and designing test cases that have a high probability of detecting faults that exist in programs. It is not concerned with the internal structure or behavior of the program.

A6.2 Primitives

List of causes: distinct input conditions.

List of effects: distinct output conditions or system transformation (effects are caused by changes in the state of the system)

$A_{existing}$ = number of ambiguities in a program remaining to be eliminated

A_{tot} = total number of ambiguities identified

A6.3 Implementation. A cause and effect graph is a formal translation of a natural language specification into its input conditions and expected outputs. The graph depicts a combinatorial logic network.

To begin, identify all requirements of the system and divide them into separate identifiable entities. Carefully analyze the requirements to identify all the causes and effects in the specification. After the analysis is completed, assign each cause and effect a unique identifier. For example, $E1$ for effect one or $I1$ for input one.

To create the cause and effect graph, perform the following steps:

(1) Represent each cause and each effect by a node identified by its unique number.

(2) Interconnect the cause and effect nodes by analyzing the semantic content of the specification and transforming it into a Boolean graph. Each cause and effect can be in one of two states: true or false. Using Boolean logic, set the possible states of the causes and determine under what conditions each effect will be present.

(3) Annotate the graph with constraints describing combinations of causes and effects that are impossible because of semantic or environmental constraints.

(4) Identify as an ambiguity any cause that does not result in a corresponding effect, any effect that does not originate with a cause as a source, and any combination of causes and effects that are inconsistent with the requirement specification or impossible to achieve.

The measure is computed as follows:

$$CE(\%) = 100 \times \left(1 - \frac{A_{existing}}{A_{tot}} \right)$$

To derive test cases for the program, convert the graph into a limited entry decision table with "effects" as columns and "causes" as rows. For each effect, trace back through the graph to find all combinations of causes that will set the effect to be TRUE. Each such combination is represented as a column in the decision table. The state of all other effects should also be determined for each such combination. Each column in the table represents a test case.

A6.4 Interpretation. When all of the causes and effects are represented in the graph and no ambiguities exist, the measure is 100%. A measure of less than 100% indicates some ambiguities still exist that have not been eliminated. Some of these ambiguities may result from incomplete graphing of cause and effect relationships or from incomplete statements in the natural language specification. Such ambiguities should be examined and reconciled.

The columns in the limited entry decision table should be used to create a set of test cases. For each test case:

(1) Establish input values or conditions for each cause that sets the effect to be true;

(2) Determine the expected value or result that should be demonstrated when the effect is true;

(3) Consider boundary conditions, incorrect values, etc.

A6.5 Considerations. Cause and effect graphing is a technique used to identify incompleteness and ambiguities in program specifications. It works best with structured specifications. It has the added capability of producing a useful set of test cases. However, this technique does not produce all the useful test cases that might be identified. It also does not adequately explore boundary conditions. This technique should be supplemented by other test design techniques addressing these areas. The graph can be processed mechanically to provide test cases.

Manual application of this technique is a tedious, long, and moderately complex process. However, the technique could be applied to selected modules with complex conditional logic. The requirements specification must be complete.

A6.6 Training. The requirement specification of the system must be clearly understood in order to successfully apply the graphing techniques to eliminate ambiguities.

Cause and effect graphing is a mathematically based technique that requires some knowledge of Boolean logic.

A6.7 Example. A database management system requires that each file in the database has its name listed in a master index that identifies the location of each file. The index is divided into ten sections. A small system is being developed that will allow the user to interactively enter a command to display any section of the index at a terminal. Cause and effect graphing is used to identify ambiguities in the specifications and to develop a set of test cases for the system.

The requirements specification for this system is as follows: To display one of ten possible index sections, a command must be entered consisting of a letter and a digit. The first character entered must be a "D" (for display) or an "L" (for list) and it must be in column 1. The second character entered must be a digit (0-9) in column 2. If this command occurs, the index section identified by the digit is displayed on the terminal. If the first character is incorrect, error message A is printed. If the second character is incorrect, error message B is printed.

The error messages are:

A = INVALID COMMAND
B = INVALID INDEX NUMBER

The causes and effects are identified as follows (see Fig A6.7-1):

Causes
  (1) Character in column 1 is a "D"
  (2) Character in column 1 is an "L"
  (3) Character in column 2 is a digit.

Effects
  (50) Index section is displayed
  (51) Error message A is displayed
  (52) Error message B is displayed.

Figure A6.7-1 was constructed through analysis of the semantic content of the specification.

In Fig A6.7-1, node 20 is an intermediate node representing the Boolean state of node 1 or node 2. The state of node 50 is true if the state of nodes 20 and 3 are both true. The state of node 20 is true if the state of node 1 or node 2 is true. The state of node 51 is true if the state of node 20 is not true. The state of node 52 is true if the state of node 3 is not true. Nodes 1 and 2 are also annotated with a constraint that nodes 1 and 2 cannot be true simultaneously (the exclusive constraint).

An ambiguity in the requirements specification results from the statement that the index section is displayed on the terminal. The specification is not clear whether the index section is listed on the printer or displayed when a valid command (eg, L7) occurs. To eliminate this ambiguity, redefine effect 50 to be effect 50A (index section is displayed), and effect 50B (index section is listed).

To derive the test cases, the graph is converted into a decision table as shown in Table A6.7-1. For each test case, the bottom of the table indicates

**Fig A6.7-1
Boolean Graph**

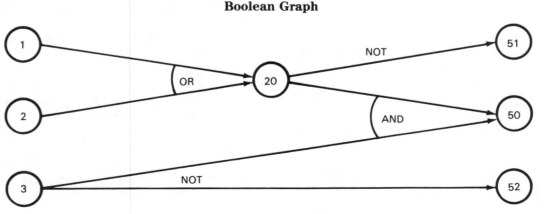

Table A6.7-1
Decision Table

Cause	Effect				
	20	50A	50B	51	52
1	1	1	0	1	
2	1	0	1		1
20				0	
3			1	1	0
*Not allowed	*	1	1	1	1	1

Table A6.7-2
Test Cases

Test Case #	Inputs	Expected Results
1	D5	Index section 5 is displayed
2	L4	Index section 4 is listed
3	B2	Invalid command
4	DA	Invalid index number

which effect will be present (indicated by a 1). For each effect, all combinations of causes that will result in the presence of the effect is represented by the entries in the columns of the table. Blanks in the table mean that the state of the cause is irrelevant.

Last, each column in the decision table is converted into test cases. Table A6.7-2 gives one example of such an approach.

A6.8 Benefits. This measure provides thorough requirements analysis, elimination of ambiguities, and a good basis for test case development.

A6.9 Experience. This technique has a modest amount of experience.

A6.10 References

[A15] ELMENDORF, W. R. *Cause-Effect Graphs on Functional Testing.* Poughkeepsie: IBM Systems Development Division, TR-00.2487, 1973.

[A16] MYERS, GLENFORD J. *The Art of Software Testing.* New York: Wiley-Interscience, 1979.

[A17] POWELL, B. P., ed. *Validation, Verification, and Testing Technique and Tool Reference Guide.* National Bureau of Standards Special Publication 500-93, 1982.

A7. Requirements Traceability

A7.1 Application. This measure aids in identifying requirements that are either missing from, or in addition to, the original requirements.

A7.2 Primitives
$R1$ = number of requirements met by the architecture.
$R2$ = number of original requirements.

A7.3 Implementation. A set of mappings from the requirements in the software architecture to the original requirements is created. Count each requirement met by the architecture ($R1$) and count each of the original requirements ($R2$). Compute the traceability measure:

$$TM = \frac{R1}{R2} \times 100\%$$

A7.4 Interpretation. When all of the original software requirements are covered in the software architecture the traceability measure is 100%. A traceability measure of less than 100% indicates that some requirements are not included in the software architecture. The architecture may contain requirements beyond the original requirements. Some of these may result naturally from stepwise refinement. Others may result from new requirements being added to the architecture. Such cases should be examined and reconciled.

A7.5 Considerations. Stepwise refinement of the requirements into the architecture produces a natural set of mappings from which to derive the measure. For large systems, automation is desirable.

A7.6 Training. Training is needed to properly interpret the results, and to make suitable decisions about reconciling architectural issues.

A7.7 Example. Suppose there is a requirement to send an alert to the supervisor console, and to print a hard copy of the alert whenever high traffic mode is entered. The architecture for such a requirement might be as follows:

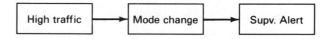

In this architecture, the hardcopy is not shown, so that complete traceability is not obtained, and the traceability will be less than 100%, with $R2 = R1 + 1$.

Alternatively, assume that there is a requirement to send an alert to the supervisor console whenever high traffic mode is entered. The architecture for this requirement might be as follows:

In this architecture, an additional requirement has been introduced that was not in the original requirements. This would result in a traceability error also, with traceability greater than 100%, and $R1 = R2 + 1$.

A7.8 Benefits. The requirements traceability measure applied to the software architecture phase can aid in identifying requirements that have not been accounted for in the architecture.

A7.9 Experience. This technique has been used extensively on large software projects [A18].

A7.10 References

[A18] HENNINGER, K. Specifying Software Requirements for Complex Systems, New Techniques and Their Application. *IEEE Transactions on Software Engineering*, vol SE-6, no 1, Jan 1980, pp 1–14.

[A19] PERRIENS, M. P. *Software Requirements Definition and Analysis with PSL and QBE*. IBM Technical Report FSD 80-0003, Bethesda: IBM Federal Systems Division, Oct 1980.

[A20] YEH, R., ZAVE, P., CONN, A., and COLE, G., Jr. *Software Requirements: A Report on the State of the Art*. Computer Science Technical Report Series TR-949, College Park, Maryland: University of Maryland, Oct 1980.

A8. Defect Indices

A8.1 Application. This measure provides a continuing, relative index of how correct the software is as it proceeds through the development cycle. This measure is a straightforward, phase dependent, weighted, calculation that requires no knowledge of advanced mathematics or statistics. This measure may be applied as early in the life cycle as the user has products that can be evaluated.

A8.2 Primitives. The following list applies to each phase in the life cycle:

D_i = Total number of defects detected during the ith phase.

S_i = Number of serious defects found.

M_i = Number of medium defects found.

PS = Size of the product at the ith phase.

T_i = Number of trivial defects found.

W_1 = Weighting factor for serious defects (default is 10).

W_2 = Weighting factor for medium defects (default is 3).

W_3 = Weighting factor for trivial defects (default is 1).

A8.3 Implementation. The measure is generated as a sum of calculations taken throughout development. It is a continuing measure applied to the software as it proceeds from design through final tests.

At each phase of development, calculate the phase index (PI_i) associated with the number and severity of defects.

$$PI_i = W_1 \frac{S_i}{D_i} + W_2 \frac{M_i}{D_i} + W_3 \frac{T_i}{D_i}$$

The defect index (DI) is calculated at each phase by cumulatively adding the calculation for PI_i as the software proceeds through development:

$$DI = \Sigma (i * PI_i)/PS$$
$$= (PI_1 + 2PI_2 + ... + iPI_i + ...)/PS$$

where each phase is weighted such that the further into development the software has progressed, such as phase 2 or 3, the larger the weight (ie, 2 or 3, respectively) assigned.

The data collected in prior projects can be used as a baseline figure for comparison.

A8.4 Interpretation. The interpretation is based on the magnitude of the defect index: the smaller the number, the better. Each organization or project should compute baseline numbers from past projects for each of the types of software produced. Then, each project should be tracked to assess the following:

(1) Whether performance has increased.

(2) Impact of programmer education programs.

(3) Impact of new programming practices.

(4) Impact of entering a new business area or performing new, unfamiliar tasks.

(5) Impact of mid-stream changes, such as major requirement changes.

This measure can be used as adjunct to either fault assessment or error cause analysis. Each user may determine a unique defect classification. For example, serious defects may be described as faults that keep the software from functioning. Medium defects may be described as faults that will cause the software to operate in a degraded mode. Trivial defects may be defined as those that will not affect functional performance, such as misspelled words on displays.

A8.5 Considerations. This measure is best applied when used with other measures because it gives an indication of what's happening, but not why. Error cause analysis in conjunction with defect index calculations can be quite enlightening.

A8.6 Training. Little or no measurement training is required.

A8.7 Example. For corresponding phases of development, calculated for three different projects, the results may be

$$DI_1 = 15 \qquad DI_2 = 20 \qquad DI_3 = 205$$

For these projects, the results show that project three has some significant problems as compared to measures of projects one and two taken at corresponding phases of development. It indicates that management action is clearly required in order to ascertain the difficulty.

A8.8 Benefits. This measure is both a process and a product measure.

As a process measure it provides an indication of whether the defect removal process employed at a given phase of development was employed in a sufficiently effective manner. It also affords the developer a means of assessing the effectiveness of phase related defect removal processes.

As a product measure, it allows the development management a means of assessing the degree of correctness of the software at a given phase, thereby providing an indication of the reliability growth as the product moves through the development phases toward final acceptance.

It is easy to use and interpret and is successively applicable across development phases. It can be done manually or automated. It can also be easily expanded to include sub-phases, with each sub-phase separately weighted. The index is weighted so that the more defects found early, the better the result. Use of the index thereafter encourages the application of early defect removal processes such as inspections.

If requirements are done in a structural requirements language, inspections can be started at the requirements level and this defect index (*DI*) measure can be adjusted to begin at the requirements phase.

A8.9 Experience. The experience base for this measure is small.

A8.10 Reference

[A21] SCHULMEYER, G., ed. Handbook for Software Quality Assurance. New York: Van Nostrand Publishing Company, 1985.

A.9 Error Distribution(s)

A9.1 Application. The search for the causes of software faults and failures involves the error analysis of the defect data collected during each phase of the software development. Distribution of the errors allows ranking of the predominant failure modes.

A9.2 Primitives. Error description notes the following points:
(1) Associated faults
(2) Types
(3) Severity
(4) Phase introduced
(5) Preventive measure
(6) Discovery mechanism including reasons for earlier non-detection of associated faults

A9.3 Implementation. The primitives for each error are recorded and the errors are counted according to the criteria adopted for each classification. The number of errors are then plotted for each class. Examples of such distribution plots are shown in Fig A9.3-1. In the three examples of Fig A9.3-1, the errors are classified and counted by phase, by the cause and by the cause for deferred fault detection. Other similar classifications could be used, such as the type of steps suggested to prevent the reoccurrence of similar errors or the type of steps suggested for earlier detection of the corresponding faults.

A9.4 Interpretation. Plots similar to Fig A9.3-1 could be analyzed by management to identify the phases that are most error prone, and to identify causes, risks, and recommend the nature and priority of corrective actions to improve error avoidance.

(a) Error Distribution by Phase

(b) Error by Cause Category

(c) Suggested Causes for Error Detection Deferral

Fig A9.3-1
Error Analysis

This measure is also useful to recommend steps to prevent the recurrence of similar errors, to eliminate known causes, and to detect faults earlier for purpose of reducing software life cycle costs.

A9.5 Considerations. Error analysis requires effective support and participation by management, because the errors usually have their origin in deficient procedures, methods, and techniques for design, inspection, and testing.

A9.6 Training. A global knowledge of the effective methodologies for the software development process for the entire life cycle phase is required to support effective error analysis and interpretation.

A9.7 Example. See Fig A9.3-1.

A9.8 Benefits. Error analysis by distributions is a key factor in understanding the areas where interventions or corrective actions or both are the most effective steps towards error and fault avoidance.

A9.9 Experience. Although there is little experience in the literature related to this measure, it is recommended as an important method for analyzing causes of errors and error prone areas.

A9.10 References

[A22] ANDRES, A. An Analysis of Errors and Their Causes in System Programs. *IEEE Transactions on Software Engineering*, Jun 1975 (reprinted in *Tutorial on Models and Metrics for Software Management and Engineering*). IEEE catalog no EHO-16-7, IEEE Computer Society, Sept 1980.

[A23] RZEVSKI, G. Identification of Factors which Cause Software Failures. Proceedings of Annual Reliability and Maintainability Symposium, Los Angeles, Jan 26–28, 1982.

A10. Software Maturity Index

A10.1 Application. This measure is used to quantify the readiness of a software product. Changes from a previous baseline to the current baseline are an indication of the current product stability. A baseline can be either an internal release or an external delivery.

A10.2 Primitives

M_T = Number of software functions (modules) in the current delivery

F_c = Number of software functions (modules) in the current delivery that include internal changes from a previous delivery

F_a = Number of software functions (modules) in the current delivery that are additions to the previous delivery

F_{del} = Number of software functions (modules) in the previous delivery that are deleted in the current delivery

A10.3 Implementation. The software maturity index (*SMI*) may be calculated in two different ways, depending on the available data (primitives).

A10.3.1 Implementation 1

(1) For the present (just delivered or modified) software baseline, count the number of functions (modules) that have been changed (F_c).

(2) For the present software baseline, count the number of functions (modules) that have been added (F_a) or deleted (F_{del}).

(3) For the present software baseline, count the number of functions (modules) that make up that release (M_T).

Calculate the maturity index using the following equation:

$$\text{Maturity Index} = \frac{\text{Number of current functions (modules)} - \text{Number of current baseline functions (modules) that have been added} + \text{Number of functions (modules) changed} + \text{Number of current baseline functions (modules) that have been deleted}}{\text{Number of current functions (modules)}}$$

ie, $$SMI = \frac{M_T - (F_a + F_c + F_{del})}{M_T}$$

Notice that the total number of current functions (modules) equals the number of previous functions (modules) plus the number of current baseline functions (modules) that were added to the previous baseline minus the number of functions (modules) that were deleted from the previous baseline. In the software maturity index calculation, the deletion of a function (module) is treated the same as an addition of a function (module).

A10.3.2 Implementation 2. The software maturity index may be estimated as

$$SMI = \frac{M_T - F_c}{M_T}$$

The change and addition of functions (modules) is tracked and the maturity index is calculated for each baseline. Problem reports that would result in the software update subsequent to the tracking period are included in the maturity analysis by estimating the configuration of the subsequent releases.

A10.4 Interpretation. The maturity index for each software release can be tracked to determine the relative impact that changes and additions are having on the software configuration and whether the software is approaching a stable configuration.

A10.5 Considerations. Additional data that is required in conjunction with the maturity index measures are as follows:

(1) The impact software function (module) changes are having on previously completed testing (see A5, Functional or Modular Test Coverage).
(2) The software release identification and date of release.
(3) Identification of the customer (producer) problems that are corrected in the release.
(4) Estimate of the configuration changes that would be required to correct the remaining customer (producer) identified problems.

The maturity index is used as a primitive in software release readiness (see A34). The functional test coverage must also be calculated in conjunction with the maturity index (see A5).

A10.6 Training. The software training required would include identification of the user requirements and the associated software functions and modules that implement the requirements. The operational user must be familiar with the system functional requirements in order to report problems in terms of those requirements.

A10.7 Example. Table A10.7-1 depicts the data and resulting maturity index for a series of software releases. Keep in mind that a series of maturity index values determined throughout a test program will be misleading unless the corresponding functional test coverage index for each release is also determined.

A10.8 Benefits. The maturity index provides a measure of the relative impact that software changes and additions are making to the total software configuration. In addition, the maturity index provides an indication of the stability of the software throughout the period of user test and evaluation.

A10.9 Experience. See Ceriani, Cicu, and Maiocchi [A11] for related experience.

A11. Manhours per Major Defect Detected

A11.1 Application. The design and code inspection processes are two of the most effective defect removal processes available. The early removal of defects at the design and implementation phases, if done effectively and efficiently, significantly improves the reliability of the developed product and allows a more controlled test environment. This measure provides a quantitative figure that can be used to evaluate the efficiency of the design and code inspection processes.

A11.2 Primitives

T_1 = Time expended by the inspection team in preparation for design or code inspection meeting.

Table A10.7-1
Example Results of a Software Maturity Index Evaluation

Release:	1	2	3	4	5	6	7
Date:	3/82	5/82	8/82	12/82	2/83	5/83	Prod
Identification of deficiency corrected	n/a	n/a	#3	#15 #16	#17	#20	#25
Modules:	99	181	181	181	183	184	185
Changes:	13	6	2	36	23	Est(6)	Est(4)
Additions	82	0	0	2	1	Est(1)	Est(0)
Deletions	0	0	0	0	0	Est(0)	Est(0)
Maturity index	.475	.966	.99	.79	.868	(.96)	(.98)
	181–95 / 181	181–6 / 181	179 / 181	181–38 / 181	183–24 / 183	184–6 / 184	181 / 185

T_2 = Time expended by the inspection team in conduct of a design or code inspection meeting.

S_i = Number of major (non-trivial) defects detected during the ith inspection.

I = Total number of inspections to date.

A11.3 Implementation. At each inspection meeting, record the total preparation time expended by the inspection team. Also, record the total time expended in conducting the inspection meeting. All defects are recorded and grouped into major/minor categories. (A major defect is one that must be corrected for the product to function within specified requirements.)

The inspection times are summarized and the defects are cumulatively added. The computation should be performed during design and code. If the design is not written in a structural design language, then this measure can be only applied during the implementation phase.

The manhours per major defect detected is

$$M = \frac{\sum\limits_{i=1}^{I} (T_1 + T_2)_i}{\sum\limits_{i=1}^{I} S_i}$$

This computation should be initiated after approximately 8,000 lines of detailed design or code have been inspected.

A11.4 Interpretation. This measure is applied to new code development, not to modification of an old code, unless the modification is a large block change.

From empirical experience, the measure (M) for new code shall fall consistently between three and five. If significant deviation from this range is experienced, the matter should be investigated. If the measure is very low, the defect density may be too high and a major product examination may be in order. If the measure is very high, the inspection process is very likely not being properly implemented and, therefore, the anticipated impact on reliability improvement expected from the inspection will not be realized.

A11.5 Considerations. This measure assumes a knowledge of the design and code inspection process. It further assumes consistent, standard data collection and recording. Experience has shown that the inspection process is quite effective, if it is strongly committed to and supported by management. The earlier the inspection process can be applied, the greater the benefit derived. It is therefore recommended that program design languages be used.

A11.6 Training. Little or no training is required for calculation of the measure. Inspections require trained personnel.

A11.7 Example

I = 2

T_1 = 28 ⎫
T_2 = 25 ⎬ i=1 T_1 = 40 ⎫
S_1 = 16 ⎭ T_2 = 50 ⎬ i=2
                       S_2 = 4 ⎭

$$M = \frac{28 + 25 + 40 + 50}{16 + 4} = \frac{143}{20} = 7.15$$

A11.8 Benefits. This measure is easy to compute. It serves as one of the index parameters to evaluate the effectiveness and efficiency of the inspection process. Deviations from the norm serve as an indicator that immediate attention is required and, therefore, gives the developer a change to make whatever modifications are necessary to maintain sufficient product correctness and reliability during early development.

A11.9 Experience. Utilization of the inspection process has been found to be highly effective in defect removal and correction.

A11.10 References. See also Dobbins and Buck [A3, A4].

[A24] FAGAN, MICHAEL E. Design and Code Inspection to Reduce Errors in Program Development. *IBM Systems Journal*, vol 15, no 3, Jul 1976, pp 182–211.

A12. Number of Conflicting Requirements

A12.1 Application. This measure is used to determine the reliability of a software system, resulting from the software architecture under consideration, as represented by a specification based on the entity-relationship-attribute model [A19].

A12.2 Primitives
(1) List of the inputs
(2) List of the outputs
(3) List of the functions performed by the program

A12.3 Implementation. The mappings from the software architecture to the requirements are identified. Mappings from the same specification item to more than one differing requirement are examined for requirements inconsistency. Mappings from more than one specification item to a single requirement are examined for specification inconsistency.

A12.4 Interpretation. If the same specification item maps to two different requirements items, the requirements should be identical. Otherwise, the requirements are inconsistent. If more than one specification item maps to a single requirement, (this should result only from application of refinement techniques) the specification items should be checked for possible inconsistency.

A12.5 Considerations. Stepwise refinement or structured analysis of the requirements into the architecture produces the best results, since there is likely to be a natural set of mappings resulting from this process. For large systems, automation is desirable.

A12.6 Training. Training is needed to interpret the results, and make suitable decisions on the adequacy of the architecture and the requirements. Experience/training in requirements analysis, the entity-relationship-attribute model, and software specification techniques are needed [A20].

A12.7 Example. Consider an example taken from the air traffic control field. Suppose there are two distinct requirements for action to be taken in the event of high traffic. These requirements might be stated as:
  (1) In the event of high traffic, send an operator alert to the supervisor console. If the supervisor console is busy, then send to the assistant.
  (2) In the event of high traffic, send an operator alert to the assistant supervisor console.
In the architecture, this could be implemented as:

A PDL representation might be as follows:
  If mode = high traffic
    Send operator alert to supervisor console
    Send operator alert to assistant console
  Endif

This example represents a potential conflicting requirement between sending an alert to both the supervisor and the assistant. This would need to be examined and resolved.

A12.8 Benefits. Identification of conflicting requirements during the software architecture phase can avoid problems later in the life cycle.

A12.9 Experience. Many large software projects informally use these techniques for determining reliability [A18].

A13. Number of Entries and Exits per Module

A13.1 Application. This measure is used to determine the difficulty of a software architecture, as represented by entry/exit points identified in a modular specification/design language.

A13.2 Primitives
  e_i = number of entry points for the ith module
  x_i = number of exit points for the ith module

A13.3 Implementation. The number of entry points and exit points for each module is

$$m_i = e_i + x_i$$

A13.4 Interpretation. Each module should have one entry and one exit point for each major function. Additional exit points may be allowed for error handling. The number of functions per module should be limited. A suggested maximum number of functions per module is five.

A13.5 Considerations. Data encapsulation should be used to optimize the number of functions and entry/exit points. If data is properly encapsulated [A27], the number of entry and exit points for each module function will be small. For large systems, automation of the count of entries and exits is desirable, so the user does not need to manually examine each module.

A13.6 Training. In both the manual and automated situations, training is needed to interpret the results and make suitable trade-off decisions.

A13.7 Example. Given a module specification (Fig A13.7-1), this method can be used. This module has four entry points, and, since it is structured, four exit points.

<u>mod</u> idset

    <u>def</u>

        hash (id) = return an index value from 1 to max as a *f*(*id*)

        <u>type</u> item = <u>rec</u>

                id: idtype

                data: datatype

          <u>cer</u>

<u>ism</u>

    <u>input</u>

        <u>var</u> in: item

        <u>var</u> searchid: idtype

    <u>output</u>

        <u>var</u> out: item

        <u>var</u> status: (OK, full, notthere, alreadythere)

    <u>state</u>

        <u>const</u> max = [maximum size of set]

        <u>var</u> s: <u>set of</u> item [s $\leq$ max]

    <u>init</u>

        [s: = ϕ]

    <u>trans</u>

        <u>entry</u> add (<u>in</u> in, <u>out</u> status)

            [(iϵs) in. id = i. id $\rightarrow$ status: = alreadythere

              <u>true</u> $\rightarrow$ (s $<$ max $\rightarrow$ s, status: = s$\cup$ (in),OK

                      <u>true</u> $\rightarrow$ status: = full)]

        <u>entry</u> delete (<u>in</u> Searchid, <u>out</u> status)

            [(iϵs) searchid = i. id $\rightarrow$ s, status: = s − (in),OK

              <u>true</u> $\rightarrow$ status: = notthere]

        <u>entry</u> has (<u>in</u> searchid, <u>out</u> status, out)

            [(iϵs) searchid = i. id $\rightarrow$ out, status: = i,OK

              <u>true</u> $\rightarrow$ status: = notthere]

        <u>entry</u> clear

            [s: = ϕ]

<u>des</u>

    (*to be added*)

<u>dom</u>

Fig A13.7-1
Program Design Language Module Specification

A13.8 Benefits. The entry/exit point measure applied to the software architecture phase can aid in identifying modules that do not exhibit proper data encapsulation, and are likely to result in high operating system overhead times (which occur when one module invokes another) and difficulty in testing.

A13.9 Experience. Minimizing the number of entry/exit points is a key feature of structured design and structured programming techniques that have been used in software architecture definition. Limited published experience is currently available.

A13.10 References

[A25] GUTTAG, J. Abstract Data Types and the Development of Data Structures. Conference on Data, Salt Lake City, 1976. *CACM*, vol 20, no 6, June 1977, pp 396–404.

[A26] LISKOV, B. H. and ZILLES, S. N. Specification Techniques for Data Abstractions. *IEEE Transactions on Software Engineering*, vol SE-2, no 1, Mar 1975, pp 7–19.

[A27] PARNAS, D. L. On the Criteria To Be Used in Decomposing Systems into Modules. *CACM*, vol 15, no 12, 1972, pp 1053–1058.

A14. Software Science Measures

A14.1 Application. These measures apply Halstead software science to the properties and structure of computer programs. They provide measures of the complexity of existing software, predict the length of a program, and estimate the amount of time an average programmer can be expected to use to implement a given algorithm.

This measure computes the program length by counting operators and operands. The measure suggests that the difficulty of a given program can be derived, based on the above counts.

A14.2 Primitives

n_1 = Number of distinct operators in a program

n_2 = Number of distinct operands in a program

N_1 = Total number of occurrences of the operators in a program

N_2 = Total number of occurrences of the operands in a program

A14.3 Implementation. Once the source code has been written, this measure can be applied to predict program difficulty and other derived quantities using the following equations (Halstead [A30]).

Program vocabulary: $l = n1 + n2$

Observed program length: $L = N1 + N2$

Estimated program length:
$$\hat{L} = n1\ (\log_2 n1) + n2\ (\log_2 n2)$$

Program volume: $V = L\ (\log_2 l)$

Program difficulty: $D = (n1/2)\ (N2/n2)$

Program level: $L1 = 1/D$

Effort: $E = \dfrac{V}{L1}$

Number of errors: $B = \dfrac{V}{3000} \simeq \dfrac{E^{2/3}}{3000}$

Time: $T = E/S$ (S = Stroud number; typical value is eighteen elementary mental discriminations per second)

An alternate expression to estimate program length is the factorial length estimator (A32):

$$\hat{L} = \log_2 ((n1)!) + \log_2 ((n2)!)$$

A14.4 Interpretation. The interpretation of these measures is illustrated in the example (A14.7); for the average PL/I program, difficulty should be less than 115. Difficulty of greater than 160 indicates serious problems. Difficulty data is available for other languages as well [A29.5, A30, A35].

A14.5 Considerations. The technique is recommended only if automated support is available. The software needed to parse the programs and accumulate data is somewhat lengthy. However, there has been some experience in writing such software.

A14.6 Training. Training is needed in the definition of operators and operands and in the interpretation of the results. The results will differ depending on the language and applications. The user should examine results obtained in some of the reference material beforehand, and, if possible, contact other users.

A14.7 Example

Program fragment (written in *PL/I*):
```
/* x becomes the maximum of A and B*/
    if A > B
    then X = A;
    else X = B;
```

Software science basic parameters:

operators and their frequencies: $n1 = 4 \quad N1 = 6$

if...then...else	1
>	1
=	2
;	2

operands and their frequencies: $n2 = 3 \quad N2 = 6$

A	2
B	2
X	2

Software science measurements:

Program vocabulary: $l = n1 + n2 = 4 + 3 = 7$

Observed program
length: $\quad L = N1 + N2 = 6 + 6 = 12$

Estimated program length:

$$\hat{L} = n1 \, (\log_2 n1) + n2 \, (\log_2 n2)$$
$$= 4(\log_2 4) + 3 \, (\log_2 3) \qquad = 12.76$$

Estimated program length using the factorial length estimator is

$$\hat{L} = \log_2((4)!) + \log_2((3)!) = 7.17$$

Program volume: $\quad V = L \, (\log_2 l)$
$$= 12 \, (\log_2 7) = 33.68$$

Program difficulty: $\quad D = (n1/2) \, (N2/n2)$
$$= (4/2) \, (6/3) = 4.0$$

Program level: $\quad L1 = \dfrac{1}{D} = \dfrac{1}{4.0} = .25$

Effort: $\quad E = V/L1 = 33.68/.25$
$$= 134.72$$

Number of errors: $\quad B = V/3000 = 33.68/3000$
$$= 0.01123$$

Time: $\quad T = E/S = 134.72/18 = 7.48$

A14.8 Benefit. Application of the software science measures to the implementation phase can aid in the identification of programs that are overly complex, and likely to result in excessive development effort.

A14.9 Experience. There has been considerable and notable experience reported concerning this measure.

A14.10 References

[A28] CONTE, S. D., DUNSMORE, H. E., and SHEN, V. Y. *Software Engineering Metrics and Models.* Menlo Park: Benjamin/Cummings Publishing Co, 1986.

[A29] COULTER, M. S. Software Science and Cognitive Psychology. *IEEE Transactions on Software Engineering*, vol SE-9, no 2, Mar 1983, pp 166–171.

[A29.5] FITZSIMMONS, A., and LOVE, T. A Review and Evaluation of Software Science. *ACM Computing Surveys*, vol 10, no 1, Mar 1978, pp 3–18.

[A30] HALSTEAD, M. H. *Elements of Software Science.* Operating and Programming Systems Series, P. J. Denning, ed, New York: Elsevier North Holland, 1977.

[A31] HALSTEAD, M. H., GORDON, R. D., and ELSHOFF, J. L. *On Software Physics and GM's PL/I Programs.* GM Research Publication GMR-2175, Warren, Michigan: GM Research Laboratories, Jun 1976.

[A32] JENSEN, H. J., and VAIRAVAN, K. An Experimental Study of Software Metrics for Real Time Software. *IEEE Transactions on Software Engineering*, vol SE-11, no 2, Feb 1985, pp 231–234.

[A33] LIND, R. K., and VAIRAVAN, K. *A Study of Software Metrics for Predicting Software Errors.* M.S. Thesis, University of Wisconsin, Milwaukee, Wisconsin, Dec 1986.

[A34] SCHNEIDER, V. Prediction of Software Effort and Project Duration. *SIGPLAN Notices*, vol 14, no 6, Jun 1978, pp 49–59.

[A35] SHEN, V. Y., CONTE, S. D., and DUNSMORE, H. E. Software Science Revisited: A Critical Analysis of the Theory and Its Empirical Support. *IEEE Transactions on Software Engineering*, vol SE-9, no 2, Mar 1983, pp 155–165.

A15. Graph-Theoretic Complexity for Architecture

A15.1 Application. Complexity measures can be applied early in the product life cycle for development trade-offs as well as to assure system and module comprehensibility adequate for correct and efficient maintenance. Many system faults are introduced in the operational phase by modifications to systems that are reliable but difficult to understand. In time, a system's entropy increases, making a fault insertion more likely with each new change. Through complexity measures the developer plans ahead for correct change by establishing initial order, and thereby improves the continuing reliability of the system throughout its operational life.

There are three graph-theoretic complexity measures for software architecture:

Static complexity is a measure of software architecture, as represented by a network of modules, useful for design tradeoff analyses. Network complexity is a function based on the countable properties of the modules (nodes) and inter-module connections (edges) in the network.

Generalized static complexity is a measure of software architecture, as represented by a network of modules and the resources used. Since resources are acquired or released when programs are invoked in other modules, it is desirable to measure the complexity associated with allocation of those resources in addition to the basic (static) network complexity.

Dynamic complexity is a measure of software architecture as represented by a network of modules during execution, rather than at rest, as is the case for the static measures. For example, modules may execute at different frequencies.

A15.2 Primitives

K = Number of resources, indexed by $k = 1$, ..., K

E = Number of edges, indexed by $i = 1, ..., E$

N = Number of nodes, indexed by $j = 1, ..., N$

c_i = complexity for program invocation and return along each edge e_i as determined by the user (such as operating system complexity).

Resource status array $R(K,E)$

$$r_{ki} = \begin{cases} 1 & \text{if } k^{th} \text{ resource is required for the } i\text{th edge } (e_i) \\ 0 & \text{otherwise} \end{cases}$$

d_k = complexity for allocation of resource k as determined by the user (eg, complexity associated with a procedure used to gain exclusive access to common data)

A15.3 Implementation.
Using nodes and edges, a strongly connected graph of the network is required. A strongly connected graph is one in which a node is reachable from any other node. This is accomplished by adding an edge between the exit node and the entry node. Each node represents a module that may or may not be executed concurrently with another module. Each edge represents program invocation and return between modules. In this case the edges are called single paths.

A15.3.1 Static Complexity. Once a strongly connected graph is constructed, with modules as nodes, and transfer of control as edges, the static complexity is calculated as

$$C = E - N + 1$$

A15.3.2 Generalized Static Complexity. Resources (storage, time, logic complexity or other measurable factors) are allocated when programs are invoked in other modules. Given a network and resources to be controlled in the network, the generalized static complexity associated with allocation of these resources is

$$C = \sum_{i=1}^{E} \left(c_i + \sum_{k=1}^{K} (d_k * r_{ki}) \right)$$

A15.3.3 Dynamic Complexity. A change in the number of edges may result from module interruption due to invocations and returns. An average dynamic network complexity can be derived over a given time period to account for the execution of modules at different frequencies and also for module interruption during execution. Dynamic complexity is calculated using the formula for static complexity at various points in time. The behavior of the measure (except time average) is then used to indicate the evolution of the complexity of the software.

A15.4 Interpretation.
For a typical subsystem, 10 represents the maximum ideal static complexity. A very complex system may be composed of a number of such subsystems. When the computed complexity is too large, one can consider more use of pipelining, fewer modules (if feasible), or more subsystems.

For a typical subsystem, $20E$ (E = number of edges) represents maximum ideal generalized static complexity, if the complexity of program invocation is 20 and no resources are needed.

The dynamic complexity is generally higher than the static complexity. Ideally, the dynamic complexity should be as close to the static complexity as possible. Addition or deletion of modules during execution affects the dynamic complexity. Minimization of the frequency of module interruption during execution reduces average dynamic network complexity. This results in an overall improvement in software reliability.

A15.5 Considerations. Pipeline architectures have lower static complexity value, since there is less overhead for transfer of control than for hierarchies. Decisions can be made on whether to implement services as distinct modules by combining the result obtained with this measure with the internal module complexity measures. For large systems, automation is desirable.

When the generalized static complexity is too large, one can consider more use of pipelining, fewer modules (if feasible), more subsystems, use of fewer resources, or less costly methods of resource acquisition.

When the dynamic network complexity is too large, one should consider reducing it by optimizing the dynamic creation and deletion of modules, or by minimizing task interruptions by timing adjustments, or both.

A15.6 Training. Training in graph theory is recommended for manual application of the measure. Training is also needed to interpret the results for suitable design trade-off decisions for software architecture design.

A15.7 Example. Static complexity measures for network hierarchies and pipelines are shown in Figs A15.7-1 and A15.7-2. Detailed examples for dynamic creation/deletion of modules, module interruption, modules in execution at different frequencies, and dynamic network complexity are illustrated in Halstead [A30].

A15.8 Benefits. These complexity measures, applied to the software architecture, can aid in identifying networks that are overly complex, and that are likely to result in high system overhead,

Fig A15.7-1
Hierarchy Network

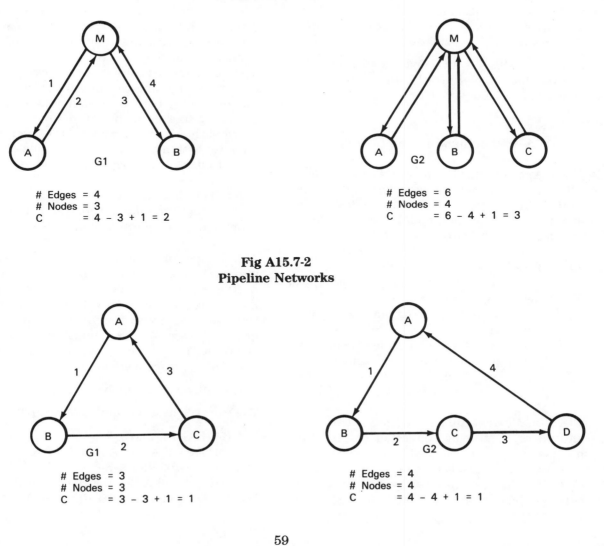

Fig A15.7-2
Pipeline Networks

difficulty in testing, and difficulty in meeting performance requirements. They can also aid in identifying areas that make excessive use of resources, and areas in which resource acquisition overhead is high.

A15.9 Experience. The static complexity measure has been used extensively for design and code [A36]. Generalized static and dynamic complexity measures have been used in experiments, [A38], but not operationally.

A15.10 References. See also Conte, Dunsmore, and Shen [A28] and Halstead [A30].

[A36] HALL, N. R. *Complexity Measures for Systems Design*. Ph.D. Dissertation, Polytechnic Institute of New York, Brooklyn, Jun 1983.

[A37] HALL, N. R. and PREISER, S. Dynamic Complexity Measures for Software Design. *Proceedings of Total Systems Reliability Symposium*, IEEE Computer Society, Dec 1983.

[A38] HALL, N. R. and PREISER, S. Combined Network Complexity Measures. *IBM Journal of Research and Development*, Jan 1984.

[A39] McCABE, T. J. A Complexity Measure. *IEEE Transactions on Software Engineering*, vol SE-2, no 4, Dec 1976, pp 308–320.

A16. Cyclomatic Complexity

A16.1 Application. This measure may be used to determine the structural complexity of a coded module. The use of this measure is designed to limit the complexity of a module, thereby promoting understandability of the module.

A16.2 Primitives

N = Number of nodes (sequential groups of program statements).

E = Number of edges (program flows between nodes).

SN = Number of splitting nodes (nodes with more than one edge emanating from it).

RG = Number of regions (areas bounded by edges with no edges crossing).

A16.3 Implementation. Using regions, or nodes and edges, a strongly connected graph of the module is required. A strongly connected graph is one in which a node is reachable from any other node. This is accomplished by adding an edge between the exit node and the entry node. Once the graph is constructed, the measure is computed as follows:

$$C = E - N + 1$$

The cyclomatic complexity is also equivalent to the number of regions (RG) or the number of splitting nodes plus one ($SN+1$). If a program contains an N-way predicate, such as a CASE statement with N cases, the N-way predicate contributes $N-1$ to the count of SN.

A16.4 Interpretation. For a typical module, ten represents a maximum ideal complexity. For a very complex system, the cyclomatic number (complexity) may be larger. If the calculated complexity number is too large, modularization of the code is required [A41].

A16.5 Considerations. Since the construction of the graph can be a tedious, error-prone process, automation of graph construction is desirable. The cyclomatic complexity method does not take into account the complexity of sequential program statements, a single program statement, or control flow caused by a multi-branching conditional statement.

The cyclomatic complexity can be used to limit intra-module complexity. However, to accomplish this one may increase the intermodule complexity by adding to the number of modules needed to accomplish a given function. The user should optimize both inter- and intra-module complexity, not one at the expense of the other.

A16.6 Training. If a tool is used, training in the use of a tool is required. If performed manually, training in graph construction is required.

A16.7 Example. Figure A16.7-1 illustrates a strongly connected graph. The nodes are labeled A (the entry node) through J (the exit node). Each node represents a block of code where control flow can only go from one statement to the next. There are 14 edges, 5 numbered regions, and 10 nodes. The complexity can be computed using either of the three methods:

C = complexity = number of regions = 5

The five regions are bounded by the paths:

A-B-C-E-G-J-A and J-A
A-B-C-E-F-I-J-A and A-B-C-E-G-J-A
A-B-C-E-F-H-J and A-B-C-E-F-I-J
A-B-C-D-J and A-B-C-E-F-H-J
D-D (this could be a DO statement)

Nodes and edges: complexity = $E - N + 1$
$$= 14 - 10 + 1 = 5$$

Splitting nodes: complexity = $SN + 1 = 4 + 1 = 5$

The four splitting nodes are: C, D, E and F

A16.8 Benefits. The cyclomatic number can be a good indicator of module complexity, and may be used to keep modules within an understandable and workable size. This measure also results in the computation of the number of distinct paths in a module without considering the complexity of an individual statement.

A16.9 Experience. There is empirical evidence [A41] that the cyclomatic complexity can reduce the difficulty encountered by programmers. There is some evidence that using the cyclomatic measure results in a module with fewer faults. Basili and Perricone [A40] provide a critical evaluation of this measure.

A16.10 References. See also Conte, Dunsmore, and Shen [A28] and McCabe [A39].

[A40] BASILI, V. R., and PERRICONE, B. T. Software Errors and Complexity: An Empirical Investigation. *Communications of the ACM*, Jan 1984.

[A41] McCABE, T. J. *Structured Testing: A Software Testing Methodology Using the Cyclomatic Complexity Metric.* National Bureau of Standards Special Publication 500-99, Dec 1982.

A17. Minimal Unit Test Case Determination

A17.1 Application. This measure determines the number of independent paths through a module so that a minimal number of covering test cases can be generated for unit test. It is applied during unit testing.

A17.2 Primitives
N = number of nodes; a sequential group of program statements.
E = number of edges; program flow between nodes.
SN = number of splitting nodes; a node with more than one edge emanating from it.
RG = number of regions; in a graph with no edges crossing, an area bounded by edges.

A17.3 Implementation. The cyclomatic complexity is first computed using the cyclomatic

Fig A16.7-1
Module Control Graph

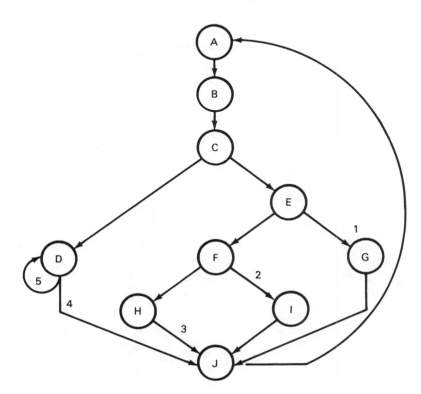

complexity measure described in A16. The complexity of the module establishes the number of distinct paths. The user constructs test cases along each path so all edges of the graph are traversed. This set of test cases forms a minimal set of cases that covers all paths through the module.

A17.4 Interpretation. The minimal set of test cases is the number of independent paths through the module. Execution of these test cases generally causes every statement and decision outcome to be executed at least once. Additional test cases may be added (eg, to test upper and lower bounds on variables).

A17.5 Considerations. The construction of the graph can be a tedious, error-prone process. Thus, automation of the graph construction is desirable. Once the graph is constructed, the generation of test cases is done by hand. Since the graph produces a minimal set of test cases, additional test cases should be generated to comprehensively test the module.

A17.6 Training. Training may be required in graph construction and interpretation in order to determine the minimal set of test cases.

A17.7 Example. Figure A17.7-1 illustrates a strongly connected graph. The nodes are labeled A (entry node) through J (exit node). Each node represents a block of code where control flow can only go from one statement to the next. Using the method for computing complexity (A16), the complexity of the module represented in Fig A17.7-1 is five. There are five distinct paths through the graph. They are:

A-B-C-E-G-J
A-B-C-E-F-I-J
A-B-C-E-F-H-J
A-B-C-D-J
A-B-C-D-D-J

The user selects five test cases causing the five distinct paths to be executed. The selection of minimal test case is demonstrated in McCabe [A41].

A17.8 Benefits. The minimal test case provides a rigorous method of determining minimal test coverage. This same set can be used, with appropriate modifications, during maintenance.

A17.9 Experience. There is empirical evidence [A41] that determining minimal test cases reduces

Fig A17.7-1
Module Control Graph

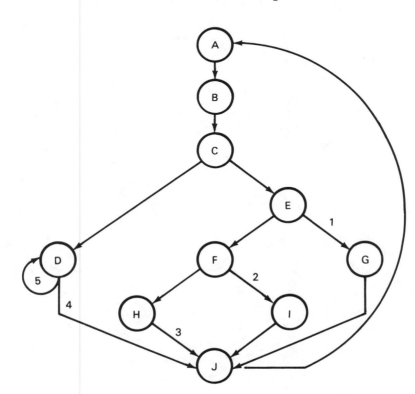

the difficulty encountered by programmers in testing every path in a module. The advantage of this approach is the completeness of the test of a module and the assurance that all segments of the module are tested.

A17.10 References. See Conte, Dunsmore, and Shen [A28] and McCabe [A39, A41].

A18. Run Reliability

Run reliability (R_k) is the probability that k randomly selected runs (corresponding to a specified period of time) will produce correct results.

A18.1 Application. The run reliability measure may be applied at any phase in the life cycle when the set of possible discrete input patterns and states can be identified. The sequence is randomly selected based on the probability assigned to selection of any one of them.

A18.2 Primitives

NR = Number of runs in a given test sample.

nc = Number of correct runs in a given test sample.

k = Number of runs for the specified period of time.

S = Sample space of possible input patterns and states. (S_i, i =1 ...) are elements in the sample space. For each input pattern and state there is a unique output pattern and state. Thus, S_i designates a given ((input, state), (output, state)) that constitutes a run.

P = Probability measure over the sample space.

P_i = Probability that the ith run is selected from the sample space.

A18.3 Implementation

A18.3.1 Sample Space (S). The sample space is viewed as the set of possible inputs into the program. In the early phases of the life cycle, the sample space consists of operational scenarios. For instance, in the early requirements phase the inputs and states are the listed requirements for the program. In the later phases of the life cycle, the sample space consists of all detailed input and state conditions of the program. For a given life cycle phase, a single sample space (S) is determined and a probability measure (P) is assigned. Runs are then generated by randomly choosing input patterns and states from the sample space according to the assigned probability P.

A18.3.2 Probability Measure (P). For each possible run i, a number p_i (between zero and one inclusive) must be assigned so that the sum of all the p_i's is 1. The simplest case is the assumption of a uniform probability distribution. However, in the operational environment some runs are more likely to occur than others, and should be weighted appropriately.

A18.3.3 Test NR Randomly Selected Runs. The accuracy of the measure R_k is determined by the number of runs NR used for estimation. The runs are randomly selected according to the probability distribution. The results of each run are examined for correctness. The number of correct runs is nc.

A18.3.4 Probability of a Successful Run (P_r). The probability of a randomly selected run being correct (P_r) is estimated by the sum of the probabilities for the correct runs, divided by the sum of the probabilities for all runs. In the case of a uniform distribution P_r = nc/NR.

A18.3.5 Run Reliability (R_k). Given k randomly selected runs during the specified period of time, the probability that all k runs give correct results is $R_k = P_r^k$.

A18.4 Interpretation. The reliability obtained using the number of runs for the specified period of time is the probability that the software will perform its intended function for the specified period of time under the stated conditions. Thus, it satisfies the standard definition for systems reliability [A42, A46] and may be combined with other components of the system, such as the hardware component, using the usual rules of probability.

A18.5 Considerations. The run reliability is not defined until the sample space and probability measure are defined for the specific application. These are not unique for the program. They must be carefully constructed by all parties with knowledge of the application environment, the program, and the test procedures, as well as the construction of probability spaces. Construction of the input sample space (A18.3.1) can be done in a number of different ways. There must be a unique output for each input. Thus attention must be given to the initialization of the variables. If more than one input channel is possible, an input pattern may be a vector over time. If a real time system is involved, the exact time of each input must be specified. When a hardware/software system is considered, there must be agreement on the accuracy of the input magnitude and timing.

During the specification or early design phase, a sample space might involve the variety of application scenarios using the various system functions in different ways. A run might be judged successful if all the functions needed in that scenario are appropriately specified.

Construction of the probability measure (P) is possibly the most difficult and potentially misleading error source. The uniform distribution on all possible inputs is the simplest and might be agreed on for test purposes, but may not be representative of the application environment. An inappropriate probability measure will not predict what happens in the field. Changes in the way in which the system is used constitute a change in the probability measure and may change the actual and predicted run reliability. A high reliability measure during one phase or period of time will be applicable to other stages only to the extent that the program remains constant and the sample space and probability measure is representative of the runs that will be made in that other phase.

A18.6 Training. Training should include the basic four chapters in Feller [A44], random sampling techniques, a beginning level of statistical knowledge, and an understanding of the application environment.

A18.7 Example

A18.7.1 Concept Phase. In order for the final system to work reliably, a list of necessary functions must be identified. Suppose a list of functions has been prepared which contains $NR = 20$ different scenarios. The list of functions and scenarios are given to a review team that traces each of the scenarios to check that all the functions required for mission success are available. Further, suppose the review team reports that in one of the scenarios a function necessary for the success of the mission was not in the list. The estimate of the system reliability at this point is .95. After adding the necessary function, one has a new system that works for these scenarios. In order to make a statement concerning the reliability of the new system, however, one would need to "randomly" select a new set of scenarios and test again. Suppose then, in this second test, that in all 20 scenarios the mission could have been performed successfully in the sense that all necessary functions were in the list. This does not mean, however, that following the next scenario through will necessarily find satisfactory results. Suppose the required reliability for the run is .9 and we

wish to demonstrate that this requirement has been met with an accepted 5% risk of failing to reject an unreliable program. That is to say, we wish to test the null hypothesis that the probability of a successful run is less than .9 at the 5% significance level. The probability of making 30 successful runs when the probability of success is less than or equal to .9 is at most $.9^{30} = .047$. Thus, by obtaining success in 30 randomly selected test cases, one could conclude that the requirement of a run reliability of .9 had been met with less than a 5% chance of making an incorrect conclusion.

A18.7.2 Implementation Phase. Suppose the software program has nautical miles (nmi) as input and the range is broken up into the following categories: (0, 500 nmi), (500, 1000 nmi), (1000, 2000 nmi), and (above 2000 nmi). In addition, suppose the associated probabilities assigned by the user are ¼, ⅛, ⅛, and ½ respectively. The user believes that ¼ of the operational time ranges will come from the interval (0, 500), ⅛ of the time from (500, 1000), etc. A random selection of ranges are generated according to the distribution where, once an interval is chosen, a range is drawn uniformly from the chosen interval. Now suppose nr_i ranges were randomly selected from interval i with nc_i being run successfully, $i = 1, 2, 3, 4$. The estimated reliability is then

$$R = \frac{nc_1}{4nr_1} + \frac{nc_2}{8nr_2} + \frac{nc_3}{8nr_3} + \frac{nc_4}{2nr_4}$$

Another example within the implementation phase is as follows:

Alphameric input patterns can be defined for use in code walk-through or computer runs. Consider a module with two input variables A and B. The range as viewed by the user for A is the alphameric characters A through Z and for B is all positive real numbers. Regardless of how the user views the ranges, an 8 bit computer will view each input as one of 2^8 possibilities. The two characters together will be one of 2^{16} possibilities, presuming here that timing is of no concern. For simplicity it might be agreed that each of the 2^{16}th possible inputs representing an input for which the algorithm was intended will have a constant probability p of being chosen, and the rest will have probability p'. One can easily develop a random number generator to randomly select among these possible inputs. One can either select from both intended and unintended inputs and weight the results, or one can develop a random number generator that will have an appropriate probability for selecting from the intended or unintended inputs. Numerical results for real numbers will not always be exactly correct, but are said to be "correct" if the difference is within some acceptable bounds of accuracy. The results computed by the computer operating on these inputs may then be compared to those calculated by hand or other "oracle", perhaps a program in double precision instead of single precision.

A18.8 Benefits. The technique is solidly based theoretically and very easy to interpret if one accepts the assumed sample space and probability measure. This measure can be integrated with a hardware reliability measure to form system reliability, maintainability, and availability estimates.

A18.9 Experience. The concepts and experiences with this measure are documented in [A43, A45, and A47-A49].

A18.10 References

[A42] ANSI/IEEE 729-1983, IEEE Standard Glossary of Software Engineering Terminology.

[A43] BROWN, J. R. and LIPOW, M. Testing for Software Reliability. Proceedings of the 1975 International Conference on Reliable Software, Apr 21-23, 1975, IEEE catalog no 75-CH0940-7CSR, pp 518-527.

[A44] FELLER, W. *An Introduction to Probability Theory and Its Applications.* New York: John Wiley and Sons, Inc, 1957, chaps I, V, VI, and IX.

[A45] LIPOW, M. *Measurement of Computer Software Reliability.* AFSC-TR-75-05, 1979.

[A46] MIL Std 721.

[A47] NELSON, E. C. *A Statistical Basis for Software Reliability Assessment.* TRW-SS-73-03, Redondo Beach, California: TRW, Mar 1973.

[A48] NELSON, E. C. *Software Reliability.* TRW-SS-75-05, Redondo Beach, California: TRW, Nov 1975.

[A49] THAYER, T. A., LIPOW, M and NELSON, E. C. *Software Reliability: A Study of Large Project Reality.* New York: North Holland Publishing Co, 1978.

A19. Design Structure

A19.1 Application. This measure is used to determine the simplicity of the detailed design of a software program. Also, the values determined for the associated primitives can be used to identify problem areas within the software design.

A19.2 Primitives

$P1$ = total number of modules in the program
$P2$ = number of modules dependent on the input or output
$P3$ = number of modules dependent on prior processing (state)
$P4$ = number of database elements
$P5$ = number of non-unique database elements
$P6$ = number of database segments (partition of the state)
$P7$ = number of modules not single entrance/ single exit.

A19.3 Implementation. The design structure measure is the weighted sum of six derivatives determined by using the primitives given above. The six derivatives are:

D_1 = design organized top down (Boolean)
D_2 = module dependence ($P2/P1$)
D_3 = module dependent on prior processing ($P3/P1$)
D_4 = database size ($P5/P4$)
D_5 = database compartmentalization ($P6/P4$)
D_6 = module single entrance single exit ($P7/P1$).

The design structure measure (DSM) can be expressed as:

$$DSM = \sum_{i=1}^{6} W_i D_i$$

The weights (W_i) are assigned by the user based on the priority of each associated derivative. Each W_i has a value between 0 and 1 ($\Sigma_i W_i = 1.0$).

A19.4 Interpretation. The value of the design structure measure is scaled between 0 and 1 by the appropriate weights. A score near 0 is considered better than a score near 1. Design structure measure values that are considered high could be traced to "offending" primitive(s) to highlight particular priority areas for change in the design. As changes are made to the design structure, the incremental design structure measure values can be plotted to show whether improvements are being made and how rapidly. Also, comparisons of design structure measures between different projects allows a relative scaling to be made for values determined.

A19.5 Considerations. Each primitive is calculated to help identify those characteristics in the design that promote simplicity in the construction of modules and databases.

A19.6 Training. Training would be necessary to understand the definitions of the primitives for the particular application. The use of a program design language (PDL) would enhance and standardize the definition procedure for primitives.

A19.7 Example. Previous to calculating the primitive (and associated derivative) values, the following steps should occur:

(1) The definitions of the primitives for the particular application must be determined. For example, if a program design language (PDL) were being used to develop the software design, then the primitives would be defined in association with the PDL constructs.

(2) Priorities should be determined for each derivative (D_i). These priorities should then be used to assign the associated weighting factors (W_i). If no priorities are established, the weight for each derivative would be one-sixth ($\frac{1}{6}$).

To arrive at a value for the design structure measure, assume that the primitives have the following values:

$$P1 = 250 \quad P3 = 50 \quad P5 = 500 \quad P7 = 10$$
$$P2 = 125 \quad P4 = 2500 \quad P6 = 50$$

The derivative values are calculated to be:

$D_1 = 0$ (assumed, top-down design)
$D_2 = .5\ (P2/P1)$
$D_3 = .2\ (P3/P1)$
$D_4 = .2\ (P5/P4)$
$D_5 = .02\ (P6/P4)$
$D_6 = .04\ (P7/P1)$

Using a weight of one-sixth ($\frac{1}{6}$) for each W_i the design structure measure value is:

$$DSM = \sum_{i=1}^{6} W_i D_i$$

$$= \tfrac{1}{6}(0) + \tfrac{1}{6}(.5) + \tfrac{1}{6}(.2) + \tfrac{1}{6}(.2) + \tfrac{1}{6}(.02) + \tfrac{1}{6}(.04)$$

$$= .16$$

A19.8 Benefits. The design structure measure will give an indication of the simplicity (value near 0) or complexity (value near 1) of the software design.

A19.9 Experience. There is limited published experience with the use of the design structure measure. This measure is similar to the completeness measure [A35]. The experience consists of the determination of the proper definitions and measurements of primitives and calculation of associated derivatives. This technique worked successfully for the completeness measure, and similar results are expected for the design structure measure.

A19.10 References

[A50] FRANCIS, J. et al. *The Application of Software Quality Metrics to Mx Operational G&C Software.* Dynamics Research Corporation, Sept 1982.

[A51] McCALL, J., RICHARDS, P., and WALTERS, G. *Factors in Software Quality*, RADC-TR-77-369, 3 vols, Nov 1977.

[A52] McCALL, J., and MATSUMOTO, M. *Metrics Enhancements.* RADC-TR-80-109, 2 vols, Apr 1980.

[A53] MILLER, D. et al. *The Application of Software Quality Metrics to PCKR Operational Guidance and Control Software.* Dynamics Research Corporation, Sept 1983.

A20. Mean Time to Discover the Next K Faults

A20.1 Application. This measure can be used to project the average length of time until the next K faults are discovered. This can provide an indication of how much time would be required until a desired level of reliability is achieved.

A20.2 Primitives

f = number of failures found from the beginning of testing to the present

t_i = observed time between the $(i-1)$st and ith failure for a given severity level $i=1,\dots$

A20.3 Implementation. The mean time to failure (see A30) should be used to estimate the mean time to discover the next K faults in the software. This can then be expressed as:

$$\begin{array}{l}\text{mean time to discover} \\ \text{the next } K \text{ faults}\end{array} = \sum_{i=f}^{f+K-1} \widehat{\mathrm{MTTF}}_i$$

where $\widehat{\mathrm{MTTF}}_i$ is an estimate of the mean time to failure between the ith and $(i+1)$st failure.

The estimate of the mean time to failure between the ith and $(i+1)$st failure can be calculated using any of the software models based upon time between failures [A56–A58]. Suppose that estimate is:

$$\widehat{\mathrm{MTTF}}_i = \hat{E}\{\text{time between the } i\text{th and the } (i+1)\text{st failures}\}\ f \le i \le f+K-1$$

Notice that if $K=1$, then we simply have the estimate of the MTFF (see A30) between the fth and $(f+1)$st failure. Then the estimate is:

$$\begin{pmatrix} \text{mean time to} \\ \text{discover the} \\ \text{next } K \text{ faults} \end{pmatrix} = \sum_{i=f}^{f-K+1} \hat{E} \begin{Bmatrix} \text{time between} \\ \text{the } i\text{th and the} \\ (i+1)\text{st} \end{Bmatrix}$$

By estimating the mean time to failure, one can then estimate how much additional time will be required to discover all, or a subset, of the estimated remaining faults. One can judge how long it will take before the software achieves a desired level of reliability.

A20.4 Interpretation. Actual numerical calculations of the estimate depends on the form of the model chosen to represent the distribution of MTTF. Within the software life cycle, the estimate is useful when planning for time necessary to achieve stabilization.

A20.5 Considerations. To apply this measure, one must collect the times between failure and then fit the data to one of the software models. For better estimates, it is desirable to have time units with as much resolution as feasible, eg, CPU execution time is especially appropriate in a software development environment. Sometimes wall-clock time is the only time available, and in this situation estimates can be made, but with much less precision. For the situations where operational or application usage requires less resolution, estimates based on wall-clock time units would be appropriate.

During the software development life cycle, evaluation of model predictions versus actual time required to achieve a certain level of reliability should be used to construct realistic schedules.

A20.6 Training. The implementation requires knowledge of the application of software models that use the time between failure data.

A20.7 Example. In the fitting of the Jelinski and Moranda "de-eutrophication" model [A56], the estimate of the mean time to failure between the ith and $(i+1)$st error is

$$\text{MTTF}_i = \hat{E}\{\text{time between } i\text{th, } (i+1)\text{st}\} = \frac{1}{\hat{Q}(\hat{NF}-i)}$$

where $\hat{Q}$ is the estimate of the proportionality constant in that model and $\hat{NF}$ is the estimate of the total number of faults in the program. The estimate of the mean time to discover the next K faults is then:

$$\sum_{i=f}^{f+K-1} \frac{1}{\hat{Q}(\hat{NF}-i)}$$

For illustrative purposes suppose $f=20$ and $\hat{Q}$ and $\hat{NF}$ were calculated as .05 and 100 respectively. If one were interested in the mean time to discover the next $K=2$ failures then the estimate becomes:

$$\sum_{i=20}^{21} \frac{1}{(.05)(100-i)} = \frac{1}{(.05)(80)} + \frac{1}{(.05)(79)} = 0.50$$

A20.8 Benefits. This measure can be plotted against K ($K=1, 2, 3,...NF$ remaining number of faults) to judge the integrity of the system at any point in time.

A20.9 Experience. Experience is a function of application of any of the given models in the references.

A20.10 References. See also Musa, Iannino, and Okumoto [A7].

[A54] GOEL, AMRIT L., and OKUMOTO, K. *A Time Dependent Error Detection Rate Model for Software Performance Assessment with Applications*. RADC #F3062-78-C-0351, Mar 1980, p 76.

[A55] LITTLEWOOD, B. A Stochastic Reliability Growth: A Model for Fault Removal in Computer Programs and Hardware Designs. *IEEE Transactions on Reliability*, vol R-30, no 4, Oct 1981, pp 313-320.

[A56] MORANDA, PAUL L., and JELINSKI, Z. *Final Report on Software Reliability Study*. McDonnell-Douglas Astronautics Company, MDC Report no 63921, 1972.

[A57] MUSA, J. D. A Theory of Software Reliability and Its Application. *IEEE Transactions on Software Engineering*, vol SE-1, no 3, 1975, pp 312-327.

[A58] SCHICK, GEORGE J., and WOLVERTON, RAY, W. An Analysis of Competing Software Reliability Models. *IEEE Transactions on Software Engineering*, vol SE-4, no 2, 1978, pp 104-120.

A21. Software Purity Level

A21.1 Application. The software purity level provides an estimate of the relative fault-freeness of a computer program at any specified point in time during the operational phase.

A21.2 Primitives

t_i = observed times between failures (eg, execution time) for a given severity level

f = total number of failures in a given time interval

A21.3 Implementation. Suppose f failures have occurred during the operational phase of the life cycle of the program. Suppose also the length of time in this phase when the fth failure is detected is t_f. Then the estimate of the purity level of the program at that point in time is

$$PL = \frac{\hat{Z}(t_0) - \hat{Z}(t_f)}{\hat{Z}(t_0)}$$

where t_0 is the start of the operations and maintenance phase and $\hat{Z}(t)$ is the estimated hazard (or failure) rate at time t. The hazard rate is defined as the conditional probability that a software failure happens in an interval of time $(t, t+\Delta t)$ given that the software has not failed up to time t. It is derived from any of the software reliability models that use time between failures data t_i. PL denotes the relative change in the hazard rate function from the beginning of the operations and maintenance phase to the time of the fth failure detection.

A21.4 Interpretation. The closer PL gets to 1 the greater the reliability of the program. Values close to 1 indicate that many of the initial faults in the program have been eliminated.

A21.5 Considerations. The application of this measure is especially applicable for those classes of models in which the total number of remaining faults in the program cannot be predicted (eg, Moranda's geometric model [A60 and A61]). Its use is restricted to those phases where significant test results can be obtained.

A21.6 Training. Familiarity with the various software reliability models employing time between failure data is essential.

A21.7 Example. For the Moranda geometric model (A60), the estimate of the hazard rate at any time t between the occurrence of the ith failure and the $(i+1)$st is:

$$\hat{Z}(t) = \hat{D}\hat{Q}^i$$

$\hat{D}$ is the estimate of the initial hazard rate at time t_o and $(0<Q<1)$ is the estimate of the proportionality constant in the model [A60]. Then the purity level using this model is

$$PL = \frac{\hat{Z}(t_0) - \hat{Z}(t_f)}{\hat{Z}(t_0)} = 1 - \hat{Q}^f$$

A21.8 Benefits. A plot of PL versus n (the number of failures) can be used to see the relative "fault-freeness" of the program as the number of detected faults increases.

A21.9 Experience. Limited experience is provided in the references.

A21.10 References. See also Musa, Iannino, and Okumoto [A7].

[A59] FARR, W. H. *A Survey of Software Reliability, Modeling and Estimation.* Dahlgren, Virginia: Naval Surface Weapons Center, NSWC TR 82-171, Sept 1983.

[A60] MORANDA, PAUL Predictions of Software Reliability During Debugging. *1975 Proceedings of the Annual Reliability and Maintainability Symposium*, 1975.

[A61] MORANDA, PAUL Event-Alerted Rate Models for General Reliability Analysis. *IEEE Transactions on Reliability*, vol R-28, no 5, 1979, pp 376–381.

A22. Estimated Number of Faults Remaining (by Seeding)

A22.1 Application. The estimated number of faults remaining in a program is related to the reliability of the program. There are many sampling techniques that estimate this number. This section describes a simple form of seeding that assumes a homogeneous distribution of a representative class of faults [A67].

This measure can be applied to any phase of the software life cycle. The search for faults continues for a determined period of time that may be less than that required to find all seeded faults. The measure is not computed unless some non-seeded faults are found.

A22.2 Primitives

N_s = the number of seeded faults

n_s = the number of seeded faults found

n_F = the number of faults found that were not intentionally seeded

A22.3 Implementation. A monitor is responsible for error seeding. The monitor inserts (seeds) N_s faults representative of the expected indigenous faults. The test team reports to the monitor the faults found during a test period of predetermined length.

Before seeding, a fault analysis is needed to determine the types of faults and their relative frequency of occurrence expected under a particular set of software development conditions [A49, A65]. Although an estimate of the number of faults remaining can be made on the basis of very few inserted faults, the accuracy of the estimate (and hence the confidence in it) increases as the number of seeded faults increases.

Faults should be inserted randomly throughout the software. Personnel inserting the faults should be different and independent of those persons later searching for the faults. The process of searching for the faults should be carried out without knowledge of the inserted faults. The search should be performed for a previously determined period of time (or effort) and each fault reported to the central monitor.

Each reported fault should be reviewed to determine whether it is in the class of faults being studied, and if so, whether it is a seeded or an indigenous fault. The maximum likelihood estimate of the number of indigenous (unseeded) faults in the specified class is:

$$\hat{NF} = \frac{n_F N_s}{n_s} \qquad \text{(eq A22-1)}$$

where $\hat{NF}$ is truncated to the integer value. The estimate of the remaining number of faults is then: $\hat{NF}_{rem} = \hat{NF} - n_F$.

The probability of finding n_F of NF indigenous faults and n_F of N_s seeded faults, given that there are $n_F + n_s$ faults found in the program is $C(N_s, n_s) C(NF, n_F) / C(NF + N_s, n_F + n_s)$ where the function $C(x, y) = x! / (x-y)! y!$ is the combination of "x" things taken "y" at a time. Using this relation one can calculate confidence intervals.

A22.4 Interpretation. The number of seeded and indigenous faults discovered enables the number of faults remaining to be estimated for the fault type being considered. The phrase "fault type being considered" means that if, for example, one was seeding typographical faults, one would not expect a good prediction of the number of omitted functions or algorithmic faults. If one were seeding faults of the type found in unit testing, one would not expect the estimate to apply to those interface faults found in integration testing.

A22.5 Considerations. This measure depends on the assumption that the seeded (inserted) faults are representative of existing (unseeded) faults.

In general, not all faults are equally likely to be found in any given test procedure. To assure that the seeded faults are representative of a specific class of faults, and the result will have the desired accuracy, enough faults of the kind expected should be inserted to provide the desired accuracy.

Faults are corrected in the original software only after the fault has been determined to be unseeded by rerunning the test case on the original unseeded software. Good configuration management practices are needed to assure that the seeded version is not the version finally released and that indigenous faults discovered are corrected only in the unseeded version.

The correction of the indigenous faults in the original version raises the problem of whether the correction introduces further faults. At this time this must be left as an engineering judgment as to whether the new (corrected) program needs to be seeded to give an estimate of its reliability or whether the estimate of the faults remaining in the new (corrected) program is $NF - n_F$ where n_F is the number of indigenous faults found and corrected.

In lieu of actually seeding faults in a program, the number of "seeded" faults may sometimes be generated by examining the results of testing by two independent test teams [A71 and A63]. The seeded faults would be those faults identified by both test teams. The unseeded faults are those identified by either, but not both, of the test teams. An estimate of the number of remaining faults can then be calculated using Eq A22-1.

A22.6 Training. No additional training is required for the developers or the testers. Training in seeding the faults and monitoring the process is needed. Some general training and practice in classifying faults is also needed.

A22.7 Example. Suppose 100 were seeded. During the prescribed test period, 50 of the 100 seeded faults and 2 unseeded faults were found.

Then:

$$N_s = 100$$
$$n_s = 50$$
$$n_F = 2$$
$$\hat{NF} = \left[\frac{n_F N_s}{n_s} \right] = \left[\frac{2(100)}{50} \right] = 4$$

Thus, it is estimated that there are $\hat{NF}_{rem} = \hat{NF} - n_F$ = 2 faults remaining.

A22.8 Benefits. This procedure encourages the reporting of faults and competition between developers and testers. Since faults are known to be there, the tester knows there is something to search for. The reporting of faults does not necessarily admit to an error on the part of the developers.

The procedure could be carried out by a customer monitor with little effort, high effectiveness, and minimal interference with the developer's normal patterns. For the cost of a second independent testing group, an estimate of the number of remaining faults can be obtained without seeding errors.

A22.9 Experience. Nippon Telephone and Telegraph reported [A73] good results applying their version of the seeding method to an operating system consisting of 150,000 lines of code. A mixture of seeding and a software reliability growth model at IBM Japan Ltd. for predicting the number of faults to be found during the operational phase is described. Techniques for seeding faults include: (1) deferring correction of actual faults by programmers; (2) mutants (eg, replacing "and" with "or") that are considered to be similar inherent defects due to misinterpretation of the specifications; and (3) transplanted defects (eg, adding or deleting a flow-control statement) simulating the design mistakes. In two experiments involving 3000 and 4000 lines of code for modules in an on-line terminal operating program, the authors claim to have predicted (to within ±10%) the fraction of defects found during testing with those remaining to be found during operation. The authors claim that seeding is practical in their experience.

In the US, a number of published papers have developed the principles and techniques for seeding [A64, A65, A67, A70, A74, A75].

A22.10 References. See also Thayer, Lipow, and Nelson [A49].

[A62] BASIN, S. L. *Estimation of Software Error Rates Via Capture-Recapture Sampling*. Palo Alto: Science Applications Inc, Sept 1973.

[A63] BASIN, S. L. *Measuring the Error Content of Software*. Palo Alto: Science Applications Inc, Sept 1974.

[A64] BOWEN, J. B. and SAIB, S. H. *Association of Software Errors, Classifications to AED Language Elements*. Prepared under Contract Number NAS 2-10550 by Hughes Aircraft Company, Ful-

lerton, and General Research Corporation, Santa Barbara, California, Nov 1980.

[A65] BOWEN, J. B. and SAIB, S. H. *Error Seeding Technique Specification*. Prepared under Contract Number NAS 2-10550 by Hughes Aircraft Company, Fullerton, and General Research Corporation, Santa Barbara, California, Dec 1980.

[A66] DACS. *Rudner Model, Seeding/Tagging*. Quantitative Software Models, DACS, SSR-1, Mar 1979, pp 3-56 to 3-58.

[A67] DURAN, J. W. and WIORKOWSKI, J. J. Capture-Recapture Sampling for Estimating Software Error Content. *IEEE Transactions on Software Engineering*, vol SE-7, Jan 1981.

[A68] FELLER, W. *An Introduction to Probability Theory and Its Applications*. New York: John Wiley and Sons, Inc, 1957, p 43.

[A69] *System Spec. ... tion for Flexible Interconnect*. Specification Number SS078779400, May 15, 1980.

[A70] LIPOW, M. *Estimation of Software Package Residual Errors*. TRW Software Series SS-72-09, Redondo Beach: TRW E & D, 1972.

[A71] McCABE, THOMAS J. *Structural Testing*. Columbia, Maryland: McCabe & Associates, Inc, 1984.

[A72] MILLS, H. D. *On the Statistical Validation of Computer Programs*. FSC-72-6015, Gaithersburg, Maryland: Federal Systems Division, International Business Machines Corporation, 1972.

[A73] OHBA, M., et al. *S-Shape Reliability Control Curve: How Good Is It?* Proceedings COMPSAC82, IEEE Computer Society, 1982, pp 38-44.

[A74] RUDNER, B. Seeding/Tagging Estimation of Software Errors: Models and Estimates. RADC-TR-15, 1977.

[A75] SEBER, G. A. F. *Estimation of Animal Abundance and Related Parameters*. 2nd ed, New York: McMillan Publishing Co, 1982.

A23. Requirements Compliance

A23.1 Application. This analysis is used to verify requirements compliance by using system verification diagrams (SVDs), a logical interconnection of decomposition elements (eg, stimulus and response) that detect inconsistencies, incompleteness, and misinterpretations.

A23.2 Primitives

*DE*s = Decomposition elements
- Stimulus = External input
- Function = Defined input/output process
- Response = Result of the function
- Label = Numerical *DE* identifier
- Reference = Specification paragraph number

Requirement errors detected using SVDs:
- N_1 = Number due to inconsistencies
- N_2 = Number due to incompleteness
- N_3 = Number due to misinterpretation.

A23.3 Implementation. The implementation of a SVD is composed of the following phases:

(1) The decomposition phase is initiated by mapping the system requirement specifications into stimulus/response elements (*DE*s). That is, all key words, phrases, functional or performance requirements or both, and expected output are documented on decomposition forms (see Fig A23.3-1).

(2) The graph phase uses the *DE*s from the decomposition phase and logically connects them to form the SVD graph.

(3) The analysis phase examines the SVD from the graph phase by using connectivity and reachability matrices. The various requirement error types are determined by experiencing the system verification diagram and identifying errors as follows:

inconsistencies. Decomposition elements that do not accurately reflect the system requirement specification.

incompleteness. Decomposition elements that do not completely reflect the system requirement specification.

misinterpretation. Decomposition elements that do not correctly reflect the system requirement

**Fig A23.3-1
Decomposition Form**

STIMULUS	LABEL	RESPONSE
	FUNCTION	
SPECIFICATION REFERENCE		

specification. These errors may occur during translation of the requirements into decomposition elements, constructing the SVD graph, or interpreting the connectivity and reachability matrices.

An analysis is also made of the percentages for the various requirement error types for the respective categories: inconsistencies, incompleteness, and misinterpretation.

Inconsistencies (%) = $N_1/(N_1+N_2+N_3) \times 100$
Incompleteness (%) = $N_2/(N_1+N_2+N_3) \times 100$
Misinterpretation (%) = $N_3/(N_1+N_2+N_3) \times 100$

This analysis can aid also in future software development efforts.

A23.4 Interpretation. The SVDs are analyzed by interpreting the connectivity and reachability matrices. The rules governing their use are as follows:

Connectivity Matrix. The rules governing the use of connectivity matrices are as follows:

Rule 1. The matrix size is $N \times N$ where N equals the number of decomposition elements in a given SVD.

Rule 2. Any (i, j) matrix element is equal to one, if DE_i transfers directly to DE_j. It is equal to zero otherwise.

Rule 3. Any matrix column of all zeros identifies a *DE* that is not transferred to or by any other *DE* and, therefore, must be an entry *DE*.

Rule 4. Any matrix row of all zeros identifies a *DE* that does not transfer to any other *DE* and, therefore, must be a terminal *DE*.

Rule 5. If there is a one along the diagonal, it indicates that a particular *DE* loops back to itself. Though possible, this is improbable at the requirement level and usually indicates a fault.

Rule 6. Any *DE* with an associated zero row and zero column indicates a stand alone system function. Though possible, they are rare and should be double checked for authenticity.

Reachability Matrix. The rules governing the use of reachability matrices include the rules 1–6 for connectivity matrices and the following reachability rule:

Rule 7. Any (i, j) matrix element is equal to one if DE_j can be reached (directly or indirectly) from DE_i. It is equal to zero otherwise.

An analysis of the percentages will aid requirements specifications and future code testing. The categories with the higher percentages should receive the most scrutiny for future requirement specifications and test case design.

A23.5 Considerations. SVDs can be implemented either manually or with the aid of automation. Automation is recommended for large SVDs. An SVD can be used during the system requirement definition phase and/or during the software requirement phase.

A23.6 Training. Training is required if automation is used. The manual approach requires a familiarization with logic methodology.

A23.7 Example. See Fig A23.7-1.

A23.8 Benefits. SVDs are good communication devices for internal and external reviews. The reachability matrix associated with SVDs can be used during the maintenance phase to assess modification impact and test direction. Requirements can be verified per life cycle phase.

A23.9 Experience. See also Fischer and Walker [A76].

A23.10 Reference

[A76] FISCHER, K. F. and WALKER, M. G. *Improved Software Reliability Through Requirement Verification.* IEEE Transactions on Reliability, vol R-28, no 3, Aug 1979, pp 233–239.

Fig A23.7-1

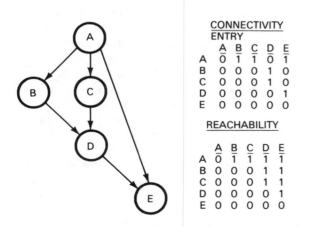

NOTE: Assume A, B, C, D, E are decomposition elements. Using the connectivity matrix rules 1–6 to identify the entry *DE* as A (Rule 3) B-to-A would not be allowed (it violates Rule 2). This results in column 1 having all zeros.

A24. Test Coverage

A24.1 Application. Test coverage is a measure of the completeness of the testing process from both a developer and a user perspective. The measure relates directly to the development, integration and operational test stages of product development: unit, system and acceptance tests. The measure can be applied by developers in unit tests to obtain a measure of thoroughness of structural tests. The developer can use the program class of primitives. The system tester can apply the measure in two ways: (1) focusing on requirement primitives, the system tester can gain a user-view of the thoroughness of functional tests, or (2) the program class of primitives can be used to measure the amount of implementation in the operational environment.

A24.2 Primitives. The primitives for test coverage are in two classes, program and requirement. For program, there are two types, functional and data. The program functional primitives are either modules, segments, statements, branches (nodes), or paths. Program data primitives are equivalence classes of data. Requirement primitives are either test cases or functional capabilities.

A24.3 Implementation. Test coverage (TC) is the percentage of requirement primitives implemented times the percentage of primitives executed during a set of tests. A simple interpretation of test coverage can be expressed by the following formula:

$$TC(\%) = \frac{(\text{Implemented capabilities})}{(\text{Required capabilities})}$$
$$\times \frac{(\text{Program primitives tested})}{(\text{Total program primitives})} \times 100$$

A24.4 Interpretation. Test coverage is only an indication of the thoroughness of test. Due to the interplay of data with function, there are usually an infinite number of cases to test. This can be significantly reduced, if equivalence relations can be logically defined on the data and functions.

Confidence in the level of test thoroughness is increased by using more refined primitives. For example, segment coverage of 100% is a stronger statement than 100% module coverage.

A24.5 Considerations. Test coverage is a measure of the testing made on two categories of the software product, the program and the requirement (Fig A24.5-1). The program is a set of coded

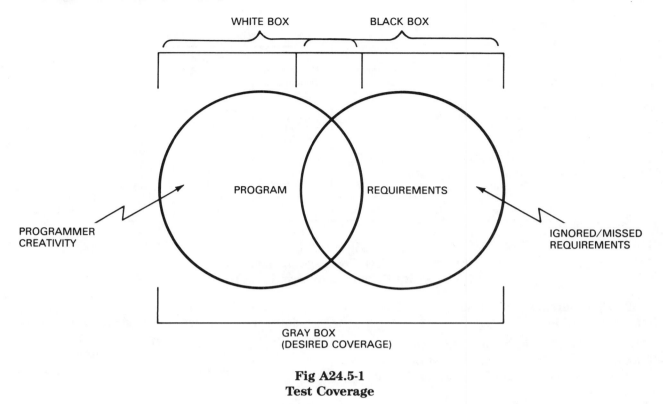

Fig A24.5-1
Test Coverage

instructions. The requirement is a set of user-intended capabilities. The intersection is the set of implemented user-intended capabilities. The left area represents either programmer creativity or those areas for which necessary implementation decisions were made due to the hardware, for example. The right area represents those user-intended capabilities that are missing in the implementation either unintentionally or intentionally due to other overriding factors such as storage. Corresponding to this model we can associate test activities and test coverage measures.

To the program, we associate a unit or functional test activity that is based on the premise that the structure of the programmed implementation is known. Hence the program primitives are known and available for a developer-oriented measure of test coverage. This is usually known as white box testing or clear box testing.

To the requirements, we associate a system test activity that in most cases assumes no knowledge of the programmed implementation. Test scenarios are designed to demonstrate correct operation from a user's view. The requirement primitives are known and can be used to give a user-oriented test coverage measure. This is usually known as black box testing.

A combination activity can be postulated. This is known as gray box testing. Test coverage in this activity is the product of the test coverage of program and requirement.

A24.6 Training. The user should understand basic testing theory.

A24.7 Example. Assuming all capabilities are implemented, Fig A24.7-1 gives the test coverage of a set of tests with segments as the primitives.

A24.8 Benefits. The test coverage measure is important in regulating effort expended to benefit achieved increasing the efficiency of the test process. Test cases can be developed to maximize the coverage measure.

A24.9 Experience. Test coverage is faciliated by code instrumented with probes to monitor usage. These, however, are programming language dependent. It is not a standard practice in program language specifications to provide this monitoring feature. Many projects are "tooling up" by customizing probes into language precompilers to automate this measure. DeMillo and Martin [A77] gives an assessment of test coverage usage in the DoD community.

No.	Module Name	Number of Segments:	(Archived) Past Tests		
			Number of Invocations	Number of Segments Hit	Percent Coverage
50:	do_one_to_one	Tio 177	12	52	29.38
51:	calculate_and_test_so	15	2	11	73.33
52:	a_to_r	7	14	4	57.14
53:	GET_CELL_FLG	3	34	2	66.67
54:	Put_txt_cell	54	20	18	33.33
55:	CUR_DOWN	5	5	3	60.00
56:	RESET_GRAPH_VARS	9	1	9	100.00
57:	set_target_loop_ctr	29	2	14	48.28
	Totals	1192	397	454	38.09

Fig A24.7-1
Example of Test Coverage Measurements*
(with Segments as Primitives)

A24.10 References. See also Ceriani, Cicu, and Maiocchi [A11].

[A77] DEMILLO, R. A. and MARTIN, R. J. *Software Test and Evaluation: Current Defense Practices Overview*. Georgia Institute of Technology, Jun 1983.

[A78] McCABE, T. *Tutorial Text: Structured Testing*. IEEE Computer Society Press, 1981.

[A79] MILLER, E. *Tutorial: Program Testing Techniques*. IEEE Computer Society Press, 1977.

A25. Data or Information Flow Complexity

A25.1 Application. This is a structural complexity or procedural complexity measure that can be used to evaluate the following:

(1) The information flow structure of large scale systems;
(2) The procedure and module information flow structure;
(3) The complexity of the interconnections between modules.

Moreover, this measure can also be used to indicate the degree of simplicity of relationships between subsystems and to correlate total observed failures and software reliability with data complexity.

A25.2 Primitives

lfi = local flows into a procedure.
datain = number of data structures from which the procedure retrieves data.

*Coverage Analyzer, Version 1.8 (80 Column).
© Copyright 1984 by Software Research Associates.

lfo = local flows from a procedure.
dataout = number of data structures that the procedure updates.
length = number of source statements in a procedure (excludes comments in a procedure.

A25.3 Implementation. Determine the flow of information between modules or subsystems or both by automated data flow techniques, HIPO charts, etc.

A local flow from module A to B exists if one of the following holds true:

(1) A calls B;
(2) B calls A and A returns a value to B that is used by B; or
(3) Both A and B are called by another module that passes a value from A to B.

Values of primitives are obtained by counting the data flow paths directed into and out of the modules.

fanin = lfi + datain
fanout = lfo + dataout.

The information flow complexity (IFC) is $IFC = (\text{fanin} \times \text{fanout})^2$.

Weighted IFC = length $\times$ (fanin $\times$ fanout)^2.

A25.4 Interpretation. A module with a high information flow complexity is assumed to be more likely to have faults than a module with a low complexity value.

Measurements taken during integration testing show possible areas for redesign or restructuring of excessively complex subsystems/modules, or where maintenance of a system might be difficult.

Procedure complexities show the following:

(1) Procedures that lack functionality (may have more than one function),

(2) Stress points in the system (high information traffic), or

(3) Excessive functional complexity of the subsystem/module.

A25.5 Considerations. Evaluation of procedural complexity is better suited for structured code. This measure generally is applied first during detailed design, and re-applied during integration to confirm the initial implementation. For large-scale systems, an automated procedure for determining data flow is essential.

A25.6 Training. Familiarity with data flow and complexity analysis and some experience in software design and development is required. A background in mathematics and statistics would aid in correlation studies.

A25.7 Example

Module A

Call Module B	1 fanout
Update global structure X	1 fanout
Read from file Y	1 fanin

End A

    fanin = 1,

    fanout = 2, therefore,

      $IFC = (1*2)**2 = 4$

A25.8 Benefits. Designers can aim toward a lower information flow complexity for reliable systems.

The complexity can be verified early in the design and again in the testing cycle, enabling changes before extensive testing has been conducted.

High information flow complexity indicates candidate modules and procedures for extensive testing or redesign. For failure correlation studies, associate the failure with a particular procedure/module.

A25.9 Experience. Limited experience is currently available [A83]. The use of this measure is being evaluated by a NASA/Goodard software group.

A25.10 References

[A80] BIEMAN, J. W., and EDWARDS, W. R. *Measuring Software Complexity.* Technical Report 83-5-1, Computer Science Department, University of Southwestern Louisiana, Feb 1983.

[A81] BIEMAN, J. W., and EDWARDS, W. R. *Measuring Data Dependency Complexity.* Technical Report 83-5-3, Computer Science Department, University of Southwestern Louisiana, Jul 1983.

[A82] BIEMAN, J. W., BAKER, A., CLITES, P. GUSTAFSON, D., and MILTON, A. A Standard Representation of Imperative Language Program for Data Collection and Software Measures Specification. *Journal of Systems and Software*, Dec 1987.

[A83] HENRY, S., and KAFURA, D. Software Structure Metrics Base on Information Flow. *IEEE Transactions on Software Engineering*, vol SE-7 (5), Sept 1981.

A26. Reliability Growth Function

A26.1 Application. This measure provides an estimate (or prediction) of the time or stage of testing when a desired failure rate or fault density goal will be acheived. It is an indicator of the level of success of fault correction.

A26.2 Primitives

NR_k = Total number of test cases during the kth stage

NS = Total number of stages

nc_k = Total number of successful test cases during the kth stage

A26.3 Implementation. Good record keeping of failure occurrences is needed to accurately document at which stage the failure occurred. Detailed failure analysis is required to determine whether a fault was inserted by previous correction efforts. This will be used to calculate the reinsertion rate of faults (r), which is the ratio of the number of faults reinserted to the total number of faults found.

A test-sequence of software is conducted in N stages (periods between changes to the software being tested). The reliability for the kth stage is:

$$R(k) = R(u) - A/k \qquad \text{(eq A26-1)}$$

where:

$$\lim_{k \to \infty} R(k) = R(u)$$

The unknown parameter A represents the growth parameter of the model. An $A > 0$ indicates the reliability is increasing as a function of the testing stage; an $A < 0$ indicates it is decreasing. The estimation of $R(u)$ and A is done using least-square estimates. The two equations used to derive the estimates are:

$$\sum_{k=1}^{NS} \left(\frac{nc_k}{NR_k} - R(u) + \frac{A}{k} \right) = 0 \qquad \text{(eq A26-2)}$$

$$\sum_{k=1}^{NS} \left(\frac{nc_k}{NR_k} - R(u) + \frac{A}{k} \right) \frac{1}{k} = 0 \qquad \text{(eq A26-3)}$$

The simultaneous solution of these two equations provides the estimates. If failure analysis was performed to determine a fault reinsertion rate (r); a third equation can be used in conjunction with (A26-2), and (A26-3) to estimate the fault insertion rate, r.

$$\sum_{k=1}^{NS} \left(\frac{nc_k}{NR_k} - R(u) + \frac{A}{k(1-r)} \right) \frac{1}{k(1-r)} = 0$$

$$\text{(eq A26-4)}$$

A26.4 Interpretation. A positive number (A) or essentially monotonic increasing function indicates positive reliability growth as well as a successful fault correction program. A negative number (A) or a monotonic decreasing function indicates reliability degradation as well as an unsuccessful fault correction program.

A26.5 Considerations. Some testing and accumulation of failure experience is necessary before a first estimate of the growth function can be made. Projecting growth when moving from one testing phase to the next will generally not be applicable unless the level of testing is comparable. Those models that use the success of test cases to project growth to some reliability goal are very dependent on the randomness of testing done and the completeness of coverage.

Determination of a significant rate of growth can be a statistically difficult task. Some models circumvent this by determining the distribution function of the parameter whose growth is being estimated. This reduces the problem to hypothesis testing [A89]. However, these models are generally more difficult to implement.

A26.6 Training. Some knowledge of software development and testing is necessary if models using test cases or the reinsertion rate of faults, r, are desired. Some statistical knowledge would aid in the interpretation of results for most models. The calculation involved in some of the models will require implementation on a digital computer.

A26.7 Example. A number of practical examples can be found in LaPadula [A88].

A26.8 Benefits. Once some initial testing experience is accumulated, this metric can be used throughout the testing phase and re-estimated as needed. Some models will estimate the distribution function of the parameter whose growth is being tracked. This often simplifies hypothesis testing to determine whether a specific goal has been achieved. Additionally, in some cases the time necessary to achieve a specific reliability goal can be calculated.

A26.9 Experience. See LaPadula [A88].

A26.10 References. See also Musa, Iannino, and Okumoto [A7].

[A84] DOWNS, T. Extensions to an Approach to the Modeling of Software Testing with Some Performance Comparisons. *IEEE Transactions on Software Engineering*, vol SE-12, no 9, Sept 1986.

[A85] DOWNS, T. An Approach to the Modeling of Software Testing With Some Applications. *IEEE Transactions on Software Engineering*, vol SE-11, 1985, pp 375–386.

[A86] GOEL, A. L., and OKUMOTA, K. *Baysian Software Prediction Models*. RADCTR-78-155 (5 vols), Jul 1978.

[A87] HECHT, H. *Measurement, Estimation and Prediction of Software Reliability*. NASA-CR-145135, Aerospace Corporation, Jan 1977.

[A88] LAPADULA, L. J. *Engineering of Quality Software Systems, Volume VIII: Software Reliability Modeling and Measurement Techniques*. RADC-TR-74-325, MITRE Corporation, Jan 1975.

[A89] LARSON, H. J. *Introduction to Probability Theory and Statistical Inference*. John Wiley & Sons, Inc, 1969.

[A90] LIPOW, M. *Some Variations of a Model for Software Time-to-Failure*. TRW Systems Group, Correspondence ML-74-2260.1.9.-21, Aug 1974.

[A91] LITTLEWOOD, B., and VERRALL, J. L. A Bayesian Reliability Model with a Stochastically Monotone Failure Rate. *IEEE Transactions on Reliability*, vol R-23, no 2, Jun 1974, pp 108–114.

A27. Residual Fault Count

A27.1 Application. This measure provides an indication of software integrity.

A27.2 Primitives

t_i = observed time between the ith and $(i-1)$st failure of a given severity level

f_i = number of failures during the ith time interval of a given severity level.

A27.3 Implementation.
The failure-rate class of models can be used to predict the remaining faults. This class of models is used to estimate the shape of a hypothesized hazard function from which an estimate of the number of remaining faults can be obtained [A96].

A27.4 Interpretation.
Ideally, the software failure rate is constant between failures. Where inter-failure times are not independent, a non-homogeneous Poisson-type model for failure count data may be used to predict the number of remaining faults [A96]. This measure is the parameter of the Poisson distribution describing the number of failures if testing is continued.

A27.5 Considerations.
Assumptions for this class of models should be verified in order to select an appropriate model to fit the data. The appropriateness of the measure depends upon the validity of the selected model. Among the most common assumptions are the following:

- Failure rate is generally decreasing.
- The numbers of failures in non-overlapping time intervals are independent and distributed exponentially with different failure rates. However, for the non-homogeneous Poisson type process, the model utilizing failure count data assumes that the number of errors has independent increments even though the times between failures are not independent.
- No two failures occur simultaneously.
- The instantaneous failure rate of software is proportional to the number of errors remaining, each of which is equally likely to cause the next failure.

A27.6 Training.
The implementation of this measure requires an understanding of probability theory and numerical analysis techniques.

A27.7 Example.
A numerical example using a set of failure times to compute the number of remaining faults with the Jelinski-Moranda "Deeutrophication" and non-homogeneous Poisson process type models are compared in [A96].

A27.8 Benefits.
The conditional distribution of remaining faults, given a number of known faults, can be used for deciding whether the software is acceptable for release [A92].

A27.9 Experience.
A case study showing an actual analysis of failure data from a Space Shuttle Software project using a non-homogeneous Poisson type process is shown in [A95]. The reference illustrates the number of failures during the mission and subsequent verification of these projections using this measure. Experience with this measure can be found also in [A97].

A27.10 References.
See also Musa, Iannino, and Okumoto [A7].

[A92] GOEL, A. L., and OKUMOTO, K. Time-Dependent Error-Detection Rate Model for Software Performance Assessment with Applications. *Annual Technical Report*, Contract Number F30602-78-C-0351, Rome Air Development Center, Griffis Air Force Base, Mar 1980.

[A93] JEWELL, W. S. *Bayesian Estimation of Undetected Errors*. Oper Res Center, University of California at Berkeley, Rep ORC 83-11.

[A94] JEWELL, W. S. Bayesian Extension to a Basic Model of Software Reliability. *IEEE Transactions on Software Engineering*, vol SE-11, no 12, Dec 1985.

[A95] MISRA, P. N. Software Reliability Analysis. IBM Systems Journal, vol 22, no 3, 1983.

[A96] *Software Reliability Modelling and Estimation Technique*. RADC-TR-82-263 Final Technical Report, Oct 1982.

[A97] SRIVASTAVA, V. K., and FARR, W. The Use of Software Reliability Models in the Analysis of Operational Systems. *1986 Proceedings of the Institute of Environmental Sciences*, 32nd Annual Technical Meeting, Dallas/Fort Worth, 1986.

A28. Failure Analysis Using Elapsed Time

A28.1 Applications.
This measure can be used to determine reliability growth based on the estimated number of remaining faults and software reliability. It can be used to:

- predict the total number of faults in the software
- predict the software reliability
- estimate required testing time for reliability goal
- estimate required resource allocation

A28.2 Primitives

t_i = Observed time between failures of a given severity level (eg, execution time).

A28.3 Implementation.
Observed failures should be recorded and the associated faults identified. The time between failures (CPU or other unit which represents actual execution time of the software) should also be recorded.

Using the maximum likelihood estimation, the method of least squares, or the Newton-Raphson optimizing scheme, the parameters and normalizing constants of candidate models can be estimated. These can be interpreted as initial fault content (N_o), normalizing constants, and initial mean time to failure (M_o) based on the model selected. Once a model has been successfully fitted to the data using any of the well-known statistical tests (eg, goodness-of-fit), then the model can be used to estimate the remaining faults (N), MTTF (M), and reliability (R).

A28.4 Interpretation.
Based on the confidence in the determination of total faults, MTTF, and reliability, decisions can be made on the need for additional testing. The testing time required to reach a specified reliability can be determined and evaluated in terms of resources required to reach the goal. Resources include testing personnel, debugging personnel and available computer time.

A28.5 Considerations.
Failures must be observed and recorded to improve reliability and obtain statistically valid results. The test coverage must be random and comprehensive, and the goodness-of-fit tests should be applied to determine the validity of the selected model. Failure analysis is required to determine severity and class of failures.

A28.6 Training.
A background in software testing procedures is needed to perform the necessary failure analysis. The model, including the assumptions and limitations, used to determine initial values and parameters must be understood. A program to perform parameters estimation must be developed, or obtained from the author of the model if it is available.

A28.7 Example.
There are many examples available in the listed references [A99, A57].

A28.8 Benefits.
This measure can be re-used throughout test and operation phases to provide continuing assessment of the quality of the software.

A28.9 Experience.
Extensive experience has been accumulated on the applicaiton of the Musa Model [A102]. The performance of various models are reported in [A97].

A28.10 References.
See also Musa, Iannino, and Okumoto [A7] and Farr [A59].

[A98] ANGUS, J. E. The Application of Software Reliability Models to a Major C3I System. *1984 Proceedings of the Annual Reliability and Maintainability Symposium*, Jan 1984, pp 268–274.

[A99] GOEL, A. L., and OKUMOTA, K. Time Dependent Error Detection Model for Software Reliability and Other Performance Measures. *IEEE Transactions on Reliability*, vol R-28, no 3, 1979, pp 206–211.

[A100] JELINSKI, Z. and MORANDA, P. B. Software Reliability Research. In *Statistical Computer Performance Evaluation*, W. Frieberger, ed, New York: Academic Press, 1972, pp 465–484.

[A101] MORANDA, P. B. An Error Detection Model for Application During Software Development. *IEEE Transactions on Reliability*, vol R-30, no 4, 1981, pp 309–312.

[A102] MUSA, J. D. The Measurement and Management of Software Reliability. *Proceedings of the IEEE*, vol 68, no 9, 1980, pp 1131–1143.

[A103] MUSA, J. D. and IANNINO, A. Software Reliability Modeling: Accounting for Program Size Variation Due to Integration or Design Changes. *ACM SIGMETRICS Performance Evaluation Review*, 10(2), 1981, pp 16–25.

[A104] ROSS, M. Software Reliability: The Stopping Rule. *IEEE Transactions on Software Engineering*, vol SE-11, no 12, Dec 1985, pp 1472–1476.

[A105] SUKERT, A. N. An Investigation of Software Reliability Models. *1977 Proceedings of the Annual Reliability and Maintainability Symposium*, Philidelphia, 1977.

A29. Testing Sufficiency

A29.1 Application.
This measure assesses the sufficiency of software-to-software integration testing by comparing actual to predicted faults.

A29.2 Primitives

NF = Total number of faults predicted in the software

F_{it} = Total number of faults detected to date in software integration testing

F_{pit} = Number of faults detected prior to software integration testing

M_{it} = Number of modules integrated

M_{tot} = Total number of modules in final configuration

A29.3 Implementation.

The fault density ($M1$) should be used to calculate the estimated total number of faults (NF) in the software. The number of faults remaining in the integrated portion of the software can then be estimated using the following equation:

$$NF_{rem} = (NF - F_{pit})\, M_{it}/M_{tot}$$

Maximum and minimum tolerance coefficients (l_1 and l_1) should be established based on user experience. Values of 0.5 and 1.5 are suggested for use as the default values.

The guidelines given in Table A29.3-1 assume that all scheduled integration tests have been run.

A29.4 Interpretation.

The interpretation of testing sufficiency is given in Table A29.3-1 under "Recommended Action" and "Comments."

A29.5 Considerations.

The total predicted faults (NF) should be calculated using either micro quantitative software reliability models [A108] based on path structure, or Halstead's software science measures [A106, A107] based on operators and operands. The usefulness of this measure hinges on the accuracy of the prediction of NF.

The measure assumes faults are evenly distributed between modules. Due to this assumption, caution should be exercised in applying it during early stages of integration testing (eg, less than 10% of modules integrated). Tolerance coefficients (l_1 and l_2) may be tailored to support the user's tolerance experience. Examples of experience factors are the degree of software reliability desired, and historical accuracy of the fault prediction measure used.

A29.6 Training.

Some mathematical and software development background is necessary to predict total faults and to determine testing sufficiency tolerance coefficients.

A29.7 Example.

Assume that 30 modules of a 100-module system are integrated for software-to-software testing. Prior to integration testing, 20 faults of a total predicted fault count of 150 were discovered. During the initial stage of integration testing, 27 more faults were discovered. The standard min/max tolerance coefficients of l_1 = 0.5 and l_2 = 1.5 were selected. Then:

$$\hat{NF}_{rem} = (150 - 20) \times (30)/100 = 39$$
$$l_1\hat{NF}_{rem} = 0.5(39) = 19.5$$
$$l_2\hat{NF}_{rem} = 1.5(39) = 58.5$$
$$F_{it} = 27$$

Therefore, the recommended action is to proceed with integration testing or the next stage of testing since 19.5<27<58.5.

A.29.8 Benefits.

The measure is relatively simple to apply, and provides an early indication of testing sufficiency.

A29.9 Experience.

No published experience is available.

A29.10 References

[A106] HALSTEAD, M. H. *Elements of Software Science.* Operating and Programming Systems

Table A29.3-1
Testing Sufficiency

Measure Result	Interpretation	Recommended Action	Comments
$l_1 NS_{rem} < F_{it} < l_2 N_{rem}$	Testing sufficiency is adequate	Proceed	—
$F_{it} > l_2 NF_{rem}$	Detected more faults than expected	Proceed, but apply fault density measure for each integrated module. Re-calculate NF.	Error-ridden modules may exist that should be replaced by a redesigned module.
$F_{it} < l_1 NF_{rem}$	Detected fewer faults than expected	Apply test coverage measure (see A24) before proceeding	May not have designed adequate number or variety of tests

Series, P. J. Denning, ed, New York: Elsevier North Holland, 1977, pp 84-91.

[A107] NASA-GODDARD, *Fortran Static Source Code Analyzer Program (SAP) User Guide (Revision 1)*, Sept 1982, pp 3-31.

[A108] SHOOMAN, M. L. *Software Engineering Design/Reliability/Management.* New York: McGraw Hill, 1983, chap 5.

A30. Mean Time to Failure

A30.1 Application. This measure is used for hypothesis testing a specified MTTF requirement.

A30.2 Primitives. Mean time to failure is the basic parameter required by most software reliability modules. Computation is dependent on accurate recording of failure time (t_i), where t_i is the elapsed time between the ith and the ($i-1$)st failure. Time units used should be as precise as feasible. CPU execution time provides more resolution than wall-clock time. Thus, CPU cycles would be more appropriate for a software development environment. For an operational environment, which might require less resolution, an estimate based on wall-clock time could be used.

A30.3 Implementation. Detailed record keeping of failure occurrences that accurately track the time (calendar or execution) at which the faults manifest themselves is essential. If weighting or organizing the failures by complexity, severity or the reinsertion rate is desired, detailed failure analysis must be performed to determine the severity and complexity. Prior failure experience or model fitting analysis (eg, goodness-of-fit test) can be used to select a model representative of a failure process, and to determine a reinsertion rate of faults.

A30.4 Interpretation. This measure gives an estimate of the mean time to the next failure. A high value implies good reliability and availability of the software. This must be balanced against severity and complexity, if such weights are used.

A30.5 Considerations. The calculation of the mean of the time-to-failure distribution is dependent upon the analytical form of the failure distribution. This, in turn, is dependent upon the underlying assumptions of the failure process.

The number, description, and weights of the levels of severity and complexity should be established prior to data gathering if these factors are to be considered. Techniques for validating statements of complexity and severity should be established. Test planning must emulate operational experience.

A30.6 Training. Depending upon the number of assumptions placed on the failure process and the extent to which severity and complexity weighting is desired, the user's basic knowledge may range from little or no background in mathematics and software development to a need for extensive background in both. The simplest models are easy to implement and apply. Those that attempt to account for input space, human factors, or imperfect debugging or all three require detailed data gathering and rigorous analysis. The references (A30.10) describe various techniques, including the relevant assumptions regarding the failure processes, for some or the more sophisticated approaches.

Training requirements depend upon the type of model used. In data gathering, some background in software development would be necessary to maximize the information obtained from failure analysis. An elementary background in mathematics and reliability theory would promote better interpretation of the results, but is not essential unless assumptions require use of a complex model. The calculation for most models will require implementation on a digital computer.

A30.7 Example. A simple estimate of the MTTF is illustrated. Through prior test exerience and analysis, the user assumes a constant failure rate, with no further correction of faults to be performed. Three levels of severity failure classes are considered. Suppose the levels are labeled SF_1, SF_2, and SF_3 respectively. Every failure is then assigned to one of the classes with the respective time between failure recorded within that class. Suppose the following data is recorded:

SF_1: 180, 675, 315, 212, 278, 503, 431
SF_2: 477, 1048, 685, 396
SF_3: 894, 1422

Then a simple estimate of the mean time to failure is

$$\text{MTTF} = \sum_{k=1}^{i} \frac{t_k}{i} \quad \text{for each class,}$$

where

t_k = time between failures

and

i = number of failures in the respective severity class. The calculated estimates are:

$$\text{MTTF}_{SF_1} = \frac{2594}{7} = 370.57,$$

$$\text{MTTF}_{SF_2} = \frac{2606}{4} = 651.5,$$

$$\text{MTTF}_{SF_3} = \frac{2316}{2} = 1158$$

These values may be compared against some specified MTTF for each severity class, by any of a number of statistical techniques.

Since the data confirms the existence of a constant failure rate, the failure distribution can be assumed to be exponential; ie, $F(t) = 1\text{-exp}(-t/\text{MTTF})$, which is the probability of failure of the software within time t.

A30.8 Benefits. This measure can be used throughout the testing and operational phase of the software, as long as data gathering efforts are maintained. A number of hardware statistical techniques are based on this measure and, if the justification for similar failure processes in the software exists, extensive modeling is available.

A30.9 Experience. Significant experience with this measure has been documented in several reports [A57, A86, A111]. The reader is cautioned to utilize the assumptions required for the various models.

A30.10 References. See also Musa, Iannino, and Okumoto [A7]; Musa [A57]; Farr [A59]; and Goel and Okumoto [A86].

[A109] CURRIT, P. A., DYER, M., and MILLS, H. D. Certifying the Reliability of Software. *IEEE Transactions on Software Reliability*, vol SE-12, no 1, Jan 1986, pp 3-11.

[A110] MUSA, J. D., and OKUMOTO, K. A. Logarithmic Poisson Execution Time Model for Software Reliability Measurement. *Proceedings of the 7th International Conference on Software Engineering*, 1984, pp 230-238.

[A111] RUSHFORTH, C., STAFFANSON, F., and CRAWFORD, A. Software Reliability Estimation Under Conditions of Incomplete Information, University of Utah, RADC-TR-230, Oct 1979.

[A112] SHOOMAN, M. L., and TRIVEDI, A. K. A Many-State Markov Model for Computer Software Performance Parameters. *IEEE Transactions on Reliability*, vol R-25, no 2, Jun 1976, pp 66-68.

[A113] SUKERT, A. N., *A Software Reliability Modeling Study*. RADC-TR-76-247, Aug 1976.

[A114] WAGONER, W. L. *The Final Report on Software Reliability Measurement Study*. Aerospace Corporation, Report Number TOR-0074 (4112), Aug 1973.

A31. Failure Rate

A31.1 Application. This measure can be used to indicate the growth in the software reliability as a function of test time.

A31.2 Primitives

t_i = Observed times between failures (eg, execution time) for a given severity level, $i=1,\ldots$

f_i = number of failures of a given severity level in the ith time interval

A31.3 Implementation. The failure rate $\lambda(t)$ at any point in time can be estimated from the reliability function, $R(t)$ which in turn can be obtained from the cumulative probability distribution, $F(t)$, of the time until the next failure using any of the software reliability growth models such as the non-homogeneous Poisson process (NHPP) [A99] or a Bayesian type model [A55, A115]. The failure rate is

$$\lambda(t) = -\frac{1}{R(t)}\left[\frac{dR(t)}{dt}\right] \qquad \text{(eq A31-1)}$$

where $R(t) = 1 - F(t)$.

A31.4 Interpretation. The failure rate $\lambda(t)$ obtained from NHPP depends only upon time t and decreases continuously. However, $\lambda(t)$ derived from Littlewood's reliability growth model depends both upon time t and the value growth function, $\psi(i)$ at the ith failure. By requiring the function $\psi(i)$ to be increasing, the condition

$$\lambda(t_i) \leq \lambda(t_{i-1})$$

is met in a probabilistic sense, ie, the programmer may introduce new errors while correcting an error.

A31.5 Considerations. The underlying assumptions for the NHPP model are the following:

(1) Equal probability of exposure of each fault.
(2) The fault count type NHPP Model assumes that the number of failures detected during the non-overlapping intervals, f_i, are independent.
(3) The time between failure type NHPP model assumes that the time between the $(i-1)$st and ith failures depends upon time to the $(i-1)$st failure.

The underlying assumptions for Bayesian reliability growth model are as follows:

(1) Successive execution time between failures with different failure rates are independently exponentially distributed

ie, $pdf(t_i | \lambda_i) = \lambda_i \exp(-\lambda_i t_i)$

(2) In the Littlewood-Verrall model [A115] the successive failure rate forms a sequence of independent random variables $\{\lambda_i\}$ with gamma distribution with parameters α and $\psi(i)$

ie, $pdf(\lambda_i | \alpha, \psi(i)) =$

$$\frac{[\psi(i)]^\alpha \lambda_i^{\alpha-1} \exp(-\psi(i)\lambda_i)}{\Gamma(\alpha)}$$

(3) The failure rate is statistically decreasing.
(4) In the Littlewood stochastic reliability growth model [A55], the failure rate of the program after removal of i errors is:

$$\lambda = \lambda_1 + \lambda_2 + \dots \lambda_{NF-i}$$

where

NF = total number of faults in the program prior to testing and $\lambda_1 \dots \lambda_{NF-i}$ are $i.i.d.$ (identically independently distributed) and each has a gamma pdf.

A31.6 Training. The development computer programs needed to compute this measure require an understanding of stochastic processes and familiarity with numerical analysis and optimization techniques.

A31.7 Examples. A practical application for both NHPP and Littlewood-Verrall reliability growth models for obtaining the measure of software failure rate is shown in the following examples.

In Misra [A95] a fitted mean value function is obtained for the data collected by testing space shuttle flight software consisting of over .5 million lines of source code. After 38 wk of testing (2454.7 cumulative hrs) the following estimate of the parameters of the NHPP model for the major error category were calculated:

"a" = 163.813   "b" = 0.28759 * 10^-3

The failure rate decrease is described by

$$\lambda(t) = ab \exp\left\{-b\left(\sum_{i=1}^{n} t_i + t\right)\right\}$$

$$\text{for } \sum_{i=1}^{n} t_i < t \qquad \text{(eq A31-2)}$$

In [A115] the probability distribution function of the ith failure rate $\{\lambda_i\}$ is assumed to be gamma (g) with parameters α and $\psi(i)$, then

$$R(t) = \int_0^\infty e^{-\lambda_i t} g(\lambda_i | \alpha, \psi(i)) d\lambda_i \qquad \text{(eq A31-3)}$$

and the failure rate after the ith failure is now obtained by using equation A31-1 and is given by

$$\lambda(t) = \frac{\alpha}{t + \psi(i)}, \quad t_i \leq t \leq t_{i+1} \qquad \text{(eq A31-4)}$$

Littlewood has examined the data set of 136 execution times reported by Musa [A57] to predict the future times to failure using a linear form of $\psi(i)$:

$$\psi(i) = \beta_1 + \beta_2 i \qquad \text{(eq A31-5)}$$

The parameters α, β_1 and β_2 obtained using maximum likelihood methods [A115] based upon the first 35 observations are:

$\alpha = 1.51890; \quad \beta_1 = -0.9956 \text{ and } \beta_2 = 7.8342$

The failure rate after the ith failure can be computed by substituting the value of the parameters α and $\psi(i)$ in equation A31-4.

$$\hat{\lambda}(t) = \frac{1.5189}{t - .9956 + 7.8342i}, \qquad \text{(eq A31-6)}$$

$$t_i \leq t \leq t_{i+1} (i=1, \dots 136)$$

A31.8 Benefits. The stepwise decrease in the failure rate at each incidence of a failure model can be used to show the improvement in software reliabiilty as a result of operational usage and can also be used to estimate the test time needed to reach target reliability.

A31.9 Experience. Experience with the use of this measure is provided by Misra [A95].

A31.10 References. See also Downs [A84, A85]; Goel and Okumoto [A54]; Littlewood [A55]; Misra [A95]; and Musa [A7, A57].

[A115] LITTLEWOOD, B. Theories of Software Reliability: How Good Are They and How Can

They Be Improved? *IEEE Transactions on Software Engineering*, vol 6, no 5, 1980, pp 489–500.

[A116] MILLER, D. R. Exponential Order Statistic Models of Software Reliability Growth. *IEEE Transactions on Software Engineering*, vol SE-12, no 1, Jan 1986.

[A117] OKUMOTO, K. A Statistical Method for Quality Control. *IEEE Transactions on Software Engineering*, vol SE-11, no 12, Dec 1985, pp 1424–1430.

[A118] SINGPURWALLA, N., and SOYER, R. Assessing (Software) Reliability Growth Using a Random Coefficient Autoregressive Process and Its Ramifications. *IEEE Transactions on Software Engineering*, vol SE-11, no 12, Dec 1985, pp 1456–1463.

[A119] YAMADA, S., and OSAKI, S. Software Reliability Growth Modeling: Models and Applications. *IEEE Transactions on Software Engineering*, vol SE-11, no 12, Dec 1985, pp 1431–1437.

A32. Software Documentation and Source Listings

A32.1 Application. The primary objective of this measure is to collect information to identify the parts of the software maintenance products that may be inadequate for use in a software maintenance environment. Two questionnaires are used to examine the format and content of the documentation and source code attributes from a maintainability perspective.

A32.2 Primitives. The questionnaires examine the following primitive product characteristics:
(1) modularity
(2) descriptiveness
(3) consistency
(4) simplicity
(5) expandability
(6) testability.
Sub-characteristics include format, interface, math models, and data/control.

A32.3 Implementation. Two questionnaires; Software Documentation Questionnaire and the Software Source Listing Questionnaire, are used to evaluate the software products in a desk audit. The questionnaires are contained in *Software Maintainability—Evaluation Guide* [A120].

For the software documentation evaluation, the resource documents should include those that contain program design specifications, program testing information and procedures, program maintenance information, and guidelines used in preparation of the documentation. These documents may have a variety of physical organizations depending upon the particular source, application, and documentation requirements. The documentation will, in general, consist of all documents that reveal the software design and implementation. A single evaluation of all the documents is done. Typical questions from the software Documentation Questionnaire include the following:

- The documentation indicates that data storage locations are not used for more than one type of data structure.
- Parameter inputs and outputs for each module are explained in the documentation.
- Programming conventions for *I/O* processing have been established and followed.
- The documentation indicates that resource (storage, timing, tape drives, disks, consoles, etc.) allocation is fixed throughout program execution.
- The documentation indicates that there is a reasonable time margin for each major time-critical program function (rate group, time slice, priority level, etc.).
- The documentation indicates that the program has been designed to accommodate software test probes to aid in identifying processing performance.

For the software source listings evaluation, the program source code is evaluated. The source code may be either a high order language or assembler. Multiple evaluations using the questionnaire are conducted for the unit (module) level of the program. The units (modules) selected should represent a sample size of at least 10% of the total source code. Typical questions from the Source Listing Questionnaire include the following:

- Each function of this module is an easily recognizable block of code.
- The quantity of comments does not detract from the legibility of the source listing.
- Mathematical models as described/derived in the documentation correspond to the mathematical equations used in the modules source listing.
- Esoteric (clever) programming is avoided in this module.
- The size of any data structure that affects the processing logic of this module is parameterized.

- Intermediate results within this module can be selectively collected for display without code modification.

A32.4 Interpretation. The average scores across evaluators, test factors, product categories, and programs are used to develop a relative degree of confidence in the software documentation and the source code.

A32.5 Considerations. The software source listings and documentation evaluation assumptions are as follows:

(1) Software source listing and documentation considerations are essentially independent of application and implementation language.

(2) The evaluators must be knowledgeable in software maintenance, but do not necessarily require detailed knowledge about the specific application software.

(3) At least five independent evaluators (with software maintenance experience) must be used to provide a 75% confidence that the resulting scores indicate the actural condition of the documentation and source listing.

(4) The software source listings selected for evaluation may be from any unit level of the program that would provide conclusions that hold for the general population of the program.

A32.6 Training. Prior to an evaluation, the evaluators must participate in a calibration exercise by completing each of the questionnaires on a sample software product. This exercise is to ensure a reliable evaluation through a clear understanding of the questions and their specific response guidelines on each questionnaire. The completed questionnaires are reviewed by the evaluator group to detect and resolve areas of misunderstanding.

A32.7 Example. Table A32.7-1 demonstrates the results of an evaluation. The questionnaires employ a six-point response scale where 6 is the highest possible score (completely agree), and 1 is the lowest subjective rating (completely disagree). The bracketed score indicates that for the documentation, the instrumentation test factor (how well the program has been designed to include test aids) scored below the minimum acceptable threshold criteria.

Table A32.7-1
Example Results of a Source Listing and Documentation Evaluation

Test Factor	Documentation	Source Listings
Modularity	4.3	5.3
Descriptiveness	3.9	4.5
Consistency	4.8	5.0
Simplicity	4.7	5.3
Expandability	4.5	5.1
Instrumentation	(3.0)	4.5
Weighted Score	4.3	5.0
Combined Score	4.7	

A32.8 Benefits. The application of the questionnaires provides an identification of potential problems in the software documentation and source listings that may affect the maintainability of the software.

A32.9 Experience. The evaluation is consistently used during operational test and evaluation for most Air Force systems.

A.32.10 References

[A120] *Software Maintainability Evaluators Guide.* AFOTEC Pamphlet 800-2, vol 3, no 2, Mar 1987.[4]

[A121] PEERCY, D. A Software Maintainability Evaluation Methodology. *IEEE Transactions on Software Engineering*, no 4, Jul 1981.

A33. RELY — Required Software Reliability

A33.1 Application. At the early planning phases of a project, RELY provides a measure that makes visible the tradeoffs of cost and degree of reliability. It is recognized that reliability may vary relative to the system purpose. Man-rated software in space applications, for example, has higher reliability requirements than game software. The development processes for high reliability software, especially integration and test, should correspondingly be greater than that of average software.

A33.2 Primitives. Required reliability ratings are as follows:[5]

---

[4] This guide can be obtained from the Air Force Operational Test and Evaluation Center (AFOTEC/DAP), Kirtland Air Force Base, NM 87117-7001.

[5] Definition of primitives and figures from Boehm [A122], reprinted by permission.

Very low. The effect of a software failure is simply the inconvenience incumbent on the developers to fix the fault. Typical examples are a demonstration prototype of a voice typewriter or an early feasibility phase software simulation model.

Low. The effect of a software failure is a low level, easily-recoverable loss to users. Typical examples are a long-range planning model or a climate forecasting model.

Nominal. The effect of a software failure is a modereate loss to users, but a situation from which one can recover without extreme penalty. Typical examples are management information systems or inventory control systems.

High. The effect of a software failure can be a major financial loss or a massive human inconvenience. Typical examples are banking systems and electric power distribution systems.

Very high. The effect of a software failure can be the loss of human life. Examples are military command and control systems or nuclear reactor control systems.

A33.3 Implementation. Depending on the required rating, the effort required for each phase of the development cycle can be adjusted to include the processes necessary to ensure that the product achieves the reliability goal. Figure A33.3-1 shows the effort factors relative to nominal necessary to achieve each of the required reliability ratings.

This technique can be used conversely to provide a reliability rating for a product through examination of the processes used to develop it (see Table A33.3-1).

A33.4 Interpretation. Differences in required reliability effort factors are relatively small for development phases prior to, and including, code unit test. The major factor difference is in the integration and test phases. The added requirements of operational and stress testing can make a 70% difference from the nominal.

A33.5 Considerations. These effort factors were developed empirically to reflect development processes used in the 1970 timeframe. They should be updated where the data exists to reflect local development processes including the productivity benefits of tools.

A33.6 Training Required. No special training is required.

Fig A33.3-1
Effort Multipliers by Phase: Required Software Reliability

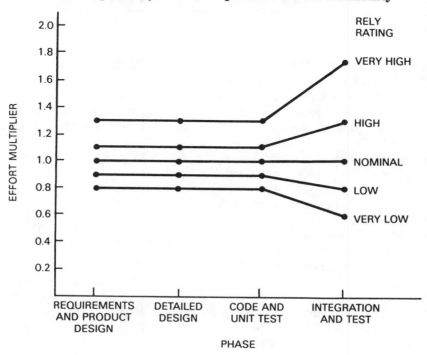

Table A33.3-1
Projected Activity Differences Due to Required Software Reliability

Rating	Requirements and Product Design	Detailed Design	Code and Unit Test	Integration and Test
Very low	Little detail Many TBDs Little verification Minimal quality assurance (QA), configuration management (CM) draft user manual, test plans Minimal program design review (PDR)	Basic design information Minimum QA, CM, draft user manual, test plans Informal design inspections	No test procedures Minimal path test, standards check Minimal QA, CM Minimal I/O and off-nominal tests Minimal user manual	No test procedures Many requirements untested Minimal QA, CM Minimal stress, off-nominal tests Minimal as-built documentation
Low	Basic information, verification Frequent TBDs Basic QA, CM, standards, draft user manual, test plans	Moderate detail Basic QA, CM, draft user manual, test plans	Minimal test procedures Partial path test, standards check Basic QA, CM, user manual Partial I/O and off-nominal tests	Minimal test procedures Frequent requirements untested Basic QA, CM, user manual Partial stress off-nominal tests
Nominal	Nominal project V & V	—	—	—
High	Detailed verification, QA, CM, standards, PDR, documentation Detailed test plans, procedures	Detailed verification, QA, CM, standards, CDR, documentation Detailed test plans, procedures	Detailed test procedures, QA, CM, documentation Extensive off-nominal tests	Detailed test procedures, QA, CM, documentation Extensive stress, off-nominal tests
Very high	Detailed verification, QA, CM, standards, PDR, documentation IV & V interface Very detailed test plans, procedures	Detailed verification, QA, CM, standards, CDR, documentation Very thorough design inspections Very detailed test plans, procedures IV & V interface	Detailed test procedures, QA, CM, documentation Very thorough code inspections Very extensive off-nominal tests IV & V interface	Very detailed test procedures, QA, CM, documentation Very extensive stress, off-nominal tests IV & V interface

A33.7 Examples. The effect of failures in an airplane control system can be the loss of human life. Hence the reliability should be specified as "Very High." To obtain this, each phase should have detailed documentation, quality assurance, adherence to standards, and verificaiton. There should be very detailed test plans and procedures, including independent verification and validation.

Suppose, however, that the Statement of Work and level of funding called for (or allowed) only basic verification, QA, draft user manuals and test plans with minimal testing. From examining Table A33.3-1, it can be seen that this corresponds to low reliability.

A33.8 Benefits. This rating is important to apply as soon as sufficient specificaiton detail is available, to justify using the intermediate level COCOMO Model for projecting costs for the software development. The ratings are consistent with a very high-level failure effects analysis and are an important input to costing and, therefore, cost-benefit tradeoffs at the earliest level.

A33.9 Experience. Experience is somewhat limited.

A33.10 References

[A122] BOEHM, B. *Software Engineering Economics.* Englewood Cliffs: Prentice-Hall, 1981, pp 374–376.

[A123] LIPOW, M. Quantitative Demonstration and Cost Consideration of a Software Fault Removal Methodology. *Journal Quality and Reliability Engineering International*, vol 1, 1985, pp 27–35.

A34. Software Release Readiness

A34.1 Application. This measure is used to quantify the user and support (consumer) risk of ownership, based on either quantitative or subjective assessments of user and support issues. Given a number of issues, one can combine them to obtain a composite risk assessment. Although the primitives described here are designed for the operation and maintenance phase, the risk assessment method is applicable during any phase of the lifecycle by the identification of appropriate issues and the selection or design of corresponding measures for assessment.

A34.2 Primitives. The measurements of effectiveness, $ME(i)$, $i=1, ..., I$, for issues relating to software risk assessment. Example issues are:
- Functional test coverage
- Software maturity
- Software source code listings quality factors
- Documentation quality factors
- Software operator–machine interface
- Software support resources assessments

A34.3 Implementation. This measure assumes that I issues can be combined to assess the readiness of software for release and the attendant consumer risk. For each issue i the measure $ME(i)$ is converted into an associated risk $RK(i)$ as it relates to the user and supporter. This risk is subjectively assigned by the evaluators and is defined to be in the range of 0 to 1.0, where zero denotes no risk and one denotes extreme risk. For the functional test coverage, maturity, and quality factor primitives, the associated risk is determined by:

$$RK(i) = 1.0 - ME(i)$$

Further, each of the primitives $ME(i)$ is assigned a subjective, relative weight that represents its importance to the user (supporter). For each $ME(i)$ value, there is a corresponding $RK(i)$ risk and a $W(i)$ relative importance weight. All the relative weights $W(i)$ for all user (supporter) measures sum to 1.0. Further, there is an influence matrix $[S]$ that provides a modification factor to the risk $RK(i)$ when a measure $ME(i)$ is influenced by another measure $ME(j)$. For example, consider the influence between software maturity (the fraction of software modified and added during a test [see A4.10]) and functional test coverage (the fraction of code demonstrated during a test [see A4.5]). It is clear that incomplete testing would reduce the confidence in the resulting maturity score because of incomplete

demonstration of the software functions. The influence matrix $S(i,j)$ coefficients are assigned values that are representative of the dependence between $ME(i)$ and $ME(j)$.

The following steps are used in calculating this measure:
(1) Evaluate each primitive $ME(i)$.
(2) Assign a risk value $RK(i)$ to the $ME(i)$ measure such that $RK(i)$ is between zero and one (eg, $RK(i) = 1.0 - ME(i)$.)

Or, for subjective assessments, note the following:

low risk = 0.0 to 33
medium risk = .34 to .66
high risk = .67 to 1.0

(3) For each measure $ME(i)$, determine the weighting $W(i)$ that reflects the importance of the measure to the total user (supporter). A suggested default value is $1/I$ giving equal weight to all issues.
(4) For each pair of measures $ME(i)$ and $ME(j)$, assign a value for the $S(i,j)$ influence coefficient that represents the subjective or quantified influence between the measures. The $S(i,j)$ coefficients vary between zero and one, with zero representing no influence (low correlation), and one representing high dependence (high correlation). Coefficient $S(i,j)$ is the measured or subjective value of measure $ME(i)$'s dependence on measure $ME(j)$. Usually matrix [S] is symmetric.

Let the apportioned risk $RK'(i)$ for measure i in relation to the other measures be:

$$RK'(i) = \frac{\sum_{j=1}^{I} RK(j) \times S(i,j)}{\sum_{j=1}^{I} S(i,j)}$$

Then combined user (supporter) risk is:

$$R_{(User/Supporter)} = \sum_{i=1}^{I} RK'(i) \times W(i)$$

A34.4 Interpretation. The value R(user) or R(supporter) is a cumulative measure of either user or supporter risk that can be compared against a predefined rating scale for reporting.

A34.5 Considerations. The quantities for $W(i)$, $S(i,j)$, and some values of $ME(i)$ are subjectively determined. It is important that the acceptance criteria be kept firmly in mind when these values

Table A34.7-1
Primitive Scores and Weighting

Measure	Measurement				Weighting $W(i)$	
	Range	Score	$ME(i)$	$RK(i)$	User $W(U)$	Supporter $W(S)$
Test coverage: $ME(1)$	0–1	0.6	0.6	0.4	0.5	0.0
Maturity index: $ME(2)$	0–1	0.83	0.83	0.17	0.5	0.0
Source listings: $ME(3)$	0–6	5.0	0.83	0.17	0.0	0.5
Documentation: $ME(4)$	0–6	4.3	0.72	0.28	0.0	0.5

Table A34.7-2
Influence Matrix (S)

User Influence Matrix			Supporter Influence Matrix		
User Primitives: $ME(1)$, $ME(2)$			Supporter Primitives: $ME(3)$, $ME(4)$		
	$ME(1)$	$ME(2)$		$ME(3)$	$ME(4)$
$ME(1)$	1	0.6	$ME(3)$	1	1
$ME(2)$	0.6	1	$ME(4)$	1	1

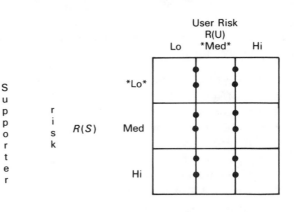

Fig A34.7-1

are established. The subjectively determined rating scale should be determined before the evaluation to avoid prejudicing the results.

A34.6 Training. Training in the evaluation/ assessment of relative weights for different quality factors and for sensitivity coefficients is required, together with an understanding of the reciprocal influence of quality factors.

A34.7 Examples. Assume the primitive data values given in Table A34.7-1 are determined during testing:

Combining $ME(1)$ and $ME(2)$ for the user and $ME(3)$ and $ME(4)$ for the supporter, the influence matrices can be defined as shown in Table A34.7-2.

The above influence matrices result in the following confidence modifiers:

For the user combining $ME(1)$ and $ME(2)$,

$$RK'(1) = ((0.4*1.0) + (0.7*0.6))/1.6 = 0.31$$
$$RK'(2) = ((0.4*0.6) + (0.17*1.0))/1.6 = 0.25$$

For the supporter combining $ME(3)$ and $ME(4)$,

$$RK'(3) = ((0.17*1.0) + (0.28*1.0))/2.0 = 0.23$$
$$RK'(4) = ((0.17*1.0) + (0.28*5.0))/2.0 = 0.23$$

Calculating the user $R(U)$ and Supporter $R(S)$ risks,

$$R(U) = (0.31*0.5) + (0.25*0.5) = 0.28$$
$$R(S) = (0.23*0.5) + (0.23*0.5) = 0.23$$

The calculated $R(U)$ and $R(S)$ values represent a low-low risk respectively. The results may be presented in the combined format shown in Fig A34.7-1.

A34.8 Benefits. This approach provides a method to combine a number of measures. As such, it can be a viable approach to use in the decision process to release or buy software.

A34.9 Experience. Use of the risk assessment reporting and evaluation technique has been limited to methodology development investigations using data obtained from operational test and evaluation programs. Current efforts include a study to identify the contributing elements to the supporter risk.

A34.10 References

[A124] *Software Operator-Machine Interface Evaluators Guide.* AFOTEC Pamphlet 800-2, vol 4, Feb 1983.

[A125] *Software Support Resources Evaluation Users Guide.* AFOTEC Pamphlet 800-2, vol 5, Feb 1983.

[A126] FISK, F. B. and MURCH, W. G. *Computer Resources Risk Assessment During Operatonal Test and Evaluation.* Journal of Operational Test and Evaluation, International Test and Evaluation Association (ITEA), Jan 1985.

A35. Completeness

A35.1 Application. The purpose of this measure is to determine the completeness of the software specification during the requirements phase. Also, the values determined for the primitives associated with the completeness measure can be used to identify problem areas within the software specification.

A35.2 Primitives. The completeness measure consists of the following primitives:

B_1 = number of functions not satisfactorily defined

B_2 = number of functions

B_3 = number of data references not having an origin

B_4 = Number of data references

B_5 = number of defined functions not used

B_6 = number of defined functions

B_7 = number of referenced functions not defined

B_8 = number of referenced functions

B_9 = number of decision points not using all conditions or options or both

B_{10} = number of decision points

B_{11} = number of condition options without processing

B_{12} = number of condition options

B_{13} = number of calling routines with parameters not agreeing with defined parameters

B_{14} = number of calling routines

B_{15} = number of condition options not set

B_{16} = number of set condition options having no processing

B_{17} = number of set condition options

B_{18} = number of data references having no destination

A35.3 Implementation. The completeness measure (CM) is the weighted sum of ten derivatives expressed as:

$$CM = \sum_{i=1}^{10} w_i D_i$$

where for each $i=1,\ldots,10$ each weight, w_i has a value between 0 and 1, the sum of the weights is equal to 1, and each D_i is a derivative with a value between 1 and 0.

To calculate the completeness measure, the definitions of the primitives for the particular application must be determined, and the priority associated with the derivatives must also be determined. This prioritization would affect the weights used to calculate the completeness measure.

Each primitive value would then be determined by the number of occurrences related to the definition of the primitive.

Each derivative is determined as follows:

$D_1 = (B_2 - B_1)/B_2$ = functions satisfactorily defined

$D_2 = (B_4 - B_3)/B_4$ = data references having an origin

$D_3 = (B_6 - B_5)/B_6$ = defined functions used

$D_4 = (B_8 - B_7)/B_8$ = referenced functions defined

$D_5 = (B_{10} - B_9)/B_{10}$ = all condition options at decision poiints

$D_6 = (B_{12} - B_{11})/B_{12}$ = all condition options with processing at decision points are used

$D_7 = (B_{14} - B_{13})/B_{14}$ = calling routine parameters agree with the called routine's defined parameters

$D_8 = (B_{12} - B_{15})/B_{12}$ = all condition options that are set

$D_9 = (B_{17} - B_{16})/B_{17}$ = processing follows set condition options

$D_{10} = (B_4 - B_{18})/B_4$ = data references have a destination

A35.4 Interpretation. The value of the completeness measure is scaled between 0 and 1 by the appropriate weights. A score near 1 is considered better than a score near 0. Those values near zero should be traced to the suspect primitive(s) to highlight any need for change in the software specification. As changes are made to the specification, the incremental specification measure values can be plotted to show if improvements are being made and how rapidly. The comparison of specification measures among different projects permits relative evaluations to be accomplished for improved completeness.

A35.5 Considerations. Each derivative helps identify characteristics in the software specification that promote completeness during the construction of the software.

A35.6 Training. Training would be necessary to understand the definitions of the primitives (which are based on the use of a specification language, eg, PSL) for the particular application.

A35.7 Example. The following example is developed to show the numerical procedure associated with the calculation of the completeness measure.

To arrive at a value for the completeness measure, assume that the primitives have been determined to have the following values:

$B_1 = 10$	$B_7 = 8$	$B_{13} = 2$
$B_2 = 50$	$B_8 = 40$	$B_{14} = 10$
$B_3 = 50$	$B_9 = 2$	$B_{15} = 4$
$B_4 = 2500$	$B_{10} = 100$	$B_{16} = 2$
$B_5 = 2$	$B_{11} = 5$	$B_{17} = 20$
$B_6 = 50$	$B_{12} = 50$	$B_{18} = 100$

These primitives are then combined to determine the derivative values.

$D_1 = .8$	$D_5 = .98$	$D_9 = .9$
$D_2 = .98$	$D_6 = .9$	$D_{10} = .98$
$D_3 = .96$	$D_7 = .8$	
$D_4 = .8$	$D_8 = .92$	

Assuming each weight as one-tenth (1/10), the completeness measure would be calculated as follows:

$$\text{Since } CM = \sum_{i=1}^{10} w_i D_i = 0.9$$

This value could be used in comparison with other completness measures or could be recalculated following improvements made within the software specification (as additions or deletions are made to the specification).

A35.8 Benefits. The completeness measure will give an indication of the completeness (value near 1) or incompleteness (value near 0) of the software specification during the early development stages.

A35.9 Experience. Validation of the completeness measure [A50, A53] consists of determining the proper definitions and measurements of primitives and calculation of associated derivatives using PSL/PSA. Other measures of completeness are also given in Murine [A127].

A35.10 References. See also Francis [A50], and Miller et al [A53].

[A127] MURINE, G. E. On Validating Software Quality Metrics. *4th annual IEEE Conference on Software Quality*, Phoenix, Arizona, Mar 1985.

[A128] SAN ANTONIO, R, and JACKSON, K. Application of Software Metrics During Early program Phases. *Proceedings of the National Conference on Software Test and Evaluation, Feb 1982.*

A36. Test Accuracy

A36.1 Application. This measure can be used to determine the accuracy of the testing program in detecting faults. With a test coverage measure, it can be used to estimate the percentage of faults remaining.

A36.2 Primitives
N_s = Number of seeded faults
$\hat{N}_s$ = Estimated number of detectable seeded faults

A36.3 Implementation. The software to be tested is seeded with faults. The number of seeded faults detected in each testing time interval is recorded along with time to detect faults, and a mathematical model is selected to represent the cumulative seeded faults detected across the total testing period. The cumulative seeded faults detected at time infinity is then estimated and test accuracy is calculated:

$$\text{ALPHA} = \hat{N}_s / N_s$$

A36.4 Interpretation. Ideally, ALPHA is independent of test duration and approaches 100%. However, ALPHA can be used in conjunction with GAMMA, a test coverage measure [A129, A131], to estimate the percentage of inherent faults remaining at the end of test.

$$NF_{\text{rem}}(\%) = (1 - \text{ALPHA} \times \text{GAMMA}) \times 100$$

A36.5 Considerations. To meet the requirement that seeded faults reflect typical ones, a scheme for categorizing seeded faults according to difficulty of detection is required. A mathematical model must be selected that accurately describes the fault detection process. The model is likely to be complex with non-trivial estimation of its parameters, thereby requiring automation. A single model may not be appropriate for all processes.

A36.6 Training. The level of training required depends on the automated tool used. Training in mathematical model fitting and tool usage is required. Experience in software testing would be applicable as well.

A36.7 Example.

A software module to be tested was seeded with 37 faults. Given the following observed fault detection profile, a model was fitted to describe the testing process.

Model estimated seeded faults detectable at time infinity = 32; ALPHA = 32/37 = .865.

A36.8 Benefits.

The test accuracy measure is an indicator of a test's ability to accurately detect faults, which will identify problem areas in testing practices.

A36.9 Experience.

Limited published experience is available.

A36.10 References

[A129] OHBA, M. Software Quality = Test Accuracy × Test Coverage. *IEEE International Symposium on Software Engineering*, Chicago, 1982, pp 287–293.

[A130] OHBA, M. *Software Quality = Test Coverage × Test Accuracy.* (In Japanese.) IPS-J, Proceedings WGSE Meeting, vol 21, 1981.

[A131] SHINODA, T., ISHIDA, T., and OHBA, M. *Control Defects and Test Accuracy.* (In Japanese.) IPS-J, Proceedings Spring conference, 5C-7, 1981.

Fig A36.7-1
Control Defect Removal Process

A37. System Performance Reliability

A37.1 Application.

This measure assesses the system's performance reliability, the probability that the value of each performance requirement will be less than or equal to a predefined threshold value. The specific performance requirements addressed in this measure are:

U = Utilization
X = Throughput
Q = Queue length distribution
WT = Waiting time distribution
SE = Mean server's efficiency
RT = Response time distribution
ST = Service time distribution

The application of these derived measures will ensure that reliability planning functions are done by all inter- and intra-organizations, periodic reliability etimations during the software life cycle are done to track reliability development, and verificaiton and validation are done on the system capacity.

A37.2 Primitives.

The following primitives quantify the basic performance attributes that are measured over a time period of length T.

A = The number of arrivals (functional jobs) during the time period T.
SB = The total amount of time "server" is busy.
J = The number of jobs completed during T.
VR = The number of requests (visits) per functional job for each server during time period T.
T = Time period over which measurements are made.

A37.3 Implementation.

These measures are applicable to operating systems and networks. Based upon the measured primitives the derived quantifiable measures are:

Γ = A/T, the average arrival rate of jobs
X = J/T, the average throughput rate
U = SB/T, the average utilization
AS = SB/J, the average service time
WT = $f(\Gamma, U, AS, VR)$, the waiting time distribution (expressed as a function of arrival rate, utilization, service time, and visit rate)
SE = $A/(AS+W)$, the server's efficiency of each job

$$R = \sum_{i=1}^{k} (VR \times S)_i + \sum_{i=1}^{k} (VR \times W)_i,$$

the total response time for each functional job over the k servers [see (5) below]

$AQ = W \times \Gamma$, the average queue length

Using any of these measures, one can derive the corresponding probability distribution of the measure under the stated assumptions of the system. The distribution can then be used to calculate the probability that the measure will achieve a desired level.

The following step by step process can be followed to calculate the probability of achieving the desired level.

(1) Determine the infrastructure of the performance model. This involves identifying the critical system resources and the system's underpinning connections in the form of a queueing network model (QNM). The basic idea of the model is that the "essential" part of the system's architecture is represented by a network of "servers" and queues that are connected by transition paths. Jobs circulate through the network, the flow being controlled by the transition probabilities.

(2) Define, qualify, and quantify the workload classes. This is to identify the resource demand characteristics of the different classes of jobs and their dynamic performance attribute matrix. This determines the apportionment of the utilization of each server by each work class.

(3) Measure the resource demands for each work class. The service time, arrival rate, and visit ratios of each system resource are measured for each class of job.

(4) Solve the QNM Model. The approximation algorithms in analytic queueing theory and operations research techniques are used to solve the model.

(5) Perform the reliability evaluation. For example, suppose the response time R must meet the goal of $R \leq R_o$ where R is given in A37.3. Calculate the system performance reliability as reliability = Probability ($R \leq R_o$) for stated assumptions during time period of length T. The system performance is not achieved if the desired reliability is not attained.

A37.4 Interpretation. In order to determine that the model did, in fact, represent the signifi-

cant dynamic behavior of the system, the monitored measures from the real system need to be compared with that of the model. The validated and verified model can then be used to develop the planning strategy by answering the following questions:

(1) Where are the bottlenecks in the system and why do they exist?

(2) What actions are required to rectify the deficiencies?

(3) What performance improvement can be expected by upgrading the system level software efficiency for a given scheduling policy?

(4) How will the addition of a new application functionality affect the current performance?

(5) What are the single failure paths in the system configuration and their effects on downtime? The system downtime is qualified and quantified as the elapsed time during which a degradation or a cessation of system performance occurs.

A37.5 Considerations. There are two basic operational techniques to the deployment of the monitors for the primitives.

(1) The event trace mode records all state transition events that can be used for a complete "reconstruction" of the critical activities via a trace driven simulation program.

(2) The sampling mode involves the gathering and sampling states of the system at predetermined times. A "steady state" condition must be assumed. The performance model must be validated via measurements before the model can be used with a high degree of confidence.

A37.6 Training. Knowledge of probability, statistics, queuing theory, hardware and operating system software architecture are required.

A37.7 Example. This example is a simple one-server queueing system taken from Denning and Buzen [A137]. This simple system could represent some type of computer device (ie, disk unit, I/O device, etc.) within a more complex computer design. See Denning and Buzen [A137] for more complex examples using these measures for performance and reliability analysis.

Fig A37.7-1 is a pictorial representation of a simple computer system in which requests are being made to a device. The device processes

Fig A37.7-1
Single Server System

those requests immediately if it is free; otherwise it files the request in a queue to be processed when it becomes free.

Suppose the device is observed over a period of $T = 20$ sec. When the device is first observed there are two requests in the queue and a third has just entered processing. During this time period seven new requests are made of the device (ie, A = 7). It is also observed that the device was busy processing the requests for a period of 16 seconds and that during this time period all ten requests were completed. Hence B = 16 and C = 10.

The basic performance measures can then be calculated as:

$\Gamma = A/T = 7/20 = .35$ jobs per second
$X = J/T = 10/20 = .5$ jobs per second for throughput
$U = SB/T = 16/20 = .8$ utilization factor
$AS = SB/J = 16/10 = 1.6$ seconds for the average service time

See Denning and Buzen [A137] for the derivation of the remaining measures.

A37.8 Benefits. These measures can be used throughout the system life cycle to ensure an effective and resource-efficient design. These measures will provide the logical and economic framework for critical tradeoff decisions, (eg, performance vs functionality, cost vs performance, etc).

A37.9 Experience. Many examples can be found in the literature on queueing theory of this network analysis approach [A133, A135, A136, and A137].

A37.10 References

[A132] ALLEN, A. O. *Probability, Statistics and Queueing Theory.* Academic Press, 1978.

[A133] ALLEN, A. O. Queueing Models of Computer Systems. *Computer*, vol 13, no 4, Apr 1980.

[A134] BARD, Y. An Analytic Model of the VM/370 System. *IBM Journal of Research and Development*, vol 22, no 5, Sept 1978.

[A135] BASKETT, F., CHANDY, K. M., and PALACIOS, F. G. Open, Closed, and Mixed Networks of Queues with Different Classes of Customers. *Communications of the ACM*, vol 22, no 2, Apr 1975.

[A136] BUZEN, J. P., and DENNING, P. J. Measuring and Calculating Queue Length Distributions. *Computer*, vol 13, no 4, Apr 1980.

[A137] DENNING, P. J., and BUZEN, J. P., The Operational Analysis of Queueing Network Models. *Computing Surveys*, vol 10, no 3, Sept 1978.

[A138] GRAHAM, G. S. Queueing Network Models of Computer System Performance. *Computing Surveys*, vol 10, no 3, Sept 1978.

[A139] TRIVEDI, K. S. and KINICKI, R. E. A Model for Computer Configuration Design. *Computer*, vol 14, no 4, Apr 1980.

A38. Independent Process Reliability

A38.1. Application. This measure provides a direct method to compute reliability (R) of certain types of software systems such as telephone switching and business transaction systems in which the programs have no loops and no local dependencies exist. This is a measure of the reliability of service that a software system provides.

A38.2 Primitives

f_{ij} = frequency of execution of intermodule transfer from module i to j.
MD = number of modules
P_i = ith process which can be generated in a user environment.
q_i = probability that P_i will be generated in a user environment.

r_i = random variable equal to 1 if the process P_i generates the correct software system output and zero otherwise.

R_i = reliability of the ith module.

A38.3 Implementation. This measure assumes that a large program is composed of logically independent modules which can be designed, implemented and tested independently.

Let L = set of processes P_i that can be generated by the software system corresponding to different input values. Then the reliability R of the software system can be computed from

$$R = \sum_{\forall P_i \,\epsilon\, L} q_i \, r_i$$

In large programs, it is infeasible to evaluate r_i and q_i for each process P_i because L could be large. To circumvent this difficulty, a simple Markov model is developed with intermodule probabilities, (f_{ij}), as the user profiles.

The reliability parameters of the program are expressed in terms of transitional probability parameters between states. The reliability R of the software system is defined as the probability of reaching the correct state [after module n] from the initial state [from module 1] of the Markov process, ie:

$$R = S\,(1, MD)\,R_n$$

where $S = [I - Q]^{-1}$;

Q is the state transition matrix spanning the entire Markov graph program; I is the identity matrix.

Elements of the matrix, $f_{ij}R_i$ represent the probability that execution of module i produces the correct result and transfers control to module j. R_i is determined from experimentation as the ratio of the number of output sets generated by module i to the number of input sets when the software system is tested by samples of representative valid input.

A38.4 Interpretation. The reliability measure provides the user with a direct estimate of the confidence in system software performance and indicates whether further testing and software updates are required for a given operational environment. In addition, this approach also indicates to the user how to improve the system reliability most effectively by evaluating the sensitivity of the system reliability with respect to that of a module [A142]. A high-sensitivity coefficient indicates a critical module that has greater impact on software reliability.

A38.5 Considerations. The underlying assumptions for the use of this measure are the following:

(1) The reliability of the modules are independent — ie, one module fault is not compensated by another.

(2) The transfer of control between program modules is a Markov process. (Next module to be executed depends probabilistically on the present module only and is independent of past history). When no modification is made on the modules, the transition probabilities are assumed constant. These characterize the user environment with respect to the reliability model.

A38.6 Training. The implementation of this methodology requires an understanding of stochastic processes.

A38.7 Examples. An example of the use of this measure is illustrated in Cheung [A142].

A38.8 Benefits. The measure gives a direct indication of the reliability of service to the user and determines whether further testing and improvement is required for the application. The sensitivity coefficient provides a scheme for correcting faults by providing priority updates to modules that have the greatest impact on software reliability.

A38.9 Experience. Limited published experience is available.

A38.10 References

[A140] CHEUNG, R. C. A Structural Theory for Improving SW Reliability. Ph.D. Dissertation, University of California at Berkeley, Dec 1974.

[A141] CHEUNG, R. C. and RAMAMOORTHY, C. V. Optimal Measurement of Program Path Frequencies and Its Applications. In Proc. 1975, *Int Fed Automat Contr Congr*, Aug 1975.

[A142] CHEUNG, R. C. A User Oriented Software Reliability Model. *IEEE Transactions on Software Engineering*, vol SE-6, no 2, Mar 1980.

A39. Combined Hardware and Software (System) Operational Availability

A39.1 Application. This measure provides a direct indication of system dependability, that is, whether it is operating or operable when required by the user.

A39.2 Primitives

λ = Observed software failure rate

β = Observed hardware failure rate

μ_i = Observed software fault correction rate with i faults in the software

γ = Observed hardware repair rate

NF = Estimated number of remaining software faults

P_s = Probability of correcting a software fault when detected ($0 \leq P_s \leq 1$)

P_h = Probability of correctly repairing a hardware failure ($0 \leq P_h \leq 1$)

A39.3 Implementation.

The basic Markovian model is used for predicting combined hardware and software (system) availability as a function of operating time. System upstate probabilities $P_{NF,n}(t)$ with n remaining faults, given that there were NF software faults at the commissioning ($t=0$) of the system, is computed for $n = 0, 1, 2, ..., N$.

System availability $A(t) = \sum_{n=0}^{NF} P_{N,n}(t)$

The expression for $P_{NF,n}(t)$, $n=1, ..., NF$ is derived as follows [A96]:

$$P_{NF,n}(t) = G_{NF,n}(t)$$

$$-\sum_{j=1}^{K} \frac{\prod\limits_{i=n+1}^{NK} (P_s \lambda_i \mu_i)(-x_j + P_h \gamma)^{NF-n} A(-x_j)(1 - e^{-x_j t})}{x_j \prod\limits_{\substack{i=1 \\ i \neq j}}^{K} (-x_j + x_i)}$$

where

$G_{NF,n}(t)$ = Cumulative distribution function of the first passage time for operational state with NF faults to operational state with n faults and is expressed as:

$$\sum_{j=1}^{K} \frac{\prod\limits_{i=n+1}^{NF} (P_s \lambda_i \mu_i)(-x_j + P_h \gamma)^{NF-n}}{\prod\limits_{\substack{i=1 \\ i \neq j}}^{K} (-x_j + x_i)} \frac{1}{-x_j}(e^{-x_j t} - 1)$$

$\lambda_i = i\lambda$

$\mu_i = i\mu$

$K = 3\,(NF-n)$

$x_1 = x_{1,(n+1)}$

$x_2 = x_{2,(n+1)}$

$x_3 = x_{3,(n+1)}$

$x_4 = x_{1,(n+2)}$

$x_5 = x_{2,(n+2)}$

$x_6 = x_{3,(n+2)}$

.

.

.

$x_{1(NF-n)} = x_{1,NF}$

$x_{2(NF-n)} = x_{2,NF}$

$x_{3(NF-n)} = x_{3,NF}$

$-x_{1,i}, -x_{2,i}$ and $-x_{3,i}$ ($i=n+1, ..., NF$) are the roots of the polynomial

$$S^3 + S^2\,(\lambda + \mu + \beta + P\,\gamma)$$

$$+ S(P\lambda\,\mu + \beta\mu + \lambda\,P\,\gamma + \mu\,P_h\gamma) + P_s\,P_h\,\gamma\,\lambda_i\,\mu_i$$

Also,

$$A(-x_j) = (-x_j\beta)\,(-x_j + \mu_n)$$

$$+ \lambda_n(-x_j + P_s\mu_n)\,(-x_j + P_h\gamma)$$

A39.4 Interpretation.

$A(t)$ will show a characteristic drop initially and then will rise, approaching a steady state value determined by the hardware availability.

A39.5 Considerations.

The underlying assumptions for the use of this measure based on *Software Reliability Modelling and Estimation Technique* [A96] are as follows:

(1) The occurrence of software and hardware failures are independent.

(2) The probability of two or more software or hardware failures occurring simultaneously is negligible.

(3) Failures and repairs of the hardware are independent of both fault detection and correction of the software.

(4) The software failure rate and the hardware failure rate are constants.

(5) The time to repair hardware failures and the time to correct software failures follow exponential distributions, each with a fixed parameter.

A39.6 Training.

The implementation of this methodology requires an understanding of stochastic processes and familiarity with programming analytical models.

A39.7 Example.

See combined HW/SW Reliability Models, Section A2.4.2 [A143] for a specific example for system availability.

A39.8 Benefits. A sampling measure for the average availabiity $A_{av}(t)$ of an operational system can be developed and compared with the theoretically computed figure for availability $A(t)$.

A39.9 Experience. Few hardware/software models have been developed that can be applied to the measurement of system operational availability (see Software Reliability Modelling and Estimation Technique [A96]). These models have not yet been tested against actual system failure data. Yet, because it is judged to have great potential for addressing the problem of measuring combined hardware/software performance, their applica-

tion to actual system failure data is encouraged. However, as other models become available, they too should be considered when system availability calculations/predictions need to be made [A144].

A39.10 References. See also *Software Reliability Modelling and Estimation Technique* [A96].

[A143] *Combined HW/SW Reliability Models*, RADC-TR-82-68, Final Technical Report, Apr 1982.

[A144] SUMITA, U., and MASUDA, Y. Analysis of Software Availability/Reliability Under the Influence of Hardware Failures. *IEEE Transactions on Software Reliability*, vol SE-12, no 1, Jan 1986.

An American National Standard

IEEE Guide for Software Quality Assurance Planning

983

Sponsor

**Software Engineering Standards Subcommittee
of the
Technical Committee on Software Engineering
of the
IEEE Computer Society**

Approved September 19, 1985

IEEE Standards Board

Approved February 20, 1986

American National Standards Institute

Foreword

(This Foreword is not a part of IEEE Std 983-1986, IEEE Guide for Software Quality Assurance Planning.)

The purpose of this guide is to recommend approaches to good Software Quality Assurance practices in support of ANSI/IEEE Std 730-1984, IEEE Standard for Software Quality Assurance Plans. This guide is meant to supplement ANSI/IEEE Std 730-1984 by presenting the current consensus of those in the software development community who have expertise or experience in generating, implementing, evaluating, and modifying Software Quality Assurance plans. This guide is not offered as a detailed procedures manual for establishing and operating Software Quality Assurance programs. This guide does not constitute further requirements than those stated in ANSI/IEEE Std 730-1984. An organization can claim compliance with ANSI/IEEE Std 730-1984 without following completely, or in part, this guide. Detailed information regarding specific software quality assurance activities may be found in other IEEE Standards. These are referenced where appropriate. While this guide quotes major portions of ANSI/IEEE Std 730-1984, the standard is not quoted in its entirety. ANSI/IEEE Std 730-1984 users are advised to consult that standard directly.

In accordance with ANSI/IEEE Std 730-1984, the practices herein are directed toward the development and maintenance of critical software, that is, where failure could impair safety or cause large financial losses. Determination of this criticality lies in the "eyes of the beholder." The specific application and situation of each user must be carefully considered. Should there be doubt, it is suggested that the software be considered critical. For software that is definitely noncritical, or software already developed, a subset of the requirements stated in ANSI/IEEE Std 730-1984 is appropriate.

This guide serves the three groups discussed in the Foreword to ANSI/IEEE Std 730-1984: the user, the developer, and the public.

(1) The user, whether external or internal to the developing organization, has a need for the software product that meets its identified requirements. Thus, the user cannot afford to rely solely on the developer's tests at the conclusion of the software development effort. Should the software product fail to meet requirements at that point, the user's need still exists and a major portion of the development time has been lost. The user, therefore, needs to have a reasonable degree of confidence that the product is in the process of acquiring required attributes during software development.

(2) The developer needs a software quality assurance standard which establishes responsibility and accountability. It is unreasonable to expect a complete reorientation from project to project. Not only is it not cost-effective, but unless there exists a stable framework on which to base changes, improvements cannot be made.

(3) The public, which may be affected by the use of the software, has a vested interest in software development. This public includes, for example, depositors at a bank and passengers using a reservation system. The public has a right to expect that software developers have acted in a reasonable and prudent professional manner to provide the required software attributes. At some later date, the user, the developer, or both may be required to show that they did, in fact, act in such a reasonable and prudent professional manner.

This guide is addressed to readers who have professional experience in quality assurance, or in software development, but not necessarily in both. For example, this guide should be useful to the following individuals:

(1) A quality assurance person with the responsibility for developing or implementing a Software Quality Assurance Plan for a project

(2) A software development project manager desiring to initiate Software Quality Assurance procedures on a project

(3) A purchaser or user of a software product who wants to evaluate a seller's Software Quality Assurance Plan or to specify a Software Quality Assurance Plan

(4) An independent evaluator, such as an EDP auditor

(5) The person with accountability for the implementation of a Software Quality Assurance Plan

In the body of this guide, the use of "shall" is to be understood as referring to an item or activity that is mandated by ANSI/IEEE Std 730-1984. The use of "should" is to be understood as referring to a recommended item or activity. The use of "may" is to be understood as referring to an item or activity that can be advised under some circumstances, but for which there is not a professional consensus. The use of "could" is to be understood as suggesting the existence of several possibilities, the selection among which will be specific to the project and not driven by specific quality assurance considerations.

This guide was prepared and balloted by the Software Engineering Standards Subcommittee of the Software Engineering Technical Committee of the IEEE Computer Society. At the time it approved this standard, the subcommittee had the following membership:

George D. Tice, Jr., *Chairperson*

Joel Hebert, *Treasurer*
A. Frank Ackerman, *Vice Chairperson*
John W. Horch, *Vice Chairperson*
Thomas M. Kurihara, *Vice Chairperson*

Laurel V. Kaleda, *Secretary*
Robert M. Poston, *Vice Chairperson*
Leonard Tripp, *Vice Chairperson*

William L. Anderson
Roy W. Bass
Nestore G. Biasi
Michael A. Blackledge
John F. Boucher
William L. Bryan
Fletcher J. Buckley
Une H. Butenhoff
C. L. Carpenter
Jung K. Chung
Won L. Chung
Corey Clinger
David Collard
Christopher M. Cooke
Gilmore G. Cooke
John D. Cooper
A. J. Cote, Jr.
Richard Cotter
Steward G. Crawford
Robert C. Crombe
George D. Darling
Noah Seth Davis
James A. Dobbins
Irving Doshay
David C. Doty
Gene E. Dufoe
Patricia W. Duggett
Robert E. Dwyer
John D. Earls
Leo G. Egan, Jr.
Caroline L. Evans
John W. Fendrich
Glenn S. Fields
Heinz H. Frey
Edward L. Gibbs
Michael J. Gooding
Robert M. Gross
Russell T. Gustin
Virl E. Haas

Carolyn M. Harrison
Clark M. Hay
Madeleine C. Heidkamp
Leslie R. Heselton, III
Charles R. Hollocker
Samual Horvitz
Lawrence M. Johmann
Harry Kalmbach
Michael R. Kirchner
George A. Klammer
Joseph J. Klock
Dwayne L. Knirk
Albert M. Lerner
Richard C. Lewis
F. C. Lim
Gary S. Lindsay
Ben Livson
Alan Cheuk-Wai Ma
Henry A. Malec
William A. Mandeville
Ben Manny
Paulo Cesar Marcondes
Philip C. Marriott
Roger J. Martin
Werner R. MaHersdorff
Leroy M. May
Belden Menkus
Walter Merenda
Dennis F. Meronek
Gene T. Morun
David G. Mullens
Saied Najafi
Jainendra K. Navlakha
Dennis E. Nickle
Olebernt Olavesen
David E. Perr
Poul Grao Petersen
Donald J. Pfeiffer
Patricia B. Powell

Jock A. Rader
Jean-Claude Rault
Lawrence K. Reed
Donald J. Reifer
Steven M. Rowan
Frank Salvia
Hans Schaefer
Robert W. Schillato
Max J. Schindler
Norman F. Schneidewind
Robert G. Schueppert
David J. Schultz
Leonard W. Seagren
Anthony E. Severino
Ronald L. Skelton
Marian P. Smith
Wayne Smith
Thomas Q. Stevenson
William G. Sutcliffe
Michael H. Taint
Barbara J. Tante
E. Frank Testa
Richard H. Thayer
J. Rush Thompson
Paul U. Thompson
Terrence L. Tillmanns
George W. Trever
Henry J. Trochesset
C. L. Troyanowski
William S. Turner, III
David Usechak
R. L. Van-Tilbury
Udo Voges
Ralph Wachter
Andrew H. Weigel
Paul A. Willis
David L. Winningham
Charles Wortz
Robert H. Yacobellis

Special representatives to the Software Engineering Standards Subcommittee were as follows:

H. R. Berlack: Electronic Industry Association
N. C. Farr: Nuclear Power Engineering Committee,
  IEEE Power Engineering Society
A. Ferlan: American Society for Quality Control

S. R. Jarocki: EDP Auditors Association
J. Milandin: ANSI Z1
W. E. Perry: Data Processing Manufacturers Association
T. L. Regulinski: IEEE Reliability Society

The working group that developed this standard had the following membership:

George D. Tice, Jr., *Chairperson*　　　　　　　　**A. Frank Ackerman,** *Co-Chairperson*

Alphonso J. Barr	Eugene Gouldman	Dennis E. Nickle
William Belke	Joseph Guidos	George O'Connell
Nestore G. Biasi	Russel Gusten	Robert M. Poston
Margaret Bornett	Carolyn M. Harrison	Patricia B. Powell
Vincent Boyer	Joel Hebert	Peter Ron Prinzivalli
Eric J. Braude	George Heblinger	Jane Radatz
Fletcher J. Buckley	John Hoelzel	Hans Reiche
Robert A. Burch	Charles R. Hollocker	Lenard B. Robertson
William Burns	Robert Hood	James Ronback
John Center	John W. Horch	Miney Roseberry
Richard Chilausky	Philip Jacobs	Hans Schaefer
Peter Clemens	Laurel V. Kaleda	Roger Scholten
Joan Colbert	Myron S. Karasik	David J. Schultz
James V. Dinkey	Robert Kessler	Robert W. Shillato
Paul Doyle	Joseph J. Klock	J. Michael Smith
Walter DuBlanica	John S. Kopec	Andi Stout
Robert L. Erickson	Richard W. Kubica	Barbara J. Taute
Charles Feather	Robert Lane	Nina C. Thomas
Arthur Ferlan	Albert M. Lerner	Don Thorne
David Gelperin	Venetta Mallory	William S. Turner, III
Jean A. Gilmore	Philip C. Marriott	Donald Willett
Shirley Gloss-Soler	Charles F. Martiny	James Zoog
Edward Gonzales	Gerald Neidhart	

When the IEEE Standards Board approved this standard on September 19, 1985, it had the following membership:

John E. May, *Chairman*　　　　　　　　**John P. Riganati,** *Vice Chairman*

Sava I. Sherr, *Secretary*

James H. Beall	Daniel L. Goldberg	Lawrence V. McCall
Fletcher J. Buckley	Kenneth D. Hendrix	Donald T. Michael*
Rene Castenschiold	Irvin N. Howell	Frank L. Rose
Edward Chelotti	Jack Kinn	Clifford O. Swanson
Edward J. Cohen	Joseph L. Koepfinger*	J. Richard Weger
Paul G. Cummings	Irving Kolodny	W. B. Wilkens
Donald C. Fleckenstein	R. F. Lawrence	Charles J. Wylie
Jay Forster		

*Member emeritus

Contents

IEEE Guide for Software Quality Assurance Planning

1. Scope and References

1.1 Scope. The purpose of this guide is to explain and clarify the contents of each section of a Software Quality Assurance Plan (SQAP) that satisfies the requirements of ANSI/IEEE Std 730-1984 [2].[1] The guide does not constitute further requirements than those stated in ANSI/IEEE Std 730-1984 [2]. An organization can claim compliance with ANSI/IEEE Std 730-1984 [2] without following completely, or in part, this guide.

This guide presents the current consensus of those in the software development community with expertise or experience in generating, implementing, evaluating, and modifying a SQAP. Section 3 of this guide describes the content of each section in a SQAP that satisfies ANSI/IEEE Std 730-1984 [2]. Each subsection of Section 3 quotes the applicable wording from the standard. Section 4 provides guidance for implementing a SQAP on a software project, or within a software development organization. Section 5 provides guidance for evaluating the contents and the implementation of a SQAP. Section 6 provides guidance for the procedures used to modify an existing SQAP. The Appendix presents a summary of the contents of a SQAP. This guide is applicable to the development and maintenance of all software, recognizing that the application of these recommendations should be tailored to the specific software product item. The user of this guide should be aware that efforts are underway to provide standards and guides that cover many areas. Prior to implementation, a check should be made with the Secretary, IEEE Standards Board, for further detailed guidance in this area.

1.2 References.

[1] ANSI/IEEE Std 729-1983, IEEE Standard Glossary of Software Engineering Terminology.

[2] ANSI/IEEE Std 730-1984, IEEE Standard for Software Quality Assurance Plans.[2]

[3] ANSI/IEEE Std 828-1983, IEEE Standard for Software Configuration Management Plans.

[4] ANSI/IEEE Std 829-1983, IEEE Standard for Software Test Documentation.

[5] ANSI/IEEE Std 830-1984, IEEE Guide to Software Requirements Specifications.

2. Definitions and Acronyms

2.1 Definitions. The definitions listed below establish meaning in the context of this guide. Other definitions can be found in ANSI/IEEE Std 729-1983 [1] and ANSI/IEEE Std 730-1984 [2].

conventions. Requirements employed to prescribe a disciplined, uniform approach to providing consistency in a software *product,* that is, uniform patterns or forms for arranging data.

practices. Requirements employed to prescribe a disciplined, uniform approach to the software development *process.*

standards. Mandatory requirements employed and *enforced* to prescribe a disciplined, uniform

---

[1] The numbers in brackets correspond to those of the references listed in Section 1.2.

[2] ANSI/IEEE publications are available from the Sales Department, American National Standards Institute, 1430 Broadway, New York, NY 10018, and the Institute of Electrical and Electronics Engineers, Service Center, 445 Hoes Lane, Piscataway, NJ 08854.

approach to software development, that is, mandatory conventions and practices are in fact standards.

techniques. Technical and managerial procedures that aid in the evaluation and improvement of the software development process.

2.2 Acronyms. The following alphabetical contractions appear within the text of this guide:

CCB	Change control board (in this document refers to change control board for a SQAP)
CDR	Critical design review
CI	Configuration item
PDR	Preliminary design review
SCM	Software configuration management
SCMP	Software configuration management plan
SDD	Software design description
SDP	Software development plan
SPM	Standards and procedures manual
SQA	Software quality assurance
SQAP	Software quality assurance plan
SRR	Software requirements review
SRS	Software requirements specification
SVVP	Software verification and validation plan
SVVPR	Software verification and validation plan review
SVVR	Software verification and validation report
UDR	User documentation review

3. Contents of a Software Quality Assurance Plan

"The organization responsible for Software Quality Assurance shall prepare a Software Quality Assurance Plan (also referred to as the Plan) that includes the sections listed below. The sections should be ordered in the described sequence. If there is no information pertinent to a section, the following statement shall appear below the section heading. *This section is not applicable to this plan,* together with the appropriate reasons for the exclusion.

(1) Purpose
(2) Reference Documents
(3) Management

(4) Documentation
(5) Standards, Practices, and Conventions
(6) Reviews and Audits
(7) Software Configuration Management
(8) Problem Reporting and Corrective Action
(9) Tools, Techniques, and Methodologies
(10) Code Control
(11) Media Control
(12) Supplier Control
(13) Records Collection, Maintenance, and Retention

"Additional sections may be added at the end, as required. Some of the material may appear in other documents. If so, then reference to those documents should be made in the body of the plan." [2][4]

For example, portions of the required information may be contained in a separate Software Configuration Management Plan (SCMP) or in a Software Development Plan (SDP). These sections should reference those particular plans. Those plans should be reviewed to ensure that they provide all the required information.

3.1 Purpose. "This section shall delineate the specific purpose and scope of the particular Software Quality Assurance Plan (SQAP). It shall list the name(s) of the software product items covered by the SQAP and the intended use of the software." [2]

The following questions should be addressed in this section:

(1) *Which software products are covered by this SQAP?* Specific names and abbreviations should be supplied for these products.

(2) *What is the intended use of the software covered by this SQAP?* How is the software to be utilized? How critical is this software? Is it part of a larger system; if so, how is it related to the system?

(3) *Why is this SQAP being written?* Is this Plan being written in response to an internal or external requirement? Why is this SQAP needed?

(4) *What documents form the basis of this SQAP?* Describe the extent to which this SQAP is based on ANSI/IEEE Std 730-1984 [2]. Identify any other documents on which this SQAP is based, eg, military or corporate quality assurance standards and guidelines.

---

[4] The quoted material appearing in this standard has been extracted from ANSI/IEEE Std 730-1984 [2].

(5) *What is the rationale behind departures from documents mentioned in 3.1(4)?* Which product or development attributes warrant additional or stricter practices or procedures? Which attributes warrant more lenient practices or procedures?

3.2 Reference Documents. "This section shall provide a complete list of documents referenced elsewhere in the text of the plan." [2]

Clearly identify the sources from which the documents can be obtained.

3.3 Management. "This section shall describe the organization, tasks, and responsibilities." [2]

Section 3.3.1 shall describe each major element of the organization which influences the quality of the software. Section 3.3.2 shall list the tasks covered by this plan. Section 3.3.3 shall identify specific organizational responsibilities for each task. This description should also identify the management position which retains overall authority and responsibility for software quality.

3.3.1 Organization. "This paragraph shall depict the organizational structure that influences the quality of the software. This shall include a description of each major element of the organization together with the delegated responsibilities. Organizational dependence or independence of the elements responsible for SQA from those responsible for software development and use shall be clearly described or depicted." [2]

The organizational element(s) responsible for the software quality assurance functions covered by the SQAP may be developers knowledgeable in quality assurance techniques and tools; a dedicated quality assurance element serving a number of projects; or a series of separate organizational elements, each of which implements one or more SQA functional activities. The SQAP should state the organizational and functional boundaries of the SQA element. This should not be construed to indicate that a specific SQA organization must be established nor that a SQA organizational element must perform specific tasks.

If the SQA element is not attached to the software development element, the plan should state this clearly and explain any interrelationships that exist between these and other elements. If the SQA element is attached to other elements, the plan should explain its structure and interrelationships.

A pictorial organizational structure should be included with a written explanation amplifying the nature and degree of relationships with all organizational elements responsible for software product quality and development. The written explanation should include:

(1) A description of each element which interacts with the SQA element

(2) Delegated responsibilities of interacting elements

(3) Reporting relationships among the interacting elements

(4) Identification of the organizational element with product release authority

(5) Identification of the organizational element which approves the SQAP

(6) The method by which conflicts are to be resolved among the elements

The written explanation may also include:

(7) The size of the SQA element

(8) An explanation of any deviations from organizational SQA policies, procedures, or standards

The description of the organizational structure should be complete so that all the tasks addressed in the SQAP can be directly related to the structure.

3.3.2 Tasks. "This paragraph shall describe the tasks associated with that portion of the software life cycle covered by this plan with special emphasis on software quality assurance activities. The sequence of the tasks shall be indicated." [2]

The basic tasks are described in 3.4 through 3.13. All of the tasks in these sections may not be applicable to a specific project, in which event they may be omitted. Any omissions or deviations from ANSI/IEEE Std 730-1984 [2] should be explained. Any additional tasks, along with additional sections to the Plan, should be included. Any deviations from corporate software quality assurance policies should be explained. This section of the SQAP should also designate the personnel responsible for publication, distribution, maintenance, and implementation of the SQAP.

Each task should be defined with entrance and exit criteria, that is, what is needed to initiate the task, and what is the output of the task. The output of each task should be defined in such a

11

way that its achievement or completion can be objectively determined in a prescribed manner. Additionally, this section could include a table indicating the staffing levels for the listed tasks.

While it is strongly recommended that a Software Development Plan (SDP) (see 3.4.3.1) be prepared, if an SDP is not available, this section should provide schedule information outlining the development cycle.

3.3.3 Responsibilities. "This paragraph shall identify the specific organizational elements responsible for each task." [2]

If two or more elements share responsibility for a task, their respective responsibilities should be identified. The management position accountable for overall software quality should be identified. This section of the SQAP should also designate the personnel responsible for publication, distribution, and maintenance of the SQAP. It should indicate the review and approval cycle, indicating signature authority as required. It should show the number of controlled copies and describe the method of control, if applicable. It should designate the personnel responsible for distributing the SQAP and describe the methods and responsibilities for the promulgation, approval, distribution, and incorporation of changes.

3.4 Documentation. "This section shall:

(1) Identify the documentation governing the development, verification, and validation, use, and maintenance of the software.

(2) State how the documents are to be checked for adequacy. The statement shall include identification of the review or audit by which the adequacy of each document shall be confirmed, with reference to Section 6 of the Plan." [2]

Section 6 of the Plan is discussed in 3.6 of this guide.

3.4.1 Purpose. The SQAP should identify the documentation that will be prepared during the development, verification and validation, use, and maintenance of the software. The SQAP should identify the organizational elements responsible for the origination, verification, maintenance, and control of the required documentation. The SQAP should also identify the specific reviews, audits, and associated criteria required for each document, including references as appropriate to 3.6, Reviews and Audits.

The following subsections should describe the format and content of each of the documents used. If this information is provided in another document, only a reference should be given. Organizational policies, procedures, and standards may determine additional information requirements.

3.4.2 Minimum Documentation Requirements. "To ensure that the implementation of the software satisfies the requirements, the following documentation is required as a minimum . . ." [2]

ANSI/IEEE Std 730-1984 [2] requires the following documents:

(1) Software Requirements Specification (SRS)

(2) Software Design Description (SDD)

(3) Software Verification and Validation Plan (SVVP)

(4) Software Verification and Validation Report (SVVR)

(5) User Documentation

These documents will provide the basis for a logical and systematic approach to the development and operation of the software. A brief description of each document follows.

3.4.2.1 Software Requirements Specification (SRS). "The SRS shall clearly and precisely describe each of the essential requirements (functions, performances, design constraints, and attributes) of the software and the external interfaces. Each requirement shall be defined such that its achievement is capable of being verified and validated objectively by a prescribed method, for example, inspection, demonstration, analysis, or test." [2]

The SRS is usually developed from one or more completed documents such as a user requirements statement, operational requirements, statement of work, or contract. It specifies in detail the requirements as agreed upon by the developer and the requester or user. The SQAP should identify what standards or guides apply to the content and format of the SRS. ANSI/IEEE Std 830-1984 [5] describes the necessary content and qualities of an SRS.

The SRS is subject to the Software Requirements Review (SRR) described in 3.6.

3.4.2.2 Software Design Description (SDD). "The SDD shall describe the major components of the software design including data bases and internal interfaces. An expansion of this description shall be included to describe each subcomponent of the major components." [2]

The SDD is a technical description of how the software will meet the requirements set forth in the SRS. Its most important function is to describe a decomposition of the system as a whole, into components (subsystems, segments, etc) that are complete and well-bounded.

The SDD describes major system features such as data bases, diagnostics, external and internal interfaces, and overall structure. It involves descriptions of the operating environment, monitors, timing, system throughput, tables, sizing, modeling, etc. The SQAP should identify the standards and conventions that apply to the content and format of the SDD, as well as the procedures to be used in developing the SDD.

The SDD is subject to the Preliminary Design Review (PDR) and the Critical Design Review (CDR) described in 3.6.

For each component in the system, the SDD should consist of items such as:

(1) A textural description of the component's:
    (a) Inputs
    (b) Outputs
    (c) Calling sequence
    (d) Function or task
    (e) Algorithms
(2) A list of other components called
(3) A list of all calling components
(4) Allowed and tolerable range of values for all inputs
(5) Allowed and expected range of values for all outputs
(6) Assumptions, limitations, and side effects

3.4.2.3 Software Verification and Validation Plan (SVVP). "The SVVP shall describe the methods (for example, inspection, demonstration, analysis, or test) to be used:

(1) To verify that
    (a) The requirements in the SRS are implemented in the design expressed in the SDD.
    (b) The design expressed in the SDD is implemented in the code.
(2) To validate that the code, when executed, complies with the requirements expressed in the SRS." [2]

The SVVP describes the overall plan for the verification and validation of the software. The tasks, methods, and criteria for verification and validation are described. The SVVP specifies minimum test documentation requirements. ANSI/IEEE Std 829-1983 [4] may be consulted.

The SQAP should identify which standards and conventions apply to the content and format of the SVVP. A section of the SVVP should include a verification matrix where requirements are listed with their corresponding SVVP section. The contents of the SVVP will be evaluated at the Software Verification and Validation Plan Review (SVVPR) described in 3.6.

3.4.2.4 Software Verification and Validation Report (SVVR). "The SVVR shall describe the results of the execution of the SVVP. This shall include the results of all reviews, audits, and tests required by the SQA plan." [2]

The SVVR summarizes the observed status of the software as a result of the execution of the SVVP. It outlines any major deficiencies found; provides the results of reviews, audits, and tests; indicates the status of planned corrective actions; and should recommended whether the software is, or is not, ready for operational use.

3.4.2.5 User Documentation. "The User Documentation (eg, manual, guide, etc) shall specify and describe the required data and control inputs, input sequences, options, program limitations, and other activities/items necessary for successful execution of the software. All error messages shall be identified and corrective actions described. A method of describing user-identified errors/problems to the developer/owner of the software shall be described." [2]

The User Documentation should be composed of the following items:

(1) User instructions which contain an introduction, a description of the user's interaction with the system, and a description of any required training for using the system (see, also, Training Manual, 3.4.4.4)
(2) A system narrative purpose and description
(3) Input/output specifications
(4) Samples of original source documents and examples of all input formats (forms or displays)
(5) Samples of all outputs (forms, reports, or displays)
(6) Data entry instructions that contain instructions for data preparation, data keying, data verification, data proofing, and error correction
(7) References to all documents or manuals intended for use by the users
(8) A description of the system's limitations
(9) A description of all error situations which can occur and how to react

A User Documentation Review (UDR) is described in 3.6.3.1

3.4.3 Other Documentation. "Other documentation may include the following:

(1) Software Development Plan
(2) Software Configuration Management Plan
(3) Standards and Procedures Manual." [2]

3.4.3.1 Software Development Plan (SDP). The SDP should identify all technical and managerial activities associated with computer program development. The SDP should specify the following items:

(1) Activity description
(2) Activity deliverables and associated completion criteria
(3) Prerequisite deliverables from prior activities, if any
(4) Schedule and interrelationships among activities
(5) Assignment of responsibility for each activity

3.4.3.2 Software Configuration Management Plan (SCMP). The SCMP should describe the methods to be used for:

(1) Identifying the software configuration items
(2) Controlling and implementing changes
(3) Recording and reporting change implementation status
(4) Conducting configuration audits

The SCMP may be a separate document or a section of the SQAP. The ANSI/IEEE Std 828-1983 [3] provides minimum acceptable requirements for the content of an SCMP.

3.4.3.3 Standards and Procedures Manual (SPM). The SPM should provide details on standards and procedures to be followed for specific activities. As a minimum, the information described in 3.5 should be included.

3.4.4 Additional Suggested Documentation. The attributes, context, and environment of the product could dictate inclusion of additional documents, such as but not limited to the following:

(1) User Requirements Statement
(2) External Interface Specification
(3) Internal Interface Specification
(4) Operations Manual
(5) Installation Manual
(6) Maintenance Manual

(7) Training Manual
(8) Training Plan

3.4.4.1 User Requirements Statement. The User Requirements Statement should include, but is not limited to:

(1) A service request which contains the identity of the requester, the software product name and title, the date the software product was requested and is required, a description of what the software product should do, an abstract of the need for the software product, privacy or security considerations, and a list of potential users of the software product.
(2) A list of the objectives that are to be satisfied by the software product, as well as any other needs (administrative, timing, SQA, etc) and restraints the user perceives as necessary.
(3) Any studies done to define resource requirements (ie, hardware, software, personnel, plant and facilities, or environmental), feasibility, or cost-benefits analyses.

3.4.4.2 External Interface Specification. The External Interface Specification should contain information about files and other interconnections to all other software products outside the system to be developed. Consideration should be given to human interfaces, hardware interfaces, environmental constraints, and files or transactions coming from or going to other systems.

3.4.4.3 Internal Interface Specification. The Internal Interface Specification should contain information about files and other interconnections among all the components within the system. Consideration should be given to such subjects as transfer of control between modules, passing of data between modules, physical interfaces, and common data bases.

3.4.4.4 Operations Manual. The Operations Manual should be composed of at least the following items:

(1) Operating instructions that contain:
   (a) An introduction
   (b) Run schedules
   (c) Setup requirements
   (d) Job control procedures
   (e) Error procedures
   (f) Security procedures
   (g) Distribution procedures
   (h) Backup and recovery procedures
   (i) Restart procedures

(2) Specifications for the system, including environmental requirements

(3) Input / output specifications

(4) Auditing controls

3.4.4.5 Installation Manual. An Installation Manual should contain instructions for the installation of the software product, file conversion instructions, use of user-controlled installation options, and instructions for performing an installation test.

3.4.4.6 Maintenance Manual. A Maintenance Manual should contain instructions for software product support and maintenance, such as procedures for correcting defects and installation of enhancements. This document should refer to the Problem Reporting System (see 3.8) and the SCMP (see 3.4.3.2).

3.4.4.7 Training Manual. The Training Manual should contain information necessary for training users and operators of the system. It should contain, but is not limited to:

(1) An introduction

(2) How to use the system

(3) Preparing input

(4) Data input descriptions

(5) Data control descriptions

(6) How to run the system

(7) Output distributions

(8) Description of output data and interpretations

3.4.4.8 Training Plan. The development of software products that require complex or unfamiliar interactions with users and operators should include a comprehensive plan for training. The Training Plan should include:

(1) A description of the population to be trained and the learning objectives for each population

(2) An estimate of the amount of resources necessary for training development, delivery, and time expenditures

(3) Procedures for evaluating the effectiveness of the training and for making modifications to the training plan

3.5 Standards, Practices, and Conventions. "This section shall:

(1) Identify the standards, practices, and conventions to be applied.

(2) State how compliance with these items is to be monitored and assured." [2]

3.5.1 Purpose. This section of the SQAP should identify the standards, practices, and conventions to be employed and specify the phases of the life cycle to which they apply. It should also indicate which individual or organizational element will be responsible for the enforcement, evaluation, and maintenance of the standards, practices, and conventions, and specify how compliance will be monitored and assured.

3.5.2 Content of Sections. "The subjects covered shall include the basic technical, design, and programming activities involved, such as documentation naming and coding, programming languages, and unit testing. As a minimum, the following information shall be provided:

(1) Documentation standards

(2) Logic structure standards

(3) Coding standards

(4) Commentary standards." [2]

The SQAP should reference or include a listing of the standards, practices, and conventions to be used on the project. As a minimum, the standards, practices, and conventions should address requirements, design, implementation, test, and documentation.

3.5.2.1 Requirements. Specify the standards, practices, and conventions to be used during requirements analysis. Use formal requirements statement languages, either textual or graphic, whenever possible. Provision should be made for a scheme that uniquely identifies each requirement. This facilitates traceability during the subsequent phases.

3.5.2.2 Design. Specify the standards, practices, and conventions to be used during the preliminary design phase where the overall structure of the software system is defined. Give serious consideration to the use of graphic techniques and top-down design.

For detailed design, state what standards, practices, and conventions will be used for specifying the internal structure of each program module, and the interfaces among them. Address such matters as naming conventions and argument list standards. Give serious consideration to requiring the use of a program design language.

3.5.2.3 Implementation. Specify the standards, practices, and conventions to be used during the implementation phase. Address such topics as the end-use computer, programming language(s), module size, declaration statement conventions, naming and labeling conventions, component layout standards, and the use of structured coding techniques (or structuring precompilers). Consider data conversion techniques for new systems that are replacing old ones. Standards for the inclusion of comment statements should also be covered here. Use standard support software and software tools whenever possible or state reasons for the use of nonstandard support software and tools.

3.5.2.4 Test. Specify the standards, practices, and conventions to be used during the testing phase. This includes unit, integration, system and acceptance testing, as well as regression testing. ANSI/IEEE Std 829-1983 [4] describes an integrated set of test documents.

Address criteria for test repeatability and test coverage such as testing every requirement, user procedure, and program statement. Specify techniques for tracing the test coverage to the test set. Indicate whether any support software will be required, and state how and from where this software will be obtained.

3.5.2.5 Documentation. Specify the standards, practices, and conventions to be used in preparing software documentation. Cite any external (eg, military, user, etc) standards with which the documents must comply. Include any standards, practices, and conventions which apply to the deliverable program source listings or executable code. Include any standards, practices, and conventions which apply to documentation for deliverable tools.

3.6 Reviews and Audits. "This section shall:

(1) Define the technical and managerial reviews and audits to be conducted.
(2) State how the reviews and audits are to be accomplished." [2]

3.6.1 Purpose. The software items produced by the software development effort should be reviewed and audited on a planned basis to determine the extent of progress and to evaluate the technical adequacy of the work and its conformance to system requirements. Technical reviews and audits should be conducted to evaluate the status and quality of the software development effort and to assure the use of required documentation. Completion of audits provides the basis for making decisions during the course of software development. Completion of reviews provides assurance that design integrity is maintained, technical deficiencies are identified, and

necessary changes have been identified and implemented.

This section should identify the specific technical and managerial reviews and audits to be conducted with respect to the software development plans, schedules, and environment. It should describe the procedures to be used in the conduct of reviews and audits, and it should identify the participants and their specific responsibilities. These review and audit procedures should identify specific responsibility for the preparation of a report upon the completion of each review. This section should identify by position or job title who is to prepare these reports, the report format, who is to receive the reports, and associated management responsibilities. The review and audit procedures should also describe the follow-up actions to assure that the recommendations made during the reviews and audits are properly implemented. This section should indicate the interval of time between performance of the review or audit and performance of the follow-up. It should also identify those responsible for performing follow-up actions.

3.6.2 Minimum Requirements. "As a minimum, the following reviews shall be conducted": [2]

(1) Software Requirements Review (SRR)
(2) Preliminary Design Review (PDR)
(3) Critical Design Review (CDR)
(4) Software Verification and Validation Plan Review (SVVPR)
(5) Functional Audit
(6) Physical Audit
(7) In-Process Audits
(8) Managerial Reviews

Tailoring or inclusion of additional reviews and audits should be made as local, contractual, or project-specific conditions dictate.

An example of the relationships and timing of these reviews and audits to the software development process is presented in Fig 1.

3.6.2.1 Software Requirements Review (SRR). "The SRR is held to ensure the adequacy of the requirements stated in the Software Requirements Specification." [2]

The SRR is an evaluation of the Software Requirements Specification (SRS). The SRR is conducted to assure the adequacy, technical feasibility, and completeness of the requirements stated in the SRS. The SRR should evaluate the SRS for the attributes required by

Typical Software Development Phases (per ANSI/IEEE Std 729-1983 [1])	Required Software Development Products (Documentation per 3.4.2)	Required SQA Audits and Reviews[2] per 3.6.2
Requirements	SQAP[1] SRS SVVP[4]	SRR In-Process Audit[3] SVVPR[4] Managerial Review[3]
Design	Preliminary SDD	PDR[5] In-Process Audit
	SDD	CDR[5]
	User Documentation[5]	UDR[5]
Implementation	Software items with documentation	In-Process Audit
Test	Test Documentation[6]	Functional Audit
Installation and Checkout[7]	Deliverable items SVVR	Physical Audit
Operation and Maintenance[8]	Products depend on scope of maintenance. Major modifications will have some or all of the above products.	Review depends on scope of required products.

Fig 1
Example of Relationships and Timing of Required Reviews and Audits

NOTES:
   [1] This includes any referenced documents.
   [2] Results of these activities are reports that identify what was reviewed, the deficiencies found, and conclusions. A report generated by a review meeting also includes recommendations as to what needs to be done to resolve the deficiencies. (The items subject to review are the software development products.)
   [3] In-process audits and managerial reviews are scheduled as required throughout the software life cycle. For additional assistance see Section 5.
   [4] The SVVP completion and SVVPR should be accomplished prior to the PDR.
   [5] A UDR may be held independently of other reviews or in conjunction with the PDR and the CDR (a UDR is not an ANSI/IEEE Std 730-1984 [2] requirement).
   [6] Refer to ANSI/IEEE Std 829-1983 [4].
   [7] In the event this phase is not utilized in the SQAP, move the required products and audit to the test phase.
   [8] This phase is in addition to typical software development phases to show that the SQA effort can be an iterative process.

ANSI/IEEE Std 830-1984 [5] (unambiguous, complete, verifiable, consistent, modifiable, traceable, and usable during the operation and maintenance phase). The review assures that sufficient detail is available to complete the software design.

The SQAP should indicate the organizational element responsible for conducting the SRR. All organizational elements that contribute or are impacted by the requirements should partici-

pate. These may include software design, software test, software quality assurance, system engineering, customers, users, marketing, manufacturing, etc.

The SQAP should indicate, but not be limited to, the following items as review requirements for the SRR:

(1) Traceability and completeness of the requirement from the next higher level specifi-

cation (such as a system specification or user requirements specification)

(2) Adequacy of rationale for any derived requirements

(3) Adequacy and completeness of algorithms and equations

(4) Correctness and suitability of logic descriptions that may be warranted

(5) Compatibility of external (hardware and software) interfaces

(6) Adequacy of the description of and approach to the human–machine interface

(7) Consistency in the use of symbols and in the specification of all interfaces

(8) Availability of constants and tables for calculations

(9) Testability of the software requirements

(10) Adequacy and completeness of the verification and acceptance requirements

(11) Completeness and compatibility of interface specification and control documentation

(12) Freedom from unwarranted design detail

Additional items to be considered as review requirements for the SRR could include:

(1) Trade-off and design studies that have applicability for decisions on:
    (a) Data base design
    (b) Programming language usage
    (c) Space allocation
    (d) Operations system or executive design, or both

(2) The general description of the size and operating characteristics of all support software (eg, operational program, maintenance and diagnostic programs, compilers, etc)

(3) A description of requirements for the operation of the software and identification of functional requirements such as functional simulation, environmental recording and analysis, exercise configuration, etc.

The results of the review should be documented in an SRR Report that identifies all deficiencies identified in the review and provides a plan and schedule for corrective action. After the SRS is updated to correct any deficiencies, it should be placed under configuration control to establish the baseline to be used for the software design effort.

3.6.2.2 Preliminary Design Review (PDR). "The PDR is held to evaluate the technical adequacy of the preliminary design of the software as depicted in a preliminary version of the Software Design Description." [2]

The PDR is held to evaluate the technical adequacy of the preliminary design before the beginning of detailed design. The review assesses the progress, consistency, and technical adequacy of the selected design approach; checks the design's compatibility with the functional and performance requirements of the SRS; and verifies the existence and compatibility of the interfaces between the software, hardware, and end users. The PDR is also conducted to determine that the preliminary SDD defines a suitable software design that fulfills the requirements contained in the SRS.

The SQAP should indicate the organizational element responsible for conducting the PDR. All organizational elements that impose requirements or are impacted by the design should participate in the review. These groups could include system engineering, software development, software test, software quality assurance, the customers, users, etc.

The following items could be specified in the SQAP as review requirements for the PDR:

(1) All detailed functional interfaces with other software, system equipment, communication systems, etc, for adequate identification of interface design and design solution adequacy

(2) The software design as a whole, emphasizing allocation of software components to functions, functional flows, storage requirements and allocations, software operating sequences, and the design of the data base

(3) An analysis of the design for compatibility with critical system timing requirements, estimated running times, and other performance requirements

(4) The human factor requirements and the human–machine interfaces for adequacy and consistency of design

(5) Testability of the design, such as the existence of data store and processes that support behavior and state determination

(6) Test concepts, requirements, documentation, and tools, for adequacy

(7) Technical accuracy and currency of all available test documentation and its compatibility with the test requirements of the SRS

The results should be documented in a PDR Report which identifies all deficiencies discovered during the review and a plan and schedule for corrective action. The updated preliminary

SDD document should be placed under configuration control to establish the baseline for the detailed software design effort.

3.6.2.3 Critical Design Review (CDR). "The CDR is held to determine the acceptability of the detailed software designs as depicted in the Software Design Description in satisfying the requirements of the Software Requirements Specification." [2]

The CDR is an evaluation of the completed Software Design Description (SDD). The CDR evaluates the technical adequacy, completeness, and correctness of the detailed design of the software before the start of coding. The purpose of the CDR is to evaluate the acceptability of the detailed design, to establish that the detailed design satisfies the requirements of the SRS, to review compatibility with the other software and hardware with which the product is required to interact, and to assess the technical, cost, and schedule risks of the product design.

The SQAP should indicate the organizational element responsible for conducting the CDR. All other organizational elements that impose requirements or are impacted by the design should participate. These groups could include system engineering, software development, software test, software quality assurance, customers, users, etc.

The following items could be specified in the SQAP as review requirements for the CDR:

(1) The compatibility of the detailed design with the SRS

(2) Available data in the form of logic diagrams, algorithms, storage allocation charts, and detailed design representations (eg, flow chart, program design language) to establish design integrity

(3) Compatibility and completeness of interface requirements

(4) All external and internal interfaces, including interactions with the data base

(5) Technical accuracy and currency of all available test documentation and its compatibility with the test requirements of the SRS

(6) The requirements for the support and test software and hardware to be used in the development of the product

(7) The final design, including function flow, timing, sizing, storage requirements, memory maps, data base, and other performance factors

The results of the review should be documented in a CDR Report which identifies all

deficiencies discovered during the review and a plan and schedule for corrective actions. The updated SDD document, when placed under configuration control, establishes the baseline for coding.

3.6.2.4 Software Verification and Validation [Plan] Review (SVVPR). "The Software Verification and Validation [Plan] Review is held to evaluate the adequacy and completeness of the verification and validation methods defined in the SVVP." [2]

The SVVPR is an evaluation of the completed Software Verification and Validation Plan (SVVP). Since the SVVP may be developed incrementally, multiple reviews may be required. These reviews are held to assure that the verification and validation methods described in the SVVP are adequate and will provide complete evaluation data.

The SQAP should indicate the organizational element responsible for conducting the Software Verification and Validation Plan Review. All organizational elements that impose requirements or are impacted by the SVVP should participate. These groups could include system engineering, software development, software design, software test, software quality assurance, customers, users, etc.

The following items should be specified in the SQAP as the SVVPR requirement criteria:

(1) All verification and validation methods, along with completion criteria to assure traceability to, and compatibility with, the functional and performance requirements expressed in the SRS

(2) Reports to adequately document results of all reviews, audits, and tests based on the requirements listed in the SVVP

(3) Adequate descriptions of the software configuration to be tested, including test support software and hardware

(4) Test plans and test designs to assure that all requirements are tested

(5) Test procedures and test cases to assure that test inputs and success criteria are adequately defined and that test instructions are clear and concise

(6) A test schedule identifying which tests are to be done, when, and by whom

The results of the review should be documented in an SVVPR Report which identifies all deficiencies discovered during the review, and which provides a plan and schedule for corrective action. The updated SVVP, when placed under configuration control, establishes the baseline for the software verification and validation effort.

3.6.2.5 Functional Audit. "This audit is held prior to the software delivery to verify that all requirements specified in the Software Requirements Specification have been met." [2]

The Functional Audit compares the code with the documented software requirements as stated in the current SRS. Its purpose is to assure that the code addresses all, and only, the documented requirements stated in the SRS.

The SQAP should indicate the organizational element responsible for the Functional Audit. The results are to be documented in the Functional Audit Minutes, which identify all discrepancies found and the plans for their resolution.

Input to the Functional Audit should consist of:

(1) Software Requirements Specification (SRS)
(2) Software Verification and Validation Report (SVVR)
(3) Software Verification and Validation Plan Review (SVVPR) Minutes

3.6.2.6 Physical Audit. "This audit is held to verify that the software and its documentation are internally consistent and are ready for delivery." [2]

The Physical Audit compares the code with its supporting documentation. Its purpose is to assure that the documentation to be delivered correctly describes the code.

The SQAP should indicate the organizational element responsible for conducting the Physical Audit. The results of the Physical Audit are to be documented in the Physical Audit Minutes which identify all discrepancies and the plans for their resolution. Once the discrepancies have been resolved, the software can be delivered.

Input to the Physical Audit should consist of:

(1) Software Design Description (SDD)
(2) Software products
(3) Associated documentation

3.6.2.7 In-Process Audits. "In-process audits of a sample of the design are held to verify consistency of the design, including:

(1) Code versus design documentation

(2) Interface specifications (hardware and software)
(3) Design implementations versus functional requirements
(4) Functional requirements versus test descriptions." [2]

In-process audits of samples of the product development items are held as required by the SQAP. The SQAP should indicate the organizational element responsible for conducting the in-process audits. Software inspections may be included as part of the in-process audit activity. The objective is to verify the consistency of the product as it evolves through the development process by determining that:

(1) Hardware and software interfaces are consistent with design requirements in the SRS
(2) The functional requirements of the SRS are fully tested by the SVVP
(3) The design of the product, as the SDD is evolving, satisfies the functional requirements of the SRS
(4) The code is consistent with the SDD

The results of all in-process audits are measures of how well the process is working. They should be documented in in-process audit reports, which identify all discrepancies found and the plans for their resolution.

3.6.2.8 Managerial Reviews. "These reviews are held periodically to assess the execution of this [SQA] plan. These reviews shall be held by an organizational element independent of the unit being audited, or by a qualified third party." [2]

The planned frequency and structure of the managerial reviews should be stated in the SQAP. They should be conducted at the direction of an appropriate level of management independent of the SQA effort.

A managerial review results in a statement as to the adequacy of the SQAP and its execution. Each review should be documented by a report summarizing the review findings, including any exceptions to the process stated in the SQAP, and any recommended changes or improvements.

Section 5 provides guidance for evaluating the contents and the implementation of a SQAP.

3.6.3 Other. Other reviews may also be conducted.

3.6.3.1 User Documentation Review (UDR). The UDR is held to determine the technical adequacy of the documentation approach and design as described in draft versions of the User Documentation.

The SQAP should indicate the organizational element responsible for conducting the UDR. All organizational elements that are affected or impacted by the User Documentation should participate in the review. These groups may include system engineering, software, development, software test, software quality assurance, customers, users, etc.

The following items could be specified in the SQAP as the UDR requirement criteria:

(1) The methods used to validate that the software product matches the user documentation

(2) Test plans, test procedures, and test cases to assure that all user documentation is tested in conjunction with the software

The UDR can be held independently of other reviews or in conjunction with the Preliminary Design Review (PDR) and the Critical Design Review (CDR).

The results of the review should be documented in a UDR Report, which identifies all deficiencies discovered during the review and which provides a plan and schedule for connective action. The updated user documentation should be placed under configuration management prior to the physical audit described in 3.6.2.6.

3.7 Software Configuration Management.
"This section shall document the methods to be used for identifying the software product items, controlling and implementing changes, and recording and reporting change implementation status. This documentation shall either be provided explicitly in this section or by reference to an existing software configuration management plan." [2]

The SQAP should describe the tasks and methodology required to assure that adequate Software Configuration Management (SCM) procedures and controls are documented and are being implemented correctly. It is not necessary that the SQA function prepare the Software Configuration Management Plan (SCMP).

The material to be supplied in this section is specified in ANSI/IEEE Std 828-1983 [3].

3.8 Problem Reporting and Corrective Action.
"This section shall:

(1) Describe the practices and procedures to be followed for reporting, tracking, and resolving software problems.

(2) State the specific organizational responsibilities concerned with their implementation." [2]

Problems encountered during software development or operation may result in defects in the software, hardware, or operations. Because of their diversity, the determination of the sources of a problem and its appropriate corrective action requires a centrally controlled system for monitoring problems and determining systemic causes.

The purposes of a software problem reporting and corrective action system are to:

(1) Assure that problems are documented, corrected, and not forgotten

(2) Assure that problem reports are assessed for their validity

(3) Provide feedback to the developer and the user on problem status

(4) Provide data for measuring and predicting software quality and reliability

These goals should be satisfied by the problem reporting and corrective action system described in the SQAP.

The SQAP should include methods to be used to assure that reported software problems are being properly controlled. The SQAP should describe the organizational element(s), provisions, and procedures for documenting, validating, tracking, and reporting the status of software problems and the appropriate corrective action.

Validating, tracking, and resolving software problems require the coordination of various groups within the organization. The SQAP should specify the groups responsible for authorizing and implementing problem reporting and corrective actions. It should also identify the point in the development process where generation of problem reports is to begin.

3.9 Tools, Techniques, and Methodologies.
"This section shall identify the special software tools, techniques, and methodologies employed on the specific project that support Quality Assurance, state their purposes, and describe their use." [2]

The SQAP shall identify the tools, techniques, and methodologies to be used to support software quality assurance. It should list or reference those tools, techniques, and methodologies which are available, and those that need to be acquired or developed. The responsible organization(s) should also be identified.

3.9.1 Tools. SQA software tools aid in the evaluation or improvement of software quality. Typical tools include, but are not limited to, operating system utilities, debugging aids, documentation aids, structuring preprocessors, file comparators, structure analyzers, standards auditors, simulators, execution analyzers, performance monitors, statistical analysis packages, test drivers, test case generators, and static or dynamic test tools.

3.9.2 Techniques. SQA techniques are technical and managerial procedures that aid in the evaluation and improvement of software quality. Such techniques include standards, software inspections, requirements tracing, requirements and design verification, reliability measurements and assessments, and rigorous or formal logic analysis.

3.9.3 Methodologies. SQA methodologies are integrated sets of the above techniques.

3.10 Code Control. "This section shall define the methods and facilities used to maintain and store controlled versions of identified software. This may be implemented in conjunction with a Computer Program Library." [2]

Code control can be interpreted as the ways and means necessary to protect or ensure the validity of a completed code. Once an appropriate baseline has been established, the code should be placed under configuration management in a computer program library. The SQAP should specify controls and security measures for software change and for protection from inadvertent alteration after the code has been baselined. It should define or reference the procedures and organizational responsibility for controlling the developed code.

The SQAP should specify a code control procedure that:

(1) Defines the specific software to be controlled

(2) Describes a standard method for identifying, labeling, and cataloging the software

(3) Lists the physical location of the software under control

(4) Describes the location, maintenance, and use of all backup copies

(5) Describes procedures for distributing a copy

(6) Identifies the documentation which is affected by changes

(7) Describes procedures for implementing a new version

3.11 Media Control. "This section shall state the methods and facilities to be used to protect computer program physical media from unauthorized access or inadvertent damage or degradation." [2]

Computer program media can be defined as those media on which computer data are stored. Typically, the storage media are disks or tapes, but could include cards, diskettes, listings, or other forms in which the data reside.

The media control methods and facilities should ensure that:

(1) The software is stored and retrieval is guaranteed

(2) Offsite storage and retrieval are provided for critical software and copies of baselined code

(3) The software is accessible only to those with the need of access

(4) The environment is controlled so that the physical media on which the software is stored do not degrade

The SQAP should reference or specify procedures and practices that pertain to the above items. For example, a backup procedure for software could indicate the schedule for backup, the type of media on which it will be placed, the location of the storage, the environment of the storage area, and the method to retrieve the backed-up software. A security system may be in place that allows access to software only through an authorization process. The SQAP should delineate the organizational elements responsible for administering and reviewing media control methods and facilities. The method for identifying, labeling, and data logging may be the same in both code and media control.

3.11.1 Unauthorized Access. Several methods are available which will provide adequate protection from unauthorized access of computer program media. The primary method is to provide a permanent labeling or identification scheme within the storage media. When the disk or tape is used on a computer, this technique can provide adequate password control or access protection. Other methods include a limited access program library, encryption, external markings, and proprietary statements identifying a controlled program. The physical security of all media must also be considered.

SQA activities to verify appropriateness and implementation of access procedures should be documented in the SQAP. Areas of concern include: identifying the programs requiring limited access, adherence to label and file restrictions, ensuring use of adequate external labeling restrictions, and providing a controlled environment such as a program library.

3.11.2 Inadvertent Damage or Degradation. Damage or degradation of the media can be minimized by providing adequate configuration management techniques, safe storage locations such as fireproof vaults, and packaging practices that are antistatic in design. Periodic reviews to ensure use of controlled environmental and cataloging practices will minimize degradation of external or physical identification of the media.

SQA activities to verify appropriateness and implementation of procedures to minimize media damage or degradation should be documented in the SQAP.

3.12 Supplier Control. "This section shall state the provisions for assuring that vendor-provided and subcontractor-developed software meets established technical requirements. As a minimum, the supplier shall be required to prepare and implement a Software Quality Assurance Plan in accordance with this standard." [2]

This section of the purchaser's SQAP should specify:

(1) The purchaser's involvement with the supplier's SQA program

(2) The purchaser's procedures for auditing the supplier's conformance to ANSI/IEEE Std 730-1984 [2] and the supplier's SQAP (an option could be to provide for an independent auditor)

(3) The actions available to the purchaser should the supplier not be in conformance with ANSI/IEEE Std 730-1984 [2] and the supplier's SQAP

3.13 Records Collection, Maintenance, and Retention. "This section shall identify the SQA documentation to be retained, shall state the methods and facilities to be used to assemble, safeguard and maintain this documentation and shall designate the retention period." [2]

3.13.1 Records Collection. The type of records to be collected are determined by the overall objectives for record keeping. These objectives should be documented in the SQAP. Possible objectives are:

(1) To provide legal or contractual evidence that the software development process was performed in conformance with established professional practice and the customer's requirements. The documents collected for legal or contractual purposes should provide evidence that:

(a) The SQAP is being followed and conforms to the requirements of applicable standards

(b) The software meets design intent and satisfies contractual requirements

(c) Corrective action is effective

(d) Testing has been performed in accordance with test plans.

(2) To provide historical or reference data that could be used to discover long-term trends in the organization's development techniques. The documents collected for historical or reference purposes should be capable of providing data for productivity, quality, and methodology studies. The documents should provide sufficient design, implementation, and testing data so as to be useful for future development.

In addition to SQA documents, records should include program media containing the exact version of programs and materials used in performing tests to assure test repeatability at any time in the future.

3.13.2 Records Maintenance. The SQAP should specify the manner in which records will be kept, that is, hard copy, microfiche, etc. Also, it should state how records will be stored to protect them from fire, theft, or environmental deterioration. The SQAP should provide for historical archiving if applicable.

3.13.3 Records Retention. The SQAP should specify the length of retention for each type of record maintained. It is important to state in the SQAP when records should be retained and when they should be destroyed.

3.13.4 Organizational Responsibilities. The SQAP should specify the organizational element responsible for originating, collecting, maintaining, storing, and protecting records. The plan should also identify the authority for access to records, and the responsibilities for changing, purging, or destroying records. Information in this section shall be compatible and consistent with information shown in 3.3.2 and 3.3.3.

4. Implementation of a Software Quality Assurance Plan

The purpose of this section is to describe the steps necessary for successfully implementing the SQAP that has been prepared for a specific project. The following items are discussed in this section:

(1) Acceptance of the SQAP by management
(2) Acceptance of the SQAP by the software developers and others whose task responsibilities are defined in the SQAP
(3) Planning and scheduling of resources and tasks for implementation of the SQAP
(4) Training of personnel to implement the SQAP
(5) Distribution of the SQAP to implementors and interfacing personnel
(6) Execution of the SQAP

4.1 Acceptance by Management. Management acceptance and commitment to the SQAP should be obtained. This will provide the support required for implementing the tasks defined. This acceptance should include commitments for the budget and resources required to implement the SQA activities.

The SQAP should be coordinated with and agreed to by each unit of the organization having responsibilities defined within the SQAP. Acceptance of the SQAP should be indicated on the cover page by an approval signature of the person in charge of each unit. Implementation of the SQAP can be effective only if all the actions called for in the SQAP are performed with the full support of management.

4.2 Acceptance by Development Personnel. It is essential to foster a spirit of cooperation between the personnel responsible for software development and the SQA activities. An effective method of achieving this is to have the development personnel participate in the preparation of the SQAP. This will tend to increase their support of SQA in general, and of the SQAP in particular. Preliminary drafts of the SQAP should therefore be circulated within the development organization for review and comments. It may also be useful to hold walkthroughs of the SQAP with all concerned personnel. During this time they will be able to ask questions directly of the authors of the SQAP, and to make their concerns and objections known before the SQAP is officially published. In this manner, the groundwork will be laid for cooperation and mutual support between all organizations responsible for activities required by the SQAP.

4.3 Planning for Implementation of the SQAP. Planning for SQAP implementation comprises three aspects:

(1) Identification of required resources
(2) Scheduling implementation resources
(3) Assessing the risks involved

4.3.1 Resources. The four types of resources required to implement a SQAP are: personnel, equipment, facilities, and tools. The quantity and quality of these resources should be made known to the appropriate level of management.

The responsible element should identify the job classifications and skill levels of the personnel required to implement and maintain the SQAP throughout the life of the project. It should identify the hardware needed to implement the SQAP and to support it throughout the project, as well as estimates of computer time and support required. It should also identify the facilities needed for storage of media and records. When resources are identified by an element other than the SQA element, the SQA element should verify compliance with this task. The tools required for implementation should already have been identified in the SQAP itself.

4.3.2 Scheduling. Once the resources involved in implementing a SQAP have been identified, the next step is to establish a schedule for the implementation. For each task identified in the SQAP, this schedule should identify the starting and completion dates for each required resource. In a similar manner, a schedule should be established for the development or acquisition of any necessary support tools.

4.3.3 Risk Assessment. The last element of planning is risk assessment. It is essential to identify the level of risk (high, medium, or low) associated with the possible failure of each required task or the unavailability of each resource. This risk assessment should identify the resulting impact on other schedules and outline alternative actions available to mitigate the risks.

4.4 Training. The need for training of personnel designated to perform the activities defined in the SQAP should be assessed. Considerations for training should include the skills of assigned personnel; special tools, techniques, and methodology that must be used; computer resources that will be used; etc.

Existing training programs should be adapted or new training programs developed to meet the needs of the plan. Training sessions should be scheduled for personnel who will be assigned to carry out the tasks. This training should be compatible with the task schedules discussed in 4.3.2.

4.5 Distribution of the SQAP. A distribution list of all personnel who are to receive the final approved copy of the SQAP should be prepared. A copy of the published SQAP should then be distributed to each individual listed, with an attached sign-off sheet that is to be initialed by the person receiving the SQAP and returned to the organization responsible for the SQAP's publication and distribution.

4.6 Execution of the SQAP. Once the SQAP is distributed, the Software Quality Assurance element shall assure that the tasks (eg, reviews and audits) documented within the SQAP are performed at the appropriate points in the life cycle. The SQAP will specify the activity to be performed, the person(s) performing the activity, and the results to be achieved. It will reference other documents as necessary. Associated work papers of the reviews and audits must provide sufficient evidence that the steps in the SQAP have been performed and reviewed by the management accountable for the SQAP. This will permit an objective determination of how well the SQA objectives have been met.

5. Evaluation of a Software Quality Assurance Plan

5.1 Purpose. The SQA element should make provision for periodic or on-going evaluation of the SQAP. Evaluating the SQAP involves examining it from two different viewpoints:

(1) Evaluating the plan's content (initially and after all revisions)
(2) Evaluating the use and management of the SQAP

The evaluation of the SQAP's content is an assessment of how the SQAP complies with ANSI/IEEE Std 730-1984 [2], internal development and quality assurance standards, and contractual documents. Evaluation of the completeness and applicability of the SQAP is facilitated by the questions presented in 5.2.1.

These questions provide an overview of the state of the SQAP.

The evaluation of the use and management of the SQAP is an assessment of the specific project's implementation of the SQAP. Section 5.2.2 contains some suggestions for this ongoing activity.

5.2 Methodology

5.2.1 SQAP Evaluation. The following questions should be asked in evaluating the overall approach of the SQAP:

(1) Are all the mandatory requirements per ANSI/IEEE Std 730-1984 [2] addressed in the SQAP?
(2) Are all contractual and company SQAP standards addressed in the SQAP?
(3) Does the SQAP specify compliance with any standards in addition to ANSI/IEEE Std 730-1984 [2]? If so, does the SQAP meet the requirements of those standards?
(4) Are all exceptions to mandatory requirements noted and adequately justified?
(5) Is the content of the SQAP adequate to achieve its stated objectives?

Additional questions which can be used in support of the evaluation of specific SQAP sections are:

(1) Purpose
 (a) Are the specific purpose and scope of the SQAP described?
 (b) Are the software product items covered by the SQAP completely described?
 (c) Is the intended use of the software items described?
(2) Referenced Documents
 (a) Are all documents referenced by the SQAP listed in this section?
(3) Management
 (a) Are the structures of all the organizations that influence the quality of the software depicted?
 (b) Are the management activities completely described?
 (c) Are the tasks and responsibilities of the organizations that influence the quality of the software listed?
(4) Documentation
 (a) Does the section describe all necessary software documentation?
 (b) Does this section describe the methodologies to be used for checking documentation adequacy with reference to 3.6?
 (c) Are the methodologies adequate?

(5) Standards, Practices, and Conventions

(a) Does this section identify all standards, practices, and conventions to be applied to the software?

(b) Are compliance and monitoring procedures identified?

(c) Are (a) and (b) adequate?

(6) Reviews and Audits

(a) Does this section define all necessary reviews and audits for the documentation described in 3.4?

(b) Are the methodologies for all reviews and audits described?

(c) Are (a) and (b) adequate?

(7) Software Configuration Management (SCM)

(a) Does the SCM information in this section, or contained in a separate SCMP, conform to ANSI/IEEE Std 828-1983 [3]?

(b) If the SCM/SCMP is not in conformance with ANSI/IEEE Std 828-1983 [3], is it adequate for this particular SQAP?

(8) Problem Reporting and Corrective Action

(a) Does this section describe problem reporting and corrective action procedures to be used for this project?

(b) Does this section state specific organizational responsibilities?

(c) Are the procedures adequate?

(9) Tools, Techniques, and Methodologies

(a) Are all tools, techniques, and methodologies to be used for SQA purposes fully described?

(b) Are they adequate?

(10) Code Control

(a) Does this section contain a description of all methods and facilities to be used for code control?

(b) Are they adequate?

(11) Media Control

(a) Does this section contain a description of all methods and facilities to be used for media control?

(b) Are they adequate?

(12) Supplier Control

(a) Are all procedures for interfacing between each supplier's SQAP and this SQAP fully described?

(b) Are they adequate?

(13) Records Collection, Maintenance, and Retention

(a) Are all records collection, maintenance, and retention procedures fully described?

(b) Are they adequate?

5.2.2 Implementation Evaluation. At several points in the product life cycle, usually major project milestones, the SQAP and its implementation should be evaluated by means of a managerial review. This will help assure that the project and its SQAP evolve together. As the project proceeds through the software life cycle, there are likely to be changes in the product scope. As the development plan changes, the SQAP and its implementation should also be reviewed to determine if any changes are required.

The use of the SQAP should be evaluated in terms of the tasks and responsibilities detailed in the SQAP (3.3.2 and 3.3.3). This evaluation should review the status of each task and the adequacy of the actions taken in terms of both product quality results and the schedules actually achieved for the tasks.

5.2.3 Evaluation Process Relationship. The evaluation process will have a cause–effect relationship as shown in Fig 2. A SQAP evalu-

**Fig 2
Cause–Effect Graph of SQAP Evaluation and Modification**

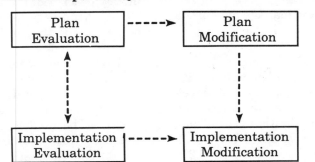

ation, whether formal or informal, may have the effect of causing SQAP modification or causing an implementation evaluation. A SQAP modification may necessitate a corresponding implementation modification. An implementation evaluation may cause an implementation change to bring the use and management into compliance with the SQAP.

6. Modification of the Software Quality Assurance Plan

The previous section addressed the evaluation of a SQAP and the determination of any necessary changes to it. This section will describe a mechanism for implementing such changes.

6.1 Purpose. The purpose of this section is to provide a method for modifying an existing SQAP. Only if there is a provision for systematic modification of a SQAP can its users have confidence in its continued usability.

There are several reasons why a SQAP, once approved and implemented, may subsequently need to be modified. First, the SQAP may contain deficiencies. Second, it may be necessary to adjust to changes in the environment of the SQAP. For example, a new set of system requirements may require stricter or more detailed testing to assure that they are satisfied. Third, changes in the management structure of the project may make portions of the SQAP (eg, reporting lines or sign-off authorities) obsolete. Finally, the advent of new technology may make modification desirable, as for example, when new SQAP tools or techniques must be incorporated.

6.2 Scope. This section addresses methods for proposing, reviewing, and instituting modifications to a SQAP. It does not cover modifications to the manner in which the SQAP is used, managed, or controlled; provisions for these are made either within the SQAP itself or in project management directives.

6.3 Methodology. As with any document, there are five steps in the modification of a SQAP:

(1) Identify alternative options
(2) Recommend proposed change
(3) Review proposed change
(4) Incorporate approved change
(5) Release and promulgate change

Steps (1) and (2) will be followed in all cases. If a project SCM organization exists, then steps (3), (4), and (5) will be accomplished according to that organization's procedures. If there is no project SCM, then steps (3), (4), and (5) will be followed as described below.

6.3.1 Identify Alternative Options. Changes to a SQAP may be proposed from any of several sources, such as project management, software development, system validation, configuration management, quality assurance, or customer. They could suggest different solutions to the same problem. It is important to provide for the results of the SQAP evaluation process (see Section 5) to be routed through all of these sources in order that each of their proposed solutions may be presented and reviewed.

6.3.2 Recommend Proposed Change. A Change Control Board (CCB) should be organized to review all alternative solutions and to determine a single recommended change (or set of changes) which they believe best addresses the acknowledged requirement. Depending upon the frequency with which SQAP changes are proposed, this CCB may be either a standing or an ad hoc organization. It may be useful to set up such a group as a standing organization at the time the SQAP is first published, if numerous change requests are expected. When such requests become fewer and farther between, the CCB may be converted to an ad hoc status.

6.3.3 Review Proposed Change. Once the CCB has agreed upon a proposed change, it should be sent to all interested or potentially affected parties for their review and comments. This step is necessary to provide agreement before the change is published and distributed. The CCB should have responsibility for evaluation and incorporation of comments received from the reviewers, and for approval or rejection of the proposed change.

6.3.4 Incorporate Approved Change. If, after studying the reviewers' comments, the CCB approves the proposed change, it is incorporated into the SQAP. Standard document control procedures should be employed here, including editorial review, printing of change pages, use of vertical bars to highlight added or modified text, and control procedures to preserve previous versions of the document.

6.3.5 Release and Promulgate Change. A management official should be designated who will have sign-off authority on SQAP changes.

Once this official has approved the change page(s) for release, standard document distribution methods may be employed. Then, all that remains is to monitor the implementation of the change. This responsibility should be assigned to the appropriate management official. At this point, the evaluation process begins again (see Section 5).

Appendix

(This Appendix is not a part of IEEE Std 983-1986, IEEE Guide for Software Quality Assurance Planning.)

Table A1
Summary of SQAP Contents

Item	Shall	Should	May	ANSI/ IEEE Std 730-1984 [2]	IEEE Std 983-1986	Other Stds
• Description of specific scope and purpose of SQAP	X			3.1		
products covered by the SQAP	X			3.1	3.1(1)	
intended use	X			3.1	3.1(2)	
reason for SQAP		X		—	3.1(3)	
base documents		X		—	3.1(4)	
rationale for departures from base documents		X		—	3.1(5)	
• Reference documents list	X			3.2	3.2	
• Description of project and plan management						
Organization	X			3.3.1	3.3.1	
Tasks	X			3.3.2	3.3.2	
Responsibilities	X			3.3.3	3.3.3	
• Identification of documents to be used for development, verification, use, and maintenance of the products covered by SQAP and how they are to be evaluated	X			3.4	3.4	
SRS	X			3.4.2.1	3.4.2.1	ANSI/IEEE 830-1984 [5]
SDD	X			3.4.2.2	3.4.2.2	
SVVP	X			3.4.2.3	3.4.2.3	
SVVR	X			3.4.2.4	3.4.2.4	
User Documentation	X			3.4.2.5	3.4.2.5	
SDP			X	3.4.3(1)	3.4.3.1	
SCMP			X	3.4.3(2)	3.4.3.2	ANSI/IEEE 828-1983 [3]
SPM			X	3.4.3(3)	3.4.3.3	
User Requirements Statement			X	—	3.4.4.1	
External Interface Specification			X	—	3.4.4.2	
Internal Interface Specification			X	—	3.4.4.3	
Operations Manual			X	—	3.4.4.4	
Installation Manual			X	—	3.4.4.5	
Maintenance Manual			X	—	3.4.4.6	
Training Manual			X	—	3.4.4.7	
Training Plan			X	—	3.4.4.8	
• Identification of Standards, Practices, and Conventions, and statement of compliance check methods	X			3.5	3.5	
Documentation Standards	X			3.5.2	3.5.2	
Logic Structure Standards	X			3.5.2	3.5.2	
Coding Standards	X			3.5.2	3.5.2	
Commentary Standards	X			3.5.2	3.5.2	
Requirements Standards		X		—	3.5.2.1	
Design Standards		X		—	3.5.2.2	
Implementation Standards		X		—	3.5.2.3	

Item	Shall	Should	May	ANSI/ IEEE Std 730-1984 [2]	IEEE Std 983-1986	Other Stds
Test Standards		X		—	3.5.2.4	ANSI/IEEE 829-1983 [4]
Documentation Standards		X		—	3.5.2.5	
• Definition of technical reviews and audits and means of accomplishment	X			3.6.1	3.6	
• Conduct the following reviews:	X			3.6.2	3.6.2	
SRR	X			3.6.2.1	3.6.2.1	ANSI/IEEE 830-1984 [5]
PDR	X			3.6.2.2	3.6.2.2	
CDR	X			3.6.2.3	3.6.2.3	
SVVPR	X			3.6.2.4	3.6.2.4	
Functional Audit	X			3.6.2.5	3.6.2.5	
Physical Audit	X			3.6.2.6	3.6.2.6	
In-Process Audits	X			3.6.2.7	3.6.2.7	
Managerial Reviews	X			3.6.2.8	3.6.2.8	
UDR			X		3.6.3.1	
• Definition of software product item control procedures	X			3.7	3.7	ANSI/IEEE 828-1983 [3]
• Document methods for identification of software product items, change control, and change reporting	X			3.7	3.7	ANSI/IEEE 828-1983 [3]
• Discussion of problem reporting and corrective action	X			3.8	3.8	
• Describe tools, techniques and methodologies to be used	X			3.9	3.9	
• Definition of code control methods and facilities	X			3.10	3.10	
• Definition of media control methods and facilities	X			3.11	3.11	
Unauthorized access	X			3.11	3.11.1	
Damage and degradation	X			3.11	3.11.2	
• Provision for supplier quality assurance methods	X			3.12	3.12	
• Identification of software SQA records collection, maintenance, and retention	X			3.13	3.13	
Document record types and objectives		X		—	3.13.1	
Maintenance	X			3.13	3.13.2	
Retention period	X			3.13	3.13.3	
Organizational responsibility		X		—	3.13.4	
• Implementing a SQAP		X			4.0	
• Evaluating a SQAP		X			5.0	
• Modifying a SQAP		X			6.0	

Acknowledgments

The following organizations provided support for the development of this standard:

AT&T Bell Laboratories
AT&T Information Systems
AT&T Technologies
Bell Canada
B. L. Rosenberg and Co
Boeing Aerospace Co
CAP Gemini/DASD
Central Institute for Industrial Research
Computer Sciences Corp
Cox Cable Communications Inc
Data General Corp
Defense Mapping Aerospace Center
E-Systems, Inc
EG&G Idaho, Inc
Federal Aviation Agency
General Electric Co
IBM Corp
Itek Applied Technology
Lockheed Electronics
Logicon, Inc
Loral Electric Systems
Martin Marietta Engineering Systems
McLaughlin Research, Inc
Medtronic, Inc
National Bureau of Standards
Naval Air Development Center
Naval Surface Weapons Center

NCR Corp
Northern Telecom Limited
Northeast Utilities
Northrop Corp
OASAS Limited
Paradyne Corp
Perkin Elmer
Planning Research Corp
Programming Environments, Inc
PRP Systems, Inc
Raytheon Data Systems
RCA
SAI Comsystems
Science Applications, Inc
Software Quality Engineering
Sperry
Tektronix, Inc
Teledyne Brown Engineering
Teledyne Geotech
Texas Instruments
Time, Inc
Union Carbide Nuclear Division
US Air Force Communications Computer Programming Center
US Army Computer Systems Command
US Nuclear Regulatory Commission
Veatch, Rich & Nadler

(This support does not constitute or imply approval or endorsement of this standard.)

31

An American National Standard

IEEE Recommended Practice for Ada*
As a Program Design Language

Sponsor

**Technical Committee on Software Engineering of the
IEEE Computer Society**

Approved December 11, 1986

IEEE Standards Board

Approved October 1, 1987

American National Standards Institute

990

*Ada is a registered trademark of the United States Government, Department of Defense (Ada Joint Program Office).

Foreword

(This Foreword is not a part of IEEE Std 990-1987, IEEE Recommended Practice for Ada As a Design Language.)

Software Engineering is an emerging field. As part of that process, the Department of Defense initiated, and ANSI approved, ANSI/MIL-STD-1815A-1983, which defines the Ada* Programming Language. In recent years, there has been a growing demand for the use of Ada as a Program Design Language (PDL). Recognizing that an adequate definition of an Ada PDL did not exist, a project was approved in March 1983 to provide that definition as part of a voluntary consensus process. This recommended practice is the result of that process.

This is one of an evolving set of integrated software engineering standards; for example,
ANSI/IEEE Std 729-1983, IEEE Standard Glossary of Software Engineering Terminology
ANSI/IEEE Std 730-1984, IEEE Standard for Software Quality Assurance Plans
ANSI/IEEE Std 828-1983, IEEE Standard for Software Configuration Management Plans
ANSI/IEEE Std 829-1983, IEEE Standard for Software Test Documentation
ANSI/IEEE Std 830-1983, IEEE Guide for Software Requirement Specifications
ANSI/IEEE Std 983-1986, IEEE Guide for Software Quality Assurance Planning
ANSI/IEEE Std 1008-1987, IEEE Standard for Software Unit Testing
This recommended practice may be used either in conjunction with those standards or separately.

As a recommended practice, this document should be helpful to PDL designers, PDL evaluators, software designers, and other members of the software engineering community concerned with the use of Ada as a PDL.

Members of the Executive Steering Committee were as follows:

Robert M. Blasewitz, *Chairman*   **Mark S. Gerhardt,** *Vice-Chairman*
Susan P. Mardinly, *Executive Chairman*
Dianna H. Peet, *Secretary*

Michael J. Devlin   Michael Gordon   Charlene Hayden
Debbie Faith   Thomas J. Walsh

*Ada is a registered trademark of the United States Government, Department of Defense, (Ada Joint Program Office`.

The Ada as a PDL Working Group had the following members:

Robert M. Blasewitz, *Chairman*

George H. Alessi
Ed Amoroso
Christine M. Anderson
John A. Anderson
Peter G. Anderson
Grebenc Andrej
Barbara Ardary
Jeannine Arsenault
John Bailey
James Baldo, Jr
Richard W. Baldwin
Leo Beltracchi
Mordechai Ben Menachem
Yechiel Ben Naftali
John C. Bennett
Victor G. Berecz
Ed Bevard
Lee Blaine
William Bogdan
Roy Bollinger
Graham D. Boose
Robert Borland
Jack Boudreaux
Carol Brade
James Bradley
Eric J. Braude
Christine L. Braun
Alton L. Brintzenhoff
Dwight R. Brooks
Jerry R. Brookshire
Al Brown
Fletcher J. Buckley
Ruck Byrne
Jim Cain
Lorie J. Call
Robert Calland
Miguel A. Carrio
Virginia L. Castor
Phil Caverly
Ann Chase Charles
R. Childress
Antonio M. Cicu
James H. Cistone
Rita Coco
Gerald Cohen
Richard L. Conn
Jack W. Crenshaw
John J. Cupak, Jr
Patricia W. Daggett
B. K. Daniels
Adriam Davidoviciv
Theodore F. DeMuro
Phil A. J. DeVicci
Michael J. Devlin
C.J. DiPietro
Jack Dozier
Einar Dragstedt
Lawrence E. Druffel
Walter DuBlanica
Robert Eachus
Michael W. Evans
Richard E. Fairley
Debbie Faith
Jeffrey K. Farmer
Sal Fazzolari
Hal C. Ferguson

Kathy A. Fieldstad
Charles A. Finnell
Herman A. Fischer
Gerald Fisher
Larry Fishtahler
A.M. Foley
Alain Fontaine
Kevin Fosso
Helene Freedman
Jean Friedman
Bob Fritz
Sigrid Fritz
Vivian M. Gaetano
Michael J. Gagnon
Michel Galinier
Gary Garb
Forrest Karl Gardner
William Gardner
Anthony Gargaro
Dale Gaumer
Charles L. Gausche
William X. Gebele
David Gelperin
Mark S. Gerhardt
Larry D. Gilchrist
Shirley A. Gloss-Soler
Philip Goldstein
Michael Gordon
D.J. Gorman
Allain Griesemer
Thomas A. Grobicki
Howard Hamer
Richard M. Hanchett
Larry E. Hanlan
Ralph V. Harris
Michele Hartman
Charlene R. Hayden
Marlow Henne Herman
Ness Richard F. Hilliard
Warren Hoffnung
Michael Olin Hogan
Maretta T. Holden
Michael Horton
Mary Inglis
Jonathan James
Vicki Johnson
Lesa Kaitz
Gilbert H. Kemp
Robert Knapper
Martin Koenekamp
Shai Koenig
John F. Kramer, Jr
Bill Krueger
Arthur F. Krummenoeh
Joseph A. Krupinski
Mike Kuchinski
Joan Kundig
Carole J. Kuruma
Frank X. Laslo
Cony Lau
C. Crissman Laubach, III
Chris Laudbach
Carol LeDoux
Raymond C. Leber
Min Lee
Roger Lee

Larry Lindley
Steven Litvintchouk
Warren Loper
Michael E. Luken
Paul Maguire
Mark Maiocco
Allen Malberg
Sue Mardinly
D.H. Martin
Robert F. Mathis
Cathy Maxson
R.D. McCamy
Robert D. McClure
Ed McCronen
Gregory McFarland
Raymond J. McGlynn
George McPherson
Loren Meck
Mike Meirink
Louis Minham
James Moloney
David Moore
John I. Moore, Jr
William L. Morrison
A.J. Murfin
J.O. Neilson
Thomas Newsome
Edward Ng
Robert F. Owens
Eddie Paramore
Bruce R. Parker
Michael Patrick
Dianna H. Peet
George Petrovay
Larry Pochetti
Tim Portor
John Privitera
Thomas S. Radi
Stan F. Ralph
Salim Ramji
Kim T. Rawlinson
Ann Reedy
Alan Reiblein
Donald J. Reifer
Patrick J. Reilly
Herbert L. Resnick
Carol Righini
John W. Roberts
Kenneth Roberts
Mike Rockenhause
Paul Rogoway
Helen E. Romanowsky
Steven M. Rowan
R.C. Roy
David Rudd
Ruth Rudolph
Richard Rupolo
John L. Rymer
Mark Sadler
Sabina Saib
Arthur E. Salwin
Burnett H. Sams
Jack Schaefer
David F. Schick
Richard Schneider
Harvey E. Schock, Jr

Joann Schultz
William M. Scott
Alfred Seita
A.E. Severin
Rod Sheffield
Sylvia B. Sheppard
Tracy G. Shoor
Jeffrey E. Simon
Dave Sloyer
Joan D. Spalding
Robert D. Spray
Donald Squires
William Stafford
David Steinberg

Putnam Texel
R.C. Thomas
Terrence L. Tillmanns
William Stephen Turner, III
M.V. Underwood
Joseph E. Urban
David Usechak
A. Vandenakker
Ralph Wachter
Larry K. Walker
Fred L. Wallace
John R. Wallace
John P. Walsh
Thomas J. Walsh

Martin M. Waxman
Robert Weissensee
Walt Whipple
B.A. Wichmann
Herbert E. Willman, Jr
Daryl R. Winters
Martin I. Wolfe
Helen Wu
Fred E. Wuebker
Lawrence Yelowitz
Michael E. York
Janusz Zalewski
George L. Zenzerovich
Sandra Zucker

The following persons were on the balloting committee that approved this standard for submission to the IEEE Standards Board:

A. Frank Ackerman
William W. Agresti
Dock Allen
Dennis R. Allison
Charles J. Antwelli
Barbara Ardary
Wolf Arfuidson
Tom Armbruster
James Baldo
Geoff R. Baldwin
Karl G. Balke
Bryce M. Bardin
John G.P. Barnes
B.C. Bass
Richard E. Batty
August A. Bauer
Leo Beltracchi
Frank Belz
Mordechai Ben-Menachem
Victor G. Berecz
H. Ronald Berlack
Brett L. Binns
Michael A. Blackledge
Robert M. Blasewitz
John J. Blyskal
Barry W. Boehm
William Bogdan
William Boyden
Carl Brandon
Jerry R. Brookshire
Al Brown
Fletcher J. Buckley
Harry Carl
David J. Carlson
Ingemar Carlson
A.J. Carvalho III
Janice A. Chelini
John Chihorek
Nhan V. Chu
Won L. Chung
Antonio M. Cicu
James H. Cistone
Suzette N. Clafton
John R. Clark
Donald R. Clarson
Corey Clinger
Richard T. Close
Peter Coad, Jr
Norman Cohen
Benjamin J. Consilvio
Chrisopher M. Cooke
Bard S. Crawford
James A. Darling
Sid David
Thomas Davis
Phil A.J. DeVicci
Vincent P. De-vito
Robert J. Decker
Michael J. Devlin
David G. Doty
Einar Dragstedt
Walter Du-Blanica
Robert E. Dwyer
Theodore J. Dzik
John D. Earls
Lange Brian Eliot
Richard E. Fairly
Raouf H. Farag
John W. Fendrich

Hal C. Ferguson
Glenn S. Fields
Gerry Fisher
A.M. Foley
Julian Forster
Kenneth A. Foster
Deborah L. Franke
Craig D. Fuget
Alfred Ganz
Leonard B. Gardner
Anthony Gargaro
David Gelperin
Edward L. Gibbs
Luther E. Gifford
Shirley A. Gloss-Soler
Marty Goldberg
Michael Gordon
Jacob Vadim Gore
Robert M. Grahm
Benjamin W. Green
Thomas A. Grobicki
Robert S. Grossman
Lawrence M. Gunther
Virl E. Haas
Harry E. Hansen, Jr
Hal M. Hart
Clark M. Hay
Paul L. Hazan
Jeffrey M. Hickey
L.J. Hoffman
Robert Hofkin
C.F. Howard
Henry B. Hoyle
Wendy J. Hudson
Charles J. Huller
James H. Ingram
Garland M. Jett, Jr
David Johnson III
Owen K. Kato
Mansour Kavianpour
Judith S. Kerner
Glenn M. Kersnick
Robert A. Kessler
Duane E. Kiefer
Genevieve M. Knight
Joseph A. Krupinski
Joan Kundig
Thomas M. Kurihara
Robert G. Kurkjian
Robin B. Lake
Robert A.C. Lane
Gregory N. Larsen
Randal Leavitt
Raymond C. Leber
David H. Lee
John A.N. Lee
James M. Lepsch
Ear Leung
Ben Livson
Paul E. MacNeil
Kartic C. Majumdar
Armand Marchesin
Sue Mardinly
Borut Maricic
Uchida Mark-Rene
Gregory C. Marr
Thomas H. Maryanski
Paul A. Mauro
C. Mazza

Maurice B. McEoy
Gregory McFarland
Raymond J. Mc-glynn
James McKelvey
Philip N. Merritt
Ben W. Miller
Robert P. Miller
Siba N. Mohanty
James Moody
Charles S. Mooney
John I. Moore, Jr
Nancy Moore
Gene T. Morun
Stephen V. Mroczek
David G. Mullens
Jose L. Munoz
W.M. Murray
Myron L. Nack
Hironobu Nagano
Jainendra K. Navlakha
Geraldine Rajcul Neidhart
States L. Nelson
Thomas Newsome
Dennis E. Nickle
T.L. Norman
John C. Norrell
Tim O'Bannon
James E. O'Day
Bruce R. Parker
Judson F. Parker
Michael Patrick
Robert L. Patton, Jr
Dianna H. Peet
Paul Peterson
Ramona Pfau
Ronald N. Pipes
Tim Porter
Ian Pyle
Edward Purvis
James E. Quelle
Sandra J. Raddue
Jock A. Rader
Thomas S. Radi
Salim Ramji
John Reddan
Larry K. Reed
T.D. Regulinski
Donald J. Reifer
Helen E. Romanowsky
Steven M. Rowan
Daniel M. Roy
Ruth Rudolph
Frances A. Ruhlman
John L. Rymer
H. Saha
Paul J. Sakson
Arthur E. Salwin
Jean E. Sammet
Burnett H. Sams
Raymond E. Sandborgh
Julio Gonzalez Sanz
Stephen R. Schach
Franz P. Schauer
Peter E. Schilling
Lee O. Schmidt
Norman F. Schneidewind
Wolf A. Schnoege
Leonard W. Seagren
Devdoot D. Sen

Gerard P. Shabe
Lawrence H. Shafer
S. Wayne Sherer
David M. Siefert
Jeffrey E. Simon
J.G. Snodgrass
Charles Snyder
Werner Sohn
Robert D. Spray
V. Srinivas
Paul D. Stachour
Manfred P. Stadel
G. Wayne Staley
Marilyn J. Stewart
Captain Mark D. Stotzer
A.W. Strohmeier
William G. Sutcliffe
Mary A. Sutton

Kou Chung Tai
Alan E. Ternstrom
Helmut E. Thiess
Booker T. Thomas
Terrence L. Tillmanns
Valentin W. Tirman, Jr
Henry J. Trochesset
C.L. Troyanowski
Kevin J. Tully
Erwin A. Ulbrich, Jr
David Usechak
Kazuo Ushijima
Howard E. Verne
Thomas Vollman
Ralph Wachter
John P. Walsh
Thomas J. Walsh
William M. Walsh III

Roger D.H. Warburton
Douglas W. Waugh
Martin M. Waxman
Peter J.D. Weyman
Thomas J. Wheeler
Walter L. Whipple
W.A. Whitaker
Paul A. Willis
Herbert E. Willman, Jr
Andrew F. Wilson
Patric J. Wilson
Paul A.T. Wolfgang
S.Y. Wong
Paul R. Work
Tom Worthington
Yung-Koh Yin
Michael E. York
Don Zeleny

Special representatives to the Software Engineering Standards Subcommittee were:

F. Gracza, ADAPSO
William C. Perry, DPMA
H. Ronald Berlack, EIA
T. D. Regulinski, IEEE Reliability
S. I. Heisler, Z1 Committee

When the IEEE Standards Board approved this standard on December 11, 1986, it had the following membership:

John E. May, *Chairman*   **Irving Kolodny,** *Vice Chairman*
                          Sava I. Sherr, *Secretary*

James H. Beall
Fletcher J. Buckley
Paul G. Cummings
Donald C. Fleckenstein
Jay Forster
Daniel L. Goldberg
Kenneth D. Hendrix
Irvin N. Howell

Jack Kinn
Joseph L. Koepfinger*
Edward Lohse
Lawrence V. McCall
Donald T. Michael*
Marco W. Migliaro
Stanley Owens
John P. Riganati
Frank L. Rose

Robert E. Rountree
Martha Sloan
Oley Wanaselja
J. Richard Weger
William B. Wilkens
Helen M. Wood
Charles J. Wylie
Donald W. Zipse

*Member emeritus

Contents

IEEE Recommended Practice for Ada As a Program Design Language

1. Introduction

1.1 Scope. This document provides recommendations reflecting the state of the art and alternate approaches to good practice for characteristics of Program Design Languages (PDLs) based on the syntax and semantics of the Ada Programming Language. In this recommended practice, these are referred to as Ada PDLs.

1.2 Scope Restrictions. This recommended practice addresses the characteristics of an Ada PDL and not the use of an Ada PDL. Although certain capabilities are recommended to be provided by an Ada PDL, this document does not state how a designer will design, nor how the design is to be documented, using an Ada PDL. While certain capabilities are recommended for an Ada PDL, specification of the ways to use those capabilities is beyond the scope of this document.

While it is widely recognized that graphic representations may enhance the design activity, there is no clear consensus concerning graphic representations at this time. As such, this document is principally concerned with the aspects of textual representations.

This recommended practice does not specify:

(1) A single PDL syntax

(2) The programming languages in which a design may be implemented

(3) A specific methodology to be used in conjunction with an Ada PDL

(4) The method by which a PDL text is represented, stored, or processed

This recommended practice does not provide:

(1) A tutorial on the use of:

(a) The Ada Programming Language, to include an exhaustive list of Ada constructs

(b) An Ada PDL

(2) A survey of PDLs or a history of their use

(3) A means for quantitatively determining the cost effectiveness of using an Ada PDL

1.3 Terminology. Where recommendations are made that represent the position of the IEEE, the verb *should* is used. Where alternate approaches are provided and no firm recommendations are made, the verb *may* is used.

1.4 Cautions. These are as follows:

(1) This document focuses on Ada PDLs. The use of a design language that is consistent with this recommended practice for other areas—for example, system requirements or hardware requirements—is not prohibited by this document. However, the reader is warned that there may very well be other substantial considerations in these uses, and that these considerations are beyond the scope of this recommended practice.

(2) An Ada PDL may be used to document a design when the implementation is projected to be in a Programming Language other than Ada. Users should be aware that an Ada PDL may not have the ability to represent such a design.

(3) Personnel associated with the use of a PDL should take special care to ensure that the designers do not become preoccupied with the details of the implementation when they should be designing. This may require special training, additional informal reviews, etc.

1.5 Examples. Examples are incorporated into the text of this recommended practice to enhance clarity and to promote understanding. All examples are explicitly identified. Examples should not be construed as recommended implementations.

2. Definitions and References

2.1 Definitions. The definitions listed in this section establish meaning in the context of this recommended practice. Other definitions can be found in: ANSI/IEEE Std 729-1983 [1][1] and ANSI/MIL-STD-1815A-1983 [2].

design element. A basic component or building block in a design.

design unit. A logically related collection of design elements. In an Ada PDL, a design unit is represented by an Ada compilation unit.

2.2 References. This standard shall be used in conjunction with the following publications:

[1] ANSI/IEEE Std 729-1983, IEEE Standard Glossary of Software Engineering Terminology.[2,3]

[2] ANSI/MIL-STD-1815A-1983 Reference Manual for the Ada Programming Language.[4]

3. Characteristics

3.1 General Methodology Support. A specific Ada PDL may support more than one design methodology. For example, both rapid prototyping and object-oriented design may be supported by the same Ada PDL. This is because no single development methodology is known to be superior for all applications and for all development organizations.

3.1.1 Abstraction. An Ada PDL should support the extraction of essential concepts while supporting the suppression of nonessential details.

3.1.2 Decomposition. An Ada PDL should support the division of a large software system into smaller, more manageable pieces while maintaining a fixed level of detail.

3.1.3 Information Hiding. An Ada PDL should support isolating and making inaccessible certain details that ought not to affect other parts of the software system.

3.1.4 Stepwise Refinement. An Ada PDL should support the progressive addition of detail to a software design.

3.1.5 Modularity. An Ada PDL should support the development of the design from standardized units.

3.2 Specific Design Support

3.2.1 Algorithm Design. An Ada PDL should support algorithm design. For example, depending on the intended usage, the PDL may support the use of structured control flow, computations, finite state machines, and Petri nets.

3.2.2 Data Structure Design. An Ada PDL should support data structure design. Specifically, an Ada PDL should support:

(1) Data structure definition

(2) Formalization of data structures

(3) Identification of constraints on acceptable values

(4) Identification of allowable operations on objects

(5) Location of points of access to data objects

(6) Modification of data objects

(7) Specification of data structure scope, duration, and storage methodology (for example, stored in shared memory, files, stack, etc) and constraints (for example, size limitations).

3.2.3 Connectivity. An Ada PDL should support the identification of explicit connections, including dependencies.

(1) The following should be formally described by the PDL:

(a) Ordering of component execution. As a part of this, the PDL should support the expression of:

(i) Sequential invocation of computational processes

(ii) Initiation and termination of parallel processes

(iii) Synchronization of parallel processes

(b) Data definition dependencies

---

[1] The numbers in brackets correspond to those of the references in 2.2 of this section.

[2] ANSI documents are available from the Sales Department, American National Standards Institute, 1430 Broadway, New York, NY 10018.

[3] See, specifically, Algorithm, Data Structure, Design, Design Language, Design Methodology, Life Cycle, Process, Program Design Language, and Software Life Cycle.

[4] See, specifically, Ada Programming Language, Compilation Unit, Generic Unit, Object, Package, Program Unit, Subprogram, Task, and Type.

(c) Data flow

(d) Possible error conditions and their associated consequences

(e) Interfaces between design units and between design elements

(f) Asynchronous interrupts

(2) The following may be formally describable by the Ada PDL:

(a) How the hardware works

(b) How interacting systems are expected to behave

3.2.4 Adaptability. The Ada PDL may have the capability to:

(1) Be adjusted under controlled forms to allow for national characters in a language other than English

(2) Implement restriction of certain syntax and semantics for particular applications (see 3.4.1.)

(3) Support graphic representations of the design being described

3.3 Other Support. The PDL may support the expression of Product and Management Information.

3.3.1 Product Information. Examples include:

(1) Performance. This may include critical timing, frequency, capacity, and other constraints.

(2) Fault Tolerance. This may include error detection/diagnosis and error handling, backup and recovery, reliability, and redundancy.

(3) Security. This may include multilevel security constraints, set/use access restrictions, breach detection and handling, and the identification of the security classification(s) of the material itself.

(4) Distribution. This may include geographic distribution of processing, data storage, and access.

(5) Adaptation. This may include accommodations to be made to support differing levels of user expertise.

(6) Assumptions. Description of a context within which an algorithm exists. For example, a function that does division may be built on the assumption that the denominator is not zero.

(7) History. This may include design decisions and alternate, rejected solutions to the chosen design, together with a rationale for the choice.

(8) Traceability. This may include traceability of:

(a) Detailed Design to Preliminary or Top-Level Design, and further to the Software Requirements specifications

(b) Preliminary, or Top-Level Design to Detailed Design

(c) Applicable standards

3.3.2 Management Information. Examples include:

(1) Organizational information, such as division of work and assignment of tasks to team members

(2) Planning information, such as milestone definitions, resource estimation, dependencies that affect the development process itself, and scheduling

(3) Status information, such as milestone completion

(4) Configuration Management information, to include Configuration Identification and Change Control restrictions

3.4 Ada Relationships. The PDL should be related to the Ada Programming Language in the following respects:

3.4.1 Conformance. An Ada PDL should conform syntactically and semantically to ANSI/MIL-STD-1815A-1983 [2]. Specifically, an Ada PDL should be processible by a validated Ada compiler without error.

(1) An Ada PDL may be processible by other tools: for example, a PDL Preprocessor. Preprocessing should not be required prior to error-free processing by a validated Ada compiler.

(2) There is no requirement that an Ada PDL provide the full capabilities of the Ada Programming Language. A conforming subset should be adequate for the application and is allowable, for example, to prevent the use of:

(a) Untranslatable Ada constructs when designing for a target language other than Ada

(b) Inefficient control structures when developing embedded computer systems software

(c) Excessively detailed design constructs during high-level design, for example, use of representation specifications

3.4.2 Extensions. Commentary text may be used to extend the expressive capability of an Ada PDL beyond the semantics of Ada.

Two forms of comments are available:

(1) Unstructured comments

(2) Structured comments

3.4.2.1 Unstructured Comments. Unstructured comments may be used for:

(1) Natural language explanation of statements made in Ada

(2) Any information required in the design process where formal structures are not required: for example, for humanto-human communication

The user of unstructured comments should be aware that tools can process unstructured comments only in very primitive ways (for example, storage, retrieval, and crossreferencing).

3.4.2.2 Structured Comments. Structured comments (also known as annotations):

(1) May be used to provide design information in additional design-oriented semantics.

(2) Should be consistent with the Ada language. For example, in compound constructs, the end of the construct should mirror the beginning:

```
--*High Level Design
--*
--*
--*End High Level Design
```

(3) Are identified by a sentinel character, word, or phrase immediately following the double dash that indicates a comment to an Ada complier, for example, "--keyword" or "--*".

(a) The sentinel has two functions:

(i) To highlight the comment as belonging to the formal structure of the PDL, alerting any reader that the information is of special significance

(ii) To direct PDL processing tools toward information upon which the tools may be required to act

(b) Associated with the sentinel are semantic rules that indicate:

(i) Whether the comment applies to the preceding or the following Ada construct

(ii) What constructs are allowed after the sentinel, based on the context in which the sentinel appears

3.4.2.3 Replication Constraints. All concepts that can be reasonably expressed in noncommentary Ada should be so expressed. Information that can be provided in the Ada portion of the PDL should not be replicated within the commentary text by Ada constructs or by any other means.

The following organizations supported working group members in the development of this recommended practice:

Ada Joint Program Office
AT&T Bell Laboratories
BDM Corporation
Bendix Corporation
Boeing-Vertol
Burroughs Corporation
Canadian Marconi Company
Comptek Research, Inc
Computer Sciences Corporation
Control Data Corporation
Convex Computer Corporation
Digital Equipment Corporation
Federal Aviation Administration
Federal Department of Transportation
Ford Aerospace & Communications Division
General Dynamics
General Electric Company
General Research Corporation
Grumman Aerospace Corporation
GTE Government Systems Division
GTE Sylvania
SSD Harris Corporation
Hughes Aircraft Company
IBM
I.C.L. Intermetrics
Johns Hopkins Applied Physics Lab

Kearfott Softech, Inc
Litton Data Systems
Lockheed Electronics Company
M/A Com—Linkabit
Magnavox
Martin Marietta Aerospace
MITRE
National Bureau of Standards
Naval Air Development Center
Naval Avionics Center
NBC
Norden Systems
Prior Data Sciences, Ltd
Raytheon Company
RCA SAI Comsystems
SDC
Singer
Sperry
SYSCON Corporation
Teledyne Brown Engineering
Texas Instruments
Transport Canada
U.S. Air Force
U.S. Army
U.S. Navy
Vitro Corporation

An American National Standard

IEEE Standard Taxonomy for Software Engineering Standards

Sponsor

**Software Engineering Subcommittee
of the
Technical Committee on Software Engineering
of the
IEEE Computer Society**

1002

Approved December 11, 1986
IEEE Standards Board

Approved June 4, 1987
American National Standards Institute

Foreword

(This Foreword is not a part of ANSI/IEEE Std 1002-1987, IEEE Standard Taxonomy for Software Engineering Standards.)

Software Engineering is an emerging field. As part of that process a set of software engineering standards is being developed. They are used to:

(1) Improve communications between and among software engineers and others.

(2) Achieve economy of cost, human effort, and essential materials.

(3) Institutionalize practical solutions to recurring problems.

(4) Achieve predictability of cost and quality.

(5) Establish norms of acceptable professional practice.

To support the development, integration, and use of software engineering standards, a need for a taxonomy is recognized. A project was approved in June 1983 to define a taxonomy as part of a voluntary consensus process. This document is the result of that process.

This is one of an evolving set of integrated IEEE Software Engineering standards, recommended practices, and guides. The set currently includes:

ANSI/IEEE Std 729-1983, IEEE Standard Glossary of Software Engineering Terminology

ANSI/IEEE Std 730-1984, IEEE Standard for Software Quality Assurance Plans

ANSI/IEEE Std 828-1983, IEEE Standard for Software Configuration Management Plans

ANSI/IEEE Std 829-1983, IEEE Standard for Software Test Documentation

ANSI/IEEE Std 830-1984, IEEE Guide to Software Requirements Specifications

ANSI/IEEE Std 983-1986, IEEE Guide for Software Quality Assurance Planning

ANSI/IEEE Std 1008-1987, IEEE Standard for Software Unit Testing

This standard may be used in conjunction with this set of standards or separately.

The taxonomy can be applied, but is not limited to, project, program, organization, industrial, national, and international standards. As a document, this standard should be useful to those who develop, use, manage, and evaluate software engineering standards. The taxonomy provides a:

(1) Comprehensive scheme for classifying software engineering standards, recommended practices, and guides.

(2) Framework for identifying the need for new software engineering standards, recommended practices, and guides.

(3) Comprehensive scheme for analyzing a set of software engineering standards, recommended practices, and guides appropriate for a given industry, company, program, project, or particular work assignment.

(4) Framework for comparing sets of software engineering standards, recommended practices, and guides to support the selection of the most useful set for a particular software product.

The application of the taxonomy to achieve the above purposes is described in the appendix.

Keywords applicable to this standard are: nomenclature standard, notation standard, software engineering.

The sponsor for this standard was the Software Engineering Standards Subcommittee of the Software Engineering Technical Committee of the IEEE Computer Society, John W. Horch, Chairman.

Special representatives to the Software Engineering Standards Subcommittee were:

P.W. Abrahams	S.R. Jarocki	W.F. Mitchell
H.R. Berlack	R.R. Jones	W.E. Perry
A. Ferlan	J.A.N. Lee	T.L. Regulinski
	J. Milandin	P.E. Schilling

The working group that developed this standard had the following membership:

Leonard L. Tripp, *Chairperson*   **Perry R. Nuhn,** *Co-Chairperson*

Ralph G. Wachter, *Co-Chairperson*

A. Frank Ackerman	Paul Howley	Robert C. Olsen
Eleanor Antreasian	John Horch	Sharon R. Cobb-Pierson
Joan P. Bateman	Harry Kalmbach	Robert B. Poston
H. Ronald Berlack	Louis B. Kiersky	Max J. Schindler
Richard L. Chilausky	Thomas M. Kurihara	David Schultz
Francois Coallier	John B. Lane	Leonard W. Seagren
Stewart Crawford	F. C. Lim	John Selman
James Darling	Phillip C. Marriott	David M. Siefert
John W. Fendrich	Virginia Marting	Dave Simkins
Mehmet Ficici	Dan G. McNicholl	R. van Tilburg
Craig D. Fuget	Mordechai Ben-Menachim	William S. Turner, III
David Gelperin	Fred Mervine	Clyde E. Willis
Jeff van Gilder	Manijeh Moghis	Paul A. Willis
	Dennis E. Nickle	

When the IEEE Standards Board approved this standard on December 11, 1986, it had the following membership:

John E. May, *Chairman*   **Irving Kolodny,** *Vice Chairman*

Sava I. Sherr, *Secretary*

James H. Beall	Jack Kinn	Robert E. Rountree
Fletcher J. Buckley	Joseph L. Koepfinger*	Martha Sloan
Paul G. Cummings	Edward Lohse	Oley Wanaselja
Donald C. Fleckenstein	Lawrence V. McCall	J. Richard Weger
Jay Forster	Donald T. Michael*	William B. Wilkens
Daniel L. Goldberg	Marco W. Migliaro	Helen M. Wood
Kenneth D. Hendrix	Stanley Owens	Charles J. Wylie
Irvin N. Howell	John P. Riganati	Donald W. Zipse
	Frank L. Rose	

*Member emeritus

The following persons were on the balloting committee that approved this document for submission to the IEEE Standards Board:

A. Frank Ackerman
Jagdish C. Agrawal
Richard L. Aurbach
K. Ramesh Babu
James Baldo, Jr
H. Jack Barnard
Roy W. Bass
Leo Beltracchi
Yechiel Ben-Naftali
Victor G. Berecz
H.R. Berlack
J. Emmett Black
Michael A. Blackledge
Ron Blair
Kevin W. Bowyer
Kathleen L. Briggs
Fletcher J. Buckley
Margaret Butler
Homer C. Carney
Ronald R. Carter
Robert N. Charette
Tsun S. Chow
Jung K. Chung
Peter Coad, Jr
Francois Coallier
Christopher M. Cooke
A.J. Cote, Jr
Stewart Crawford
George D. Darling
Taz Daughtrey
P.O. Denny
Harpal S. Dhama
Mike Dotson
William P. Dupros
Michael Dutton
Robert E. Dwyer
Mary Eads
John D. Earls
Michael Edward
L.G. Egan
Steven R. Eisen
Caroline L. Evans
David W. Favor
John W. Fendrich
Robert G. Ferreol
Glenn S. Fields
Gordon Force
J. Forster
Deborah L. Franke
C.R. Frederick
Carl Friedlander

Ismael Fuentes-Crespo
Micheel Galinier
Leonard B. Gardner
David Gelperin
James L. Gildersleeve
Shirley Gloss-Soler
Ole Golubjatnikov
J. Kaye Grau
Andrej Grebenc
Thomas Griest
Victor M. Guarnera
Lawrence M. Gunther
David A. Gustafson
Russell Gustin
Howard Hamer
Hans-Ludwig Hansen
George B. Hawthorne
Clark M. Hay
Terry L. Hengl
Charles P. Hollocker
John W. Horch
Cheng Hu
Shang-Sheng Jeng
David Johnson, III
Laurel V. Kaleda
Constantine Kaniklidis
Myron S. Karasik
Adi N. Kasad
Ron Kenett
R.A. Kessler
Joseph A. Krupinski
Hirayr M. Kudyan
Joan Kundig
T.M. Kurihara
Robin B. Lake
Lak-Ming Lam
John B. Lane
Robert A.C. Lane
William P. LaPlant, Jr
Greg Larsen
Jack A. Latimer
Jay Levenson
Leon S. Levy
Paul Lieberaz
F.C. Lim
Bertil Lindberg
David Linsson
William M. Lively
John M. Long
John Lowell
L.J. Mablack

Bill Macre
Andy Mahindru
Henry Malec
Paulo Cesar Marcondes
Stuart Marcotte
Philip C. Marriott
Nicholas L. Marselos
Roger J. Martin
Robert F. Martini
Ivano Mazza
J.A. McCall
John McKissick, Jr
Glen A. Meldrum
Belden Menkus
Ben W. Miller
Manijeh Moghis
Charles S. Mooney
Joyce E. Mortison
Gene T. Morun
Dale N. Murray
Myron L. Nack
Hironobu Nagano
Saied Najafi
Gerry Neidhart
Brian Nejmeh
Dennis E. Nickle
I.H. Obbink
Wilma Osborne
D.J. Ostrom
David G. Owens
Thomas D. Parrish
M.T. Perkins
Donald J. Pfeiffer
R.M. Poston
Peter Ron Prinzivalli
Thomas S. Radi
Meir Razy
John Reddan
Larry K. Reed
Matthias F. Reese, III
T.D. Regulinski
Donald J. Reifer
Steven M. Rowan
R. Waldo Roth
Hom Sack
Julio Gonzalez Sanz
Stephen R. Schach
Franz P. Schauer
Max Schindler
Norman Schneidewind
Nolf A. Schnoege

Robert G. Schueppert
David J. Schultz
Gregory D. Schumacher
Leonard W. Seagren
Devdoot Sen
Gerard P. Share
Robert W. Shillato
David M. Siefert
David J. Simkins
Jacob Slonim
Marion P. Smith
Harry M. Sneed
J.G. Snodgrass
Al R. Sorkowitz
Hugh B. Spillane
Lee Sprague
G. Wayne Staley
Alan N. Sukert
William G. Sutcliffe
Richard H. Thayer
Booker T. Thomas
Paul U. Thompson
E.O. Tilford
Terrence L. Tillmanns
Lawrence F. Tracey
Glendon R. Trebble
Robert Troy
C.L. Troyanowski
Dana L. Ulery
R.L. Van Tilburg
P.M. Vater
Osmo Vikman
R. Wachter
Dolores R. Wallace
Andrew H. Weigel
R.W. Werlwas
Walter L. Whipple
Paul A. Willis
Patrick J. Wilson
Paul Wolfgang
W. Martin Wong
Dennis L. Wood
Paul R. Work
Tom Worthington
Charles Wortz
Stephen D. Yaste
Natalie C. Yopconka
Michael E. York
Marvin Zelkowitz
Peter F. Zoll

Contents

An American National Standard
IEEE Standard Taxonomy for Software Engineering Standards

1. Introduction

1.1 Scope.
This document describes the form and content of a software engineering standards taxonomy. Applicability is not restricted by software application, size, complexity, criticality, or hardware environment. This taxonomy applies to standards (from the related disciplines of engineering management, systems engineering, computer hardware engineering, computer science, and information science) with which a software engineer would be reasonably acquainted. This taxonomy is application independent. For example, an accounting test standard would be placed under test standards, but the qualifier, accounting, has no significance. The document explains the various types of software engineering standards, their functional and external relationships, and the role of various functions participating in the software life cycle. The taxonomy may be used as a method for planning the development or evaluation of standards for an organization. It could also serve as a basis for classifying a set of standards or for organizing a standards manual.

1.2 Terminology.
The word *shall* identifies the mandatory material within this standard. The words *should* and *may* identify optional material.

1.3 References.
This standard shall be used in conjunction with the following reference:

[1] ANSI/IEEE Std 729-1983, IEEE Standard Glossary of Software Engineering Terminology.[1]

---

[1] ANSI/IEEE publications can be obtained from the Sales Department, American National Standards Institute, 1430 Broadway, New York, NY 10018, or from the Service Center, The Institute of Electrical and Electronics Engineers, 445 Hoes Lane, P.O. Box 1331, Piscataway, NJ 08855-1331.

2. Definitions

The definitions listed below establish meaning in the context of this standard. Other definitions can be found in ANSI/IEEE Std 729-1983 [1].[2] **See specifically: audit, certification, configuration management, conversion, debugging, design, design phase, implementation phase, installation and checkout phase, integration, maintenance, operation and maintenance phase, quality assurance, requirements analysis, requirements phase, retirement phase, review, software engineering, software maintenance, test phase, and testing.** For the purpose of this standard, the term "software" includes the computer programs, data, and documentation portions of both software and firmware.

code of ethics standard. A standard that describes the characteristics of a set of moral principles dealing with accepted standards of conduct by, within, and among professions.

coding. The transforming of logic and data from design specifications into a programming language.

component standard. A standard that describes the characteristics of data or program components.

concept phase. The period of time in the software life cycle during which the user needs are described and evaluated through documentation (for example, statement of needs, advance planning report, project initiation memo, feasibility studies, system definition documentation, regulations, procedures or policies relevant to the project).

---

[2] The numbers in square brackets refer to those of the references listed in 1.3.

curriculum standard. A standard that describes the characteristics of a course of study on a body of knowledge that is offered by an educational institution.

description standard. A standard that describes the characteristics of product information or procedures provided to help understand, test, install, operate, or maintain the product.

design standard. A standard that describes the characteristics of a design or a design description of data or program components.

job function. A group of engineering processes that is identified as a unit for the purposes of work organization, assignment, or evaluation. Examples are design, testing, or configuration management.

language standard. A standard that describes the characteristics of a language used to describe a requirements specification, a design, or test data.

licensing standard. A standard that describes the characteristics of an authorization given by an official or a legal authority to an individual or organization to do or own a specified thing.

manufacturing phase. The period of time in the software life cycle during which the basic version of a software product is adapted to a specified set of operational environments and is distributed to a customer base.

measurement standard. A standard that describes the characteristics of evaluating a process or product.

method standard. A standard that describes the characteristics of the orderly process or procedure used in the engineering of a product or performing a service.

nomenclature standard. A standard that describes the characteristics of a system or set of names, or designations, or symbols.

notation standard. A standard that describes the characteristics of formal interchanges within a profession.

occupational title standard. A standard that describes the characteristics of the general area of work or profession.

plan standard. A standard that describes the characteristics of a scheme for accomplishing

defined objectives or work within specified resources.

process management. The direction, control, and coordination of work performed to develop a product or perform a service. Example is quality assurance.

process standard. A standard that deals with the series of actions or operations used in making or achieving a product.

product analysis. The process of evaluating a product by manual or automated means to determine if the product has certain characteristics.

product engineering. The technical processes to define, design, and construct or assemble a product.

product management. The definition, coordination, and control of the characteristics of a product during its development cycle. Example is configuration management.

product standard. A standard that defines what constitutes completeness and acceptability of items that are used or produced, formally or informally, during the software engineering process.

product support. The providing of information, assistance, and training to install and make software operational in its intended environment and to distribute improved capabilities to users.

professional standard. A standard that identifies a profession as a discipline and distinguishes it from other professions.

report standard. A standard that describes the characteristics of describing results of engineering and management activities.

representation standard. A standard that describes the characteristics of portraying aspects of an engineering or management product.

requirement standard. A standard that describes the characteristics of a requirements specification.

resource management. The identification, estimation, allocation, and monitoring of the means used to develop a product or perform a service. Example is estimating.

software life cycle. The period of time that starts when a software product is conceived and ends when the product is no longer available for use. The software life cycle typically includes a concept phase, requirements phase, design phase, implementation phase, test phase, manufacturing phase, installation and checkout phase, operation and maintenance phase, and sometimes, retirement phase.

taxonomy. A scheme that partitions a body of knowledge and defines the relationships among the pieces. It is used for classifying and understanding the body of knowledge.

technical management. The application of technical and administrative resources to plan, organize, and control engineering functions.

technique standard. A standard that describes the characteristics of applying accumulated technical or management skills and methods in the creation of a product or performing a service.

verification and validation. The process of determining whether the requirements for a system or component are complete and correct, the products of each development phase fulfill the requirements or conditions imposed by the previous phase, and the final system or component complies with specified requirements.

3. Taxonomy of Software Engineering Standards

The taxonomy shall consist of a standards partition, software engineering partition, and a framework that relates the two partitions. Each partition results in the definition of a set of categories wherein each category has a name and a membership rule. The standards partition characterizes the roles of standards. The software engineering partition characterizes the aspects of software engineering with which a standard can be associated. The framework combines the two partitions into a two-dimensional scheme, which describes the set of possible software engineering standards. The taxonomy framework also describes how the categories are organized for classification purposes. Section 3.1 describes the standards partition, Section 3.2 describes the software engineering partition, and Section 3.3 describes the taxonomy framework and its relationships.

3.1 Standards Partition. The standards partition shall be organized by type of standard. The

Fig 1
Partition of Standards by Type

four types are process, product, professional, and notation standards. See Fig 1 for the complete partition.

Process standards deal with the series of actions or operations used in engineering a product or delivering a service. The actions or operations make use of methods, tools, and techniques. They give the "whos," "whats," "hows," "wheres," "whens," and levels of the work done in software engineering. Product standards are concerned with the format and content of things. The products are the documented results of the software development and maintenance activities and provide a baseline for future activities. Professional standards deal with all aspects of software engineering that identify it as a profession. An example is a curriculum for a Master of Software Engineering degree. Notation standards deal with the communication of common items among the software engineering professionals in a uniform manner. An example is a glossary. The output of a process is a product; the process is performed by people using tools and techniques within the profession.

3.2 Software Engineering Partition. The software engineering partition shall consist of two parts: job functions and software life cycle. These two parts or perspectives are used in order to compare, judge, evaluate, and determine the scope and content of software engineering standards. See Fig 2 for the software engineering

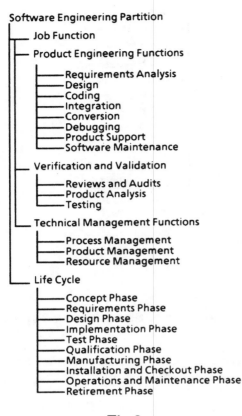

Software Engineering Partition
└─ Job Function
└─ Product Engineering Functions
   └─ Requirements Analysis
   ├─ Design
   ├─ Coding
   ├─ Integration
   ├─ Conversion
   ├─ Debugging
   ├─ Product Support
   └─ Software Maintenance
└─ Verification and Validation
   ├─ Reviews and Audits
   ├─ Product Analysis
   └─ Testing
└─ Technical Management Functions
   ├─ Process Management
   ├─ Product Management
   └─ Resource Management
└─ Life Cycle
   ├─ Concept Phase
   ├─ Requirements Phase
   ├─ Design Phase
   ├─ Implementation Phase
   ├─ Test Phase
   ├─ Qualification Phase
   ├─ Manufacturing Phase
   ├─ Installation and Checkout Phase
   ├─ Operations and Maintenance Phase
   └─ Retirement Phase

Fig 2
**Partition of Software Engineering by
Function and Life Cycle**

partition. Job functions are the identifiable processes of software engineering. Job functions often occur in parallel. For example, designs are updated as software elements are developed. No strict temporal sequence exists among the job functions since planning, execution, or follow-up within a function will certainly overlap other job functions.

Job functions are divided into three parts: product engineering functions, verification and validation functions, and technical management functions. The three parts contain the major ongoing, parallel activities of producing, checking, and controlling that are not concentrated in a single life cycle phase. The product engineering functions includes those processes that are necessary to define, produce, and support the final software product. Verification and validation functions are the technical activities that check the quality of the product. Technical management functions are those processes that structure and control the engineering functions. Project management is viewed as being related

to technical management in the following way: Typically, project management is the use, by one or more organizations, of the technical management functions of process management, product management, and resource management to develop a product within specified resources.

3.3 Taxonomy Framework. The taxonomy framework shall consist of:

(1) Names of the categories in the standards partition and the relationships among the names

(2) Names of the categories in the software engineering partition and the relationships among the names

(3) Rules for composing the framework

(4) Presentation format for the framework

The taxonomy may be presented in different ways, depending on how it can be used most effectively. The rows and columns may be reversed, higher or lower levels of classification can be shown, or only part of the table may be used.

This standard presents three versions of the taxonomy framework for use. The three versions are titled:

(a) Basic Taxonomy Framework (Version A)

(b) Basic Taxonomy Framework (Version B)

(c) Comprehensive Taxonomy Framework

The two Basic Taxonomy Frameworks have the same column labels with the row labels being somewhat different. The row labels for Version A are a selection from the job function portion of the software engineering partition that generally are present in all software life phases and the software life cycle phases. The column labels are the major categories of the standards partition. The row labels for Version B are the complete job function portion of the software engineering partition.

The two Basic Taxonomy Frameworks are illustrated in Figs 3 and 4. The frameworks are presented in the form of a two-dimensional table. An entry in one of the tables is defined by the names from the respective row label and column label of the entry. For example, in Fig 4, the most upper left table entry would be process standards for requirements analysis.

The Comprehensive Taxonomy Framework (see Fig 5) uses the full depth of both the standards partition and the software engineering partition. For presentation purposes, the framework is organized into two parts with the row labels from the standards partition and the column labels from the software engineering partition. For this framework, the entry name is defined by the names of the respective column label and row label of the entry.

The framework composition rules define the layout for the framework and how the entries in the table are composed. The rules are:

(1) The framework is displayed as a two-dimensional table with a set of labels for the rows and a set of labels for the columns.

(2) The names from either the standards partition or the software engineering partition are assigned as the source for the row labels. The remaining partition is the source for the column labels.

(3) A suitable set of names for the row and column labels is selected from the lists shown in Figs 1 and 2, starting at the left and proceeding to the desired level of detail.

(4) The scope of the framework is defined by eliminating those row-column pairs that are not feasible.

(5) An entry in the table is defined by names from the respective row and column of the entry.

Examples of how to classify standards using this taxonomy are contained in Appendix A.

			Type of Standard			
			Process Standard	Product Standard	Professional Standard	Notation Standard
Job Function	Ver & Val	Reviews & Audits				
		Product Analysis				
		Testing				
	Tech Mgmt	Process Management				
		Product Management				
		Resource Management				
S/w Life Cycle		Concept				
		Requirement				
		Design				
		Implementation				
		Test				
		Manufacturing				
		Operation and Maintenance				
		Retirement				

**Fig 3
Basic Taxonomy Framework (Version A)**

13

	Type of Standard			
	Process Standard	Product Standard	Professional Standard	Notation Standard
Requirements Analysis				
Design				
Coding				
Integration				
Conversion				
Debugging				
Product Support				
Software Maintenance				
Reviews and Audits				
Product Analysis				
Testing				
Process Management				
Product Management				
Resource Management				

Fig 4
Basic Taxonomy Framework (Version B)

			Job Function													
		Product Engineering								Verification & Validation			Technical Management			
		Requirements Analysis	Design	Coding	Integration	Conversion	Debugging	Product Support	Software Maintaince	Reviews and Audits	Product Analysis	Testing	Process Management	Product Management	Resource Management
P r o c e s s	Method														
	Technique														
	Measurement														
T y p e O f S t a n d a r d	**P r o d u c t**	Requirements														
	Design														
	Component														
	Description														
	Plan														
	Report														
P r o f e s s i o n	Occupational Title														
	Code of Ethics														
	Certification														
	Licensing														
	Curriculum														
N o t a t i o n	Nomenclature														
	Representation														
	Language														

Fig 5
Comprehensive Taxonomy Framework
(Part 1)

Software Life Cycle

	Concept	Requirements	Design	Implementation	Test	Manufacturing	Installation & Checkout	Operation & Maintenance	Retirement
Process									
Method									
Technique									
Measurement									
Product									
Requirements									
Design									
Component									
Description									
Plan									
Report									
Profession									
Occupational Title									
Code of Ethics									
Certification									
Licensing									
Curriculum									
Notation									
Nomenclature									
Representation									
Language									

Type Of Standard

**Fig 5 (Cont'd)
Comprehensive Taxonomy Framework
(Part 2)**

Appendix
Taxonomy Usage Examples

(This Appendix is not a part of ANSI/IEEE Std 1002-1987, IEEE Standard Taxonomy for Software Engineering Standards, but is included for information only.)

This Appendix illustrates how the taxonomy can be used to:

(1) Classify a set of software engineering standards

(2) Annotate software engineering standards with keywords

(3) Characterize a software engineering standards program

(4) Correlate functions and software life cycle viewpoints

A1. Classification of Selected Standards

This section presents a selection of references on software engineering standards. The key for selection was that the reference is publicly available through a trade association, government agency, or national society other than IEEE. The references are listed below with their identifier. The identifiers are placed in the two tables (Figs A1 and A2). The selected standards were classified using the job function table of the Comprehensive Taxonomy Framework organized by software life cycle phase. In a complete example, there would be a job function table for each software life cycle phase. The example presented contains two tables. The first table (see Fig A1) depicts those standards that essentially have equal applicability over most software life cycle phases. The second table (see Fig A2) depicts those standards that are of special importance for the design phase of the software life cycle.

Identifier	Title
ICAM	Air Force Materials Laboratory, ICAM Documentation Standards, IDS 150120000A, December 28, 1981.
480	Department of Defense, Configuration Control-Engineering Changes, Deviations, and Waivers, DOD-STD-480A, 1978.[3]
483	Department of Defense, Configuration Management Practices for Systems, Equipment, Munitions, and Computer Programs, MIL-STD-483A, June 4, 1985.[4]
499	Department of Defense, Engineering Management, MIL-STD-499, May 1, 1974.
52779	Department of Defense, Software Quality Assurance Program Requirements, MIL-S-52779A, August 1, 1979.
490	Department of Defense, Specification Practices, MIL-STD-490, June 4, 1985.
RADC	Rome Air Development Center, RADC Computer Software Development Specification, CP 0787796100E, May 1979.
TADSTAD9	Department of Defense, Tactical Digital System Standard, Software Quality Assurance Testing Criteria, TADSTAD 9, 1978.[5]
1521	Department of Defense, Technical Reviews and Audits for Systems, Equipment, and Computer Software, MIL-STD-1521B, June 4, 1985.
2167	Department of Defense, Defense System Software Department, DOD-STD-2167, June 4, 1985.

[3] DOD and MIL publications are available from the Director, US Navy Publications and Printing Service, Eastern Division, 700 Robbins Avenue, Philadelphia, PA 19111.

[4] See footnote 3.

[5] Information on this publication can be obtained by writing to TAD, Chief of Materiel Command Headquarters, Washington, DC 20360.

Identifier	*Title*	
2167.1	Section 5.1	Requirements Analysis
2167.2	Sections 5.2, 5.3	Design
2167.3	Section 5.4	Coding
2167.4	Sections 5.5, 5.6	Integration and Testing
2167.5	Section 5.7	Configuration Management
2167.6	Section 5.8	Quality Evaluation
2167.7	Section 5.8.1.5	Installation and Checkout
2167.8	Sections 4.1, 4.2, 5.9	Project Management

FIPS 38 — National Bureau of Standards, Guidelines for Documentation of Computer Programs and Automated Data Systems, Federal Information Processing Standards (FIPS) Publication (PUB) 38, February 15, 1976.[6]

FIPS 64 — National Bureau of Standards, Guidelines for Documentation of Computer Programs and Automated Data Systems for the Initiation Phase, FIPS PUB 64, August 1, 1979.

FIPS 99 — National Bureau of Standards, Guideline: A Framework for the Evaluation and Comparison of Software Development Tools, FIPS PUB 99, March 1983.

FIPS 101 — National Bureau of Standards, Guideline for Lifecycle Validation, Verification, and Testing of Computer Software, FIPS PUB 101, June 1983.

FIPS 105 — National Bureau of Standards, Guideline for Software Documentation Management, FIPS PUB 105, June 1984.

FIPS 106 — National Bureau of Standards, Guideline on Software Maintenance, FIPS PUB 106, July 1984.

NSAC-39 — Nuclear Safety Analysis Center, Verification and Validation for Safety Parameter Display Systems, NSAC-39, December 1981.

178 — Radio Technical Commission for Aeronautics, Software Considerations in Airborne Systems and Equipment Certification, RTCA/DO-178A, March 22, 1985.[7]

178.1	Section 6	Development Verification and Validation
178.2	Sections 7.1, 7.2	Configuration Management
178.3	Sections 7.1, 7.3	Software Quality Assurance

9650 — MITRE, Software Reporting Metrics, ESD-TR-85-145, MTR 9650, Revision 2, November 1985.

---

[6] FIPS publications are available from the Standards Processing Coordinator, Institute for Computer Sciences and Technology, National Bureau of Standards, Gaithersburg, MD 20899.

[7] RTCA publications are available from the Radio Technical Commission for Aeronautics (RTCA), 1425 K Street, NW, Suite 500, Washington, DC 20005.

Type of Standard

Job Functions		Process Standard	Product Standard	Professional Standard	Notation Standard
Product Engineering	Requirement Analysis	FIPS 99			
	Design	FIPS 99			
	Coding	FIPS 99			
	Integration	FIPS 99			
	Conversion	FIPS 99			
	Debugging	FIPS 99			
	Product Support	FIPS 99			
	Software Maintenance	FIPS 99			
V & V	Reviews and Audits	1521, 178.1, FIPS 101 NSAC-39			
	Product Analysis	178.1, FIPS 101 NSAC-39			
	Testing	TADSTAD 9, 178.1, FIPS 101, NSAC-39			
Mgt Tech	Process Management	52779, 2167.6, 1521, FIPS 105, RADC, 2167.8, 178.3	2167		
	Product Management	480, 483, 178.2, 2167.5	483, 2167		
	Resource Management	2167.8, 9650			

Fig A1
Example of General Standard Classification (Phase Independent)

Type of Standard

Job Functions		Process Standard	Product Standard	Professional Standard	Notation Standard
Product Engineering	Requirement Analysis	499*, 2167.1*	2167.1*, FIPS 64*, ICAM*		
	Design	2167.2, RADC	2167.2, FIPS 38, ICAM, 490		
	Coding	2167.3*, RADC*	2167.3*, ICAM*		
	Integration	2167.4	2167.4		
	Conversion				
	Debugging				
	Product Support				
	Software Maintenance	FIPS 106*			
V&V	Reviews and Audits	1521, 178.1, FIPS 101, NSAC-39			
	Product Analysis	178.1, FIPS 101 NSAC-39			
	Testing	TADSTAD 9, 178.1, FIPS 101, NSAC-39			
Mgmt	Process Management	52779, 2167.6, 1521, FIPS 105, RADC, 2167.8, 178.3	2167		
	Product Management	480, 483, 178.2, 2167.5	483, 2167		
	Resource Management	2167.8, 9650			

Legend *Examine for planning purposes

Fig A2
Example of General Standard Classification (Design Phase)

A2. An Approach to Annotating Software Engineering Standards with Keywords

The process of analysis, selection, and comparing of standards will benefit from a systematic means of keyword identification, which may then be incorporated into an organization's classification and retrieval procedures. An example set of keyword formation rules follows:

(1) Software engineering standards shall be classified with keywords. This shall be accomplished as part of a standard's development.

(2) Keywords shall be included in a standard's introduction. Keyword inclusion shall use the following format: "Keywords applicable to this standard are: Keyword 1, Keyword 2, . . ., Keyword n."

(3) Keywords shall be limited to words or phrases as contained in IEEE Std 1002-1987.

(4) Multiple keywords may be used in classifying a standard.

(5) Commas shall be used to separate keywords. The keyword shall will be terminated with a period.

(6) A standard shall be assigned at least one keyword from both the standards partition and software engineering partition. Within the categories of function and life cycle, multiple primary keywords may be selected.

The application of the keyword rules to some of the IEEE software engineering standards is illustrated in the following list:

Example #1. ANSI/IEEE Std 729-1983, IEEE Standard Glossary of Software Engineering Terminology. Keywords applicable to this standard are: nomenclature standard, notation standard, software engineering.

Example #2. ANSI/IEEE Std 730-1984, IEEE Standard for Software Quality Assurance Plans. Keywords applicable to this standard are: process management, product standard, software engineering, technical management.

Example #3. ANSI/IEEE Std 828-1983, IEEE Standard for Software Configuration Management Plans. Keywords applicable to this standard are: product management, product standard, technical management, software engineering.

Example #4. ANSI/IEEE Std 829-1983, IEEE Standard for Software Test Documentation. Keywords applicable to this standard are: product standard, software engineering, testing, verification and validation.

Example #5. ANSI/IEEE Std 830-1984, IEEE Guide to Software Requirements Specifications. Keywords applicable to this standard are: product engineering, product standard, requirements analysis, software engineering.

Example #6. ANSI/IEEE Std 983-1986, IEEE Guide to Software Quality Assurance Planning. Keywords applicable to this standard are: process standard, process management, technical management, software engineering.

Example #7. ANSI/IEEE Std 1008-1987, IEEE Standard for Software Unit Testing. Keywords applicable to this standard are: process standard, testing, verification and validation, software engineering.

A3. Application of Taxonomy to IEEE Software Engineering Standards (SES) Program

The IEEE Technical Committee on Software Engineering has an active program for software engineering standards. Listed below are the standards that are complete and those that are still in progress. The list of standards has been categorized by the taxonomy. To do that, three tables were created. The first table (see Fig A3) consists of the job function portion of the software engineering partition down the side and standards partition across the top. This orientation was chosen for presentation purposes.

Each entry on the standards list below was placed in the appropriate table entry. The S, R, and G refer to standard, recommended practice, and guide, respectively. The empty entries indicate possible areas for future standards.

The second and third tables use the standards partition down the side and functions across the top. The next lower level of detail was added for the standards partition. See Figs A4 and A5.

Approved Software Engineering Standards

Ref	Description
729	IEEE Standard Glossary or Software Engineering Terminology
730	IEEE Standard for Software Quality Assurance Plans
828	IEEE Standard for Software Configuration Management Plans

Ref	Description
829	IEEE Standard for Software Test Documentation
830	IEEE Guide to Software Requirements Specifications
983	IEEE Guide for Software Quality Assurance Planning
990	IEEE Guide for the Use of Ada* As a PDL
1002	IEEE Standard Taxonomy for Software Engineering Standards
1008	IEEE Standard for Software Unit Testing
1012	IEEE Standard for Software Verification and Validation Plans
1016	IEEE Recommended Practice for Software Design Descriptions

Approved Software Engineering Standards Projects

Ref	Description
P982	Standard for Software Reliability Measurement
P1028	Standard for Software Reviews and Audits
P1042	Guide for Software Configuration Management
P1044	Standard Classification of Software Errors, Faults, and Failures
P1045	Standard for Software Productivity Metrics
P1058	Standard for the Software Project Management Plan
P1059	Guide for Software Verification and Validation

Ref	Description
P1060	Standard for Software Maintenance
P1061	Standard for Software Quality Metrics
P1062	Guide for Third Party Software Acquisition
P1063	Standard for User Documentation
P1074	Standard for the Software Life Cycle Processes

A4. Job Function to Software Life Cycle Correlation

In some sense, job functions and phases can be correlated to each other. The purpose of this section is to illustrate that relationship. See Fig A6.

Note that in the product engineering and verification and validation categories each row is filled in to indicate where

(1) the planning or monitoring activity takes place (empty square)

(2) the focus of the phase and job function partially coincide (shaded square)

(3) the focus of the phase and job function directly coincide (dark square)

For product engineering and verification and validation activities, this indicates the respective phases for which these activities build, reach and stay at peak effort, and then taper off. The maintenance phase is typically a repeat of the basic software life cycle, and this is denoted in the respective column by an asterisk.

Note that for the technical management functions, activities generally happen across all phases. This is indicated by dark squares for all phases for these job functions.

---

* Ada is a registered trademark of the U.S. Government, AJPO.

Type of Standard

		Process Standard	Product Standard	Professional Standard	Notation Standard
Product Engineering	Requirement Analysis	1074(S)	830(G)		729, 1002(S)
	Design	1074(S)	1016(R)		729(S), 990(R), 1002(S), 1016(R)
	Coding	1074(S)			729(S), 1002(S)
	Integration	1074(S)			729(S), 1002(S)
	Conversion	1074(S)			729(S), 1002(S)
	Debugging	1074(S)			729(S), 1002(S)
	Product Support	1074(S)	1063(S)		729(S), 1002(S)
	Software Maintenance	1060(S), 1074(S)			729(S), 1002(S)
V & V	Review and Audits	1028(S), 1074(S)	1012(S)		729(S), 1002(S)
	Product Analysis	1059(G)			729(S), 1002(S)
	Testing	829(S), 1008(S), 1012(S), 1074(S), 1059(G)	829(S), 1012(S)		729(S), 1002(S)
Mgmt Tech	Process Management	1028(S), 1062(S), 1074(S), 983(G), 1061(S)	730(S), 1058(S)		729(S), 1002(S)
	Product Management	982(S), 1028(S), 1042(G), 1044(S), 1074(S)	828(S), 1063(S)		729(S), 1002(S)
	Resource Management	1045(S)			729(S), 1002(S)

Job Functions

Fig A3
Classification of IEEE Software Engineering Standards (Gross Level)

		Job Function							
		Product Engineering						Software Maintenance	Product Support
		Requirements Analysis	Design	Coding	Integration	Conversion	Debugging		
Process	Method	1074	1074	1074	1074	1074	1074	1060, 1074	1074
	Technique								
	Measurement								
Product	Requirement	830							
	Design		1016						
	Component								
	Description								1063
	Plan								
	Report								
Profession	Occupational Title								
	Code of Ethics								
	Certification								
	Licensing								
	Curriculum								
Notat	Nomenclature	729,1002	729,1002	729,1002	729,1002	729,1002	729,1002	729,1002	729,1002
	Representation		1016						
	Language		990						

Type of Standard

Fig A4

Classification of IEEE Software Engineering Standards (Refined Level—Part I)

ANSI/IEEE
Std 1002-1987

Type of Standard		Job Function					
		Technical Management Functions			Verification & Validation		
		Process Management	Product Management	Resource Management	Review and Audits	Product Analysis	Testing
Process	Method	983,1028,1062,1074	1028,1042,1074	1074	1028,1074	1074	829,1008,1074
	Technique						
	Measurement	1061	982, 1044	1045			
Product	Requirement						
	Design						
	Component		1063				
	Description						829
	Plan	730, 1058	828		1012	1012	829,1012
	Report						829
Profession	Occupational						
	Code of Ethics						
	Certification						
	Licensing						
	Curriculum						
Notat	Nomenclature	729,1002	729,1002	729,1002	729,1002	729,1002	729,1002
	Representation						
	Language						

Fig A5

Classification of IEEE Software Engineering Standards (Refined Level—Part II)

Software Life Cycle

Job Function		Concept	Requirements Definition	Design	Implementation	Test	Manufacturing	Installation & Checkout	Operation & Maintenance	Retirement
Product Engineering Function	Requirements Analysis	■	■	▨	□	□	■	□	*	
	Design	▨	▨	■	▨	□	▨	□	*	
	Coding	□	□	▨	■	▨	▨	□	*	
	Integration	□	▨	▨	▨	■	■	□	*	
	Conversion	□	▨	▨	▨	■	▨	■	*	
	Debugging	□	□	▨	▨	■	▨	▨	*	
	Product Support	□	▨	▨	▨	▨	▨	■	■	■
	Software Maintenance	□	□	□	□	□	▨	▨	■	▨
V&V	Review and Audits	▨	■	■	■	▨	▨	■	*	□
	Product Analysis	□	■	▨	■	■	▨	▨	*	
	Testing	□	□	□	▨	■	▨	▨	*	
Mgt	Process Management	■	■	■	■	■	■	■	■	□
	Product Management	▨	■	■	■	■	▨	■	■	□
	Resource Management	■	■	■	■	■	■	■	■	□

Legend:

■ Primary Role

▨ Support Role

□ Planning/Monitoring role

* Repeat of Life Cycle

Fig A6
Job Function–Software Life Cycle Correlation

ANSI/IEEE
Std 1002-1987

Acknowledgements

The following organizations provided support for the development of this standard:

AccuRay Corporation
Applied Physics Laboratory
AT&T Bell
Canada Bell
Northern Research
The Boeing Company
Bradley University
Computer Sciences Corporation
E-Systems
Edinboro University of Pennsylvania
Hewlett-Packard
Hughes
IBM
INCO, Inc.
ITT Corporation
McDonnell Douglas
Mervine and Pallesen
MIV-MEDA Ltd.
NCR Corporation
Northern Telecom
Pratt & Whitney Aircraft
Programming
Environments, Inc.
Sanders Associates Software
Engineering Associates Software
Quality Engineering
Teledyne Brown Engineering
Tennessee Valley Authority
The Algoma Steel Corporation, Ltd.
U.S. Department of Housing and Urban Development
U.S. Department of Transportation

This support does not constitute or imply approval or endorsement of this standard.

An American National Standard

IEEE Standard for
Software Unit Testing

Sponsor

**Software Engineering Technical Committee
of the
IEEE Computer Society**

Approved December 11, 1986
IEEE Standards Board

1008

Approved July 28, 1986
American National Standards Institute

Foreword

(This Foreword is not a part of ANSI/IEEE Std 1008-1987, IEEE Standard for Software Unit Testing.)

Objectives

This standard's primary objective is to specify a standard approach to software unit testing that can be used as a basis for sound software engineering practice.

A second objective is to describe the software engineering concepts and testing assumptions on which this standard approach is based. This information is contained in Appendix B. Note that Appendix B is not a part of this standard.

A third objective is to provide guidance and resource information to assist with the implementation and usage of the standard unit testing approach. This information is contained in Appendixes A, C, and D. Note that these Appendixes are not a part of this standard.

Motivation

A consensus definition of sound unit testing provides a baseline for the evaluation of specific approaches. It also aids communication by providing a standard decomposition of the unit testing process.

Audience

The primary audience for this standard is unit testers and unit test supervisors. This standard was developed to assist those who provide input to, perform, supervise, monitor, and evaluate unit testing.

Relationship with Other Software Engineering Standards

ANSI/IEEE Std 829-1983, IEEE Standard for Software Test Documentation, describes the basic information needs and results of software testing. This unit testing standard requires the use of the test design specification and test summary report specified in ANSI/IEEE Std 829-1983.

This standard is one of a series aimed at establishing the norms of professional practice in software engineering. Any of the other software engineering standards in the series may be used in conjunction with it.

Terminology

Terminology in this standard is consistent with ANSI/IEEE Std 729-1983, IEEE Standard Glossary of Software Engineering Terminology. To avoid inconsistency when the glossary is revised, its definitions are not repeated in this standard.

The *test unit* referred to in this standard is a specific case of the *test item* referred to in ANSI/IEEE 829-1983. The term *test unit* is used because of this standard's narrower scope.

The use of the term *specification, description,* or *document* refers to data recorded on either an electronic or paper medium.

The word *must* and imperative verb forms identify mandatory material within the standard. The words *should* and *may* identify optional material.

Overview

The unit testing process is composed of three *phases* that are partitioned into a total of eight basic *activities* as follows:

(1) *Perform the test planning*
  (a) Plan the general approach, resources, and schedule
  (b) Determine features to be tested
  (c) Refine the general plan
(2) *Acquire the test set*
  (a) Design the set of tests
  (b) Implement the refined plan and design

(3) *Measure the test unit*
    (a) Execute the test procedures
    (b) Check for termination
    (c) Evaluate the test effort and unit

The major dataflows into and out of the phases are shown in Fig A.

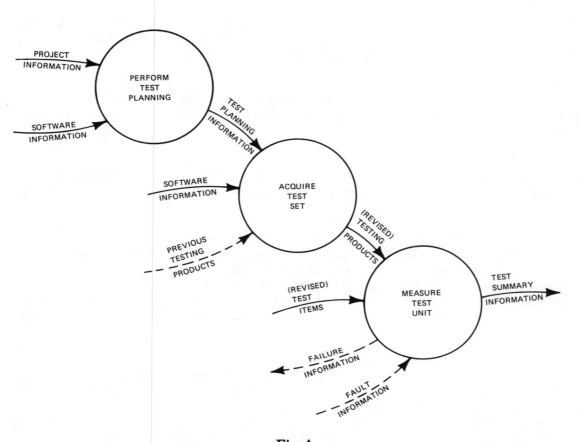

Fig A
Major Dataflows of the Software
Unit Testing Phases

Within a phase, each basic activity is associated with its own set of inputs and outputs and is composed of a series of tasks. The inputs, tasks, and outputs for each activity are specified in the body of this standard.

The set of outputs from all activities must contain sufficient information for the creation of at least two documents—a test design specification and a test summary report. Both documents must conform to the specifications in ANSI/IEEE Std 829-1983.

History

Work on this standard began in February 1983, following announcement of the formation of the task group in the technical and commercial press in late 1982. The project authorization request was approved by the IEEE Standards Board on June 23, 1983 following the second meeting. A total of seven meetings held throughout the United States at three month intervals produced the draft submitted for ballot in March 1985. A total of over 90 persons contributed to the initial development of this standard. Contributors are those individuals who either attended a working-group meeting, submitted written comments on a draft, or both.

This standard was developed by a working group with the following members:

David Gelperin, *Chairperson*   **Pat Wilburn,** *Cochairperson*

A. Frank Ackerman
Craig Adams
David Adams
Jack Barnard
Wanda Beck
Boris Beizer
K. Mack Bishop
Jill E. Boogaard
Milt Boyd
Nathan B. Bradley
Martha Branstad
Fletcher Buckley
John W. Cain
Christopher Cooke
L. L. Doc Craddock
Palmer Craig
Michael Cramer
Dave Dahlinghaus
Noah Davids
Henry Davis
Bruce Dawson
Claudia Dencker
Michael Deutsch
Judie Divita
Jim Dobbins
David C. Doty
Bill Dupras
Jim Edwards
Karen Fairchild
Peter Farrell-Vinay
Thom Foote-Lennox

Ken Foster
John Fox
Roger Fujii
Ross Gagliano
Mark Gerhard
Ed Gibson
Therese Gilbertson
Gary Girard
Keith Gordon
Paul Grizenko
Jeff Grove
Ismet Gungor
Mark Heinrich
Rudolph Hodges
R. A. Kessler
Tom Kurihara
Costas Labovites
Frank LaMonica
F. C. Lim
Philip C. Marriott
Debra L. McCusker
Charlie McCutcheon
Rudolf van Megen
Denis Meredith
Edward Miller, Jr
William Milligan
Marcus Mullins
W. M. Murray
Bruce Nichols
Dennis Nickle
Larry Nitzsche

John Owens
William Perry
Gerald Peterson
Bob Poston
Patricia Powell
Samuel T. Redwine, Jr
Sanford Rosen
Hans Schaefer
Eric Schnellman
Harvey Schock
Al Sema, Jr
Harlan Seyfer
Victor Shtern
Rick Simkin
Wayne Smith
Harry Sneed
Hugh B. Spillane
Ben Sun
Murray Tabachnick
Barbara Taute
Leonard Tripp
William S. Turner III
John Vance
Guy Vogt
Dolores Wallace
John Walter
John C. Wang
Cheryl Webb
William Wilson
Ed Yasi
Natalie C. Yopconka

The following persons were on the balloting committee that approved this document for submission to the IEEE Standards Board:

Frank Ackerman
Leo Beltracchi
Ron Berlack
William Boll, Jr
F. Buckley
Douglas Burt
Homer Carney
Skip Carpenter, Jr
Jung Chung
Won Lyang Chung
Francois Coallier
Richard Coates
A.J. Cote, Jr
Patricia Daggett
Jim Darling
N.S. Davids
Henry Davis
Peter Denny
A. Dniestrowski
David Dobratz
David Doty
Walter DuBlanica
R.E. Dwyer
Mary Eads
John Earls
L.G. Egan
John Fendrich
Glenn Fields
Charles Finnell
Jim Flournoy
Violet Folds
Julian Forster
Rick Fredrick
Lee Gagner
M. Galinier
David Gelperin
L.M. Gunther
David Gustafson

Russell Gustin
Virl Haas
William Hanrahan
Carolyn Harrison
G.B. Hawthorne
Clark Hay
Leslie Heselton, III
Mark Holthouse
John Horch
Frank Jay
Laurel Kaleda
Adi Kasad
Ron Kenett
Bob Kessler
Gary Kroc
Robert Lane
Greg Larsen
F.C. Lim
Bertil Lindberg
Gary Lindsay
Ben Livson
M. Malagarois
W.A. Mandeville
Stuart Marcotte
Philip C. Marriott
Roger Martin
Paul Mauro
Belden Menkus
Jerome Mersky
Gene Morun
Hironobu Nagano
Geraldine Neidhart
G.A. Niblack
Dennis Nickle
Larry Nitzsche
Peter Olsen
Wilma Osborne

Bill Perry
Poul Grav Peterson
Donald Pfeiffer
Sharon Cobb-Pierson
Robert Poston
Thomas Radi
Meir Razy
Larry Reed
R. Waldo Roth
Raymond Sandborgh
Hans Schaefer
Norm Schneidewind
Eric Schnellman
Wolf Schnoege
Robert Schueppert
David Schultz
Leonard Seagren
Gary Shea
Craig Shermer
Robert Shillato
David Siefert
David Simkins
Shirley Gloss-Soler
William Sutcliffe
K.C. Tai
Barbara Taute
Paul Thompson
Terrence Tillmanns
R.L. Van Tilburg
Dolores Wallace
M.L. Weisbein
Joseph Weiss
N.P. Wilburn
Paul Wolfgang
Charles Wortz
Edward Yasi
Zhou Zhi Ying
Natalie Yopconka

When the IEEE Standards Board approved this standard on December 11, 1986, it had the following membership:

John E. May, *Chairman*   **Irving Kolodny,** *Vice Chairman*
Sava I. Sherr, *Secretary*

James H. Beall
Fletcher J. Buckley
Paul G. Cummings
Donald C. Fleckenstein
Jay Forster
Daniel L. Goldberg
Kenneth D. Hendrix
Irvin N. Howell

Jack Kinn
Joseph L. Koepfinger*
Edward Lohse
Lawrence V. McCall
Donald T. Michael*
Marco W. Migliaro
Stanley Owens
John P. Riganati

Frank L. Rose
Robert E. Rountree
Martha Sloan
Oley Wanaselja
J. Richard Weger
William B. Wilkens
Charles J. Wylie
Donald W. Zipse

*Member emeritus

Contents

An American National Standard

IEEE Standard for
Software Unit Testing

1. Scope and References

1.1 Inside the Scope. Software unit testing is a process that includes the performance of test planning, the acquisition of a test set, and the measurement of a test unit against its requirements. Measuring entails the use of sample data to exercise the unit and the comparison of the unit's actual behavior with its required behavior as specified in the unit's requirements documentation.

This standard defines an integrated approach to systematic and documented unit testing. The approach uses unit design and unit implementation information, in addition to unit requirements, to determine the completeness of the testing.

This standard describes a testing process composed of a hierarchy of phases, activities, and tasks and defines a minimum set of tasks for each activity. Additional tasks may be added to any activity.

This standard requires the performance of each activity. For each task within an activity, this standard requires either that the task be performed, or that previous results be available and be reverified. This standard also requires the preparation of two documents specified in ANSI/IEEE Std 829-1983 [2][1]. These documents are the Test Design Specification and the Test Summary Report.

General unit test planning should occur during overall test planning. This general unit test planning activity is covered by this standard, although the balance of the overall test planning process is outside the scope of this standard.

This standard may be applied to the unit testing of any digital computer software or firmware. However, this standard does *not* specify

any class of software or firmware to which it must be applied, nor does it specify any class of software or firmware that must be unit tested. This standard applies to the testing of newly developed and modified units.

This standard is applicable whether or not the unit tester is also the developer.

1.2 Outside the Scope. The results of some overall test planning tasks apply to all testing levels (for example, identify security and privacy constraints). Such tasks are not considered a part of the unit testing process, although they directly affect it.

While the standard identifies a need for failure analysis information and software fault correction, it does not specify a software debugging process.

This standard does not address other components of a comprehensive unit verification and validation process, such as reviews (for example, walkthroughs, inspections), static analysis (for example, consistency checks, data flow analysis), or formal analysis (for example, proof of correctness, symbolic execution).

This standard does not require the use of specific test facilities or tools. This standard does not imply any particular methodology for documentation control, configuration management, quality assurance, or management of the testing process.

1.3 References. This standard shall be used in conjunction with the following publications.

[1] ANSI/IEEE Std 729-1983, IEEE Standard Glossary of Software Engineering Terminology.[2]

[2] ANSI/IEEE Std 829-1983, IEEE Standard for Software Test Documentation.

---

[1] The numbers in brackets correspond to the references listed in 1.3 of this standard.

[2] These publications are available from American National Standards Institute, Sales Department, 1430 Broadway, New York, NY 10018 and from IEEE Service Center, 445 Hoes Lane, Piscataway, NJ 08854.

2. Definitions

This section defines key terms used in this standard but not included in ANSI/IEEE Std 729-1983 [1] or ANSI/IEEE Std 829-1983 [2].

characteristic. *See:* **data characteristic** or **software characteristic.**

data characteristic. An inherent, possibly accidental, trait, quality, or property of data (for example, arrival rates, formats, value ranges, or relationships between field values).

feature. *See:* **software feature.**

incident. *See:* **software test incident.**

nonprocedural programming language. A computer programming language used to express the parameters of a problem rather than the steps in a solution (for example, report writer or sort specification languages). Contrast with **procedural programming language.**

procedural programming language. A computer programming language used to express the sequence of operations to be performed by a computer (for example, COBOL). Contrast with **nonprocedural programming language.**

software characteristic. An inherent, possibly accidental, trait, quality, or property of software (for example, functionality, performance, attributes, design constraints, number of states, lines of branches).

software feature. A software characteristic specified or implied by requirements documentation (for example, functionality, performance, attributes, or design constraints).

software test incident. Any event occuring during the execution of a software test that requires investigation.

state data. Data that defines an internal state of the test unit and is used to establish that state or compare with existing states.

test objective. An identified set of software features to be measured under specified conditions by comparing actual behavior with the required behavior described in the software documentation.

test set architecture. The nested relationships between sets of test cases that directly reflect the hierarchic decomposition of the test objectives.

test unit.[3] A set of one or more computer program modules together with associated control data, (for example, tables), usage procedures, and operating procedures that satisfy the following conditions:

(1) All modules are from a single computer program

(2) At least one of the new or changed modules in the set has not completed the unit test[4]

(3) The set of modules together with its associated data and procedures are the sole object of a testing process

unit. *See:* **test unit.**

unit requirements documentation. Documentation that sets forth the functional, interface, performance, and design constraint requirements for the test unit.

3. Unit Testing Activities

This section specifies the activities involved in the unit testing process and describes the associated input, tasks, and output. The activities described are as follows:

(1) Perform test planning phase
   (a) Plan the general approach, resources, and schedule
   (b) Determine features to be tested
   (c) Refine the general plan
(2) Acquire test set phase
   (a) Design the set of tests
   (b) Implement the refined plan and design
(3) Measure test unit phase
   (a) Execute the test procedures
   (b) Check for termination
   (c) Evaluate the test effort and unit

When more than one unit is to be unit tested (for example, all those associated with a software project), the Plan activity should address the total set of test units and should not be repeated for each test unit. The other activities must be performed at least once for each unit.

Under normal conditions, these activities are sequentially initiated except for the Execute and Check cycle as illustrated in Fig 1. When per-

---

[3] A test unit may occur at any level of the design hierarchy from a single module to a complete program. Therefore, a test unit may be a module, a few modules, or a complete computer program along with associated data and procedures.

[4] A test unit may contain one or more modules that have already been unit tested.

Fig 1
Unit Testing Activities

forming any of the activities except Plan, improper performance of a preceding activity or external events (for example, schedule, requirements, or design changes) may result in the need to redo one or more of the preceding activities and then return to the one being performed.

During the testing process, a test design specification and a test summary report must be developed. Other test documents may be developed. All test documents must conform to the ANSI/IEEE Std 829-1983 [2]. In addition, all test documents must have identified authors and be dated.

The test design specification will derive its information from the Determine, Refine, and Design activities. The test summary report will derive its information from all of the activities.

3.1 Plan the General Approach, Resources, and Schedule. General unit test planning should occur during overall test planning and be recorded in the corresponding planning document.

3.1.1 Plan Inputs
(1) Project plans
(2) Software requirements documentation

3.1.2 Plan Tasks
(1) *Specify a General Approach to Unit Testing.* Identify risk areas to be addressed by the testing. Specify constraints on characteristic determination (for example, features that must be tested), test design, or test implementation (for example, test sets that must be used).

Identify existing sources of input, output, and state data (for example, test files, production files, test data generators). Identify general techniques for data validation. Identify general techniques to be used for output recording, collection, reduction, and validation. Describe provisions for application software that directly interfaces with the units to be tested.

(2) *Specify Completeness Requirements.* Identify the areas (for example, features, procedures, states, functions, data characteristics, instructions) to be covered by the unit test set and the degree of coverage required for each area.

When testing a unit during software development, every software feature must be covered by a test case or an approved exception. The same should hold during software maintenance for any unit testing.

When testing a unit implemented with a procedural language (for example, COBOL) during software development, every instruction that can be reached and executed must be covered by a test case or an approved exception, except for instructions contained in modules that have been separately unit tested. The same should hold during software maintenance for the testing of a unit implemented with a procedural language.

(3) *Specify Termination Requirements.* Specify the requirements for normal termination of the unit testing process. Termination requirements must include satisfying the completeness requirements.

Identify any conditions that could cause abnormal termination of the unit testing process (for example, detecting a major design fault, reaching a schedule deadline) and any notification procedures that apply.

(4) *Determine Resource Requirements.* Estimate the resources required for test set acquisition, initial execution, and subsequent repetition of testing activities. Consider hardware, access time (for example, dedicated computer time), communications or system software, test tools, test files, and forms or other supplies. Also consider the need for unusually large volumes of forms and supplies.

Identify resources needing preparation and the parties responsible. Make arrangements for these resources, including requests for resources that require significant lead time (for example, customized test tools).

Identify the parties responsible for unit testing and unit debugging. Identify personnel requirements including skills, number, and duration.

(5) *Specify a General Schedule.* Specify a schedule constrained by resource and test unit availability for all unit testing activity.

3.1.3 Plan Outputs

(1) General unit test planning information (from 3.1.2(1) through (5) inclusive)

(2) Unit test general resource requests—if produced from 3.1.2(4)

3.2 Determine Features To Be Tested

3.2.1 Determine Inputs

(1) Unit requirements documentation

(2) Software architectural design documentation—if needed

3.2.2 Determine Tasks

(1) *Study the Functional Requirements.* Study each function described in the unit requirements documentation. Ensure that each function has a unique identifier. When necessary, request clarification of the requirements.

(2) *Identify Additional Requirements and Associated Procedures.* Identify requirements other than functions (for example, performance, attributes, or design constraints) associated with software characteristics that can be effectively tested at the unit level. Identify any usage or operating procedures associated only with the unit to be tested. Ensure that each additional requirement and procedure has a unique identifier. When necessary, request clarification of the requirements.

(3) *Identify States of the Unit.* If the unit requirements documentation specifies or implies multiple states (for example, inactive, ready to receive, processing) software, identify each state and each valid state transition. Ensure that each state and state transition has a unique identifier. When necessary, request clarification of the requirements.

(4) *Identify Input and Output Data Characteristics.* Identify the input and output data structures of the unit to be tested. For each structure, identify characteristics, such as arrival rates, formats, value ranges, and relationships between field values. For each characteristic, specify its valid ranges. Ensure that each characteristic has a unique identifier. When necessary, request clarification of the requirements.

(5) *Select Elements to be Included in the Test-*

ing. Select the features to be tested. Select the associated procedures, associated states, associated state transitions, and associated data characteristics to be included in the testing. Invalid and valid input data must be selected. When complete testing is impractical, information regarding the expected use of the unit should be used to determine the selections. Identify the risk associated with unselected elements.

Enter the selected features, procedures, states, state transitions, and data characteristics in the *Features to be Tested* section of the unit's Test Design Specification.

3.2.3 Determine Outputs

(1) List of elements to be included in the testing (from 3.2.2(5))

(2) Unit requirements clarification requests—if produced from 3.2.2(1) through (4) inclusive

3.3 Refine the General Plan

3.3.1 Refine Inputs

(1) List of elements to be included in the testing (from 3.2.2(5))

(2) General unit test planning information (from 3.1.2(1) through (5) inclusive)

3.3.2 Refine Tasks

(1) *Refine the Approach.* Identify existing test cases and test procedures to be considered for use. Identify any special techniques to be used for data validation. Identify any special techniques to be used for output recording, collection, reduction, and validation.

Record the refined approach in the *Approach Refinements* section of the unit's test design specification.

(2) *Specify Special Resource Requirements.* Identify any special resources needed to test the unit (for example, software that directly interfaces with the unit). Make preparations for the identified resources.

Record the special resource requirements in the *Approach Refinements* section of the unit's test design specification.

(3) *Specify a Detailed Schedule.* Specify a schedule for the unit testing based on support software, special resource, and unit availability and integration schedules. Record the schedule in the *Approach Refinements* section of the unit's test design specification.

3.3.3 Refine Outputs

(1) Specific unit test planning information (from 3.3.2(1) through (3) inclusive)

(2) Unit test special resource requests—if produced from 3.3.2(2).

3.4 Design the Set of Tests

3.4.1 Design Inputs

(1) Unit requirements documentation

(2) List of elements to be included in the testing (from 3.2.2(5))

(3) Unit test planning information (from 3.1.2(1) and (2) and 3.3.2(1))

(4) Unit design documentation

(5) Test specifications from previous testing—if available

3.4.2 Design Tasks

(1) *Design the Architecture of the Test Set.* Based on the features to be tested and the conditions specified or implied by the selected associated elements (for example, procedures, state transitions, data characteristics), design a hierarchically decomposed set of test objectives so that each lowest-level objective can be directly tested by a few test cases. Select appropriate existing test cases. Associate groups of test-case identifiers with the lowest-level objectives. Record the hierarchy of objectives and associated test case identifiers in the *Test Identification* section of the unit's test design specification.

(2) *Obtain Explicit Test Procedures as Required.* A combination of the unit requirements documentation, test planning information, and test-case specifications may implicitly specify the unit test procedures and therefore minimize the need for explicit specification. Select existing test procedures that can be modified or used without modification.

Specify any additional procedures needed either in a supplementary section in the unit's test design specification or in a separate procedure specification document. Either choice must be in accordance with the information required by ANSI/IEEE Std 829-1983 [2]. When the correlation between test cases and procedures is not readily apparent, develop a table relating them and include it in the unit's test design specification.

(3) *Obtain the Test Case Specifications.* Specify the new test cases. Existing specifications may be referenced.

Record the specifications directly or by reference in either a supplementary section of the unit's test design specification or in a separate document. Either choice must be in accordance with the information required by ANSI/IEEE Std 829-1983 [2].

(4) *Augment, as Required, the Set of Test-Case Specifications Based on Design Information.* Based on information about the unit's design, update as required the test set architecture in accordance with 3.4.2(1). Consider the characteristics of selected algorithms and internal data structures.

Identify control flows and changes to internal data that must be recorded. Anticipate special recording difficulties that might arise, for example, from a need to trace control flow in complex algorithms or from a need to trace changes in internal data structures (for example, stacks or trees). When necessary, request enhancement of the unit design (for example, a formatted data structure dump capability) to increase the testability of the unit.

Based on information in the unit's design, specify any newly identified test cases and complete any partial test case specifications in accordance with 3.4.2(3).

(5) *Complete the Test Design Specification.* Complete the test design specification for the unit in accordance with ANSI/IEEE Std 829-1983 [2].

3.4.3 Design Outputs

(1) Unit test design specification (from 3.4.2(5))

(2) Separate test procedure specifications—if produced from 3.4.2(2)

(3) Separate test-case specifications—if produced from 3.4.2(3) or (4)

(4) Unit design enhancement requests—if produced from 3.4.2(4)

3.5 Implement the Refined Plan and Design

3.5.1 Implement Inputs

(1) Unit test planning information (from 3.1.2(1), (4), and (5) and 3.3.2(1) through (3) inclusive)

(2) Test-case specifications in the unit test design specification or separate documents (from 3.4.2(3) and (4)

(3) Software data structure descriptions

(4) Test support resources

(5) Test items

(6) Test data from previous testing activities—if available

(7) Test tools from previous testing activities—if available

3.5.2 Implement Tasks

(1) *Obtain and Verify Test Data.* Obtain a copy of existing test data to be modified or used without modification. Generate any new data required. Include additional data necessary to ensure data consistency and integrity. Verify all data (including those to be used as is) against

the software data structure specifications. When the correlation between test cases and data sets is not readily apparent, develop a table to record this correlation and include it in the unit's test design specification.

(2) *Obtain Special Resources.* Obtain the test support resources specified in 3.3.2(2).

(3) *Obtain Test Items.* Collect test items including available manuals, operating system procedures, control data (for example, tables), and computer programs. Obtain software identified during test planning that directly interfaces with the test unit.

When testing a unit implemented with a procedural language, ensure that execution trace information will be available to evaluate satisfaction of the code-based completeness requirements.

Record the identifier of each item in the *Summary* section of the unit's test summary report.

3.5.3 Implement Outputs

(1) Verified test data (from 3.5.2(1))

(2) Test support resources (from 3.5.2(2))

(3) Configuration of test items (from 3.5.2(3))

(4) Initial summary information (from 3.5.2(3))

3.6 Execute the Test Procedures

3.6.1 Execute Inputs

(1) Verified test data (from 3.5.2(1))

(2) Test support resources (from 3.5.2(2))

(3) Configuration of test items (from 3.5.2(3))

(4) Test-case specifications (from 3.4.2(3) and (4))

(5) Test procedure specifications (from 3.4.2 (2))—if produced

(6) Failure analysis results (from debugging process)—if produced

3.6.2 Execute Tasks

(1) *Run Tests.* Set up the test environment. Run the test set. Record all test incidents in the *Summary of Results* section of the unit's test summary report.

(2) *Determine Results.* For each test case, determine if the unit passed or failed based on required result specifications in the case descriptions. Record pass or fail results in the *Summary of Results* section of the unit's test summary report. Record resource consumption data in the *Summary of Activities* section of the report. When testing a unit implemented with a procedural language, collect execution trace summary information and attach it to the report.

For each failure, have the failure analyzed

and record the fault information in the *Summary of Results* section of the test summary report. Then select the applicable case and perform the associated actions.

Case 1: *A Fault in a Test Specification or Test Data.* Correct the fault, record the fault correction in the *Summary of Activities* section of the test summary report, and rerun the tests that failed.

Case 2: *A Fault in Test Procedure Execution.* Rerun the incorrectly executed procedures.

Case 3: *A Fault in the Test Environment (for example, system software).* Either have the environment corrected, record the fault correction in the *Summary of Activities* section of the test summary report, and rerun the tests that failed OR prepare for abnormal termination by documenting the reason for not correcting the environment in the *Summary of Activities* section of the test summary report and proceed to check for termination (that is, proceed to activity 3.7).

Case 4: *A Fault in the Unit Implementation.* Either have the unit corrected, record the fault correction in the *Summary of Activities* section of the test summary report, and rerun all tests OR prepare for abnormal termination by documenting the reason for not correcting the unit in the *Summary of Activities* section of the test summary report and proceed to check for termination (that is, proceed to activity 3.7).

Case 5: *A Fault in the Unit Design.* Either have the design and unit corrected, modify the test specification and data as appropriate, record the fault correction in the *Summary of Activities* section of the test summary report, and rerun all tests OR prepare for abnormal termination by documenting the reason for not correcting the design in the *Summary of Activities* section of the test summary report and proceed to check for termination (that is, proceed to activity 3.7).

NOTE: The cycle of Execute and Check Tasks must be repeated until a termination condition defined in 3.1.2(3) is satisfied (See Fig 3). Control flow within the Execute activity itself is pictured in Fig 2.

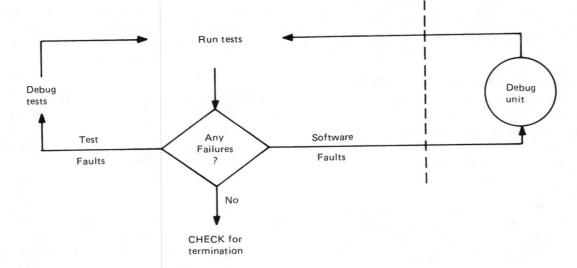

**Fig 2
Control Flow Within the Execute Activity**

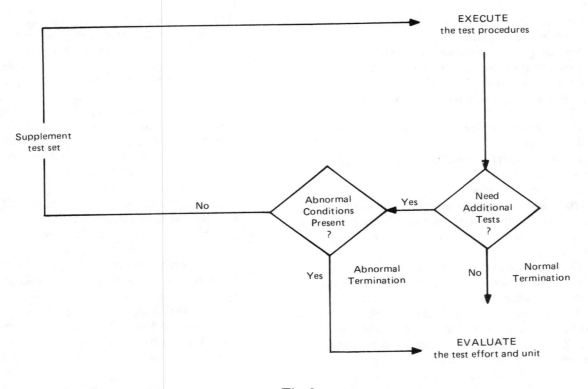

**Fig 3
Control Flow Within the Check Activity**

3.6.3 Execute Outputs

(1) Execution information logged in the test summary report including test outcomes, test incident descriptions, failure analysis results, fault correction activities, uncorrected fault reasons, resource consumption data and, for procedural language implementations, trace summary information (from 3.6.2(1) and (2))

(2) Revised test specifications—if produced from 3.6.2(2)

(3) Revised test data—if produced from 3.6.2(2)

3.7 Check for Termination
3.7.1 Check Inputs

(1) Completeness and termination requirements (from 3.1.2(2) and (3))

(2) Execution information (from 3.6.2(1) and (2))

(3) Test specifications (from 3.4.2(1) through (3) inclusive)—if required

(4) Software data structure descriptions—if required

3.7.2 Check Tasks

(1) *Check for Normal Termination of the Testing Process.* Determine the need for additional tests based on completeness requirements or concerns raised by the failure history. For procedural language implementations, analyze the execution trace summary information (for example, variable, flow).

If additional tests are *not* needed, then record normal termination in the *Summary of Activities* section of the test summary report and proceed to evaluate the test effort and unit (that is, proceed to activity 3.8).

(2) *Check for Abnormal Termination of the Testing Process.* If an abnormal termination condition is satisfied (for example, uncorrected major fault, out of time) then ensure that the specific situation causing termination is documented in the *Summary of Activities* section of the test summary report together with the unfinished testing and any uncorrected faults. Then proceed to evaluate the test effort and unit (that is, proceed to activity 3.8).

(3) *Supplement the Test Set.* When additional tests are needed and the abnormal termination conditions are not satisfied, supplement the test set by following steps (a) through (e).

(a) Update the test set architecture in accordance with 3.4.2(1) and obtain additional test-case specifications in accordance with 3.4.2(3).

(b) Modify the test procedure specifications in accordance with 3.4.2(2) as required.

(c) Obtain additional test data in accordance with 3.5.2(1).

(d) Record the addition in the *Summary of Activities* section of the test summary report.

(e) Execute the additional tests (that is, return to activity 3.6).

3.7.3 Check Outputs

(1) Check information logged in the test summary report including the termination conditions and any test case addition activities (from 3.7.2(1) through (3) inclusive)

(2) Additional or revised test specifications—if produced from 3.7.2(3)

(3) Additional test data—if produced from 3.7.2(3)

3.8 Evaluate the Test Effort and Unit
3.8.1 Evaluate Inputs

(1) Unit Test Design Specification (from 3.4.2(5)

(2) Execution information (from 3.6.2(1) and (2))

(3) Checking information (from 3.7.2(1) through (3) inclusive)

(4) Separate test-case specifications (from 3.4.2(3) and (4))—if produced

3.8.2 Evaluate Tasks

(1) *Describe Testing Status.* Record variances from test plans and test specifications in the *Variances* section of the test summary report. Specify the reason for each variance.

For abnormal termination, identify areas insufficiently covered by the testing and record reasons in the *Comprehensiveness Assessment* section of the test summary report.

Identify unresolved test incidents and the reasons for a lack of resolution in the *Summary of Results* section of the test summary report.

(2) *Describe Unit's Status.* Record differences revealed by testing between the unit and its requirements documentation in the *Variances* section of the test summary report.

Evaluate the unit design and implementation against requirements based on test results and detected fault information. Record evaluation information in the *Evaluation* section of the test summary report.

(3) *Complete the Test Summary Report.* Complete the test summary report for the unit in accordance with ANSI/IEEE Std 829-1983 [2].

(4) *Ensure Preservation of Testing Products.* Ensure that the testing products are collected,

organized, and stored for reference and reuse. These products include the test design specification, separate test-case specifications, separate test procedure specifications, test data, test data generation procedures, test drivers and stubs, and the test summary report.

3.8.3 Evaluate Outputs

(1) Complete test summary report (from 3.8.2(3))

(2) Complete, stored collection of testing products (from 3.8.2(4))

Appendixes

(These Appendixes are not a part of ANSI / IEEE Std 1008-1987, IEEE Standard for Software Unit Testing, but are included for information only.)

Appendix A

Implementation and Usage Guidelines

This section contains information intended to be of benefit when the standard is being considered for use. It is therefore recommended that this section be read in its entirety before any extensive planning is done.

A1. Use of the Standard

The standard can be used
(1) As a basis for comparison to confirm current practices
(2) As a source of ideas to modify current practices
(3) As a replacement for current practices

A2. Additional Testing Requirements

Requirements such as the amount of additional test documentation (for example, test logs), the level of detail to be included, and the number and types of approvals and reviews must be specified for each project. Factors, such as unit criticality, auditing needs, or contract specifications will often dictate these requirements. The standard leaves it to the user to specify these requirements either by individual project or as organizational standards. If the requirements are project specific, they should appear in the project plan, quality assurance plan, verification and validation plan, or overall test plan.

A3. Additional Test Documentation

The information contained in the test design specification and the test summary report is considered an absolute minimum for process visibility. In addition, it is assumed that any test information need can be satisfied by the set of test documents specified in ANSI / IEEE Std 829-

1983 [2], either by requiring additional content in a required document or by requiring additional documents.

A4. Approvals and Reviews

If more control is desired, the following additional tasks should be considered:
(1) Approval of general approach at the end of Plan
(2) Approval of identified requirements at the end of Determine
(3) Approval of specific plans at the end of Refine
(4) Approval of test specifications at the end of Design
(5) Review of test readiness at the end of Implement
(6) Review of test summary report at the end of Evaluate

A5. Audit Trails

It is assumed that auditing needs are taken into account when specifying control requirements. Therefore, the set of test documents generated together with the reports from test reviews should be sufficient to supply all required audit information.

A6. Configuration Management

Configuration management should be the source of the software requirements, software architectual design, software data structure, and unit requirements documentation. These inputs must be managed to ensure confidence that we have current information and will be notified of any changes.

The final unit testing products should be provided to configuration management. These outputs must be managed to permit thorough and economical regression testing. See ANSI/IEEE Std 828-1983, IEEE Standard for Software Configuration Management Plans, for details.

A7. Determination of Requirements-Based Characteristics

Psychological factors (for example, self-confidence, a detailed knowledge of the unit design) can make it very difficult for the unit developer to determine an effective set of requirements-based elements (for example, features, procedures, state transitions, data characteristics) to be included in the testing. Often, this determination should be made by someone else.

There are several ways to organize this separation.

(1) Developers determine these elements for each other.

(2) Developers fully test each other's code. This has the added advantage that at least two developers will have a detailed knowledge of every unit.

(3) A separate test group should be available The size of the project or the criticality of the software may determine whether a separate group can be justified.

If developers determine requirements-based elements for their own software, they should perform this determination *before* software design begins.

A8. User Involvement

If the unit to be tested interacts with users (for example, menu displays), it can be very effective to involve those users in determining the requirements-based elements to be included in the testing. Asking users about their use of the software may bring to light valuable information to be considered during test planning. For example, questioning may identify the relative criticality of the unit's functions and thus determine the testing emphasis.

A9. Stronger Code-Based Coverage Requirements

Based on the criticality of the unit or a shortage of unit requirement and design information

(for example, during maintenance of older software), the code-based coverage requirement specified in 3.1.2(2) could be strengthened. One option is to strengthen the requirement from instruction coverage to branch coverage (that is, the execution of every branch in the unit).

A10. Code Coverage Tools

An automated means of recording the coverage of source code during unit test execution is highly recommended. Automation is usually necessary because manual coverage analysis is unreliable and uneconomical. One automated approach uses a code instrumentation and reporting tool. Such a tool places software probes in the source code and following execution of the test cases provides a report summarizing data and control-flow information. The report identifies unexecuted instructions. Some tools also identify unexecuted branches. This capability is a feature in some compilers.

A11. Process Improvement

To evaluate and improve the effectiveness of unit testing, it is recommended that failure data be gathered from those processes that follow unit testing, such as integration test, system test, and production use. This data should then be analyzed to determine the nature of those faults that should have been detected by unit testing but were not.

A12. Adopting the Standard

Implementing a new technical process is itself a process that requires planning, implementation, and evaluation effort. To successfully implement a testing process based on this standard, one must develop an implementation strategy and tailor the standard. Both activities must reflect the culture and current abilities of the organization. Long-term success will require management commitment, supporting policies, tools, training, and start-up consulting. Management can demonstrate commitment by incorporating the new process into project tracking systems and performance evaluation criteria.

A13. Practicality of the Standard

This standard represents consensus on the definition of good software engineering practice. Some organizations use practices similar to the process specified here while others organize this work quite differently. In any case, it will involve considerable change for many organizations that choose to adopt it. That change involves new policies, new standards and procedures, new tools, and new training programs. If the differences between the standard and current practice are too great, then the changes will need to be phased in. The answer to the question of practicality is basically one of desire. How badly does an organization want to gain control of its unit testing?

Appendix B

Concepts and Assumptions

B1. Software Engineering Concepts

The standard unit testing process specified in this standard is based on several fundamental software engineering concepts which are described in B1.1 through B1.8 inclusive.

B1.1 Relationship of Testing to Verification and Validation. Testing is just one of several complementary verification and validation activities. Other activities include technical reviews (for example, code inspections), static analysis, and proof of correctness. Specification of a comprehensive verification and validation process is outside the scope of this standard.

B1.2 Testing As Product Development. Testing includes a product development process. It results in a *test set* composed of data, test support software, and procedures for its use. This product is documented by test specifications and reports. As with any product development process, test set development requires planning, requirements (test objectives), design, implementation, and evaluation.

B1.3 Composition of Debugging. The debugging process is made up of two major activities. The objective of the first activity, *failure analysis,* is to locate and identify all faults responsible for a failure. The objective of the second, *fault correction,* is to remove all identified faults while avoiding the introduction of new ones. Specification of the process of either failure analysis or fault correction is outside the scope of this standard.

B1.4 Relationship of Testing to Debugging. Testing entails attempts to cause failures in order to detect faults, while debugging entails both failure analysis to locate and identify the associated faults and subsequent fault correction. Testing may need the results of debugging's failure analysis to decide on a course of action. Those actions may include the termination of testing or a request for requirements changes or fault correction.

B1.5 Relationship Between Types of Units. A one-to-one relationship between design units, implementation units, and test units is not necessary. Several design units may make up an implementation unit (for example, a program) and several implementation units may make up a test unit.

B1.6 Need for Design and Implementation Information. Often, requirements information is not enough for effective testing, even though, fundamentally, testing measures actual behavior against required behavior. This is because its usually not feasible to test all possible situations and requirements often do not provide sufficient guidance in identifying situations that have high failure potential. Design and implementation information often are needed, since some of these high-potential situations result from the design and implementation choices that have been made.

B1.7 Incremental Specification of Elements To Be Considered in Testing.
Progressively more detailed information about the nature of a test unit is found in the unit requirements documentation, the unit design documentation, and finally in the unit's implementation. As a result, the elements to be considered in testing may be built up incrementally during different periods of test activity.

For procedural language (for example, COBOL) implementations, element specification occurs in three increments. The first group is specified during the Determine activity and is based on the unit requirements documentation. The second group is specified during the Design activity and is based on the unit design (that is, algorithms and data structures) as stated in a software design description. The third group is specified during the Check activity and is based on the unit's code.

For nonprocedural language (for example, report writer or sort specification languages) implementations, specification occurs in two increments. The first is during the Determine activity and is based on requirements and the second is during Design and is based on the nonprocedural specification.

An incremental approach permits unit testing to begin as soon as unit requirements are available and minimizes the bias introduced by detailed knowledge of the unit design and code.

B1.8 Incremental Creation of a Test Design Specification.
Information recorded in the test design specification is generated during the Determine, Refine, and Design activities. As each of these test activities progress, information is recorded in appropriate sections of the specification. The whole document must be complete at the end of the final iteration of the Design activity.

B1.9 Incremental Creation of the Test Summary Report.
Information recorded in the test summary report is generated during all unit testing activities expect Plan. The report is initiated during Implement, updated during Execute and Check, and completed during Evaluate.

B2. Testing Assumptions

The approach to unit testing specified in this standard is based on a variety of economic, psychological, and technical assumptions. The significant assumptions are given in B2.1 through B2.7 inclusive.

B2.1 The objective of unit testing is to attempt to determine the correctness and completeness of an implementation with respect to unit requirements and design documentation by attempting to uncover faults in:

(1) The unit's required features in combination with their associated states (for example, inactive, active awaiting a message, active processing a message)

(2) The unit's handling of invalid input

(3) Any usage or operating procedures associated only with the unit

(4) The unit's algorithms or internal data structures, or both

(5) The decision boundaries of the unit's control logic

B2.2 Testing entails the measurement of behavior against requirements. Although one speaks informally of *interface testing, state testing,* or even *requirement testing,* what is meant is measuring actual behavior associated with an interface, state, or requirement, against the corresponding required behavior. Any verifiable unit testing process must have documented requirements for the test unit. This standard assumes that the documentation of unit requirements exists before testing begins.

B2.3 Unit requirements documentation must be thoroughly reviewed for completeness, testability, and traceability. This standard assumes the requirements have been reviewed either as a normal part of the documentation review process or in a special unit requirements review.

B2.4 There are significant economic benefits in the early detection of faults. This implies that test set development should start as soon as practical following availability of the unit requirements documentation because of the resulting requirements verification and validation. It also implies that as much as practical should be tested at the unit level.

B2.5 The levels of project testing (for example, acceptance, system, integration, unit) are specified in project plans, verification and validation plans, or overall test plans. Also included is the unit test planning information that is applicable to all units being tested (for example, completeness requirements, termination requirements, general resource requirements). Subsequently, based on an analysis of the software design, the test units will be identified and an integration sequence will be selected.

B2.6 The availability of inputs and resources to do a task is the major constraint on the sequencing of activities and on the sequencing of tasks within an activity. If the necessary resources are available, some of the activities and some of the tasks within an activity may be performed concurrently.

B2.7 This standard assumes that it is usually most cost-effective to delay the design of test cases based on source-code characteristics until the set of test cases based on requirements and design characteristics has been executed. This approach minimizes the code-based design task. If code-based design is started before test execution data is available, it should not start until the test cases based on unit requirements and design characteristics have been specified.

Appendix C

Sources for Techniques and Tools

C1. General

Software tools are computer programs and software techniques are detailed methods that aid in the specification, construction, testing, analysis, management, documentation, and maintenance of other computer programs. Software techniques and tools can be used and reused in a variety of development environments. Their effective use increases engineering productivity and software quality.

The references given in C2 of this Appendix contain information on most of the testing techniques and tools in use today. The set of references is not exhaustive, but provides a comprehensive collection of source material. To keep up to date, the reader is encouraged to obtain information on recent IEEE tutorials and recent documents in the Special Publications series of the National Bureau of Standards.[5] Current information on test tools can be obtained from the Federal Software Testing Center[6] and software tool data bases are accessible through the Data & Analysis Center for Software.[7]

A set of general references on software testing is listed in Appendix D.

C2. References

BEIZER, BORIS. *Software Testing Techniques.* New York: Van Nostrand Reinhold, 1983. This book presents a collection of experience-based test techniques. It describes several test design techniques together with their mathematical foundations. The book describes various techniques (decision tables and formal grammars) that provide a precise specification of the input and software. It also discusses a data-base-driven testing technique. Many techniques are based on the author's first-hand experience as director of testing and quality assurance for a telecommunications software producer. The inclusion of experiences and anecdotes makes this book enjoyable and informative.

HOUGHTON, Jr, RAYMOND C. Software Development Tools: A Profile. *IEEE Computer* vol

[5] The NBS publications and software tools survey may be obtained from Superintendent of Documents, US Government Printing Office, Washington, DC 20402.

[6] Information regarding test tools may be obtained by contacting Federal Software Testing Center, Office of Software Development, General Services Administration, 5203 Leesburg Pike, Suite 1100, Falls Church, VA 22041.

[7] Information regarding the tools data base may be obtained from Data & Analysis Center for Software (DACS), RADC/ISISI, Griffiss AFB NY 13441.

16, no 5, May 1983.[8] The Institute of Computer Science and Technology of the National Bureau of Standards studied the software tools available in the early 1980's. This article reports the results of that study and analyzes the information obtained. Various categorizations of the tools are presented, with tools listed by their characteristics. The lists incorporate percentage summaries based on the total number of tools for which information was available.

OSD/DDT & E Software Test and Evaluation Project, Phases I and II, Final Report, vol 2, *Software Test and Evaluation: State-of-the-Art Overview*. School of Information and Computer Science, Georgia Institute of Technology, June 1983, 350 pp.[9] This report contains a concise overview of most current testing techniques and tools. A set of references is provided for each one. A set of test tool data sheets containing implementation details and information contacts is also provided.

POWELL, PATRICIA B. (ed). *Software Validation, Verification, and Testing Technique and Tool Reference Guide*. National Bureau of Standards Special Publication 500–93, 1982. Order from GPO SN-003-003-02422-8.[5] Thirty techniques and tools for validation, verification, and testing are described. Each description includes the basic features of the technique or tool, its input, its output, and an example. Each description also contains an assessment of effectiveness and usability, applicability, an estimate of the learning time and training, an estimate of needed resources, and associated references.

PRESSON, EDWARD. *Software Test Handbook: Software Test Guidebook*. Rome Air Develop-

ment Center RADC-TR-84-53, vol 2 (of two) March 1984. Order from NTIS A147-289. This guidebook contains guidelines and methodology for software testing including summary descriptions of testing techniques, typical paragraphs specifying testing techniques for a Statement of Work, a cross-reference to government and commercial catalogs listing automated test tools, and an extensive bibliography.

REIFER, DONALD J. *Software Quality Assurance Tools and Techniques*. John D. Cooper and Matthew J. Fisher (eds). Software Quality Management, New York: Petrocelli Books, 1979, pp. 209–234. This paper explains how modern tools and techniques support an assurance technology for computer programs. The author first develops categories for quality assurance tools and techniques (aids) and discusses example aids. Material on toolsmithing is presented next. Finally, an assessment is made of the state of the technology and recommendations for improving current practice are offered.

SOFTFAIR 83. *A Conference on Software Development Tools, Techniques, and Alternatives*. IEEE Computer Society Press, 1983.[8] This is the proceedings of the first of what is likely to be a series of conferences aimed at showing the most promising approaches within the field of software tools and environments. It is a collection of 42 papers covering a broad range of software engineering tools from research prototypes to commercial products.

Software Aids and Tools Survey. Federal Software Management Support Center, Office of Software Development, Report OIT/FSMC-86/002, 1985.[6] The purpose of this document is to support management in various government agencies in the identification and selection of software tools. The document identifies and categorizes tools available in the marketplace in mid 1985. Approximately 300 tools are presented with various data concerning each one's function, producer, source language, possible uses, cost, and product description. The survey is expected to be updated periodically.

---

[8] Information regarding IEEE Computer Society publications may be obtained from IEEE Computer Society Order Department, PO Box 80452, Worldway Postal Center, Los Angeles, CA 90080.

[9] The Georgia Technology report may be obtained from Documents Librarian, Software Test and Evaluation Project, School of Information and Computer Science, Georgia Institute of Technology, Atlanta, Georgia 30332.

Appendix D

General References

This section identifies a basic set of reference works on software testing. While the set is not exhaustive, it provides a comprehensive collection of source material. Additional references focusing specifically on testing techniques and tools are contained in Appendix C.

CHANDRASEKARAN, B. and RADICCHI, S., (ed) *Computer Program Testing,* North-Holland, 1981. The following description is from the editors Preface:

> "The articles in this volume, taken as a whole, provide a comprehensive, tutorial discussion of the current state of the art as well as research directions in the area of testing computer programs. They cover the spectrum from basic theoretical notions through practical issues in testing programs and large software systems to integrated environments and tools for performing a variety of tests. They are all written by active researchers and practitioners in the field."

DEUTSCH, MICHAEL S. *Software Verification and Validation.* ENGLEWOOD CLIFFS: Prentice-Hall, 1982. The following description is taken from the Preface.

> "The main thrust of this book is to describe verification and validation approaches that have been used successfully on contemporary large-scale software projects. Methodologies are explored that can be pragmatically applied to modern complex software developments and that take account of cost, schedule, and management realities in the actual production environment. This book is intended to be tutorial in nature with a 'This is how it's done in the real world' orientation. Contributing to this theme will be observations and recounts from actual software development project experiences in industry."

Guideline for Lifecycle Validation, Verification, and Testing of Computer Software. Federal Information Processing Standards (FIPS) Publication 101.[10] Order from NTIS FIPSPUB101 1983 (See Appendix C). This guideline presents an integrated approach to validation, verification, and testing that should be used throughout the software lifecycle. Also included is a glossary of technical terms and a list of supporting ICST publications. An Appendix provides an outline for formulating a VV & T plan.

HETZEL, WILLIAM, *The Complete Guide to Software Testing.* QED Information Sciences,

1984. This book covers many aspects of software verification and validation with a primary emphasis on testing. It contains an overview of test methods and tools including sample reports from several commercially available tools. The book is especially useful when used for viewing testing from a management perspective and discussing many of the associated management issues. An extensive bibliography is included.

McCABE, THOMAS J. (ed). *Structured Testing.* IEEE Computer Society Press, Cat no EHO 200–6, 1983.[8] This IEEE Tutorial is a collection of papers focusing on the relationship between testing and program complexity. The first two papers define cyclomatic complexity and describe an associated technique for developing program test cases. The third paper describes a systematic approach to the development of system test cases. The fourth paper provides general guidelines for program verification and testing. The balance of the papers deal with complexity and reliability.

MILLER, EDWARD and HOWDEN, WILLIAM E. (ed). Tutorial: *Software Testing & Validation Techniques* (2nd ed) IEEE Computer Society Press, Cat no EHO 180–0, 1981.[8] This IEEE Tutorial is a collection of some significant papers dealing with various aspects of software testing. These aspects include theoretical foundations, static analysis, dynamic analysis, effectiveness assessment, and software management. An extensive bibliography is included.

MYERS, GLENFORD J. *The Art of Software Testing.* New York: Wiley–Interscience, 1979. This book contains practical, *How To Do It* technical information on software testing. The main emphasis is on methodologies for the design of effective test cases. It also covers psychological and economic issues, managerial aspects of testing, test tools, debugging, and code inspections. Comprehensive examples and checklists support the presentation.

---

[10] The FIPS VV & T Guideline may be obtained from National Technical Information Service, 5285 Port Royal Road, Springfield, VA 22161.

POWELL, PATRICIA B. (ed). *Plan for Software Validation, Verification, and Testing.* National Bureau of Standards Special Publication 500–98, 1982.[5] Order from GPO SN-003-003-02449-0 (See Appendix C). This document is for those who direct and those who implement computer projects. It explains the selection and use of validation, verification, and testing (VV & T) tools and techniques. It explains how to develop a plan to meet specific software VV & T goals.

Acknowledgment

Appreciation is expressed to the following companies and organizations for contributing the time of their employees to make possible the development of this text:

Algoma Steel
Applied Information Development
AT & T Bell Labs
AT & T Information Systems
Automated Language Processing Systems
Bank of America
Bechtel Power
Bell Canada
Boeing Computer Services
Boston University
Burroughs, Scotland
CAP GEMINI DASD
Central Institute for Industrial Research, Norway
Communications Sciences
Conoco
Digital Equipment Corp
US Department of the Interior
US Department of Transportation
Data Systems Analysts
E-Systems
K.A. Foster, Inc
General Dynamics
Georgia Tech
General Services Administration
Honeywell
Hughes Aircraft
IBM
IBM Federal Systems Division
International Bureau of Software Test
Johns Hopkins University Applied Physics Laboratory
Lear Siegler
Logicon

Management and Computer Services
Martin Marietta Aerospace
McDonald-Douglas
Medtronic
Micom
Mitre
M. T. Scientific Consulting
NASA
National Bureau of Standards
NCR
Product Assurances Consulting
Professional Systems & Technology
Programming Environments
Quality Assurance Institute
RCA
Reynolds & Reynolds
Rolm Telecommunications
Rome Air Development Center
Sallie Mae
Seattle—First National Bank
SHAPE, BELGIUM
Software Engineering Service, Germany
Software Quality Engineering
Software Research Associates
Solo Systems
Sperry
SQS GmbH, Germany
Tandem Computers
Tektronix
Televideo
Tenn Valley Authority
Texas Instruments
Time
University of DC
University of Texas, Arlington
US Army Computer Systems Command
Warner Robins ALC
Westinghouse Hanford

An American National Standard

IEEE Standard for Software Verification and Validation Plans

Sponsor

**Software Engineering Technical Committee
of the
IEEE Computer Society**

Approved September 18, 1986

IEEE Standards Board

Approved February 10, 1987

American National Standards Institute

1012

Foreword

(This Foreword is not a part of IEEE Std 1012-1986, IEEE Standard for Software Verification and Validation Plans.)

This standard provides uniform and minimum requirements for the format and content of Software Verification and Validation Plans (SVVPs). Performing software verification and validation (V&V) as defined in this standard provides for a comprehensive evaluation throughout each phase of the software project to help ensure that:

(1) Errors are detected and corrected as early as possible in the software life cycle

(2) Project risk, cost, and schedule effects are lessened

(3) Software quality and reliability are enhanced

(4) Management visibility into the software process is improved

(5) Proposed changes and their consequences can be quickly assessed

This standard applies to both critical and noncritical software.

(1) For critical software, this standard:

    (a) Requires that minimum V&V tasks, inputs, and outputs specified in this standard be included in SVVPs

    (b) Permits the SVVP to be extended by selecting additional V&V tasks from the optional tasks described in this standard or new tasks identified by the V&V planner

(2) For noncritical software, this standard:

    (a) Recommends the use of minimum V&V tasks

    (b) Permits the SVVP to be tailored to V&V efforts by selecting any of the V&V tasks (minimum, optional, new)

This standard applies to all phases of the software life cycle from the Concept Phase to the Operation and Maintenance Phase. Maximum benefits are derived when V&V is started early in the software life cycle, preferably at project initiation during the Concept Phase. Benefits can be derived for software already in development or in the Operation and Maintenance Phase if the V&V requirements from this standard are invoked consistent with cost and schedule constraints. When V&V is invoked for software in development or in operation and maintenance, required V&V inputs may not exist. Under these conditions, this standard permits the V&V tasks to be tailored to adjust for missing V&V inputs. In some instances, this may require the generation of appropriate software documentation.

V&V is performed in parallel with software development. Each V&V life-cycle phase ends when the V&V tasks of that phase are completed and the software development products are determined to be adequate. V&V life-cycle phases may overlap as activities of the new life-cycle phase are beginning and activities of the previous life-cycle phase are completing.

V&V tasks are iterative: as changes are made to the software product, selected V&V tasks from the previous life-cycle phases are reperformed, or additional V&V tasks are performed to address the changes. V&V tasks are reperformed if errors are discovered in the V&V inputs or outputs. The complexity and scope of changes determine the level of detail covered by the iteration. The SVVP identifies the criteria for performing the iterative V&V tasks.

This standard defines a V&V reporting structure by identifying format and content of the Software Verification and Validation Report (SVVR). The standard for Software Quality Assurance Plans (SQAP, ANSI/IEEE Std-730-1984) requires the SVVR to include both V&V and other quality assurance results. The SVVR defined here is flexible enough to include both types of results. The interim phase reports, final summary report, and optional SQAP-related activity reports defined by the SVVP provide visibility into the development and V&V processes.

This standard considers both the software and its system or operating environment. It can be used where software is the system or where software is part of a larger system. V&V should have a total system scope (that is, including interfaces between software, hardware, and operators) during the product life cycle. Embedded software is strongly coupled to hardware and other subsystems, and requires a system-level SVVP.

This standard was written to provide direction to organizations responsible for preparing or assessing a Software Verification and Validation Plan. This standard may be used by project management, software developers, quality assurance organizations, purchasers, end users, maintainers, and verification and validation organizations. If V&V is performed by an independent group, then the SVVP should specify the criteria for maintaining the independence of the V&V effort from the software development and maintenance efforts.

Suggestions for the improvement of this standard will be welcomed. They should be sent to

Secretary
IEEE Standards Board
Institute of Electrical and Electronics Engineers, Inc
345 East 47th Street
New York, New York 10017

The working group that developed this standard consisted of the following members:

Roger U. Fujii, *Chairman*   **Doug McMann,** *Vice Chairman*
Dolores R. Wallace, *Secretary*

Stephen Benz	Ralph A. Kubek	David M. Siefert
Julian O. Blosiu	Joyce Lewis	Hugh Spillane
Martha Branstad	Roger J. Martin	George Tice
Fletcher J. Buckley	Jerome W. Mersky	Richard Thayer
François Coallier	Dennis E. Nickle	David Turner
James A. Darling	Larry E. Nitszche	William S. Turner
Taz Daughtrey	A.E. Nountor	Adam Valentine
David C. Doty	Jane W. Radatz	Robert A. Walker
Sam Dugdale	Don J. Robbins	Jay W. Wiley
William Dupras	J. A. Ronbeck	Andrea Williams
Michael Edwards	Hans Schaefer	Laurence Wilson
John Horch	David Schultz	Helen M. Wood

When the IEEE Standards Board approved this standard on September 18, 1986, it had the following membership:

John E. May, *Chairman*   **Irving Kolodny,** *Vice Chairman*
Sava I. Sherr, *Secretary*

James H. Beall	Jack Kinn	Robert E. Rountree
Fletcher J. Buckley	Joseph L. Koepfinger*	Martha Sloan
Paul G. Cummings	Edward Lohse	Oley Wanaselja
Donald C. Fleckenstein	Lawrence V. McCall	J. Richard Weger
Jay Forster	Donald T. Michael*	William B. Wilkens
Daniel L. Goldberg	Marco W. Migliaro	Helen M. Wood
Kenneth D. Hendrix	Stanley Owens	Charles J. Wylie
Irvin N. Howell	John P. Riganati	Donald W. Zipse
	Frank L. Rose	

*Member emeritus

The standard was approved by the Software Engineering Standards Subcommittee of the IEEE Computer Society. At the time it approved this standard, the Ballot Group had the following membership:

John W. Horch, *Chairman*

A. Frank Ackerman
Jagdish Agrawal
Tom Armbruster
Richard L. Aurbach
James Baldo, Jr
Geoff Baldwin
H. Jack Barnard
Roy W. Bass
Leo Beltracchi
Yechiel Ben-Naftau
H.R. Berlack
Matt Biewer
J. Emmett Black
Michael A. Blackledge
Ronald M. Blair
Walter DuBlanica
Kevin W. Bowyer
Ingar Brauti
Michael F. Brennter
Kathleen L. Briggs
William L. Bryan
Fletcher J. Buckley
Douglas Burt
Homer C. Carney
C.L. Carpenter, Jr
Ronald R. Carter
R.L. Chilavsky
Tsun S. Chow
Jung K. Chung
Peter Coad, Jr
François Coallier
Sharon R. Cobb
William J. Cody
Christopher M. Cooke
Gail A. Cordes
A.J. Cote
Patricia W. Daggett
James A. Darling
George D. Darling
Taz Daughtrey
P.A. Denny
James H. Dobbins
David C. Doty
Einar Dragstedt
Robert Dunn
William P. Dupras
Robert E. Dwyer
Mary Eads
John D. Earls
Michael Edwards
L.G. Egan
Wolfgang Ehrenberger
Steven R. Eisen
Caroline L. Evans
David W. Favor
John Fendrich
Robert G. Ferreol
Glenn S. Fields
Wayne Fischer
Gordon Force
Julian Forster
C.R. Frederick
Carl Friedlander
Richard C. Fries
Ismael Fuentes
Roger U. Fujii
Michel Galinier
Leonard B. Gardner
David Gelperin
J. Kaye Grau
Andres Grebenc
Thomas Griest
James L. Gildersleeve
Shirley A. Gloss-Soler
Victor M. Guarnera
Lawrence M. Gunther

David A. Gustafson
Russell Gustin
Howard Hamer
Harry E. Hansen
Allen L. Hankinson
Robert M. Haralick
Hans Ludwig Hausen
Clark M. Hay
Herb Hecht
Terry L. Hengl
Charles P. Hollocker
John W. Horch
James W. Howatt
Cheng Hu
Peter L. Hung
Don L. Jackson
Shang-Sheng Jeng
Laurel Kaleda
Constantine Kaniklidis
Myron S. Karasik
Adi Kasad
Ron Kenett
R.A. Kessler
John M. Kinn
Shaye Koenig
Edward E. Kopicky
Joseph A. Krupinski
Joan Kundig
Tom Kurihara
Lak Ming Lam
John B. Lane
Robert A. Lane
William P. LaPlant
Greg Larsen
John A. Latimer
Paul Lebertz
J.A.N. Lee
Leon S. Levy
F.C. Lim
Bertil Lindberg
Gary Lindsay
David P. Linssen
Steven Litvintchouk
John M. Long
Donald C. Loughry
John K. Lowell
Bill Macre
Harold T. Maguire
Andy Mahindru
Kartik C. Majumdar
Henry A. Malec
Paulo C. Marcondes
Stuart Marcotte
Philip C. Marriott
Nicholas L. Marselos
Roger J. Martin
Paul Mauro
L.J. Mazlack
Ivano Mazza
J.A. McCall
Paul E. McKenney
Jack McKissick
Stanley E. McQueen
Glen A. Meldrum
Mordechai Ben Menachen
Belden Menkus
Jerome W. Mersky
W.F. Mitchell
Celia Modell
Charles S. Mooney
Gary Moorhead
Gene T. Morun
David G. Mullens
Myron L. Nack
Hironobu Nagano
Saied Najafi

G.R. Neidhart
Dennis E. Nickle
Perry R. Nuhn
J.H. Obbink
Deene Ogden
Wilma Osborne
D.J. Ostrom
Thomas D. Parrish
William E. Perry
Donald J. Pfeiffer
Harpal S. Phama
Robert M. Poston
Peter Prinzivalli
I.C. Pyle
Jane W. Radatz
Thomas S. Radi
Jock Rader
Wendy Rauch-Hindein
Meir Razy
John Reddan
Larry K. Reed
Matthias F. Reese
T.D. Regulinski
Paul Renaud
John P. Riganati
Gary S. Robinson
Hom Sack
J. Gonzales Sanz
Lawrence R. Satz
Franz P. Schauer
Peter E. Schilling
Max J. Schindler
Norman Schneidewind
Wolf A. Schnoege
Robert Schueppert
David J. Schultz
Gregory D. Schumacher
Leonard W. Seagren
Craig L. Shermer
Robert W. Shillato
Victor Shtern
David M. Siefert
David J. Simkins
Jacob Slonim
Jean-Christopher Slucki
Marion P. Smith
Harry M. Sneed
Al Sorkowitz
Hugh B. Spillane
Lee Sprague
G. Wayne Staley
Robert G. Stewart
Vegard Stuan
Alan N. Sukert
William G. Sutcliffe
Robert A. Symes
Richard H. Thayer
Paul U. Thompson
Michael H. Thursby
George Tice
R.L. Van Tilburg
Terrence L. Tillmanns
Lawrence F. Tracey
Henry J. Trochesset
Robert Troy
C.L. Troyanowski
Dana L. Ulery
David Usechak
P.M. Vater
Osmo Vikman
R. Wachter
Dolores R. Wallace
Thomas J. Walsh
William M. Walsh
Roger Warburton
Robert Werlwas

(Continued on next page)

(Continued from preceding page)

Charles J. Wertz
N.P. Wilburn
Andrew F. Wilson
Patrick J. Wilson
Paul A. Willis
Walter L. Whipple
Theodore J. Wojcik

Paul Wolfgang
Tom Worthington
W. Martin Wong
Dennis L. Wood
Helen M. Wood
Charles Wortz
A.W. Yonda

Natalie C. Yopconka
Michael E. York
Janusz Zalewski
Donald J. Zeleny
Marvin Zelkowitz
Hugh Zettel
Peter F. Zoll

Contents

IEEE Standard for Software Verification and Validation Plans

1. Scope and References

1.1 Scope. This standard has a threefold purpose:

(1) To provide, for both critical and noncritical software, uniform and minimum requirements for the format and content of Software Verification and Validation Plans (SVVPs)

(2) To define, for critical software, specific minimum verification and validation (V&V) tasks and their required inputs and outputs that shall be included in SVVPs

(3) To suggest optional V&V tasks to be used to tailor SVVPs as appropriate for the particular V&V effort

This standard requires that an SVVP be written for both critical and noncritical software. Critical software is software in which a failure could have an impact on safety or could cause large financial or social losses.

This SVVP shall include V&V tasks to:

(1) Verify that the products of each software life-cycle phase:

(a) Comply with previous life-cycle phase requirements and products (for example, for correctness, completeness, consistency, accuracy)

(b) Satisfy the standards, practices, and conventions of the phase

(c) Establish the proper basis for initiating the next life-cycle phase activities

(2) Validate that the completed end product complies with established software and system requirements.

For critical software, this standard requires that minimum V&V tasks and their inputs and outputs be included in all SVVPs. For noncritical software, this standard does not specify minimum required V&V tasks; however, all other requirements of this standard shall be satisfied. This standard does recommend that the minimum V&V tasks for critical software also be employed for noncritical software.

This standard defines optional V&V tasks that permit V&V planners to tailor an SVVP for a V&V effort. For critical software, the minimum tasks may be supplemented with tasks selected from the optional tasks. For noncritical software, tasks may be selected from the minimum and optional tasks. Additional tasks identified by the user of this standard may be included in the SVVP for critical and noncritical software.

The life cycle used in this standard serves as a model and consists of the following life-cycle phases:

(1) Concept
(2) Requirements
(3) Design
(4) Implementation
(5) Test
(6) Installation and checkout
(7) Operation and maintenance

Compliance with this standard does not require use of the life-cycle model presented here. If a different model is used, the SVVP shall include cross-references to this standard's life cycle and to the V&V tasks, inputs, and outputs specified here for each life-cycle phase.

This standard requires that the following be defined for each phase:
(1) Verification and validation tasks
(2) Methods and criteria
(3) Inputs and outputs
(4) Schedule
(5) Resources
(6) Risks and assumptions
(7) Roles and responsibilities

This standard requires a management effort that encompasses all life-cycle phases. The management section of the SVVP defines information necessary to manage and perform the V&V effort, and to coordinate V&V with other aspects of the project. The standard requires the SVVP to specify how the V&V results shall be documented in the Software Verification and Validation Report (SVVR).

When this standard is invoked for existing software, the SVVP shall describe how V&V will be performed when required inputs do not exist. The standard does not prohibit the incorporation of additional content into an SVVP.

The SVVP standard derives its scope from ANSI/IEEE Std 730-1984 [2].[1] The SVVP standard may be applied in conjunction with, or independent of, other IEEE software engineering standards. This standard uses the definitions of ANSI/IEEE Std 729-1983 [1]. This SVVP standard contains V&V configuration analysis tasks that, in part or in whole, are reflected in ANSI/IEEE Std 828-1983 [3]. Test documentation is compatible with that in ANSI/IEEE Std 829-1983 [4].

1.2 References. This standard shall be used in conjunction with the following publications:

[1] ANSI/IEEE Std 729-1983, IEEE Standard Glossary of Software Engineering Terminology.[2]

[2] ANSI/IEEE Std 730-1984, IEEE Standard for Software Quality Assurance Plans.

[3] ANSI/IEEE Std 828-1983, IEEE Standard for Software Configuration Management Plans.

[4] ANSI/IEEE Std 829-1983, IEEE Standard for Software Test Documentation.

---

[1] Numbers in brackets correspond to those of the references in 1.2 of this standard.

[2] ANSI documents are available from the Sales Department, American National Standards Institute, 1430 Broadway, New York, NY 10018.

2. Conventions, Definitions, and Acronyms

2.1 Conventions. The use of the term *documentation* rather than *document* indicates that the information may exist in several documents or may be embedded within a document addressing more than one subject.

2.2 Definitions. The following terms, including those defined in other standards, are used as indicated in this standard.

acceptance testing. Formal testing conducted to determine whether or not a system satisfies its acceptance criteria and to enable the customer to determine whether or not to accept the system. (See ANSI/IEEE Std 729-1983 [1].)

anomaly. Anything observed in the documentation or operation of software that deviates from expectations based on previously verified software products or reference documents. A critical anomaly is one that must be resolved before the V&V effort proceeds to the next life-cycle phase.

component testing. Testing conducted to verify the implementation of the design for one software element (for example, unit, module) or a collection of software elements.

concept phase. The initial phase of a software development project, in which user needs are described and evaluated through documentation (for example, statement of needs, advance planning report, project initiation memo, feasibility studies, system definition documentation, regulations, procedures, or policies relevant to the project).

critical software. Software whose failure could have an impact on safety, or could cause large financial or social loss.

design phase. The period of time in the software life cycle during which the designs for architecture, software components, interfaces, and data are created, documented, and verified to satisfy requirements. (See ANSI/IEEE Std 729-1983 [1].)

implementation phase. The period of time in the software life cycle during which a software product is created from design documentation and debugged. (See ANSI / IEEE Std 729-1983 [1].)

installation and checkout phase. The period of time in the software life cycle during which a software product is integrated into its operational environment and tested in this environment to ensure that it performs as required. (See ANSI / IEEE Std 729-1983 [1].)

integration testing. An orderly progression of testing in which software elements, hardware elements, or both are combined and tested until the entire system has been integrated. (See ANSI / IEEE Std 729-1983 [1].)

life-cycle phase. Any period of time during software development or operation that may be characterized by a primary type of activity (such as design or testing) that is being conducted. These phases may overlap one another; for V&V purposes, no phase is concluded until its development products are fully verified.

minimum tasks. Those V&V tasks applicable to all projects. V&V planning for critical software shall include all such tasks; these tasks are recommended for the V&V of noncritical software.

operation and maintenance phase. The period of time in the software life cycle during which a software product is employed in its operational environment, monitored for satisfactory performance, and modified as necessary to correct problems or to respond to changing requirements. (See ANSI / IEEE Std 729-1983 [1].)

optional tasks. Those V&V tasks that are applicable to some, but not all, software, or that may require the use of specific tools or techniques. These tasks should be performed when appropriate. The list of tasks provided in Table 2 is not exhaustive.

required inputs. The set of items necessary to perform the minimum V&V tasks mandated within any life-cycle phase.

required outputs. The set of items produced as a result of performing the minimum V&V tasks mandated within any life-cycle phase.

requirements phase. The period of time in the software life cycle during which the requirements, such as functional and performance capabilities for a software product, are defined and documented. (See ANSI / IEEE Std 729-1983 [1].)

software design description. A representation of software created to facilitate analysis, planning, implementation, and decision making. The software design description is used as a medium for communicating software design information, and may be thought of as a blueprint or model of the system.

software requirements specification. Documentation of the essential requirements (functions, performance, design constraints, and attributes) of the software and its external interfaces. (See ANSI / IEEE Std 730-1984 [2].)

software verification and validation plan. A plan for the conduct of software verification and validation.

software verification and validation report. Documentation of V&V results and appropriate software quality assurance results.

system testing. The process of testing an integrated hardware and software system to verify that the system meets its specified requirements. (See ANSI / IEEE Std 729-1983 [1].)

test case. Documentation specifying inputs, predicted results, and a set of execution conditions for a test item. (See ANSI / IEEE Std 829-1983 [4].)

test design. Documentation specifying the details of the test approach for a software feature or combination of software features and identifying the associated tests. (See ANSI / IEEE Std 829-1983 [4].)

test phase. The period of time in the software life cycle in which the components of a software product are evaluated and integrated, and the software product is evaluated to determine whether or not requirements have been satisfied. (See ANSI / IEEE Std 729-1983 [1].)

test plan. Documentation specifying the scope, approach, resources, and schedule of intended testing activities. (See ANSI/IEEE Std 829-1983 [4].)

test procedure. Documentation specifying a sequence of actions for the execution of a test. (See ANSI/IEEE Std 829-1983 [4].)

validation. The process of evaluating software at the end of the software development process to ensure compliance with software requirements. (See ANSI/IEEE Std 729-1983 [1].)

verification. The process of determining whether or not the products of a given phase of the software development cycle fulfill the requirements established during the previous phase. (See ANSI/IEEE Std 729-1983 [1].)

2.3 Acronyms. The following acronyms appear in this standard:

SDD	Software Design Description
SRS	Software Requirements Specification
SVVP	Software Verification and Validation Plan
SVVR	Software Verification and Validation Report
V&V	Verification and Validation

3. Software Verification and Validation Plan

The Software Verification and Validation Plan (also referred to as the Plan) shall include the sections shown below to be in compliance with this standard. If there is no information pertinent to a section or a required paragraph within a section, the following shall appear below the section or paragraph heading together with the appropriate reason for the exclusion: *This section/paragraph is not applicable to this plan.* Additional sections may be added at the end of the plan as required. Some of the material may appear in other documents. If so, reference to those documents shall be made in the body of the Plan.

Software Verification and Validation Plan Outline
1. Purpose
2. Referenced Documents
3. Definitions
4. Verification and Validation Overview
    4.1 Organization

    4.2 Master Schedule
    4.3 Resources Summary
    4.4 Responsibilities
    4.5 Tools, Techniques, and Methodologies
5. Life-Cycle Verification and Validation
    5.1 Management of V&V
    5.2 Concept Phase V&V
    5.3 Requirements Phase V&V
    5.4 Design Phase V&V
    5.5 Implementation Phase V&V
    5.6 Test Phase V&V
    5.7 Installation and Checkout Phase V&V
    5.8 Operation and Maintenance Phase V&V
6. Software Verification and Validation Reporting
7. Verification and Validation Administrative Procedures
    7.1 Anomaly Reporting and Resolution
    7.2 Task Iteration Policy
    7.3 Deviation Policy
    7.4 Control Procedures
    7.5 Standards, Practices, and Conventions

3.1 Purpose. (Section 1 of the Plan.) This section shall delineate the specific purpose and scope of the Software Verification and Validation Plan, including waivers from this standard. The software project for which the Plan is being written and the specific software product items covered by the Plan shall be identified. The goals of the verification and validation efforts shall be specified.

3.2 Referenced Documents. (Section 2 of the Plan.) This section shall identify the binding compliance documents, documents referenced by this Plan, and any supporting documents required to supplement or implement this Plan.

3.3 Definitions. (Section 3 of the Plan.) This section shall define or provide a reference to the definitions of all terms required to properly interpret the Plan. This section shall describe the acronyms and notations used in the Plan.

3.4 Verification and Validation Overview. (Section 4 of the Plan.) This section shall describe the organization, schedule, resources, responsibilities, and tools, techniques, and methodologies necessary to perform the software verification and validation.

    3.4.1 Organization. (Section 4.1 of the Plan.) This section shall describe the organization of the V&V effort. It shall define the relationship of V&V to other efforts such as development, project management, quality assurance, configuration or data management, or end user. It shall define the lines of communication within the V&V effort, the authority for resolving issues raised by V&V tasks, and the authority for approving V&V products.

3.4.2 Master Schedule. (Section 4.2 of the Plan.) This section shall describe the project life cycle and milestones, including completion dates. It shall summarize the scheduling of V&V tasks and shall describe how V&V results provide feedback to the development process to support project management functions (for example, comments on design review material).

If the life cycle used in the Plan differs from the life-cycle model in the standard, this section shall show how all requirements of the standard are satisfied (for example, cross-reference for life-cycle phases, tasks, inputs, and outputs). When planning V&V tasks, it should be recognized that the V&V process is iterative. The summary of tasks may be in narrative, tabular, or graphic form (for example, Fig 1). The life-cycle model in Fig 1 is a sample model used for this standard.

3.4.3 Resources Summary. (Section 4.3 of the Plan.) This section shall summarize the resources needed to perform the V&V tasks, including staffing, facilities, tools, finances, and special procedural requirements such as security, access rights, or documentation control.

3.4.4 Responsibilities. (Section 4.4 of the Plan.) This section shall identify the organizational element(s) responsible for performing each V&V tasks. It shall identify the specific responsibility of each element for tasks assigned to more than one element. This section may be a summary of the roles and responsibilities defined in each of the life-cycle phases (see 3.5 of this standard).

3.4.5 Tools, Techniques, and Methodologies. (Section 4.5 of the Plan.) This section shall identify the special software tools, techniques, and methodologies employed by the V&V effort. The purpose and use of each shall be described. Plans for the acquisition, training, support, and qualification for each shall be included. This section may reference a V&V Tool Plan.

3.5 Life-Cycle Verification and Validation. (Section 5 of the Plan.) This section of the Plan shall provide the detailed plan for the V&V

tasks throughout the life cycle. The detailed plan (Section 5.1—Management, and Sections 5.2 through 5.8—Life-Cycle Phases) shall address the following topics:

(1) Verification and Validation Tasks. Identify the V&V tasks for the phase. Describe how each task contributes to the accomplishment of the project V&V goals. For all critical software, the SVVP shall include all minimum V&V tasks for the management of V&V and for each life-cycle phase. Any or all of these minimum tasks may be used for noncritical software. These minimum V&V tasks are referenced in the management and life-cycle phases sections of the standard (3.5.1 through 3.5.8), and are described in Table 1. The minimum tasks are also consolidated in graphic form in Fig 1.

Optional V&V tasks may also be selected to tailor the V&V effort to project needs for critical or noncritical software. Optional V&V tasks are defined in the Appendix and a suggested application for the management of V&V and for each life-cycle phase is presented in Table 2. The optional V&V tasks identified in this standard may be applicable to some, but not all, critical software. These tasks may require the use of specific tools or techniques. The list in Table 2 is illustrative and not exhaustive. The standard allows for the optional V&V tasks and any others identified by the planner to be used as appropriate.

Testing requires advance planning that spans several life-cycle phases. Test documentation and its occurrence in specific life-cycle phases are shown in Fig 2 as a recommended approach. To be in compliance with this standard, the test documentation and test execution specified in Fig 2 shall be required. If the V&V planner uses different test documentation or test types (for example, component, integration, system, acceptance) from those in this standard, the SVVP shall contain a mapping of the proposed test documentation and execution to the items shown in Fig 2. Test planning criteria defined in Table 1 (Tasks 5.3 (4a), 5.3 (4b), 5.4 (4a), 5.4 (4b)) shall be implemented in the test plan, test design(s), test case(s), and test procedure(s) documentation, and shall be validated by test execution.

(2) Methods and Criteria. Identify the methods and criteria used in performing the V&V tasks. Describe the specific methods and procedures for each task. Define the detailed criteria for evaluating the task results.

(3) Inputs/Outputs. Identify the inputs re-

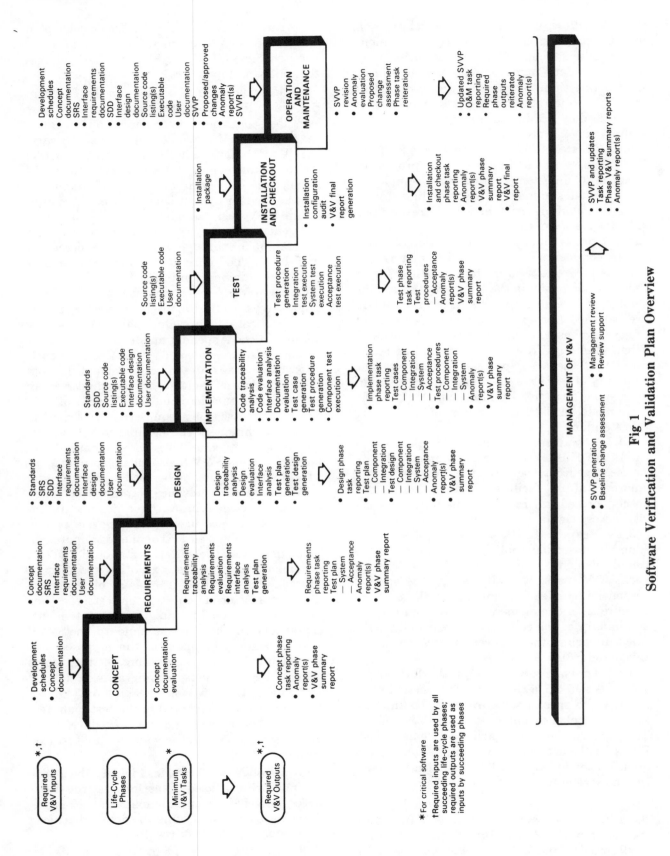

Fig 1
Software Verification and Validation Plan Overview

TP: Test Plan
TD: Test Design(s)
TC: Test Cases
TPr: Test Procedures
TE: Test Execution
TR: Test Reporting *
[Task Report(s), V&V Phase Summary Report(s), and Anomaly Report(s)-produced throughout the test activity]

Requirements · **Design** · **Implementation** · **Test** · **Installation & Checkout**

Component Test
- Verifies design/implementation
- Test
  — Units
  — Modules
  — Subelements
- Uses programmer and development test environment

TP · TD · TC · TPr · TE · TR

Integration Test
- Integrates subelements
- Tests
  — Subelements with subelements
  — Hardware interfaces
  — External software interfaces
  — Functional requirements
- Uses subelement integration test environment

TP · TD · TC · TPr · TE · TR

System Test
- Verifies compliance with system objectives
- Tests
  — End item functional requirements
  — System requirements
- Uses system test environment

TP · TD · TC · TPr · TE · TR

Acceptance Test
- Supports acceptance
- Tests
  — Software against acceptance criteria
- Uses operational test environment

TP · TD · TC · TPr · TE · TR

Fig 2
V&V Test Tasks and Documentation

*This test planning documentation need not be individual documents. The placement of test outputs in specific life-cycle phases indicates a recommended approach.

15

quired for each V&V task. Specify the source and format of each input. The inputs required for each of the minimum V&V tasks are identified in Table 1. The required inputs are used, as appropriate, by subsequent life-cycle phase V&V tasks. Only the primary inputs are listed in Table 1.

Identify the outputs from each V&V task. Specify the purpose and format for each output. The outputs from each of the minimum V&V tasks are identified in Table 1.

The outputs of the management of V&V and of the life-cycle phases shall become inputs to subsequent life-cycle phases, as appropriate.

Anomaly report(s), task report(s), and phase summary report(s) provide feedback to the software development process regarding the technical quality of each life-cycle phase software product. Each critical anomaly shall be resolved before the V&V effort proceeds to the next life-cycle phase.

(4) Schedule. Identify the schedule for the V&V tasks. Establish specific milestones for initiating and completing each task, for the receipt of each input, and for the delivery of each output.

(5) Resources. Identify the resources for the performance of the V&V tasks. Specify resources by category (for example, staffing, equipment, facilities, schedule, travel, training). If tools are used in the V&V tasks, specify the source of the tools, their availability, and other usage requirements (for example, training).

(6) Risks and Assumptions. Identify the risks and assumptions associated with the V&V tasks, including schedule, resources, or approach. Specify a contingency plan for each risk.

(7) Roles and Responsibilities. Identify the organizational elements or individuals responsible for performing the V&V tasks. Assign specific responsibilities for each task to one or more organizational element.

3.5.1 Management of V&V. (Section 5.1 of the Plan.) This section of the Plan shall address the seven topics identified in 3.5 of this standard. The management of V&V spans all life-cycle phases. The software development may be a cyclic or iterative process. The V&V effort shall reperform previous V&V tasks or initiate new V&V tasks to address software changes created by the cyclic or iterative development process. V&V tasks are reperformed if errors are discovered in the V&V inputs or outputs.

For all software, management of V&V shall include the following minimum tasks:

(1) Software Verification and Validation Plan (SVVP) Generation

(2) Baseline Change Assessment

(3) Management Review of V&V

(4) Review Support

Table 1 describes the minimum management V&V tasks and identifies the required inputs and outputs. The inputs and outputs required for each V&V task shall include, but not be limited to, those listed in Table 1.

3.5.2 Concept Phase V&V. (Section 5.2 of the Plan.) This section of the Plan shall address the seven topics identified in 3.5 of this standard.

For critical software, Concept Phase V&V shall include the following minimum V&V task:

Concept Documentation Evaluation. Table 1 contains a description of the minimum Concept Phase V&V task and identifies the required inputs and outputs. The inputs and outputs required to accomplish the minimum V&V task shall include, but not be limited to, those listed in Table 1.

3.5.3 Requirements Phase V&V. (Section 5.3 of the Plan.) This section of the Plan shall address the seven topics identified in 3.5 of this standard.

For critical software, Requirements Phase V&V shall include the following minimum tasks:

(1) Software Requirements Traceability Analysis

(2) Software Requirements Evaluation

(3) Software Requirements Interface Analysis

(4) Test Plan Generation

  (a) System Test

  (b) Acceptance Test

Table 1 contains a description of the minimum Requirements Phase V&V tasks and identifies the required inputs and outputs. The inputs and outputs required to accomplish the minimum V&V tasks shall include, but not be limited to, those listed in Table 1.

3.5.4 Design Phase V&V. (Section 5.4 of the Plan.) This section of the Plan shall address the seven topics identified in Section 3.5 of this standard. For critical software, Design Phase V&V shall include the following minimum V&V tasks:

(1) Software Design Traceability Analysis

(2) Software Design Evaluation

(3) Software Design Interface Analysis

(4) Test Plan Generation

(a) Component Test
(b) Integration Test
(5) Test Design Generation
(a) Component Test
(b) Integration Test
(c) System Test
(d) Acceptance Test

Table 1 contains a description of the minimum Design Phase V&V tasks and identifies the required inputs and outputs. The inputs and outputs required to accomplish the minimum V&V tasks shall include, but not be limited to, those listed in Table 1.

3.5.5 Implementation Phase V&V. (Section 5.5 of the Plan.) This section of the Plan shall address the seven topics identified in 3.5 of this standard.

For critical software, Implementation Phase V&V shall include the following minimum V&V tasks:

(1) Source Code Traceability Analysis
(2) Source Code Evaluation
(3) Source Code Interface Analysis
(4) Source Code Documentation Evaluation
(5) Test Case Generation
(a) Component Test
(b) Integration Test
(c) System Test
(d) Acceptance Test
(6) Test Procedure Generation
(a) Component Test
(b) Integration Test
(c) System Test
(7) Component Test Execution

Table 1 contains a description of the minimum Implementation Phase V&V tasks and identifies the required inputs and outputs. The inputs and outputs required to accomplish the minimum V&V tasks shall include, but not be limited to, those listed in Table 1.

3.5.6 Test Phase V&V. (Section 5.6 of the Plan.) This section of the Plan shall address the seven topics identified in 3.5 of this standard.

Testing activities and their interrelationships with previous V&V phases are shown in Fig 2.

For critical software, Test Phase V&V shall include the following minimum V&V tasks:

(1) Acceptance Test Procedure Generation
(2) Test Execution
(a) Integration Test
(b) System Test
(c) Acceptance Test

Table 1 contains a description of the minimum Test Phase V&V tasks and identifies the required inputs and outputs. The inputs and outputs required to accomplish the minimum V&V tasks shall include, but not be limited to, those listed in Table 1.

3.5.7 Installation and Checkout Phase V&V. (Section 5.7 of the Plan.) This section of the Plan shall address the seven topics identified in Section 3.5 of this standard.

For critical software, Installation and Checkout Phase V&V shall include the following minimum V&V tasks:

(1) Installation Configuration Audit
(2) Final V&V Report Generation

Table 1 contains a description of the minimum Installation and Checkout Phase V&V tasks and identifies the required inputs and outputs. The inputs and outputs required to accomplish the minimum V&V tasks shall include, but not be limited to, those listed in Table 1.

3.5.8 Operation and Maintenance Phase V&V. (Section 5.8 of the Plan.) This section of the Plan shall address the seven topics identified in Section 3.5 of this standard.

Any modifications, enhancements, or additions to software during this phase shall be treated as development activities and shall be verified and validated as described in 3.5.1 through 3.5.7. These modifications may derive from requirements specified to correct software errors (that is, corrective), to adapt to a changed operating environment (that is, adaptive), or to respond to additional user requests (that is, perfective).

If the software was verified under this standard, the standard shall continue to be followed in the Operation and Maintenance Phase. If the software was not verified under this standard, the V&V effort may require documentation that is not available or adequate. If appropriate documentation is not available or adequate, the SVVP shall comply with this standard within cost and schedule constraints. The V&V effort may generate the missing documentation.

For critical software, Operation and Maintenance Phase V&V tasks shall include the following minimum V&V tasks:

(1) Software Verification and Validation Plan Revision
(2) Anomaly Evaluation
(3) Proposed Change Assessment
(4) Phase Task Iteration

Table 1 contains a description of the minimum Operation and Maintenance Phase V&V tasks. The inputs and outputs required to accomplish the minimum V&V tasks shall include, but not be limited to, those listed in Table 1.

3.6 Software Verification and Validation Reporting. (Section 6 of the Plan.) This section shall describe how the results of implementing the Plan will be documented. V&V reporting shall occur throughout the software life cycle. This section of the Plan shall specify the content, format, and timing of all V&V reports. These V&V reports shall constitute the Software Verification and Validation Report (SVVR).

3.6.1 Required Reports. The following reports shall be generated for each software V&V effort.

(1) Task Reporting. These shall report on the individual V&V phase tasks and shall be issued as necessary. They may document interim results and status. They may be in a format appropriate for technical disclosure (for example, technical reports or memos).

(2) V&V Phase Summary Report. A Phase Summary Report shall summarize the results of V&V tasks performed in each of the following life-cycle phases: Concept, Requirements, Design, Implementation, Test, and Installation and Checkout. For the Operation and Maintenance Phase, V&V phase summary reports may be either updates to previous V&V phase summary reports or separate documents. Each V&V Phase Summary Report shall contain the following:

(a) Description of V&V tasks performed
(b) Summary of task results
(c) Summary of anomalies and resolution
(d) Assessment of software quality
(e) Recommendations

(3) Anomaly Report. An Anomaly Report shall document each anomaly detected by the V&V effort. Each Anomaly Report shall contain the following:

(a) Description and location
(b) Impact
(c) Cause
(d) Criticality
(e) Recommendations

(4) V&V Final Report. The Verification and Validation Final Report shall be issued at the end of the Installation and Checkout phase or at the conclusion of the V&V effort. The Final Report shall include the following information:

(a) Summary of all life-cycle V&V tasks
(b) Summary of task results
(c) Summary of anomalies and resolutions

(d) Assessment of overall software quality
(e) Recommendations

3.6.2 Optional Reports
The following reports are optional.

(1) Special Studies Report. This report shall describe any special studies conducted during any life-cycle phase. The report shall document technical results and shall include, at a minimum, the following information:

(a) Purpose and objectives
(b) Approach
(c) Summary of results

(2) Other Reports. These reports shall describe the results of tasks not defined in the SVVP. These other activities and results may include quality assurance results, end user testing results, or configuration and data management status results.

3.7 Verification and Validation Administrative Procedures. (Section 7 of the Plan). This section of the Plan shall describe, at a minimum, the V&V administrative procedures described in 3.7.1 through 3.7.5.

3.7.1 Anomaly Reporting and Resolution. (Section 7.1 of the Plan.) This section shall describe the method of reporting and resolving anomalies, including the criteria for reporting an anomaly, the anomaly report distribution list, and the authority and time lines for resolving anomalies. The section shall define the anomaly criticality levels. Each critical anomaly shall be resolved satisfactorily before the V&V effort can formally proceed to the next life-cycle phase.

3.7.2 Task Iteration Policy. (Section 7.2 of the Plan.) This section shall describe the criteria used to determine the extent to which a V&V task shall be reperformed when its input is changed. These criteria may include assessments of change, criticality, and cost, schedule, or quality effects.

3.7.3 Deviation Policy. (Section 7.3 of the Plan.) This section shall describe the procedures and forms used to deviate from the Plan. The information required for deviations shall include task identification, deviation rationale, and effect on software quality. The section shall define the authorities responsible for approving deviations.

3.7.4 Control Procedures. (Section 7.4 of the Plan.) This section shall identify control procedures applied to the V&V effort. These procedures shall describe how software products and results of software V&V shall be configured, protected, and stored.

These procedures may describe quality assurance, configuration management, data management, or other activities if they are not addressed by other efforts. At a minimum, this section shall describe how SVVP materials shall comply with existing security provisions and how the validity of V&V results shall be protected from accidental or deliberate alteration.

3.7.5 Standards, Practices, and Conventions. (Section 7.5 of the Plan.) This section shall identify the standards, practices, and conventions that govern the performance of V&V tasks, including internal organizational standards, practices, and policies.

Table 1
Required V&V Tasks, Inputs, and Outputs for Life-Cycle Phases[3]

Minimum V&V Tasks	Required Inputs	Required Outputs*
5.1 MANAGEMENT OF V&V		
(1) Software Verification and Validation Plan (SVVP) Generation. Generate SVVP (during Concept Phase) for all life-cycle phases in accordance with this standard based upon available documentation. Include estimate of anticipated V&V activities for Operation and Maintenance Phase. Update SVVP for each life-cycle phase, particularly prior to Operation and Maintenance. Consider SVVP to be a *living document,* and make changes as necessary. A baseline SVVP should be established prior to the Requirements Phase.	Development Schedules Concept Documentation SRS Interface Requirements Documentation SDD Interface Design Documentation Source Code Listing(s) Executable Code User Documentation Proposed Changes	SVVP and Updates
(2) Baseline Change Assessment. Evaluate proposed software changes (for example, anomaly corrections, performance enhancements, requirement changes, clarifications) for effects on previously completed V&V tasks. When changes are made, plan iteration of affected tasks which includes reperforming previous V&V tasks or initiating new V&V tasks to address the software changes created by the cyclic or iterative development process.	Proposed Changes	Updated SVVP
(3) Management Review. Conduct periodic reviews of V&V effort, technical accomplishments, resource utilization, future planning, risk management. Support daily management of V&V phase activities, including technical quality of final and interim V&V reports and results. Review the task and V&V phase summary reports of each life-cycle phase. Evaluate V&V results and anomaly resolution to determine when to proceed to next life-cycle phase and to define changes to V&V tasks to improve the V&V effort.	Development Schedules V&V Outputs	Task Reporting V&V Phase Summary Reports
(4) Review Support. Correlate V&V task results to support management and technical reviews (for example, Software Requirements Review, Preliminary Design Review, Critical Design Review). Identify key review support milestones in SVVP. Schedule V&V tasks to meet milestones. Establish methods to exchange V&V data and results with development effort.	V&V Outputs	Task Reporting Anomaly Report(s)
5.2 CONCEPT PHASE V&V		
(1) Concept Documentation Evaluation. Evaluate concept documentation to determine if proposed concept satisfies user needs and project objectives (for example, performance goals). Identify major constraints of interfacing systems and constraints or limitations of proposed approach. Assess allocation of functions to hardware and software items, where appropriate. Assess criticality of each software item.	Concept Documentation (for example, Statement of Need, Advance Planning Report, Project Initiation Memo, Feasibility Studies, System Definition Documentation, Governing Regulations, Procedures, Policies, and customer acceptance criteria/ requirements)	Task Reporting Anomaly Report(s)
5.3 REQUIREMENTS PHASE V&V		
(1) Software Requirements Traceability Analysis. Trace SRS requirements to system requirements in concept documentation. Analyze identified relationships for correctness, consistency, completeness, accuracy.	Concept Documentation SRS Interface Requirements Documents	Task Reporting Anomaly Report(s)
(2) Software Requirements Evaluation. Evaluate SRS requirements for correctness, consistency, completeness, accuracy, readability, and testability. Assess how well SRS satisfies software system objectives. Assess the criticality of requirements to identify key performance or critical areas of software.	Concept Documentation SRS Interface Requirements Documentation	Task Reporting Anomaly Report(s)

* Outputs from phase tasks are used to develop corresponding V&V phase summary reports and are ongoing inputs to the SVVR. Outputs of V&V tasks become inputs to subsequent life-cycle V&V tasks.

[3] The section numbers referred to in this Table refer to Section 5 of the Plan.

Table 1 *(Continued)*

Minimum V&V Tasks	Required Inputs	Required Outputs*
5.3 REQUIREMENTS PHASE V&V *(Continued)*		
(3) Software Requirements Interface Analysis. Evaluate SRS with hardware, user, operator, and software interface requirements documentation for correctness, consistency, completeness, accuracy, and readability.	SRS Interface Requirements Documentation	Task Reporting Anomaly Report(s)
(4a) System Test Plan Generation. Plan system testing to determine if software satisfies system objectives. Criteria for this determination are, at a minimum: (a) compliance with all functional requirements as complete software end item in system environment (b) performance at hardware, software, user, and operator interfaces (c) adequacy of user documentation (d) performance at boundaries (for example, data, interface) and under stress conditions. Plan tracing of system end-item requirements to test design, cases, procedures, and execution results. Plan documentation of test tasks and results.	Concept Documentation SRS Interface Requirements Documentation User Documentation	System Test Plan Anomaly Report(s)
(4b) Acceptance Test Plan Generation. Plan acceptance testing to determine if software correctly implements system and software requirements in an operational environment. Criteria for this determination are, at a minimum: (a) compliance with acceptance requirements in operational environment (b) adequacy of user documentation. Plan tracing of acceptance test requirements to test design, cases, procedures, and execution results. Plan documentation of test tasks and results.	Concept Documentation SRS Interface Requirements Documentation User Documentation	Acceptance Test Plan Anomaly Report(s)
5.4 DESIGN PHASE V&V		
(1) Design Traceability Analysis. Trace SDD to SRS and SRS to SDD. Analyze identified relationships for correctness, consistency, completeness, and accuracy.	SRS SDD Interface Requirements Documentation Interface Design Documentation	Task Reporting Anomaly Report(s)
(2) Design Evaluation. Evaluate SDD for correctness, consistency, completeness, accuracy, and testability. Evaluate design for compliance with established standards, practices, and conventions. Assess design quality.	SDD Interface Design Documentation Standards (standards, practices, conventions)	Task Reporting Anomaly Report(s)
(3) Design Interface Analysis. Evaluate SDD with hardware, operator, and software interface requirements for correctness, consistency, completeness, and accuracy. At a minimum, analyze data items at each interface.	SDD Interface Design Documentation	Task Reporting Anomaly Report(s)
(4a) Component Test Plan Generation. Plan component testing to determine if software elements (for example, units, modules) correctly implement component requirements. Criteria for this determination are, at a minimum: (a) compliance with design requirements (b) assessment of timing, sizing, and accuracy (c) performance at boundaries and interfaces and under stress and error conditions (d) measures of test coverage and software reliability and maintainability. Plan tracing of design requirements to test design, cases, procedures, and execution results. Plan documentation of test tasks and results.	SRS SDD Interface Requirements Documentation Interface Design Documentation	Component Test Plan Anomaly Report(s)
(4b) Integration Test Plan Generation. Plan integration testing to determine if software (for example, subelements, interfaces) correctly implements the software requirements and design. Criteria for this determination are, at a minimum: (a) compliance with increasingly larger set of functional requirements at each stage of integration (b) assessment of timing, sizing, and accuracy (c) performance at boundaries and under stress conditions (d) measures of functional test coverage and software reliability. Plan tracing of requirements to test design, cases, procedures, and execution results. Plan documentation of test tasks and results.	SRS SDD Interface Requirements Documentation Interface Design Documentation	Integration Test Plan Anomaly Report(s)

* Outputs from phase tasks are used to develop corresponding V&V phase summary reports and are ongoing inputs to the SVVR. Outputs of V&V tasks become inputs to subsequent life-cycle V&V tasks.

Table 1 *(Continued)*

Minimum V&V Tasks	Required Inputs	Required Outputs*
5.4 DESIGN PHASE V&V *(Continued)*		
(5) Test Design Generation. Design tests for: (a) component testing (b) integration testing (c) system testing (d) acceptance testing. Continue tracing required by the Test Plan.	SDD Interface Design Documentation User Documentation	Component Test Design(s) Integration Test Design(s) System Test Design(s) Acceptance Test Design(s) Anomaly Report(s)
5.5 IMPLEMENTATION PHASE V&V		
(1) Source Code Traceability Analysis. Trace source code to corresponding design specification(s) and design specification(s) to source code. Analyze identified relationships for correctness, consistency, completeness, and accuracy.	SDD Interface Design Documentation Source Code Listing(s)	Task Reporting Anomaly Report(s)
(2) Source Code Evaluation. Evaluate source code for correctness, consistency, completeness, accuracy, and testability. Evaluate source code for compliance with established standards, practices, and conventions. Assess source code quality.	Source Code Listing(s) Standards (standards, practices, conventions) SDD Interface Design Documentation User Documentation	Task Reporting Anomaly Report(s)
(3) Source Code Interface Analysis. Evaluate source code with hardware, operator, and software interface design documentation for correctness, consistency, completeness, and accuracy. At a minimum, analyze data items at each interface.	Source Code Listing(s) User Documentation	Task Reporting Anomaly Report(s)
(4) Source Code Documentation Evaluation. Evaluate draft code-related documents with source code to ensure completeness, correctness, and consistency.	Source Code Listing(s) User Documentation	Task Reporting Anomaly Report(s)
(5) Test Case Generation. Develop test cases for: (a) component testing (b) integration testing (c) system testing (d) acceptance testing. Continue tracing required by the Test Plan.	SDD Interface Design Documentation Source Code Listing(s)	Component Test Cases Integration Test Cases System Test Cases Acceptance Test Cases Anomaly Report(s)
(6) Test Procedure Generation. Develop test procedures for: (a) component testing (b) integration testing (c) system testing. Continue tracing required by the Test Plan.	SDD Interface Design Documentation Source Code Listing(s) User Documentation	Component Test Procedures Integration Test Procedures System Test Procedures Anomaly Report(s)
(7) Component Test Execution. Perform component testing as required by component test procedures. Analyze results to determine that software correctly implements design. Document and trace results as required by the Test Plan.	Source Code Listing(s) Executable Code SDD Interface Design Documentation	Task Reporting Anomaly Report(s)
5.6 TEST PHASE V&V		
(1) Test Procedure Generation. Develop test procedures for acceptance test. Continue tracing required by the Test Plan.	SDD Interface Design Documentation Source Code Listing(s) User Documentation	Acceptance Test Procedures Anomaly Report(s)

* Outputs from phase tasks are used to develop corresponding V&V phase summary reports and are ongoing inputs to the SVVR. Outputs of V&V tasks become inputs to subsequent life-cycle V&V tasks.

Table 1 (Continued)

Minimum V&V Tasks	Required Inputs	Required Outputs*
5.6 TEST PHASE V&V (Continued)		
(2a) Integration Test Execution. Perform integration testing in accordance with test procedures. Analyze results to determine if software implements software requirements and design and that software components function correctly together. Document and trace results as required by the Test Plan.	Source Code Listing(s) Executable Code	Task Reporting Anomaly Report(s)
(2b) System Test Execution. Perform system testing in accordance with test procedures. Analyze results to determine if software satisfies system objectives. Document and trace all testing results as required by the Test Plan.	Source Code Listing(s) Executable Code User Documentation	Task Reporting Anomaly Report(s)
(2c) Acceptance Test Execution. Perform acceptance testing in accordance with test procedures under formal configuration control. Analyze results to determine if software satisfies acceptance criteria. Document and trace all testing results as required by the Test Plan.	Source Code Listing(s) Executable Code User Documentation	Task Reporting Anomaly Report(s)
5.7 INSTALLATION AND CHECKOUT PHASE V&V		
(1) Installation Configuration Audit. Audit installation package to determine that all software products required to correctly install and operate the software are present, including operations documentation. Analyze all site-dependent parameters or conditions to determine that supplied values are correct. Conduct analyses or tests to demonstrate that installed software corresponds to software subjected to V&V.	Installation Package (for example, Source Code Listing(s), Executable Code, User Documentation, SDD, Interface Design Documentation, SRS, Concept Documentation, Installation Procedures, and Installation Tests)	Task Reporting Anomaly Report(s)
(2) V&V Final Report Generation. Summarize all V&V activities and results, including status and disposition of anomalies in the V&V final report (see 3.6.1 of this standard).	All V&V Phase Summary Report(s)	V&V Final Report
5.8 OPERATION AND MAINTENANCE PHASE V&V		
(1) Software V&V Plan Revision. For software verified and validated under this standard, revise SVVP to comply with new constraints based upon available documentation. For software not verified and validated under this standard, write new SVVP.	Development Schedules Concept Documentation SRS Interface Requirements Documentation SDD Interface Design Documentation Source Code Listing(s) User Documentation Installation Package Proposed Changes	Updated SVVP
(2) Anomaly Evaluation. Evaluate severity of anomalies in software operation. Analyze effect of anomalies on system.	Anomaly Report(s)	Task Reporting
(3) Proposed Change Assessment. Assess all proposed modifications, enhancements, or additions to determine effect each change would have on system. Determine extent to which V&V tasks would be iterated.	Proposed Changes	Task Reporting
(4) Phase Task Iteration. For approved software changes, perform V&V tasks necessary to ensure that: planned changes are implemented correctly; all documentation is complete and up to date; and no unacceptable changes have occurred in software performance.	Approved Changes	Task Reporting from Iterated Tasks Anomaly Report(s) Required Phases Outputs of Iterated Tasks

* Outputs from phase tasks are used to develop corresponding V&V phase summary reports and are ongoing inputs to the SVVR. Outputs of V&V tasks become inputs to subsequent life-cycle V&V tasks.

Table 2
Optional V&V Tasks and Suggested Applications

Optional V&V Tasks	Life-Cycle Phases							
	Management	Concept	Requirements	Design	Implementation	Test	Installation and Checkout	Operation and Maintenance
Algorithm Analysis			●	●	●	●		●
Audit Performance								
Configuration Control					●	●	●	●
Functional					●	●	●	●
In-Process			●	●	●	●	●	●
Physical						●	●	●
Audit Support								
Configuration Control					●	●	●	●
Functional					●	●	●	●
In-Process			●	●	●	●	●	●
Physical						●	●	●
Configuration Management	●	●	●	●	●	●	●	●
Control Flow Analysis			●	●	●			●
Database Analysis			●	●	●	●		●
Data Flow Analysis			●	●	●			●
Feasibility Study Evaluation		●						●
Installation and Checkout Testing*			●	●	●	●	●	●
Performance Monitoring								●
Qualification Testing*			●	●	●	●	●	●
Regression Analysis and Testing			●	●	●	●	●	●
Reviews Support								
Operational Readiness							●	●
Test Readiness					●	●	●	●
Simulation Analysis			●	●	●	●	●	●
Sizing and Timing Analysis				●	●	●	●	●
Test Certification						●	●	●
Test Evaluation			●	●	●	●	●	●
Test Witnessing						●	●	●
User Documentation Evaluation		●	●	●	●	●	●	●
V&V Tool Plan Generation	●							●
Walkthroughs								
Design				●				●
Requirements			●					●
Source Code					●			●
Test					●	●	●	●

* Test plan, test design, test cases, test procedures, and test execution.

Appendix

(This Appendix is not a part of IEEE Std 1012-1986, IEEE Standard for Software Verification and Validation Plans, but is included for information only.)

Description of Optional V&V Tasks

The descriptions of optional V&V tasks listed in Table 2 of this standard are defined in this Appendix. These V&V tasks are not mandatory for all V&V projects because they may apply to only selected software applications or may force the use of specific tools or techniques. These optional V&V tasks are appropriate for critical and noncritical software. By selecting V&V tasks from these optional V&V tasks, one can tailor the V&V effort to project needs and also achieve a more effective V&V effort.

algorithm analysis. Ensure that the algorithms selected are correct, appropriate, and stable, and meet all accuracy, timing, and sizing requirements.

audit performance. Conduct independent compliance assessment as detailed for configuration control audit, functional audit, in-process audit, or physical audit.

audit support. Provide documentation for, or participate in, any audits performed on the software development (for example, configuration control, functional, in-process, physical).

configuration control audit. Assess the configuration control procedures and the enforcement of these procedures.

configuration management. Control, document, and authenticate the status of items needed for, or produced by, activities throughout the software life cycle.

control flow analysis. Ensure that the proposed control flow is free of problems, such as design or code elements that are unreachable or incorrect.

database analysis. Ensure that the database structure and access methods are compatible with the logical design.

data flow analysis. Ensure that the input and output data and their formats are properly defined, and that the data flows are correct.

design walkthrough. Participate in walkthroughs of the preliminary design and updates of the design to ensure technical integrity and validity.

feasibility study evaluation. Evaluate any feasibility study performed during the concept phase for correctness, completeness, consistency, and accuracy. Trace back to the statement of need for the user requirements. Where appropriate, conduct an independent feasibility study as part of the V&V task.

functional audit. Prior to delivery, assess how well the software satisfies the requirements specified in the Software Requirements Specifications.

in-process audit. Assess consistency of the design by sampling the software development process (for example, audit source code for conformance to coding standards and conventions and for implementation of the design documentation).

installation and checkout testing. Generate the test plan, test design, test cases, and test procedures in preparation for software installation and checkout. Place the completed software product into its operational environment, and test it for adequate performance in that environment.

operational readiness review. Examine the installed software, its installation documentation, and results of acceptance testing to determine that the software is properly installed and ready to be placed in operation.

performance monitoring. Collect information on the performance of the software under operational conditions. Determine whether system and software performance requirements are satisfied.

physical audit. Assess the internal consistency of the software, its documentation, and its readiness for delivery.

qualification testing. Generate the test plan, test design, test cases, and test procedures in preparation for qualification testing. Perform formal testing to demonstrate to the customer that the software meets its specified requirements.

regression analysis and testing. Determine the extent of V&V analysis and testing that must be repeated when changes are made to any software products previously examined.

requirements walkthrough. Ensure that the software requirements are correct, consistent, complete, unambiguous, and testable by participating in a walkthrough of the requirements specification.

review support. Provide the results of applicable V&V tasks to support any formal reviews. The results may be provided in written form or in a presentation at the formal review meeting (for example, operational readiness, test readiness).

simulation analysis. Simulate critical aspects of the software or system environment to analyze logical or performance characteristics that would not be practical to analyze manually.

sizing and timing analysis. Obtain program sizing and execution timing information to determine if the program will satisfy processor size and performance requirements allocated to software.

source code walkthrough. Ensure that the code is free from logic errors and complies with coding standards and conventions by participating in a walkthrough of the source code.

test certification. Ensure that reported test results are the actual findings of the tests. Test-related tools, media, and documentation shall be certified to ensure maintainability and repeatability of tests.

test evaluation. Confirm the technical adequacy of test plans, test design, test cases, test procedures, and test results.

test readiness review. Evaluate the code, software documentation, test procedures, test reporting, error detection, and correction procedures to determine that formal testing may begin.

test walkthrough. Ensure that the planned testing is correct and complete and that the test results are properly interpreted by participating in walkthroughs of test documentation.

test witnessing. Observe testing to confirm that the tests are conducted in accordance with approved test plans and procedures.

user documentation evaluation. Examine draft documents during the development process to ensure correctness, understandability, and completeness. Documentation may include user manuals or guides, as appropriate for the project.

V&V tool plan generation. Produce plans for the acquisition, development, training, and quality assurance activities related to tools identified for support of V&V tasks (for example, test bed software used in validation).

walkthrough. Participate in the evaluation processes in which development personnel lead others through a structured examination of a product. See specific descriptions of requirements walkthrough, design walkthrough, source code walkthrough, and test walkthrough.

Acknowledgements

The following organizations supported employee participation in the development of this standard:

ACEx Technology
Army Computer Systems Command
AT&T Technologies
Babcock & Wilcox
Bechtel Power Corporation
Bell Canada
The Boeing Company
Booz Allen Hamilton
Central Institute For Industrial Research
Computer Science Corporation
Data Logic
E-Systems
Gemini
Hewlett Packard
Jet Propulsion Laboratory

Johns Hopkins University Applied Physics Laboratory
Logicon, Inc
Lucas Micro, Ltd
National Bureau of Standards
NCR Corporation
RCA
STC - Standard Telecommunications
Teledyne Brown Engineering
Televideo Systems
TRW
U.S. Department of Agriculture
U.S. Department of Transportation
Veatch, Rich, & Nadler
Walt Disney World
Worldwide Service Technologies, Ltd

ANSI/IEEE
Std 1016-1987

An American National Standard

IEEE Recommended Practice for Software Design Descriptions

Sponsor

**Software Engineering Subcommittee
of the
Technical Committee on Software Engineering of the
IEEE Computer Society**

Approved March 12, 1987

IEEE Standards Board

Approved October 6, 1987

American National Standards Institute

1016

Foreword

(This Foreword is not a part of IEEE Std 1016-1987, IEEE Recommended Practice for Software Design Descriptions.)

Purpose

This recommended practice specifies the necessary information content and recommends an organization for software design descriptions. This document does not explicitly support, nor is it limited to, any particular software design methodology or descriptive technology. It will guide the production of anything from paper design documents to an automated database of design information. For an organization in the process of developing a design description standard, use of this document will help the new standard meet the needs of all of its users. For an organization with a mature design description standard, it should prove useful in evaluating and modifying that standard in light of the informational and organizational needs of the design description user community.

This practice can be applied to commercial, scientific, and military software. Applicability is not restricted by size, complexity, or criticality of the software. This practice considers both the software and its system operational environment. It can be used where software is the system or where software is part of a larger system that is characterized by hardware and software components and their interfaces.

Overview

This document consists of six sections. Section 1 defines the scope of the recommended practice and Section 2 references other ANSI/IEEE standards that should be followed when applying this practice. Section 3 provides definitions of terms within the context of the practice. Section 4 places the Software Design Description into the framework of the software development life cycle. Section 5 describes the minimum information that shall be included in a software design description and Section 6 gives a recommended organization for software design descriptions. The Appendix shows a sample table of contents for a software design description.

Audience

This document is intended for those in technical and managerial positions who prepare and use software design descriptions. It will guide a designer in the selection, organization, and presentation of design information. It will help standards developers ensure that a design description is complete, concise, and well organized.

Software design descriptions play a pivotal role in the development and maintenance of software systems. During its lifetime, a given design description is used by project managers, quality assurance staff, configuration managers, software designers, programmers, testers, and maintainers. Each of these users has unique needs, both in terms of required design information and optimal organization of that information. Hence, a design description must contain all the design information needed by those users.

Terminology

This recommended practice follows the IEEE Guide to Standards Development. In particular, the word *shall* and the imperative form identify mandatory material within the recommended practice. The words *should*, *might*, and *may* identify advisory material.

History

The project authorization request for development of this recommended practice was approved by the IEEE Standards Board on September 22, 1983. Modification of the authorization request to change the title and scope was approved on March 13, 1986. A series of 10 meetings were held within the United States and internationally between March, 1983 and March, 1986. These meetings produced the draft submitted for balloting in April, 1986.

Suggestions for the improvement of this practice will be welcome. They should be sent to
Secretary
IEEE Standards Board
Institute of Electrical and Electronics Engineers, Inc
345 East 47th Street
New York, NY 10017

Contributors

This document was developed by the Software Design Description Working Group of the Software Engineering Standards Subcommittee of the IEEE Computer Society. The Software Design Description Working Group Steering Committee had the following members:

H. Jack Barnard, *Chairman*   **James A. Darling,** *Vice Chairman*
Robert F. Metz, *Secretary*

Chris Beall	H. Gregory Frank	John McArdle
Patricia Cox	Manoochehr Ghiassi	Arthur L. Price
Leo Endres	Daniel E. Klingler	Basil Sherlund

The Software Design Description Working Group had the following members:

A. Frank Ackerman	Yair Gershkovitch	Walter Merenda
Jim Anderson	Tom Gilb	Randy Peterson
Sandro Bologna	Shirley A. Gloss-Soler	Robert Poston
Fletcher Buckley	Larry J. Hardouin	Ian C. Pyle
Lori J. Call	Fredrick Ho	Ann S. Ping
Wan P. Chiang	David M. Home	Hans Schaefer
Francois Coallier	William S. Junk	David Schultz
Cliff Cockerham	Laurel Kaleda	David Siefert
Patricia W. Daggett	Tom Kurihara	Peter Smith
Jim DeLeo	Jim Lemmon	Richard H. Thayer
Cammie Donaldson	F. C. Lim	T. H. Tse
Euiar Dragstedt	Oyvind Lorentzen	David Weiss
Laurence E. Fishtahler	Bert Martin	Charles J. Wertz
David Gelperin	Lindsay McDermid	G. Robert Zambs
	Glen Meldrum	

The following persons were on the balloting committee that approved this document for submission to the IEEE Standards Board:

A. Frank Ackerman	William P. Dupres	Harry E. Hansen, Jr
Jagdish Agrawal	Michael Dutton	Robert M. Haralick
Richard L. Aurbach	Robert E. Dwyer	Haus-Ludis Hauser
James Baldo, Jr	Mary L. Eads	Clark M. Hay
H. Jack Barnard	John D. Earls	H. Hect
Leo Beltracchi	Mike Edwards	Terry L. Hengl
Yechiel Ben-Naftali	L. G. Egan	Maretta T. Holden
H. R. Berlack	W. D. Ehrenberger	Charles P. Hollocker
Michael A. Blackledge	Steven R. Eisen	Mark Holthouse
Ron Blair	Caroline L. Evans	John Horch
Kevin W. Bowyer	John W. Fendrich	Cheng Hu
Kathleen L. Briggs	Robert G. Ferreol	Peter L. Hung
A. Winsor Brown	Glenn S. Fields	Sheng-Sheng Jeng
F. Buckley	Gordon Force	Laurel Kaleda
Homer C. Carney	Julian Forster	Charles F. Kaminski
Ronald G. Carter	Deborah L. Franke	Constantine Kaniklidis
Richard L. Chilausky	C. R. Frederick	Myron S. Karasik
Robert N. Chorette	Carl Friedlander	Adi N. Kasad
T. S. Chow	Richard Fries	Ron Kenett
Slucki Jean Christophe	Michael Galinier	R. A. Kessler
Jung K. Chung	Leonard B. Gardner	Shaye Koenig
Peter Coad, Jr	David Gelperin	Edward E. Kopicky
François Coallier	Tom Gilb	Joseph A. Krupinski
Sharon R. Cobb-Pierson	James L. Gildersleeve	H. M. Kudyan
Christopher M. Cooke	Shirley Gloss-Soler	Joan Kundig
A. J. Cote, Jr	Ole Golubjatnikov	Lak-Ming Lam
Ismael Fuentes Crespo	J. Kaye Grau	John B. Lane
Patricia W. Daggett	Andrej Grebenc	Robert Lane
George D. Darling	Thomas Griest	William P. LaPlant
Taz Daughtry	Robert S. Grossman	Greg Larsen
Peter A. Denny	Victor M. Guarnera	John A. Latimer
Harpal S. Dhama	Lawrence M. Gunther	John A. N. Lee
Mike Dotson	David A. Gustafson	Leon S. Levy
David C. Doty	Russell Gustin	Paul Liebertz
Einar Dragstedt	Michael Haggerty	F. C. Lim
W. DuBlanica	Howard Hamer	Bertil Lindberg

David P. Linssen
Steven Lituintchouk
William Lively
John M. Long
John Lowell
Bill Macre
Andy Mahindru
Kartik C. Majumdar
Henry A. Malec
Paulo C. Marcondes
Stuart Marcotte
Gregory Mark
Phillip C. Mariott
Nicholas L. Marselos
Roger Martin
Paul A. Mauro
Jean I. Maxwell
L. J. Mazlack
Ivano Mazza
John McArdle
J. A. McCall
John McKissick, Jr
Glen A. Meldrum
Belden Menkus
Ben W. Miller
Charles S. Mooney
Gary D. Moorhead
Joyce E. Mortison
Gene T. Morun
David G. Mullens
Myron L. Nack
Hironobu Nagano
Saied Najafi
Gerry Neidhart
Brian A. Nejmeh
Dennis E. Nickle
J. T. L. Obbink
Wilma M. Osborne
D. J. Ostrom
Thomas D. Parrish
William Perry

Donald J. Pfeiffer
Robert M. Poston
Peter Ron Prinzivalli
James E. Quelle
Thomas S. Radi
Edward B. Rawson
Meir Razy
John Reddan
Larry K. Reed
Matthais F. Reese II
T. D. Regulinski
R. T. Reiner
Paul Renaud
Steven M. Rowan
John Rymer
Hom Sack
Julio Gonzalez Samz
Stephen R. Schach
Franz P. Schauer
Max Schindler
Norman Schneidewind
Wolf A. Schnoege
Robert G. Schueppert
David J. Schultz
Gregory D. Schumacher
Leonard W. Seagren
Gary T. Shea
Craig Shermer
Robert W. Shillato
Victor Shtern
David M. Siefert
David J. Simkins
William G. Singer
Jacob Slonim
H. Bennett Smith
Harry M. Sneed
J. G. Snodgrass
A. R. Sorkowitz
Hugh B. Spilhne
G. Wayne Staley
Mary Jane Stoughton

Alan N. Sukert
Robert A. Symes
Michael Taint
Richard H. Thayer
Paul U. Thompson
Michael H. Thursby
Terrence L. Tillmanns
Lawrence F. Tracey
Illeana Trandafir
Henry J. Trochesset
Robert Troy
C. L. Troyanowski
Dana L. Ulery
David Usechok
R. L. Vantilburg
P. M. Vatez
Osmo Vikman
R. Wachter
Dolores R. Wallace
William M. Walsh III
Thomas J. Walsh
Roger D. H. Warburton
Andrew H. Weigel
R. W. Werlwas
Charles J. Wertz
W. L. Whipple
Patrick J. Wilson
T. J. Wojcik
Paul Wolfgang
W. Martin Wong
Dennis L. Wood
Tom Worthington
Charles Wortz
Zhou Zhi Ying
A. W. Yonda
Natalie C. Yoptanka
Michael E. York
Don Zeleny
Marvin Zelkowitz
Hugh Zettel
Peter F. Zoll

When the IEEE Standards Board approved this standard on March 12, 1987, it had the following membership:

Donald C. Fleckenstein, *Chairman*   **Marco W. Migliaro,** *Vice-Chairman*

Sava I. Sherr, *Secretary*

James H. Beall
Dennis Bodson
Marshall L. Cain
James M. Daly
Stephen R. Dillon
Eugene P. Fogarty
Jay Forster
Kenneth D. Hendrix
Irvin N. Howell

Leslie I. Kerr
Jack Kinn
Irving Kolodny
Joseph L. Koepfinger*
Edward Lohse
John May
Lawrence V. McCall
L. Bruce McClung

Donald T. Michael*
L. John Rankine
John P. Riganati
Gary S. Robinson
Frank L. Rose
Robert E. Rountree
William R. Tackaberry
William B. Wilkens
Helen M. Wood

* Member emeritus

Contents

IEEE Recommended Practice for Software Design Descriptions

1. Scope

This is a recommended practice for describing software designs. It specifies the necessary information content, and recommended organization for a software design description. A software design description is a representation of a software system that is used as a medium for communicating software design information.

The practice may be applied to commercial, scientific, or military software that runs on any digital computer. Applicability is not restricted by the size, complexity, or criticality of the software.

This practice is not limited to specific methodologies for design, configuration management, or quality assurance. It is assumed that the quality design information and changes to the design of description will be managed by other project activities. Finally, this document does not support nor is it limited to any particular descriptive technique. It may be applied to paper documents, automated databases, design description languages, or other means of description.

2. References

This standard shall be used in conjunction with the following publications:

[1] ANSI/IEEE Std 729-1983, IEEE Standard Glossary of Software Engineering Terminology.[1]

[2] ANSI/IEEE Std 730-1984, IEEE Standard for Software Quality Assurance Plans.

[3] ANSI/IEEE Std 828-1983, IEEE Standard for Software Configuration Management Plans.

[4] ANSI/IEEE Std 830-1984, IEEE Guide to Software Requirements Specifications

[5] Freeman, P. and A. I. Wasserman. *Tutorial on Software Design Techniques*. 4th Edition, IEEE Computer Society Press, Annotated Bibliography, pp 715–718, 1983.

3. Definitions

The definitions listed here establish meaning in the context of this recommended practice. Definitions of other terms used in this document can be found in ANSI/IEEE Std 729-1983 [1].[2]

design entity. An element (component) of a design that is structurally and functionally distinct from other elements and that is separately named and referenced.

design view. A subset of design entity attribute information that is specifically suited to the needs of a software project activity.

entity attribute. A named characteristic or property of a design entity. It provides a statement of fact about the entity.

software design description (SDD). A representation of a software system created to facilitate analysis, planning, implementation, and decision making. A blueprint or model of the software system. The SDD is used as the primary medium for communicating software design information.

4. Considerations for Producing a Software Design Description (SDD)

This section provides information to be considered before producing an SDD. How the SDD fits

---

[1] ANSI/IEEE publications can be obtained from the Sales Department, American National Standards Institute, 1430 Broadway, New York, NY 10018, or from the Service Center, The Institute of Electrical and Electronics Engineers, 445 Hoes Lane, Piscataway, NJ 08855-1331.

[2] Numbers in brackets correspond to those of the references in Section 2 of this standard.

into the software life cycle, where it fits, and why it is used are discussed.

4.1 Software Life Cycle. The life cycle of a software system is normally defined as the period of time that starts when a software product is conceived and ends when the product is no longer available for use. The life cycle approach is an effective engineering management tool and provides a model for a context within which to discuss the preparation and use of the SDD. While it is beyond the scope of this document to prescribe a particular standard life cycle, a typical cycle will be used to define such a context for the SDD. This cycle is based on ANSI/IEEE Std 729-1983 [1] and consists of a concept phase, requirements phase, design phase, implementation phase, test phase, installation and checkout phase, operation and maintenance phase, and retirement phase.

4.2 Software Design Description (SDD) within the Life Cycle. For both new software systems and existing systems under maintenance, it is important to ensure that the design and implementation used for a software system satisfy the requirements driving that system. The minimum documentation required to do this is defined in ANSI/IEEE Std 730-1984 [2]. The SDD is one of these required products. It records the result of the design processes that are carried out during the design phase.

4.3 Purpose of a Software Design Description (SDD). The SDD shows how the software system will be structured to satisfy the requirements identified in the software requirements specification ANSI/IEEE Std 830-1984 [4]. It is a translation of requirements into a description of the software structure, software components, interfaces, and data necessary for the implementation phase. In essence, the SDD becomes a detailed blueprint for the implementation activity. In a complete SDD, each requirement must be traceable to one or more design entities.

5. Design Description Information Content

5.1 Introduction. A software design description is a representation or model of the software system to be created. The model should provide the precise design information needed for planning, analysis, and implementation of the software system. It should represent a partitioning of the system into design entities and describe the important properties and relationships among those entities.

The design description model used to represent a software system can be expressed as a collection of design entities, each possessing properties and relationships.[3] To simplify the model, the properties and relationships of each design entity are described by a standard set of attributes. The design information needs of project members are satisfied through identification of the entities and their associated attributes. A design description is complete when the attributes have been specified for all the entities.

5.2 Design Entities. A *design entity* is an element (component) of a design that is structurally and functionally distinct from other elements and that is separately named and referenced.

Design entities result from a decomposition of the software system requirements. The objective is to divide the system into separate components that can be considered, implemented, changed, and tested with minimal effect on other entities.

Entities can exist as a system, subsystems, data stores, modules, programs, and processes; see ANSI/IEEE Std 729-1983 [1]. The number and type of entities required to partition a design are dependent on a number of factors, such as the complexity of the system, the design technique used, and the programming environment.

Although entities are different in nature, they possess common characteristics. Each design entity will have a name, purpose, and function. There are common relationships among entities such as interfaces or shared data. The common characteristics of entities are described by design entity attributes.

5.3 Design Entity Attributes. A *design entity attribute* is a named characteristic or property of a design entity. It provides a statement of fact about the entity.

Design entity attributes can be thought of as questions about design entities. The answers to those questions are the values of the attributes. All the questions can be answered, but the content of the answer will depend upon the nature of the entity. The collection of answers provides a complete description of an entity.

---

[3] The design description model is similar to an entity-relationship model, a common approach to information modeling.

The list of design entity attributes presented in this section is the minimum set required for all software design descriptions. The selection of these attributes is based on three criteria:

(1) The attribute is necessary for all software projects

(2) An incorrect specification of the attribute value could result in a fault in the software system to be developed

(3) The attribute describes intrinsic design information and not information related to the design process. Examples of attributes that do not meet the second and third criteria are designer names, design status, and revision history. This important process information is maintained by other software project activities as described in ANSI/IEEE Std 730-1984 [2] and ANSI/IEEE Std 828-1983 [3].

All attributes shall be specified for each entity. Attribute descriptions should include references and design considerations such as tradeoffs and assumptions when appropriate. In some cases, attribute descriptions may have the value *none*. When additional attributes are identified for a specific software project, they should be included in the design description. The attributes and associated information items are defined in 5.3.1 through 5.3.10.

5.3.1 Identification. *The name of the entity.* Two entities shall not have the same name. The names for the entities may be selected to characterize their nature. This will simplify referencing and tracking in addition to providing identification.

5.3.2 Type. *A description of the kind of entity.* The type attribute shall describe the nature of the entity. It may simply name the kind of entity, such as subprogram, module, procedure, process, or data store. Alternatively, design entities may be grouped into major classes to assist in locating an entity dealing with a particular type of information. For a given design description, the chosen entity types shall be applied consistently.

5.3.3 Purpose. *A description of why the entity exists.* The purpose attribute shall provide the rationale for the creation of the entity. Therefore, it shall designate the specific functional and performance requirements for which this entity was created; see ANSI/IEEE Std 830-1984 [4]. The purpose attribute shall also describe special requirements that must be met by the entity that are not included in the software requirements specification.

5.3.4 Function. *A statement of what the entity does.* The function attribute shall state the transformation applied by the entity to inputs to produce the desired output. In the case of a data entity, this attribute shall state the type of information stored or transmitted by the entity.

5.3.5 Subordinates. *The identification of all entities composing this entity.* The subordinates attribute shall identify the *composed of* relationship for an entity. This information is used to trace requirements to design entities and to identify parent/child structural relationships through a software system decomposition.

5.3.6 Dependencies. *A description of the relationships of this entity with other entities.* The dependencies attribute shall identify the *uses* or *requires the presence of* relationship for an entity. These relationships are often graphically depicted by structure charts, data flow diagrams, and transaction diagrams.

This attribute shall describe the nature of each interaction including such characteristics as timing and conditions for interaction. The interactions may involve the initiation, order of execution, data sharing, creation, duplicating, usage, storage, or destruction of entities.

5.3.7 Interface. *A description of how other entities interact with this entity.* The interface attribute shall describe the *methods* of interaction and the *rules* governing those interactions. The methods of interaction include the mechanisms for invoking or interrupting the entity, for communicating through parameters, common data areas or messages, and for direct access to internal data. The rules governing the interaction include the communications protocol, data format, acceptable values, and the meaning of each value.

This attribute shall provide a description of the input ranges, the meaning of inputs and outputs, the type and format of each input or output, and output error codes. For information systems, it should include inputs, screen formats, and a complete description of the interactive language.

5.3.8 Resources. *A description of the elements used by the entity that are external to the design.* The resources attribute shall identify and describe all of the resources *external* to the design that are needed by this entity to perform its function. The interaction rules and methods for using the resource shall be specified by this attribute.

This attribute provides information about items such as physical devices (printers, disc-partitions, memory banks), software services (math libraries, operating system services), and processing resources (CPU cycles, memory allocation, buffers).

The resources attribute shall describe usage characteristics such as the process time at which resources are to be acquired and sizing to include quantity, and physical sizes of buffer usage. It should also include the identification of potential race and deadlock conditions as well as resource management facilities.

5.3.9 Processing. *A description of the rules used by the entity to achieve its function.* The processing attribute shall describe the algorithm used by the entity to perform a specific task and shall include contingencies. This description is a refinement of the function attribute. It is the most detailed level of refinement for this entity.

This description should include timing, sequencing of events or processes, prerequisites for process initiation, priority of events, processing level, actual process steps, path conditions, and loop back or loop termination criteria. The handling of contingencies should describe the action to be taken in the case of overflow conditions or in the case of a validation check failure.

5.3.10 Data. *A description of data elements internal to the entity.* The data attribute shall describe the method of representation, initial values, use, semantics, format, and acceptable values of internal data.

The description of data may be in the form of a data dictionary that describes the content, structure, and use of all data elements. Data information shall describe everything pertaining to the use of data or internal data structures by this entity. It shall include data specifications such as formats, number of elements, and initial values. It shall also include the structures to be used for representing data such as file structures, arrays, stacks, queues, and memory partitions.

The meaning and use of data elements shall be specified. This description includes such things as static versus dynamic, whether it is to be shared by transactions, used as a control parameter, or used as a value, loop iteration count, pointer, or link field. In addition, data information shall include a description of data validation needed for the process.

6. Design Description Organization

6.1 Introduction. Each design description user may have a different view of what is considered the essential aspects of a software design. All other information is extraneous to that user. The proportion of useful information for a specific user will decrease with the size and complexity of a software project. The needed information then becomes difficult or impractical to extract from the description and impossible to assimilate. Hence, a practical organization of the necessary design information is essential to its use.

This section introduces the notion of *design views* to aid in organizing the design attribute information defined in Section 5. It does not supplement Section 5 by providing additional design information nor does it prescribe the format or documentation practice for design views.

A recommended organization of design entities and their associated attributes are presented in this section to facilitate the access of design information from various technical viewpoints. This recommended organization is flexible and can be implemented through different media such as paper documentation, design languages, or database management systems with automated report generation, and query language access. Since paper documentation is currently the primary design description medium, a sample table of contents is given in the Appendix.

6.2 Design Views. Entity attribute information can be organized in several ways to reveal all of the essential aspects of a design. In so doing, the user is able to focus on design details from a different perspective or viewpoint. A *design view* is a subset of design entity attribute information that is specifically suited to the needs of a software project activity.

Each design view represents a separate concern about a software system. Together, these views provide a comprehensive description of the design in a concise and usable form that simplifies information access and assimilation.

A recommended organization of the SDD into separate design views to facilitate information access and assimilation is given in Table 1. Each of these views, their use, and representation are discussed in detail.

6.2.1 Decomposition Description

6.2.1.1 Scope. The decomposition description records the division of the software system into design entities. It describes the way the system has been structured and the purpose and function of each entity. For each entity, it provides a reference to the detailed description via the identification attribute.

Table 1
Recommended Design Views

Design View	Scope	Entity Attributes	Example Representations
Decomposition Description	Partition of the system into design entities	Identification, type, purpose, function, subordinates	Hierarchical decomposition diagram, natural language
Dependency Description	Description of the relationships among entities and system resources	Identification, type, purpose, dependencies, resources	Structure charts, data flow diagrams, transaction diagrams
Interface Description	List of everything a designer, programmer, or tester needs to know to use the design entities that make up the system	Identification, function, interfaces	Interface files, parameter tables
Detail Description	Description of the internal design details of an entity	Identification, processing, data	Flowcharts, N-S charts, PDL

The attribute descriptions for identification, type, purpose, function, and subordinates should be included in this design view. This attribute information should be provided for all design entities.

6.2.1.2 Use. The decomposition description can be used by designers and maintainers to identify the major design entities of the system for purposes such as determining which entity is responsible for performing specific functions and tracing requirements to design entities. Design entities can be grouped into major classes to assist in locating a particular type of information and to assist in reviewing the decomposition for completeness. For example, a module decomposition may exist separately from a data decomposition.

The information in the decomposition description can be used by project management for planning, monitoring, and control of a software project. They can identify each software component, its purpose, and basic functionality. This design information together with other project information can be used in estimating cost, staff, and schedule for the development effort.

Configuration management may use the information to establish the organization, tracking, and change management of emerging work products; see ANSI/IEEE Std 828-1983 [3]. Metrics developers may also use this information for initial complexity, sizing, staffing, and development time parameters. The software quality assurance staff can use the decomposition description to construct a requirements traceability matrix.

6.2.1.3 Representation. The literature on software engineering describes a number of methods that provide consistent criteria for entity decomposition [5]. These methods provide for designing simple, independent entities and are based on such principles as structured design and information hiding. The primary graphical technique used to describe system decomposition is a hierarchical decomposition diagram. This diagram can be used together with natural language descriptions of purpose and function for each entity.

6.2.2 Dependency Description

6.2.2.1 Scope. The dependency description specifies the relationships among entities. It identifies the dependent entities, describes their coupling, and identifies the required resources.

This design view defines the strategies for interactions among design entities and provides the information needed to easily perceive how, why, where, and at what level system actions occur. It specifies the type of relationships that exist among the entities such as shared information, prescribed order of execution, or well defined parameter interfaces.

The attribute descriptions for identification, type, purpose, dependencies, and resources should be included in this design view. This attribute information should be provided for all design entities.

6.2.2.2 Use. The dependency description provides an overall picture of how the system works in order to assess the impact of requirements and design changes. It can help maintainers to isolate entities causing system failures or resource bottlenecks. It can aid in producing the system integration plan by identifying the entities that are needed by other entities and that must be developed first. This description can also be used by integration testing to aid in the production of integration test cases.

6.2.2.3 Representation. There are a number of methods that help minimize the relationships among entities by maximizing the relationship among elements in the same entity. These methods emphasize low module coupling and high module cohesion [5].

Formal specification languages provide for the specification of system functions and data, their interrelationships, the inputs and outputs, and other system aspects in a well-defined language. The relationship among design entities is also represented by data flow diagrams, structure charts, or transaction diagrams.

6.2.3 Interface Description

6.2.3.1 Scope. The entity interface description provides everything designers, programmers, and testers need to know to correctly use the functions provided by an entity. This description includes the details of external and internal interfaces not provided in the software requirements specification.

This design view consists of a set of interface specifications for each entity. The attribute descriptions for identification, function, and interfaces should be included in this design view. This attribute information should be provided for all design entities.

6.2.3.2 Use. The interface description serves as a binding contract among designers, programmers, customers, and testers. It provides them with an agreement needed before proceeding with the detailed design of entities. In addition, the interface description may be used by technical writers to produce customer documentation or may be used directly by customers. In the later case, the interface description could result in the production of a human interface view.

Designers, programmers, and testers may need to use design entities that they did not develop. These entities may be reused from earlier projects, contracted from an external source, or produced by other developers. The interface description settles the agreement among designers, programmers, and testers about how cooperating entities will interact. Each entity interface description should contain everything another designer or programmer needs to know to develop software that interacts with that entity. A clear description of entity interfaces is essential on a multiperson development for smooth integration and ease of maintenance.

6.2.3.3 Representation. The interface description should provide the language for communicating with each entity to include screen formats, valid inputs, and resulting outputs. For those entities that are data driven, a data dictionary should be used to describe the data characteristics. Those entities that are highly visible to a user and involve the details of how the customer should perceive the system should include a functional model, scenarios for use, detailed feature sets, and the interaction language.

6.2.4 Detailed Design Description

6.2.4.1 Scope. The detailed design description contains the internal details of each design entity. These details include the attribute descriptions for identification, processing, and data. This attribute information should be provided for all design entities.

6.2.4.2 Use. This description contains the details needed by programmers prior to implementation. The detailed design description can also be used to aid in producing unit test plans.

6.2.4.3 Representation. There are many tools used to describe the details of design entities. Program design languages can be used to describe inputs, outputs, local data and the algorithm for an entity. Other common techniques for describing design entity logic include using metacode or structured English, or graphical methods such as Nassi-Schneidermann charts or flowcharts.

Appendix

(This Appendix is not a part of IEEE Std 1016-1987, IEEE Recommended Practice for Software Design Descriptions, but is included for information only.)

The following example of a table of contents shows only one of many possible ways to organize and format the design views and associated information presented in Section 6 of this standard.

Table of Contents for an SDD

The following organizations supported working group members in the development of this recommended practice:

AT&T Bell Laboratories
AT&T Information Systems
Atkinson System Technologies Co
Bell Canada
Bendix Field Engineering Corp
California State University, Sacramento
Center for Industrial Research (Norway)
Computer Sciences Corp
Computer Systems & Sciences
Douglas Aircraft Co
Digital Equipment Corp
Erisoft AB, Sweden
GEAC Computers International, Inc
General Electric Co
Grumman-CTEC, Inc
Harris Corp
Hewlett Packard
Hughes Aircraft
ITT-Chernow Communications, Inc

Jet Propulsion Laboratory
John Fluke Mfg Co
London School of Economics
McDonald Dettwiler & Associates
National Semiconductor
NCR
Northern Telecom
Ortho Pharmaceutical Corp
Programming Environments, Inc
Raytheon
RCA
Santa Clara University
Storage Technology Corp
Systems Designers
Unisyn Inc
University of Hong Kong
University of Idaho
U.S. Dept of Transportation
Zilog Corp

An American National Standard

IEEE Standard for
Software Reviews and Audits

Corrected Edition
June 30, 1989

Corrections have been made on pages 5, 8, 10, 11, 12, 25, 26, 27, 29, and 35. A black bar has been added opposite each correction to aid in identifying the changes made to this printing.

Sponsor

**Software Engineering Technical Committee of the
IEEE Computer Society**

Approved June 9, 1988

IEEE Standards Board

Approved June 29, 1989

American National Standards Institute

1028

Foreword

(This Foreword is not a part of IEEE Std 1028-1988, IEEE Standard for Software Reviews and Audits.)

This Foreword provides the user with the rationale and background of the review and audit procedures outlined in this standard, and their relation to other IEEE standards.

Purpose. This standard defines the review and audit processes applicable to critical and noncritical software, and the specific procedures required for the execution of the reviews and audits described. Also, this standard supports ANSI/IEEE Std 730-1984 by defining review and audit procedures.

This standard does not establish measures or mechanisms for judging individual contributions to product development. Conformance to this standard may be claimed where reviews and audits are performed using procedures defined by this standard.

Additional documents that should be referenced for specific application of this standard are as follows:

(1) ANSI/IEEE Std 729-1983, IEEE Standard Glossary of Software Engineering Terminology.
(2) ANSI/IEEE Std 730-1984, IEEE Standard for Software Quality Assurance Plans.
(3) ANSI/IEEE Std 828-1983, IEEE Standard for Software Configuration Management Plans.
(4) ANSI/IEEE Std 983-1986, IEEE Guide for Software Quality Assurance.
(5) ANSI/IEEE Std 1012-1986 IEEE Standard for Software Verification and Validation Plans.

These standards address specific applications to this standard. Although only IEEE standards are referenced in this standard, this standard can be applied in concert with local standards requiring reviews and audits.

Moreover, to support the use of this standard by ensuring uniform classification and codes, use of IEEE Std 1044-1988, IEEE Standard Classification for Software Errors, Faults, and Failures, is suggested.

General Application Intent. This standard applies to all phases of typical software life cycles and provides a standard against which review and audit plans can be prepared and assessed. Maximum benefit can be derived from this standard by planning for its application early in the project life cycle.

This standard can be used with different life cycles provided its intent is followed. ANSI/IEEE Std 730-1984 identifies specific (and minimum) review and audit applications for critical software, while this standard defines the specific processes available to meet these application needs. Planning for reviews and audits, as part of an integrated verification and validation approach, can be aided by following ANSI/IEEE Std 1012-1986.

This standard for software reviews and audits was written in consideration of both the software and its system operating environment. It can be used where software is the total system entity or where it is part of a larger system. Care should be taken to integrate software review and audit activities into any total system development planning; they should exist in concert with hardware system reviews and audits to the benefits of the entire system. To broaden the application possibilities of this standard, simply replace *software element* with *system element* when reading.

This standard was written with the assumption that organizations are void of corruption. This may become an issue where, for example, during the course of an audit, theft or embezzlement is discovered. In such a case, although the audit may proceed, the applicability of this standard is removed.

Appendixes. Although not considered part of this standard, appendixes are provided to assist the reader in understanding:

(1) Specific process applications required by ANSI/IEEE Std 730-1984.
(2) How processes defined in this standard might be applied to meet those application needs.

Audience. This standard was written for those who are responsible for defining, planning, implementing, or supporting software reviews and audits.

Conformance. Conformance to this standard can be claimed when review and audit processes, wherever performed, are performed as defined in this standard.

The following persons were on the balloting committee that approved this document for submission to the IEEE Standards Board.

At the time this standard was approved, the Software Reviews and Audits Working Group of the Software Engineering Technical Committee of the IEEE Computer Society had the following members:

Charles P. Hollocker, Chairman   **Tim Kasse,** Cochairman

William A. Hoberg, Secretary

A. Frank Ackerman	Violet Foldes	Stan McQueen
Jack Barnard	Gordon Grunewald	Belden Menkus
William Bryan	Clark Hay	William Perry
Ronald L. Cariola	Peter Hung	William N. Sabor
Francois Coallier	David R. Janson	Isaac Shadman
Christopher M. Cooke	Harry Kalmbach	David J. Schultz
Rudy Corbett	Myron Karasik	Richard H. Thayer
Stewart Crawford	Adi Kasad	William S. Turner, III
Vince Dowd	Robert A. Kessler	Marian Wysocki
Robert G. Ebenau	Tom Kurihara	Natalie C. Yopconka
Michael Fagan	Philip C. Marriot	

When the IEEE Standards Board approved this standard on June 9, 1988, it had the following membership:

Donald C. Fleckenstein, *Chairman*   **Marco W. Migliaro,** *Vice Chairman*

Andrew G. Salem, *Secretary*

Arthur A. Blaisdell	John W. Horch	L. Bruce McClung
Fletcher J. Buckley	Jack M. Kinn	Donald T. Michael*
James M. Daly	Frank D. Kirschner	Richard E. Mosher
Stephen R. Dillon	Frank C. Kitzantides	L. John Rankine
Eugene P. Fogarty	Joseph L. Koepfinger*	Gary S. Robinson
Jay Forster*	Irving Kolodny	Frank L. Rose
Thomas L. Hannan	Edward Lohse	Helen M. Wood
Kenneth D. Hendrix	John E. May, Jr	Karl H. Zaininger
Theodore W. Hissey, Jr	Lawrence V. McCall	Donald W. Zipse

*Members Emeriti

Contents

IEEE Standard for Software Reviews and Audits

1. Scope and References

1.1 Scope. The purpose of this standard is to provide definitions and uniform requirements for review and audit processes. It does not establish the need to conduct specific reviews or audits; that need is defined by local policy. Where specific reviews and audits are required, standard procedures for their execution must be defined.

This standard provides such definition for review and audit processes that are applicable to products and processes throughout the software life cycle. Each organization shall specify where and when this standard applies and any intended deviations from this standard.

1.2 References. This standard shall be used in conjunction with the following publications:

[1] ANSI/IEEE Std 729-1983, IEEE Standard Glossary of Software Engineering Terminology.[1]

[2] ANSI/IEEE Std 829-1983, IEEE Standard for Software Test Documentation.

2. Definitions

audit. An independent evaluation of software products or processes to ascertain compliance to standards, guidelines, specifications, and procedures based on objective criteria that include documents that specify

(1) The form or content of the products to be produced
(2) The process by which the products shall be produced
(3) How compliance to standards or guidelines shall be measured

review. An evaluation of software element(s) or project status to ascertain discrepancies from planned results and to recommend improvement. This evaluation follows a formal process (for example, management review process, technical review process, software inspection process, or walkthrough process).

software element. A deliverable or in-process document produced or acquired during software development or maintenance. Specific examples include but are not limited to

(1) Project planning documents (for example, software development plans, and software verification and validation plans)
(2) Software requirements and design specifications
(3) Test effort documentation (ie, as described in ANSI/IEEE Std 829-1983 [2])[2]
(4) Customer-deliverable documentation
(5) Program source code
(6) Representation of software solutions implemented in firmware
(7) Reports (for example, review, audit, projectect status) and data (for example, defect detection, test)

For other definitions, including verification and validation, see ANSI/IEEE Std 729-1983 [1].

---

[1] ANSI/IEEE publications are available from IEEE Service Center, 445 Hoes Lane, PO Box 1331, Piscataway, NJ 08855-1331, or from the Sales Department, American National Standards Institute, 1430 Broadway, New York, NY 10018.

[2] The numbers in brackets correspond to those of the references in 1.2.

3. Introduction

Reviews and audits can be used in support of objectives associated with software quality assurance, project management, and configuration management, or similar control functions, as shown in Table 1. Those quality objectives, valid throughout software development and maintenance, include the need for evaluation, verification, validation, and compliance confirmation. For the sake of completeness, Test is identified in Table 1 as the principal process of validation. Testing, however, is outside the scope of this standard. Processes defined in this standard include

(1)   Management review
(2)   Technical review
(3)   Software inspection
(4)   Walkthrough
(5)   Audit

To support compliance confirmation, auditing activities may include performing reviews and tests to determine product consistency with respect to established baselines (ie, software requirements specifications or design descriptions) or to witness the correctness of implementation.

Moreover, since quality assurance deals with products and processes, Fig 1 provides a view of how various quality assurance pro-

Table 1
Some Principal Processes for Achieving Quality Objectives

Objectives	Principal Processes Include
Evaluation	Management review, Technical review
Verification	Inspection, Walkthrough
Validation	Test
Compliance, Confirmation	Audit

cesses can be mapped to examine product and project issues.

The examination of project issues (both technical and managerial) occurs at various phases during the project life cycle. The results of such examinations are meant to permit improvement of the methods of ensuring software quality and the ability to meet time and cost constraints. The evaluation of software elements occurs during the production of the element(s) and on its completion. This ensures that the element(s) completely and correctly embodies its baseline specifications.

Any standard process has prerequisite conditions; those conditions necessary, though not in themselves sufficient for the process to reach completion. For reviews and audits, these conditions are identified in 3.1 and 3.2 respectively.

Fig 1
Relation of Some Quality Assurance Processes to Products and Projects

Section 3.3 presents the template used to define review and audit processes in the following sections.

3.1 Review Process Prerequisites. The objective of reviewing software elements is to evaluate software or project status to identify discrepancies from planned results and to recommend improvement where appropriate.

The following managerial offices are to achieve that objective:

3.1.1 Management
(1) Responsible for reviews, and the anticipated product rework
(2) Responsible for performance of reviews and reporting of review results against project milestone events
(3) Provides the necessary resources of time, personnel, budget, and facilities required to plan, define, execute, and manage the reviews

3.1.2 Development Staff
(1) The staff has a level of development expertise and product knowledge sufficient to comprehend the software under review.
(2) Training and orientation in the use of the review processes are provided to the staff.

3.1.3 Development Process Planning
(1) Standard entry and exit criteria have been defined for development phases.
(2) The product criteria (such as readability and modularity) are sufficiently defined by development standards.
(3) The product is partitioned into manageable, reviewable units.
(4) The software elements to be reviewed and the review process to be employed are identified in the project planning documents (for example, Software Quality Assurance Plan, Software Verification Plan, and Software Project Management Plan.

3.1.4 Review Process Planning
(1) Each type of review to be employed is fully specified.
(2) Administrative procedures are defined to enable the review to be initiated, executed, recorded, and acted on.
(3) The responsibility is assigned for the planning, specification, administration, and maintenance of the review process.

3.2 Audit Process Prerequisites. The objective of software auditing is to provide an objective evaluation of products and processes to confirm compliance to standards, guidelines, specifications, and procedures. The following requirements are prerequisite to achieve that objective:
(1) Objective audit criteria exist (for example, contracts, requirements, plans, specifications, standards) against which software elements and processes can be evaluated.
(2) Audit personnel are selected to promote team objectivity. They are usually independent of any direct responsibility for the products and processes examined and may be from an external organization.
(3) Audit personnel are given sufficient authority by appropriate management to perform the audit.

3.3 Procedural Description Template. The following descriptions establish the minimum template used to plan, prepare, and execute any review or audit. The review and audit process descriptions in this standard follow this common template:

().1 *Objective:* Process goals.
().2 *Abstract:* Process overview.
().3 *Special Responsibilities:* Roles unique to this specific process.
().4 *Input:* Products to which the process is applied, and supporting information.
().5 *Entry Criteria:* Conditions that must be satisfied before the process can begin.
().6 *Procedures:* Standard steps followed in performing the process.
().7 *Exit Criteria:* Conditions that must be satisfied before this process is considered complete.
().8 *Output:* The minimum set of deliverables resulting from process completion.
().9 *Auditability:* Description of evidence needed to determine at a later date that the process was followed.

Additional template sections have been added to these basic nine sections when needed.

Procedure descriptions in section "().6" will be presented as to include, but not be limited to, the following steps:

().6.1 Planning ().6.3 Preparation
().6.2 Overview ().6.4 Examination

Additional procedure subsections have been added where needed.

4. The Management Review Process

4.1 Objective. The objective of a management review is to provide recommendations for the following:

(1) Making activities progress according to plan, based on an evaluation of product development status;

(2) Changing project direction or to identify the need for alternative planning;

(3) Maintaining global control of the project through adequate allocation of resources.

The management review process can be applied to new development or to maintenance activities.

4.2 Abstract. A management review is a formal evaluation of a project level plan or project status relative to that plan by a designated review team.

During the review meeting the entire review team examines plans or progress against applicable plans, standards, and guidelines, or both. Each problem area identified by the review team is recorded. When critical data and information cannot be supplied, then an additional meeting shall be scheduled to complete the management review process.

4.3 Special Responsibilities. The review leader is responsible for the administrative tasks pertaining to the review, for assuring that the review is conducted in an orderly manner, and for issuing the management review report (see 4.8).

The individual(s) responsible for formally reporting the status of the project under review will ensure that the project status and all supporting documentation are available for distribution.

Each member of the review team is responsible for the following:

(1) Being adequately prepared for the meeting;

(2) Ensuring that the review meets its objectives.

4.4 Input. The minimum input to the management review process is as follows:

(1) A statement of objectives for the management review

(2) A list of issues to be addressed

(3) Current project schedule and cost data

(4) Reports (for example, managerial review reports, technical review reports, audit reports) from other reviews or audits, or both, already completed

(5) Reports of resources assigned to the project

(6) Data on the software elements completed or in progress

Additional applicable reference material can be supplied by project management or requested by the review leader.

4.5 Entry Criteria

4.5.1 Authorization. The need for conducting certain management reviews is initially established in the appropriate project planning documents (for example, Software Quality Assurance Plan, Software Development Plan, or Software Verification and Validation Plan). Under these plans, completion of a specific software element (for example, a Planning Document, a Requirements Specification, a Design Document, and Code Specification), or completion of a phase can trigger a management review.

In addition to those management reviews required by a specific plan, other management reviews may be formally announced and held at the request of software quality management, functional management, project management or the customer, according to local procedures.

4.5.2 Initiating Event. A management review is conducted when a selected review leader does the following:

(1) Establishes or confirms a statement of objectives for the meeting;

(2) Judges that the software element(s) and any other documentation or reports pertinent to the review are sufficiently complete and their status available to support the review objectives.

4.6 Procedures

4.6.1 Planning. During the planning step, the review leader, in conjunction with project management, does the following:

(1) Identifies the review team
(2) Schedules the meeting and identifies a meeting place
(3) Distributes input materials to the participants, allowing adequate time for preparation

4.6.2 Overview. A qualified person from the project under examination shall conduct an overview session for the review team when requested by the review leader. This overview can occur as a part of the examination meeting (see 4.6.4) or as a separate meeting.

4.6.3 Preparation. Each person on the review team individually studies the material and prepares for the review meeting. Any required presentations to the review team are prepared.

4.6.4 Examination. During the management review the review team holds one or more meetings to do the following:

(1) Examine project status and determine if it complies with the expected status according to a predefined plan;
(2) Examine project status and determine if it is overly constrained by external and internal factors not originally considered in the project plan;
(3) Record all deviations from the expected status accenting risks;
(4) Generate a list of issues and recommendations to be addressed by higher level management;
(5) Generate a list of issues and recommendations to be addressed by other responsible individuals, or organizations who affect the project;
(6) Recommend what course of action should be taken from this point on;
(7) Recommend authorization for additional reviews or audits;
(8) Identify other issues that must be addressed.

4.6.5 Rework. Any plan adjustments or product rework resulting from the management review is not considered as part of the management review process, except where needed as additional input to complete the examination process.

4.7 Exit Criteria. The management review is considered complete when

(1) All issues identified in the review Statement of Objectives have been addressed.
(2) The management review report has been issued (see 4.8).

4.8 Output. The output from the management review process is a Management Review Report that identifies the following:

(1) The project being reviewed;
(2) The review team;
(3) Inputs to the review;
(4) Review objectives;
(5) Action item ownership and status;
(6) A list of issues and recommendations identified by the review team that must be addressed for the project to meet its milestone;
(7) Recommendations regarding any further reviews and audits, and a list of additional information and data that must be obtained before they can be executed.

Although this standard sets minimum requirements for report content, it is left to local standards to prescribe any report format requirements.

4.9 Auditability. The management review report is an auditable item. It is recommended that this report be traceable to and from the appropriate project planning documents (for example, Software Development Plan, Software Quality Assurance Plan, or other applicable plans, or a combination of these).

5. The Technical Review Process

5.1 Objective. The objective of a technical review is to evaluate a specific software element(s) and provide management with evidence that

(1) The software element(s) conform to its specifications;
(2) The development (or maintenance) of the software element(s) is being done according to plans, standards, and guidelines applicable for the project;
(3) Changes to the software element(s) are properly implemented, and affect only those system areas identified by the change specification.

Moreover, to further tailor this review process for an individual software element, specific objectives are to be identified in a Statement of Objectives made available before the review meeting. The technical review concept can be applied to new development or to maintenance activities.

5.2 Abstract. A technical review is a formal team evaluation of a software element(s). It identifies any discrepancies from specifications and standards or provides recommendations after the examination of alternatives, or both. This examination may require more than one meeting.

5.3 Special Responsibilities. Roles for the technical review include:

5.3.1 Leader. The review leader is responsible for conducting a specific review. This includes administrative tasks pertaining to the review and ensuring that the review is conducted in an orderly manner. The review leader is also responsible for issuing the review report.

5.3.2 Recorder. The recorder is responsible for documenting findings (for example, defects, inconsistencies, omissions, and ambiguities), decisions, and recommendations made by the review team.

5.3.3 Team Member. Each team's members is responsible for their own preparation, and for ensuring that the review meets its objectives. Together, they are responsible for formulating recommendations in such a way that management can act on them promptly.

Management is responsible for acting on the review team recommendations in a timely manner.

5.4 Input. The minimum input to the technical review process is as follows:

(1) A statement of objectives for the technical review
(2) The software element(s) being examined
(3) Specifications for the software element(s) being examined
(4) Any plans, standards, or guidelines against which the software element(s) are to be examined

Additional applicable reference material can be made available by the individual(s) responsible for the software element, when requested by the review leader.

5.5 Entry Criteria

5.5.1 Authorization. The need for conducting technical reviews of specific software elements is defined by project planning documents.

Unscheduled technical reviews may be conducted at the request of functional management, project management, software quality management, or software engineers, according to local procedures.

5.5.2 Initiating Event. A technical review may not be conducted until

(1) A statement of objectives for the review is established;
(2) The responsible individual(s) for the software element(s) indicate readiness for review;
(3) The technical review leader is satisfied that the software element(s) are sufficiently complete for a technical review to be worthwhile

5.6 Procedures

5.6.1 Planning. A review leader is assigned responsibility for the following planning activities:

(1) Identify, with appropriate management support, the review team
(2) Schedule and announce the meeting place
(3) Distribute input materials to participants, allowing adequate time for their preparation

5.6.2 Overview. A technically qualified person shall conduct an overview session for the review team when requested by the review leader. This overview can occur as a part of the review meeting (see 5.6.4) or as a separate meeting.

5.6.3 Preparation. During the preparation step, each review team member individually examines the software element(s) and related materials in preparation for the review meeting.

5.6.4 Examination. At the review meeting the entire team reviews the software element, evaluating its condition relative to applicable guidelines, specifications and standards, or evaluating alternative problem solutions. Specifically, the review team performs the following tasks:

(1) Examines the software element(s) under review and verifies that it complies with the specifications and standards to which it must adhere. All deviations from the specifications and standards are recorded.

(2) Documents technical issues, related recommendations, and the individual responsible for getting the issues resolved.

(3) Identifies other issues that must be addressed.

After the software element(s) have been reviewed, a report is generated to document the meeting, list deficiencies found in the software element, and describe any recommendations for management.

When deficiencies are sufficiently critical or numerous, the review leader must recommend that an additional review process (that is, management review, technical review, or walkthrough) be applied to the reworked software element(s) after the deficiencies have been resolved. This, at a minimum, covers areas changed to resolve deficiencies.

5.7 Exit Criteria. A Technical Review is complete when

(1) All issues identified in the review Statement of Objectives have been addressed

(2) The technical review report (see 5.8) has been issued

5.8 Output. The output from the technical review process is a technical review report that identifies the following:

(1) The review team members

(2) The software element(s) reviewed

(3) Specific inputs to the review

(4) A list of unresolved software element(s) deficiencies

(5) A list of management issues

(6) Action item ownership and status

(7) Any recommendations made by the review team on how to dispose of unresolved issues and deficiencies

Although this standard sets minimum requirements for report content, it is left to local standards to prescribe any report format requirements.

5.9 Auditability. The technical review report is an auditable item. It is recommended that this report be traceable to/from the appropriate project planning documents (for example, Software Development Plan, Software Quality Assurance Plan).

6. The Software Inspection Process

6.1 Objective. The objective of a software inspection is to detect and identify software element defects. This is a rigorous, formal peer examination that does the following:

(1) Verifies that the software element(s) satisfy its specifications

(2) Verifies that the software element(s) conform to applicable standards

(3) Identifies deviation from standards and specifications

4) Collects software engineering data (for example, defect and effort data)

(5) Does not examine alternatives or stylistic issues

6.2 Abstract. Software inspections are conducted by peers, and typically comprise three to six participants. The process is led by a moderator impartial to the software element(s) under examination. The moderator is not the author. Defect resolution is mandatory, and rework is formally verified.

Defect data shall be systematically collected and stored in an inspection data base. Minimum requirements for data collection are presented in 6.10. When this data is analyzed, steps can be taken to improve both the product and the development process, and to assess the effectiveness of the inspection process.

6.3 Special Responsibilities. All team members, including those with special roles, are inspectors. Special roles required for the inspection process include

6.3.1 Moderator. The moderator is the chief planner and meeting manager for the inspection process, and is responsible for issuing the inspection reports (see 6.8). The moderator may also perform the role of recorder.

6.3.2 Reader. At the meeting(s), the reader leads the inspection team through the software element(s) in a comprehensive and logical fashion, generally paraphrasing sections of the work and by reading line-by-line where required by local standards.

6.3.3 Recorder. The recorder is charged with documenting defects detected at the meeting(s) and recording inspection data required for process analysis.

6.3.4 Inspector. The role of inspector is to identify and describe defects in the software element. Inspectors must be knowledgeable of the inspection process. They are chosen to represent different viewpoints at the meeting (for example, requirements, design, code, test, independent test, project management, quality management). Only those viewpoints pertinent to the inspection of the element are present.

6.3.5 Author. The author is responsible for the software element(s) meeting its inspection entry criteria, for contributing to the inspection based on special understanding of the software element, and for performing any rework required to make the software element(s) meet its inspection exit criteria. The author is not allowed to perform any other (that is, moderator, reader, or recorder) role.

6.4 Input. The necessary inputs to the inspection consist of the following:

(1) The software element(s) to be inspected; They must satisfy the inspection entry criteria;
(2) The approved software element(s) specification;
(3) The inspection checklist. See Appendix B for sample checklists;
(4) Any standards and guidelines against which the software element is to be inspected;
(5) All necessary inspection reporting forms.

For a reinspection, the previous inspection defect list is also required.

6.5 Entry Criteria

6.5.1 Authorization. Inspections are planned for, and documented in the appropriate project planning documents (for example, the overall project plan, software quality assurance plan, or software verification and validation plan).

6.5.2 Initiating Event. The software inspection process can be triggered by the following:

(1) Software element(s) availability
(2) Project plan compliance

(3) SQAP or SVVP schedule compliance
(4) Scheduled reinspection
(5) At the request of functional management, project management, software quality management, or software engineering

6.5.3 Minimum Entry Criteria Before Pannning Inspection. Before planning the inspection, the following minimum entry criteria must be met:

(1) The software element(s) conform to project standards of content, and format
(2) All prior milestones are satisfied, as identified in the the appropriate planning documents
(3) All required supporting documentation is available
(4) For a reinspection, all items noted on the defect list must be satisfied

6.6 Procedures

6.6.1 Planning. During the planning step, the author assembles the inspection package materials for the moderator.

The moderator is responsible for assuring that the materials meet the inspection entry criteria. The moderator is also responsible for assuring the selection of the inspection team and the assignment of their inspection meeting roles, for scheduling the inspection meetings, and for the distribution of the inspection materials.

6.6.2 Overview. If scheduled, an overview presentation of the software element(s)to be inspected is conducted by the moderator, and the author makes the presentation. This overview is used to educate the other inspectors concerning the software element(s) and may also be attended by other project personnel who could profit from the presentation.

6.6.3 Preparation. It is the individual responsibility of all inspectors to become thoroughly familiar with the software element, using the inspection checklist, the information provided in the overview, and the software specification.

6.6.4 Examination. The inspection meeting shall follow this agenda:

6.6.4.1 Introduce Meeting. To open the meeting, the moderator introduces the participants, and describes their roles. The moderator states the purpose of the inspection and directs the inspectors to focus their efforts toward defect detection, not solution-hunting.

The moderator reminds the inspectors to direct their remarks to the reader and to comment only on the product, not the author. It may also be useful to resolve any special procedural questions raised by the inspectors.

6.6.4.2 Establish Preparedness. The moderator asks for individual preparation times and records the total on the inspection report. It is the moderator's responsibility to reschedule the meeting if the inspectors are not adequately prepared.

6.6.4.3 Review the Inspection Checklist. The moderator reviews the inspection checklist with the team to ensure that the product has been adequately studied before the inspection meeting.

6.6.4.4 Read Software Elements and Record Defects. The reader presents the materials to the inspection team. The inspection team examines the software objectively, and the moderator focuses this part of the meeting on creating the defect list. The recorder enters each defect, location, description, and classification on the defect list. During this time, the author answers any specific questions and contributes to defect detection based on his/her special understanding of the software element.

6.6.4.5 Review the Defect List. At the end of the inspection meeting, the moderator must have the defect list reviewed with the team to ensure its completeness and accuracy.

6.6.4.6 Make Exit Decision. The purpose of the exit decision is to bring an unambiguous closure to the inspection meeting. The exit decision determines if the materials meet the inspection exit criteria and prescribes any appropriate rework verification. Specifically, the inspection team identifies the software element(s) disposition as one of the following:

(1) *Accept.* The software element is accepted *as is* or with only minor rework (for example, that would require no further verification)
(2) *Verify Rework.* The software element is to be accepted after the moderator verifies rework.
(3) *Reinspect.* Schedule a reinspection to verify rework after revision.

At a minimum, a reinspection examines the product areas changed to resolve defects identified in the last inspection.

6.6.5 Rework. During rework, the author revises the materials, addressing all items on the inspection defect list.

6.6.6 Follow-Up. The software inspection process provides follow-up on two levels:
(1) Verifying rework per inspection disposition
(2) Reporting inspection data

6.7 Exit Criteria. A single exit criterion applied to all inspections is that all of the defects that have been detected are resolved. Each project shall develop its own criteria to meet the needs of its specific products and development environment.

The moderator will ensure that the materials comply with the exit criteria and that the inspection results have been reported before certifying that the inspection is complete.

6.8 Output. For each software element(s), the reports produced by the inspection are:
(1) The defect list, containing the defect location, description, and categorization
(2) The inspection defect summary summarizing the number of defects identified by each defect category
(3) The inspection report, containing
   (a) The number of participants
   (b) The inspection meeting duration
   (c) The size of the materials inspected
   (d) The total preparation time of the inspection team
   (e) The disposition of the software element
   (f) An estimate of the rework effort and rework completion date

Information reports are retained for subsequent analysis as prescribed in the appropriate project planning documents. Although this standard sets minimum requirements for report content, it is left to local standards to prescribe any report format requirements.

6.9 Auditability. Auditability is provided by the following:
(1) Documented inspection procedures
(2) Retained inspection reports
(3) Retained inspection defect data

6.10 Data Collection Requirements. Software inspections provide data for the analysis of the quality of the software elements, the effectiveness of the development procedures, and the efficiency of the inspection process. To enable these analyses, defects that are identified at an inspection meeting are categorized by defect type, class, and severity.

6.10.1 The defect type identifies software element(s) attribute, and for example may be identified as affecting the software element's conformance to

(1) Standards compliance
(2) Capability
(3) Procedure
(4) Interface
(5) Description

6.10.2 Defect class characterizes evidence of nonconformance, and for example, may be categorized as

(1) Missing
(2) Wrong
(3) Extra

6.10.3 Additional defect classes used when inspecting documents could include

(1) Ambiguous
(2) Inconsistent

6.10.4 Defects are then ranked by severity, for example, as

(1) *Major*. Defects that would result in failure of the software element(s) or an observable departure from specification
(2) *Minor*. Defects that would affect only the nonfunctional aspects of the software element

In addition to counts of defects by type, class, and severity, retained inspection data shall contain the identification of the software element, the date and time of the inspection, the moderator, the preparation and inspection times, the volume of the materials inspected, and the disposition of the inspected software element. The recording of this information is required in setting local guidance for inspection effort and volume. Common practice would suggest up to 1.5 h preparation, up to 2 h meeting time, and whatever volume might be comfortably handled in that period of time.

The management of inspection data requires capabilities for the storage, entry, access, updating, and summarization and reporting of the categorized defects. The frequency and types of the inspection analysis reports, and their distribution, are left to the users of this standard.

7. The Walkthrough Process

7.1 Objective. The objective of a walkthrough is to evaluate a software element. Although long associated with code examinations, this process is also applicable to other software elements (for example, architectural design, detailed design, test plans/procedures, and change control procedures). The major objectives are to find defects, omissions, and contradictions; to improve the software element(s); and to consider alternative implementations.

Other important objectives of the walkthrough process include exchange of techniques and style variations, and education of the participants. A walkthrough may point out efficiency and readability problems in the code, modularity problems in design or untestable design specifications.

The walkthrough may be used in either new development or maintenance activities.

7.2 Abstract. During the walkthrough meeting, the author makes an overview presentation of the software element(s) under review. This is followed by a general discussion from the participants after which the presenter *"walks through"* the software element in detail. As the walkthrough progresses, errors, suggested changes, and improvements are noted and written. When the walkthrough is finished, the notes are consolidated into one report, which is distributed to the author and other appropriate personnel. A copy of the report is placed in the project file for auditability.

7.3 Special Responsibilities. The following roles are established for the walkthrough:

7.3.1 Moderator. The walkthrough moderator is responsible for conducting a specific walkthrough, handling the administrative tasks pertaining to the walkthrough, and ensuring that the walkthrough is conducted in an orderly manner. The moderator is also responsible for preparing the statement of objectives to guide the team through the walkthrough.

7.3.2 Recorder. The recorder is responsible for writing all comments made during the walkthrough that pertain to errors found, questions of style, omissions, contradictions, suggestions for improvement, or alternative approaches.

7.3.3 Author. The author is the person responsible for the software element(s) being examined, and presents the materials.

Each member of the walkthrough team is responsible for reviewing any input material prior to the walkthrough, and participating during the walkthrough to ensure that it meets its objective.

Roles may be shared among the walkthrough members. The author and walkthrough moderator may be the same person.

7.4 Input. The minimum input to the walkthrough process is as follows:
(1) A statement of objectives for the walkthrough
(2) The software element under examination
(3) Standards that are in effect for the development of the software element
(4) Specifications for the software element(s) under review

7.5 Entry Criteria

7.5.1 Authorization. The need for conducting walkthroughs shall be established in the appropriate planning documents, (for example, a software quality assurance plan (SQAP) or a software development plan). In addition, under either of these plans, completion of a specific software element(s) trigger the walkthrough for that element. Additional walkthroughs should be conducted during development of the software element(s) at the request of functional management, quality management, or the author, according to local procedures.

7.5.2 Initiating Event. A walkthrough is conducted when
(1) The author of the software element(s) to be reviewed indicates it is ready, and is prepared to present the materials.
(2) The moderator is appointed per local standards or practices and has concluded that the software element is sufficiently complete to conduct a walkthrough.

7.6 Procedures

7.6.1 Planning. During the planning phase, the walkthrough moderator does the following:

(1) Identifies the walkthrough team
(2) Schedules the meeting and selects the meeting place
(3) Distributes all necessary input materials to the participants, allowing for adequate preparation time

7.6.2 Overview. An overview presentation is made by the author as part of the walkthrough meeting. Before that meeting, however, individual preparation is still required.

7.6.3 Preparation. During the preparation phase participants shall review the input material that was distributed to them and prepare a list of questions and issues to be discussed during the walkthrough.

7.6.4 Examination. During the walkthrough meeting
(1) The presenter makes an overview presentation of the software element(s) under examination.
(2) The author walks through the specific software element(s) so that members of the walkthrough team may ask questions or raise issues regarding the software element, or document their concerns, or both.
(3) The recorder writes comments and decisions for inclusion in the walkthrough report.

At the completion of the walkthrough, the walkthrough team may recommend a follow-up walkthrough. This follow-up would follow the standard for walkthroughs, and would, at a minimum, cover areas changed by the author.

Within a reasonable time after the walkthrough, the walkthrough leader shall issue a walkthrough report detailing the walkthrough findings. Minimum content requirements are stated in 7.8.

7.7 Exit Criteria. The walkthrough process is complete when
(1) The entire software element(s) have been *"walked through"* in detail
(2) All deficiencies, omissions, efficiency issues, and suggestions for improvement have been noted
(3) The walkthrough report has been issued

7.8 Output. The output of the walkthrough process is a walkthrough report listing those deficiencies, omissions, efficiency issues, and suggestions for improvement that were recorded during the walkthrough.

The walkthrough report contains the following:
(1) Identification of the walkthrough team
(2) Identification of the software element(s) being examined
(3) The statement of objectives that were to be handled during this walkthrough meeting
(4) A list of the noted deficiencies, omissions, contradictions, and suggestions for improvement
(5) Any recommendations made by the walkthrough team on how to dispose of deficiencies and unresolved issues

If follow-up walkthroughs are suggested, this suggestion shall also be mentioned in the report.

Although this standard sets minimum requirements for report content, it is left to local standards to prescribe any report format requirements.

7.9 Auditability. The walkthrough report, meeting minutes, and other materials upon which conclusions are based shall be included in project documentation files. The walkthrough moderator files these documents.

8. The Audit Process

8.1 Objective. The objective of software auditing is to provide an objective compliance confirmation of products and processes to certify adherence to standards, guidelines, specifications, and procedures.

8.2 Abstract. Audits are performed in accordance with documented plans and procedures. The audit plan establishes a procedure to conduct the audit and for follow-up action on the audit findings.

In performing the audit, audit personnel evaluate software elements and the processes for producing them against objective audit criteria, such as contracts, requirements, plans, specifications, or procedures, guidelines, and standards.

The results of the audit are documented and are submitted to the management of the audited organization, to the entity initiating the audit, and to any external organizations identified in the audit plan. The report includes a list of the items in noncompliance or other issues for subsequent review and action. When stipulated by the audit plan, recommendations are reported in addition to the audit results.

8.3 Special Responsibilities. It is the responsibility of the audit team leader to organize and direct the audit and to coordinate the preparation and issuance of the audit report. The audit team leader shall ensure that the audit team is prepared to conduct the audit, and that audit procedures are performed and reports (see 8.8) issued in accordance with audit scope.

The entity initiating the audit is responsible for authorizing the audit. Management of the auditing organization assumes responsibility for the audit, and the allocation of the necessary resources to perform the audit.

Those whose products and processes are being audited provide all relevant materials and resources and correct or resolve deficiencies cited by the audit team.

8.4 Input. The following inputs are required to ensure the success of the audit:
(1) The purpose and scope of the audit.
(2) Objective audit criteria, such as contracts requirements, plans, specifications, procedures, guidelines, and standards.
(3) The software elements and processes to be audited and any pertinent histories.
(4) Background information regarding the organization responsible for the products and processes being audited (for example, organization charts).

8.5 Entry Criteria. The need for an audit is established by one of the following events:
(1) A special project milestone has been reached. The audit is initiated per earlier plans (for example, the software quality assurance plan, software development plan).
(2) External parties (for example, regulatory agencies, or end users) demand an audit at a specific calendar date or project milestone. This may be in fulfillment of a contract requirement, or as a prerequisite to contractual agreement.

(3) A local organizational element(s) (for example, project management, functional management, systems engineering, internal quality assurance/control) has requested the audit, establishing a clear and specific need.

(4) A special project milestone, calendar date, or other criterion has been met and, as part of the auditing organization's charter, it is to respond by initiating an audit.

8.6 Procedures

8.6.1 Planning. The auditing organization shall develop and document an audit plan for each audit. This plan shall, in addition to restating the audit scope, identify the following:

(1) Project processes to be examined (provided as input) and the time frame for audit team observation.

(2) Software required to be examined (provided as input) and their availability. Where sampling is used, a statistically valid sampling methodology shall be used to establish selection criteria and sample size.

(3) Reports shall be identified (that is, results report, and optionally, the recommendations report and their general format defined). Whether recommendations are required or excluded shall be explicitly stated.

(4) Report distribution

(5) Required follow-up activities

(6) Requirements: necessary activities, elements and procedures to meet the scope of the audit

(7) Objective audit criteria: provides the basis for determining compliance (provided as input)

(8) Audit procedures and checklists

(9) Audit personnel: required number, skills, experience, and responsibilities

(10) Organizations involved in the audit (for example, the organization whose products and processes are being audited)

(11) Date, time, place, agenda, and intended audience of *overview* session (optional)

The audit team leader shall ensure that the audit team is prepared and includes members with the necessary experience and expertise.

Notification of the audit shall be provided to the involved organizations at a reasonable amount of time before the audit is performed, except for unannounced audits. The notification shall be written and shall include the scope and the identification of processes and products to be audited, and to identify the auditors.

8.6.2 Overview. An optional overview meeting with the audited organization is recommended to *kick-off* the examination phase of the audit. The overview meeting, led by the audit team leader, provides the following:

(1) Overview of existing agreements (for example, audit scope, plan, related contracts);

(2) Overview of production and processes being audited;

(3) Overview of the audit process, its objectives, and outputs;

(4) Expected contributions of the audited organization to the audit process (that is, the number of people to be interviewed, meeting facilities, etc);

(5) Specific audit schedule.

8.6.3 Preparation

8.6.3.1 The following preparations are required by the audit team:

(1) Understand the organization: it is essential to identify functions and activities performed by the audited organization, and to identify functional responsibility.

(2) Understand the products and processes: it is a prerequisite for the team to learn about the products and processes being audited through readings and briefings.

(3) Understand the objective audit criteria: it is important that the audit team become familiar with the objective audit criteria to be used in the audit.

(4) Prepare for the audit report: it is important to choose the administrative reporting mechanism that will be used throughout the audit to develop the report that follows the layout identified in the audit plan.

(5) Detail the audit plan: choose appropriate methods for each step in the audit program.

8.6.3.2 In addition, the audit team leader shall make the necessary arrangements for

(1) Team orientation and training as needed

(2) Facilities for audit interviews
(3) Materials, documents, and tools required by the audit procedures
(4) The software elements to be audited (for example, documents, computer files, personnel to be interviewed)
(5) Scheduling interviews

8.6.4 Examination. Elements that have been selected for audit shall be evaluated against the objective audit criteria. Evidence shall be examined to the depth necessary to determine if these elements comply with specified criteria.

The audit shall, as appropriate to its scope:
(1) Review procedures and instructions
(2) Examine the work breakdown structures
(3) Examine evidence of implementation and balanced controls
(4) Interview personnel to ascertain the status and functioning of the processes and the status of the products
(5) Examine element documents
(6) Test the element(s)

8.6.5 Reporting. Subsequent to the audit examination, the audit team will issue a draft audit report to the audited organization for review and comments.

Audit team rework of the audit report occurs before formal results reporting. This rework is performed, in concert with the draft report review, resolve any misunderstandings or ambiguities while maintaining objectivity and correctness. It also serves to ensure report usability by adding consistency to the level of report details and by adding any freshly verified information. The recommended practice is to involve representatives of the audited organization in reviewing audit results, as
(1) An ongoing, periodic activity integrated into the overall examination schedule, or
(2) As a closure step to the examination period

Involving the audited organization contributes to report quality through interaction and the possible delivery of any further evidence.

The audit team shall conduct a post audit conference to review with audited organization staff the deficiencies, findings, and (if applicable) recommendations. Comments and issues raised by the audited organization must be resolved.

The final audit report shall then be prepared, approved, and issued by the audit team leader to the organizations specified by the audit plan.

8.7 Exit Criteria. An audit shall be considered complete when
(1) Each element(s) within the scope of the audit has been examined;
(2) Findings have been presented to the audited organization;
(3) Response to draft findings have been received and evaluated;
(4) Final findings have been formally presented to the audited organization and initiating entity;
(5) The audit report has been prepared and submitted to recipients designated in the audit plan;
(6) The recommendation report, if required by plan, has been prepared and submitted to recipients designated in the audit plan;
(7) All of the auditing organization's follow-up actions included in the scope (or contract) of the audit have been performed.

8.8 Output. As a standard framework for audit reports, the draft and final audit reports shall, as a minimum, contain the following:
(1) *Audit identification.* Report title, audited organization, auditing organization, date of the audit.
(2) *Scope.* Scope of the audit, including an enumeration of the standards, specifications, practices, and procedures constituting the objective audit criteria against which the audit was conducted of the software elements and processes audited.
(3) *Conclusions.* A summary and interpretation of the audit findings including the key items of nonconformance.
(4) *Synopsis.* A listing of all the audited software elements, processes, and associated findings.
(5) *Follow-up.* The type and timing of audit follow-up activities.

Additionally, when stipulated by the audit plan, recommendations shall be provided to the audited organization, or the entity that initiated the audit. Recommendations shall be reported separately from results.

8.9 Auditability. The materials documenting the audit process must be maintained by the audit organization for a stipulated period of time subsequent to the audit and include the following:

(1) All work programs, checklists, etc are fully annotated

(2) Team staffing

(3) Interview notes, observation notes

(4) Compliance test evidence

(5) Copies of examined items, annotated

(6) Report draft(s) with response by audited organization

(7) Follow-up memo(s) as necessary

Appendixes

(These Appendixes are not a part of IEEE Std 1028-1988, IEEE Standard for Software Reviews and Audits, but are included here for information only.)

Appendix A

Guide to Process Applications for Critical Software

A1.

ANSI/IEEE Std 730-1984 [A1] has identified a minimum set of review and audit process applications for critical software (for example, where failure could impact safety, or cause large financial or social losses).

(1) Software requirements review (SRR)
(2) Preliminary design review (PDR)
(3) Critical design review (CDR)
(4) Software verification and validation plan review (SVVPR)
(5) Functional audit (FA)
(6) Physical audit (PA)
(7) In-process audit (IPA)
(8) Managerial review (MR)

A2.

A2.1 The goal of this Appendix is to provide one possible mapping of specific process application needs identified in that standard, to candidate processes for meeting those needs. Selection of a specific process should be made as local, contractual, or project specific conditions dictate.

For example:
(1) The software inspection process may be used to meet the software verification and validation plan review application need.
(2) The management review process may be used to meet the managerial review application need.

Table A1
Critical Software Examination

ANSI/IEEE Std 730-1984 Requirements	SRR	PDR	CDR	SVVPR	FCA	PCA	IPA	MR
Management review			X					X
Technical review	X	X	X	X				
Software inspection	X	X	X	X				
Walkthrough	*	*	*	*				
Audit					X	X	X	**

* As common practice in many companies, walkthroughs are allowed wherever software inspections might be applied. It is suggested however, that for critical software as presented in ANSI/IEEE Std 730-1984, only more formal/rigorous techniques be used. One significant difference is disallowing the author from presenting the work.

** The audit process may be tailored in its application or administration to meet the need for a managerial review.

A particular process need not be prescribed for all applications. For example, using the same process for all the SRR, PDR, and CDR might not be cost effective or might unwisely be biased toward either technical or business concerns.

A2.2 Similarly, a combination of distinct processes may be applied to meet the needs of a specific application. An example is providing adequate examination of an SRR for a very large and complex system. SRR concerns could be subdivided into three categories:

(1) Customer satisfaction with functionality and performance with consideration for technical and business feasibility

(2) Technical completeness and correctness of requirements

(3) Fitness-for-use of the specifications document(s) as viewed by development, test, and maintenance organizations

In this example, it may be appropriate to use a management review to examine the first category, a technical review for the second category, and a software inspection to verify fitness-for-use of the document itself.

Table A1 shows possible mappings of review and audit processes to the applications referenced in ANSI/IEEE Std 730-1984 [A1].

A3.

The following references apply to Appendixes A through C:

[A1] ANSI/IEEE Std 730-1984, IEEE Standard for Software Quality Assurance Plans.

[A2] ANSI/IEEE Std 1016-1987, IEEE Recommended Practice for Software Design Descriptions.

Appendix B

Guide to Specific Review Applications

This Appendix is added to guide in the application of review processes, and to delineate some specific applications.

Although review processes defined by this standard have distinct objectives, Table B1 is provided to further accent process distinctions.

In addition, the following review process applications are presented:

(1) Software requirements review (SRR)
(2) Preliminary design review (PDR)
(3) Critical design review (CDR)
(4) Software verification and validation plan review (SVVPR)
(5) Managerial reviews (MR)

B1. Software Requirements Review (SRR)

The SRR is held to ensure the adequacy of the requirements stated in the software requirements specification. See ANSI/IEEE Std 730-1984 [A1].

The SRR is an evaluation of the software requirements specification (SRS) to ensure adequacy, technical feasibility, and completeness. Moreover, the SRR is held with user participation to examine the SRS to verify that is is unambiguous, verifiable, consistent, modifiable, traceable, and usable during the operation and maintenance phase. All organizational elements (for example, software design, software test, software quality assurance, systems engineering, marketing, manufacturing, and field service) that are directly affected by the requirements should participate.

The review checklist for the software requirements review may include but is not limited to the following:

(1) Traceability and completeness of the requirement from the next higher level specification (such as a system specification or user requirements specification)
(2) Adequacy of rationale for any derived requirements
(3) Compatibility of external (hardware and software) interfaces

(4) Adequacy of requirements for the man-machine interface
(5) Availability of constants and tables for calculations
(6) Testability of the functional requirements
(7) Adequacy and completeness of the verification and acceptance requirements
(8) Conformance to requirements specification standards
(9) Adequacy and feasibility of performance requirements
(10) Adequacy of consideration for human factors

B2. Preliminary Design Review (PDR)

B2.1 The PDR is held to evaluate the technical adequacy of the preliminary design of the software as depicted in a preliminary version of the Software Design Description. See ANSI/IEEE Std 730-1984 [A1].

Specifically, the need is to apply a review process to assess the progress, consistency, and technical adequacy of the selected design approach.

All organizational elements (for example, software test, software quality assurance, systems engineering, marketing, manufacturing, and field service) that are directly affected by the software design description should participate.

The following items may be included in the review checklist for the preliminary design review (PDR):

(1) Compatibility of the interfaces between the software, hardware, and end users.
(2) Fulfillment of the requirements contained in the SRS.
(3) Conformance to design documentation standards.

B2.2 Concerns that may be addressed by the checklist for preliminary design review

Table B1

Category and Attributes	Management Review	Technical Review	Software Inspection	Walkthrough
Objective	Ensure progress. Recommend corrective action. Ensure proper allocation of resources.	Evaluate conformance to specifications and plans. Ensure change integrity.	Detect and identify defects. Verify resolution.	Detect defects. Examine alternatives. Forum for learning.
Delegated Controls				
Decision making	Management team charts course of action. Decisions are made at the meeting or as a result of recommendations.	Review team petitions. Management or technical leadership to act on recommendations.	Team chooses from predefined product dispositions. Defects must be removed.	All decisions made by producer. Change is the prerogative of the producer.
Change verification	Change verification left to other project controls.	Leader verifies as part of review report.	Moderator verifies rework.	Change verification left to other project controls.
Group Dynamics				
Recommended size	Two or more persons.	Three or more persons.	Three to six persons.	Two to seven persons.
Attendance	Management, technical leadership, and peer mix.	Technical leadership and peer mix.	College of peers meet with documented attendance.	Technical leadership and peer mix.
Leadership	Usually the responsible manager.	Usually the lead engineer.	Trained moderator.	Usually producer.
Procedures				
Matrial volume	Moderate to high, depending on the specific *statement of objectives* for the meeting.	Moderate to high, depending on the specific *statement of objectives* for the meeting.	Relatively low.	Relatively low.
Presenter	Project representative.	Software element representative.	Presentation by *reader* other than producer.	Usually the producer.
Data collection	As required by applicable policies, standards, or plans.	Not a formal project requirement. May be done locally.	Formally required.	Not a formal project requirement. May be done locally.
Outputs				
Reports	Management review report.	Technical review reports.	Defect list and summary. Inspection report.	Walkthrough report.
Data base entries	Any schedule changes must be entered into the project tracking database.	No formal data base required.	Defect counts, characteristics, severity, and meeting attributes are kept.	No formal data base requirement.

(PDR) include (but are not limited to):
(1) Software interfaces
(2) Hardware interfaces
(3) Baseline for configuration
(4) Functional overview
(5) Design alternative selection rationale
(6) Standard operating environments
(7) Human factors requirements
(8) Documentation requirements
(9) Testing considerations
(10) Manufacturability
(11) Maintainability
(12) Assumptions
(13) Risks

More information is available in ANSI/IEEE Std 1016-1987 [A2].

B3. Critical Design Review (CDR)

The CDR is held to determine the acceptability of the detailed software designs as depicted in the software design description in satisfying the requirements of the software requirements specification. See ANSI/IEEE Std 730-1984 [A1].

The CDR is an evaluation of the completed software design description (SDD) to evaluate its technical adequacy, completeness, and correctness. Other concerns include its compatibility with the other software and hardware (where the product is required to interact), and the technical, cost, and schedule risks of the product design.

All other organizational elements that impose requirements or are affected by the design should participate (for example, software design, software test, and systems engineering).

The following items may be included in the review checklist for the critical design review:
(1) The compatibility of the detailed design with the SRS
(2) Available data in the form of logic diagrams, algorithms, storage allocation charts, and detailed design representations (for example, flow chart, program design language) to establish design integrity
(3) Compatibility and completeness of interface design requirements
(4) Adequacy and completeness of algorithms and equations

(5) Correctness and suitability of logic descriptions that may be warranted
(6) Technical accuracy and currency of all available test documentation and its compatibility with the test requirements of the SRS
(7) The requirements for the support and test software and hardware to be used in the development of the product
(8) The inclusion in the final design of function flow, timing, sizing, storage requirements, memory maps, data base, and other performance factors

B4. Software Verification and Validation Plan Review (SVVPR)

The software verification and validation plan review is held to evaluate the adequacy and completeness of the verification and validation methods described in the SVVP. See ANSI/IEEE Std 730-1984 [A1].

The SVVPR is an evaluation of the completed software verification and validation plan (SVVP). Since the SVVP may be developed incrementally, multiple reviews may be required. These reviews are held to ensure that the verification and validation methods described in the SVVP are adequate and will provide complete evaluation data.

All organizational elements that impose requirements or are impacted by the SVVP should participate. These groups may include system engineering, software marketing, software design, software test, software quality assurance, customers, and users.

The following items may be included as review requirements for the software verification and validation plan review:
(1) All verification and validation methods, along with completion criteria to assure traceability to, and compatibility with, the functional and performance requirements expressed in the SRS.
(2) The methods to be used to verify and validate that the product satisfies the requirements of the SRS; these should include review process applications (for example, technical review, inspection, or walkthrough), demonstration, analysis, and test.

(3) Reports that adequately document the results of all reviews, audits, and tests based on the requirements listed in the SVVP.

(4) Adequate descriptions of the software configuration to be tested including test support software and hardware.

(5) Test plans, test procedures, test cases, and test data to ensure that all specification requirements are tested and that test instructions are clear and concise.

(6) Test procedures and test cases to ensure that test inputs and success criteria are adequately defined.

(7) A test plan and test case schedule identifying tests to be done, when, and by whom.

(8) Conformance to test documentation standards.

B5. Managerial Reviews

These reviews are held periodically to assess the execution of (the SQA) plan. These reviews shall be held by an organizational element(s) independent of the unit being audited, or by a qualified third party. See ANSI/IEEE Std 730-1984 [A1].

The planned frequency and structure of the (SQA Plan) managerial reviews should be stated in the SQA Plan. They should be conducted at the direction of the program manager.

Although the application of the *Management Review Process* meets this review requirement, an alternative is to perform the *Quality Systems Audit* (as presented in Appendix C) to the extent possible given the particular degree of independence and authority.

Appendix C

A Guide to Specific Audit Applications

To guide in the application of the audit process, and to delineate some specific applications, this Appendix has been added. The following audit process applications are presented:

(1) Functional audit (FA)
(2) Physical audit (PA)
(3) In-process audit (IPA)
(4) Quality systems audit (QSA)

Where self-examination (that is, application of the audit process by an element(s) not organizationally independent of the area audited) is desired, the general audit process is applied, with the independence requirement waived.

C1. The Functional Audit (FA)

The objective of the functional audit (FA) is to provide an independent evaluation of software products, verifying that its configuration items' actual functionality and performance is consistent with the requirement specifications. Specifically, this audit is held prior to the software delivery to verify that all requirements specified in the Software Requirements Specification have been met. See ANSI/IEEE Std 730-1984 [A1].

C1.1 Central to the FA is the identification of software elements to be audited by:

1) Nomenclature
2) Specification identification number
3) Configuration item number

C1.2 In addition, materials to be provided by the audited organization include:

(1) The software requirements specification
(2) Object copy of code
(3) Current listing of waivers against specific configuration items
(4) When available, the status of test programs to test configured items with automatic test equipment
(5) The software verification and validation report
(6) All in-process audit reports for items under audit (see C3)

(7) Any other test documentation (for example, plans, specifications, procedures, and reports) for the configuration item
(8) Listing of all successfully accomplished functional testing
(9) Listing of all planned, yet unexecuted, functional testing

C1.3 The following activities are required to conduct a functional audit:

(1) An audit of the formal test documentation shall be performed against test data. Results shall be checked for completeness and accuracy, and all deficiencies documented.
(2) An audit of the software verification and validation report shall be made to validate that the reports are accurate and completely describe the testing effort. All approved changes (problem reporting and corrective action) shall be reviewed to ensure that they have been technically incorporated and verified.
(3) Updates to previously delivered documents shall be reviewed to ensure accuracy and consistency.
(4) Preliminary design review and critical design review outputs shall be sampled to ensure that all findings have been incorporated and completed.

The audit team shall compare the code with the documented software requirements as stated in the current specifications document, to determine that the code addresses all (and only) the documented requirements.

C1.4 This audit is concerned not only with functionality, but also with performance as follows: Testing accomplished with appropriate test documentation and validated data shall sufficiently establish configuration item performance. For performance parameters that can not be verified completely during testing, simulations or other analysis shall be accomplished to establish confidence that the configuration item does meet performance criteria when in operation as stated in its specifications.

The FA report should include an evaluation of each software element(s) examined, and provides this evaluation within the standard audit report framework. The evaluation shall take the form of

(1) *Approval.* If the software element(s) had been observed as having all required functions and shows evidence of meeting minimum performance standards.

(2) *Contingent Approval.* If the evaluation of the software element(s) would result in approval given successful completion of specific, well-defined (observable) corrective action.

(3) *Disapproval.* If the software element(s) were observed to be seriously inadequate.

C2. The Physical Audit (PA)

The objective of the physical sudit (PA) is to provide an independent evaluation of a software product configuration item to confirm that components in the *as-built version* map to its specifications. Specifically, this audit is held to verify that the software and its documentation are internally consistent and are ready for delivery. See ANSI/IEEE Std 730-1984 [A1].

C2.1 Central to the PA is the identification of software elements to be audited by
(1) Nomenclature
(2) Specification identification number
(3) Configuration item number

C2.2 In addition, materials to be provided by the audited organization include
(1) Current listing of waivers against specific configuration items
(2) Requirements and architectural and detailed design specifications
(3) Listing of approved changes against the configuration with outstanding changes identified
(4) Acceptance test documentation (for examplee, plans, specifications, procedures, and reports) for the configuration item
(5) Appropriate customer deliverable documentation (for example, operating manuals, and maintenance manuals)

(6) Approved nomenclature, markings, and nameplates
(7) Software version description document
(8) FA reports

In addition, the audited organization shall identify any differences between the configuration of the system in the development environment, and the specific configuration of the system under examination. Moreover, they shall certify or otherwise demonstrate that any differences do not degrade the functional or performance characteristics of the system.

C2.3 To provide evidence of adequate control of system content and consistency, the audit team should as a minimum, examine
(1) The system specification document(s) for format and completeness
(2) Functional (FA) reports for discrepancies and actions taken
(3) Design descriptions (at least on a sampling basis) for proper symbols, labels, references, and data descriptions
(4) Design descriptions at various levels of abstraction, cross-checking for consistency
(5) Manuals (for example, user's manuals, programmer's manuals, and operator's manuals,) for format completeness and conformance with data item descriptions. Formal verification or acceptance of these manuals shall be waived until all other system testing is completed to ensure that procedural contents are correct.
(6) The software element(s) delivery media (and media controls) to ensure proper transfer or transmittal.

The audit team shall examine the system for vendor-provided or supplier-developed software elements, and seek evidence that any such software elements were produced under reasonable and prudent quality controls.

C2.4 The audit team shall examine the engineering release and change control function (and associated documentation) for evidence that it can
(1) Identify the composition of any configuration in terms of its subordinate units
(2) Determine, given a unit identifier, the parent element

(3) Describe the composition of a configuration item or its identifier with respect to other configuration items or identifiers

(4) Identify specifications relating to a given configuration item

(5) Identify outstanding changes against a given configuration item

(6) Identify changes and retain records of earlier configurations

C2.5 The PA report should include an evaluation of all software elements as a whole, and shall provide this evaluation within the standard audit report framework. The evaluation shall take the form of

(1) Approval. When the system of software elements has been observed as having all deliverable components accounted for, and of compatible issue.

(2) Contingent Approval. When the evaluation of the system of software elements results in approval given successful completion of specific, well-defined (observable) corrective action.

(3) Disapproval. When the system of software elements was observed to be seriously inadequate.

C2.6 The audit team shall examine the engineering release and change control function (and associated documentation) for evidence that it can

(1) Identify the composition of any configuration in terms of its subordinate units

(2) Determine, given a unit identifier, the parent element

(3) Describe the composition of a configuration item or its identifier with respect to other configuration items' identifiers

(4) Identify specifications relating to a given configuration item

C3. In-Process Audits

In-process audits are held during the design and development phases prior to the functional audit to verify the consistency of the design.

The objective is to verify the consistency of the product as it evolves through the development process by determining, on a sampling basis, that

(1) Hardware and software interfaces are consistent with design requirements in the software requirements specification (SRS)

(2) The code is fully tested by the SVVP to ensure that the functional requirements of the SRS are satisfied

(3) The design of the product, as the software design description (SDD) is evolving, satisfies the functional requirements of the SRS

(4) The code is consistent with the SDD

Moreover, in-process audits can be applied to determine compliance with applicable process standards (for example, auditing of the inspection process, on a sampling basis, to determine if inspection process rules are being followed).

Input material should include formal process descriptions and a product sample evidencing process execution.

In-process audit procedures are unique to the process and product examined. Specific procedures should be established locally, using the general steps found in Section 8.

The results of all in-process audits shall be documented in in-process audit reports, which identify all discrepancies found, and provide an overall opinion accordingly. The opinion should take the form of approval, contingent approval, or disapproval. Significant compliance deviations are noted and must be followed up to ensure their correction or waiver. This occurs during or before the functional audit.

C4. The Quality Systems Audit (QSA)

The purpose of a quality systems audit, or quality program evaluation, is to provide an independent assessment of the compliance to a software quality assurance plan.

C4.1 Specifically, the QSA objective is to determine, based on observable (verifiable) evidence, that

(1) The software quality program documentation established by the development organization addresses as a minimum, the basic elements of ANSI/IEEE Std 730-1984 [A1], or other appropriate standards.

(2) The software development organization follows its documented software quality program.

The SQA plan must incorporate all objective organizational performance criteria; internal standards and procedures; process requirements mandated by law, contract, or other policy; and conform to the ANSI/IEEE 730-1984 [A1] or other appropriate standards for software quality assurance.

C4.2 Central to the QSA is the identification of quality program documentation, and its availability to the audit team.

The following activities are required:

(1) A preaudit conference with audited organization personnel is held to familiarize them with audit goals and procedures

(2) Examination of quality program documents and related items for com

pleteness, traceability, and consistency

(3) Perform selective compliance testing to objectively ascertain that SQA procedures and standards are implemented correctly

(4) Interview staff

(5) Perform in-process audits as appropriate (for example, observing inspections and their documented evidence)

(6) Examine reports from any recent functional and physical configuration audits.

The QSA report should include an evaluation of the quality program as a whole, and should provide this evaluation within the standard audit report framework.

The evaluation (following the general format of Section 8) shall take the form of approval, contingent approval, or disapproval for each major program element(s) identified in the audit plan.

Acknowledgments

The following organizations supported the development of this standard:

A. Frank Ackerman Associates
AT&T Bell Laboratories
AT&T Information Systems
AT&T Technologies
Bell Canada
Bell Communications Research
Burroughs Corporation
C.S. Draper Laboratory
CAP GEMINI/DASD
Coldframe, Inc
Combustion Engineering
Computer Sciences Corporation
DP Auditing Report
Grumman-CTEC
IBM Corp
Intermetrics, Inc
Martin-Marietta
McDonnell Douglas Corporation
Motorola
Naval Weapons Center
NCR Corporation
Northern Telecom, Ltd
Northern Telecom, Inc
OASAS, Ltd
Pacific Gas and Electric
Pansophic Systems, Inc
Pinpoint Retail Systems, Inc
Quality Assurance Institute
RCA
RGE Software Methodologies, Inc
Sperry
US Department of Transportation
University of California, Sacramento
Worldwide Service Technologies, Inc

ANSI/IEEE
Std 1042-1987

An American National Standard

IEEE Guide to
Software Configuration Management

Sponsor

**Technical Committee on Software Engineering of the
Computer Society of IEEE**

Approved September 10, 1987

IEEE Standards Board

Approved March 10, 1988

American National Standards Institute

1042

Foreword

(This Foreword is not a part of ANSI/IEEE Std 1042-1987, IEEE Guide for Software Configuration Management.)

The purpose of this guide is to provide guidance in planning software configuration management (SCM) practices that are compatible with ANSI/IEEE Std 828-1983, IEEE Standard for Software Configuration Management Plans. Three groups are served by this guide: developers of software, software management community, and those responsible for preparation of SCM Plans. The developers of software will be interested in the different ways SCM can be used to support the software engineering process. The management community will be interested in how the SCM Plan can be tailored to the needs and resources of a project. Those preparing plans for SCM will be interested in the suggestions and examples for preparation of a Plan.

The introduction of this guide presents a technical and philosophical overview of the SCM planning process. Subsequent paragraphs in the body of the guide contain general statements of principles, commentary on issues to consider, and *lessons learned* for the corresponding paragraph in the outline of the ANSI/IEEE Std 828-1983 Plan. Four Appendixes illustrate how the ANSI/IEEE Std 828-1983 can be used for a variety of different projects. A fifth Appendix lists current references that may be useful in planning SCM.

This guide was prepared by a working group chartered by the Software Engineering Subcommittee of the Technical Committee on Software Engineering of the Computer Society of IEEE. This guide represents a consensus of individual working-group participants with broad expertise in software engineering and configuration management, staffed with both members within the Institute and from other groups that have expertise and interest in participating.

The following individuals contributed to the writing of this guide by attendance to two or more working sessions, or by substantial written commentary, or both.

Richard L. Van Tilburg, *Chairman*   **David Schwartz,** *Cochairman*

Bakul Banerjee	David Gelperin	Brian F. Rospide
H. Ronald Berlack	Curtis F. Jagger	Margaret Rumley
Grazyna Bielecka	Allen T. L. Jin	Edward Showalter
Jack L. Cardiff	Dwayne Knirk	Jean Stanford
Larry Cummings	Nancy Murachanian	William S. Turner, III
Michael A. Daniels	Sarah H. Nash	Albert T. Williams
	Wilma Osborne	

When the IEEE Standards Board approved this standard on September 10, 1987, it had the following membership:

Donald C. Fleckenstein, *Chairman*   **Marco W. Migliaro,** *Vice Chairman*

Andrew G. Salem, *Secretary*

James H. Beall	Leslie R. Kerr	Donald T. Michael*
Dennis Bodson	Jack Kinn	L. John Rankine
Marshall L. Cain	Irving Kolodny	John P. Riganati
James M. Daly	Joseph L. Koepfinger*	Gary S. Robinson
Stephen R. Dillon	Edward Lohse	Frank L. Rose
Eugene P. Fogarty	John May	Robert E. Rountree
Jay Forster	Lawrence V. McCall	William R. Tackaberry
Kenneth D. Hendrix	L. Bruce McClung	William B. Wilkens
Irvin N. Howell		Helen M. Wood

*Member emeritus

The following person were on the balloting committee that approved this document for submission to the IEEE Standards Board:

Acknowledgment

Appreciation is expressed to the following companies and organizations for contributing the time of their employees to make possible the development of this text:

Boeing
Burroughs
General Dynamics
Hughes Aircraft Co
Intel Corporation
IBM
Goodyear Atomic Corporation
GTE
National Bureau of Standards

MITRE
Motorola
Programming Environments, Inc
RCA Astro Electronics
Sperry
Telos
Texas Instruments
ZTROW Software Inc

Contents

Contents

An American National Standard

IEEE Guide to
Software Configuration Management

1. Introduction

1.1 Scope. This guide describes the application of configuration management (CM) disciplines to the management of software engineering projects. Software configuration management (SCM) consists of two major aspects: planning and implementation. For those planning SCM activities, this guide provides insight into the various factors that must be considered.

Users implementing SCM disciplines will find suggestions and detailed examples of plans in this guide. This guide also presents an interpretation of how ANSI/IEEE Std 828-1983 [2][1] can be used for planning the management of different kinds of computer program development and maintenance activities.

The guide is presented in two parts. The first part, the main body of the guide, presents issues to consider when planning software configuration management for a project or organization. The second part of the guide presents, for those preparing SCM Plans, a series of sample Plans illustrating different concepts discussed in the body of the guide.

The text of the guide introduces the essential concepts of SCM, particularly those of special significance (for example, libraries and tools) to software engineering. It then presents the plan-

---

[1] The numbers in brackets correspond with those of the references in 1.2.

ning for SCM in terms of documenting a Plan following the outline of ANSI/IEEE Std 828-1983 [2] so that a user who is unfamiliar with the disciplines of software configuration management can gain some insight into the issues. For those preparing SCM Plans, the second part of the guide provides sample plans for consideration.

The sample SCM Plans include a variety of software configuration management applications for different types of projects and organizations. Appendix A illustrates a software configuration management plan (SCMP) for a project developing a complex, critical computer system. It describes a Plan for managing a typical software development cycle where the development is contracted to an organization that does not have responsibility for its maintenance or use. Appendix B illustrates a SCMP for a small software development project. It describes a Plan for supporting a prototype development activity where the goal of the project is to demonstrate the feasibility of a concept. Appendix C illustrates a SCMP used by an organization where the emphasis is on maintaining programs developed by other activities or organizations. Appendix D illustrates a SCMP for an organization developing and maintaining computer programs embedded in a hardware product line. It describes a Plan for managing both software development and maintenance of a commercial product line. Some of the different characteristics illustrated are shown in Table 1.

Table 1
Characteristics of Appendixes*

Appendix Number	Emphasis of Control (Life Cycle Phase)	Type of Project	Relative Size (Dollar/Manhour)	SCM Tools Available	Life Span of Plan	Writing for Plan
1	Development	Critical	Medium	Advanced	Short	Highly structured
2	Concept	Prototype	Small	Basic	Short	Informal
3	Operations	Support sw	Large	On-line	Full life cycle	Structured
4	All	Commercial	Small	Integrated	Full life cycle	Organizational Informal

*NOTE: The purpose of the Appendixes is not to provide an illustration for every possible combination of project characteristics but rather to show that the ANSI/IEEE Std 828-1983 [2] can be applied to a wide variety of projects.

1.2 References. This guide shall be used in conjunction with the following publications:

[1] ANSI/IEEE Std 729-1983, IEEE Standard Glossary of Software Engineering Terminology.[2]

[2] ANSI/IEEE Std 828-1983, IEEE Standard for Software Configuration Management Plans.

Additional references useful in understanding software configuration management are given in Appendix E.

1.3 Mnemonics. The following acronyms are used in the text of this guide:

CCB	Configuration Control Board
CDR	Critical Design Review
CI	Configuration Item
CM	Configuration Management
CPC	Computer Program Component
CPCI	Computer Program Configuration Item
CSC	Computer Software Component
CSCI	Computer Software Configuration Item
[EP]ROM	[Electrically Programmable] Read Only Memory
FCA	Functional Configuration Audit
OEM	Original Equipment Manufacturer
PCA	Physical Configuration Audit
PDR	Preliminary Design Review
RAM	Random Access Memory
ROM	Read Only Memory
SCA	System/Software Change Authorization
SCCB	Software Configuration Control Board
SCM	Software Configuration Management
SCMP	Software Configuration Management Plan
SCR	System/Software Change Request
SQA	Software Quality Assurance
VDD	Version Description Document

1.4 Terms. Some terms used in SCM circles have restricted meanings or are not defined in the guide. General statements of the contextual meanings are given to aid in understanding the concepts in the guide. These are not formal definitions, subject to review and approval as in a standard, but contextual definitions serving to augment the understanding of configuration management activities as described within this guide.

As used here, the term **baseline**[3] represents the assignment of a documented identifier to each software product configuration item (CI) and associated entities. That is, the source code, relocatable code, executable code, files controlling the process of generating executable code from source code, documentation, and tools used to support development or maintenance of the software product should all be captured, labeled and somehow denoted or recorded as parts of the same baseline. As computer programs move from an initial idea to the maintenance phase, it is common for a series of developmental baselines of increasing complexity to be established during the various internal and external reviews conducted by management (and customers) to determine progress and technical suitability. The baseline concept is as useful to engineering during development as it is after release for use and maintenance.

The various SCM functions are dependent on the baseline concept. Several valuable uses of the baseline concept include

(1) To distinguish between different internal releases for delivery to a customer (that is, successive variants of the same product baseline)

(2) To help to ensure complete and up-to-date technical product documentation

(3) To enforce standards (SQA)

(4) To be used as a means of promoting (that is, internally releasing) each CI from one phase of development or test to another

(5) To identify customer involvement in internal (developmental) baselies

Since SCM disciplines are an integral part of the engineering process they guide the management of internal developmental baselines as well as the more formal functional, allocated, and product baselines. The SCM disciplines, as applied to developmental baselines, are used (implicitly or explicitly) to coordinate most engineering activities that occur within the context of each baseline. Varying levels of formality provide flexibility and responsiveness to the engineering process, yet maintain the benefits of recognizing SCM disciplines.

---

[2] ANSI/IEEE publications are available from IEEE Service Center, 445 Hoes Lane, Piscataway, NJ 08855-1331 and from the Sales Department, American National Standards Institute, 1430 Broadway, New York, NY 10018.

[3] A specification or product that has been formally reviewed and agreed to by responsible management, that thereafter serves as the basis for further development, and can be changed only through formal change control procedures.

The term **promotion** is used here to indicate a transition in the level of authority needed to approve changes to a controlled entity, such as a baseline CI.

Promotions typically signify a change in a CI's internal development state. The term **release** is used to designate certain promotions of CI that are distributed outside the development organization.

In general, as the development process continues, there are more constraints imposed on the change process (coordination with interfacing hardware, user's adaptations, etc) and correspondingly higher levels of authority are needed for approving the changes. When an entity is finally released as a formal baseline, a high level of authority is needed to approve changes. When internal or developmental baselines are created as a part of the engineering process and entitites are moved or released to another internal activity for additional work, integration, or testing the term **promotion** is used to distinguish this type of release from the more formal releases to users.

Promotion from one developmental baseline to another represents the visibility granted to some organizations for a given baseline. As developmental baselines are promoted within an organization, they tend to become more stable. The more stable a baseline is, the higher the level of visibility it is granted.

The term **version** is used here to indicate a software CI having a defined set of functional capabilities. As functional capabilities are added, modified, or deleted the CI is given a different version identifier. It is common and recommended practice to use a configuration identification scheme that permits easy and automatic identification of particular version labels.

The term **revision** is commonly associated with the notion of *bug fixing*, that is, making changes to a program that corrects only errors in the design logic but does not affect documented functional capabilities since none of the requirements have changed. The configuration identification scheme must provide for clear identification of revisions and versions of each specific promotion and release.

2. SCM Disciplines in Software Management

2.1 The Context of SCM. This guide discusses SCM as a set of management disciplines within

the context of the software engineering process rather than as a set of specific activities performed, or as functions within an organization. The reason for this approach is that software CM, as contrasted with hardware CM, tends to be more deeply involved in the software engineering process and, while the same general CM functions are performed, the disciplines are extended to include the process of developing a baseline.

Software CM and release processing are performed within the context of several basic CM functions: configuration identification, baseline management, change control and library control, status accounting, reviews and audits, and release processing. In practice, the ways in which these functions are performed are different for the different kinds of programs being developed (commercial, embedded, OEM, etc), and may vary in the degree of formal documentation required within and across different life-cycle management phases (research phase, product development, operations, and maintenance).

Software CM also provides a common point of integration for all planning, oversight and implementation activities for a project or product line. These functions are performed within the context of a project — providing the framework (labeling and identification) for interfacing different activities and defining the mechanisms (change controls) necessary for coordinating parallel activities of different groups. SCM provides a framework for controlling computer program interfaces with their underlying support hardware, coordinating software changes when both hardware and software may be evolving during development or maintenance activities.

Finally, SCM is practiced within the context of management, providing management with the visibility (through status accounting and audits) of the evolving computer products that it needs to perform effectively.

2.1.1 SCM is a Service Function. Software CM is a support activity that makes technical and managerial activities more effective. Effectiveness of the SCM processes increases in proportion to the degree that its disciplines are an explicit part of the normal day-to-day activities of everyone involved in the development and maintenance efforts, (as opposed to a separate SCM organization or activity). This holds true whether SCM is administered by a separate SCM group, distributed among many projects, or a mixture of both.

2.1.2 SCM is a Part of the Engineering Process. The disciplines of SCM apply to the development of programmed logic, regardless of the form of packaging used for the application. Software engineering technology is effectively used in the generation of stored programmed logic when the complexity of the function is large. SCM disciplines assist in the identification and evolution of changes during the engineering process, even though the final package may be ROM, and managed as a hardware configuration item.

Configuration management is practiced in one form or another as a part of every software engineering activity where several individuals or organizations have to coordinate their activities. Although the basic disciplines of configuration management are common to both hardware and software engineering activities, there are some differences in emphasis due to the nature of the design activity. Software products (as compared to hardware products) are easy to change[4] (little if any lead time is needed for parts procurement and production setup).

Software CM is a discipline for managing the evolution of computer program products, both during the initial stages of development and during all stages of maintenance. The designs of programs are not easily partitioned into independent tasks due to their complexity. Therefore, configuration management disciplines are more valuable during the design (and redesign during maintenance) phases. This is when using techniques of multiple levels of baselines and internal releases (or promotions) to a larger degree than is typically practiced by hardware CM really pays off.

Whether software is released for general use as programs in RAM or embedded in ROM, it is a form of logic. Therefore, SCM disciplines can and should be extended to include development of the computer programs' component parts (for example, source code and executable code) whereas hardware CM focuses mainly on the management of documentation.

The differences between hardware and software CM, of importance to software CM, include

(1) Software CM disciplines are used to simultaneously coordinate configurations of many different representations of the software product (source code, relocatable code and executable code) rather than just their *documentation*. The nature of computer programs requires this extension and the SCM disciplines and related SCM support software adapt readily to this task.

(2) The use of interactive software development environments extends the concepts of software CM to managing evolutionary changes that occur during the routine generation of specifications, designs, and implementation of code, as well as to the more rigidly documented and controlled baselines defined during development and system maintenance.

(3) Software development environments are rapidly becoming automated with interactive tool sets. This modifies many of the traditional methods used in hardware CM but the fundamental concepts of CM still apply.

2.1.3 SCM Manages all Software Entities.
Software CM extends the management disciplines of hardware CM to include all of the entities of the product as well as their various representations in documentation. Examples of entities managed in the software engineering process include

(1) Management plans
(2) Specifications (requirements, design)
(3) User documentation
(4) Test design, case and procedure specifications
(5) Test data and test generation procedures
(6) Support software
(7) Data dictionaries and various cross-references
(8) Source code (on machine-readable media)
(9) Executable code (the run-time system)
(10) Libraries
(11) Data bases:
   (a) Data which are processed,
   (b) Data which are part of a program
(12) Maintenance documentation (listings, detail design descriptions, etc)

All supporting software used in development, even though not a part of the product, should also be controlled by configuration management disciplines.

Not all entities are subject to the same SCM disciplines at the same time. When the software product is under development, the documentation entities (baselined specifications and user requirements) are the most important. When coding begins, the documentation representing the design is the most important entity to be

---

[4] Even what is traditionally thought of as *hard* software—that is, firmware, is becoming easier to modify. An example is card edge programming where the programs in a ROM are easily modified, though not under program control during execution.
NOTE: While the time to change a design may be the same for hardware engineering as for software engineering, implementation and installation time is greater and consequently more expensive for hardware configuration items.

managed. Finally, when the product is ready for general use, the source code is the most accurate representation of the real product and the documentation is related so that representation is most important. These transitions of disciplinary focus over time are common to all SCM disciplines and need to be recognized in planning systems for effectively supporting project management.

Firmware[5] raises some special considerations for configuration management. While being developed, the disciplines of software CM apply; but when made a part of the hardware (*burned* into [EP]ROM), the disciplines of hardware CM apply. Testing may vary but the SCM requirements are generally the same. The packaging of [EP]ROM versus RAM code also introduces and necessitates different identification procedures, which are noted in 3.3.1.

2.1.3.2 The issue of what entities are to be managed often arises in the practical context of what gets captured in each library, and when. Consideration need also be given to the hierarchy of entities managed during this process. There are several different ways of looking at this hierarchy of entities; one, for example, is a three-level hierarchy:

(1) Configuration item (CSCI, CPCI, System, System Segment, Program package, module)

(2) Component (CPC, CSC, Subsystem, Unit, Package, Program function)

(3) Unit (Procedure, function Routine, Module)

The configuration control boards (CCB) that are oriented to business type management decisions usually select one level in this hierarchy as the level at which they will control changes. Other CCB may focus on more technical issues and would each select other levels, the module for example, as the control level for reviewing changes. See 2.2.5 for further discussion of control levels.

---

[5]**Firmware.** Computer programs and data loaded in a class of memory that cannot by dynamically modified by the computer during processing. Used here to generically refer to any programmed code implemented in nonvolatile memory such as [EP]ROM, regardless of its function; contrasts with code designed to execute out of volatile memory, such as RAM. There are differences between software intensive firmware and hardware intensive firmware. The key is ease of adaptability or degree with which programmed instructions are used, and the size of the program. Software intensive firmware denotes an activity that has available a set of tools commonly used in software engineering. Hardware intensive firmware denotes a development activity that has available a minimum of tools necessary for creation (*burn in*) of the firmware.

Another way of looking at entities to be managed is in terms of the interrelationships between the computer programs being developed and the other software entities used during development and testing of that program. This hierarchy is illustrated in Table 2.

Table 2
Hierarchy of Controlled Entities

Entity	Layer
Released entities	Product layer
Promoted entities	Test layer
Modifiable unique entities and support software	Invocation layers
Product development environment	Support software layer
Operating system	Run-time software layer

The SCM process should support each of these layers.

2.1.3.3 Still another way of viewing the entities is in terms of the intermediate products generated in the process of building the computer program product. Each of these intermediate products may be viewed as:

(1) *Modifiable entities.* These items are the individually modifiable units that are required to produce the deliverable entities. They are the source code, control files, data descriptions, test data, documents, etc, that constitute the focus of SCM. The entities at this level are referenced as *units* or *components* in this guide.

(2) *The compilation or assembly entities, such as compilers.* These are needed to develop, test and maintain the program throughout the life cycle of the product. These entities are referenced as *support software* in this guide.

(3) *Application-specific entities.* These are the different representations that are created in the process of producing the deliverables. Examples are the results produced by the compilation and assembly entities, and link/load entities, such as a link editor/locator. These culminate in the product that is released for general use. These entities are referenced as *configuration items* (CI) in this guide.

2.2 The Process of SCM

2.2.1 Management Environment of SCM. Software engineering, and therefore SCM, takes place within an organizational business environment. To be effective, SCM must blend in with and reflect the organization. It must take into account the management style — entrepreneurial, very disciplined, etc. The technical skills of the implementing organization must be taken into account as well as available resources when specifying whether SCM is to be performed by a single organization or distributed among several. The organization must also be responsive to the kinds of controls needed by the organization that will ultimately be using the product.

SCM management provides support to the organization by working within it to define implement policies, techniques, standards, and tools that facilitate their control of the SCM process. These processes assist other managers (and customers as required) by supporting effective configuration identification, change controls, status accounting, audits, and reviews.

2.2.2 Dynamics of SCM. The cornerstone activity of SCM is managing the change process and tracking changes to ensure that the configuration of the computer program product is accurately known at any given time. The change management is accomplished by completely identifying each baseline and tracking all subsequent changes made to that baseline. This process is used whether the baseline represents preliminary documentation, such as requirements, or a fully documented program including source and object code. All entities (specifications, documents, text data, and source code) are subject to this change management discipline.

Effectively managing baseline changes requires that a scheme for identifying the *structure* of the software product must be established. This structure relates to the hierarchical organization of the computer program and is extended to include all entities or work-products associated with the program. This identification scheme must normally be maintained throughout the full life of the computer program product. Usually a numbering scheme or file name scheme is associated with the structure, and unique and appropriate labels are assigned to each entity of the product.

As new baselines are created in transition by a promotion or release, the aggregate of entities is reviewed or audited to verify consistency with the old baseline, and the identification labeling is modified to reflect the new baseline. Changes to the different versions and revisions of each baseline are maintained. The history of changes to baselined configurations is maintained and made available to engineering and management in status reports. Figure 1 illustrates a model of the SCM process.

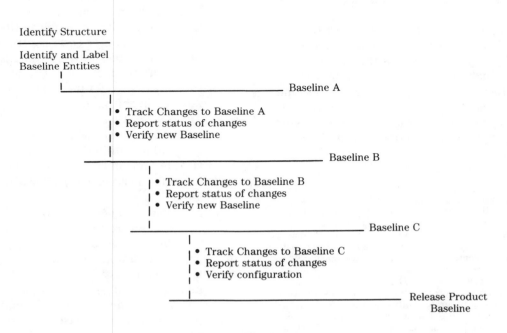

Fig 1
Model of Change Management

2.2.3 Role of Source Code in SCM. A key entity to be managed is the source code, since it is the basic representation in readable form of the product being controlled. Other forms of documentation and data are verified by comparison to this entity. At different phases in a development cycle, source code may not be available and different baselined entities may be defined as the basic representation. However, for most of the software life cycle, the source code provides the key entity for verification. The creation of executable code for the machine is directly derived (in the majority of computer systems) from the source code by various mechanized tools, such as assemblers, compilers, link/loaders, and interpreters. Recreation of source code (and object code) from design documentation can be costly. Therefore, to control only design documentation does not usually fully capture the implementation of the software. If the source code were to be lost because of improper, unreliable, or insufficient controls, the cost of recreating all of the source code would (in the majority of cases) be very expensive because of the typically incomplete state of the documentation.

Design documentation is verified against the product represented by the source code. The test entities (test design, text cases and procedures), test data (including data generation procedures) and test reports, are used to verify that the executable code (produced by the source code) matches the documentation. Documentation needed for maintenance (programming notebooks, etc) and user documentation are also verified against the source code.

Depending on the difficulty of rebuilding a complete set of executable code, the relocatable code may also be identified and considered an entity. However, the source code is generally considered to be the primary, if not sole source in establishing the product configuration.

Since source code can be interpreted differently by different compilers, it is necessary to control the versions of the support software used for a specific released product so as to have full control over the computer program product.

2.2.4 Different Levels of Control. Management delegates the authority for action downward to and including the work done by nonmanagement personnel. Management also selectively delegates aspects of control to nonmanagement personnel. In this guide, the term **levels of control** includes all control exercised by both management and nonmanagement. The term **authority** refers to control reserved by management for

management decisions relative to allocation of resources: schedule, production cost, customer requirements for product cost, performance, delivery, etc. Nonmanagement provides technical data to support these evaluations. Since the SCM Plan must identify all software CI (or classes thereof) that will be covered by the Plan, it must also define the level of management needed to authorize changes to each entity. As the software product evolves, it may be wise or necessary to increase the management authorization level (that is, level of control) needed. This can be accomplished through the internal part promotion hierarchy.

A general-use facility, which has many released software CI as well as CI under development, will often require many separate levels of control, and possibly different levels of authority for approving changes. For example, software CI that are used by several organizations may require change approval by management that is in charge of all those organizations. Not only the CI that will be delivered by the development group but also the level of authority for all vendor-supplied or internally developed software tools, utilities, operating systems, etc, used in the development need to be identified. Software CI used within any intermediate organization may usually require change approval by that organization's management. These intermediate organizations may have unique design or analysis tools for their own use on the project and can have change control authority over these tools.

2.3 The Implementation of SCM

2.3.1 Using Software Libraries. The techniques and methods used for implementing control and status reporting in SCM generally center around the operation of software libraries. Software libraries provide the means for identifying and labeling baselined entities, and for capturing and tracking the status of changes to those entities.

Libraries have been historically composed of documentation on hard copy and software on machine readable media, but the trend today is towards all information being created and maintained on machine-readable media.[6] This trend, which encourages the increased use of automated tools, leads to higher productivity. The trend also

---

[6]There may still be valid *legal* needs for maintaining hard copy versions of all baselined materials. The ability to eliminate hard copy media should not be construed as a necessary or even wise thing for an organization to do.

means that the libraries are a part of the software engineering working environment. The SCM functions associated with the libraries have to become a part of the software engineering environment, making the process of configuration management more transparent to the software developers and maintainers.

The number and kind of libraries will vary from project to project according to variations in the access rights and needs of their users, which are directly related to levels of control. The entities maintained in the libraries may vary in physical form based on the level of technology of the software tooling. When the libraries are automated, the libraries that represent different levels of control may be functionally (logically) different even though they are physically the same. The insertion of entities and changes to entities in a controlled library should produce an auditable authorization trail.

The names of libraries may vary, but fundamentally three kinds should be considered, as outlined in Fig 2.

The **dynamic library**, sometimes called the *programmer's library*, is a library used for holding newly created or modified software entities (units/modules or data files and associated documentation). This is the library used by programmers in developing code. It is freely accessible to the programmer responsible for that unit at any time. It is the programmers' workspace and controlled by the programmers.

The **controlled library**, sometimes called the *master library*, is a library used for managing the current baseline(s) and for controlling changes made to them. This is the library where the units and components of a configuration item that have been promoted for integration are maintained.

Entry is controlled, usually after verification. Copies may be freely made for use by programmers and others. Changes to units or components in this library must be authorized by the responsible authority (which could be a configuration control board or other body with delegated authority).

The **static library**, sometimes called the *software repository*, is a library used to archive various baselines released for general use. This is the library where the master copies plus authorized copies of computer program configuration items that have been released for operational use are maintained. Copies of these masters may be made available to requesting organizations.

2.3.2 Controlling Changes to Libraries. Several possible methods for controlling access to libraries are illustrated in the Appendixes. Appendix B prescribes formal change control of several configuration items at the component level within established baselines. Another approach is having rather informal methods for authorizing changes to configuration items. This method is used for fast integration of changes in a research type environment, as in Appendix B. For libraries having several configuration items including both external (third-party software) and internal (in-house developments) sources of supply, a mixture of formal methods for authorizing changes is applicable, as illustrated in Appendix C. Externally developed computer programs may be controlled at CI levels, whereas internally developed computer programs may be controlled at more discrete component levels. The procedures for authorizing changes may be integrated with the software tools in an integrated environment, as illustrated in Appendix D.

In summary, the levels of control described in each appendix are illustrated in Table 3.

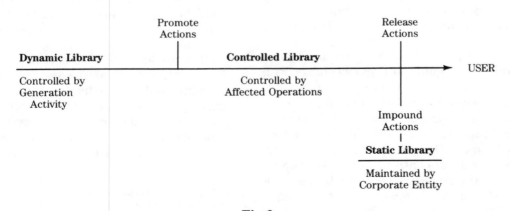

**Fig 2
Three Types of Libraries**

Table 3
Levels of Control in Sample Plans

	Appendix A	Appendix B	Appendix C	Appendix D
Number of CI	Several CI (internal)	3 CI (internal)	Internal CI External CI	2 CI (internal)
Components (CSC)	All components	NA	Internal components	Unit
Type of control	Formal	Informal	Formal	Formal (automated)

2.3.3 Using Configuration Control Boards. Another functional concept of SCM is the extended use of configuration control boards (CCB). This concept provides for implementing change controls at optimum levels of authority. Configuration control boards can exist in a hierarchical fashion (for example, at the program, system design, and program product level), or one such board may be constituted with authority over all levels of the change process. In most projects, the CCB is composed of senior level managers. They include representatives from the major software, hardware, test, engineering, and support organizations. The purpose of the CCB is to control major issues such as schedule, function, and configuration of the system as a whole.

The more technical issues that do not relate to performance, cost, schedule, etc, are often assigned to a software configuration control board (SCCB). The SCCB discusses issues related to specific schedules for partial functions, interim delivery dates, common data structures, design changes and the like. This is the place for decision-making concerning the items that must be coordinated across CI but which do not require the attention of high level management. The SCCB members should be technically well-versed in the details of their area; the CCB members are more concerned with broad management issues facing the project as a whole and with customer issues.

2.4 The Tools of SCM. The SCM software tools selected for use by a project and described in a Plan need to be compatible with the software engineering environment in which the development or maintenance is to take place.

SCM tools are beginning to proliferate and choices have to be made as to the tool set most useful for supporting engineering and management. There are many different ways of examining available SCM tools. One way is to categorize them according to characteristics of their products: a filing system, a data-base management system, and an independent knowledge-based system.[7] Another way is to examine the functions they perform: clerical support, testing and management support, and transformation support.[8] A third way of categorizing the SCM tools is by how they are integrated into the software engineering environment on the project. The current set of available SCM tools is classed in terms of the level of automation they provide to the programming environment on a project.

2.4.1 Basic Tool Set. This set includes:
(1) Basic data-base management systems
(2) Report generators
(3) Means for maintaining separate dynamic and controlled libraries
(4) File system for managing the check-in and check-out of units, for controlling compilations, and capturing the resulting products

This set is compatible with a programming environment that is relatively unsophisticated.

The tools control the information on hard copy regarding a program product. They assume a capability for maintaining machine processable libraries that distinguish between controlled and uncontrolled units or components. The tools simplify and minimize the complexity, time, and methods needed to generate a given baseline. Appendix B illustrates a project using such a tool set.

2.4.2 Advanced Tool Set. This set includes:
(1) Items in the basic tool set
(2) Source code control programs that will maintain version and revision history
(3) Compare programs for identifying (and helping verify) changes

---

[7] Reference: British Alvey Programme.

[8] Reference: *Life Cycle Support in the Ada*[9] *Environment* by Mc Dermid and Ripken.

[9] Ada is a registered trademark of the US Government, AJPO.

(4) Tools for building or generating executable code

(5) A documentation system (word processing) to enter and maintain the specifications and associated user documentation files

(6) A system/software change request/authorization (SCR/SCA) tracking system that makes requests for changes machine readable

This set provides a capability for a SCM group to perform more efficiently on larger, more complex software engineering efforts. It assumes a programming environment that has more computing resources available.

It provides the means of efficiently managing information about the units or components and associated data items. It also has rudimentary capabilities for managing the configurations of the product (building run-time programs from source code) and providing for more effective control of the libraries. Appendix A illustrates use of such a tool set.

2.4.3 On-Line Tool Set. This set includes:

(1) Generic tools of the advanced tool set integrated so they work from a common data base

(2) An SCR/SCA tracking and control system that brings generation, review, and approval of changes on-line

(3) Report generators working on-line with the common data base, and an SCR/SCA tracking system that enables the SCM group to generate responses to on-line queries of a general nature

This set of tools requires an interactive programming environment available to the project. It also provides an organization with the minimal state-of-the-art SCM capabilities needed to support the typical interactive programming environment currently available in industry. It assumes on-line access to the programming data base and the resources necessary for using the tools. Appendix C illustrates use of such a SCM tool set.

2.4.4 Integrated Tool Set. This set includes:

(1) On-line SCM tools covering all functions

(2) An integrated engineering data base with SCM commands built into the on-line engineering commands commonly used in designing and developing programs (most functions of CM are heavily used during design and development phases)

(3) The integration of the SCM commands with on-line management commands for building and promoting units and components

This set integrates the SCM functions with the software engineering environment so that the SCM functions are transparent to the engineer. The software engineer becomes aware of the SCM functions only when he/she attempts to perform a function or operation that has not been authorized (for example, changing a controlled entity when the engineer does not have the required level of authority or control). Appendix D illustrates a project having such an approach to SCM.

2.5 The Planning of SCM. Planning for SCM is essential to its success. Most of the routine activities associates with SCM are repetitious, clerical-type activities, which can be automated fairly easily. Effective SCM involves planning for how activities are to be performed, and performing these activities in accordance with the Plan. The more important disciplines of SCM, such as defining a scheme for identifying the configuration items, components, and units, or the systematic review of changes before authorizing their inclusion in a program, are management activities that require engineering judgment. Relating engineering judgment with management decisions, while also providing the necessary clerical support without slowing the decision-making process, is the critical role of SCM personnel and tools, or both.

SCM defines the interaction between a number of activities extending throughout the life cycle of the product. The SCM Plan functions as a centralized document for bringing together all these different points of view. The cover sheet of the Plan is usually approved by all of the persons with responsibilities identified in the Plan. This makes the Plan a living document, to be maintained by approved changes throughout the life of the computer programs.

Maintenance of the Plan throughout the life of the software is especially important as the disciplines of identification, status reporting, and record keeping apply throughout the maintenance part of the life cycle. Differences may be expected in how change processing is managed; and these need to be understood by all participants.

It should be clear from the information given above, but it is stated explicitly here, that the application (and thus the planning) of SCM is very sensitive to the context of the project and the organization being served. If SCM is applied as a corporate policy, it must not be done blindly, but rather it should be done in such a way that the details of a particular SCM application are reexamined for each project (or phase for very large projects). It must take into consideration the size, complexity, and criticality of the software system being managed; and the number of individuals, amount of personnel turnover, and organizational form and structure that have to interface during the life of the software system being managed.

This guide provides suggestions as to how ANSI/IEEE Std 828-1983 [2] can be interpreted for specific projects, and items to be considered in preparing a plan. The objective of the planner is to prepare a document that

(1) Clearly states the actions to be performed by software engineering and supporting activities that are required to maintain visibility of the evolving configuration of the computer program products

(2) Supports management in the process of evaluating and implementing changes to each configuration

(3) Assures that the changes have been properly and completely incorporated into each computer program product.

3. Software Configuration Management Plans

3.1 Introduction. Because SCM extends throughout the life cycle of the software product, the SCM Plan is the recommended focal point for integrating and maintaining the necessary details for software CM. Projects do differ in scope and complexity and a single format may not always be applicable. ANSI/IEEE Std 828-1983 [2] describes a minimum format for plans with a maximum amount of flexibility. If a section of the format is not applicable, the sentence *There is no pertinent information for this section* should be inserted to indicate that the section has not been overlooked.

It is desirable to provide a synopsis for users of the Software Configuration Management Plan and for the managers who must approve it. In each Appendix to this guide, a synopsis has been prepared to set the context surrounding the generation of the sample SCM Plan. For purposes of this guide, the viewpoint of each synopsis in the Appendixes is directed towards the user of the guide.

3.1.1 Purpose. The theme here is to inform the reader of the specific purpose of the SCM activity(ies) to be defined in the SCM Plan. It is sufficient to write a brief paragraph identifying

the system to which the particular SCM Plan applies, noting any dependencies on other SCM or CM Plans. For example, Appendix A emphasizes thoroughness of audits and reviews to assure conformance to contractual requirements for a computer program product; the theme is rigorous control of the configuration during development. Appendix B is directed towards low cost, quick response to changes, and documentation of the as-built versions of the computer programs. In Appendix C the theme is maintaining configuration control of many computer program products after development and while they are in use. This is complicated by the necessity to manage third-party software and subcontracted software along with internally developed software. Appendix D is directed towards the complex process of generating computer programs, and includes third-party software and subcontracted software in an environment where changes to configurations are driven by marketing, engineering, vendor changes, and customer demands, as well as the normal iteration of engineering changes.

3.1.2 Scope. The scope of the Plan encompasses the tasks of SCM. The function of the subsection is to

(1) Identify the specific SCM concerns

(2) Define what the Plan will and will not address

(3) Identify the items to be managed.

3.1.2.1 It is also important to identify the

(1) Lowest entity in the hierarchy (the control element) that will be reviewed by the top level project or system management CCB

(2) Smallest useful entity that will be reviewed (a module, a unit, a line of code) by technical management (SCCB)

(3) Deliverable entities or configuration item(s) to be released for use as separate entities

The definition and scope of each entity of the configuration item and the kind of control to be considered for each type of entity is also needed. A short description of relationships among configuration items may be appropriate. The boundary of the SCM activities may be described here with the help of graphics (block diagrams, tables, engineering drawing) as necessary.

**Issues to Consider in Planning
Section 1.2 — Scope**

(1) What are the characteristics of the configuration items to be controlled?

(a) Only one application program[10]
(b) Many separate small application programs
(c) An integrated set of application and support programs embedded in a system
(d) Computer programs as an integral part of a hardware system
(2) What are the different high-level interfaces to be managed?
  (a) People, organization interfaces
  (b) Subcontractor interfaces
  (c) Specification interfaces
  (d) Contractor interfaces
  (e) Hardware interfaces
  (f) Life cycle phase interfaces
  (g) Software interface
(3) What are the time frames of the project
  (a) Life cycle phases
  (b) Calendar time
(4) What resources will be available or required for the SCM activities?
  (a) Machine resources
  (b) Space resources
  (c) People resources
  (d) Schedule dependencies
(5) What are the software engineering entities to be controlled?
  (a) Contractual documents
  (b) Specifications
  (c) Other documentation
  (d) Test procedures, data, verification reports
  (e) Source code
  (f) Support software

3.1.3 Definitions. Subsection 1.3 of the Plan is used to capture all definitions needed for understanding the Plan or helpful for communication.

**Issues to Consider in Planning
Section 1.3 — Definitions**
(1) Are the definitions easily understood?
(2) Is there a list of definitions that can be easily referenced?
(3) Do you really need to define a new term?
(4) Can a glossary of acronyms be used?

---

[10]Throughout the guide, when lists are added to questions in the *issues to consider* NOTES, the lists are to be considered as suggested items, not an exhaustive checklist as in a standard.

It is best to use standard definitions that are common to the industry. For example, terms defined in ANSI/IEEE Std 729-1983 [1] have been arrived at by a consensus of professionals in the industry; it is a good source to use. Numerous new definitions tend only to make understanding the Plan more difficult. Define only those new terms that have to be defined — usually specific to the computer program product. Also duplicating definitions used elsewhere leads to unnecessary work to maintain them current — another configuration management task.

3.1.4 References. Subsection 1.4 of the Plan lists the documents cited elsewhere in the Plan. References made here refer to existing documents and, when customers are involved, the contractual standards and directives cited in the Plan. Having all the references in one place eliminates duplication of citing different sources. This makes a Plan that is more readable and supports general standardization of work instructions.

**Issues to Consider in Planning
Section 1.4 — References**
(1) Can policies, practices, and procedures that already exist within the organization be referenced?
(2) Is each reference necessary for the Plan?
(3) Are some references a part of the organization's directive system?

Large, critical software developments, such as illustrated in Appendix A, tend to rely on a set of standards that are shared with other projects. This makes for better communication among those using the same general system but at the cost of some flexibility. Smaller projects, such as cited in Appendix B do not need the cross-checks and redundancy of these generalized standards and tend to rely on fewer documented standards.

Referencing helps to reduce the bulk of the document that must be maintained. Care should be taken to reference only those documents that are directly applicable to the Plan. Excessive references will lessen the effectiveness of the more important references. A distinction should be made between references that are necessary for *execution* of the Plan and those documents that are included as *general or supplementary* information.

3.2 Management. Section 2 of the Plan has the theme of relating the elements of the SCM discipline to specific activities of the project's or company's management organization. It also provides an opportunity to specify budgetary, schedule, and resource requirements necessary to carry out the Plan.

3.2.1 Organization. In 2.1 of the Plan, functions are allocated to organizational entities. Interfaces between organizations are handled in a separate section (2.3). The functions of the SCM department itself (if it will exist) are defined in more detail in 2.2. It is not necessary or desirable in most cases to allocate all SCM functions to an SCM department; SCM is a part of the entire software engineering process and as such may best be accomplished by the various organizations actually performing the systems engineering or integration. Software Development, Systems Engineering, Test and Quality Assurance departments all may assume significant roles in carrying out SCM functions. The *Issues to Consider* listed below are designed to provide a starting point in looking at the project's work-flow in relation to the current management structure and to support consideration of how the SCM activities can be best allocated or coordinated.

**Issues to Consider in Planning
Section 2.1 — Organization**

(1) What kind of product interfaces have to be supported within the project itself?
  (a) Software — hardware
  (b) Software — software
  (c) Software maintained at multiple sites
  (d) Software developed at different sites
  (e) Dependencies on support software
  (f) Maintenance changes generated from different sites

(2) What are the capabilities of the staff available to perform CM specific activities?

(3) What is the management style of the organization within which the software is being developed or maintained?

(4) Who will be responsible for maintaining the support software?

(5) What organizational responsibilities are likely to change during the life of the Plan?
  (a) Project management organization

  (b) Organizational interfaces
  (c) Configuration management organization

(6) Who has the authority to capture data and information and who has authority to direct implementation of changes?

(7) What are the plans for maintaining current organization charts(s)?

(8) What level of management support is needed forimplementing various portions of the SCM discipline?

(9) Will the project management be confined to a single organization or will it be distributed among several organizations?

(10) Are responsibilities for processing changes to baselines clearly indicated, including who
  (a) Originates changes
  (b) Reviews changes
  (c) Signs-off changes
  (d) Approves changes
  (e) Administers the process
  (f) Validates and checks for completion?

(11) Who has the authority to release any software, data, and associated documents?

(12) Who has the responsibility for various SCM activities?
  (a) Ensuring the integrity of the software system
  (b) Maintaining physical custody of the baselines
  (c) Performing product audits (versus quality audits)
  (d) Library management
  (e) Developing and maintaining specialized SCM tools

(13) How is authority vested for handling exceptional situations and waivers?

If the plan for maintaining organizational charts shows a certain organization or management group (such as the program office or the business management office) assuming this responsibility, it may be wise to reference those charts in the Plan rather than placing the actual chart in the document, which must then be maintained every time another group of charts is updated. Alternatively, the organizational chart may be shown in the initial version of the Plan with a footnote directing readers to the proper official source for updates. It is usually best to include organizational charts that refer only to functional names (such as department names) rather than to individuals responsible for managing them. This information is quite dynamic in most organizations, and it is probably not worth updating a Plan every time a department is assigned a new manager.

Consider advantages of alternative forms of organizing activities. Appendix A illustrates a complex, critical software development where there is a strong need for independence and centralization of SCM duties in a functional type organization. Appendix C also illustrates a functional type organization but for a different reason: in a software maintenance environment, SCM plays a stronger role in managing the change processing, even to the scheduling of work — more so than in a typical development environment.

Another point to consider is the management support for the various SCM disciplines. Note, for example, in Appendix B the management supported some concepts of SCM but wanted the process to be as *painless* as possible for the software developers and customers. The SCM administrator established a method of collecting information necessary to achieve the purpose without interfering with the flow of changes to the sites. Similarly, the other Appendixes illustrate SCM practices that are tailored to the reality of the situations in which they are found.

For ease of reading, organize the tasks and the owners in terms of the classical set of CM functions: identification, configuration control, status accounting, and audits and reviews. The matrix in Appendix A, Table 1 illustrates how this kind of information can easily be presented.

3.2.2 SCM Responsibilities. If a specific SCM department or group is identified in the management structure, this section provides a specific description of the role this organization will play in the overall SCM process.

**Issues to Consider in Planning
Section 2.2 — SCM Responsibilities**
(1) Are there any special considerations for this project that require the SCM department to change its standard method of doing business?
(2) What explicit assumptions is the SCM group making in planning their part of the project?

---

(3) Are there specific expectations on the part of the customer or client (such as contractual requirements) for an SCM group that need to be taken into account?

While the major considerations may center on responsibilities of the configuration control boards (CCB), there is the need to consider the responsibilities of other activities such as software quality assurance (SQA), users of the system, other system or hardware configuration control boards, and other management activities.

3.2.3 Interface Control. The theme of subsection 2.3 of the Plan is how SCM disciplines are coordinated and how they are used to manage interfaces throughout the project's life. This is the place to define the roles and composition of the various CCB, SCCB, and other activities and practices used for interface control. All types of interfaces should be considered.

The scope of the SCM Plan (1.2) specifies the boundaries of the CI and the jurisdiction of the Plan, but this boundary is often not as clear as it should be and the control mechanisms are even fuzzier. The definition of interfaces is one of the most important planning elements for ensuring a smooth operation. Every possible effort should be made to reach a common agreement regarding each organization's responsibility regarding the interface(s), and then document them in this subsection. The basic types of interfaces to consider here include organization, phase, software, and hardware.

Organizational interface elements include interfaces between various organizations involved with the product; for example, vendor to buyer, subcontractor to contractor, and co-developer to co-developer. It is typical that different organizations have different views of a product and will apply different expectations to it. Effective SCM disciplines can help minimize and resolve these differences whenever and wherever they may arise.

Phase interface elements include transition interfaces between those life cycle phases of the product that are included in the Plan. They are often coincident with a transition in control of the product between different organizations; for example, promotion from a development group to a formal testing group. Effective SCM disciplines can support these transitions with all the documentation, code, data, tools, and records that are needed for management to smoothly continue SCM on the product.

Software interface elements are the agreements shared between the computer program product and other software entities (for example, operating system, utilities, communication system). These agreements involve the structure and meanings assigned to data passing and operational coordination of the data and the results. The other software may already exist or may be concurrently developed. Effective SCM disciplines can make these agreements generally known and assist management in maintaining the integrity of the product(s).

Hardware interface elements are the agreements shared between the computer program product and characteristics of any hardware in the environment with which the program product interacts. These agreements involve capabilities provided by the hardware and operations defined by the computer programs. Effective SCM disciplines help make these agreements known and support their evaluation for consistency throughout the evolution of both hardware and software.

**Issues to Consider in Planning
Section 2.3 — Interface Control**

(1) What are the organizational interfaces?
(2) What are the important interfaces between adjacent phases of the life cycle?
(3) What are the interfaces between different entities of the computer programs?
(4) What are the dependent hardware interfaces?
(5) Where are the documents defined and maintained that are used in interface control?
(6) What are the procedures for making changes to these interface documents?

Interface control should be extended to include more than just documentation. If the hardware configuration and its supporting software interfaces are complex, then the Plan must also include or reference controls for hardware drawings and equipment as well. The sample Plan in Appendix D illustrates the interface between multiple kinds of computer programs in a variable hardware configuration. In real-time system environments, the interface controls may involve tracking changes to configurations of external sensors, valves, etc. Typically, in a software modification and maintenance situation, human operator interface controls may play a significant role in this section. In

some organizations, [EP]ROM are considered hardware, yet the programs residing in them must be explicitly dealt with in this section of the Plan. The guiding principle of SCM is that any proposed changes to the product or to its expected use be considered and evaluated in an open, documented, deliberate, and mutually acceptable fashion.

3.2.4 SCM Plan Implementation. Subsection 2.4 of the Plan has the theme of providing details concerning the implementation of the key SCM milestones identified in the Plan. These details include:

(1) Identification of prerequisites or required activities that affect the Plan and the sequencing of events in the Plan
(2) Schedules for accomplishing these items
(3) Resource requirements (for example, machine time, disk space, specialized tool availability, and staff support)

The implementation section's level of detail and complexity are dependent on the level of complexity of the system being controlled. Small software development activities, particularly those that focus primarily on software and are not currently tied to hardware systems development, may need relatively simple implementation schedules. SCM Plans that support more complex activities, such as software maintenance (Appendix C) or development and maintenance of product line software (Appendix D), will have more complex implementation schedules but will focus more on events such as release for use, new product baselines, audits, and reviews.

**Issues to Consider in Planning
Section 2.4 — SCM Plan Implementation**

(1) Are the resources planned for SCM commensurate with the size and complexity of the system being controlled?
(2) How will the SCM activities be coordinated with other project activities?
(3) How will the different phases (development, maintenance) be managed throughout the software life cycle?

Resource requirements should be carefully considered and included here only when they are important factors in implementing the Plan. If there are any separate project documents that contain the necessary information (for example, department budgets, development laboratory implementation Plans), include them here by reference to avoid unnecessary document maintenance. Items to include are:

(1) People resources
(2) Computer and computer-related resources
(3) Library space
(4) Storage space (including electronic media)

It is usually impractical to put actual dates in the Plan for events. In general, it is better from the maintenance perspective to put actual dates in a schedule chart kept in an appendix or a separate document. In this section it is more appropriate to refer to significant events in terms of their relationships to other milestones (for example, a controlled library for source code will be established following the completion of the critical design review), or in terms of their relationship in time to other events (for example, the physical configuration audit will be held 90 days after the functional qualification test).

Requirements for implementation should be discussed in the same sequence in this section as they are discussed in the body of your Plan (for example, configuration identification is followed by product baselines). This should make correlating the Plan with the implementation considerations easier for the user.

Keep in mind that this section should be updated as the project continues. Consider reviewing this section and making any necessary additions or changes upon the achievement of each major milestone in the system development life cycle (for example, completion of functional design) or on a periodic basis (for example, once per quarter).

Project managers are often asked to provide a budget for SCM separate from the development budget. Little historical data are reported in the literature, primarily because every SCM activity has a slightly different organizational structure. In the example given in Appendix B, the project defined 0.5 full time equivalent man-months. Other types of projects, such as illustrated in Appendix A, will require a larger portion of dedicated SCM personnel. In general, however, as more effective automated tools are deployed and used, the need for dedicated personnel will diminish.

3.2.5 Applicable Policies, Directives, and Procedures. Subsection 2.5 of the Plan has the theme of identifying and defining the degree to which existing and future SCM policies and procedures apply to the Plan. The actual identification of referenced documents, and information on how to obtain them should be cited in Section 1.4 of the Plan. Subsection 2.5 provides the opportunity to *interpret the use* of reference document(s) and to describe any new document(s) that may be planned or are under development (which, obviously, cannot be cited in Section 1.4 of the Plan).

**Issues to Consider in Planning
Section 2.5 — Applicable Policies,
Directives and Procedures**

(1) Are any standard identification procedures available?
  (a) Standard labels for products
  (b) Identification of the hierarchical structure of computer programs
  (c) Component and unit naming conventions and limitations
  (d) Numbering or version level designations
  (e) Media identification methods (including [EP]ROM)
  (f) Data-base identification methods
  (g) Documentation labeling and identification standards
(2) Are any specific procedures existing for interacting with the dynamic libraries?
  (a) Promoting from one type of library to another
  (b) Documentation releases
  (c) Releasing computer program products
  (d) Releasing firmware products
(3) Are there standard procedures for managing the change process?
  (a) Handling change or enhancement requests
  (b) Provisions for accepting changes into a controlled library
  (c) Processing problem reports
  (d) Membership in CCB
  (e) Operating CCB
  (f) Capturing the audit trail of changes
(4) Are any status accounting procedures available?
  (a) Reporting procedures for summarizing problem reports

(b) Standard reports and other formatted management information
(c) Distributing status data
(5) Are there procedures for audits?
(a) Procedures for functional configuration audits
(b) Procedures for physical configuration audits
(6) Are there procedures for other general SCM activities?
(a) Standards for accessing and controlling libraries, including security provisions, change processing, backups and long-term storage
(b) Forms or file definitions for problem reports, change requests, documentation change notices, etc

The set of procedures need not be developed at one time; but effort consistently applied over a period of time can generate an adequate set of policies and procedures that are effective. The kinds of policies, directives, and procedures that are part of an organization's general practices and procedures might also be considered a part of the Plan.

3.3 SCM Activities. The SCM organizational descriptions in Section 2 of the Plan describe who has what responsibilities for software configuration management. Section 3 of the Plan describes how these groups accomplish their responsibilities.

3.3.1 Configuration Identification. The theme of this subsection is to document an identification scheme that reflects the structure of the product. This is a critical task of SCM, a most difficult task but one that is necessary for a smoothly running SCM operation. It is critical because the flow of management control must follow the structure of the software being managed. It is important because the identification scheme carries forth through the life of the computer program(s). It is difficult because at the time the identification scheme is constructed, the structure of the product is rarely known to the level of detail required during the development process.

Relating the identification scheme to the structure of the computer programs is complicated because there are generally two levels of identification that SCM has historically kept separate. The first level, the identification of configuration items and components recognized by management and users, is identified traditionally by

documentation. This is the level associated with released programs. The second level, the labeling of files (parts), is more unique to software and is constrained by the support software used in generating code. File nomenclature must support the structure of the product. Typically, these files are identified with mnemonics unique to a project and need to be correlated back to the identification scheme. This is the level associated with the parts of a released program. SCM not only must set identification schemes for both of these levels, but also must devise a method for relating the two different views of the same product.

Project management generally determines the criteria for identifying CI and subordinate control level items. SCM then devises the identification numbering or labeling structure for tracking those entities.

Other kinds of problems that should be considered include legal responsibilities. Some contracts require that all new code added to a program belongs legally to the owner of the original computer programs. Problems of third-party software acquisition must also be considered. The legal status of each program should be accurately identifiable before the computer programs are released for use. Usually some controls must be placed on the number of copies of third-party software *passed through* and delivered to customers as royalty payments might even be required.

**Issues to Consider in Planning
Section 3.1 — Configuration Identification**
(1) What scheme is to be used to relate the identification of files to the formal (document based) identification scheme?
(2) How does one relate the software identification scheme to the hardware identification scheme when the computer programs are deeply embedded in the system (for example, device controller firmware, code and data split between ROM firmware and loadable RAM image code)?
(3) How does one identify computer programs embedded in [EP]ROM?
(4) What specifications and management plans need to be identified and maintained under configuration management?
(5) What timing is involved in naming documents as CI?

(a) When does a document enter into controlled status (for example, when presented by author, when reviewed, when rework is verified, or when the document is formally distributed)?

(b) When and how does a document get removed from the CI status?

(6) Is a separate identification scheme needed to track third-party software?

(7) Is a special scheme needed to identify reusable/reused software as different from other software parts?

(8) Are there differences in identification across projects that have different fiscal accounting?

(9) How does one identify support software such as language translators, linkers, and cross-support tools?

(10) Is a special identification scheme needed to identify test data (transaction files, data-bases, etc) that must be kept for regression testing?

(11) Is there a need to identify tables and files for data driven systems?

One practice for identification of parts of a CI (as illustrated in Appendix A) is to use a version description document to relate the different files to the component or configuration item scheme. A suggested practice for embedding computer programs into hardware systems is illustrated in Appendix D where the system index type of project identification is used.

The management of firmware changes can become difficult when the package becomes a part of the hardware item. The problem remains to relate functional capabilities to physical part identifiers, especially when changes to the firmware are closely coupled to changes in the system or application software (for example, boot loaders, device controllers, and high-level ROM-resident system debuggers).

Third-party software needs to be tracked even though it is not changed in the same manner as other software. This is especially important if you, as a reseller, accept responsibility of collecting and dealing with problem reports generated by your customers for these products. It may be necessary too for compliance with legal restrictions on copies and distribution accounting. Appendix C describes this identification situation.

The successful reuse of pieces of software

in a (controlled) production library requires a standardized identification scheme to retrieve packages or units and account for their use in different configurations. Appendix C, 3.1 references identification of reused software. It should be noted that it is important to control the test procedures and test cases needed for regression testing in an environment that maintains such software or has extensive dynamic libraries of reusable software.

The identification scheme needs to reference dependent supporting software. Therefore, provisions must be made for identifying the internal documentation, data, and programs used in the generation of the computer program product(s).

3.3.1.2 Identify Project Baselines. Baselines are an effective mechanism to allow many people to work together at the same time. They are a way of synchronizing people working on the same project. The SCM discipline, as in all CM, focuses its activity around the construction and maintenance of baselines. The modifiable units need an identifying mechanism, and a way of describing what is contained in their aggregates is needed. Even if the program is small, a baseline is used to let the other, nonprogramming people, know what is taking place.

Issues to Consider in Defining Baselines

(1) Are baselines other than, for example, the traditional three required[11] to support the project?

(2) Who is needed to authorize the creation of new baselines?

(3) Who approves a baseline for promotion?

(4) How and where are the baselines created and who is responsible for them?

(5) How will the numbering system account for different baselines?

---

[11] The traditional baselines used in CM (functional, allocated, product) are defined in ANSI/IEEE Std 828-1983 [2] along with the minimal requirements for identifying and establishing those baselines. Additional internal or developmental baselines can be defined and included in the Plan when necessary. For example, in making multiple builds, it is useful to define separate baselines for each build to keep the status of changes straight. The sample SCM Plan in Appendix B illustrates the use of multiple builds. These developmental baselines are very helpful for integrating and testing large software systems.

(a) Different versions (functional changes)
(b) Different revisions (something to make the existing functions work)
(6) How are baselines verified?
(a) Reviews
(b) Customer approval
(c) Developer test reports
(d) Independent verification and validation
(7) Are baselines tied to milestones?
(a) Developmental milestones
(b) New versions

Baselines tie documentation, labeling, and the program together. Developmental baselines define a state of the system at a specific point in time, usually relative to an integration level, and serve to synchronize the engineering activity and documentation that occurs at that time.

Promotions are basically a change in the informal authority required to effect changes in developmental baselines. The new authority commonly represents a higher level of engineering management. The programmer cannot change a unit that has been promoted and integrated with other programmer's units without notifying the others involved, and gaining their (explicit or implicit) approval by way of an SCCB (or CCB).

The more formal baselines (functional, allocated, and product) define a product capability associated with performance, cost, and other user interests. These baselines relate the product to contractual commitments.

3.3.1.3 Delineate Project Titling, Labeling, Numbering. This part of the Plan defines the procedures and labels for identifying the CI, components, and units. This is important for identifying and retrieving information, reporting status and for legal protection of data rights.

Issues to Consider in Labeling and Numbering

(1) Is there a (corporate) standard for labeling that must be used?
(2) Does the identification scheme provide for identification of versions and revisions for each release?
(3) How can or will the physical media be identified?
(4) Are specific naming conventions available for all modifiable entities?

---

(5) Does the identification scheme need to identify the hierarchy of links between modifiable entities?
(6) Are there constraints on unit and file names?
(a) Compiler and file system limitations on name length and composition
(b) Mnemonic requirements
(c) Names that cannot be used

It is often useful to have the identification label indicate the level (that is, release, version, and revision) of the product it identifies. Labeling the components or units of computer programs can be accomplished in several ways. Numbering schemes can be devised to identify the components. A hierarchy of names can be devised that organizes and identifies parts using mnemonic or English labels. Naming conventions that are associated with the compilation system and are significant for a project are most easily used.

[EP]ROM labeling has special problems and will require a different scheme than that used for RAM-based packages shipped on disk or tape. In developing embedded computer programs, there is the additional consideration of labeling the media ([EP]ROM) with the correct version of the programs. This means that the identification scheme of some computer program packages must somehow relate to the hardware identification scheme. One possible solution is to use the version description document (VDD) form for relating the computer program identification documents to the altered item drawings conventionally used for identifying the [EP]ROM parts.

3.3.2 Configuration Control. Subsection 3.2 of the Plan describes how the configuration control process is managed. The theme here deals with identifying the procedures used to process changes to known baselines. An appropriate level of authority for controlling changes must be identified or delegated for each baseline. The organizations assigned responsibilities for control in Section 2 of the Plan have to manage changes made to the entities identified as defined in Section 3.1 of the Plan. Procedures for processing the requests for changes and approvals must be defined.

3.3.2.1 Levels of Authority. The levels of authority required to make changes to configuration items under SCM control can vary. The system or contract may often dictate the level of authority needed. For example, internally controlled software tools may require less change controls than man-rated or critical software developed under contract. The levels of authority may vary throughout the life cycle. For example, changes to code in the development cycle usually require a lower level of control to be authorized than changes to the same code after it has been released for general use. The level of authority required can also depend on how broadly the change impacts the system. A change affecting specifications during the requirements analysis phase has less ramifications than a change affecting software in operational use. Likewise, changes to draft versions of documents are less controlled than changes to final versions. Changes to a product distributed to several sites and used by many different users requires a different level of authority than products with a very restricted or minimal user base.

The level of control needed to authorize changes to developmental baselines depends on the level of the element in relation to the system as a whole (for example, a change in logic affecting one or a few units usually has less impact on the system than an interface between CI, especially if the CI are developed by different organizations.

Issues to Consider in Defining Levels of Authority

(1) Is the level of authority consistent with the entities identified in subsection 3.1 of the Plan?

(2) When are levels of control assigned to the modifiable units (parts) of the computer programs during top level and detail design stages (technical engineering phase) for developmental baselines?

(3) Do control levels assigned for developmental baselines (for both components and configuration items) need to be reviewed by management?

(4) Are there significant increases in levels of control for transitions between developmental baselines?

   (a) During design

   (b) For promotion from design to implementation

   (c) For unit testing

   (d) For integration

(5) Does management need to know specifically who requested a change?

(6) Do changes originating from outside the organization, such as customers or general users, require different authority for approval than changes from a technical development group?

(7) Do changes that do not impact formal baselines require coordination and approval by a CCB or can they be authorized by a SCCB?

The Plan should clearly define the level of authority to be applied to the baselined entities throughout the life cycle of the system, and should distinguish between controls applied to processing technical changes that do not impact formal baselines and the authority needed to approve changes to formal baselines. For example, during maintenance or in the latter stages of preparing multiple builds for a project, authority for making changes to all entities at all levels is typically restricted. However, when beginning development of a new version or build, the controls on the dynamic library and testing with the controlled library can be relaxed.

Table 4 suggests some ideas for assigning different levels of change authority to different SCM elements during the life cycle.

3.3.2.2 Processing Changes. The theme of these paragraphs is to describe the methods to be used for processing change requests. Generally, no single procedure can meet the needs of all levels of change management and approval levels. These paragraphs must concentrate on

(1) Defining the information needed for approving a change

(2) Identifying the routing of this information

**Table 4
Variable Levels of Control**

Element	Internal Coordination	Developmental Baselines	Formal Baselines
Specifications	Supervision	CCB	CCB
Test data	Supervision	SCCB	CCB
Unit code	Supervision	SCCB	CCB
Configuration Item code	SCCB	CCB	CCB

(3) Describe the control of the library(ies) used in processing the changes

(4) Describe or refer to the procedure for implementing each change in the code, in the documentation, and in the released program (for example, field upgrades).

The change initiator should analyze the proposed change to assess its impact on all configuration items (documentation, software, and hardware) and the CCB should satisfy themselves that this has been done and interface with the CCB in the impacted areas (if any).

Another area that is often overlooked (and not specifically covered) is that of the maintenance of design documentation. The documentation hierarchy should be fully defined and a change to any level should be analyzed to ensure that the higher levels of documentation have been considered and that the change is *rippled through* the lower levels to implementation in the code.

Source code changes, and indeed hardware changes, should first be implemented in the highest level of documentation and the change implemented through the subsequent levels. Provisions for backing up of changes and maintaining their history need to be considered.

A more critical issue centers on managing controlled libraries. This configuration management concept grew out of the SCM experience with managing source code and has been expanded to include all of the baseline items (including associated documentation and reports) that relate to the computer programs. One can observe that as the interactive programming environments continue to evolve, most of the procedural controls associated with SCM will probably be integrated into the programming environment. The procedures for processing changes are the same, whether for approval by a designated management authority or approval by a control activity (SCCB) delegated by management. The procedure needs to distinguish the proper channels for making the decisions, defining the flow for changes made to an established formal baseline, and the flow for changes made to developmental baselines. Most of this capability is now available in SCM and software engineering tools in one form or another.

Issues to Consider in Processing Changes

(1) What is the information necessary for processing a software/system change request (SCR) or authorizing a change (SCA)?

(2) What kind of information will a CCB or SCCB need in order to make a decision?

(3) What is the overall processing cycle of changes?

(4) What SCM support is provided by automated tools available in the environment?

(5) Will changes in procedures be required to support different kinds of reviews during each of the phases of the life cycle?

(6) When there are multiple CCB in a hierarchy, what are the procedures for information exchange and approval chains?

(7) Is there a need for dynamic libraries and controlled library interfaces?

(8) Is there a need for controlling all access to a library or just controlling changes made to the information in the libraries?

(9) Does the library system provide an audit trail, such as change histories?

(10) Are back-up and disaster files taken into account?

(11) Are there provisions for archive procedures to provide the static library support to the full life cycle?

(12) How are source items (source code) associated with their derived object (executable code) programs?

(13) What are the provisions for *draw down* or *check out* to get units from the controlled library?

(14) What are the provisions for keeping the data files synchronized with the program(s) using them?

(15) How does the change process itself support or accommodate the development of new versions or revisions?

Some library tools maintain *deltas* to base units of source code. Procedures for maintaining version histories of units as well as derived configuration items need to be established along with archiving maintenance.

A CCB concerned with project management may need information regarding estimated cost and schedules for a change, as illustrated in Appendix B. Other CCB may be interested only in the technical interfaces affected by a change, as illustrated in the sample Plan in Appendix C. Still others may need, in addition, information on proprietary rights and copyrights affected, as illustrated in Appendix D.

Some CCB review a proposed change to validate it (approve it as a necessary change; to expend time and resources for investigating feasibility of the change) while others may simply want completed (programmed and documented) changes to be approved prior to inclusion in released computer programs. There are different functions of SCCB responsibility, extending from coordinating engineering technical changes to allocating the work to a work group. Some organizations design, code and test all proposed changes with preliminary CCB approval before submitting them for final CCB approval. This technique may reduce total time to produce a change. The process for granting change approvals must guarantee that unauthorized changes do not contaminate baselined software.

Some advanced tools provide capabilities for formatting change requests, routing to different sets of individuals for approvals, and authorizing work to be done; reviewing changes and tests while in a holding area; and releasing a baseline to a controlled library for operational use. Others provide only for the recording of change information and a history of past versions of source code.

If secure procedures are not in place or feasible for controlling a library system, the library may necessarily be divided into physical entities that control access.

3.3.2.3 The Configuration Control Board.

The theme of these paragraphs is identifying the authorities needed for granting change approvals. Subsection 2.2 of the management section of the Plan identifies the general role(s) of each CCB. These paragraphs go into detail on the roles and authority. It should be remembered that the CCB has traditionally been concerned with managing changes to established baselines of documented configuration items and the components of those configuration items. There may be other change control bodies (SCCB) that authorize changes subordinate to the CCB described here. The CCB described in these paragraphs of the Plan have the role of authorizing changes to baselined configuration items and components from the point of view of entrepreneurial management. They reflect concerns over the costs, schedules, and resources available to implement changes in response to user desires for change.

Issues to Consider in Identifying Configuration Control Boards

(1) Can the limits of authority be defined?
    (a) Limited to contractual baselines as in Appendix A
    (b) Limited to developmental baselines (noncontractual) as in Appendix D
(2) Will the project mix computer programs that are controlled by other CCB?
(3) Is there a need to limit the CCB tabling actions by setting time limits?
(4) Are there contractual requirements imposed on a CCB that must be reflected in the Plan?
(5) How are the different levels of authority determined?
(6) How are different organizational bodies phased in when transitioning from one phase of the life cycle to another?
(7) How are changes to a baselined product to be batched together for release?
    (a) For a new version
    (b) For a revision
(8) Does the CCB membership reflect the management style of the organization?
    (a) For a functional organization
    (b) For a matrixed organization

Large, complex systems require ongoing configuration control authorities to coordinate the technical work involved in generating specifications and code, and in continuing the work of technical coordination required for maintaining interacting software systems (such as defined in Appendix C). Such projects use the same principles of configuration management and perform the same generic approval and scheduling functions as the CCB concerned with smaller-scale entrepreneurial management, particularly where automated SCM tools are used to support both types of activities.

Large software systems are frequently not completely new. They are often mixtures of software in public domain, vendor-supplied products, vendor supplied but modified by a contractor, subcontracted software, proprietary software, and software paid for on another project but reused or adapted. The procedures of how the CCB handles the special nature of proprietary software and reusable software are important and need to be specifically addressed in a Plan.

It may be noted that the CCB concept is another one of those functional concepts of SCM. On a small project, the CCB could be the *chief programmer* and the system will function quite adequately.

Any other change approval activities, such as the SCCB that supports the CCB, also needs to be identified and their roles defined. In some installations, the CCB may need to have the technical expertise to make the final decision on whether a requested change is technically feasible. Other CCB must be supported by technical experts or be prepared to delegate a level of change authorization to qualified subordinate bodies. *In general, decision making that affects the allocation and scheduling of development or maintenance resources should be separated from decision making motivated by various technical and marketing issues.*

3.3.2.4 Interface With Other CCB. Large or complex systems can have many hardware-software interfaces (as documented in the Interface Control [2.3] subsection of the Plan) that require continued ongoing change coordination. Sometimes these boards are called program change review boards (PCRB). The Plan needs to include a description of how these interfaces are handled and documented so all of the people on the projects know how to get the job done (this will probably involve both formal and informal organizational structures and interfaces).

**Issues to Consider in Describing
CCB Interfaces**

(1) Are there a number of CCB that have to work together, as illustrated in Appendix C, or is there only one that has total responsibility for the software configuration items?

(2) Is there a hierarchy of CCB that have authority for making business-type management decisions such as illustrated in Appendixes A and D?

(3) Who has the responsibility and authority for maintaining communications with these CCB?

(4) What body or authority has been designated to arbitrate deadlocks when two parallel CCB are unable to resolve an issue?

(5) What are the procedures for resolving differences of opinion?

---

(6) What needs to be done to maintain responsive communication and time limits on decision making?

3.3.2.5 Support Software. The theme of these paragraphs has to do with managing all the other software needed to build and maintain the computer program products throughout their life cycle. Specifically, this focus is on describing the necessary controls used to manage support software. Support software, which may be user-furnished, developed in-house, leased from a vendor or purchased off-the-shelf, is the class of software which may or may not be delivered with a product, but yet is necessary for designing, enhancing, or testing the changes made during the life of a delivered computer program product. The developer or maintainer needs to ensure that the support software is available for use for as long as may be necessary. For example, compilers need to be archived for use later *as is* when implementing enhancements to prevent subtle compiler dependencies from turning simple enhancements into major upgrades. Host systems, when used, and utility programs and test drivers are also needed.

**Issues to Consider in Planning
SCM of Support Software**

(1) What is the total set of support software used to design, develop, and test the software controlled under this Plan?

(2) Is this set of software archived and maintained for the full life cycle of the computer program products?

(3) What procedures are to be followed to introduce new versions of support software that impact the software within the scope of the Plan?

(4) How are problems resolved and changes made in the support software that impact the configurability or maintainability of the software within the scope of the Plan?

(5) How is the hardware configuration used to develop and maintain the software product identified and maintained for the full life cycle of the computer program product?

It is necessary to determine the appropriate level of software support needed for maintenance of the product throughout its full life cycle. What is sufficient and necessary for the job but not prohibitive in terms of support software costs for maintenance? In some situations, it can be very costly to actually maintain or enhance some of the support tools. For example, fixing bugs in a compiler may trigger unknown changes in production software after it is simply recompiled. *Whenever a production baseline is established, it is very important to archive all environment and support tools along with the production code.*

3.3.3 Configuration Status Accounting. The theme of this subsection is identifying what information is needed for various activities, obtaining the information and reporting it. The concern is with the acquisition of the right information at the right time so reports may be made when they are needed. In essence, this is a typical data management problem. Status accounting may be literally thought of as an accounting system; many of the concepts used to track the flow of funds through accounts may be used to track the flow of software through its evolution. Using this accounting analogy, separate accounts can be established for each CI. Individual transactions can then be tracked through each account as they occur. The configuration status accounting function, at a minimum, is basically reporting the transactions occurring between SCM-controlled entities.

The functional capabilities of the library system (or the software programming environment), in conjunction with the SCM tools, determine in a large way the capabilities of the status accounting function. As well as providing *live* information regarding the development process, the configuration of each released baseline needs to be documented, together with the exact configuration of the released system (that is, historical records). The definition of the *Build Standard* of systems is an important tool for maintenance teams. Because of its impact on maintaining operational software, support software must be addressed in status accounting.

Status accounting reports need to be addressed in detail in the Plan. The theme should be able to answer queries as to *What is the status of SCR 21, 37, 38, 39 and 50?* when one is not always sure of the query in advance. More sophisticated SCM tools that capture transaction data in the library data base can use data management systems and report generators to provide flexibility. Other systems need to anticipate common queries by capturing information in a form where it is easily accessible.

**Issues to Consider in Planning
Section 3.3 — Configuration
Status Accounting**

(1) What types of information needs to be reported?

(2) What is the degree of control required by the customer (typically management)?

(3) Who are the different audiences for each report?

(4) What is the formality required by the organization's standards and procedures for requesting or obtaining reports, or both?

(5) What kind of reports are needed to support integration of units and the tracing of error sources?

(6) What information is needed to produce reports?

   (a) Any problem report number included in a release or promotion

   (b) Units that have been delivered within a given time to integration and test activity

   (c) Changes made and released as a result of a particular problem report

   (d) Units that have been through various types of testing but have not been promoted or released

   (e) Units that have been promoted as a result of a design change

(7) For large systems, is there a need for handling rollover of identification sequences?

Many different types of reports can and do prove useful. The project's managers may, for example, make use of the status accounting data to keep track of the project's progress. Typically the report requests must evolve over a period of time. For some projects, status reporting can be extended to include the status of data items and reviews that are more strictly management scheduling information rather than just configuration management status.

The basic information needed by a CCB relates to transactions applied to the baseline(s), particularly the operational (product) baselines. The disciplines involved in controlling computer programs complement traditional CM for this process. Information needed for more detailed technical management between baseline events should also be collected somehow. Interfaces with available software engineering tools can provide much of this information.

The procedure for tracking the status of CI should be established early enough in the software development process to allow data gathering when it is most easily generated (that is, at the decision and response points) rather than after the fact. The desirable amount of automation depends in large part on the tools available, the size of the project and the maturity of the existing procedures.

Status accounting for multiple sites represents a more complex reporting procedure. The sample Plan in Appendix B describes this problem. Other general requirements for reporting must anticipate management needs for various combinations of information. An ad hoc query capability is often most useful.

3.3.4 Audits and Reviews.

The theme of subsection 3.4 of the Plan involves the procedures used to verify that the software product (executable code) matches the configuration item descriptions in the specifications and documents, and that the package being reviewed is complete. It should be noted that, as a general division of labor, the organization performing quality assurance functions also usually performs the audits that address change processing functions, operation of the library(ies), and other activities associated with the processes of software configuration management. This constrasts with the reviews and audits performed within the scope of a SCM activity or organization that verify that a software or firmware product is a consistent, well-defined collection of parts.

Audits are one means by which an organization can ensure that the developers have done all their work in a way that will satisfy any external obligations. Audits vary in formality and rigor, depending on the legal liability of external obligations. They are a check on the completeness of a computer program product. Any anomalies found during audits should not only be corrected but the root cause of the problem should be identified and corrected to ensure that the problem does not resurface.

Generally, there should be a physical configuration audit (PCA) and a functional configuration audit (FCA) of configuration items prior to the release of a product baseline or an updated version of a product baseline. The PCA portion of the audit consists of determining that all items identified as being part of the configuration are present in the product baseline. The audit must also establish that the correct version and revision of each part are included in the product baseline and that they correspond to information contained in the baseline's configuration status report.

The FCA portion is similar, in that someone acknowledges having inspected or tested each item to determine that it satisfies the functions defined in the specifications or contract(s) for which it was developed. The objectives of a PCA/FCA are for the developers to provide notice that contractual obligations are nearing completion, and to provide sufficient evidence for the clients or user organization to accept the product and initiate the transition into operational usage.

This section of the Plan should define ways to ensure that established configuration management procedures are followed:

(1) Test specifications are maintained current
(2) Test reports are properly prepared
(3) Test procedures explicitly define tests to be conducted
(4) Test results comply with acceptance criteria in the test procedure
(5) Test data package contents are complete and comply with approved formats

---

**Issues to Consider in Planning
Section 3.4 — Audits and Reviews**

(1) Are there needs or provisions for more than one audit of each product baseline?
(2) Is there a single, separate audit trail for each component and for the personnel working on them?
(3) How are subcontractors involved in an audit (if part of project)?
(4) Are provisions made for auditing the SCM process?
(5) Are periodic reviews held to determine the progress and technical quality of a computer program product?

Audits of a configuration as it evolves can prevent massive problems at the time of release for operational use.

A higher-level audit trail for business-type management that reflects the real-time relationships and status of CI changes, component changes and individuals responsible for development is often very useful. When addressing subcontractor audits, reference Section 5, Supplier Control, in the Plan.

When addressing internal audits, the Plan should identify who will be performing these audits and exactly what is to be audited. For example, the SQA group may audit the SCM group's adherence to change control procedures (assuming an SCM group exists — otherwise the general use of tools is audited).

Although SCM functions generally do not initiate or direct reviews, quite often the mechanisms used by SCM to process changes are used to organize and process items in a review conducted by other functions such as software quality assurance (SQA). The mechanisms of status reporting are often useful in maintaining detailed action items from reviews of complex systems. SCM supports reviews in this way as any other support provided to management.

There should always be an audit of the configuration items at the time a product is released. This will vary according to the baseline being released and the criteria for the audit stated in the Plan. At a minimum, when the product baseline is established and whenever it is subsequently changed due to the release of a new version of the computer program, the configuration should be audited. Again, the roles of the SCM organization and its participation in the audit should be established in the Plan.

3.3.5 Release Process. Major releases of software must be described so that the recipient understands what has just been delivered. Often the recipient will need installation instructions and other data concerning the use of the new system. The installation instructions should define the environment on which the software will run. This is to cover both hardware (for example, machine type, peripherals needed, and extra memory required) and software (for example, operating system version, and utilities not provided) environments. SCM verifies that the release package is complete and ready to be handed over to the user.

A short outline of the documentation (often referred to as the version description document, or VDD) typically associated with the release package is given in 3.3.5.1. It may be modified to suit the project. The more critical or the larger the application, the more complete the documentation needs to be.

3.3.5.1 Version Description Document. The version description document describes the tapes, diskettes, or other media used to provide the software.

(1) *Release Media.* List the labels on each tape, diskette or [EP]ROM and provide some guidance as to the contents of each volume. For example, *Tape FG301 contains the executable load unit library required to run FRED.*

When one has a more complex system with many CI and associated data files, it may be necessary to describe each file on the tape in this section.

(2) *Functional Description.* When the release contains any functions not previously released, describe them briefly to inform the users of new capabilities. This is not intended to be a user's manual — just the summation of the new capabilities.

(3) *User Considerations.* If there are any special actions the users must take in using the new release, describe them here. Examples may be changes in the use of a new function key, a special procedure needed to complete a certain action, hardware limitations, etc.

In this section, also list any open problem reports (SCR) against the system. Typically the open reports are listed by short title and number in this section. This is for user reference. It may prevent users from filing duplicate problem reports and will give them a better understanding of the system's status.

(4) *Closed Problem Reports.* List in this section all SCR closed out in this release.

(5) *Inventory.* If necessary, provide in this section an inventory of the source and executable load units and data objects (typically at the file level) that are contained in this release. This inventory is generally necessary for those systems that must be tightly controlled. The units are usually listed in alphabetical order by CI, with a designation of version, revision, and date changed. In some cases, the SCR initiating the change is listed against each unit.

(6) *Installation Instructions.* This section may be used when the installation is made at a remote site, at numerous sites or when there are special actions to be taken. The instructions should be specific for each site.

The most important aspect of writing installation instructions is to walk through each step that the installer will have to perform and ensure that he/she will have the information necessary to perform it.

3.4 Tools, Techniques and Methodologies. The theme of Section 4 of the Plan is making it all happen—the easy way. A well planned project typically takes advantage of planning tools such as PERT charts and Gantt charts.

The audit trail reports should reflect directly back to milestones and other activities on the planning charts, thus giving management a tool for tracking progress on a project. An automated system for software configuration management may include some way of integrating these classical planning tools with the SCM data base to provide all parties (management, designers, developers, testers, quality assurance, etc) with an on-line tool for creating products and observing their current development status dynamically in real-time, correlated automatically with a predefined Plan to yield a quantitative performance-against-schedule measures. The group that is responsible for specific tools should be identified.

The tools, techniques, and methods used to implement SCM are usually discussed in terms of a (set of) libraries and the methods and techniques used to capture, store, and promote or release the items of each type of library in a controlled manner. The concept of *software library* varies according to the level of technology available for generating software. The degree to which all entities of the product are machine accessible is a rough measure of the level of automation for a particular project.

**Issues to Consider in Planning
Section 4—Tools, Techniques,
and Methodologies**
(1) What are the number and types of libraries to be established?
   (a) A dynamic library (or programmer's library)
   (b) A controlled library (or master library)
   (c) A static library (or software repository)
   (d) Other libraries
(2) What is the amount of change activity anticipated for the project?
(3) Can the SCM tools in the library be used to manage documentation and source code?

---

(4) What kinds and amounts of training (for example, orientation and learning time) are needed to make the tools and procedures an effective solution for the organization?

Definition and use of a minimal set of libraries are illustrated in Appendix C and in 2.3.1. These libraries can accomplish all of the necessary functions of baseline control but usually need to be supplemented with other kinds of libraries to provide the necessary flexibility for smooth operation on larger projects. The libraries have to be structured in such a way that the source code associated with a given executable unit is promoted at the same time that the executable unit is. The source and executable load unit libraries should **always** be kept in synchronization. There are numerous technical methods for achieving this, depending on the development environment and the tools available.

For run-time efficiency, it may be necessary to merge various CI executable units into an integrated run-time environment. When this is done, it is also advisable to maintain the source separately that created the load units.

Note that the corresponding data files are included in the various levels of libraries. When table driven software is used, it is critical to maintain that data at the same level as the corresponding code. This can be handled by carefully structuring the libraries and using appropriate naming conventions.

Manual SCM methods may be perfectly adequate for a small project. However, if the tools and equipment are already in place, they may well be cost effective. The characteristics of the project must guide tool selection. A small project may not need the detailed planning and overhead supported by a complex set of integrated SCM tools. Problems in turnover of software developers may make automation attractive even though its initial cost is high.

In the selection of SCM tools, one needs to consider the cost effectiveness of their use for the given project, product, or site. New SCM tools and methods may be good, but if the engineering staff does not trust them, understand them, or is unwilling to learn new ways of working, they may hinder rather than support the performing organizations in getting the job done.

Current commercially available SCM tools focus primarily on controlling source code. They are written by programmers and code is the important element in programming. Due consideration should be made to bring documentation under control of the same tools as the code. Good SCM systems work on files, and files can consist of paragraphs of a document as well as code.

The kinds of SCM tools recommended in a Plan should also be considered in relation to the probable availability of the tools for use within the project's environment. That is, one should not make the entire Plan dependent on a tool set that may never materialize.

3.5 Supplier Control. The theme of Section 5 of the Plan is how to place effective CM on the computer programs over which you have no direct CM control. Computer program suppliers are considered to fall into one of two classes:

(1) Subcontracted software, or those contractors that develop unique or dedicated software under contract to a developer

(2) Vendor software, or those contractors that provide privately developed and existing software, and bundled application software such as operating systems, compilers, word processing tools, software configuration management tools, and data-base management systems.

Issues to Consider in Planning Section 5 — Supplier Control

(1) Is the product being procured to be used internally, delivered as part of your organization's product, or both?

(2) What post-delivery defect correction requirements and procedures need to be established?

(3) What changes is the purchaser permitted to make after delivery without invalidating the warranty or violating legal constraints?

(4) When should audits be performed?
   (a) When subcontractor or vendor releases parts to the buyer
   (b) After successful integration in buyer's system

(5) Is there a need to *pass through* SCM tools to a supplier or a vendor?

---

(6) Consider the use of *software in escrow*[12] as a method of enforcing SCM and quality

(7) What periodic reviews of the subcontractor's work will be needed?

3.5.1 Subcontractor Software. If a portion of a software development project is to be subcontracted to another organization, the responsibility for SCM is generally passed to that organization. However, the subcontractor can only be responsible for the portion of the work that his organization is tasked to perform, not for the integration of the subcontracted work with the final product.

Possible methods for integrating subcontractor SCM include

(1) Specifying or providing a library management tool and monitoring its use

(2) Letting the subcontractor(s) promote code to your software generation system and controlling it in the same fashion as is done in-house.

(3) Obtaining the source for all subcontractor deliveries and recompiling and relinking it using the buyer's software generation tools

To ease integration and maintenance, the subcontractor should be required to implement a system of configuration management based on the buyer's requirements — one that is compatible with the buyer's configuration management system or a subset thereof. Identification schemes should be compatible. A system for effectively managing interfaces should be developed. The subcontractor should have an internal configuration control system that is equivalent to the systems and procedures described by the buyer. The format and frequency of status reports also should be agreed upon.

Not all contractor-subcontractor relationships are easily identifiable. Sometimes, the contractual relationship does not afford the buyers any control over the subcontractor SCM processes and the buyer has to bound the relationship of the subcontracted software by alternate identification and by accepting the configuration as given, verified by testing the delivered product (as illustrated in Appendix C). Generally, it is possible to tailor the SCM requirements passed on to the subcontractor, using specifications or statements of work.

---

[12] If the executable code is the only code obtained, it may be advisable to have the supplier place the source code in *escrow* as a warranty that the source will be available if the supplier goes out of business.

Issues to Consider in Defining Subcontractor Relationships

(1) What SCM concerns need to be added to or removed from the contract?

(2) Who is responsible for auditing versus enforcing SCM for contractual products?

(3) What audits and procedures need to be established where the subcontractor has no documented SCM practices or procedures?

If the buyer's organization is developing the computer programs for a customer, the contract should be reviewed for any specific legal requirements that need to be passed on to the subcontractor, or special actions that have to be taken by the buyer to ensure the performance of the subcontractors' product.

Integration of subcontractor software is very difficult unless communication is kept open. One way is to allow subcontractor representatives to attend SCCB meetings to ensure that they are aware of all important technical issues. It may also be useful to accept incremental versions of the code for integration and test with the rest of the code, rather than waiting until the end of the development cycle.

In specifying delivery, identify all items that are to be a part of the deliverable. Possibilities include

(1) Source code

(2) Executable code

(3) Load units

(4) Data files

(5) Test cases

(6) Any JCL or other procedures used in running or creating the software

(7) Compilation listings or link-edit maps (for debugging)

(8) Documentation

Another concern for SCM is the subcontractor's actual performance to an agreed-upon Plan or statement of work. A preselection or purchase audit of the potential subcontractor's configuration management policies and procedures can provide an indication of the potential for the organization to perform satisfactorily. If possible, the buyer's software configuration management group should perform an in-process SCM audit of all project subcontractors to ensure satisfactory compliance. As part of this audit, a specific approved change should be traced through the subcontractor's system to the point of verifying the implementation.

A critical role for SCM is in the inspection (FCA/PCA) of the product as it is prepared for delivery to the buyer. This is most important as it determines the effort and resources that may be needed to integrate and maintain the product once it has been incorporated in the buyer's system. There are still compatibility problems and problems of error correction, and updates that have to be provided for even if the program is a stand-alone product (as for a compiler). If the program received is not well identified and documented, then the task of maintenance is generally increased.

3.5.2 Vendor Software. Warranties contained in purchase orders may be difficult to enforce. The specific criterion is that the vendor should furnish the computer program *media* as specified by a purchase order or as specified by the supplier's documentation referenced in the purchase order. Test documentation confirming compliance is desirable but often unavailable.

Issues to Consider in Defining Vendor Interfaces

(1) How is the vendor software identified?

(2) How are license agreements and data rights protected and enforced? Are there limitations on
   (a) Duplication of documentation
   (b) Your customer making copies of the program

(3) How will vendor support be provided over the life cycle of the computer program product being purchased?

(4) How will copyright interests be protected?

(5) How will legal copies of leased software be controlled?

The handling of vendor software can be very complex, particularly in a maintenance environment, such as described in Appendix C, where the vendor software is intermixed with internally developed software. More importantly, if you release the vendor product as a part of your organization's product, your organization may be responsible for ensuring its maintenance as part of your released product. An organization embedding third party software in a product delivered to a customer can be open to financial and legal liabilities if a vendor fails to perform — that is, making required changes in a timely manner. One possible consideration is the use of an escrow account with a vendor agreement tied to performance of his product.

3.6 Records Collection and Retention. The theme of Section 6 of the Plan is to *keep the information necessary only for the time required.* This is another service aspect of configuration management. Good configuration management practices include maintaining copies of released material for backup and disaster protection. Also the liability and warranty provisions and responsibilities make considering the retention of test and approval records a necessity. If a master disaster recovery plan exists for the company, the Plan needs to disclose all information regarding the location of backups and records that are impounded in relation with that plan.

Records collection can also be a part of risk management. Part of the trade-off must consider whether personnel will be available to recover lost software. Trade-offs can be made concerning the cost of capturing and maintaining records versus the potential cost savings for

(1) Recovering programs in the event of a disaster for
  (a) Software developed for internal use
  (b) Delivered products for which warranty is still in effect
  (c) Support software necessary for maintaining computer program products under warranty
(2) Liability for not being able to certify the reliability of delivered products
(3) Information gathered that may lead to performance or productivity improvements in development or maintenance activities.

Record keeping begins in planning the capture of all data that needs to be maintained. In addition to all other considerations, archiving the software should be done in a manner acceptable to any legal contracts that may affect the computer programs. Static libraries, disaster planning, and storage should consider the legal status of the software involved (for example, whether it has trade secret status) and the impact on the provisions made for the care and storage of the software components. Special attention should be given to the retention of support software associated with software on target machines.

**Issues to Consider in Planning
Section 6 — Records Collection
and Retention**

(1) What type of information needs to be retained?
(2) What data need to be maintained over a period of time for trend data analysis?
(3) Is all the information, support software, and equipment needed to recreate the product available from archives?
(4) Is media protected from disaster?
(5) Is there a need to maintain copies of software licensed for use and distribution?
(6) What activities need to be recorded (and data captured) for maintaining a product after the project is completed?
  (a) Copyright records
  (b) Distribution records
  (c) Benchmarks
  (d) Change history (CCB activity, SPR, etc)
  (e) Audits, reviews, status reports
(7) For whose use are the records being maintained?
  (a) Engineering
  (b) Management
  (c) Software Quality Assurance
  (d) Legal, customer
(8) How are the records to be kept?
  (a) On line versus off line
  (b) Media and format (hard copy document versus electronic media, deterioration rate versus time needed)
  (c) Location (preservation conditions, accessibility both off site and on site)
  (d) Tools used on the project that affect data capture
(9) How long will the data be kept?

The information collected need not mirror that collected for hardware bit for bit. For example, serial information on production that is kept to identify configurations in hardware may not be necessary for software. Plan to keep only the data that will be of use in maintenance, disaster recovery, or which has other justification. Is the deterioration rate of the storage medium sufficient for the needed time span? Media can deteriorate in storage; also, work in-progress should be backed-up at specific intervals to protect the investment for projects that have long development periods or are of high cost.

Appendixes

(The following Appendixes are not a part of ANSI/IEEE Std 1042-1987, IEEE Guide to Software Configuration Management, but are included for information only.)

Appendix A

Software Configuration Management Plan for Critical Software for Embedded Systems

Version 1.0

Approved

_____

Mgr, SCM Dept

_____

Project Mgr

_____

Contracts

_____

Customer

Date: ___ /___ /___

Synopsis

This example contains a discussion of a hypothetical contract to provide a medium-sized real-time control system for the management of advanced vehicles. Sensors are used for input of information to the system; displays are used to support a man-machine interface. The contract for the system consists of eight software configuration items being developed concurrently with five new and seven off-the-shelf hardware configuration items. The project is expected to have at most three hundred and fifty-six personnel, with an average of thirty-four and peak of fifty software development personnel over the estimated three and a half year development cycle.

Most of the development work is performed in the contractor's main facility with some work being performed at a nearby subsidiary. Testing and acceptance is performed at the mock-up in the contractor's facility. Some commercial software is procured from a vendor for the support software and the firmware for the vehicle is subcontracted to the builder of the vehicle. This is a turnkey contract. The customer takes over all maintenance of the software after delivery of the first system.

The customer's procurement organization has a large staff for monitoring the contract and is expected to perform frequent audits. The contractor's project office wishes to minimize friction with the customer and is willing to perform most, but not all, of the necessary record keeping and in-process inspections. The configuration management department of the contractor has a long history of involvement in projects with the customer and there is a general familiarity and comfortableness in *doing business* in this manner. The software configuration management activity is relatively new but is strongly supported by the old line configuration management department.

In this environment, the software configuration management activity will be a very disciplined operation, logging and maintaining accurate records of *all* transactions against established baselines.

Contents

Appendix A

Software Configuration Management Plan for Critical Software for Embedded Systems

1. Introduction

This document is the Software Configuration Management (SCM) Plan for the *Critical Software for Embedded Systems* (CSES). The CSES system performs functions critical to the life and safety of human beings. The configuration management of this software during development is essential to the delivery of error-free and reliable software configuration items.

1.1 Purpose. This plan provides information on the requirements and procedures necessary for the configuration management activities of the CSES project. It identifies the software configuration management requirements and establishes the methodology for generating configuration identifiers, controlling engineering changes, maintaining status accounting, and performing audits and reviews during the design and development of software configuration items.

1.2 Scope. This plan applies to all software and associated documentation used in the production of computer programs produced under the critical software for embedded systems contract including, but not limited to, source, object, and executable load images. Software configuration items referenced in the contract and controlled by this plan include

  CSES Operational System
  CSES Training Program
  CSES Test Program
  CSES Hardware Acceptance Programs

  CSES Diagnostic Software
  CSES Software Support System
  CSES Simulation System
  CSES Utilities

The organizations involved in this project are identified in Fig 1.

This plan applies to all phases of the software development life cycle, up to and including the time of delivery to the customer. Maintenance of the software after delivery is covered by another contract.

1.3 Definitions and Mnemonics

1.3.1 Definitions. The definitions used in this plan conform to the company standards as set forth in Vol II of the company *Configuration Practices Manual.* Other definitions will conform to those found in ANSI/IEEE Std 729-1983, IEEE Standard Glossary of Software Engineering Terminology. See specifically: baseline, configuration item, configuration management, configuration control, configuration control board, configuration audit, configuration identification, configuration status accounting, and software library. Unique definitions used in this document include:

interface control. The process of

(1) Identifying all functional and physical characteristics relevant to the interfacing of two or more configuration items provided by one or more organizations.

(2) Ensuring that proposed changes to these characteristics are evaluated and approved prior to implementation.

1.3.2 Mnemonics. The following mnemonics are referred to within the text of this standard:

Fig 1
Program Organization Chart

41

CCB	Configuration Control Board
CDR	Critical Design Review
CI	Configuration Item
CM	Configuration Management
CSES	Critical Software in Embedded System
ECN	Engineering Change Notice
FCA	Functional Configuration Audit
I&T	Integration and Test
PCA	Physical Configuration Audit
SCA	Software Change Authorization
SCM	Software Configuration Management
SCMP	Software Configuration Management Plan
SCR	Systems/Software Change Request
SQ&C	Software Quality and Control
SQA	Software Quality Assurance
SQAP	Software Quality Assurance Plan
SRR	System Requirements Review
SSR	Software Specifications Review

1.4 References. The standards listed here will be considered when applying this plan. The latest revisions apply:

[1] ANSI/IEEE Std 729-1983, IEEE Standard Glossary of Software Engineering Terminology.

[2] ANSI/IEEE Std 730-1984, IEEE Standard for Software Quality Assurance Plans.

[3] ANSI/IEEE Std 828-1983, IEEE Standard for Software Configuration Management Plans.

[4] ANSI/IEEE Std 829-1983, IEEE Standard for Software Test Documentation.

[5] Company Standard *Configuration Management Practices Manual*, Vol II.

[6] CSES Software Development Plan

Reference documents are available for use in the company library.

2. Management

2.1 Organization. The critical software for embedded systems program organization is designed to ensure clear lines of authority and to provide a framework within which administrative and technical control of software activities can be cost-effectively integrated into a quality product.

Primary responsibilities for various configuration management tasks are assigned as shown in Table 1. Within the CSES project organization, the program manager has total responsibility for the project. With this project, the program manager will have overall responsibility for configuration management of this project. The program manager serves as the project configuration control board (CCB) chairperson. The SCM project authority from the SCM organization cochairs the CCB. The SCM authority assists the program manager with planning and tailoring of the software configuration management plan (SCMP) and related CM procedures and is responsible for overseeing their implementation. The software configuration management authority reports functionally to the critical software for embedded systems program manager for the implementation of this plan. Administratively, the SCM authority reports to the SCM Department, which performs the necessary activities for the project.

Table 1
Responsibility Assignments

Responsibilities	Program Manager	Software Engineer	SCM Authority	SQA	Drafting
Configuration identification			Originate		
Approve/release tech documentation	Approve	Originate	Review	Review	
Change preparation		Originate			
Change control		Approve			
Change implementation		Approve	Review		Originate
Documentation maintenance		Approve			
Status accounting			Originate	Review	
Formal SCM audits		Approve	Originate	Review	
Baseline definition	Approve	Originate	Review	Review	Review

2.2 SCM Responsibilities. The software configuration management authority has the authority to require changes in practices and procedures that do not meet contract requirements. The general responsibilities of the software configuration management authority are outlined in Table 1. The software configuration management authority's functions include, but are not limited to the following tasks:

(1) Configuration control
(2) Status accounting
(3) Configuration identification
(4) Implementation and maintenance of the software configuration management plan
(5) Configuration control board cochairperson
(6) Establishment and maintenance of engineering baselines
(7) Cochairperson for formal audits
(8) Participation in reviews

2.2.1 Configuration Identification. Configuration identification is applied to all critical software for embedded software, both code and associated documentation. Associated documentation (that is, specifications, design documents, and program/procedure listings) along with the actual produced software makes up the configuration item. The software configuration management authority originates the identification scheme, with the approval of program management.

Configuration identification of computer programs and documentation during the development effort consists of established baselines and releases that are time-phased to the development schedules as described in the CSES software development plan.

2.2.1.1 Baselines. Baselines are established for the control of design, product, and engineering changes and are time-phased to the development effort. Baselines are established by the authority of the program manager. The software configuration management authority administers application of the baselines. Baselines defined for CSES include

(1) Functional baseline
(2) Allocated baseline
(3) Developmental baseline
(4) Product baseline

More details on baselines are presented in 2.4.2.

2.2.1.2 Releases. Throughout the development life cycle, at the discretion of the program manager, software manager, and SCM, baseline releases are performed. The releases fall into one of three categories

(1) Developer release (engineering release)

(2) Release to SCM (preliminary release)
(3) Final release (formal release to customer).

It is the responsibility of SCM to establish the release, version, and update number identifiers.

2.2.1.3 Documentation. All relevant specifications and documentation are given an identifier by SCM.

2.2.2 Configuration Control. All documentation and software entities are released to and maintained by software configuration management in a controlled library. SCM administers the change control process.

2.2.2.1 Systems/Software Change Request (SCR). The SCR is the mechanism by which change requests are presented to the CCB. This action allows a developer to check out software/documentation from SCM controlled libraries. The mechanism for requesting authorization is to present the SCR to the CCB and request approval for work to begin. The SCR form shown in Attachment A is used.

2.2.2.2 Software Change Authorization (SCA). The SCA is used to request SCM to place a new version of software/documentation into the controlled libraries. The approvals necessary are as follows: software manager, software quality assurance, and SCM. The SCA form shown in Attachment B is used.

2.2.3 Status Accounting. A software change authorization data base is used for generating reports that track changes to all of the controlled baselines. At project request, SCM generates reports that track the status of documentation and the software.

2.2.4 Audits. The SCM authority is responsible for cochairing, with the customer, all formal audits.

2.2.4.1 SQA Audits. It is the responsibility of SCM to assist SQA with their audit of the development effort. SCM maintains all documentation and software under strict controls to minimize the effort required by SQA to perform their function.

2.2.5 Configuration Control Board (CCB). The CSES project CCB is established by the program manager and SCM authority.

The program manager is the CCB chairperson and has the final responsibility for CCB actions relative to program SCM policies, plans, procedures, and interfaces. The software configuration management authority acts as cochair. In addition to the chairpersons and the CCB secretary, the CCB may include: development personnel; hardware representative; drafting representative; testing representative; customers; and always will include a representative from software quality assurance. CCB meetings are held on a regular basis determined by the CSES program manager, or when required at the call of the CCB chairperson. The system/software change request that is generated is reviewed by the CCB and one of the following actions taken: approved, disapproved, or tabled.

2.3 Interface Control. Interface control is handled in the same manner as other types of hardware, software, or documentation. Any differences between the SQAP and the SCMP must be resolved prior to the establishment of any baselines.

2.4 SCMP Implementation. The SCMP is implemented as soon as it is signed off by the CSES program manager but prior to holding any formal reviews with the customer. Any unresolved issues found once the SCMP is written must be resolved as soon as possible during the development period and prior to any baselines being established.

2.4.1 Configuration Control Board. The CCB is established at the time of SCMP approval but prior to the establishment of any baselines.

2.4.2 Configuration Baselines. Baselines are established by the following events:

2.4.2.1 Functional Baseline. The functional baselines are established by the acceptance, or customer approval of the CSES system/segment specification. Normally this occurs at the completion of the CSES system requirement review (SRR).

2.4.2.2 Allocated Baseline. The allocated baseline is established with the customer approval of the CSES software requirement specification. Normally this corresponds to the completion of the software specification review (SSR). The specification(s) and associated documentation define the allocated configuration identification.

2.4.2.3 Developmental Baseline. The developmental baseline is established by the approval of technical documentation that defines the top-level design and detailed design (including documentation of interfaces and data bases for the computer software). Normally, this corresponds to the time frame spanning the preliminary design review (PDR) and the critical design review (CDR).

2.4.2.4 Product Baseline. The product baseline is established upon customer approval of the product specification following completion of the last formal audit (FCA).

2.4.3 Schedules and Procedures for SCM Reviews and Audits. Reviews and audits are held as defined by CSES software development plan.

2.4.4 Configuration Management of Software Development Tools. The configurations of all support software used in development and test on the CSES project software is controlled in the same manner as the critical software. Nondeliverable support software baselines do not need customer approval.

2.5 Applicable Policies, Directives, and Procedures. The complete SCM policies, directives, and procedures that apply to this program are included as part of the procedures section of this document or are part of the referenced documents or one of the appendixes.

3. SCM Activities

3.1 Configuration Identification

3.1.1 Documentation. All supporting documentation generated for this project is identified by the use of the following convention: CSES, an abbreviation for the document nomenclature, a unique four digit number assigned by the CSES software configuration manager, and the product's version-revision-update number.
EXAMPLE: CSES-SDP-0024-1.2.1

Table 2
Baseline Objectives

Baseline	Purpose	Reviews & Audits
Functional	Functions established	SRR
Allocated	Requirement defined	SSR
Developmental	Top level design complete	PDR
Developmental	Detailed design complete	CDR
Product	Approval of product spec	FCA/PCA

Document Nomenclature	Mnemonic
Software Configuration Management Plan	SCMP
Software Detailed Design Document	SDD
Software Development Plan	SDP
Software Test Procedures	SPP
Software Product Specification	SPS
Software Quality Assurance Plan	SQAP
Software Requirements Specification	SRS
Software System Specification	SSS
Software Top-Level Design Document	STD
Software Test Plan	STP
Software Test Report	STR

3.1.2 Software Parts. The software configuration items, components, and units are identified by unique identification labels.

3.1.3 Configuration Identification of the Functional Baseline. The functional baseline is identified by the approval of the CSES system segment specification.

3.1.4 Configuration Identification of the Allocated Baseline. The allocated baseline is identified by the approval of the software requirement specification.

3.1.5 Configuration Identification of the Developmental Baselines. The developmental baselines are identified by the approved technical documentation that defines the top level design and detailed designs. The process by which the initial developmental baselines are established is shown in Attachment C, Create Initial Baseline.

3.1.6 Configuration Identification of the Product Baseline. The product baseline is identified by the approval of the CSES software product specification. This baseline specification is made up of the top level specification, detailed design specification, and the computer listings.

3.2 Configuration Control. Software configuration management and change control is applied to all documents and code, including CSES critical operational software and support software. Control is effected through the implementation of configuration identification, the CCB, change control, and status accounting functions.

3.2.1 Function of the Configuration Control Board. The configuration control board reviews proposed changes for assuring compliance with approved specifications and designs, and evaluates impacts on existing software. Each engineering change or problem report that is initiated against a formally identified configuration item is evaluated by the CCB to determine its necessity and impact. The CCB members electronically sign the document to indicate that they have reviewed the changes and provided their recommendations to the chairperson. The CCB approves, disapproves, or tables all changes. The mechanism for submitting changes to the software or documentation is the systems/software change request.

3.2.2 The System/Software Change Request. The SCR system is one of the major tools for identifying and coordinating changes to software and documentation. The SCR system is a minicomputer based tool used to track the status of a change from its proposal to its eventual disposition and assist in documenting important information about the change. The SCR form (Attachment A) contains a narrative description of the change or problem, information to identify the source of the report and some basic information to aid in evaluating the report. SCR is submitted only against baselined software or documentation. SCR may be submitted by anyone associated with the project effort or its products, but usually is submitted by a member of the software development team. SCM provides the single point for receiving and processing SCR. SCM, using the report writer feature of the SCR system, is capable of producing reports that provide change control tracking. A SCR is *closed* when

(1) Integration testing has shown that the changes have been correctly made
(2) No unexpected side-effects have resulted from making the change
(3) Documentation has been updated and reviewed

3.2.3 Software Change Authorization. The software change authorization form (Attachment B) is used to control changes to all documents and software under SCM control and for documents and software that have been released to SCM. The SCA is an on-line form that the software developers use to submit changes to software and documents to SCM for updating the master library. Approvals required for baselining or updating baselined software are as follows. The developer(s) first obtain the manager's signature, I&T signature, and an SCM signature. These approvals can either be written or added electronically. SCM signature testifies that the action has occurred. SQA signature signifies that they have verified that the change has been incorporated. SCM notifies the software developer through the electronic mail system that the change has occurred so the developer can delete extra copies of the changed parts. The SCA data base, along with the SCR data base, is used for status accounting needs.

The process by which changes are made is shown in Attachment D, change procedure.

3.2.4 Change Control Automated SCM Tools. The libraries of the CSES system are used to control all textual files containing the specifications, documentation, test plans and procedures, and source code. The support software (listed below) is also under configuration management by SCM. The library structure that is used is as follows:

(1) The CSES master library
(2) The program library
(3) The development library

3.2.4.1 For this mini-computer based development effort, the change control tools are as follows:

(1) *The Source Management System* The mechanism for creating and maintaining delta files (changes only) for the CSES master library. Only SCM has access to the CSES master libraries. The CSES master library data base is accessible by the SCM status accounting system.

(2) *The Package Management System* is used to automate the build process and is used to assist SCM with the generation of software.

(3) *SCM Get* is the function invoked by software developers to acquire software modules, or parts from the program libraries.

(4) *SCM Send* is the function invoked by software developers to impound a software module into the SCM program libraries. The use of this function implicitly and automatically generates an SCA.

3.3 Configuration Status Accounting. The status accounting system is capable of generating the following reports:

(1) *Report 1.* A list of all SCR with a status of *not closed* (that is, the same as *open*)

(2) *Report 2.* A cross-reference of SCA, engineering change notices (ECN), and drawings, per SCA

(3) *Report 3.* A monthly summary of the SCR and SCA data bases

(4) *Report 4.* A total of all SCR submitted per unit within a user-selected range of submittal dates

(5) *Report 5.* A list of all SCR which are *open*, *closed*, or *all* (selected by the user)

(6) *Report 6.* A summary of all SCR submitted by unit

(7) *Report 7.* A summary of the current approval status of all SCR with a status of *not closed*

(8) *Report 8.* A short summary of all SCR within a particular software component with a status of either open, closed, or all

(9) *Report 9.* A version description document

(10) *Report 10.* A report that gives the status of all documentation under SCM control

(11) *General Report.* Allows the user to define his/her own reports. The user must first specify which fields to include in the report.

(12) *On-Line Inquiry.* Allows the user to interactively view fields within the SCM data bases. The user specifies the fields that he/she wishes displayed and conditions for searching the data base

3.4 Audits and Reviews. The SCM authority cochairs, with the customer, the formal CM audits: the functional configuration audit (FCA) and the physical configuration audit (PCA).

3.4.1 Functional Configuration Audit. The functional configuration audit is performed on the software configuration items when the acceptance tests have been completed. Both the functional baseline and the allocated baselines have previously been approved by the customer.

The audit is made on the formal test plans, descriptions, and procedures and compared against the official test data. The results are checked for completeness and accuracy. Deficiencies are documented and made a part of the FCA minutes.

Completion dates for all discrepancies are clearly established and documented. An audit of both draft and final test reports is performed to validate that the reports are accurate and completely describe the development tests.

Preliminary and critical design review minutes are examined to assure that all findings have been incorporated and completed.

3.4.2 Physical Configuration Audit. A physical examination is made of the CI to verify that the first article conforms *as-built* to its technical documentation. The SCM authority assembles and makes available to the PCA team at the time of the audit all data describing the item configuration. This includes a current set of listings and the final draft of the product baseline specifications. Customer acceptance or rejection of the CI and the CI product specification presented for the PCA is furnished to the project manager in writing by the responsible customer representative after completion of the PCA.

3.4.3 Reviews. The SCM authority participates in all formal reviews with the customer.

In addition, the SCM activity conducts two informal audits of the developing CI during the development cycle. The first informal audit is just prior to CDR. The second informal audit is performed at the discretion of the SCM authority midpoint between the CDR and final acceptance test.

4. Tools, Techniques, and Methodologies

4.1 Configuration Control Tools. An integrated set of SCM tools is used for configuration control and status accounting for this project. The particular tools are as follows:

(1) *Source Management System* (SMS). This tool is a file system for checking out vendor-supplied and internal software. A license agreement has been purchased from the vendor of this tool for use on this project.

(2) *Package Management System* (PMS). This tool is a vendor supplied data management tool used to automatically generate software. A license agreement has been secured from the vendor for use on this project.

(3) *Systems/Software Change Request Tool.* This is a proprietary piece of CSES software. This tool has two parts: the input form and its data base.

(4) *Software Change Authorization* (SCA) *Tool.* The SCA is a proprietary piece of CSES software. This tool has two parts: the input form and its data base.

(5) *Status Accounting Report Generator Tool.* This is a proprietary piece of CSES software. This is a report generation tool that gathers input from the following subsystems:

(a) Source management system
(b) Package management system
(c) System/software change request
(d) Software change authorization

5. Supplier Control

5.1 Vendor-Provided Software. Vendor-provided software that is to be used by this project must conform to *good business practice* SCM. The vendor provides to this project a copy of its SCM Plan for evaluation. This project must ensure that the vendor SCM system is adequate. If the vendor system is found to be inadequate, or if no vendor SCM Plan is available, then at the program manager's discretion, the vendor can be disqualified from providing software for this project.

5.2 Subcontracted Software. Any subcontractor wishing to do business with this project must provide a copy of its SCMP for evaluation by project SCM or agree to follow and abide by this SCMP. If the subcontractor SCMP is found inadequate, all other provisions of this SCMP apply. Any subcontractor not willing to abide by the above provision may be disqualified at the program manager's discretion.

5.3 Vendor and Subcontractor Software. All vendors and subcontractors are audited for compliance with *good business practice* SCM. The frequency and methods of audits are determined by the size, dollar value, and critical nature of the software.

6. Records Collection and Retention

All formal documentation produced for and by this project is retained and safeguarded for 20 years. A second copy of all software and documentation is stored in an off-site facility. This off-site facility is 21 mi from primary storage.

Attachment A
System/Software Change Request

SCR NUM.: _____

1.   Submitted by: _____   DATE: _____ /_____ /_____

     Project Name: _____

2.   Software Program/Document Name: _____

     Version/Revision _____

3.   SCR Type: (1-Development, 2-Problem, 3-Enhancement)

4.   Short Task Description:

5.   Detail Description:

6.   Submitter's Priority [   ]   1 = Critical   2 = Very Important   3 = Important   4 = Inconvenient   5 = Interesting

7.   CCB Action: _____   CCB Priority [   ]

8.   Assigned to: _____   Target Release Date_____

9.   Solution Comments:

10. Software Programs affected:

11. I&T Approval _____   Date: _____ /_____ /_____

     SCM Approval _____   Date: _____ /_____ /_____

12. Actual Release _____   Date: _____ /_____ /_____

13. Closed by: _____   Date: _____ /_____ /_____

     SCA Reference No: _____

14. SQA Approval: _____   Date: _____ /_____ /_____

Attachment B
Software Change Authorization

SCA Number: XXXXXX
Sheet Number: 1

Submitter:_____ System: _____ Date: ____/____/____ Time: ____/____/____ 00:00:00

Product Version ID: _____ Computer Name_____

Input Names	Release Names	Module Types	L N	A C	System/Software Change Request Numbers

Comments: _____

_____

_____

_____

_____

Approvals	I & T	SCM	SQA
Signature			
Date			

Attachment C

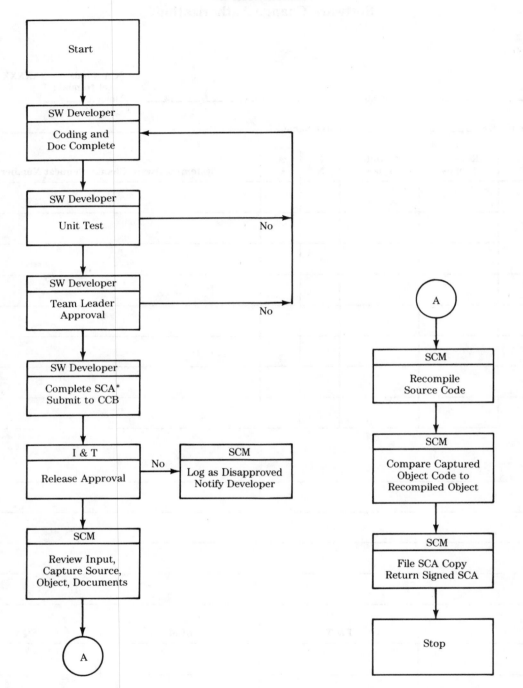

*NOTE: Developer's work files are retained until an approved SCA is received from SCM.

Fig 1
CSES Procedure for Creating Initial Baseline

Attachment D

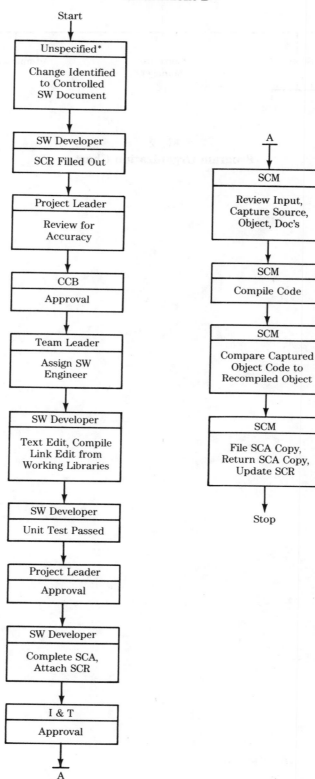

NOTE: If type of change is unspecified, submit SCR to SW Development.

Fig 1
CSES Procedures for Changes to Controlled Software/Documentation

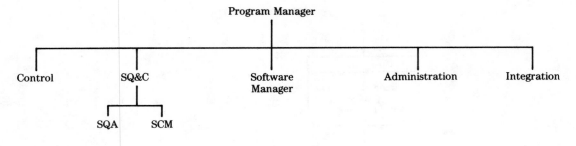

Fig 2
Program Organization Chart

Appendix B

Software Configuration Management Plan for Experimental Development Small System

Version 1.0

Approved

_____

Project Manager

_____

SCM Manager

_____

Customer

Date: ___ / ___ / ___

Synopsis

This example contains a hypothetical contract to provide a prototype minicomputer-based system for a research-oriented customer. The system consists of three software programs, to be developed by a project team of twenty persons (of which ten are programmers) and is considered a prototype for installation in one field site. The software is written in COBOL. If the system is considered successful at that site, it will be expanded to an additional two sites for further evaluation. These sites may be supported by different hardware (for example, a transition may have to be made from hardware configuration A to hardware configuration B) or by different versions of the code (for example, one site may be a data input-processing installation and another a centralized data-gathering installation; each may use slightly different logic or data elements). The development time frame for the prototype system is two years. The expected life of the system is not known as the production system becomes part of a major procurement sometime in the future when the management of the first three sites agree on the requirements.

The contracting company and the customer are very end-user oriented, willing to sacrifice rigor in configuration management and specifications in the interest of speedy delivery of software to the sites and rapid response to changes. Because of this orientation, the configuration control board functions are administered by the project manager alone. All change requests are reviewed by the manager and an immediate ruling is made as to whether and when to implement them. The project manager meets with the customer technical representative regularly to review change requests that require consultation, making disposition of the requests quite rapid.

In this environment, the software configuration management (SCM) activity must be very supportive of the customer and manager or all SCM records will be lost. The SCM coordinator attends meetings between users and the project staff and prepares change requests on the spot. These are provided to the project manager and customer technical representative for resolution. The project emphasis is on intensive support to management in performing SCM — it is literally transparent to management since the SCM organization completes all of the required paperwork. The managers' and customers' responsibility is to review and authorize the resulting documentation.

Contents

Appendix B

Software Configuration Management Plan for
Experimental Development Small System

1. Introduction

This document describes the software configuration management activities to be performed in support of the Experimental Development Small System (EDSS) Project. The EDSS project is charged with developing and demonstrating an advanced data processing concept, which, at a later date, may be converted to a fully functional system for processing special data. The project is considered to be a research/development program.

1.1 Purpose of the Plan. The software configuration management plan (SCMP) for the EDSS system describes how the software development activity supports EDSS management in the rapid iteration of software builds necessary for efficient development of the prototype demonstration software at site A. It also describes how this demonstration baseline is to be captured to provide for adaptation of the operational program to sites B and C and for subsequent up-grade of the software to full production quality for support of operational sites.

1.2 Scope. Three software configuration items (CI) are being developed as part of this contract:
(1) The Operational Program
(2) The Data Reduction Program
(3) The Test Generator Program
The development of these three CI is the responsibility of the contractor's software engineering organization. The internal build testing, the conduct of integration testing and demonstration of the prototype at site A is the responsibility of the contractor's test and control organization. The test and control organization is also responsible for demonstrations at sites B and C under this contract and possible subsequent upgrade testing of the software during later contracts.

The configuration of the operational program is managed at the unit level with all changes reviewed and approved as each unit comes under configuration management in the master library. The configuration of the data reduction program and test generator program is managed at the component level after being released for use with the operational program.

This SCMP specifically covers the configuration management support provided by the software configuration management department to the EDSS project office for
(1) The development of software used for different builds in test
(2) The prototype demonstration at site A
(3) The demonstrations at sites B and C.

1.3 Definitions and Mnemonics

1.3.1 Standard Definitions. Definitions used are found in ANSI/IEEE Std 729-1983, IEEE Standard Glossary of Software Engineering Terminology. Specifically, attention is called to definitions of
configuration item
configuration identification
configuration status accounting
master library
software library

1.3.2 Other Definitions
prototype system. The software developed for demonstrating the feasibility of the system concept.

1.3.3 Mnemonics. The following mnemonics are used within this document:

AXCESS	Vendor Software Company
CCB	Configuration Control Board
CI	Configuration Item
CM	Configuration Management
DRP	Data Reduction Program
EDSS	Experimental Development Software System
OP	Operational Program
SCA	Software Change Authorization
SCI	Software Configuration Item
SCM	Software Configuration Management
SCMP	Software Configuration Management Plan
SCR	System/Software Change Request
SDG	Software Development Group
SPR	Software Promotion Request
T & CG	Test and Control Group
TGP	Test Generation Program

1.4 References

[1] ANSI/IEEE Std 729-1983, IEEE Standard Glossary of Software Engineering Terminology.[13]

[2] ANSI/IEEE Std 828-1983, IEEE Standard for Software Configuration Management Plans.

[3] Contractor Software Engineering Organization Labeling Standards for EDSS System.

[4] Contractor Test and Control Malfunction Reports.[14]

[5] EDSS Software Development Plan

2. Management

2.1 Organizations. All authority for managing the EDSS system is vested in the EDSS project office. The software engineering organization and the test and control organization provide personnel on loan to the EDSS project office for the duration of the project. The configuration management department provides qualified personnel to the EDSS project office to perform the necessary SCM coordination. Figure 1 illustrates the major organizations.

The working organization is divided into two main groups
    (1) EDSS software development group (SDG)
    (2) EDSS test and control group (T & CG)

---

[13] IEEE publications are available in the company technical library.

[14] Organizational standards are available from the EDSS project office secretary.

Both groups report to the EDSS project manager. The SCM coordinator is provided by the CM department to the EDSS project office to help support both the software development group and the test and control group.

The EDSS project office has full responsibility for program management functions, including configuration management, until the demonstrations at all three sites are concluded. The SDG has responsibility for preparing and maintaining requirements specifications, designing the software, and performing the unit testing needed for all builds. The T & CG is responsible for integration tests, field installations, and all demonstrations. The SCM coordinator is responsible for processing all changes affecting the documentation (including test data and test procedures) and programs after their release to the T & CG.

The EDSS project manager is responsible for approving/denying all changes to the program, whether originating from the T & CG or from the customer. The project manager functions as the configuration control board (CCB).

2.2 SCM Responsibilities. The general responsibilities of the SCM coordinator are to process the information needed to control changes in the prototype software as it develops and to capture the as-built documentation, test data and reports, and code that represent each successful site demonstration. The emphasis is placed on supporting the project change activities by independently handling all of the required paperwork —making the CM process transparent to management.

Specific organizational responsibilities of the SCM coordinator are as follows:

2.2.1 Identification. Naming conventions are established for

Fig 1
Project Organization Chart

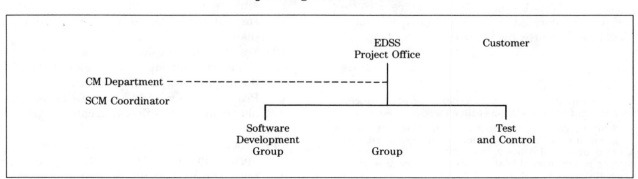

(1) *Unit Names.* These are designed so that unique identification of each item is possible. In addition, the unit naming conventions are structured so that it is possible to determine which SCI each unit belongs to by simply looking at the unit name.
(2) *File Names.* These are designed with the same mnemonic capability as the units.
(3) *Component Names.* These are given unique names so the source code can be matched to the supporting documentation.
(4) *Configuration Item Names.* These are defined in the same manner as in the contract statement of work.

2.2.2 Control. Control of all changes is maintained by
(1) Preparing and tracking approved system/software change requests (SCR), including all problem reports originatingfrom the customer, throughout implementation and testing
(2) Acting as software librarian, controlling the release of code to
  (a) The integration library for integration and testing by the T & CG at the contractor's development facility
  (b) The master library for installation and demonstrations at the site(s)

2.2.3 Status Accounting. The SCM coordinator provides the necessary status reports to the groups and project management. Typically, the reports cover
(1) SCR opened during period XXXX-XXXX[15]
(2) SCR closed for period XXXX
(3) Major SCR remaining open for three or more weeks
(4) SPR made during period XXXX
(5) SCR included in SPR, by date of promotion

2.2.4 Audits and Reviews. There is no pertinent information for this section.[16]

2.3 Interface Control. The EDSS system interfaces with the *AXCESS* software being developed by the *AXCESS Company.* The interface with this software is defined in an interface specification developed jointly by representatives from the

software development activities of each company. The specification is approved by the responsible project managers of each company.

The EDSS interfaces with the hardware configurations found at customer sites are defined in a memorandum of agreement between the customer and EDSS project manager. Where agreement is not mutual, resolution is reached by contract negotiations. For changes to the EDSS system, the EDSS project manager initiates all change requests. For necessary changes to the *AXCESS* system, the *AXCESS* project manager initiates the change requests.

2.4 SCMP Implementation. The CM Department supports the EDSS project office with the services of a qualified SCM coordinator on the basis of 50% of one person's services per month.

One four-drawer file cabinet in the library is used for storage for the period of time specified in Section 6.

One workstation for execution of the data management system is used for the duration of the project.

Key events in the SCM planning phase are
(1) Establishing the integration library upon release of the first unit to T & CG for integration
(2) Establishing the EDSS master library upon release of the first software system configuration for demonstration at site A
(3) Impounding the master libraries from the three sites, along with the associated documentation and test data and reports, at the end of the final site demonstrations

2.5 Applicable Policies, Directives, and Procedures. The following standards and procedures apply for the duration of the contract:
(1) Labeling standards used for documentation, test data, and software media are in accordance with the standards in the software engineering organization's standards and procedures manual, modified as necessary in the EDSS software development plan.
(2) Version level designations are sequential numbers following a dash, appended to the documentation/media label.
(3) Problem report (SCR) processing is done according to the flow diagram in Attachment B.
(4) Procedures for operating the integration library and the EDSS master library are documented and distributed as a part of

---

[15]The period *XXXX* is left to the discretion of the program manager but is no less frequent than three-week intervals.

[16]No audits are performed as there is no contractual requirements. All reviews are informally conducted. Since there is no formal delivery, the software quality assurance activity is not involved in the configuration management of the software.

the EDSS software development plan prior to establishing the integration library

3. SCM Activities

3.1 Configuration Identification

3.1.1 EDSS Project Baselines. The requirements baseline (functional baseline) is established as the list of functional capabilities set forth in Addendum 2 of the statement of work in the contract.

The design baseline (allocated baseline) is established as the source code and associated design documentation, and all test procedures of the *as built* configuration items are successfully demonstrated to the customer at site A.

The prototype system baseline (product baseline) is established by the current design baseline of site A and versions of the configuration items for sites B and C at the end of the final demonstration.

Integration baselines are used to maintain successive builds during the development of the prototype demonstration at site A. A significant number of software builds at site A can be expected.

3.1.2 EDSS Project Labeling. The basis for labeling is by mnemonic labels assigned to each unit. In addition, each source unit shall have a prologue embedded in it. This prologue shall contain the following elements:

(1) Unit name
(2) Component name or identifier
(3) CI identifier
(4) Programmer name
(5) Brief description of the function of the module
(6) Change history
    (a) Date of each change
    (b) Reason for change (see SCR)
    (c) Change level (version being changed)

For example, the initial version of a unit is A-0, the second is A-1, etc. The change level is incremented each time the code is revised. The change level and the unit name are used to uniquely identify the version of the source code that incorporated a given problem correction, for example, ABC (3) for revision 3 of the unit ABC.

3.2 Configuration Control

3.2.1 Configuration Control Board. The EDSS project manager performs the functions of the change control board. The SCM coordinator supports the project manager by preparing SCR for the manager's review and processing the SCR subsequent to the manager's decision.

3.2.2 Processing SCR. The procedure for handling SCR is described in Attachment B.

3.2.3 CCB Interfaces. The EDSS project manager performs all of the coordination necessary with the customer in reviewing and in accepting, rejecting and negotiating changes. The manager also performs the liaison with the AXCESS vendor. Changes originating from the EDSS project are processed by the SCM coordinator. The two project managers provide coordination between projects and mutually resolve differences.

Changes to a system that result from these agreements are initiated by the responsible project manager.

3.3 Configuration Status Accounting.
Status accounting is accomplished by tracking the changes to units through the use of the SCR form. This manually generated form (reference Attachment C) is updated (upon release) with the version number of each release.

Status of each CI is reported periodically to the project manager or at the manager's request. The status of the revisions to the units and components is reported weekly to the managers of the SDG and T & CG. When a software system is released to a site, the release and version are recorded and the units contained in the system are listed, along with their current change level.

3.4 Audits and Reviews.
No audits are scheduled to be held for the EDSS system. Instead, the system is verified through the customer's functional testing. Parallel operation using the site's previous manual system and the new system is maintained until the users are confident that the system is producing accurate reports and displays. The SCM coordinator attends performance/functional reviews to record action items and change status.

Functional reviews are held periodically during the software development cycle. The principle document used is the *User Interface Guide*. This document contains the layouts of each of the displays and reports the users have available from the system. Each data element in each display or report is defined there, along with the method by which the element is derived (if any).

4. Tools, Techniques, and Methodologies

The primary technique for SCM is the manual processing of SCR, SCA, and SPR. The SCR form (see Attachment C) is used to record all customer requests for changes, their disposition, and eventual implementation. The same form is used to record enhancements or changes requested by the SDG. These forms later become the basis for updating the requirements specifications and for resolving questions concerning the origin of a change or the status of a requirement that arise during implementation, during integration, installation and checkout at site(s) and during the demonstrations.

A set of basic SCM tools is available for use. A data management system is used for recording and reporting status of the units, components, and CI.

The integration library uses a file system to check in and check out units for revision and test. The project master library uses the same system to impound master copies of the units and components.

Release of code to the integration library is made through software promotion requests (SPR) shown in Attachment A. The software is compiled and built into a protected integration package owned by the T & CG. Software successfully demonstrated at the sites is placed in the EDSS master library for future demonstrations and upgrades.

5. Supplier Control

There is no pertinent information for this section.

6. Records Collection and Retention

Copies of each status report are maintained as a historical record for the EDSS project until the project is terminated or the prototype demonstration system is replaced by the production system. These records are transferred to microfiche as they age over six months.

The prototype system baseline code, test data and reports, and documentation shall be maintained at the termination of the project for a period of two years or until replaced by a production system. The software media for retention of this baseline code is magnetic tape. The documentation for this is retained on microfiche.

Test procedures and test data resulting from the successful demonstrations shall be retained as a part of the data for use in defining the production system.

Attachment A

Software Promotion Requests

Table 1 defines the list of data elements included in the Transaction file for release of each unit.

Table 1
Data for Software Release

Element Name	Definition
CI number	Number assigned for CI identification
Sub-application	The name or number assigned to the unit or portion of the CI being released
Release request	Data release was requested
Action requested	The control action requested by the development activity (builds, move to test library)
Members	Names of modules, units to be included in the release
Change level	The change level or version number of the units being released
Justification	The number or the statement of justification concerning the reason for release
From library	The library location of the units before the release
Member type	The type of the unit being released (procedures, macros, test drivers)
Load module	The load module with which the units are linked
Time tag	The time tag for the version of the unit being promoted

Attachment B

IEEE Guide for
Processing System Software Change Requests

System/Software Change Request (SCR) forms are used to document three types of situations:

(1) Requests for changes to the software by the customer (whether these requests result from tests, demonstrations, or from experience at the sites).

(2) Requests for changes by the designers or coders (generated within the company) that affect code already in use at the sites.

(3) Problems or errors in the code in test or at the sites that were clearly not requests for new or different functions — documented *bugs* in the released code

1.1 Processing steps are

(1) All SCR are logged in by the SCM coordinator and assigned a number on receipt. After logging, the SCR is forwarded to appropriate manager for action or resolution.

(2) When an SCR results in a software change (whether a correction or a new function), the software manager annotates the SCR form at the time of release of the new software to the sites and forwards the SCR to the SCM coordinator who then updates the master file.

1.2 SCM Coordinator.
The SCM coordinator attends all customer/designer meetings and acts as the recorder of change requests. Signature approvals are obtained at that time.

When a release of software to sites is being prepared, the SCM coordinator meets with the project manager and review all outstanding SCR against the released software.

The SCR closed at that time are documented by the SCM coordinator.

Attachment C

System/Software Change Request Form

The following data elements are included on the SCR form.

Table 1
SCR Data Elements

Element	Values
CI	The name of the configuration item involved
Environment	The hardware site involved (may be more than one as project uses three different types of minicomputers)
Change type	Legal values: new function, error correction, design change
Date requested	DD/MM/YR
Narrative description	Description of the change desired in language as explicit as possible; description of the problem in the case of error reports
Disposition	Final disposition: fixed, accepted but delayed, rejected.
	If fixed, description of changes made are included here
Requester	Person making the request for the change
Requester site	Location of the person making the request
Release and version	The release and version number in which the problem existed
Implementation data	List of modules involved in the change on system/software change request form
Implementation release and version	Release and version number in which change appears
Implementation ship date	Date on which the change is shipped to the sites
Responsible manager signature	
Customer approval signature	(Used only for changes to software already released for field use)

Appendix C

Software Configuration Management Plan for a
Software Maintenance Organization

Version 1.0

Approved

_____

Mgr SPLIT Facility

_____

Mgr SCM Dept

Date: ___ /___ /___

Synopsis

This example contains a discussion of a hypothetical programming facility that manages the support software systems used in the design, development, test and maintenance of the software systems for a large software engineering company. The company has approximately twenty-seven hundred employees of whom nine hundred are professional software engineers with degrees in computer science, computer systems or electrical engineering. The average experience of the professional engineers is five and one-half years. The software products they build and maintain are primarily real-time systems for many applications, some critical and some not. The company has an extensive investment in software engineering facilities. There are software engineering work stations for a third of the professional programming staff and terminals available for the support staff. The work stations are attached to a local area network that is integrated with a large number of mini-computers and two mainframes.

The programming facility, SPLIT, is staffed with one hundred and thirty-five people. Fifty are systems and maintenance programmers. There is a software configuration management department within the company that performs all of the configuration management activities for the facility and the software engineering groups. Special emphasis is placed on the management of the products in the SPLIT facility since the productivity and reputation of the company directly depends on the efficiency and reliability of the support software used by the engineering groups. A special software configuration management group is permanently assigned to the SPLIT facility with the responsibility for controlling the company's support software. The company management supports this focus — as long as the software engineering activities do not complain too loudly about the service they receive.

In this environment, the software configuration management group in the facility has a direct role in the control of the support software. This group processes all changes made to the support software by the system programmers, builds the run-time systems and performs all the other normal configuration management activities. The role of configuration management in maintenance makes this group a major part of the facility's management team.

Since the company has a considerable investment in the support software and data records, the disaster control practice requires that the support software in the production library have copies in the software archival repository. The company maintains the software repository in a protected shelter thirty-five miles from the main facility.

Contents

Appendix C

Software Configuration Management Plan for a
Software Maintenance Organization

1. Introduction

This plan describes the standard operating procedures for managing the configuration of all the support software available to the users of the SPLIT facility. The SPLIT facility provides the supporting software used in the design, development and maintenance of software products produced by the company. All of the support software products available to the users of the SPLIT facility are maintained under configuration management to ensure that users have continual and reliable service from the software products in the run-time environment, and that errors in the support software and requests for enhancements are handled accurately, completely, and in a timely manner.

1.1 Purpose of the Plan. This operating plan specifies procedures whereby software configuration management supports the entire software change/enhancement process.

1.2 Scope. This plan defines the SCM activities necessary for maintaining all support software items being procured, tested, sustained and kept in the production environment in the facility. The list of the software configuration items will vary over time. The consolidated list of configuration items and their status is maintained by the SCM group within the SPLIT facility and published monthly in the SPLIT configuration summary.

1.3 Definitions and Mnemonics
1.3.1 Definitions. The terms used in this plan conform to the definitions found in ANSI/IEEE Std 729-1983, IEEE Standard Glossary of Software Engineering Terminology.
1.3.2 Mnemonics. The following mnemonics are used within this document:

CCB	Configuration Control Board
CCM	Configuration Change Management [system]
CI	Configuration Item
CM	Configuration Management
COMM	Communications Software
EWS	Engineering Work Stations

HW	Hardware
LAN	Local Area Network
SCA	Software Change Authorization
SCM	Software Configuration Management
SCMG	Software Configuration Management Group
SCMP	Software Configuration Management Plan
SSQAG	SPLIT Software Quality Assurance Group
SCR	System/Software Change Request
SQA	Software Quality Assurance
SQAG	Software Quality Assurance Group
STEG	SPLIT Test and Evaluation Group
SDT	Software Development Tools
TFR	Transfer File Request

1.4 References[17]

[1] ANSI/IEEE Std 729-1983, IEEE Standard Glossary of Software Engineering Terminology.

[2] ANSI/IEEE Std 828-1983, IEEE Standard for Software Configuration Management Plans.

[3] GP:25, Software Configuration Management.

[4] GP:26, Software Change Request Processing.

[5] SF:39, Vendor License Identification and Accountability.

[6] SF:27, Inspection and Test of Support Software Products.

[7] SF:15, Test and Evaluation Group Activities.

[8] CMP:13, Identification and Labeling of Software.

[9] CMP:25.3, Unit Naming Conventions.

[10] CMP:25.4, Version Level Designation.

[11] CMP:37, Computer Program Media Identification and Marking.

[12] CMP:12, Software Auditing.

[13] SP:17, Support Software Status Reporting.

---

[17]Referenced documents are available for use in the SPLIT software reference library.

67

[14] SP:12, Operation of SPLIT Configuration Control Board.

[15] SP:5, User Documentation Maintenance.

[16] SP:7, SPLIT Production Library Maintenance.

[17] SP:95, Work Station Request and Allocation.

[18] SCMG-WP:19, Data Retention—SCR/SCA.

[19] SCMG-WP:1, Software Release Procedures.

2. Management

2.1 Organization. The vice-president managing the SPLIT facility reports to the company president along with the vice-president in charge of the product effectiveness group and the vice-president in charge of the operations division (engineering). The configuration management (CM) department is part of the product effectiveness group. The software configuration management group (SCMG) is administratively a part of the CM department and their activities are responsive to the policies set by the CM department; but, functionally, they report to the manager of the SPLIT facility.

The organizational structure of the SPLIT facility is shown in Fig 1.

2.1.1 Operations Group. The operations group maintains the processing and communications systems, installs and reconfigures hardware installations, and performs the day-to-day operations of the processing environments.

2.1.2 Systems Software Programmers. The systems software programmers perform the main-tenance on the support software developed in-house (generally by the engineering division) and subcontracted software acquired by the facility. Third party software acquired from vendors is not maintained by the SPLIT facility.

2.1.3 Test and Evaluation Group. The test and evaluation group performs the acceptance tests for vendor and subcontracted software and also all new releases for in-house support software maintained by the systems software programmers.

2.1.4 User Consultants. The user consultants provide training to that portion of the company that does not include Section 2.1.3 in the use of the support software systems, and consulting services to the software engineers as needed. They are the primary source of change requests for support software.

2.1.5 SPLIT Software Quality Assurance Group. The SSQAG is functionally a part of the product effectiveness group. They perform evaluations of new software as an incoming QA function, and periodic audits of the operations of the facility.

2.1.6 Multiple Configuration Control Boards. There are multiple configuration control boards (CCB) within the facility. The senior CCB, called the SPLIT CCB, has overall responsibility for managing the hardware and software configurations in the facility. This responsibility includes

(1) Allocating SPLIT resources for use on company projects
(2) Setting overall schedules for support software updates and new version releases
(3) Allocating resources to update configurations of mainframe processors, the minicomputer nodes, and the LAN/Hi-Speed data bus configurations.

Fig 1
SPLIT Facility Organization

Fig 2
Structure of CCB

(4) Providing resources to subordinate CCB that manage software product lines

The manager of the SPLIT facility chairs the SPLIT CCB. The head of the SCMG is the alternate chairman and attends all meetings of the SPLIT CCB.

The in-house software is grouped by function into three separate CCB

    (a) Software development (SWDEV) tools

    (b) Programming environments (PROG)

    (c) Communications (COMM) software

These subordinate CCB have configuration management responsibility for support software developed in-house, and managing the changes approved for software acquired from outside sources. Individual product line CCB are assigned to software products developed by the company, but their operation is independent of the SPLIT facility CCB. When these company software products are used in the SPLIT facility, they are controlled in the same way any product purchased from an outside vendor is controlled. The software used in the engineering work stations has a separate work station CCB for tracking the volatile hardware and software configuration.

Each SPLIT facility CCB is responsible for allocating resources needed for maintaining their assigned software products. Where changes affect interfaces with other hardware or software within the facility, or both, the issue must be brought before the SPLIT facility CCB. The head of the SCMG cochairs the SPLIT facility CCB and work station CCB with their respective managers.

Each project making use of a software product has representation on the CCB controlling that product.

2.2 SCM Responsibilities. The primary SCM responsibilities involve supporting the change process as it affects existing software product baselines; maintaining an accounting of the status

of *all* the software configuration items in the facility; and auditing physical configurations (CI) received from subcontractors, vendors of commercial software used in the facility, and support software from the company engineering division.

2.2.1 Identification. The SCMG is responsible for maintaining the identification (numbering, labeling, and integrity of documentation) for all the support software in the facility. Responsibility also extends to identifying the configuration items that are acquired from commercial vendors.

2.2.2 Configuration Control. The SCMG is responsible for supporting the change process for all of the support software used in the SPLIT facility.

2.2.3 Configuration Status Accounting. The SCMG maintains the data base used to prepare reports on the status of all support software products and hardware configurations used in the facility.

2.2.4 Audits and Reviews. Audits are performed by two groups

    (1) The SCMG performs physical configuration audits of all support software acquired by the facility. Periodic inventory audits of the support software are also performed as directed by the SPLIT facility manager

    (2) The SCMG supports SSQAG in performing functional configuration audits of incoming subcontracted and vendor-provided support software. The SCMG also provides SSQAG with summary data on probable causes of failure

The SCMG works directly with the STEG in evaluating software changes being released to the production library.

2.3 Interface Control. One of the most critical activities is controlling the interfaces between the different software systems in the facility and between the software and changing hardware configurations.

The SCMG supports the interfaces between the multiple CCB by recording action items affecting each interface and following up on them to see that they are accomplished in a timely manner.

The SCMG maintains configuration control of the specifications and standards controlling the interfaces between the software elements of the workstations. The workstation configuration must include both hardware and support software for each installation. This includes accounting for leased and licensed software used on personal computers and in workstations.

The SCMG maintains the operating system configuration used in the SPLIT facility as a means for enforcing control of the interfaces with the applications programs.

2.4 SCMP Implementation. The staff of the SCMG is composed of one group head, who acts as coordinator, and one qualified SCM administrator for each separate SPLIT facility CCB (one per CCB). One additional person has the function of tracking the EWS configuration(s).

Computer resources and work space are provided by the SPLIT facility manager for the SCMG.

Milestones for SCMG activity are set by the manager of the SPLIT facility and reflect the ongoing continuous support activities required for managing the various support software configurations.

2.5 Applicable Policies, Directives, and Procedures

  2.5.1 Policies
  (1) Company Policy
    (a) GP:25, Software Configuration Management
    (b) GP:26, Software Change Request Processing
  (2) SPLIT Policies
    (a) SF:39, Vendor License Identification and Accountability
    (b) SF:27, Inspection and Test of Support Software Products
    (c) SF:15, Test and Evaluation Group Operations

  2.5.2 Directives
  (1) Company Bulletin, GB:87, *Use of Licensed Software*
  (2) Company Directive, CD:34, *Copyright Protection*
  (3) Company Bulletin(s), GB:(various), *CCB Membership*

  2.5.3 Procedures
  (1) Company Procedures
    (a) CMP:13, Identification and Labeling of Software
    (b) CMP:25.3, Unit Naming Conventions
    (c) CMP:25.4, Version Level Designations
    (d) CMP:37, Computer Program Media Identification and Marking
    (e) CMP:12, Software Auditing
  (2) SPLIT Procedures
    (a) SP:17, Support Software Status Reporting
    (b) SP:12, Operation of SPLIT Configuration Control Board
    (c) SP:5, User Documentation Maintenance
    (d) SP:7, SPLIT Production Library Maintenance
    (e) SP:95, Work Station Request and Allocation
  (3) SCMG Procedures
    (a) SCMG-WP:19, Data Retention — SCR/SCA
    (b) SCMG-WP:1, Software Release Procedure

3. SCM Activities

3.1 Configuration Identification. Each support software product in the facility is identified by configuration item title, specifications, user documentation, and media labels in accordance with established company procedures.

Since the software being managed has already had a product baseline established, the identification schema is already set. The SCMG uses the identification and labeling standards in the product baseline. In-house software identification follows company procedures CMP-13; 25.3; 25.4; and 37. Third-party software is labeled with company-defined labels for record-keeping purposes.

The elements of software (programs, documentation, test data, etc) in the production library (the library of software released for running on hardware in the facility) is organized as in Table 1.

Table 1
Hierarchy of Elements

Generic Term	Alternate Terms
Configuration item	Package, product
Component	Segment, program
Unit	Module, routine

The level of control applied by the SCMG will generally be to the component level. Components are considered to be the *controlled item* in managing the operation of the SPLIT facility. A given programming library used by systems programmers may have a system for managing configurations of software units previously used in the development and maintenance of other programs. Sometimes the units in these libraries are referred to as packages, following the concepts of *reusable software* being advocated.

3.1.1 Baseline Identification. Support software product baselines are established during incoming inspections of the product at the facility. New releases to a product baseline are labeled in accordance with 2.5.3(1)(c). New releases include changes or updates as necessary to the product package—specifications, user documentation, design documentation (listings), test procedures, and associated test and inspection reports. The procedure 2.5.3(1)(a) is followed for each new release of a support software product.

A new release of a support software product is made in accordance with 2.5.3(3)(b).

The scheduling of a new release is determined by the SPLIT CCB.

3.1.2 Product Baseline Cataloging. Labeling of product CI is in accordance with 2.5.3(1)(a). The SCMG reviews each request to be released for conformance to company procedures. The SCMG then checks the release package against the transfer file and the CCB authorization for completeness and STEG/SSQAG approvals.

3.2 Inspection and Receiving. New products entering into the facility for use are inspected for conformance to 2.5.3(1)(a) by the SCMG. Vendor software parts (configuration items) are given company CI part numbers in the 7000 series for maintaining separate accountability within the status accounting system.

3.3 Configuration Control
3.3.1 Levels of Authority for Approvals. All software is tested by the STEG prior to its promotion into the integration library or the production

library. Both STEG approval and SCMG approval is required before the software is promoted to the integration library or production library.

The promotion of changes into the integration library is authorized by the SPLIT facility and work station CCB and approved by the SCMG after design checks by the STEG.

The release of changes to the production library is authorized by the SPLIT CCB. Prior to entering changes into the production library, each change is tested and verified as correct by the STEG, checked for conformance to packaging standards by SSQAG, and administratively approved by the head of the SCMG before being placed into the library.

3.3.2 Change Proposal Processing
3.3.2.1 SCR Processing. Software change requests are prepared using the form C-1049, software/system change request, or use of the SCR ENT command in the interactive configuration change management (CCM) system. Manually prepared forms (C-1049) are entered into the CCM system by the SCMG librarian. The same form used to initiate a problem report is used for requesting an enhancement to the system. All changes are concurrently routed to the SCMG files in the CCM system for administrative checks and to the appropriate product line manager for verification. Each SCR is reviewed by technical personnel and their evaluation is forwarded to the appropriate SPLIT CCB for action.

The SPLIT CCB can approve, reject, or table (with an action date) a request pending further information.

Action in response to a SCR is scheduled by the CCB in response to the severity of the problem reported or the need for enhancement. Problem reports are given priority over change requests not associated with an operating problem. Problem reports (as indicated on the SCR form) are processed on an expedited basis.

Problem reports that are determined to be valid errors in the performance of the system and given priority for solution with temporary fixes are incorporated into the subject system—along with publication of a bulletin notifying all users of the

Table 2
Problem Criteria

Category	Symptom
"C"	A software item cannot be executed by a user
"M"	Users have problems with a program but can work around with temporary fix
"S"	Minor irritation but users can still accomplish work

change in the system. Permanent modifications to correct the error are incorporated with the next upgrade released to all users.

Requests for system enhancements that are valid and within the scope and resources allocated to the software product are scheduled for incorporation in the next scheduled upgrade to that product.

Approvals are incorporated in the maintenance schedule and a release date tentatively identified for a scheduled upgrade or correction to the affected support software product(s). Status of these SCR is indicated as *approved*.

The SCR may be returned to the user when additional clarification is needed or when the results of the design review may necessitate additional design analysis or even modification to the change request. The SCR is held with the status *pending* until a course of action has been determined.

Testing for promotion to the integration library or release to the production library may result in additional design changes or recoding. In that event, the status of the SCR reflects *approved* and the status of the SCA reflects *in-work*. The status of the SCR/SCA action is changed to *implemented* only if the change has been completed, verified, and released into the production library.

3.3.2.2 SCA Processing. Approved SCR are forwarded by the CCM system to the appropriate programming activity for implementation. Similar changes that are grouped together for an upgrade are worked on at the same time. Emergency changes (needed to keep the system in operation) are expedited through the system. The programming activity extracts necessary files for work from the production library and makes the changes. When the supervisor is ready to integrate the file, the SCA and the code are completed and passed to the CCM_HLD/INT area for administrative checks by SCMG before being released to the integration library for integration and test.

STEG performs the integration and testing, requesting modifications from the programming activity as appropriate. When it has been demonstrated that the change package is correct and introduces no additional errors into the system, the SPLIT CCB is informed of the pending update whereby STEG initiates a transaction file request (TFR). Upon approval by the SPLIT CCB, the SCMG enters the change into the production library. The status of the SCR/SCA is then changed to *closed*.

The SCMG performs the systems generation of the run-time programs used in the facility, and loads, after verification by the STEG, into the necessary hardware configurations.

Failure of the users to accept the changes in the support software system may result in it being returned to a previous step or cancellation of the task.

3.3.2.3 Changes to EWS. The processing of changes to work station support software is the same as the above procedure except that the run-time software generation and allocation to HW configuration is controlled by the EWS CCB network manager.

3.3.2.4 Changes to Supplier Software. Change processing for subcontracted software is performed in the same manner described above when the source code is in-house and maintenance is being performed by the SPLIT systems software programmers. When the software product is under subcontractor warranty, the SCR is passed to the subcontractor and the new version is accepted into the production library in the usual manner. In the event where the subcontractor has a maintenance contract for the product, the SCR is passed on to them for processing.

3.3.2.5 Licensed Software. Licensed software is given a company label with a unique identifier to indicate limited use. Periodic audits are conducted by the SCMG to determine adherence to the license limitations by users.

3.3.2.6 Purchased Commercial Software. Purchased commercial software is relabeled with company identifying numbers and released for use and configuration management in the same manner as in-house developed software.

3.3.3 CCB Roles. The CCB evaluation takes into consideration, among other things, the staff resources available versus the estimated workload of the request; the estimated additional computing resources that are required for the design, test, debug, and operation of the modified system, and the time and cost of updating the documentation.

An essential function of each CCB is to coordinate the flow of information between the users of the software product and the maintenance organization supporting the product. This function is executed when the CCB representatives of the project use the products and monitor the evaluation of the significance of problem reports and requests for enhancements. The result of the CCB review is the assignment of a priority to each request.

3.3.4 Control of Interfaces. There is no pertinent information for this subsection.

3.4 Configuration Status Accounting. The SCMG supports the following reports:

(1) *SPLIT Software Configuration Report.* An accounting of the software and hardware configurations of all the systems within the SPLIT facility. This report is kept current at all times. Weekly reports are made to the SPLIT facility manager, including changes just completed and changes scheduled for the next week.

(2) *SPLIT Performance Summary.* A monthly summary of the up-time of all systems and an analysis of all problems causing unscheduled down-time.

(3) *SCR/SCA Summary.* For each configuration item, a summary of the current status of SCR/SCA activity is given on a weekly basis to the SPLIT facility manager. The SCR summary includes problem type and severity, priority given by the CCB, activity or programmer assigned, and target release date for either the fix or new release.

(4) *EWS Configuration Status.* This configuration status is maintained in a data base for general access. Status and configuration summaries are presented to the SPLIT facility manager on a weekly basis.

3.5 Audits and Reviews. The SCMG performs a physical configuration audit on all incoming third-party software.

The SCMG performs functional and physical configuration audits on each new release of software in the system.

The SCMG performs periodic audits of the software and hardware configurations in the facility to ascertain that no unauthorized changes have been made. Particular attention is paid to licensed software.

4. Tools, Techniques, and Methodologies

4.1 Use of the CCM System. The CCM system is used to manage and track all changes to the software in the SPLIT facility. The system provides for initiating changes, review and approval by management, assigning and monitoring work status, and the testing and releasing of all changes. Status reporting is provided as an output from the CCM data base. This configuration management tool is one of the set of software tools used

in the SPLIT facility by all of the operating activities.

4.2 Inspections. Releases to the production library are inspected to confirm inclusion of scheduled SCR/SCA.

4.3 Library Management. The SCMG makes disciplined use of programming libraries to manage the changes to support software configuration items. The SCMG and the STEG cooperate in promoting software modifications from the development library into the integration library and from there releasing them to the production library.

4.3.1 Development Library. The development library is used by the systems software programmers as they develop their code. The units and components are controlled by the individual programmers. Criteria for allowing promotions into the integration library includes the successful completion of unit testing and approval by the group's supervisor.

4.3.2 Integration Library. The integration library is used by the SCMG to capture and build the code that is designated for promotion to the STEG for integration and test. This library contains the source code and executable load modules created as a result of a system build. The source code is placed in a special controlled library in preparation for a build. Then the code is recompiled and link edited before it is placed in the integration library. Criteria for releasing to the production library includes

(1) Submission of a software release request by the SPLIT CCB

(2) Completion of status accounting audits and resolution of issues by SCMG

(3) Acknowledgment of regression and integration test completion by the STEG and SQA

All test data and routines used to verify software released for use are also maintained under configuration control in the integration library.

4.3.3 Production Library. The production library contains the master copies of all the support software configuration items used in the SPLIT facility. Copies are made from the masters by the SCMG for use on other systems. The production library acts as backup for the run-time configurations used on the systems. Only current master copies of support software configuration items are maintained in the production library.

4.3.4 Software Repository. Current copies of all support software configuration items from the production library are maintained in the software repository. Historical copies of support software released for use outside the facility are maintained in the repository for a period of ten years after release.

5. Supplier Control

Since the SCMG does not have responsibility for supporting the development of subcontracted software, the SCMG has no interface with the support software developed in this way.

The SCMG does participate with the STEG in the receiving inspection of commercial software and subcontracted software to ascertain that

(1) All physical items are available as required by contract
(2) The proper labels are on the media to be placed in the integration library, and subsequently, in the production library

The SCMG is responsible for the physical configuration audit of subcontracted and vendor-supplied software. The SQA activity performs the functional configuration audit.

6. Records Collection and Retention

Records of SCR/SCA processing are retained for a period of five years to support fiscal standards of records. Status reports of the SPLIT facility configurations are also maintained for a period of five years.

Records defining the product baselines of all support software products released for use outside the facility (in conjunction with engineering division sales) are maintained for a period of twenty years to protect product warranties. The product baselines of all other support software products developed in-house but not released for use outside the facility are maintained for a period of ten years.

Records of licensed vendor software integrated, or otherwise used, with internal configurations are maintained for a period of five years after their removal from the system.

Biweekly backups of the systems are archived for a period of six months to protect the data files of the ongoing engineering division development activities. Backups of the systems processing company financial records are archived for a period of seven years, as required by law.

Attachment A

System/Software Change Request
(SPLIT Form C-1049)

Table 1
Definitions of Elements in SCR

Element	Values
Originator	Name of the person making the request
Product	Originator's subject support software product
Date	Date of change request (option: date of anomaly detection for the SCR
SCR number	Sequential number assigned for the product in question
SCR title	A concise descriptive title of the request
SCR type	One of the following types: AR — Anomaly Report SCN — Specification Change Notice ECR — Engineering Change Request ER — Enhancement Request IR — Impound Request
Program	Identification of the support software product for which the change is requested
System version	Version identifier of the system for which the change is requested
Description of change	Originator's description of the need for a change
Disposition	CCB indicates one of the following dispositions: Approved — Date approved and assigned for implementation _____ Deferred — Date deferred to _____ Rejected — Date rejected _____
User class	Indicates organization/activity using the software
Date needed	Indicates date the change is needed in the production system

For those SCR referencing anomalies detected in a product baseline, the CCB must verify that the problem exists and the following data should be added:

Optional Data for Anomaly Reports

Item	Data
1	System configuration on which the anomaly was detected.
2	Performance effect — The effect the anomaly has on the performance of the system [c] critical; [m] major; or [s] small

Attachment B

Software Change Authorization

Table 1 defines the list of data elements included in the SCA file for releasing each unit. The SPLIT facility CCB may add to the list of elements. Deletions are made only with explicit approval of the SPLIT CCB.

Table 1
Definitions of Elements in SCA

Element Name	Definition
CI number	Number assigned for CI identification
Date	(1) Date change was released to the integration library
	(2) Date change was released to the production library
SCR number	The SCR number of the request/authority for making the change
Subapplication	The name or number assigned to the unit or portion of the CI being released
Release request	Date release was requested
Action requested	The control action requested by the development activity (builds, move to integration library, etc)
Programmer(s)	The names of the programmer(s) making the changes
Members	Names of modules, units affected by the change in the release
Change level	The change level or version number of the units being released
Justification	The number or the statement of justification concerning the reason for release
From library	The library location of the units before the release
Member type	The type of the unit being released (procedures, macros, test drivers)
Load module	The load module with which the unit will be linked
Verified by	Name of the person approving the verification
Verified system name	Identification of system used for testing change
Time tag	The time tag for the version of the unit being released

Appendix D

Software Configuration Management Plan for a
Product Line System

Version 1.0

Approved

_____

Director, Engineering

_____

PLAS Program Manager

Date: ___ / ___ / ___

Synopsis

This example Plan contains a discussion of a hypothetical project in a microelectronics company that makes microprocessors and microprocessor-based systems that are later embedded within other hi-tech electronic systems. The company has approximately nineteen hundred employees, of which one hundred and thirty-four are in the engineering division and the remainder are in the production division, marketing, and administration group. There is an extensive investment in hardware CAD/CAM to make the operation productive and a lesser investment in computer-aided engineering (CAE). Office automation is used to minimize the costly handling of paper; therefore, most of the communication within the company uses electronic media. Customers buy hardware or systems — receiving software products only as part of a system.

There is no independent software development activity. Software technology is considered a basic skill that electronic engineers and system designers use in their day-to-day work. The engineers design software for execution within their system's RAM or ROM with the same ease as they use the silicon compilers to design chips. There are two focal points where the different engineering design technologies interact with the configuration management discipline. The first focal point is in the system's computer aided engineering system where the engineering libraries (where functional logic and piece/part information is maintained) or data bases and VLSI design systems are maintained. The second focal point is in the production computer aided manufacturing system where the programmed logic is transformed from compiled into deliverable products. The two focal points are separate as the mode of implementation demands different interfaces — the production system interfaces directly with the hardware CAD/CAM systems in production; the engineering system with the software/firmware development stations and prototype-testing stations. The configuration management software to support management of these data bases is largely embedded within the program management system, which schedules work and manages the changes to baselines.

In this environment, the software configuration management disciplines are just another one of the tools used by engineering and production management for performing their daily tasks. The software configuration management plan focuses primarily on establishing unique project data base structures in the engineering systems, routing the change management materials to named organizational positions for approvals, and defining data-base baselines. Software configuration management is a service provided by the engineering, production, and management systems to help management more effectively perform their tasks.

Contents

Appendix D

Software Configuration Management Plan for a
Product Line System

1. Introduction

This guide describes the plan for managing the configurations of stored program logic used in manufacturing the product line analysis system (PLAS) module. This module performs the computational, communications, and device-controller functions of a larger system — *The Quick Stretch*, which performs stress analysis for mechanical structures. This system is sold as a proprietary company product to customers and is maintained by field representatives of the company. The company intends that the PLAS module have functional flexibility through its use of computer programs to make the module adaptable to other company proprietary systems and possibly for sale to other systems manufacturers.

1.1 Purpose. This plan identifies the procedures for managing the configurations of the PLAS computer programs during their development and for maintenance of the programs throughout the time period the company sells and has warranty responsibility for the products that incorporate the PLAS as an embedded system.

1.2 Scope. This plan is applicable to the development and maintenance of all the computer programs embedded in ROM, loaded into EPROMS, or loaded into RAM for use in the PLAS module. Configuration management of the hardware associated with the PLAS module is covered in a PLAS hardware configuration management plan — PLAS-CMP. These computer programs, packaged in different media, are collectively managed under the single configuration item *PLAS software configuration item* regardless of their function. The computer programs packaged for ROM or EPROM are managed as hardware components, identified under their prime hardware configuration item identification. The support software used in production and test of the PLAS module components (both hardware and computer programs) is also controlled by this plan.

1.3 Definitions and Mnemonics

1.3.1 Definitions. The terms used in this plan conform to the definitions found in ANSI/IEEE Std 729-1983, *IEEE Standard Glossary of Software Engineering Terminology*.

hard logic. Programmed logic that is embedded as circuit logic in a chip. The logic is developed using the general software engineering tools and disciplines. Packaging of the logic uses silicon compilers for generating the geometry of the chip.

P-CAMS. The product computer aided manufacturing system (P-CAMS) environment that contains

(1) The engineering data bases of hard logic and stored-programmed logic defining the products in the production environment (the controlled libraries)
(2) The support software used in converting the controlled engineering data bases into instructions and data for
  (a) Production of chips, software and firmware
  (b) Test programs and data for verifying that the produced entities have been correctly implemented

User documentation is also produced using P-CAMS. Configuration management disciplines relating to product serialization, change labeling and tracking, and verification tests are a part of this environment.

project-management system (PMS). The PMS provides the capability for management to

(1) Define an identification schema for projects at start-up time and to make changes to the different schemes
(2) Authorize and control the release of project drawings and engineering data bases from the dynamic libraries in systems computer-aided engineering system (SCAES) to the controlled project libraries in P-CAMS

(3) Schedule the production and release of product changes, and coordinate the production schedules within the production division

In general, this system supports the configuration management change control board (CCB) and production scheduling activities.

stored program logic. Computer program instructions and data that are executed out of RAM, ROM, and EPROM in the PLAS module. The instructions and data are developed using general software engineering tools and disciplines. Packaging of the instructions and data uses technology appropriate for the media.

systems computer aided engineering system (SCAES). The SCAES environment is composed of

(1) A variety of engineering support software including different simulators, prototyping tools, modeling programs, engineering design aids, documentation tools, test generators, test simulators, utilities and compilers
(2) Engineering libraries (the **dynamic** libraries) that contain general algorithms that have widespread utility, reusable stored-programmed logic, reusable hard-logic functions, and access to selected product designs
(3) Design data bases representing the dynamic working libraries for product developments that are currently in progress (such as the PLAS module development)

The commands that are used in SCM disciplines for supporting identification of entities relating to a specific project and for tracking current versions of those entities are an integral part of SCAES.

1.3.2 Mnemonics. The following mnemonics are used within this document:

APM	Associate Program Manager
CAD/CAM	Computer-Aided Design/Computer-Aided Manufacturing
CAE	Computer-Aided Engineering
CAES	Computer-Aided Engineering Systems
CCB	Configuration Control Board
CI	Configuration Item
CM	Configuration Management
CMP	Configuration Management Plan
CMS	Change Management System
CSCI	Computer Software Configuration Item
DP&S	Data Processing and Support

EPROM	Erasable Programmable Read Only Memory
EWS	Engineering Work Stations
EWSW	Engineering Work Stations Environment
LSI	Large Scale Integration
MSI	Medium Scale Integration
P-CAM	Product Computer-Aided Manufacturing System
PLAS	Product Line Analysis System
PMS	Project Management System
QC	Quality Control
ROM	Read Only Memory
SCA	System Change Authorization
SCR	System Change Request
SCAES	Systems Computer-Aided Engineering System
TD	Technical Director
VDD	Version Description Document
VLSI	Very Large Scale Integration

1.4 References

[1] PLAS Functional Requirements.[18]

[2] Engineering Work Station and Environment User's Manual.

[3] Programming Standards Manual.

[4] Product Line Identification Numbering Standard.

[5] Software Quality Assurance Policy.

[6] Production Test Standards.

2. Management

2.1 Organization. The PLAS program manager of the product line has financial and administrative responsibility for all PLAS module engineering and production. He is part of the administration and reports directly to the general manager of the company. The company uses a matrix organization for managing projects.

The PLAS program manager has final responsibility for the business success of the program. The project staff consists of the financial staff, the technical director (TD), an associate program manager (APM), and a quality representative from the quality control (QC) department. The PLAS APM is functionally a part of the production division and attends all PLAS project meetings.

---

[18]All referenced documentation is available from the SCAES library.

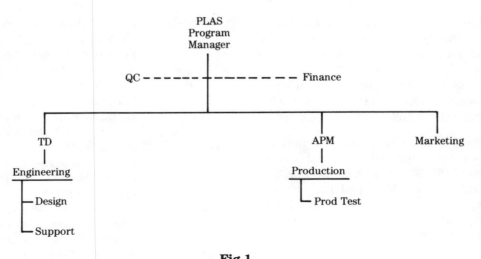

Fig 1
PLAS Organization Chart

The major elements in the administration, engineering division, and production division that support the PLAS product line include

(1) Marketing (administration) provides the sales and marketing support to
 (a) Perform market analyses and prepare functional requirements for the Quick Stretch System that indirectly determine the functional requirements for engineering the PLAS module
 (b) Maintain customer liaison for product maintenance and improvement and
 (c) Sell the Quick Stretch Systems
(2) The PLAS engineering design group (engineering division) is an ad hoc organization under the direction of the PLAS technical director, which provides engineering expertise to
 (a) Manage the overall system design activity
 (b) Develop the hard logic, the stored program logic, and drawings for PLAS assemblies
 (c) Review all proposed changes for feasibility, cost, and design integrity
 (d) Perform all necessary engineering design and logic changes
(3) The PLAS engineering support group (engineering division) provides the technicians and technical resources to
(a) Maintain the SCAES_PLAS engineering data base
(b) Perform product engineering based on design prototypes to be released for production

(c) Support TD and PLAS program manager in verifying design changes prior to release to P-CAMS.
(4) The PLAS production group (production division) activity, under direction of the PLAS APM, provides the capability to
 (a) Manufacture hardware in accordance with PLAS drawings released for production
 (b) Compile, verify, and package programmed logic released as software for PLAS RAM
 (c) Compile, verify, and burn-in programmed logic released as firmware for PLAS EPROM
 (d) Compile, verify, and coordinate mask production or programmed logic released as firmware for PLAS ROM
 (e) Compile, verify, and coordinate production of hard logic released as VLSI chips
 (f) Test complete assemblies of PLAS modules
 (g) Maintain inventories
 (h) Ship PLAS modules to customers as directed by the PLAS program manager

The functions that are generally performed by a separate SCM activity and not supported by SCAES and PMS are shared between the quality control representative and the APM. This is possible because most of the detailed SCM processing activities and library interface management are accomplished by the PMS.

The PLAS technical director is the chairperson of the configuration control board (CCB). The PLAS identification scheme implemented in the SCAES control system is approved by the chairperson of the CCB. The responsibility for reviewing and approving all changes to established baselines and scheduling releases belongs to the CCB chairperson. Release of PLAS engineering data base(s) to P-CAMS and all changes to the P-CAMS data base for PLAS is authorized by the CCB chairperson.

2.2 SCM Responsibilities

(1) The PLAS program manager provides general direction to the TD for establishing the identification scheme, to the APM for production scheduling, and authorizes the establishment of baselines. The PLAS program manager also provides general direction to the TD for CCB actions and issues requests for QC to audit and review the integrity of the SCAES_PLAS engineering data base and the P-CAMS_PLAS production data base.

(2) The PLAS TD establishes the contract identification schema used by the PLAS project engineers and performs (or delegates to engineering support group) the duties of updating the P-CAMS_PLAS production data base when authorized by CCB actions. All changes to the P-CAMS_PLAS production data base are approved by the TD.

(3) The PLAS associate program manager (or a delegated assistant, such as a librarian) has overall responsibility for maintaining the P-CAM PLAS data base, PLAS unit and module tests, and production schedules.

(4) The production test group is responsible for testing the hardware assemblies, including the units containing the packages of programmed logic (ROM and EPROM), and verifying that the correct version of the logic is embedded in the device. The group also verifies that the diskettes containing the dynamically loadable software for the PLAS module is the correct version for shipment. Final assembly tests of these units along with VLSI chips are also conducted by this group.

(5) The PLAS quality control representative is responsible for reviewing the production test group's verification activities, and auditing the integrity and use of SCAES_PLAS engineering data base and P-CAMS_PLAS production data base. The QC representative verifies the physical configuration of the PLAS module, its associated user documentation, and its functional capabilities (review of module acceptance testing) as a part of the quality review prior to shipment.

(6) The engineering support group provides special extractions from the SCAES, P-CAMS and PMS systems data bases showing status of the various baselines when information other than that provided by general project status commands is required.

(7) The marketing organization provides the functional requirements for the system and is the major source of high-level system changes and improvements. In effect, this organization defines the functional baseline. Customers purchasing a PLAS module for their own use or for the PLAS module integration in the Quick Stretch System have no direct interface or review authority over PLAS baseline activities or product capabilities.

2.3 Interface Control. The data bases for the PLAS module are maintained in two different library systems: the SCAES_PLAS engineering data base and the P-CAMS_PLAS production data base. The interface between these two data bases is controlled by PLAS CCB authorizations.

The SCAES_PLAS engineering data base is made up of several parts representing

(1) Top-level drawing of the PLAS module
(2) Detail design representations of the programmed logic as it is to be packaged for implementation in ROM, EPROM, and RAM based software
(3) Detail designs for implementation in chips (LSI and VLSI designs)
(4) Electrical engineering drawings for cards and assemblies and
(5) Mechanical drawings for the module assemblies

The interfaces between these subdata bases are managed as developmental baselines during the engineering development phase of a PLAS module.

The interface with the Quick Stretch System, or with customer defined systems using the PLAS module, is defined by the top-drawing design data base. Changes in this interface are made only with the authority of the TD. In case of conflict, the PLAS program manager negotiates the changes with the appropriate system representative.

Interfaces with the P-CAMS_PLAS production data base and the computer-aided manufacturing software are managed by the APM in production division, as long as the changes do not affect the CAES_PLAS engineering data-base interface.

2.4 SCMP Implementation

2.4.1 PLAS Configuration Baselines.
The functional baseline is established when the system level description for the PLAS module is approved by the general manager for prototype development. Marketing surveys and analyses of potential customer applications provide a description of the desired functional capabilities of the proposed system. The functional baseline is documented with the marketing analysis report, supplemented by a preliminary top-level drawing of a proposed system. This baseline is considered obsolete after acceptance of the preproduction baseline.

The allocated baseline is established upon approval of the top-level drawing and preliminary detailed designs, verified by simulation runs, by the PLAS program manager. This baseline is obsoleted after acceptance of the preproduction baseline.

The developmental baselines are established by the TD at his/her discretion as needed for coordinating the changing allocated baselines during development. The developmental baselines represent incremental software builds needed to develop the prototype system and to verify revisions to the production baseline or different models of the production baseline for various customer applications.

The preproduction baseline is established with the successful demonstration of a prototype system and an absence of any priority 1 (emergency) error reports or changes outstanding. The PLAS program manager authorizes development of the preproduction baseline when given the go-ahead by Marketing management.

The production baseline is established with the concurrence of the PLAS APM and PLAS TD that the design is functionally adequate and that the production facilities of the production division can produce the design in an economical way. The production baseline is a formal agreement between the PLAS program manager and the production division manager.

2.4.2 The Configuration Control Board.
The PLAS technical director is the chairperson of the PLAS CCB. This review activity is established at the initiation of preproduction model development.

2.4.3 The Support Environment.
The SCAES environment consists of a compatible set of engineering and software development tools that can work with the general engineering data base and special data bases set up for different projects, such as PLAS. The configuration of this support software environment is most carefully controlled by the company data processing and support (DP & S) organization. The support software that interfaces with the data-base management system is most rigidly controlled but there is latitude for engineers to develop special programs restricted to engineering work stations (EWS), that do not generate data for entry into the dynamic engineering data bases. Access keys for controlling entry to the SCAES_PLAS engineering data base are assigned to responsible engineers at the onset of allocated baseline development.

The P-CAMS environment interfaces with a wide variety of CAM and computer-aided test (CAT) systems. These interfaces are critical for the reliable management and administration of company operations. The company DP & S organization manages these interfaces. Any changes must be approved (among other approvals) by the PLAS APM. This review activity is initiated with the development of the preproduction baseline.

Vendor software is used extensively in the supporting software environments of CAES and P-CAMS. Vendor software is also used extensively in the EWS environment supporting SCAES. The management of the vendor software in the EWS environment that is not under the control of the company DP & S organization is initiated by the PLAS TD after the preproduction baseline is established.

2.4.4 SCM Resource Requirements.
The resources required for providing configuration management of the PLAS module development and production are embedded in the requirements for training, management oversight, computer resources, administrative support from the engineering support group and DP & S maintenance.

(1) *Training requirements.* Approximately two days training is needed for a new hire engineer to become familiar with use of the data bases and control programs relative to managing configurations. This time is allocated as a part of the overall training program for new hires.

(2) *Management oversight.* Approximately two hours a week are spent on CCB reviews and six hours a week using the PMS control program to schedule analysis and imple-

mentation of system change requests (SCR).

(3) *Computer resources.* Storage requirements for configuration data are a small part of the engineering and production data bases for PLAS modules. The requirements for processor time varies from day to day, but generally does not exceed three minutes of CPU time per day for processing each SCR.

(4) *Support software maintenance.* DP & S is budgeted three man-years effort per year for maintaining the software used for PLAS module configuration management.

2.5 Applicable Policies, Directives, and Procedures

2.5.1 Existing Policies and Procedures. The following company policies are used for configuration management on the PLAS subsystem:

(1) Product Line Identification Numbering — Supplement 2

(2) Corporate Software Protection Policy (Rev 3)

(3) Quality Control Policy for Engineering Data Bases

(4) Production Test Standards

(5) Engineering Standards for Detail Design and Drawings

(6) User's Manual for SCAES

(7) User's Manual for EWS

(8) User's Manual for P-CAMS

2.5.2 New Policies and Procedures To Be Written. The following procedure(s) will be developed for the PLAS project:

(1) Managing of Third-Party Software: Proprietary Marking

(2) PLAS Project Naming Standards

3. SCM Activities

3.1 Configuration Identification. The identification scheme for the PLAS project is developed by the engineering support group and approved by the PLAS TD. The numbering and labeling standards are distributed for project use in the *PLAS Project Naming Standards document.*

3.1.1 Naming Conventions. All data in the SCAES_PLAS engineering data base is arranged and retrievable under the collective identifier PLAS-1800000.

All control level items (programmed logic components and hardware assemblies) are identified within a block of numbers beginning with 532000 and ending with 554000. The engineering support group allocates the numbers for the control level items.

Programmed-logic components have a version description document (VDD) associated with their assigned number. Each assigned number has a preceeding letter identifying the media in which the logic is embedded:

ROM = R
EPROM = E
Diskette[19] = S
Gate arrays = G
PLA = P

Programmable microcontrollers = M

Hardware drawing numbers are assigned to a control level drawing. Parts list for the drawing is made up of part numbers assigned from the 700000 series of numbers.

Reprogrammed logic components keep their basic 1000 number assigned to them in the general SCAES engineering data base. Dash numbers, referencing appropriate VDD, tracks embedded CI, and associated SCR.

3.1.2 Implementation. Identification is assigned to each component and unit defined in the top-level drawing. When an engineer defines a unit, he/she indicates to the program the type of component he/she is defining and the system assigns the appropriate number. Programmed login associated with a defined hardware component or unit is linked to that component's identifier in a *packaging list* associated with the top-level drawing.

Components and units are identified by form, fit, and function (data flow). The engineer defining a component or unit is automatically made *owner* of that component or unit. Changes in the form, fit, or function cannot be made without his/her consent and approval of change. The CAES design tools automatically flag conflicts and force resolution before another of the iterative development baselines can be created.

All system entities associated with the design (specifications, drawings, detail documentation, test data, test procedures, etc) are assigned the appropriate component or unit identifier with which they are associated.

The identifiers assigned in the SCAES_PLAS engineering data base are transferred to the P-CAMS_PLAS production data base at the time

---

[19]Used for shipping software that executes out of RAM. Software media characteristics may vary but the implementation designator is always *S.*

the preproduction baseline definition effort is initiated.

3.1.3 Ownership Notification Procedures. Filing of software copyright notices for proprietary programmed logic developed for the PLAS project will be performed by Marketing.

Notification to users of the PLAS module copyright will be included in the load module of the software released to the user on the PLAS module diskette. Visual indication of ownership and copyright registration will be displayed at the console when the system is booted, in accordance with Revision 3 (current) of the corporate software protection policy.

All documentation released to customers will be marked with a proprietary notice, vendor license number, or both.

3.2 Configuration Control. Authority for approving changes to baselines varies in accordance with the baseline being changed and the phase of the project.

(1) Authority for approving changes to the *functional baseline* is vested in the PLAS program manager. The PLAS program manager coordinates all changes with the production department manager and with the PLAS TD. This baseline is obsoleted with the initiation of the production baseline.

(2) Authority for approving changes to the *allocated baseline* is vested in the PLAS TD. The PLAS TD coordinates all changes in the allocated baseline with the PLAS program manager and PLAS APM for production. This baseline is shared by SCAES and P-CAMS during the period after the preproduction demonstration is accepted and the production baseline is formally defined.

(3) Authority for approving changes to *developmental baselines* is vested in the PLAS TD. The PLAS TD establishes the developmental baseline criteria, resolves conflicts in allocation and ownership of components or units, and sets schedules for iteration of these baselines.

(4) Authority for approving changes to the *preproduction baseline* is vested in the PLAS TD. The PLAS TD makes changes in allocation and detail design to fit the production facilities on the recommendation of the PLAS APM from production division. Conflicts are resolved by the PLAS program manager.

(5) Authority for approving changes to the *PLAS production baseline* is vested in the PLAS CCB, chaired by the PLAS TD. The PLAS APM and PLAS marketing representative are members of the PLAS CCB. Technical representation from PLAS engineering and PLAS production activities are made when necessary. The PLAS QC representative and production test group representative are permanent members of the PLAS CCB.

Technical review of the system change requests (SCR) is provided by members of the engineering support group who assemble engineering analyses as required, and by members of the PLAS production team who assemble information on the impact of a proposed SCR as required

3.2.1 Change Processing. Changes to the system may originate from the marketing organization (in response to customer desires), from the test group in the production division, or from within the engineering division. Requests for changes are submitted by way of electronic mail using the SCR format provided in the EWS environment. Changes originating from outside the company are entered into the program management system (PMS) by marketing representatives. Internally originated changes are submitted by way of local engineering work stations.

The PMS control system routes SCR to the originator's supervisor for verification when appropriate, and then queues it for review and disposition by the appropriate change authority for the affected baseline. When change requests require further analysis, the change authority routes the SCR (electronically) to the appropriate support group for gathering information. When the support group has assembled a complete analysis package, it is again queued to the appropriate review authority or CCB for disposition. This authority then disposes of the request by indicating approval (providing a schedule and effectivity date of change), deferring it for further analysis or allocation of resources, or disapproving it with reason(s) for disapproval noted.

Approved changes are electronically routed to the PLAS engineering group for implementation.

The tracking of changes is performed in the PMS control system, based on the SCR approval flow status and system change authorizations (SCA), or by extractions from the PLAS data bases in SCAES or P-CAMS to which it has access.

3.2.2 Production Baseline Changes. Changes to the production baseline are made only after changes have been verified in a test environment on a test model of the PLAS module, using simulated test drivers or mock-ups to test the system.

Table 1
Processing Approved Changes

Baseline	Entity	Implemented By	Verified By	Scheduled By
Functional	Document	Engineering	Eng check	Various
Allocated	Document	Engineering	Eng check	Various
Developmental	Document	Engineering	Eng check	TD
	Design data	Engineering	Simulation	TD
	Drawings	Engineering	Eng check	TD
Preproduction	Document	Eng or prod	Eng check	TD
	Design data	Engineering	Simulation	TD
	Drawings	Engineering	Eng check	TD
Production	Document	Production	Test Gp	APM
	Design data	Engineering	Test Gp	APM
	Drawings	Engineering	Eng check	APM

The production test group verifies the changes as operational and authorizes release of the change data from the SCAES_PLAS engineering data base to the P-CAMS_PLAS production data base. The transfer of data is performed by the engineering support group.

3.2.3 PLAS Module Release. Each PLAS module version is released for use in a Quick Stretch System or to individual customers for incorporation into their systems, along with a technical data kit containing the top-level drawings of the system, associated parts lists, and the VDD for control level programmed logic components.

Since PLAS software, released on diskettes, provides the most flexible means of adaptation, provisions exist to release the software VDD independently of the rest of the data packages. This way, revisions to the PLAS functions can be made to PLAS modules in systems released previously. This requires that the configuration of all released modules be maintained in an archive, along with an extraction from the P-CAMS configuration environment containing all support software used in the production and test of that delivery.

3.3 Configuration Status Accounting. The following PLAS configuration status reports are regularly available:

(1) *PLAS Module Development Status.* This is a listing of all configuration items, control level items, and units that are being designed or modified by engineering. The report identifies each unit/control-level-item/CI, status of technical work, outstanding SCR, SCA ready for release, and units or changes released since the last reporting period. This report is generated weekly for the PLAS management team.

(2) *PLAS Module Production Status.* This is a listing of all configuration items, control level items and units that are in production. The report identifies all units in production during the period, SCR/SCA incorporated, scheduled release date (by contract number), and schedule variance. The report is generated weekly for the PLAS management team.

(3) *SCR Status Summary.* This report lists all outstanding SCR that have not been resolved or incorporated into delivered modules. The report lists, for each SCR: CCB action date and disposition; group or department presently responsible for action; status of activity; and schedule for completion. The report is prepared weekly but is available any time the PLAS management team requests it.

(4) *Special Queries.* The report generator of the PMS program provides a query capability that allows anyone to extract the status of:
  (a) Any one SCR
  (b) All open SCR
  (c) All SCR in engineering
  (d) All SCR in production
  (e) PLAS modules in production with associated SCR number

The general query capability for the data-management systems allow formulation of special queries in the PMS control program for interrogating the SCAES_PLAS engineering data base and the P-CAMS_PLAS production data base for information relative to any changes that are in process or that have been released to customers.

3.4 Audits and Reviews

3.4.1 Audits. The PLAS module configuration is audited each time a baseline is established.

(1) *Functional Baseline.* The PLAS program manager is responsible for ascertaining if the reports and design descriptions are complete enough to present to management.

(2) *Allocated Baselines.* The PLAS technical director is responsible for reviewing the designs to ascertain if the designs are complete enough to present to the PLAS program manager. The engineering support group assists the TD in this review.

(3) *Developmental Baselines.* The engineering support group uses the PMS control program to

    (a) Generate set/use type analyses of the detailed designs to uncover outstanding discrepancies and

    (b) Establish design activity cut-offs for a specific iteration.

This group also supports the changes by modifying access codes to the new baseline to restrict entry of changes. The TD reviews the summaries of design activities to estimate technical progress in the design.

(4) *Preproduction Baseline.* Prior to establishing the preproduction baseline, the configuration is again audited by the engineering support group to ascertain that the design of the demonstration meets all functional requirements established by the functional baseline and that all entities generated in the developmental baselines are present or accounted for in the demonstration. The QC representative assists in the review of entities for this baseline.

(5) *Production Baseline.* The QC representative reviews the entities in the P-CAMS_ PLAS production data base to ascertain that all functional capabilities demonstrated for the preproduction model and all changes stemming from the review of the demonstration are present in the data base. The production test group reviews the entities to verify that all changes and modifications to the preproduction demonstration have been made to the production data base. The engineering support group performs a comparison of the engineering data base with the production data base to verify that the transfer of data is complete. The PLAS TD is responsible for preparing this audit.

(6) *Shipping Review.* The PLAS module and its associated documentation package is audited prior to shipment to a customer, either as a part of the Quick Stretch System or as an independent line item to a customer.

The functional audit is performed by the QC representative who reviews the PLAS module against the appropriate extracted data from the P-CAM_PLAS library for that item. A representative from the PLAS engineering support group reviews the product to ascertain that the physical configuration of the module and its associated documentation represents

    (a) The specified configuration ordered by the customer

    (b) The corresponding configuration in the P-CAMS_PLAS data base and

    (c) Accurately reflects any changes that have been made to the data base by the PLAS CCB

Discrepancies or problems uncovered in reviews and audits are reported to the PLAS program manager for resolution.

4. Tools, Techniques, and Methodologies

The basic configuration management tool used for PLAS module is the change management program (CMP), which is a part of the PMS. This program supports change management by

(1) Providing the means to enter system/software change requests (SCR)

(2) Forcing reviews by appropriate supervision by way of the electronic mail system

(3) Deriving analytical data from each SCR

(4) Providing for supervision or CCB review and approval, as appropriate

(5) Directing authorized changes to engineering or production supervision

(6) Providing for authorizing of changes to the P-CAMS_PLAS data base

(7) Providing for transfering data from the PLAS engineering data base to the production data base

The SCM tool for establishing the identification scheme for PLAS data bases is resident in the SCAES system. This information is transferred to the production data base during the preproduction phase. It is verified when the production baseline is established.

Order information from marketing is entered into the PLAS production schedule by way of the program management system. The detailed configuration is formatted by the configuration management program in CMS, passed on to the P-CAMS_ PLAS data base upon approval of the PLAS program manager, and reviewed for schedule and resource consumption by the PLAS APM. Upon his/her approval, resources are committed to the production configuration. Extractions of this configuration are released for inspection and auditing at time of shipment.

5. Supplier Control

Subcontracted PLAS support software is placed under configuration management after inspection and acceptance by the QC representative.

6. Records Collection and Retention

6.1 Backup Data Base. The engineering data base from SCAES_PLAS is backed-up on a weekly basis and stored in Beskin's storage building during the engineering phase (up to the time the production baseline is established). Following establishment of the production baseline, the engineering data base is backed-up on a monthly basis.

The production data base from P-CAMS_PLAS is backed-up on a weekly basis.

6.2 Archive Data Base. Archive data is maintained for purposes of warranty protection, proprietary data production, and liability insurance. The following data are maintained in on-line optical storage media:

(1) Copies of each baseline data base extracted at the time the baseline is established
(2) Copies of order and configuration data passed from PMS to the production data base for each order and
(3) Copies of each configuration of the data base used for production of customer order
(4) Copies of reviews and audits performed on each production item

Appendix E

References Bibliography

Preface

This Appendix contains selected bibliography pertaining to the subject of software configuration management. The list of publications contains both government and private sector references so users may find material applicable to their situation. Because of the scarcity of literature pertaining to configuration management, and especially to software configuration management, the fullest possible list of references will be useful to the practitioner.

Most of the references contain some information regarding software configuration management. The topic of software configuration management plans is addressed in a subset of these references.

References Bibliography

E1. General Bibliography

[1] BERSOFF, E., HENDERSON, V., and SIEGEL, S. *Software Configuration Management, An Investment in Product Integrity.* Englewood, N.J.: Prentice-Hall, 1980.

[2] BERSOFF, E., HENDERSON, V., and SIEGEL, S. *Software Configuration Management: A Tutorial.* Computer, *IEEE Computer Society Magazine*, vol 12 no 1, Jan 1979.

[3] *Configuration Management Procedures (CMP)*, Global Engineering Documents, 1984.

[4] *IEEE Transactions on Software Engineering*, IEEE Computer Society, vol SE-10, nr 1, Jan 1984.

[5] BUCKLE, J. K. *Software Configuration Management*, New York: The Macmillan Press Ltd, 1982.

[6] DANIELS, M. A. *Principles of Configuration Management*, Advanced Applications Consultants, Inc, 1987.

[7] BABICH, W. A. *Software Configuration Management*: Coordination for Team Productivity, New York: Addison-Wesley, 1986.

E2. Military Standards for SCM[20]

[8] MIL-STD-481A Configuration Control—Engineering Changes, Deviations, and Waivers (Short Form).

[9] MIL-STD-482A Configuration Status Accounting Data Elements and Related Features.

[10] MIL-STD-483A Configuration Management Practices for Systems Equipment, Munitions, and Computer Programs.

[11] MIL-STD-490A Specification Practices.

[12] MIL-STD-499A Engineering Management.

[13] MIL-STD-881A Work Breakdown Structure.

[14] MIL-STD-962A Outline of Forms and Instructions for the Preparation of Military Standards and Military Documents.

[15] MIL-STD-1456 Contractor Configuration Management Plan.

---

[20] Military Standards may be ordered from the Commanding Officer (Code 301) Naval Publications and Forms Center, 5801 Tabor Avenue, Philadelphia, PA 19120.

[16] MIL-STD-1521B Technical Reviews and Audits for Systems, Equipments, and Computer Programs.

E3. Department of Defense Standards

[17] DoD-STD-480 Configuration Control-Engineering Changes, Deviations and Waivers.

[18] DoD-STD-1467 Software Support Environment.

[19] DoD-STD-2167 Defense System Software Development.

[20] DoD-STD-2168 Software Quality Evaluation.

[21] DoD-STD-7935 Automated Data Systems Documentation.

E4. Military Specification

[22] MIL-D-1000B Drawings, Engineering, and Associated List.

[23] MIL-S-83490 Specifications, Types and Forms.

E5. Department of Defense Directives

[24] DoDD 4120.21 Specifications and Standards Applications.

[25] DoDD 5000.1 Major Systems Applications.

[26] DoDD 5000.19L Acquisition Management Systems and Data Requirements Control List.

[27] DoDD 5000.39 Acquisition and Management of Integrated Logistic Support for Systems and Equipment.

[28] DoDD 5010.19 Configuration Management.

[29] DoDD 7920.1 Life Cycle Management of Automated Information Systems (AIS).

E6. Department of Defense Instructions

[30] DoDI 5000.2 Major Systems Acquisition Process.

[31] DoDI 5000.38 Production Readiness Reviews.

[32] DoDI 7045.7 The Planning, Programming and Budgeting System.

[33] DoDI 7935.1 DoD Automated Data Systems Documentation Standards.

E7. US Government Publications[21]

[34] DoD Configuration Management Standardization Program, (CMAM) Plan.

[35] DoD Trusted Computer System Evaluation Criteria, CSC-STD-001-83, 15 Aug 1983.

[36] *NASA Handbook 8040.2.* System Engineering Management Guide, Defense System Management College, 1983. Configuration Management, Management Instruction, GMI8040.1A. NASA Goddard Space Flight Center.

[37] Federal Information Processing Standards (FIPS) *Publication 106.* Guideline on Software Maintenance, National Bureau of Standards. Institute for Computer Sciences and Technology, 1984.

[38] MARTIN, R. and OSBORNE, W. *Special Publication 500-106,* Guidance on Software Maintenance. National Bureau of Standards, Institute for Computer Sciences and Technology, 1983.

[39] McCALL, JIM, HERNDON, MARY, and OSBORNE, WILMA. *Special Publication 500-129,* Software Maintenance Management, National Bureau of Standards, Institute for Computer Sciences and Technology, 1985.

---

[21] Copies of these publications can be obtained from the Superintendent of Documents, US Governmental Printing Office, Washington, DC 20402.

E8. Electronic Industries Association Publications[22]

[40] EIA CMB 4-1a (Sept 1984), Configuration Management Definitions for Digital Computer Programs.

[41] EIA CMB 4-2 (June 1981), Configuration Identification for Digital Computer Programs.

[42] EIA CMB 4-3 (Feb 1981), Computer Software Libraries.

[43] EIA CMB 4-4 (May 1982), Configuration Change Control for Digital Computer Programs.

[44] EIA CMB 5 (April 1973), Subcontractor/ Vendor Configuration Management and Technical Data Requirements.

E9. American Defense Preparedness Association Publications[23]

[45] Proceedings of the 24th Annual Meeting, Technical Documentation Division, May 1982, Denver, Colorado.

[46] Proceedings of the 25th Annual Meeting, Technical Documentation Division, May 1983, Ft. Monroe, Virginia.

[47] Proceedings of the 26th Annual Meeting, Technical Documentation Division, May 1984, San Antonio, Texas.

---

[22] EIA publications can be obtained from the Standards Sales Department, Electronics Industries Association, 2001 Eye Street, NW, Washington DC 20006.

[23] Copies of these publications can be obtained from the American Defense Preparedness Association, 1700 N. Monroe St, Suite 900, Arlington, VA 22209.

ANSI/IEEE
Std 1058.1-1987

An American National Standard

IEEE Standard for
Software Project Management Plans

Sponsor

**The Software Engineering Technical Committee
of the
Computer Society of the IEEE**

Approved December 10, 1987

IEEE Standards Board

Approved October 6, 1988

American National Standards Institute

1058.1

Foreword

(This Foreword is not a part of IEEE Std 1058.1-1987, IEEE Standard for Software Project Management Plans.)

Purpose

This standard specifies the format and contents of software project management plans. It does not specify the exact techniques to be used in developing project plans, nor does it provide examples of project management plans. Each organization that uses this standard should develop a set of practices and procedures to provide detailed guidance for preparing and updating software project management plans based on this standard. These detailed practices and procedures should take into account the environmental, organizational, and political factors that influence application of the standard.

Not all software projects are concerned with development of source code for a new software product. Some software projects consist of a feasibility study and definition of product requirements. Other projects terminate upon completion of product design, and some projects are concerned with major modifications to existing software products. This standard is applicable to all types of software projects; applicability is not limited to projects that develop operational versions of new products. Application of this standard is not limited by project size. Small projects may require less formality in planning than large projects, but all components of this standard should be addressed by every software project.

Software projects are sometimes component parts of larger projects. In these cases, the software project management plan may be a separate component of a larger plan or it may be merged into the system level project management plan.

Overview

This standard contains three sections. Section 1 defines the scope of the standard and provides references to other IEEE standards that should be followed when applying this standard. Section 2 provides definitions of terms that are used throughout the standard. Section 3 contains an overview and a detailed specification of the standard, including required components that must be included, and optional components that may be included in project plans based on this standard. The sequence of project plan elements presented in Section 3 does not imply that project plans should be developed in the order of presentation. In most instances, project plans based on this standard will be developed by repeated iteration and refinement of the various elements in the plan.

Audience

This standard is intended for use by software project managers and other personnel who prepare and update project plans and monitor adherence to those plans.

Evolution of Plans

Developing the initial version of the software project management plan should be one of the first activities to be completed on a software project. As the project evolves, the nature of the work to be done and the decomposition of work will be better understood. The project management plan must be updated periodically to reflect the evolving situation. Thus, each version of the plan should be placed under change control, and each version should contain a schedule for subsequent updates to the plan.

Terminology

This standard follows the IEEE Guide to Standards Development. In particular, the words shall, must, and the imperative form identify mandatory material within the standard. The words should, might, and may identify optional material.

History

The project authorization request for development of this standard was approved by the IEEE Standards Board on December 13, 1984. Modification of the authorization request was approved in September, 1986. Ten meetings were held within the United States and internationally between September, 1984, and September, 1986. These meetings produced the draft submitted for balloting in December, 1986.

Contributors

This standard was developed by the Software Project Management Plans Working Group of the Software Engineering Standards Subcommittee of the Computer Society of the IEEE. The following individuals contributed to the development of this standard:

Richard H. Thayer, *Chairman*   **Richard E. Fairley,** *Co-Chairman*

Gary L. Whitten, *Secretary*

Steering Committee

Ronald L. Atchley	Hosein Fallah	Robert F. Metz
H. Jack Barnard	Richard Johansson	Patrick A. Rich
François Coallier	Kari Kansala	Hans Schaefer

Working Group

Bakul Banerju	Galwin Ferwin	Robert Poston
George J. Bozoki	Cheng Hu	David Schultz
V. Churchill	John A. King	Robert Shillato
Peter Coad	Thomas M. Kurihara	Daniel Solis
P. I. Davis	F. C. Lim	George Spidel
Raymond Day	Richard W. MacDonald	Richard Van Tilburg
T. Debling	Roger Martin	Delores Wallace
J. Deleo	Randy Paddock	David Weiss
Ake Dovstram	Francoise Perrodeau	Lauri Werth
R. Ferreol		Janusz Zalweski

Supporting Organizations

The following organizations provided support for development of this standard:

AT&T Bell Laboratories	National Bureau of Standards
AT&T Information Systems	NCR Corporation
Bell Canada	Programming Environments, Inc.
California State University, Sacramento	Standard Telecommunications Labs
Center for Industrial Research, Norway	System Development Corporation
Compagnie D'Informatique Militaire, France	Technical Research Centre of Finland
Computer Sciences Corporation	Teleindustrier AB, Sweden
Goodyear Atomic Corporation	U.S. Department of Commerce
Hughes Aircraft Company	U.S. Department of Transportation
Institute of Atomic Energy, Poland	U.S. Naval Research Laboratories
Intercon Systems Corporation	University of Nevada, Las Vegas
Lockheed Missiles & Space Co.	University of Texas, Austin
Mirror Systems, Inc.	Wang Institute of Graduate Studies

The Software Engineering Standards Subcommittee comprised the balloting committee that approved this document for submission to the IEEE Standards Board, and at the time of balloting was composed of the following persons:

A. F. Ackerman
Richard L. Aurbach
Motoei Azuma
H. J. Barnard
J. Behm
H. Ronald Berlack
Michael A. Blackledge
Giles Bracon
J. Joseph Brandt
Kathleen L. Briggs
A. Winsor Brown
F. Buckley
L. J. Call
H. Carl
John W. Center
John Chihorek
T. S. Chow
J. K. Chung
Won L. Chung
Antonio M. Cicu
Judith Clapp
Peter Coad, Jr.
François Coallier
Christopher M. Cooke
Richard Cotter
T. Daughtrey
Peter Denny
F. M. Discenzo
David A. Dobraiz
David Doty
Einar Dragstedt
William Dupres
Albert D. DuRee
Mary Eads
L. E. Egan
W. D. Ehrenberger
Steven R. Eisen
Walter Ellis
Caroline Evans
Richard E. Fairley
David W. Favor
Joan Feld
John Fendrich
Glenn S. Fields
Violet Foldes
T. Foote-Lennox
Joel Forman
Julian Forster
Richard C. Fries
F. K. Gardner
L. B. Gardner

David Gilperin
Shirley Gloss-Soler
J. G. Glynn
Andrej Grebenc
Victor Guarnera
Lawrence M. Gunther
David A. Gustafson
J. A. Haksi
Jeffrey Hickey
John W. Horch
Cheng Hu
Laurel V. Kaleda
Harry Kalmbach
Daniel E. Klingler
Shaye Koenig
Joseph A. Krupinski
Joan Kundig
T. Kurihara
Lak Ming Lam
John B. Lane
Robert A. C. Lane
G. Larsen
F. C. Lim
Bertil Lindberg
B. Livson
Austin Maher
Paulo Cesar Marcondes
Nicholas Marselos
Roger Martin
John McArdle
J. A. McCall
R. McDowell
Manijeh Moghis
Charles S. Mooney
Gary D. Moorhead
D. D. Morton
G. T. Morun
Hiranobu Nagano
Geraldine Neidhart
Dennis Nickle
Wilma M. Osborne
Michael T. Perkins
W. E. Perry
John Petraglia
Donald J. Pfeiffer
I. C. Pyle
Thomas S. Radi
Salim Ramji
Jean-Claude Rault
Meir Razy
Donald Reifer

Patrick A. Rich
R. San Roman
John C. Rowe
Margaret Rumley
Julio G. Sanz
Steven Schach
Wolf A. Schnoege
Norman Schneidewind
David Schultz
Gregory D. Schumacker
Leonard W. Seagren
Gerard P. Shabe
Robert Shillato
David Siefert
William J. Singer
Jacob Slonim
H. M. Sneed
V. Srinivas
G. Wayne Staley
Franklin M. Sterling
Mary Jane Stoughton
W. G. Sutcliffe
Michael H. Taint
Richard H. Thayer
Paul U. Thompson
Terrence L. Tillmans
Valentin Tirman
G. R. Trebble
C. L. Troyanowski
William S. Turner, III
Robert Urling
David Usechak
Thomas E. Vollman
Dolores R. Wallace
John P. Walter
Dale R. Webdale
Charles J. Wertz
Peter J. Weyman
Allan Whitaker
Gary L. Whitten
Andrea S. Williams
Patrick J. Wilson
W. Martin Wong
Dennis L. Wood
Paul R. Work
Nancy Yavne
Natalie C. Yopronka
Leon Young
Donald Zelenu
Hugh Zettel
Peter Zoll

When the IEEE Standards Board approved this standard on December 10, 1987, it had the following membership:

Donald C. Fleckenstein, *Chairman*   **Marco W. Migliaro,** *Vice Chairman*

Andrew G. Salem, *Secretary*

Contents

IEEE Standard for
Software Project Management Plans

1. Scope and References

1.1 Scope. This standard prescribes the format and content of software project management plans. A software project management plan is the controlling document for managing a software project; it defines the technical and managerial processes necessary to satisfy the project requirements.

This standard may be applied to all types of software projects. Use of this standard is not restricted by the size, complexity, or criticality of the software product. This standard is applicable to all forms of product delivery media, including firmware, embedded systems code, programmable logic arrays, and software-in-silicon. This standard can be applied to any and all segments of a software product lifecycle.

This standard identifies the minimal set of elements that shall appear in all software project management plans. In order to conform to this standard, software project management plans must adhere to the format and content for project plans specified in the standard. However, users of this standard may incorporate other elements by appending additional sections or subsections to their project management plans. In any case, the numbering scheme of the required sections and subsections must adhere to the format specified in this standard. Various sections and subsections of a software project management plan may be included in the plan by direct incorporation or by reference to other plans and documents.

This standard for software project management plans incorporates and subsumes the software development plans described in ANSI/IEEE Std 729-1983 [1][1] and ANSI/IEEE Std 730-1984 [2].

---

[1]The numbers in brackets correspond to those of the references in 1.2.

1.2 References. The standards listed here should be consulted when applying this standard. The latest revisions shall apply.

[1] ANSI/IEEE Std 729-1983, IEEE Standard Glossary of Software Engineering Terminology.[2]

[2] ANSI/IEEE Std 730-1984, IEEE Standard for Software Quality Assurance Plans.

[3] ANSI/IEEE Std 828-1983, IEEE Standard for Software Configuration Management Plans.

[4] ANSI/IEEE Std 829-1983, IEEE Standard for Software Test Documentation.

[5] ANSI/IEEE Std 983-1986, IEEE Guide for Software Quality Assurance Planning.

[6] ANSI/IEEE Std 1012-1986, IEEE Standard for Software Verification and Validation Plans.

2. Definitions

The definitions listed here establish meanings within the context of this standard. Definitions of other terms that may be appropriate within the context of this standard can be found in ANSI/IEEE Std 729-1983 [1].

activity. A major unit of work to be completed in achieving the objectives of a software project. An activity has precise starting and ending dates, incorporates a set of tasks to be completed, consumes resources, and results in work products. An activity may contain other activities in a hierarchical manner.

---

[2]ANSI/IEEE publications are available from the Sales Department, American National Standards Institute, 1430 Broadway, New York, NY 10018; or from the IEEE Service Center, 445 Hoes Lane, P.O. Box 1331, Piscataway, NJ 08855-1331.

baseline. A work product that has been formally reviewed and agreed upon, and that can be changed only through formal change control procedures. A baseline work product may form the basis for further work activity(s).

customer. The individual or organization that specifies and accepts the project deliverables. The customer may be internal or external to the parent organization of the project, and may or may not be the end user of the software product. A financial transaction between customer and developer is not necessarily implied.

project agreement. A document or set of documents agreed to by the designated authority for the project and the customer. Documents in a project agreement may include some or all of the following: a contract, a statement of work, system engineering specifications, user requirement specifications, functional specifications, the software project management plan, a business plan, or a project charter.

project deliverables. The work product(s) to be delivered to the customer. The quantities, delivery dates, and delivery locations are specified in the project agreement.

project function. An activity that spans the entire duration of a software project. Examples of project functions include project management, configuration management, quality assurance, and verification and validation.

review. A meeting at which a work product or a set of work products is presented to project personnel, managers, users, customers, or other interested parties for comment or approval.

software project. The set of all project functions, activities, and tasks, both technical and managerial, required to satisfy the terms and conditions of the project agreement. A software project may be self-contained or may be part of a larger project. A software project may span only a portion of the software product lifecycle.

software project management. The process of planning, organizing, staffing, monitoring, controlling, and leading a software project.

software project management plan. The controlling document for managing a software project. A software project management plan defines the technical and managerial project functions, activities, and tasks necessary to satisfy the requirements of a software project, as defined in the project agreement.

SPMP. Software project management plan.

task. The smallest unit of work subject to management accountability. A task is a well-defined work assignment for one or more project members. The specification of work to be accomplished in completing a task is documented in a work package. Related tasks are usually grouped to form activities.

work package. A specification for the work to be accomplished in completing an activity or task. A work package defines the work product(s), the staffing requirements, the expected duration, the resources to be used, the acceptance criteria for the work products, the name of the responsible individual, and any special considerations for the work.

work product. Any tangible item that results from a project function, activity, or task. Examples of work products include customer requirements, project plan, functional specifications, design documents, source and object code, users' manuals, installation instructions, test plans, maintenance procedures, meeting minutes, schedules, budgets, and problem reports. Some subset of the work products will form the set of project deliverables.

3. Software Project Management Plans

The individual or organization responsible for a software project shall also be responsible for the software project management plan (hereafter referred to as the SPMP). This section of the standard describes each of the essential elements of a SPMP. These elements shall be ordered in the sequence of sections and subsections prescribed in Table 1.

Table 1
Software Project Management Plan Format

Title Page
Revision Chart
Preface
Table of Contents
List of Figures
List of Tables

1. Introduction
   1.1 Project Overview
   1.2 Project Deliverables
   1.3 Evolution of the SPMP
   1.4 Reference Materials
   1.5 Definitions and Acronyms

2. Project Organization
   2.1 Process Model
   2.2 Organizational Structure
   2.3 Organizational Boundaries and Interfaces
   2.4 Project Responsibilities

3. Managerial Process
   3.1 Management Objectives and Priorities
   3.2 Assumptions, Dependencies, and Constraints
   3.3 Risk Management
   3.4 Monitoring and Controlling Mechanisms
   3.5 Staffing Plan

4. Technical Process
   4.1 Methods, Tools, and Techniques
   4.2 Software Documentation
   4.3 Project Support Functions

5. Work Packages, Schedule, and Budget
   5.1 Work Packages
   5.2 Dependencies
   5.3 Resource Requirements
   5.4 Budget and Resource Allocation
   5.5 Schedule

Additional Components

Index

Appendices

The ordering of SPMP elements presented in Table 1 is not meant to imply that the sections and subsections must be developed in that order. The order of presentation is intended for ease of use, not as a guide to the order of preparing the various elements of a SPMP. The sections and subsections of a SPMP may be included by direct incorporation or by reference to other plans and documents.

Detailed descriptions of each section and subsection in a SPMP are presented in sections 3.1 through 3.5 of this standard. Certain additional components may be included in a SPMP. Additional components are described in section 3.6.

Each version of a SPMP based on this standard shall contain a title and a revision notice sufficient to uniquely identify the document. Revision information may include the project name, version number of the plan, date of release, approval signature(s), a list of pages that have been changed in the current version of the plan, and a list of version numbers and dates of release of all previous versions of the plan.

The preface of a SPMP based on this standard shall describe the purpose, indicate the scope of activities, and identify the intended audience for the SPMP. A Table of Contents, and lists of the Figures and Tables in the SPMP shall be included in every SPMP, as indicated in Table l.

3.1 Introduction (Section 1 of the SPMP). This section of the SPMP shall provide an overview of the project and the product, a list of project deliverables, the plan for development and evolution of the SPMP, reference materials for the SPMP, and definitions and acronyms used within the SPMP.

3.1.1 Project Overview (1.1 of the SPMP). This subsection of the SPMP shall provide a concise summary of the project objectives, the product to be delivered, major work activities, major work products, major milestones, required resources, and master schedule and budget. The project overview shall also describe the relationship of this project to other projects, as appropriate. This overview shall not be construed as an official statement of product requirements. Reference to the official statement of product requirements shall be provided in this subsection of the SPMP.

3.1.2 Project Deliverables (1.2 of the SPMP). This subsection of the SPMP shall list all of the items to be delivered to the customer, the delivery dates, delivery locations, and quantities required to satisfy the terms of the project agreement. This list of project deliverables shall not be construed as an official statement of project requirements.

3.1.3 Evolution of the SPMP (1.3 of the SPMP). This subsection of thc SPMP shall specify the plans for producing both scheduled and unscheduled updates to the SPMP. Methods of disseminating the updates shall be specified. This subsection shall also specify the mechanisms used to place the initial version of the SPMP under change control and to control subsequent changes to the SPMP.

3.1.4 Reference Materials (1.4 of the SPMP). This subsection of the SPMP shall provide a complete list of all documents and other sources of information referenced in the SPMP. Each document should be identified by title, report number, date, author, and publishing organization. Other sources of information, such as electronic files, shall be identified in an unambiguous manner using identifiers such as date and version number. Any deviations from referenced standards or policies shall be identified and justifications shall be provided.

3.1.5 Definitions and Acronyms (1.5 of the SPMP). This subsection of the SPMP shall define, or provide references to the definition of all terms and acronyms required to properly interpret the SPMP.

3.2 Project Organization (Section 2 of the SPMP). This section of the SPMP shall specify the process model for the project, describe the project organizational structure, identify organizational boundaries and interfaces, and define individual responsibilities for the various project elements.

3.2.1 Process Model (2.1 of the SPMP). This subsection of the SPMP shall define the relationships among major project functions and activities by specifying the timing of major milestones, baselines, reviews, work products, project deliverables, and sign-offs that span the project. The process model may be described using a combination of graphical and textual notations. The process model must include project initiation and project termination activities.

3.2.2 Organizational Structure (2.2 of the SPMP). This subsection of the SPMP shall describe the internal management structure of the project. Graphical devices such as hierarchical organization charts or matrix diagrams may be used to depict the lines of authority, responsibility, and communication within the project.

3.2.3 Organizational Boundaries and Interfaces (2.3 of the SPMP). This subsection of the SPMP shall describe the administrative and managerial boundaries between the project and each of the following entities: the parent organization, the customer organization, subcontracted organizations, or any other organizational entities that interact with the project. In addition, the administrative and managerial interfaces of the project support functions, such as configuration management, quality assurance, and verification and validation shall be specified in this subsection.

3.2.4 Project Responsibilities (2.4 of the SPMP). This subsection of the SPMP shall identify and state the nature of each major project function and activity, and identify the individuals who are responsible for those functions and activities. A matrix of functions and activities versus responsible individuals may be used to depict project responsibilities.

3.3 Managerial Process (Section 3 of the SPMP). This section of the SPMP shall specify management objectives and priorities; project assumptions, dependencies, and constraints; risk management techniques; monitoring and controlling mechanisms to be used; and the staffing plan.

3.3.1 Management Objectives and Priorities (3.1 of the SPMP). This subsection of the SPMP shall describe the philosophy, goals, and priorities for management activities during the project. Topics to be specified may include, but are not limited to, the frequency and mechanisms of reporting to be used; the relative priorities among requirements, schedule, and budget for this project; risk management procedures to be followed; and a statement of intent to acquire, modify, or use existing software.

3.3.2 Assumptions, Dependencies, and Constraints (3.2 of the SPMP). This subsection of the SPMP shall state the assumptions on which the project is based, the external events the project is dependent upon, and the constraints under which the project is to be conducted.

3.3.3 Risk Management (3.3 of the SPMP). This subsection of the SPMP shall identify and assess the risk factors associated with the project. This subsection shall also prescribe mechanisms for tracking the various risk factors and implementing contingency plans. Risk factors that should be considered include contractual risks, technological risks, risks due to size and complexity of the product, risks in personnel acquisition and retention, and risks in achieving customer acceptance of the product.

3.3.4 Monitoring and Controlling Mechanisms (3.4 of the SPMP). This subsection of the SPMP shall define the reporting mechanisms, report formats, information flows, review and audit mechanisms, and other tools and techniques to be used in monitoring and controlling adherence to the SPMP. Project monitoring should occur at the level of work packages. The relationship of monitoring and controlling mechanisms to the project support functions shall be delineated in this subsection of the SPMP (see 3.4.3).

3.3.5 Staffing Plan (3.5 of the SPMP). This subsection of the SPMP shall specify the numbers and types of personnel required to conduct the project. Required skill levels, start times, duration of need, and methods for obtaining, training, retaining, and phasing out of personnel shall be specified.

3.4 Technical Process (Section 4 of the SPMP). This section of the SPMP shall specify the technical methods, tools, and techniques to be used on the project. In addition, the plan for software documentation shall be specified, and plans for project support functions such as quality assurance, configuration management, and verification and validation may be specified.

3.4.1 Methods, Tools, and Techniques (4.1 of the SPMP). This subsection of the SPMP shall specify the computing system(s), development methodology(s), team structure(s), programming language(s), and other notations, tools, techniques, and methods to be used to specify, design, build, test, integrate, document, deliver, modify or maintain or both (as appropriate) the project deliverables. In addition, the technical standards, policies, and procedures governing development or modification or both of the work products and project deliverables shall be included, either directly or by reference to other documents.

3.4.2 Software Documentation (4.2 of the SPMP). This subsection of the SPMP shall contain either directly or by reference, the documentation plan for the software project. The documentation plan shall specify the documentation requirements, and the milestones, baselines, reviews, and sign-offs for software documentation. The documentation plan may also contain a style guide, naming conventions and documentation formats. The documentation plan shall provide a summary of the schedule and resource requirements for the documentation effort. ANSI/IEEE Std 829-1983 [4] provides a standard for software test documentation.

3.4.3 Project Support Functions (4.3 of the SPMP). This subsection of the SPMP shall contain, either directly or by reference, plans for the supporting functions for the software project. These functions may include, but are not limited to, configuration management [3]; software quality assurance [2] and [5]; and verification and validation [6]. Plans for project support functions shall be developed to a level of detail consistent with the other sections of the SPMP. In particular, the responsibilities, resource requirements, schedules, and budgets for each supporting function shall be specified. The nature and type of support functions required will vary from project to project; however, the absence of a software quality assurance, configuration management, or verification and validation plan shall be explicitly justified in project plans that do not include them.

3.5 Work Packages, Schedule, and Budget (Section 5 of the SPMP). This section of the SPMP shall specify the work packages, identify the dependency relationships among them, state the resource requirements, provide the allocation of budget and resources to work packages, and establish a project schedule.

3.5.1 Work Packages (5.1 of the SPMP). This subsection of the SPMP shall specify the work packages for the activities and tasks that must be completed in order to satisfy the project agreement. Each work package shall be uniquely identified; identification may be based on a numbering scheme and descriptive titles. A diagram depicting the breakdown of activities into subactivities and tasks (a work breakdown structure) may be used to depict hierarchical relationships among work packages.

3.5.2 Dependencies (5.2 of the SPMP). This subsection of the SPMP shall specify the ordering relations among work packages to account for interdependencies among them and dependencies on external events. Techniques such as dependency lists, activity networks, and the critical path method may be used to depict dependencies among work packages.

3.5.3 Resource Requirements (5.3 of the SPMP). This subsection of the SPMP shall provide, as a function of time, estimates of the total resources required to complete the project. Numbers and types of personnel, computer time, support software, computer hardware, office and laboratory facilities, travel, and maintenance requirements for the project resources are typical resources that should be specified.

3.5.4 Budget and Resource Allocation (5.4 of the SPMP). This subsection of the SPMP shall specify the allocation of budget and resources to the various project functions, activities, and tasks. An earned value scheme may be used to allocate budget and resources, and to track expenditures and resource utilization.

3.5.5 Schedule (5.5 of the SPMP). This subsection of the SPMP shall provide the schedule for the various project functions, activities, and tasks, taking into account the precedence relations and the required milestone dates. Schedules may be expressed in absolute calendar time or in increments relative to a key project milestone.

3.6 Additional Components. Certain additional components may be required. These may be included by appending additional sections or subsections to the SPMP. However, the numbering scheme for the required sections and subsections must adhere to the format specified in this standard. Additional items of importance on any particular project may include subcontractor management plans, security plans, independent verification and validation plans, training plans, hardware procurement plans, facilities plans, installation plans, data conversion plans, system transition plans, or the product maintenance plan. If present, additional components must be developed in a format and to a level of detail consistent with the required sections of the SPMP.

3.6.1 Index. An index to the key terms and acronyms used throughout the SPMP is optional, but recommended to improve usability of the SPMP.

3.6.2 Appendices. Appendices may be included, either directly or by reference, to provide supporting details that could detract from the SPMP if included in the body of the SPMP.

An American National Standard

IEEE Standard for
Software User Documentation

Sponsor

**Software Engineering Technical Committee of the
IEEE Computer Society**

Approved December 10, 1987

IEEE Standards Board

Approved February 2, 1989

American National Standards Institute

1063

Foreword

(This Foreword is not a part of IEEE Std 1063-1987, IEEE Standard for Software User Documentation.)

Two factors motivated the development of this standard: The concern of the software user communities over the poor quality of much user documentation, and a need for requirements expressed by producers of documentation.

This standard applies only to traditional documentation, either printed on paper or stored in some other medium in the format of a printed document and used in a manner analogous to the way a printed document is used. On-line documentation is not addressed (documentation designed for interactive access via computer) because such information is processed and used differently from printed documents.

This standard does not cover the actual writers and publishers of user documentation. The responsibility for ensuring that satisfactory software user documentation is produced rests with the organization that generates the software. Responsibility for ensuring that software user documentation is satisfactorily updated rests with the organization that repairs or modifies the software. Configuration management of the documentation is outside the scope of this standard.

Sections 4 and 5 are written as directions. An audit checklist for compliance with this standard can be compiled by identifying each direction and setting up a "yes/no/nonapplicable" condition for the direction. For example, this standard states "identify and describe all data required for the correct processing of each function," in 5.7.2.4. A checklist entry for this condition would then be as follows:

All data is identified and described:

    yes   no   nonapplicable

A successful user document is the result of proper audience determination, careful document planning, and good writing style, in addition to the contents requirement addressed by this standard. However, the ultimate test of any software document is that it is easily usable by its intended audience for its intended purpose.

At the time of approval, the Working Group on Software User Documentation which prepared this standard, had the following membership:

Christopher M. Cooke, *Chairman*   **Ruth L. Oldfield,** *Vice-Chairman & Editor*

A. Frank Ackerman	Tom Kurihara	Ian C. Pyle
George W. Barton, Jr	Joel Lang	Annette D. Reilly
Mordechai Ben-Menachem	Richard Alan Lee	Luke J. Rheaume
Jill Boogaard	F. C. Lim	Horst P. Richter
Ingar Brauti	William Lyon	Richard A. Ries
Fletcher Buckley	Borut Maričić	Lois K. Rosstedt
Lorie J. Call	Phillip C. Marriott	Julio Gonzalez Sanz
François Coallier	Roger J. Martin	Hans Schaefer
Elizabeth Connolly	Alicia McCurdy	Mitzi Sokol
Margaret Daniel	Sandra L. Merscher	Peter Stein
J. T. Deignan	Carolyn J. Mullins	William Sutcliffe
Claudia Dencker	Sarah H. Nash	Jan Tanzer
Mary Jane Dodgen	Frank Nellis	Peter Thorp
Henry H. Fong	Françoise Perrodeau	William S. Turner III
Yair Gershkovitch	William E. Perry	Clifford Way
John W. Horch	Polly Perryman	Andrew H. Weigel
Ed Humphries	Sherwood F. Prescott, Jr	Edmond H. Weiss
Tim Kalisz		Timothy Whalen

The following persons were on the balloting committee that approved this document for submission to the IEEE Standards Board:

When the IEEE Standards Board approved this standard on December 10, 1987, it had the following membership:

Contents

IEEE Standard for
Software User Documentation

1. Scope

This standard provides minimum requirements on the structure and information content of user documentation. It addresses editorial and stylistic considerations only when they impact structure and content. It applies primarily to technical substance rather than to style. Users of this standard may want to develop a style manual for use within their own organizations to complement the guidance provided in the standard. They may also select an industry-recognized style manual such as the *Chicago Manual of Style* [2][1] or the *GPO Style Manual* [3].

Adherence to the standard does not preclude the application of additional, more stringent requirements or standards, or the inclusion of additional topics or materials not required by this standard.

1.1 Applicability.
This standard applies to documentation that guides users in installing, operating, and managing software of any size, and conducting those aspects of software maintenance that do not involve modification of the software source code.

This standard does not apply to the following:

(1) Requirements, design, development, and manufacturing specifications

(2) Marketing materials

(3) Specialized course materials intended primarily for use in formal training programs

(4) User materials to be presented interactively via terminals, and other nontraditional media, such as videotape or slide presentations with recorded narration

(5) Instructions needed to install hardware or prepare it for operation

(6) Configuration management of software user documentation

(7) Verification of software user documentation

1.2 Organization.
The six sections in this standard cover the following topics:

Section 1 describes the scope of this standard, including its applicability.

Section 2 defines terms used in this standard.

Section 3 covers how to determine required document sets by defining product and audience, and describes how to determine usage modes.

Section 4 gives the requirements for information inclusion.

Section 5 covers what shall be contained in each document, including topics such as placement of title page, list of illustrations, etc.

Section 6 covers how to present material in document sets so that user documents are easy to read and understand.

2. Definitions

Certain key terms used in this standard are defined in this section. Other key terms used this standard are defined generally in ANSI/IEEE Std 729-1983 [1], or in *Webster's Third New International Dictionary of the English Language (unabridged)* [4].

action. Step a user takes to complete a task; a step that cannot be subdivided further. A single user action may invoke one or more functions but need not invoke any.

audience. Persons who are expected to need a given software user document.

caution. Advisory in a software user document that performing some action may lead to consequences that are unwanted or undefined. Compare *warning*.

document set. Document or group of documents that offers an audience the information it needs about a software product.

function. A specific purpose of an entity, or its characteristic action.

---

[1] The numbers in brackets correspond to those of the bibliography in Section 7.

illustration. Material that is labeled, numbered, set apart from the main body of text, and, normally, cited within the main text. In this standard, the term *illustration* is used as the generic term for table, figure, drawing, exhibit, and equivalent terms.

note. Helpful hint(s) and other material that may assist the user.

procedure. Ordered series of instructions that a user follows to do one or more tasks.

software user document. Body of material that provides information to users; typically printed or stored on some medium in the format of a printed document.

style. Set of editorial conventions covering grammar, terminology, punctuation, capitalization, etc, of a software user document.

task. Piece of work that a user does, following a given procedure, to achieve a specific goal. A task may include one or more actions.

usage mode. Primary manner in which the document issuer expects that document to be used. This standard recognizes two usage modes, instructional and reference, described in Section 3.

user. Person who uses software to perform some task.

warning. Advisory in a software user document that performing some action will lead to serious or dangerous consequences. Compare *caution.*

3. Identifying Required User Documents

To identify the required user documents; the software product, its applications, and the audiences that will use the product must first be identified. The document set for the audiences, and the usage mode for each document, can then be determined.

3.1 Identifying the Software. The software, its user interfaces, and the tasks that users perform with the software, shall be identified at the start of documentation planning.

3.2 Determining the Document Audience. A software user document shall be keyed to its audience. The different ways that users interact with software shall be considered when preparing user documents: for example, amount of interaction, level of interaction, direct or indirect interaction. Users can form different audiences.

Each intended audience shall be identified before the document (or set of documents) is planned and written. The identified audience will dictate the document presentation style and level of detail. Audience determination is especially important in instructional mode documents.

3.3 Determining the Document Set. A document set may consist of one or more documents, depending on the amount of information to be presented and the needs of the intended audience. Each document of a document set may be one or more volumes depending upon the amount of information to be presented. For example, a command manual might have one volume covering half the commands and a second volume covering the other half of the commands. When a document contains both instructional and reference material, the two shall be clearly separated.

A document set shall contain the information needed by each audience. Depending on the nature of the software and hardware, the software user documentation set may need to be integrated with system-level documentation. The presentation style and level of detail shall be tailored for the intended audience. When a document set must be prepared for audiences with widely differing needs, at least one of the following approaches shall be used:

(1) Separate materials devoted to the needs of specific audiences. The audiences and their needs shall be covered specifically in the introduction, allowing each user to pick out the sections of interest.

(2) Separate documents or document sets for each specific audience.

3.4 Determining Document Usage Modes. Users of software need documents either to learn about the software (instructional mode) or to refresh their memory about it (reference mode). Instructional mode documents may be either information- or task-oriented. Information-oriented documents give the reader information needed to understand the computer software and its functions; task-oriented documents show the reader how to complete a task or reach a goal.

3.4.1 Instructional Mode. An instructional mode document shall

(1) Provide the background and information needed to understand the system.

(2) Provide the information needed to learn what can be done with the software and how to use it (for example, what goals it supports).

(3) Provide examples to reinforce the learning process.

Information-oriented instructional documents provide the user with background or technical information (for example, models and algorithms) needed to use the software properly. Examples of typical information-oriented instructional mode documents include

(1) overview
(2) theory of operation manual
(3) tutorial

Task-oriented instructional mode documents provide the user with procedures to achieve specific goals. Examples of task-oriented instructional mode documents include

(1) diagnostic procedures manual
(2) operations manual
(3) software installation manual

3.4.2 Reference Mode. A reference mode document shall

(1) Organize and provide necessary information
(2) Facilitate random access to information

Examples of typical reference mode documents include

(1) command manual
(2) error message manual
(3) program calls manual
(4) quick reference guide
(5) software tools manual
(6) utilities manual

4. User Document Inclusion Requirements

This section summarizes the information required in user documents. The mandatory information described in this section shall be included in all documents, unless it is not applicable. The sequence, location grouping, and labeling of this information are left to the judgment of the document preparer. (For example, information suggested for the introduction could go in a section labeled "Preface.")

Table 1 specifies 12 basic components of a software user document. Additional information may be added as required.

Table 2 is a matrix of inclusion requirements for specific components of a document. If a component listed as mandatory contains information not applicable to a specific document, that component may be omitted (for example, a description of conventions may not be applicable in an overview document).

Table 1
Software User Document Components

User Document Components	See Paragraph:
Title page	5.1
Restrictions	5.2
Warranties	5.3
Table of contents	5.4
List of illustrations	5.5
Introduction	5.6
Body of document	5.7
Error conditions	5.8
Appendixes	5.9
Bibliography	5.10
Glossary	5.11
Index	5.12

5. User Document Content Requirements

This section describes the required content of user documents. Specific information and the level of detail for each document are determined by the audience and the usage mode of the document. The information specified in this section shall be included in a user document, unless it is not applicable or otherwise noted.

For convenience, this standard uses generic titles or labels to identify parts of a user document. As noted in Section 4, the user document itself need not use these labels. For example, in an introduction the audience description and applicability statement need not be specifically labelled "Audience Description" and "Applicability Statement."

5.1 Title Page. On the title page of a user document include at least the following information:

(1) Document name
(2) Document version and date
(3) Software covered
(4) Issuing organization

The design and arrangement of these items on the title page are at the discretion of the organization preparing the document. The identification of the document and the software shall be consistent with the configuration management system of the issuing organization.

5.2 Restrictions. When restrictions apply to using or copying the document or software product, describe these on the title page or immediately following the title page. Ensure that any proprietary markings, such as trademarks, meet appropriate accepted practices and legal conventions.

Table 2
Inclusion Requirements

Component	Single-Volume Document		Multi-Volume Document	
	8 Pages or Less	More Than 8 Pages	First Volume	Other Volume
Title page	M	M	M	M
Restrictions	M	M	M	M
Warranties	R	R	R	R
Table of contents	O	M	M	M
List of illustrations	O	O	O	O
Introduction				
Audience description	R	M	M	R
Applicability	M	M	M	M
Purpose	R	M	M	R
Document usage	R	M	M	R
Related documents	R	R	R*	R
Conventions	M	M	M	R
Problem reporting	R	M	M	R
Body				
Instruction mode	1	1	1	1
Reference mode	1	1	1	1
Error conditions	R	R	R	R
Appendixes	O	O	O	O
Bibliography	M	M	M**	M**
Glossary	M	M	M**	M**
Index	2	2	M**	M**

Key:

M   Mandatory—Shall be included when information exists.

O   Optional

R   Reference—Either include the section or a reference to where the information can be found within the document set.

*   Shall address relationship to other volumes.

**   Mandatory in at least one volume in the document set, with references to information in other volumes.

1   Every document has a body; each document set shall address the instructional and reference needs of the audience. Required content is in 5.7.1 and 5.7.2.

2   An index is manditory for documents of 40 pages or more and optional when under 40 pages.

5.3 Warranties and Contractual Obligations. Specify any warranties and contractual obligations or disclaimers.

5.4 Table of Contents. Include a table of contents in every document over eight pages long. For single-volume documents, this requirement shall be met in one of two ways:

(1) A comprehensive table of contents for the whole document

(2) A simplified table of contents, with a comprehensive section table of contents preceding each section

For multi-volume documents (a single document in multiple volumes), meet this requirement by including a simple table of contents for the entire document in the first volume. In addition each subsequent volume shall contain either

(1) A comprehensive table of contents for the volume, or

(2) A simplified table of contents for the volume, with a comprehensive table of contents preceding each section.

5.4.1 Comprehensive Table of Contents. Construct a comprehensive table of contents, for a complete document or for a section, as follows:

(1) Carry entries to at least the third level of the document structure hierarchy

(2) Give page numbers for every entry

(3) Choose a method to assist the reader in matching entries with their corresponding page numbers, such as

(a) Leader strings (strings of dots in the form "...") or equivalent, connecting entries and corresponding page numbers

(b) Double-spacing between entries

5.4.2 Simple Table of Contents. In a simple table of contents include at least the first level of the document structure hierarchy with the corresponding page numbers.

5.5 List of Illustrations. Optionally, include one or more lists of the titles and locations of all illustrations in the document. Use separate lists for figures, tables, and exhibits, or merge all types of illustrations into a single list. In each list, include

(1) Number and title of each illustration

(2) Page numbers for each illustration

(3) A method to assist the user in matching entries with their corresponding page numbers, such as

(a) Leader strings (strings of dots in the form "...") or equivalent, connecting entries and corresponding page numbers

(b) Double-spacing between entries

5.6 Introduction. Include the following information in the introduction:

(1) Audience description

(2) Applicability statement

(3) Purpose statement

(4) Document usage description

(5) Related documents list or information

(6) Conventions description

(7) Problem reporting instructions

5.6.1 through 5.6.7 describe the topics further.

5.6.1 Audience Description. Describe the intended audience. If different sections of a document (or a document set) are for different audiences, indicate the intended audience for each section. In the audience section, specify the

(1) Experience level expected of the user

(2) Previous training expected of the user

5.6.2 Applicability Statement. State the software version covered by the document the document version number, and the environment (hardware and software) in which this software runs.

5.6.3 Purpose Statement. Explain why the document was written and summarize the pur-

pose of the software. Include typical intended applications of the software.

5.6.4 Document Usage Description. Describe what each section of the document contains, its intended use, and the relationship between sections. Also provide any other directions necessary for using the document.

5.6.5 Related Documents. List related documents and give the relationship of the document to the others. In document sets comprised of may volumes, this information may be provided in a separate "roadmap" or guide to the document set.

5.6.6 Conventions. Summarize symbols, stylistic conventions, and command syntax conventions used in the document.

5.6.6.1 Symbols. Describe symbols and their usage in the document, illustrating each.

5.6.6.2 Stylistic Conventions. Describe conventions unfamiliar to the intended audience that allow users to understand text or illustrations, such as highlighting or use of boldface or italic type.

5.6.6.3 Command Syntax Conventions. Explain the conventions used for command syntax. Include examples showing options, variable parameters, and required parameters.

5.6.7 Problem Reporting Instructions. Tell the users how to report documentation or software problems. Also describe how users can suggest changes in the software or documentation. List the name and contact information for the organization responsible for responding to the problem reports or suggestions for improvements.

5.7 Body of Document. Determine the content, organization, and presentation of the body of the document after determining whether the document is an instructional mode or reference mode document. In either mode, use a consistent organizational structure based on the expected use of the document, providing examples as necessary.

5.7.1 Body of Instructional Mode Documents. Information-oriented instructional documents give the reader background information or theory needed to understand the software. Include a scope as described in 5.7.1.1 before giving the information forming the major portion of the document. Use topics to organize an information-oriented instructional document; for example, organize the document by

(1) Theory

(2) Software features

(3) Software architecture

Task-oriented instructional documents give the reader the necessary information to carry out a specific task or attain a specific goal. Include the information described in 5.7.1.1 through 5.7.1.7. Use task relations to organize a task-oriented document or section; for example, organize by

(1) Task groups
(2) Task sequence

5.7.1.1 Scope. Begin this section by indicating to the user the scope of the material to be discussed.

5.7.1.2 Materials. Describe any materials the user will need to complete the task (for example, input manuals, passwords, computers, peripherals, cabling, software drivers, interfaces, and protocols). Optionally, describe separately materials common to all or many functions and refer to that description.

5.7.1.3 Preparations. Describe any actions, technical or administrative, that must be done before starting the task (for example, obtain system passwords, access authorization, disk space). Optionally, describe in a separate section preparations common to all or many functions and refer to that section.

5.7.1.4 Cautions and Warnings. Describe general cautions and warnings that apply to the task. Place specific cautions and warnings on the same page and immediately before the action that requires the caution or warning. (See Section 2 for definitions of *caution* and *warning*.)

5.7.1.5 Method. Describe each task, including
(1) What the user must do.
(2) What function, if any is invoked (including how to invoke the function and how to recognize normal termination).
(3) Possible errors, how to avoid them, and how to resolve them.
(4) What results to expect.

5.7.1.6 Related Information. Provide other useful information about the task, such as
(1) Tasks frequently performed together and their relationship.
(2) Other tasks customarily performed by users of this document that could be supported by the methods described in this section. Describe this support.
(3) Notes, limitations, or constraints (notes may also be placed in the specific area to which they apply).

5.7.2 Body of Reference Mode Documents. Organize a reference mode document the way a user accesses a software function. Examples of the ways users access functions include

(1) By command
(2) By menu
(3) By system calls

Within this organization, arrange the functions for easy access and random user access (for example, alphabetical order or a menu-tree hierarchy). For each function, include in the body of a reference mode document the information described in 5.7.2.1 through 5.7.2.11.

5.7.2.1 Purpose. Describe the purpose of the function.

5.7.2.2 Materials. Describe materials needed to use the function or command (for example, input manuals, passwords, computers, peripherals, cabling, software drivers, interfaces, and protocols). Optionally, describe separately materials common to all or many functions and refer to that description.

5.7.2.3 Preparations. Describe any actions, technical or administrative, that must be completed before using the function or command (for example, obtain system passwords, access authorization, disk space). Optionally, describe separately preparations common to all or many functions and refer to that description.

5.7.2.4 Input(s). Identify and describe all data required for the correct processing of each function. Use one of the following methods:
(1) Describe inputs used only by a single function in the section devoted to that function.
(2) Describe in a single section or in an appendix inputs used by multiple functions. Refer to that section or appendix when describing these functions.

5.7.2.5 Cautions and Warnings. Describe general cautions and warnings that apply to each function. Place specific cautions and warnings on the same page and immediately before the action that requires a caution or warning.

5.7.2.6 Invocation. Provide all information needed to use and control the function. Describe all parameters. Include:
(1) Required parameters
(2) Optional parameters
(3) Default options
(4) Order and syntax

5.7.2.7 Suspension of Operations. Describe how to interrupt the function during execution and how to restart it.

5.7.2.8 Termination of Operations. Describe how to recognize function terminations, including abnormal terminations.

5.7.2.9 Output(s). Describe the results of executing the function, such as

(1) Screen display

(2) Effect on files or data

(3) Completion status vaues or output parameters

(4) Outputs that trigger other actions (such as mechanical actions in process control applications).

Provide a complete results description for each function. If several results are possible, explain the situations that produce each.

5.7.2.10 Error Conditions. Describe common error conditions that could occur as a result of executing the function, and describe how to detect that the error has occurred. For example, list any error messages that the system displays. (Error recovery instructions need not be provided here if they are covered in the "Error Messages, Known Problems, and Error Recovery" listing described in 5.8.)

5.7.2.11 Related Information. Provide other useful information about the function that does not readily fit under any of the sections previously described. Such information might include

(1) Limitations and constraints

(2) Notes

(3) Related functions

Notes may also be placed in the specific area to which they apply.

5.8 Error Messages, Known Problems, and Error Recovery. Describe error messages in an easily accessed location (for example, in a separate section, chapter, appendix, or a separate document). For each error message, describe in detail the error that caused it, the procedures needed to recover from it, and the action(s) required to clear it. Describe known software problems here or in a separate document and provide alternative methods or recovery procedures.

5.9 Appendixes. Include in the appendixes any supporting material, arranged for ease of access. For example, the appendixes might include

(1) Detailed input and output data or formats used in common by multiple functions

(2) "Codes" used in input or output (for example, country codes or stock number codes)

(3) Interactions between tasks or functions

(4) Global processing limitations

(5) Description of data formats and file structures

(6) Sample files, reports, or programs

5.10 Bibliography. List all publications specifically mentioned in the text. Other publications containing related information may also be listed.

5.11 Glossary. List alphabetically in the glossary definitions of

(1) All terms, acronyms, and abbreviations used in the document that may be unfamiliar to the audience

(2) All terms, acronyms, and abbreviations used in a manner that may be unfamiliar to the audience

If desired, the acronyms and abbreviations may be listed in a separate section.

5.12 Index. Develop an index, based on key words or concepts, for user documents over eight pages. Construct this index as follows:

(1) Indicate importance of information; place minor key words under major ones.

(2) Give location references for each entry, to the right of the entry.

(3) List location references in one of the following ways:

  (a) By page number

  (b) By section or paragraph number

  (c) By illustration number

  (d) By another index entry

(4) Use only one level of index reference. (For example, if an entry points to a second index entry, the second entry shall give a page number, section or paragraph number, or illustration number. The second entry shall not point to a third index entry.)

6. User Document Presentation Requirements

This section discusses the required presentation methods for user documents. The information in this section shall be included unless it is not applicable.

The method of presenting material, in addition to the style of writing and the level of detail, contributes to making a user document easy to read and understand. Presentation considerations include highlighting, consistency, terminology, and references to other material.

6.1 Highlighting. For every user document or set of documents, find a method to highlight selected material of special importance, especially cautions and warnings. Select highlighting methods that provide prominence and segregation to the material being emphasized. Describe the highlighting method in the introduction.

Choice of a specific highlighting method is left to the users of this standard, consistent with the practices or their organizations. Common highlighting methods include the use of bold and italic typefonts, the enclosure of material within lines or boxes, or the use of color.

6.2 Consistency. Use terminology and typographic and stylistic conventions consistently throughout a user document or set of documents. Identify any deviations from the conventions the first time they appear.

6.3 Terminology. Define all terms requiring a glossary entry, acronyms, and abbreviations when first used in the document.

6.4 Referencing Related Material. If related material is placed in separate parts of a document or in separate documents of a document set, repetition of the information can be avoided by providing specific references to the related information.

7. Bibliography

[1] ANSI/IEEE Std 729-1983, IEEE Standard Glossary of Software Engineering Terminology.[2]

[2] The Chicago Manual of Style, 13th ed, The University of Chicago Press, 1982.

[3] Government Printing Office (GPO) Style Manual, Government Printing Office, Washington, DC, 1984.

[4] Webster's Third New International Dictionary of the English Language (unabridged), Springfield, MA: Merriam-Webster, Inc, 1986.

---

[2] ANSI/IEEE publications are available from IEEE Service Center, 445 Hoes Lane, PO Box 1331, Piscataway, NJ 08855-1331, or from the Sales Department, American National Standards Institute, 1430 Broadway, New York, NY 10018.

Index

A

Action, 6
Appendixes, 12
  error messages, 12
Applicability, 6
  statement of, 10
Audience, 6, 7
  description, 10
  determination, 7

B

Bibliography, 12,13
Body of document, 10
  body of instruction mode document, 10
  body of reference mode document, 11

C

Caution, 6
Cautions and warnings, 6, 7, 11
  highlighting, 12
Commands, 10, 11
Consistency, 13
Content requirements, 8
Contractual obligations, 9
Conventions, 10
  command syntax, 10
  stylistic, 10
  symbols, 10

D

Definitions, 6
Detail, level of, 7, 8
Disclaimers, 9
Document
  appendixes, 12
  applicability statement, 10
  audience, 7, 10
  bibliography, 12
  body of, 10
  cautions and warnings, 11
  components, 8
  conventions, 10
  error messages, 12
  glossary, 12
  index, 12
  information-oriented, 8, 10
  illustrations, list of, 8, 9, 10
  inclusion requirements, 8, 9
  information requirements, 8

  input(s), 11
  introduction, 10
  instructional mode, 7
    body of, 10
  materials, 11
  method, 11
  multi-volume, 7, 9
  output(s), 11
  parameter(s), 11
  preparations, 11
  purpose, 11
  reference mode, 8
    body of, 11
  related documents or information, 10, 11, 12, 13
  required, 7, 8
  requirements, 8, 9
  restrictions, 8
  table of contents, 9
  task-oriented, 8, 11
  usage modes, 7
  version, 8
Document set, 6, 7

E

Error conditions, 12

F

Function, 6, 11

G

Glossary, 12

H

Highlighting, 12

I

Illustration, 7
Illustrations, list of, 10
Index, 12
Information-oriented instructional document, 8, 10
Input(s), 11
Instructional mode document, 7
  body of, 10
  information-oriented, 8, 10
  task-oriented, 8, 11
Introduction, 8, 9, 10
Invocation, 11

Acknowledgements

Working group members were individually supported by their organizations with travel expenses and working days to attend meetings. This support does not constitute or imply approval or endorsement of this standard. These organizations were:

Apollo Computer
Army Materials Technology Laboratory
AT&T Bell Laboratories
Bell Canada (Canada)
Bell Communications Research
Boeing Computer Services
Burroughs Corp.
International Bureau of Software Testing
Martin Marietta Aero and Naval Systems
3M
Mitre Corp
NCR Systems Engineering b.v.
PDA Engineering
Pratt & Whitney, Inc
Ross Laboratories
SAGE Federal Systems, Inc
Texas Instruments, Inc
US Department of Transportation
Virginia Polytechnic Institute & State University